D1212316

MEDIEVAL LINCOLN

TO
MY MOTHER

MEDIEVAL LINCOLN

BY

James William Francis Hill

SIR FRANCIS HILL

KT, C.B.E., M.A., LL.M., F.S.A.

CAMBRIDGE

AT THE UNIVERSITY PRESS

1965

PUBLISHED BY
THE SYNDICS OF THE CAMBRIDGE UNIVERSITY PRESS
Bentley House, 200 Euston Road, London, N.W.1
American Branch: 32 East 57th Street, New York, N.Y. 10022
West African Office: P.O. Box 33, Ibadan, Nigeria

First printed 1948
Reprinted 1965

First printed in Great Britain at the University Press, Cambridge
Reprinted by offset-lithography by John Dickens & Co. Ltd, Northampton

CONTENTS

ILLUSTRATIONS

LIST OF PLATES

LIST OF FIGURES IN THE TEXT

ABBREVIATIONS AND AUTHORITIES

B.M.	British Museum.
D. & C.	Dean and Chapter of Lincoln, Muniment Room.
H.M.C.	Historical Manuscripts Commission.
L.R.S.	Lincoln Record Society.
P.R. & P.R.S.	Publications of the Pipe Roll Society.
P.R.O.	Public Record Office.
R.C.	Record Commission.
R.S.	Rolls Series.

MANUSCRIPTS

Adversaria	'Collections for an history of the city of Lincoln. Indigesta Moles. March 25th 1737' (Bodleian Library, MS. Gough, Linc. I).
Bardney Cartulary	Cartulary of Bardney Abbey (B.M., Cotton MS., Vespasian E, xx).
Barlings Cartulary	Cartulary of Barlings Abbey (B.M., Cotton MS., Faustina B, i).
B.B.	Lincoln Burwarmote Book (Lincoln Cathedral Library, No. 169(8)).
Blickling Homilies	In collection of Mr John H. Scheide, Titusville, Pennsylvania. See infra, pp. 291–2.
Blickling Psalter	Pierpont Morgan Library, New York. See infra, p. 292.
C.C.M.	Minutes of the Common Council of the City of Lincoln.
Chapter Acts	Acts of the Dean and Chapter of Lincoln.
Fosse Charter	Charter granted to Fosse Nunnery in 1331 (calendared in *C.P.R.* 1330–4, p. 215).
Gild Certificates	P.R.O. Chancery Miscellanea, Bundle 40, nos. 135–59.
Goxhill Leiger	Dean and Chapter of Peterborough, Muniment Room.
Harl. Cart.	Harleian Charters (B.M.).
Kirkstead Cartulary	Cartulary of Kirkstead Abbey (B.M., Cotton MS., Vespasian E, xviii).
Lib. Cant.	Liber de Ordinationibus Cantariarum (D. & C., A/1/8).
Lincoln Cordwainers MS.	Lincoln Public Library.
Lincoln Corporation MSS.	Lincoln Corporation, Muniment Room.
Lincoln Fields Terrier	In collection of Captain W. A. Cragg, F.S.A.
Ross MSS.	Collection of John Ross, now at Burton Hall, Lincoln.
Thurgarton Cartulary	Cartulary of Thurgarton Priory (Chapter of Southwell, Muniment Room).
Welbeck Cartulary	Cartulary of Welbeck Abbey (B.M., Harleian MS., 3640).
White Book	White Book of Lincoln (Lincoln Corporation MSS.).

PRINTED BOOKS

A.A.S.R.	*Reports and Papers of the Associated Architectural and Archaeological Societies.*
Anc. Corr.	*Ancient Correspondence* in *P.R.O. Lists and Indexes.*
Arch. Journ.	*Archaeological Journal.*
B.B.C. (1)	Ballard, *British Borough Charters,* 1042–1216.
B.B.C. (2)	Ballard and Tait, *British Borough Charters,* 1216–1307.
Birch	*Royal Charters of the City of Lincoln,* edited by W. de Gray Birch.
C.A.D.	*Calendar of Ancient Deeds.*
Cal. Inq. Misc.	*Calendar of Inquisitions, Miscellaneous.*
Cal. Inq. p.m.	*Calendar of Inquisitions post mortem.*
C.C.R.	*Calendar of Close Rolls.*
C. Chart. R.	*Calendar of Charter Rolls.*
C.F.R.	*Calendar of Fine Rolls.*
C.P.R.	*Calendar of Patent Rolls.*
C.R. Rolls	*Curia Regis Rolls.*
D.B.	*Domesday Book* (R.C.).
D.C.	*Documents illustrative of the Social and Economic History of the Danelaw,* edited by F. M. Stenton.
E.H.R.	*English Historical Review.*
F.C. I	*Abstracts of Final Concords,* vol. I, edited by W. O. Massingberd.
F.C. II	*Final Concords of the County of Lincoln,* vol. II, edited by C. W. Foster (L.R.S.).
H.M.C. Lincoln	*Historical Manuscripts Commission,* 14th Report, Appendix, Part VIII. Manuscripts of Lincoln Corporation, edited by W. D. Macray.
Inq. A.Q.D.	*Inquisitions ad quod damnum.*
L.A.S.R.	*Lincoln Architectural Society's Reports and Papers.*
L.C.S.	*Lincoln Cathedral Statutes,* edited by Bradshaw and Wordsworth.
L.D.	*The Lincolnshire Domesday and the Lindsey Survey,* edited by C. W. Foster and T. Longley (L.R.S.).
Lincs N. & Q.	*Lincolnshire Notes and Queries.*
R.A.	*Registrum Antiquissimum of the Cathedral Church of Lincoln,* vols. I–III, edited by C. W. Foster; IV, edited by C. W. Foster and Kathleen Major; V, edited by Kathleen Major (L.R.S.).
R.H.	*Rotuli Hundredorum* (R.C.).
Rot. Lit. Claus.	*Rotuli Litterarum Clausarum* (R.C.).
Rot. Lit. Pat.	*Rotuli Litterarum Patentium* (R.C.).
Rot. Parl.	*Rotuli Parliamentorum.*
Sempringham Charters	From *The Genealogist,* vol. XV, pp. 158, 223.
V.C.H.	*Victoria History of the Counties of England.*

PREFACE

FOR twenty years many of my leisure moments have gone to the making of this book. The accidents of life and the pressure of other work have ensured that progress has at best been slow, and have often stopped it altogether, sometimes for long periods. Such delays, exasperating as they are, are not wholly lost time, for when research and reading are arrested, reflection, aided by occasional talk with friends, can go on, bringing a more balanced view. Nor has my other work been wholly irrelevant, for practice as a solicitor affords unusual opportunities of studying topography, and participation in local government brings contact with problems of administration which throw light upon their medieval counterparts. It is a fascinating experience to live, as it were, in the past and the present at the same time and in the same sphere; and for me there can be no more convincing proof of the continuity of history and its value in the understanding of affairs.

My chosen field, though apparently small, is nevertheless rich; how rich I have been slow to realise. I have had to go far beyond the limits originally planned, and as I look back I doubt whether I should ever have begun at all if I had known the size of the task. There is no logical reason why I should have stopped when I did. The quest for evidence might have continued indefinitely but for the war, which put original documents out of reach. I was confirmed in my decision to make do with the materials already gathered by the strictures of Sir Charles Oman (published in 1939) upon the worker, who, for the sake of some desideratum not yet discovered, goes on searching for ever, and finally dies, leaving behind him a pile of disconnected scraps and notebooks of half-arranged material. With this encouragement, and the further thought that the scraps and notebooks themselves might be destroyed by the Luftwaffe, I put most of my chapters into their final form during the war years. With a few exceptions it has not been possible to incorporate the results of more recent work, the most important of which are embodied in the Report of the meeting of the Royal Archaeological Institute at Lincoln in 1946. The shortcomings of the book are becoming increasingly obvious to me, but even so I hope that besides being a piece of local history it will be of some interest to the student of English history in general and of boroughs in particular.

My debt to printed books on Lincoln is sufficiently shown in the footnotes. Two serious attempts at a history of the city still lie in manuscript. The author of the first was Thomas Sympson (born, Great Salkeld,

Cumberland, 1702, died 1749, buried in the Consistory Court of Lincoln Minster), an antiquary who became clerk of the Minster fabric in 1738. His enquiries led him to the bishops' registers, at least one of the cartularies of the dean and chapter, and the city records. His collection, written in a folio volume called 'Adversaria', is now in the Bodleian Library. There is a notice of his work in *Appendix to the History of the Gentlemen's Society at Spalding*, p. xxxvi n.; some letters of his have been printed (from B.M. Add. MSS 5833, 5841) in *Lincolnshire Notes and Queries*, IX (1906–7), 65–90, with a portrait; and the probate of his will, which lately passed through my hands in the course of professional practice, shows him as a collector of coins, drawings and prints. As the sources of much of his material are now in print, the chief remaining interest of his manuscript is in the light which it throws upon the history of his own times.

The second and more important manuscript history of Lincoln is that of John Ross, which is now in Lord Monson's library at Burton Hall. Ross (*c.* 1800–1870) was a native of South Carlton, and was apprenticed to a Lincoln bookseller. At the end of his apprenticeship he opened a school at Edmonton. After some years there he lived in London, working at the British Museum and the Bodleian Library. From 1853 onwards he made his home in Lincoln, studying the records of the city (as witness his *Civitas Lincolnia*), though like Sympson he worked over a wider field, including some of the archives of the dean and chapter. Canon Foster used the five volumes of his 'Annals of Lincoln', and paid tribute to these beautifully written books, compiled with amazing industry, and complete with illuminated capitals and illustrations by his own hand. As with Sympson, much of the material he collected is now in print, and his history is not likely ever to be published in full, though it will always remain of value for reference. His notebooks and scrapbooks show that he was planning a history of Lincolnshire on a large scale, a task in which he still awaits a successor. There is an appreciation of Ross in the *Lincoln, Rutland and Stamford Mercury* for 28 January 1870.

Two other workers in the same field call for mention. In 1785 Samuel Lyon, the town clerk of Lincoln, compiled an account of the charters of the city which is still in the muniment room. Most of his work has been superseded by Dr Birch's *Royal Charters of the City of Lincoln* (1911), but fortunately he included a translation of the missing 'Provisions' or 'Constitutions' of the city, *c.* 1300, which has not been found elsewhere. It is printed in Appendix VII.

About 1900, Colonel J. G. Williams, a Lincoln solicitor, then mayor, undertook to investigate the history of the civic insignia, and his enquiries brought him to the early history of the mayoralty. His papers, which were given to me after his death by his daughter Miss Mabel Williams, show that he made abstracts of some hundreds of charters of the dean and chapter, and studied the Kirkstead cartulary and the city records and many printed sources. He was a shrewd observer, and little that was of moment missed his eye. He had, however, come to the subject late in life without a very full background of historical knowledge, and his writing can only be used with care. His best work was done upon the Civil War in Lincolnshire; it is printed in *Lincolnshire Notes and Queries*, vol. VIII.

If there are few references to these manuscript sources in the chapters that follow it is because direct reference to originals has been made again, but nevertheless such secondary evidence has been of value, especially in the earlier stages of my work, in pointing both to sources and to conclusions. I should certainly have missed some pieces of evidence but for the fact that my predecessors had been there before.

In writing the book I found one of the most difficult problems was that of arrangement of materials. Some chapters had to be devoted to particular subjects and some to a chronological record, and after many experiments I adopted the plan of chronology to the Norman Conquest, turned in chapters IV to VIII to a survey of the city, castle and Bail, Minster and Close, and then resumed the chronological record, adding where necessary additional chapters. The plan may be open to various objections, but it has seemed to me open to fewer than any other. As to the limits of the subject I have adopted the year 1500 as marking the end of the chronological chapters, though it has not been rigidly observed. In the treatment of subjects such as the Bail, the Close and the open fields, it has seemed better to complete their history, for in them the Middle Ages lasted into the nineteenth century. I hope some day to continue the history of Lincoln to modern times, and have already done part of the necessary work, because it helped an understanding of the medieval period.

Few students can have been more fortunate in their friends than I have been. Professor H. D. Hazeltine and Mr (now Professor) H. A. Hollond, teaching in the school of Maitland, first whetted my appetite for a piece of work of my own. The late Arthur C. Newsum, a friend of scholars whose memory is still fragrant in Lincoln, gave me the freedom of his library. Canon C. W. Foster, whose historical work it would be impertinence in me to praise, led me gradually from one subject to another with the gentle persistence that his friends (and others) found irresistible. He was always ready to produce original documents, or transcripts, or printed books, which might bear upon the problem of the moment, and no trouble was ever too great for him. I recall with lively pleasure my visits to him at Timberland Vicarage, and his calls at my firm's office on the weekly market day, when he came to Lincoln on a variety of missions, domestic, ecclesiastical and historical, all discharged with his usual care. One of his greatest kindnesses was to introduce me to Professor and Mrs Stenton. What their stimulus and help have meant cannot be put into words, but those with a like experience will understand. I hope that part of my debt to Professor Stenton is made plain in the text, but the text does not show what guidance he has given in matters which I found difficult, when a single hint from his vast learning has been enough to start a new line of enquiry.

Miss Kathleen Major, who fills the place which was created in Lincolnshire by so formidable an *antecessor* as Canon Foster, has been untiring in helping me at every stage, and I am grateful to her for letting me make such large drafts upon her time and patience. Dr Helen Cam has read the text and made many valuable suggestions. I have discussed a variety of problems with Mr F. W. Brooks, and have found his own Lincoln researches, the fruits of which he put at my disposal, and his acquaintance with other towns of great value. At an early stage I had useful advice and stimulating enquiries from Professor Carl Stephenson, and the late Dr James Tait helped me upon a number of points. Dr Ian Richmond has advised on chapter I; Professor C. F. C. Hawkes, Mr J. N. L. Myres and Mr F. T. Baker on parts of chapter II; Dr Srawley and Canon Larken on the Minster; Canon Cook on Boston; Sir Alfred Clapham and Canon Harding on architectural matters; Sir Maurice Powicke on chapter X; Professor Bruce Dickins on the inscription at St Mary le Wigford; Mr Neil Ker on the Blickling Homilies; and Mr R. Somerville on the records of the Duchy of Lancaster.

Many acknowledgments are due for help given in the collection of evidence. The Lincoln Corporation have allowed the freest access to the city muniments; the Dean and Chapter of Lincoln lent their transcripts of the Chapter Act Books; Canon Foster's Literary Executors and the Lincoln Record Society their transcripts of charters in the Chapter archives; Mr Brooks his calendar of the Burwarmote Book in the Cathedral Library; Mr E. E. Rich his lists of the mayors of the Lincoln and Boston staples; Mr C. L. Exley his collections from local newspapers; Mr John H. Scheide allowed me to have photostats of the Lincoln entries in the Blickling Homilies; the Pierpont Morgan Library sent photographs of entries in the Blickling Psalter; Captain W. A. Cragg lent his terrier of lands in the Lincoln fields; and with characteristic kindness Professor Hamilton Thompson copied the Lincoln charters in the Welbeck cartulary. The late Lord Monson encouraged me to use his library, including the Ross MSS., at Burton Hall, and I am grateful to his son, the present Lord Monson, for allowing me to continue to do so.

Valuable practical help has been rendered by successive Town Clerks of Lincoln, Mr Need, Mr Banwell and Mr J. H. Smith; by successive City Librarians, Mr Corns and Mr Cooper; by the Lindsey and Holland County Librarian, Mr Curtis; and by their respective staffs, of whom Mr Rawlinson, of the Town Clerk's Department, Miss M. L. Smith, of the Usher Art Gallery, and Miss E. Jahn, of the City Library, must be especially mentioned. The Librarians of Nottingham, Newark and University College, Nottingham, have all helped with books. Miss Thurlby, formerly Canon Foster's Secretary, and now of the Lindsey and Holland County Library, has put her knowledge of the Foster Collection at my disposal, and has transcribed many documents for ease of reference.

The sources of the illustrations are given in the Lists of Plates and Figures, and thanks are due to the custodians of the collections there mentioned for permission to use the illustrations selected. Mr R. L. Stirling and Mr H. Mills have helped in the preparation of maps, and my secretary Miss W. O. Hunt has relieved me of much clerical work. The typescript was read by Mr G. S. Dixon and Mr E. I. Abell, and Mr A. Sutcliffe helped to prepare it for the press. Miss Major read the proofs and advised on the index, which was prepared by Miss Thurlby. To all of them, and to other unnamed helpers, I offer my sincere thanks.

To the Syndics of the Press for their encouragement, and to their officers for exemplary patience and care, I am deeply grateful.

J. W. F. HILL

LINCOLN
Michaelmas 1947

CHAPTER I

THE ROMAN PATTERN

THERE is a common belief, said to have been expressed by George III, that Lincolnshire is all fens and flats. Such a belief will not survive a glance at a physical map. Besides the fenland, which occupies the south-eastern area of the county, the marshes upon the eastern seaboard, and the Trent Valley to the west, there are wolds and heaths forming part of the pattern of the lowlands of England. From the centre of the pattern, the chalk plateau formed by Salisbury Plain and the White Horse Hills, there extend two parallel ridges to the north-east.

The easterly chalk ridge forms the Chiltern Hills and the East Anglian Ridge; this fades out in Norfolk, just reaching the sea at Hunstanton, but appears in Lincolnshire and Yorkshire respectively as the Lincoln Wolds and the Yorkshire Wolds; terminating at Flamborough Head, a well-known landmark of the chalk. The westerly ridge forms the Cotteswold Hills, limestone, fading out in the Northampton Uplands; reappearing—as Lincoln Edge—on the flank of the Vale of Trent, and—as the North York Moors—on the sea's margin, overlooking the Vale of York, and forming the cliffs adjoining Whitby and Robin Hood's Bay.[1]

The Lincoln Edge is part of this limestone ridge. It is about 200 ft. high, and extends from the north nearly 80 miles towards the south of Lincolnshire: on the western side it falls away sharply and to the east more gently. North of Lincoln it is called the Cliff, to the south the Heath. The range is broken near the middle by a gap, the Lincoln Gap, through which the river Witham, after flowing northward up the western side of the ridge, turns east and flows east and south-east to the sea. It is a wide gap for so puny a stream, a fact which geologists explain by saying that it was made by what is now called the Trent, which flowed through it until the diversion of the greater river to the Humber.[2] The theory has also been advanced that in later times the principal course of the Witham below Dogdyke was to the sea at Wainfleet, and that it was only after the Roman occupation that the subsidiary channel entering the Wash became the main river.[3]

Drainage engineers can form some idea of conditions in and near the Lincoln Gap before any Roman works were undertaken. To the west were

[1] Sir Cyril Fox, *The Personality of Britain* (3rd ed. 1938), p. 28.

[2] H. H. Swinnerton, 'The Problem of the Lincoln Gap' in *Lincolnshire Naturalists' Union Transactions* (1937), pp. 145 et seq.

[3] S. B. J. Skertchley, *Geology of the Fenland* (*Memoirs of the Geological Survey*) (1877), pp. 12, 13.

great pools (or perhaps before the time of the Romans they were one vast pool) which received the waters of the upper Witham and its tributary the Till, and sometimes the overflow from the unbanked river Trent. After passing through the gap the Witham widened out into an enormous expanse of fenland.[1] Up to what level the waters used to reach it is very difficult to say, but there are stories, supported by some evidence, of boats being found on the Lincoln hillside in the region of the 50 ft. contour line: it is difficult to believe that the river ever reached this level in historic times.[2]

The strategic value of the Lincoln site could hardly be overlooked. The Romans advanced from London in three columns, moving west, north-west and north respectively. The Ninth Legion formed the right wing of the invading force, and its route lay through Cambridgeshire and round the edge of the fens.[3] The perilous and unknown fenland might well make the legionary commander uneasy about the safety of his right flank, and it would be some relief to take the higher ground of the Lincoln Edge in the parts of Kesteven. At the north end of the modern Kesteven, the first element of whose name (from the British *céto*, Welsh *coed*, meaning wood) suggests that it was a wooded district,[4] he would come upon the Witham Gap and discover an ideal site for a camp across the river. The camp could be placed on the crest of a steep hill, where it would command the waterway; it would provide a good starting point for a new northward advance; and it was the first point for some sixty miles in the march from London at which the invader could get round the head of the fens and recover contact with the coast.

There is no proof that the legionary camp occupied the same site as the future Roman *colonia*, but in spite of speculation, no other camp site has

[1] F. H. Tomes, 'Drainage of the Witham Fens' in *Lincolnshire Magazine*, II (1934–6), p. 160, and map on p. 156.

[2] 'The fact of a boat being found chained to a post in digging a cellar in Dernstall Lock is well known, and another such is said to have been discovered in building a house in front of the City Gaol (? Ald. Colton). These places are 40 ft. or more above the level of the river, so that the water must have flowed up to a height sufficient to flood the valley to a vast extent.' Colonel J. G. Williams' notes (in the writer's possession) copying a note found in Drury's *History of Lincoln*, 1816, in the British Museum, attributed to Edward James Willson, a Lincoln architect and antiquary who is entitled to respect. It is widely believed in Lincoln (as it was in Stukeley's time, see *Itinerarium Curiosum* (1724), p. 84) that the Greestone Stairs once led down to the water—in the eighteenth century they were called Greecing Staiths—but (apart from the fact that the purpose of the Stairs is to provide a short way from the Close to the lower city) this is incredible.

[3] Collingwood and Myres, *Roman Britain and the English Settlements* (1936), p. 90.

[4] See Ekwall, *Oxford Dictionary of English Place Names*. In the sixteenth century the country was still wooded from Stamford to Grantham. Leland, *Itinerary* (ed. Toulmin Smith), v, 33.

ever been found, and strategic considerations point to the one occupied by the *colonia*. As a modern observer has commented, 'the extreme cleverness of the Roman engineers becomes manifest when one studies the contour lines of the city. The centre of the Roman city is the highest point of the ridge (approximately 225 ft.) and centres on the line of the Ermine Street. The square lay-out of the original city fits most exactly the top of the hill, and its boundaries are all at approximately 215 ft., a level almost 200 ft. above the meadows below'.[1] Moreover, the city was laid out upon lines that have a military look. In plan it was rectangular, and divided into quarters by main roads intersecting at the centre, with a gateway in the middle of each side. The smaller streets have been lost, but the town probably conformed to the familiar chess-board plan in common use in the Roman Empire.[2]

It was about A.D. 47, four years after the Roman invasion began, that the Ninth Legion arrived in the Witham Gap. The first recorded name of the place is the British *Lindon*, which is cognate with the Welsh *llyn*, a lake, and refers to the widening of the Witham, still evidenced in Brayford pool.[3] This name suggests that the site had been occupied by the Britons before the Romans arrived; and the inference receives some support from the discovery of a number of objects of the early Iron Age in the river Witham near Lincoln.[4] The British name was Latinised as *Lindum*, and after the troops had resumed their northward advance to York in A.D. 71 the town became a *colonia*—a place for the settlement of time-expired legionaries—and its name was extended to *Lindum colonia*. The Roman name passed by a normal succession of British and English sound changes through the British form *Lindocolina* recorded by Bede to the Anglo-Saxon *Lindcylene*. As Professor Stenton points out, this influence of contemporary British speech in the days of the English conquest is an indication that British inhabitants of the district were not exterminated.[5]

It is important for the study of medieval Lincoln to trace the lines of the Roman walls of the city and to note their later history. The famous Newport Arch, which still spans the Ermine Street as it leaves Lincoln for the Humber, is the inner member of the Roman north gate. The eastern side

[1] Mr Robert Atkinson's Report to Lincoln Corporation on Town Planning, 1934–9.

[2] Haverfield, *Ancient Town Planning* (1913), pp. 41, 118; F. T. Baker, *Roman Lincoln* (Lincoln Branch of the Historical Association, 1938), p. 18.

[3] See Ekwall, op. cit.

[4] Baker, *Roman Lincoln*, p. 7. They include two boat-shaped *fibulae* of Hallstatt type, a shield decorated with coral, and iron swords of La Tène type. For the Witham shield, see *British Museum Guide to Early Iron Age Antiquities* (1925), pp. 101, 104.

[5] 'Historical Bearing of Place Names; England in the Sixth Century' in *Transactions of the Royal Historical Society*, 4th series, XXI, 17.

arch remains, and the springing of the western side arch was uncovered in 1937. The gateway has a squat appearance now, because the ground-level has risen about 8 ft. above the Roman level. To the east of the arch a piece of the wall remains, though its stone facings have gone, leaving the rubble core; and a length of the ditch can be seen between East Bight and Church Lane. The wall turns south in the grounds of a private house where a considerable length of the ditch survives: a piece of wall with its ditch remains in the garden of Eastgate Court. The eastern gateway of the city stood slightly to the north of the present street called Eastgate, and thence the line of the wall passes southwards through the lesser transepts of the Minster, and turns west along the northern boundary of the Bishop's Palace. Although the wall has been rebuilt, its successor on the same site serves as the boundary of the Old Palace grounds and the Leeke School. It is also the boundary of the Close, and above it are the south walls of the Subdeanery and the Precentory. The point at which the Roman south gate spanned the Steep Hill (just below the crest of the hill) is indicated by a section of masonry embedded in the front of the house No. 26, Steep Hill. In the south-western quarter of the Roman city the wall, for the greater part, is either buried under, or was removed to make room for, the walls, banks and ditch of the castle. The foundations of part of the south wall were removed from the castle ditch about 1821; another section of the south wall was uncovered in Wordsworth Street in 1898; and in 1836 the Roman west gate was discovered in the castle bank. The gate collapsed after exposure, but not before a drawing was made of it.[1] In the north-western quarter fragments of wall can still be seen here and there in the boundary walls of modern houses and gardens.

The area enclosed by the wall is 41 acres. This is small compared with the area of other Roman towns in England: London, 330 acres; Cirencester, 240; Verulam, 200; Wroxeter, 170; Colchester, 108; Silchester, 100; Caerwent, 44: among smaller towns Caistor by Norwich had an area of 35 acres.[2] It was not, however, small when compared with some other *coloniae*: Timgad had an area of 29 acres; Emona (Lubljana), 53; Lucca, 60; Gloucester, 46. Gloucester grew little, and Timgad relatively little, but at Lincoln the Roman settlement overflowed the original defences, and the extension of the occupied area, as might be expected, was in the downhill direction towards the river. The Ermine Street served as the north and south axis of the extension. Continuous occupation of both the

[1] *Gentleman's Magazine*, June 1836. For the drawing, see *R.A.* I, facing p. 269.

[2] Collingwood, *Archaeology of Roman Britain* (1930), p. 92. Compare some continental Roman towns: Nîmes, 790 acres; Autun, 494; Milan, 329; Lyons, 314; Vienna, 214; Turin, 127.

original and the added area since the English settlement has made systematic excavation impossible, but building activity has from time to time uncovered many remains of the Roman settlement. The finds on the

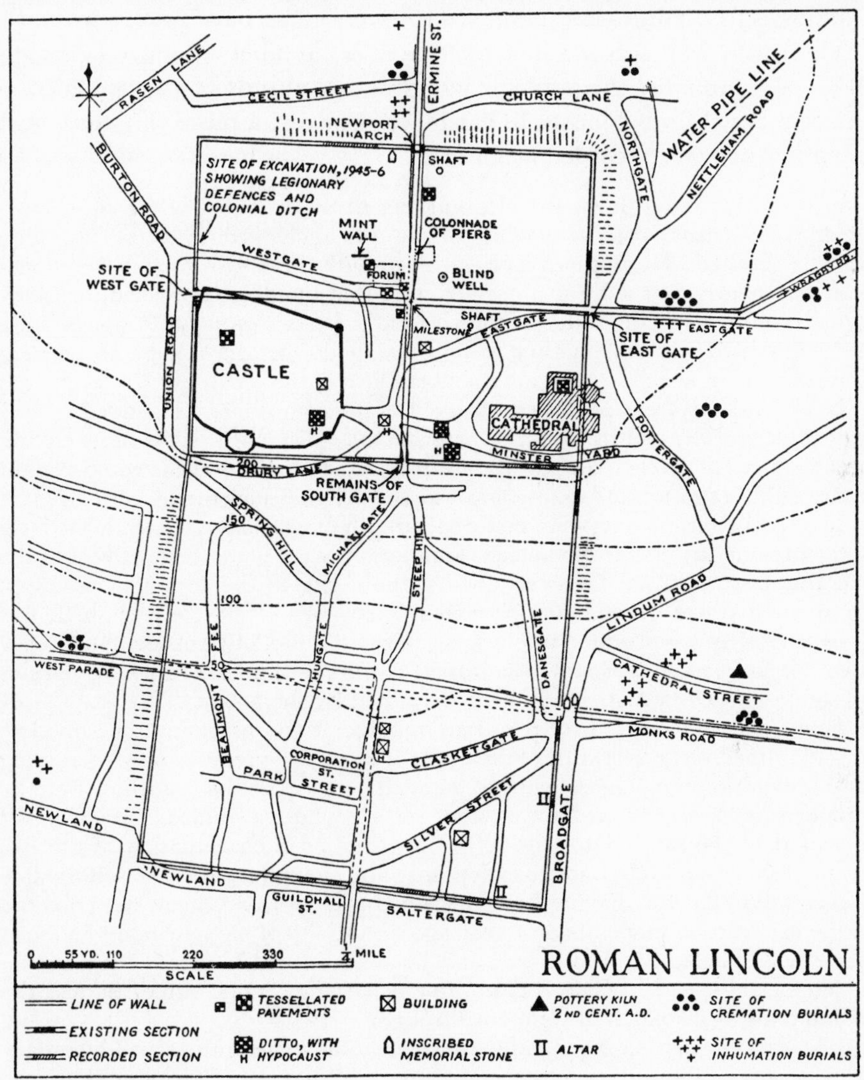

Fig. 1.

hillside indicate that the area was settled in the second century and perhaps a little earlier;[1] and at a date which is difficult to determine the Roman

[1] See plan supra. A valuable list of references to finds is given by Mr C. W. Phillips in his 'Present State of Archaeology in Lincolnshire' in *Arch. Journ.* XCI (1934), p. 173. See also Baker, *Roman Lincoln*, and A. Smith, *A Catalogue of the Roman Inscribed Stones found in the City of Lincoln* (1929).

extension was enclosed by a wall. The new enclosure is generally called the second or lower Roman city. It has an area of 56 acres, and was made by extending the east and west walls of the upper city southwards and building a new south wall parallel to the river.

The south wall was washed by the river, at least in times of flood; and it was probably the Romans who lowered the river level by cutting a new channel from Lincoln to Bardney.[1] The discovery of this south wall a century ago was recorded as follows:

In recently taking down the old building at the east end of the Stonebow, which was formerly used as the City prison, the ancient south wall of the City became exposed. Its southern face was even with the north front of the Stonebow, and nearly, but not quite, parallel with that building: the deviation being a tendency towards the south at the east end. Its thickness could not be fully ascertained without endangering a high warehouse in Mrs Coleman's occupation (the end of which stood upon the north face of the wall), but it was proved to be at least five feet. It was constructed of unhewn stones, embedded in clay instead of mortar, and its south, or external face, displayed traces of its having been repaired at divers times; the reparations being generally made with wrought stones, and better mortar than composed the original structure.

The recent excavations were made to a depth of eleven feet beneath the level of the present pavement; the ancient foundations were found below this, but the actual depth could not be ascertained without risk to the adjoining premises. At about five feet beneath the pavement a stratum of muscle [*sic*] shells was discovered firmly embedded in black silt, at least a foot in thickness; and below this, the soil as far as it was penetrated, consisted of thin laminae of various substances which had obviously been deposited by the action of water.

Again, more recently, I have had an opportunity of inspecting the same line of wall immediately westward of the Stonebow, on the premises now rebuilding for Mr Waddington. The remains of the wall on this side the Stonebow were by no means so perfect as on the east side; but they bore a similar character, and appeared of the same date; the soil also exhibited a continuation of the like strata of shells, and other aqueous deposits; and the same indications of the line of this wall of the City having formed the bed of a river or a moat, were obvious in the excavations made about a year ago on the site of the new house in Newland, belonging to Mr Dickinson; and likewise across the piece of ground on which the Independent Chapel has been erected; and, in the latter instance, the foundations of the old wall were cut through.

The wall in question is generally esteemed to have been the south boundary of the Roman Lindum; its construction, however, was not of the same character which other Roman remains in this City display. This may perhaps be accounted for by the repairs it has undergone at various periods in the interval that has elapsed since its first construction. How high the wall was originally, or how finished at the top, no evidence remained to show; but in some of the parts that

[1] F. H. Tomes in *Lincolnshire Magazine*, II (1934–6), p. 195. Mr W. G. Watkins has suggested that the original course of the river is that taken by Sincil Dyke, and that the channel from Brayford to Stamp End lock was cut by the Romans.

have lately been exposed, the vestiges existed for at least fifteen feet in height above the soil on the south side; though, as in all similar walls, the ground within the enclosed City was several feet higher than on the outside: thus making the attack of a hostile party more difficult, while the defence of the place became more easy. The difference in the level of the soil on the north and south sides, or within and without the wall, is clearly traceable from the Falcon Inn on the east, to the full extent of the wall on the west, as far as its intersection with the west wall of the City in the garden in Newland belonging to Mr Hewson, and opposite to his house.[1]

In the rebuilding of the Falcon Hotel in Saltergate in 1937 the foundations of the wall were found again, slightly to the north of the line of the Stonebow. Steps up to a few older houses along this line (as in Newland between Mint Street and Park Street) still indicate that the ground level within the walls had risen in the course of the centuries.

The lateral walls of the lower Roman city are not difficult to trace. On the west the ditch can be seen between the Park and Orchard Street, and higher up the hill to the west of Motherby Hill. On the east a piece of the Roman wall still divides the Bishop's Palace grounds, within the walled city, from Vicars' Court without; and there is a fragment of the wall in the Girls' High School garden and a section of the ditch in Temple Gardens (the grounds of the Usher Art Gallery). Farther south the wall passed down the west side of Broadgate, which is itself the ditch, and indeed served as such until it was levelled in a more sanitary age.

To turn to the later history of the Roman walls. The gates of the upper city survived into modern times. Stukeley, writing in 1724, hailed Newport Arch as 'the noblest remnant of this sort in Brittan that I know'. In 1825 a subscription was raised and the arch was preserved and a foot-road made through the postern.[2] The south gate of the upper city, said Stukeley, had been pulled down about fifteen years earlier by Mr Houghton the gaoler, and years later he noted in his diary that the huge stones of the piers had been pulled down by 1745. He also recorded that the west gate had been pulled down not beyond memory;[3] but here he must be referring to the medieval west gate erected after the street called Westgate had been pushed northwards by the castle works, the Roman west gate being buried there-

[1] W. A. Nicholson, 'The Advantage of Recording the Discovery of Local Antiquities' in *A Selection of Papers relative to the County of Lincoln read before the Lincolnshire Topographical Society* (1841, 1842), pp. 89, 90. This seems to have been the only volume published by the Society.

[2] A copy of the appeal is preserved in the Bromhead Collection in the possession of Captain W. A. Cragg. St Paul's parish was required to lower the level of the ground to the south of the arch: hence the fall in the level of East Bight (*ex inf.* Rev. E. R. Milton).

[3] Stukeley, *Itinerarium Curiosum* (1724), pp. 83, 84; *Diaries and Letters* (Surtees Society), II, 317.

under and rediscovered after Stukeley's time. The eastern Roman gateway stood slightly to the north of the present Eastgate: Lord Burlington cleared it of rubbish in 1730. According to Sir Henry Englefield it stood until about 1760;[1] the *Lincoln Date Book*[2] says it was removed in 1764.

This eastern arch was taken down by Sir Cecil Wray, who lived near by. Wray, who is now remembered chiefly as the opponent of Charles Fox in the famous Westminster election of 1784, apparently also had designs on the Newport Arch, for in 1774 Thomas Scrope of Coleby wrote:

> Sir Cecil Wray, the Solomon of these parts, I much fear is doing all he can to pull down the finest Roman antiquity in the Island, a Roman Arch belonging to the old Roman Station Lindum, near Lincoln, and all this to break apieces to mend the turnpike roads. If he carries his point, I'll hand him down to posterity with Attila, Alaric &c in a strong English or Latin inscription on some building at Coleby, on the old Roman road straight from Sandwich across the Humber through my Lordship.[3]

Happily Scrope's sound views prevailed.

Practically nothing is known about Roman gateways in the lower city. It is uncertain whether the immediate predecessor of the present Stonebow, an arch which (like the present one) had over it the Guildhall, and which was pulled down some time before 1390,[4] was the Roman gateway, but it seems doubtful. There is no direct evidence of other Roman gates in the lower Roman city, though finds suggest a road from east to west about the level of West Parade and Monks Road.[5]

It is clear, however, that the Roman walls of both upper and lower enclosures fixed the lines and provided the core of the medieval walls, and that the greater part of them survived into modern times. That careful antiquary John Ross, writing about 1850, said that part of the Werkdyke (the name of the eastern ditch) was still recognisable, and that fragments of the east wall were removed within the memory of persons then living. It was probable, he thought, that the whole wall, except what was removed for cathedral or castle, was nearly entire until a recent period.[6]

Where so much survived into recent times still more must have existed throughout the Middle Ages, before the destruction wrought by Cavalier and Roundhead, and the depredations of turnpike trustees. It is a striking

[1] *Archaeologia*, VI (1782), p. 379. Ross MSS. I, 29. Ross says that the south gate was taken down in 1710.

[2] A local chronicle compiled from a variety of sources by R. E. Leary, a Lincoln printer who brought it down to 1866.

[3] Gibbons, *Notes on the Visitation of Lincolnshire*, 1634 (1898), p. 138. And see *Lincoln Date Book*, sub anno 1778.

[4] *C.C.R.* 1389–92, p. 135.

[5] Baker, *Roman Lincoln*, p. 21.

[6] Ross MSS. I, 33, 35.

fact that the boundaries of the Bail (including the castle) defined in 1390[1] are exactly the boundaries of the upper Roman city. Whatever the state of repair of the wall may have been at the Norman Conquest, the strongest and most easily defensible part of the city was detached from the remainder and annexed to the castle as an outer bailey. It was and is still called the Bail, its main street being in these times called Bailgate. Its inhabitants lived under the jurisdiction of the constables of the castle, and its leet jury continued to meet until 1861.[2] The Bail and Close together formed a petty sessional division of Lindsey, being outside the city and the county of the city altogether. The Reform Bill of 1832 brought the Bail and Close into the parliamentary constituency of Lincoln, and the Municipal Corporations Act of 1835 brought them into the municipality also. In the main the parish boundaries conform to the old walls, that part of the Minster within the upper Roman city being in the parish of St Mary Magdalene, and the east end, built astride and beyond the wall and ditch, being in the parish of St Margaret.

Whilst the upper Roman enclosure became the Bail, the lower Roman enclosure became the medieval city proper. The important settlement of Wigford, south of the river, and the settlements on the hillside to the east and west of the city were regarded as suburbs throughout the Middle Ages: they were in the liberty of the city, but not in the city itself. When Domesday Book speaks of land in the city or near the city or outside the city it defines the situation of the land with reference to the Roman walls. Some of the old parish boundaries are lost owing to the union of parishes in the sixteenth century and earlier, but medieval charters show which parishes were formed within and which without the walls. The men of Wigford, outside the city and across the river, never acquired rights of common in the city fields: they had instead to intercommon with the men of Canwick upon the Canwick fields and the waste now represented by the South Common.

Continuous occupation of the city since the English settlement has made systematic excavation impossible, but though the archaeologist may regret that continued human occupation of the site limits his opportunities, the historian and the student of town planning cannot fail to be excited by the interest and importance of the walls bequeathed by the Roman *colonia* to the medieval city.

The walls are not the only Roman legacy: there are also roads and canals. The Ermine Street comes north from London, skirts the fenland, climbs

[1] *C.P.R.* 1388–92, p. 220.

[2] The leet jury minutes in the possession of Major G. R. Sills, Steward of the Bail, end at this date.

the Lincoln Edge south of Ancaster, and travels along the higher land until it reaches the Witham Gap. It then continues north along the ridge to the Humber which was crossed by ferry, and from the north bank of the Humber to York. Four miles north of Lincoln another road, known as Tillbridge Lane, leaves the northbound road, goes north-west to the Trent, which it used to cross by a stone-built ford at Littleborough, making thence a wide circuit through Doncaster, Castleford, and Tadcaster, in order to avoid the marshes of Thorne and Hatfield, to York. The direct road was, however, the original road to York, as is proved by the early Roman settlement at Brough on the north bank of the Humber.[1] The Fosse Way, 'the one great Roman road which does not lead to London', follows a course from Exeter through Bath, Cirencester and Leicester to Lincoln, where it meets the Ermine Street. Unlike the Ermine Street, the Fosse Way seems to have been mainly a strategic road, and it may have served for a time as a frontier south of the Trent and Severn.[2] It is a notable fact in the history of the city that these two roads belonged to a group of four which enjoyed special eminence in later times. 'Late in the eleventh century', says Professor Stenton, 'there emerges a tradition of four great roads, Watling Street, Ermine Street, the Fosse Way and the Icknield Way, on each of which travellers enjoyed the king's special peace. The tradition is interesting, for it suggests that from a time which was already remote in the eleventh century, these roads had formed continuous lines of travel.'[3]

The part of the combined Ermine Street and Fosse Way which crosses the Witham Gap, and is now St Catherine's, High Street, the Strait and Steep Hill, is of especial interest. Clearly the Romans had to raise a causeway across the valley to protect their roads from flood-waters, and there is evidence of more than one attempt to span the valley, as the following record indicates:

> In the autumn of 1847, when a sewer was constructed for the station of the Great Northern Railway, the works being carried under the High Street, a good opportunity occurred for examining the structure of the Roman road. The depth to which the excavation was carried was about 9 feet below the present [1860] surface. The upper portion of 4 feet consisted of the paving of the street with a substratum of rubbish, below which lay a regular road paved with blocks

[1] Corder and Romans, *Excavations at the Roman Town at Brough Petuaria*, 1933–7.

[2] *Historical Geography of England before* 1800 (ed. Darby, 1936), pp. 34, 80. Collingwood, *Archaeology of Roman Britain* (1930), p. 66. The discovery of a Claudian fort at Margidunum between Bingham corner and East Stoke confirms this view.

[3] 'The Road System of Medieval England' in *Economic History Review*, VII, 3. Another Roman road left Lincoln to the north-east, and curved round the northern end of the fen to Burgh le Marsh, near which contact was probably made by ferry with the Norfolk coast.

of stone, about 6 inches thick, and 5 or 6 inches square. Under this pavement was a mass of concrete 2½ feet thick, so hard that much labour was required in breaking through it. Beneath lay a bed of gravel, etc., about one foot thick, and under this was found to be another ancient road, having exactly the appearance, as the surface was partly laid bare, of a well-worn Macadamised road, the stones broken small, and with traces of ruts. This way could be traced for a width of about 4 feet, occupying nearly the centre of the present street, as it lay also under the centre of the Roman road, which had been found 4 feet above it. Its thickness was 8 or 9 inches: it rested on a bed of peaty matter containing drift wood and a few bones of cattle; some beds of sand and clay appeared about 1½ feet below it. No relics or pottery were found in these excavations.[1]

A Lincoln surveyor, Mr J. S. Padley, recorded that on the construction of sewerage works about 1879, the raised causeway on which High Street was built was found to be 13 ft. high upon a layer of sand 20 ft. deep. He added:

Undoubtedly the ground on which the street stands was originally on the same level as the land on both sides, viz.: Boultham on the west and Canwick on the east; most probably this was first raised by those great road-makers—the Romans—in fact, on digging out the foundations of a house at the corner of Alfred Street in St Peter-at-Gowts Parish, a few years ago, a stone yard, full of slabs and great stones, up to five feet in height, evidently intended for this purpose, was discovered.[2]

What the common level of the valley was is illustrated by the survival to the west of High Street of the Brayford pool, which in the Middle Ages reached as far south as St Peter at Gowts parish, and to the south-west of it the Swanpool; and place-names such as the Holmes, Spike Island, Hartsholme, recall that there was a chain of pools stretching towards the Trent. In times of flood these pools united to form one vast mere, and many pictures exist that show the Minster from the south-west with Boultham parish under water in the foreground. When in 1795 the Trent bank broke at Spalford, and the flood-water found its way to Lincoln, the High Street, being then more than 10 ft. above the level of the adjoining

[1] Note by P. N. Brockedon in *Arch. Journ.* XVII (1860), p. 21.

[2] Padley, *Fens and Floods of Mid-Lincolnshire* (1882), p. 11. 'In excavating at Lincoln for the purpose of laying the pipes for the city water company, the workmen at the south toll-gate unbared the stone pavement of the old Herman road. All the way up to the High Bridge, the hard pavement which lies about two feet below the present surface had to be cut through. The stones were pretty large, and were cemented together so as to form a compact and even surfaced road. In passing by the Corn Hall, a long wheel rut to the extent of 200 yards was bared. It would thus appear that the colonised Romans carried out here the same plan of narrow streets which only one vehicle at a time could pass in, as it is found at Pompeii. The rut showed that the vehicles used were narrow-wheeled, and in some places the depth worn in the stone was greater than in others, the stone not being uniformly hard.' August 1847. Justin Simpson, *Obituary and Records for the Counties of Lincoln, Rutland and Northampton* (1800–60), p. 371. The south toll-gate stood on or near the site of Bargate.

lands, dammed the flood, keeping it above Lincoln, with the result that the water spread over 20,000 acres of lowland.[1]

The land east of High Street beyond the Sincil Dyke (to be mentioned later) was not fit for building until the middle years of the nineteenth century. Then, under the Witham Act of 1812 the Sincil Dyke, which had joined the Witham at Stamp End lock, was carried down to Bardney, and the river level was lowered by the amount of the fall of two locks. The drainage of the low-lying areas was thus made possible; and soon afterwards the road from Broadgate was carried over an iron bridge (built in 1858) to join with the new line Melville Street—Pelham Street—Canwick Road.

The condition of the valley until recent times explains the lack of outlets from Lincoln to the east and west. Eastwards there was no road between that to Greetwell above the hill, and that to Washingborough near the South Common; and westwards no road between Newark Road (the Fosse Way) and Carholme Road, to the north of the Fossdyke.

As it crosses the valley, the High Street is flanked by the river to the west and Sincil Dyke to the east. The dyke leaves the river in the southern part of the gap; it flows eastward under the High Street, and turns north, running parallel with the street. The course of the dyke has been altered, but it used to turn eastward at a sharp angle, and after running parallel with the river for a short distance, join the river at Stamp End. Two channels, the Great and Little Gowts, run from the Witham to the dyke under the High Street.

The necessity of a raised causeway across the valley to carry the Ermine Street suggests that the river was embanked and the Sincil Dyke cut in order to protect the street and the adjacent land from flooding. There is evidence that this adjacent land was drained in the Roman period in the remains of an extensive Roman cemetery along the roadside, and in the tessellated pavements of a villa near Monson Street.[2] Though there is no positive evidence of the Roman origin of Sincil Dyke, it is difficult to see how the street and the adjoining land could have been protected from flooding without such a catch-water drain, and it is also difficult to imagine who but the Romans could have made it. There is little doubt that it existed before the Norman Conquest. As a drainage operation it was a small matter compared with others to which reference must be made.

Until within living memory Lincoln remained a long, narrow, essentially one-street town. It was not until the recent industrial expansion that the

[1] Padley, op. cit. p. 4. The flood mark was nearly 10 ft. above the level of the land.

[2] The site of the villa was described as being 'slightly elevated'. *Lincoln, Rutland and Stamford Mercury*, 23 January 1846.

city began to spread east and west. The explanation of its earlier shape is to be found in the Ermine Street. Ribbon-building is not the invention of the modern speculative builder. It is easier and cheaper to build along an existing road than to go to the trouble and expense of making a new, and probably less convenient and less important one. Many villages straggle for long distances along an old 'street'; and legislative resource has not yet devised a satisfactory remedy for what has now become a social problem and a blot on the countryside. In medieval Lincoln there was the added reason for building along the road across the valley, that the river and the Sincil Dyke provided some protection against flooding and attack.

Apart from the Sincil Dyke there were two waterways of probably Roman origin which have benefited Lincoln. One was the Cardyke. This was about 56 miles in length, and ran from the Witham to the east of Washingborough to the Nene at Peterborough. It must be acknowledged that there is no positive proof of its Roman origin, but the evidence points to that conclusion. There is some difference of opinion whether the cut was made primarily for purposes of navigation or for purposes of drainage: Stukeley thought that the Romans made it as a means of carrying corn, and Mr Phillips is inclined to agree with him. But whatever its primary purpose, it is clear that winding as it does under the eastern side of the high land, catching the upland waters and preventing them from flooding the fens, it is well adapted for the purpose of a catch-water drain.[1] Rennie, the famous engineer, wrote of it in the course of his work in the fens, that 'a more judicious and well-laid out work I have never seen...to the bad condition of this drain much of the injury done by the floods to the first district of the North Level is to be attributed'.[2]

The other waterway, and from the point of view of the economic history of Lincoln the greatest of the works attributed to the Romans, is the Foss-dyke, a canal which unites Brayford pool at Lincoln to the Trent at Torksey. The cutting of this channel would present no great difficulties. It passes through low-lying land liable to flooding: and for the first four miles of its 11-mile course from Lincoln the engineers were able to use and

[1] The lawyer Callis thought otherwise. He calls it 'an old forlorn Dike', 'more ancient than profitable', because it ran across the ordinary currents of water from east to west. *Reading on Sewers* (1st ed. 1647), pp. 58–9.

[2] Smiles, *Lives of the Engineers* (1861), I, 20 n. Phillips, op. cit. pp. 119–22. For the Cardyke generally, see Trollope, *Sleaford and the Wapentakes of Flaxwell and Aswardhurn* (1872), pp. 64 et seq. Colonel King-Fane has reviewed the evidence of its origin in *Lincs N. & Q.* XXI, 89–96. Skertchley, *Geology of the Fenland* (*Memoirs of the Geological Survey*) (1877), p. 6, regards the Cardyke as a catch-water drain. It was used as a canal until the advent of railways. In 1789 a boat with a cargo of coal was burnt at Timberland wharf. *Lincoln, Rutland and Stamford Mercury*, 13 November 1789. It had doubtless come from Sleaford by way of the river Slea and the Cardyke.

perhaps to straighten the bed of the Witham's tributary river the Till, which now runs into the canal.

There are several pieces of evidence of the Roman origin of the Fossdyke. A bronze statuette of Mars (now in the British Museum) was found in its channel before 1774,[1] and a sepulchral tablet with an inscription has been found on the side of the dyke towards Saxilby;[2] and recent excavation at Little London, at the junction of the Fossdyke with the Trent, has unearthed Roman pottery kilns.[3]

The fact that the Fossdyke forms the boundary of Lindsey and Kesteven for nearly four miles from Lincoln is consistent with the theory of an early origin of the canal,[4] though it has to be remembered that this is the part of the canal which may represent the original course of the river Till from the point of its present junction with the Fossdyke to Brayford pool. As will be noticed later, the intimate connection between Lincoln and Torksey at the time of the Norman Conquest seems in itself to imply the existence of easy communication between the two places.[5]

The service which the Fossdyke rendered to Lincoln is that it linked the city with the vast system of waterways created by the Trent, the Humber and the Yorkshire Ouse. From the twelfth to the fourteenth century it carried the wool of the midland counties to Lincoln for export to Flanders, and qualified the city to be first a port and then a staple town; in later days it carried corn, wool and malt bound for the West Riding, and brought to Lincoln linseed-cake, bone and rape-manure, coal and manufactured goods: and it was not until the advent of the railways, one of them lying along its southern bank, that it ceased to be Lincoln's chief commercial highway.

[1] This statuette, the 'finest Roman object ever found in Lincolnshire' (Phillips, op. cit. p. 117), is depicted in the *British Museum Guide to the Antiquities of Roman Britain* (1922), p. 90, and in Gough's edition of Camden's *Britannia* (1806 ed.), II, 392, where it is said to have been in the possession of Mr Ellison of Thorne. Ellison took a lease from the Lincoln Corporation of the Fossdyke navigation in 1740, and carried out considerable works for the restoration of the channel.

[2] *Proceedings of Archaeological Institute* (The Lincoln Volume), 1848, p. xxviii. The dyke is wrongly called the Witham.

[3] Oswald, *The Roman Pottery Kilns at Little London, Torksey, Lincs* (1937), p. 13. Phillips, op. cit. p. 117.

[4] This was pointed out by Professor Stenton in 'Lindsey and its Kings' in *Essays in History presented to R. Lane Poole* (1927), p. 148.

[5] Infra, p. 186.

CHAPTER II

THE ENGLISH AND DANISH SETTLEMENTS

COINS provide the only evidence of the date when Lindum was abandoned by the Romans. Taking Britain as a whole, there is a striking contrast between the abundance of fourth-century coins minted down to the year 395, and the rarity of those of late date.[1] The Lincoln coin list as compiled by the Lincoln Museum has these closing entries: Valens (364–78), 40 coins; Gratian (375–83), 18; Theodosius (379–95), 3. Only one coin is recorded of Honorius (393–423), and it was found in Bailgate in the upper Roman city. The list ends there.[2] The coin evidence, however, is not conclusive, for in 395 the western mints of the empire ceased to issue copper, and the coins of the period might therefore continue in circulation longer than usual.

There are several hints that the Roman occupation came to a violent end and that Lindum was burnt. When a Roman colonnade was found in Bailgate, the stone was seen to be reddened, like the postern of Newport Arch; and lumps of molten lead and pieces of charred wood found among the debris point to the same conclusion.[3] Similarly a tessellated pavement was found in the castle covered with a layer of cinders;[4] and the bronze leg of a horse, thought to be part of an equestrian statue, found in Lincoln, was bespattered with molten metal.[5] Perhaps it was because of this destruction that the symmetrical lines of the Roman roads in the upper city began to be lost: Bailgate follows a wavy course, and Eastgate has drifted southwards at its western end. The deflection of Westgate is no doubt due to the making of the castle.

Whether the site of the city was ever completely deserted it is impossible to say. The Anglian invaders probably first settled in open country in order to follow their agricultural pursuits, and only gradually reoccupied the site. It has been noted already that they took over and adapted the Roman name of *Lindum*, through the British *Lindocolina* to the Anglo-Saxon Lindcylene;[6] clearly the British inhabitants of the district were not exterminated.

[1] Collingwood and Myres, *Roman Britain and the English Settlements* (1936), p. 295.

[2] List kindly supplied by Mr F. T. Baker, Curator of Lincoln Museum.

[3] Venables in *Arch. Journ.* XLIX (1892), p. 134.

[4] *Lincs N. & Q.* I, 161.

[5] I. A. Richmond, 'Three Fragments of Roman Official Statues' in *Antiquaries Journal*, XXIV (1944), pp. 5–7.

[6] Supra, p. 3.

There are two sources of information concerning the Anglian invasion: archaeology and place-names. Mr C. W. Phillips has assembled the evidence of Anglo-Saxon finds of the pagan period in Lincolnshire, and concludes that

> three features of the map are striking, first the close association of most of the known cemeteries with the lines of Roman communication, and especially those consisting of urns with cremations; second, plain signs of the occupation of the Wolds after a very long period of apparent neglect; third, the use once more made of the valley of the Slea as in the Bronze Age.[1]

The study of place-names has led to the conclusion that names ending in *-ingham* can be attributed to the early part of the sixth century. When the Lincolnshire examples are plotted on the map it appears that they conform to the general conclusions of Mr Phillips. To them can be added the three archaic names *Barlings*, (*Holton*) *Beckering* and *Minting*, which all occur within a radius of four miles a little distance to the east of Lincoln, and all near to the Roman road from Lincoln to Horncastle.[2]

The evidence of some other districts points to the use of rivers by the invaders, and in Lincolnshire two tributaries of the Witham, the Slea, leading to Ancaster, and the Bain, leading to the south Lincolnshire Wolds, may have been used. Settlement by way of the Trent and the Humber may be doubted. As to the river Ancholme,

> it has been plausibly argued that the pattern of the existing parish boundaries in north Lincolnshire indicates a progressive extension of the riverside settlement up these tributary streams, giving way southwards, as the rivers ceased to be conveniently navigable, to the series of villages whose lands are carefully aligned upon both sides of the Roman road from the Humber to Lincoln.[3]

Similarly the Roman Ermine Street, south of Lincoln, serves as a parish boundary for some distance. These parish boundaries have, however, also been used to support an argument for Roman land settlement, and there are so many later people who could have drawn their boundaries in straight lines that any theory based on these boundaries alone is unconvincing.

Occupation by way of waterways or Roman roads naturally points to settlement in Lincoln, but for the city the evidence of early settlement is almost non-existent. It has until lately been recorded that an Anglo-Saxon urn in the Lincoln Museum was found in Eastgate, Lincoln, about 1850. It came from the collection of Captain Arthur Trollope, who lived

[1] 'Present State of Archaeology in Lincolnshire' in *Arch. Journ.* XCI (1934), p. 138.

[2] Stenton, *Anglo-Saxon England* (1943), pp. 48–9. And see Ekwall, *Place-Names in -Ing* (Lund, 1923).

[3] Collingwood and Myres, op. cit. p. 414, quoting W. Page in *Antiquity*, I (1927), pp. 454–61.

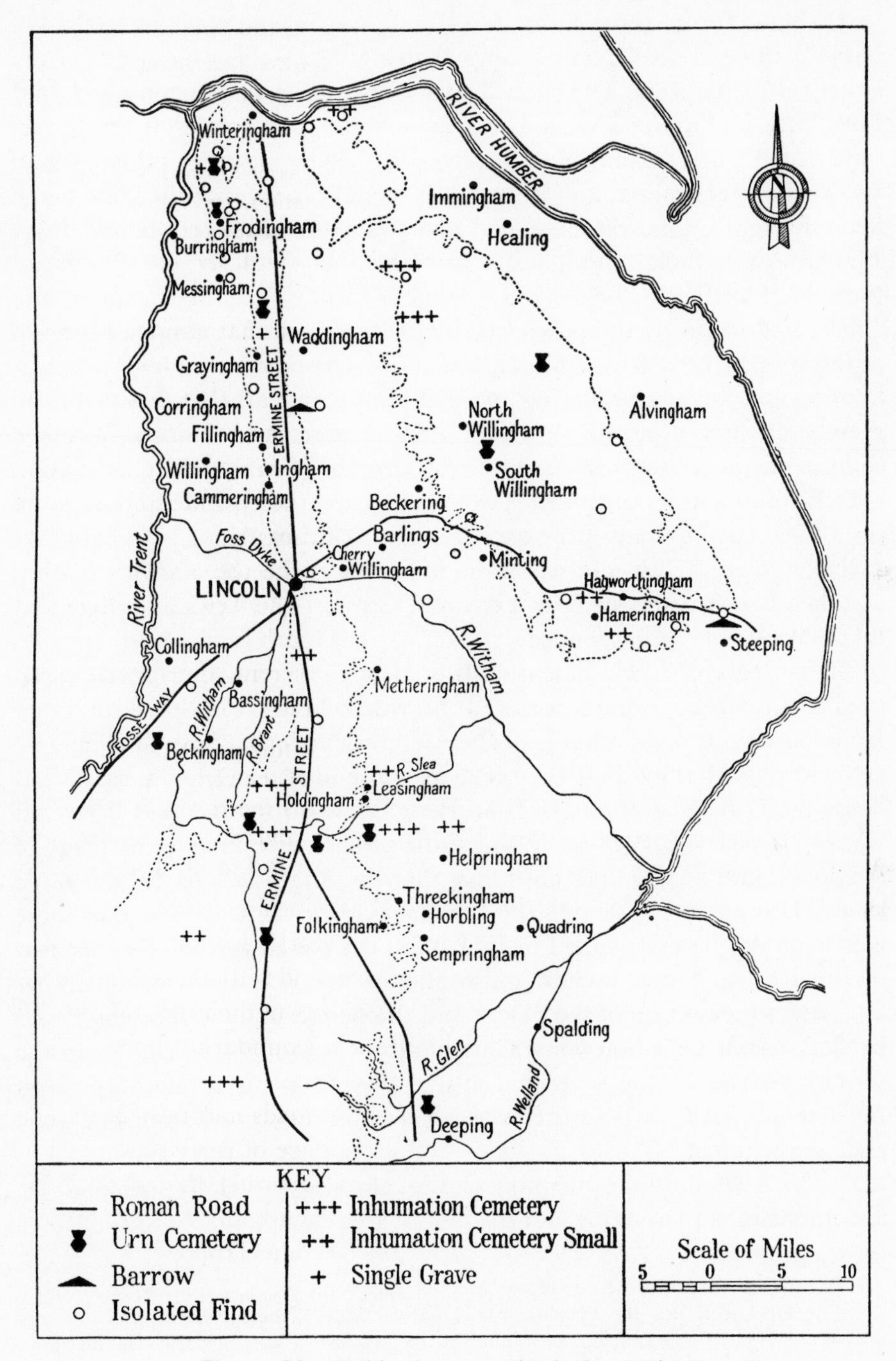

Fig. 2. Lincolnshire in pagan Anglo-Saxon times.

at Eastgate House (now Eastgate Court); this house stands immediately without the eastern Roman gateway astride the ditch to the north of the street called Eastgate. The central part of the house, now demolished, had been built by Sir Cecil Wray.[1] It is now found, however, that the provenance of the urn was incorrectly recorded. There were two other urns in the Trollope collection, and it was once thought likely that they also came from Eastgate. One of them has now been identified as coming from Elmham in Norfolk,[2] and it seems probable that the other was also found there. A fourth urn, bearing the label 'Lincoln', has been sent to the Lincoln Museum by the public-spirited action of the Dorchester Museum authorities. Where it was found, and how it reached Dorchester, is unknown, and when considering the evidence of the label it has to be remembered that 'Lincoln' may and often does refer to the county rather than to the city. Another Anglo-Saxon urn has been found in association with Roman pottery at the Roman villa at Greetwell, a mile to the east of the upper city.[3] At any time excavation may bring evidence to light: an early cemetery at Lincoln would be in keeping with the known situation at other Roman sites such as York and Caistor by Norwich. Judgement must meanwhile be suspended.

The absence of Anglo-Saxon finds in Lincoln or any other town can be used to support opposing theories. It may be held to mean that a surviving Romano-British population kept the English invaders at bay; or it may be thought only to show that the invaders chose to stay outside, perhaps because they preferred the open country or because the town had been laid waste. To each theory must be added the proviso that the non-discovery of Anglo-Saxon remains does not prove that the Anglo-Saxons did not settle there. Disappointing though the Lincoln evidence is, it is clear that there was some Anglian settlement in Lincoln in the pagan period. The survival of the Roman name in new guise and of the Roman defences argues against long desertion of the place; and the period of uncertainty is closed by Bede's statement that when Christianity was brought to Lincoln in the second quarter of the seventh century there was an Anglian *praefectus Lindocolinae civitatis*, whose presence implies not only population but some civic government.[4]

At this early date the mention of Lincolnshire is, strictly speaking, an anachronism, for the name and the unit of area do not appear until a later

[1] Supra, p. 8.

[2] This urn is figured in the group on p. 45 of Jacquetta Hawkes, *Early Britain* (1945).

[3] The Greetwell pot fits in with Mr J. N. L. Myres' theory of the possibility of British survival in the Lincoln area followed by peaceful absorption into the kingdom of Lindsey. See Collingwood and Myres, op. cit. pp. 414–15.

[4] Infra, p. 20.

date. The future county was divided into two parts, with the more northerly and better defined of which the city was closely associated. This part was the ancient kingdom of Lindsey, whose boundaries were the same as those of the modern administrative county of that name. The relation between the city and the kingdom is implied by the connection between their names: *Lindsey* is made of a British derivative of *Lindon*, the old name of Lincoln, and the Old English *eg*, an island. Bede mentions that Lindsey is the first province to the south of the Humber, extending to the sea. On the south the fens of the river Witham extended as far inland as Lincoln, separating Lindsey from Holland and Kesteven. West of the city the Fossdyke serves as the boundary for four miles: beyond this,

> the boundary, which now separates Lindsey from Nottinghamshire, passes irregularly over a belt of sandy country, much of which was only reclaimed in the eighteenth century, until it meets the Trent. For the next fifteen miles the Trent itself forms the boundary, which then curves westwards to include the Isle of Axholme within Lindsey. The course actually taken by the boundary as it crosses the Hatfield Moors and the low ground between Trent and Ouse has been determined by slow processes of reclamation. In early times Axholme was a true island, more readily accessible from Lindsey across the broad channel of the Trent than from Deira across a wilderness of flooded moors. Finally, after devious meanderings, the boundary rejoins the Trent by way of the ancient channel of the Don, and so passes to the Humber, the great barrier between the northern and southern English already in the age of Bede. Among all the earliest English kingdoms, only Sussex is surrounded by more definite and formidable barriers than those which enclose Lindsey.

Professor Stenton adds that 'the number and distribution of the archaic Anglian place-names which have survived the flood of Scandinavian immigration into Lindsey prove that the region had been thoroughly settled at a very early date'.[1]

An ancient genealogy of the kings of Lindsey yields a little information about their kingdom. The last of the line was Aldfrith, whom Professor Stenton believes to have been contemporary with Offa of Mercia. He was probably dead before 800, but if he was born about 750, and thirty years are allowed for a generation, the birth of one of the earlier kings, Biscop Beding, could be placed about 660, and that of another, Caedbaed, about 570. The name of Biscop suggests that its bearer was born after the conversion to Christianity. The first element in *Caedbaed* is the British *cad*, meaning 'battle', from which it may be inferred that he was born after the migration to England and after there had been some intercourse between the Britons of Lindsey and their Anglian conquerors. The genealogy goes back seven generations further (which suggests that the dynasty came over with the

[1] 'Lindsey and its Kings' in *Essays...presented to R. Lane Poole* (1927), pp. 148–9.

invaders), until it comes to Woden.[1] There is nothing to show where the kings lived, nor that the first Christian mission converted the royal house or even attempted to do so. The existence of the dynasty would never have been known to scholars but for the survival of lists of the names of the kings.

The kingdom of Lindsey being bounded on the south by the Witham and the Fossdyke, the walled city of Lincoln lay within it, though upon its very edge. The future transpontine suburb of Wigford lay without its bounds in the region which became Kesteven, which, with the future Holland, belonged to the kingdom of Middle Anglia. The early ecclesiastical history of this kingdom connects it with Mercia. Professor Stenton gives several examples of this connection. The Mercian saint Werburh, who was the head of many monasteries, was particularly associated with Hanbury in Staffordshire and Threekingham in Kesteven; Guthlac, the founder of Crowland, belonged to the Mercian royal house; and Headda, bishop of Lichfield, dedicated Guthlac's new church a little before 706.[2]

The recorded history of Lincoln after the English settlement begins with Bede. His *Ecclesiastical History* was completed about 731, and in his references to Lindsey he was helped by Cynebert bishop of Lindsey and Deda abbot of Partney. In a narrative which relates, perhaps, to the year 627, he tells that Paulinus, who came from the church of York, preached to the province of Lindsey, and converted Blaecca, the reeve (*praefectus*) of the city of Lincoln, and his household. In Lincoln Paulinus built a beautiful stone church. This, the first Christian church in Lindsey, in its chief town, with a famous founder, was greatly reverenced; and when, a century later, its roof had fallen, whether by time or the action of heathen Mercian raiders, miraculous cures were said to be wrought there. In it Paulinus consecrated Honorius the fifth archbishop of Canterbury. Bede gives the source of his information:

A certain priest and abbot of the monastery of Partney (*Peartaneu*), a man of singular veracity, whose name was Deda, told me concerning the faith of this province that an old man had informed him that he himself had been baptised at noon-day, by Bishop Paulinus, in the presence of King Edwin, and with him a great multitude of the people, in the river Trent, near the city which in the English tongue is called Tiouulfingacaestir; and he was also wont to describe the person of the same Paulinus, saying that he was tall of stature, stooping somewhat, his hair black, his visage thin, his nose slender and aquiline, his aspect both venerable and

[1] *Essays...presented to R. Lane Poole* (1927), p. 143. The divine descent of the early kings may have been real in the sense that they were descended from priest-kings who were regarded as incarnations of the gods whom they served.

[2] Stenton, *Anglo-Saxon England*, p. 49.

awe-inspiring. He had also with him in the ministry James, the deacon, a man of zeal and great fame in Christ and in the Church, who lived even to our days.[1]

Where was this place of uncouth name at which Deda's informant and a multitude of others were baptised in the presence of Edwin, king of Northumbria, himself a recent convert? The name does not help, but the latest and most convincing suggestion is that the place is Littleborough. The Roman Ermine Street and Tillbridge Lane make it the most accessible point on the Trent to Lincoln, and if the ceremony took place on the Lindsey bank of the river, the spot could be described as near Tiouulfingacaestir, for Littleborough is situate on the Nottinghamshire bank. There was a Roman ford here: Paulinus seems to have had a preference for Roman sites.[2]

Bede's narrative implies that at the time of Paulinus' mission (in spite of the apparent existence of its own dynasty) Lindsey owned the sway of Edwin of Northumbria. In 633, it seems, its overlordship passed to Penda of Mercia, for Oswald of Northumbria recovered it, and almost certainly by war. When Oswald was defeated at Maserfelth in 641, Penda again became overlord until he in turn was overthrown by Oswy at Winwaed in 654. Lindsey must have been recovered by Wulfhere, son of Penda of Mercia, for when he was defeated by Oswy's son Ecgfrith Lindsey was annexed to Northumbria; though in 678 he was defeated by Wulfhere's brother Æthelred, and Lindsey returned again to the overlordship of Mercia.

Whilst Lindsey was under the rule of Ecgfrith of Northumbria, archbishop Theodore of Canterbury divided the vast diocese of Northumbria, and he also formed Lindsey, which had been part of the original diocese of Lichfield, into a separate see in 677. The new see survived the Mercian reconquest which followed immediately, and continued until about 869 when its separate existence was ended by the Danish invasion. Then the sees of Lindsey and Leicester passed, at least in name, under the authority of the bishop seated at Dorchester on Thames.[3]

[1] *Historia Ecclesiastica*, II, 16. The translation is that of Hodgkin, *History of the Anglo-Saxons*, I (1935), p. 278. Wordsworth gives the passage describing Paulinus thus:

> 'Mark him, of shoulders curved, and stature tall,
> Black hair, and vivid eye, and meagre cheek,
> His prominent feature like an eagle's beak:
> A man whose aspect doth at once appal
> And strike with reverence.'

[2] *Place-Names of Nottinghamshire* (English Place-Name Society), pp. 35–6. For the claims of Torksey, see Cole, 'Royal Burgh of Torksey' in *A.A.S.R.* XXVIII (1906), pp. 452–6. Stukeley favoured Torksey; *Diaries and Letters* (Surtees Society), II, 274.

[3] Stenton, op. cit. pp. 134, 432.

Bede gives the following account of the see of Lindsey:

> Eadhed was ordained bishop in the province of Lindsey, which king Egfrid had but newly subdued, having overcome and vanquished Wulfhere; and this was the first bishop of its own which that province had; the second was Ethelwin; the third Edgar; the fourth Cynebert, who is there at present. Before Eadhed, Saxulf was bishop as well of that province as of the Mercians and Midland Angles.[1]

In 685 Eadhed's name and title are given as *Eadhaed* (or *Eadhert*) *Lindissi Episcopus*.[2] Only one piece of evidence has been found bearing upon the question where the bishop of Lindsey had his seat: it would be irony to call it a clue. The signature attributed to Eadulf bishop of Lindsey in the solemn act of the Council of Cloveshoe in 803 is *Eadwulf Syddensis civitatis episcopus*.[3] This strange attestation goes unnoticed by the *Anglo-Saxon Chronicle*, Henry of Huntingdon and Roger Howden, but it spread confusion among a number of post-Conquest historians. As Dr Mansel Sympson says:

> the various forms of the name, Sinacester (Roger of Wendover), Sinacestrensis, Sidnacestrensis (William of Malmesbury), Sidnacestrenses (Camden), and 'in civitate quae vocabatur Siddena' (Florence of Worcester), seem to be later translations, corruptions or adaptations of the original signature 'Syddensis Civitas', and consequently to have little or no independent authority whatever.[4]

The word *civitas* was generally used of places known to have been sites of Roman occupation, though it does not imply any considerable number of inhabitants;[5] the act of 803 so described Worcester and Dunwich as well as London, Winchester, Canterbury and Leicester. The best-known identification of *Syddensis* is that of Edmund Gibson (later bishop successively of Lincoln and London), who suggested Stow in his edition of Camden's *Britannia*, published in 1695.[6] Though it is hardly possible to prove a negative it may be noted that no evidence of Roman settlement has been found at Stow,[7] nor is there any evidence that the place existed until a later date. Caistor is a possibility: the name may have lost a prefix, and the place was certainly a Roman settlement. Professor Hamilton Thompson believes that 'Sidnaceaster' was simply a careless manuscript corruption of 'Lindaceaster' or some allied form of 'Lindum colonia'.[8] Canon Foster was inclined to think that there might have been a continuous tradition

[1] *Historia Ecclesiastica*, IV, 12.
[2] Kemble, *Codex Diplomaticus*, I, 29.
[3] Birch, *Cartularium Saxonicum*, I, 436.
[4] 'Where was Sidnacester?' in *A.A.S.R.* XXVIII (1905), p. 91.
[5] Stenton, op. cit. p. 518.
[6] Col. 480. On the Stow claim, see Appendix III.
[7] A Roman tessellated pavement was found in 1928 at Sturton-by-Stow on Tillbridge Lane.
[8] *Memorials of Lincolnshire* (1911), p. 71 n.

which regarded Lincoln as the true seat of the bishops of Lindsey, though he was careful not to rule out the possibility that excavation might discover an extinct Roman town.[1] It would be dangerous to assume a clerical error in a solemn and formal document, but among all the other possibilities is one that *Syddensis* may have been an alternative name for Lincoln, or a name of a particular part or suburb of it. The problem of *Syddensis* remains unsolved.

The see of Lindsey, with the Saxon institutions of the district, was swept away by the Danish invasion. The *Anglo-Saxon Chronicle* records that in 838 the alderman Herebryht was slain by heathen men, and with him many of the marsh-dwellers; and that in Lindsey and East Anglia and among the Kentish people many men were slain by the army.[2] In 868 the heathen army went from East Anglia across the Humber to York, and no doubt left a trail of devastation behind it; the following year it took up winter quarters at Nottingham, where Burhred, king of the Mercians, aided by the king of the West Saxons, besieged it, though he later came to terms. A year later the Danes went into East Anglia, defeated and slew King Edmund, and destroyed all the monasteries they could reach. Medeshamstede (Peterborough) is specially mentioned, but probably Bardney, Crowland and Ely perished at the same time.[3] In 873 the invaders fixed their winter quarters at Torksey and in the following year drove Burhred of Mercia overseas. The Danes set up Ceolwulf, one of Burhred's thegns, as a puppet king, until a few years later, when the army took half of the Mercian kingdom for division among its members, leaving the other half to Ceolwulf. The region so divided certainly included the medieval shires of Lincoln, Nottingham, Derby and Leicester.[4] About 886 Alfred the Great, who had become the leader of all the Englishmen who were free to give him their allegiance, made terms with the Danish leader Guthrum and his followers in East Anglia: apparently Guthrum's kingdom did not extend north of the Welland, and therefore did not include the army settlements beyond the river.[5]

Each of these Danish armies settled on the land was grouped round a fortified centre or *burh*,

which formed a convenient meeting-place in time of peace, and a defensible post against attack by English or Norwegians. Whatever the origin of these *burhs* may have been, they influenced the whole history of the Danelaw in the following generations, and, with the solitary exception of Stamford, they appear as county towns in the eleventh century. The great campaigns of Edward the Elder turned on the necessity for their reduction, and long after the Danish armies had

[1] *Lincolnshire Magazine*, II (1934–6), p. 229.
[2] (R.S.), I, 118, 119.
[3] Ibid. pp. 132–7.
[4] Stenton, op. cit. pp. 249, 251.
[5] Ibid. pp. 257–8.

accepted English rule the connexion between the army and its *burh* was still maintained....It was this function of the *burh* which explains the remarkable fact that one of the largest and most populous divisions of the whole Danelaw derived its name from the five principal boroughs of Lincoln, Leicester, Stamford, Nottingham and Derby. The common assembly of the Five Boroughs, which in the tenth century gave to the district between Humber and Welland such administrative unity as it possessed, must originally have been a meeting of the 'armies' settled in the country around these five strong places.[1]

The military nature of the Danish settlement made it desirable that the host could be easily collected and quickly moved. 'The chief means of communication were the Roman roads, and it is evidently not due to chance that there seems to be a certain connection between Scandinavian place-names and the Roman roads.'[2] There is no sign of a dense Danish settlement near Lincoln such as there is on the western slopes of the Wolds, east of the river Ancholme, and in the south riding of Lindsey round Horncastle. Danish names appear along the Ermine Street from Stamford to Lincoln near the south of the county, but as the road approaches Lincoln there are fewer. There are Coleby, Boothby and Navenby at a little distance from the city, but nearer to it are the English Harmston and Waddington. On King Street, from Castor by Sleaford to Lincoln, there is a group of Danish names between Bourne and Sleaford, but nearer to Lincoln are the English Blankney, Metheringham, Mere and Branston. On the Ermine Street towards the north, Danish names are scattered on both sides of the road, but nearest to Lincoln is Burton (Old English *burh -tun*), a farm by a *burh*. On or near the city boundary are the English Greetwell, Nettleham, Riseholme, Cherry Willingham, Washingborough, Canwick and Boultham. Even so, however, there is some evidence of Scandinavian settlement close at hand. The two Carltons, north of Burton, are probably settlements of Scandinavian carls. To the west, Skellingthorpe is apparently a Scandinavianised form of the English *Scheldingas*. On this side and near the Trent, Scandinavian settlement is more marked. On the Fossdyke is the Danish Saxilby, the English population having perhaps retired to an adjoining site, now represented by the hamlet of Ingleby, the *by* of the English: a name of no significance save in a district where the English are a minority. Near Saxilby and the Fossdyke are the Scandinavian Kettlethorpe, Broxholme, Bransby, Broadholme, Harby, Whisby, Thorpe and Hartsholme.[3]

[1] Stenton, *Danes in England* (1927), pp. 6, 7. (Reprinted from *Proceedings of the British Academy*, XIII.)

[2] Ekwall in *Introduction to Survey of English Place-Names*, p. 83.

[3] See Ekwall, 'Scandinavian Settlement' in *Historical Geography of England before* 1800 (ed. Darby, 1936), pp. 145–7.

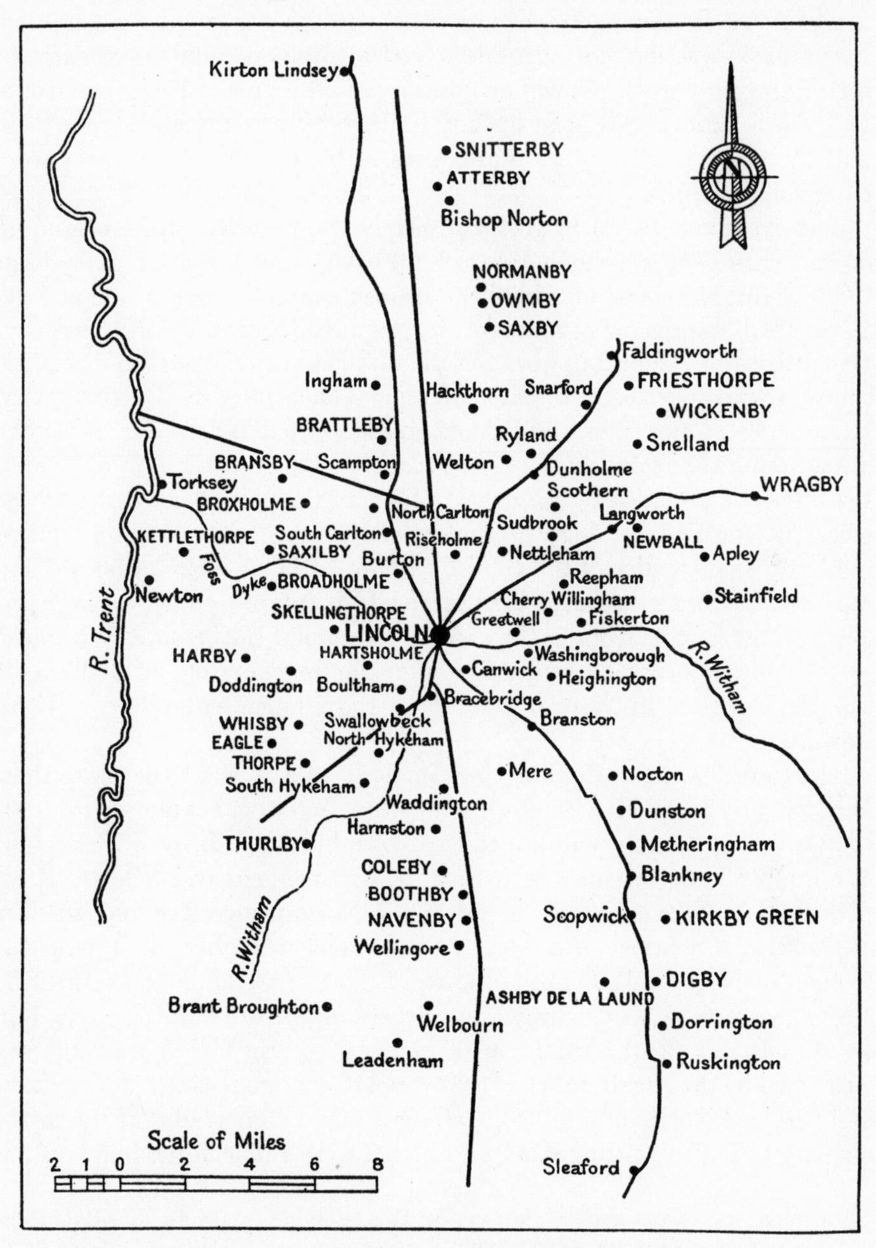

Fig. 3. Place-names in the neighbourhood of Lincoln. Names showing Scandinavian influence are printed in capitals.

The survival of many English names round the city in spite of extensive Scandinavian settlement suggests a considerable population which absorbed its conquerors. As will be noticed presently, many English personal and place-names survived in the city itself. Several centuries were to pass, and there were to be other admixtures of blood, before the races were completely merged.

The struggle between English and Danes was renewed at the beginning of the tenth century, when Edward the Elder and his sister Æthelflæd, Lady of the Mercians, following the Danish example, built a line of *burhs* across their frontier in preparation for an advance into Danish territory. Derby fell to Æthelflæd in 917, and the military region of which it was the centre was annexed to English Mercia. The armies of Northampton, Huntingdon, Cambridge and East Anglia submitted to Edward. A further inroad upon the region of the Five Boroughs was made early in 918 when Leicester was occupied by Æthelflæd. Edward then marched on Stamford, where he fortified the high ground to the south of the Welland, and so induced the surrender of the Danish *burh* to the north of it. After a delay due to Æthelflæd's death Edward received the submission of Nottingham. The surrender of Lincoln is not expressly recorded but its fate is 'implied by the contemporary statement that after the surrender of Nottingham all the people settled in Mercia, Danes and Englishmen, submitted to King Edward'.[1]

The lordship of the English kings in the Danelaw was little more than nominal, and in the Five Boroughs they were content to act mainly through the Danish jarls, who maintained their own customs. In 934, if the date of a doubtful charter may be trusted, a Witenagemot was held by King Æthelstan at Nottingham.[2] Meanwhile, a Norse prince Regnold, the son of Godfrey, a member of a Norse family ruling in Dublin, had gained a footing in Northumbria and conquered York. An alliance of English, Norse and Scots was overthrown by Æthelstan at Brunanburh in 937, but on Æthelstan's death Anlaf son of Godfrey returned to York and was welcomed by the Northumbrians. He seems to have gone south immediately and besieged Northampton, from which it may be inferred that the intermediate *burhs* like Nottingham and Lincoln were either in the hands of his

[1] Stenton, *Anglo-Saxon England*, pp. 323–7. It is tempting to surmise that the superstition which appears in the twelfth century that an evil fate awaited a crowned head that entered Lincoln's walls (see infra, pp. 180, 182) had its origin in the separatism of the Danish *burh* population.

[2] Farrer, *Early Yorkshire Charters*, I, 1–5. It is pleasant to record that in the medieval romance Sir Guy of Warwick fought a great battle with a dragon, cut off its head in spite of its impenetrable scales, and carried the head in triumph to King Æthelstan at Lincoln. Ellis, *Early English Metrical Romances* (1848), p. 218.

people or incapable of resistance. He failed at Northampton, but destroyed Tamworth, and after a general devastation returned to Leicester and met King Edmund and his army. Edmund came to terms with him and left Mercia north of Watling Street (that is to say, the shires of Leicester, Derby, Nottingham and Lincoln) in the hands of a Norse king ruling at York. When Anlaf Godfreyson was succeeded by Anlaf Sihtricsson, Edmund took advantage of the change, overran Mercia, and recovered the Five Boroughs. The story of their recovery is told in the Song of Edmund in the *Anglo-Saxon Chronicle*:

> King Edmund, prince of the English, protector of kinsfolk, beloved doer of deeds, overran Mercia as bounded by Dore, Whitwell Gate and the river Humber, broad ocean stream, the five boroughs, Leicester and Lincoln and Nottingham, likewise Stamford also and Derby. The Danes were before this subject for a long time by force under the Norsemen, in bonds of captivity under the heathen, until, through his valour, the protector of warriors, the son of Edward, King Edmund, redeemed them again.[1]

Whether the poet correctly interpreted the sympathies of the men of the Five Boroughs there is nothing to show. It is clear, however, and significant, that the laws of Edgar (959–75) most scrupulously acknowledge the distinctive customs of the Danish districts within the English custom. After legislating for his English subjects he adds:

> And it is my will that the rights of the laity be maintained among the Danes in accordance with the best constitution which they can determine upon. Among the English, however, the additions which I and my councillors have made to the laws of my ancestors shall be observed, for the benefit of the whole nation.

He acknowledged the loyalty of his Danish subjects:

> Further, it is my will that the Danes continue to observe the best constitution which they can determine upon. I have always granted you such a concession and will continue to do so, as long as my life lasts, because of the loyalty which you have constantly professed to me.

Even when he insists that laws intended to suppress traffic in stolen cattle shall apply alike to Danes and English, he leaves the Danes free to assess their own penalties.[2]

Æthelred II (the 'Unready') (979–1016) does, however, legislate for the Danelaw, though in a different code from that for the English district. The penalty for a breach of the peace is graduated according to the place in which the breach is committed. For a breach of the peace established by the ealdorman or the king's reeve in the court of the Five Boroughs, the penalty is 1,200 of silver; in the court of one borough, 600; and in that of

[1] A. Mawer, 'The Redemption of the Five Boroughs' in *E.H.R.* XXXVIII (1923), p. 551.

[2] 4 Edgar, c. 2*a*, 12, 13. Robertson, *Laws of the Kings of England from Edmund to Henry I* (1925), pp. 33, 37.

a wapentake or country district, 100.[1] The regulation gives an impression of the relative importance of the federal court of the Five Boroughs, that of the individual borough, and that of the ordinary country district. About the turn of the century (the presumed date of this law) the region of the Five Boroughs was still, it seems, undivided into shires, but the *Anglo-Saxon Chronicle* mentions Lincolnshire and Nottinghamshire under 1016.[2] At some date before the Norman Conquest the lands which must once have belonged to the army of Stamford had gone to make the shire of Lincoln its present great size, and the practice of assigning the district known as Rutland to the king's wife in dower had begun the process which in turn created the county of that name: the only one in this region of England which does not take its name from its chief borough.[3]

Under Æthelred nominal English rule in the Danelaw broke down again. The coasts of Northumbria and Lindsey were ravaged by Danes and Norsemen under Olaf Tryggvason, and the only method which Æthelred could devise to obtain relief from the raiders was to buy them off. In 993, after storming Bamburgh, the Danes came to the mouth of the Humber and did great damage on both sides of it. An army was assembled against them, but the three leaders, Fraena, Frithgist and Godwine, fled, apparently because they were of Danish descent. Of these three, Fraena witnessed two charters of Æscwig bishop of Dorchester, which suggests that he belonged to Lindsey; and Godwine may be the Godwine, ealdorman of Lindsey, who died at Ashingdon in 1016, in the fight between Swein's son Cnut and Æthelred's son Edmund Ironside.[4]

In 1013 Swein king of Denmark invaded England, choosing the Humber as his landing place, no doubt because he looked to the Danelaw for a friendly reception. If so, he was not disappointed, for before he left Gainsborough, where he disembarked, he received the submission of the leading men of Northumbria, Lindsey, the Five Boroughs, and Danish England south of the Welland and east of Watling Street. Æthelred fled to Normandy, but, when Swein died in February 1014, returned to England and marched northwards to meet the Danes. As he entered Lindsey, Swein's son Cnut, now in command of the Danes, sailed from the Trent. The men of Lindsey were left to the tender mercies of Æthelred, who ravaged the district ruthlessly.[5]

[1] 3 Æthelred II, c. i. Robertson, op. cit. p. 65.

[2] I, 278–9. See Tait, *Medieval English Borough* (1936), pp. 36, 39 n.

[3] Stenton, *Anglo-Saxon England*, p. 334.

[4] Kemble, *Codex Diplomaticus*, III, 288, 289; Freeman, *Norman Conquest*, I, 283, 637.

[5] Professor Stenton points out (op. cit. p. 381 n.) that the chronicler of Abingdon, in the south of England, remarks uncompromisingly that 'the poor people' of Lindsey were 'betrayed' by Cnut.

The Five Boroughs returned to their English allegiance, and were represented at a gemot held by Æthelred at Oxford in 1015, when Siferth and Morcar, two leading Danish thegns from north of the Welland, were put to death and their estates seized by the king.[1]

Cnut returned to England in 1015 and Æthelred died the following year, leaving his son Edmund Ironside to carry on the struggle with Cnut. After the battle of Ashingdon the parties came to terms, and divided England between them, Cnut taking London and the whole country north of the Thames. When in the same year Edmund died, Cnut became sole king. He died in 1035, and was followed by his sons Harold I (Harefoot) and Harthacnut. When the latter died in 1042, Edward the Confessor was elected king, and he occupied the throne until his death in 1066. The brief reign of Harold II came to an end on the field of Hastings.

This outline of the history of the region which included Lincoln yields little concerning the city itself, but fortunately it can be supplemented from a few other sources. Among these are the coins which were struck there. Perhaps the earliest are a few pennies which bear the name of Alfred and *Lincolla* in monogram, with the name of Heribert the moneyer. These can hardly belong to a regular coinage of Alfred the Great, as he never had authority there, and they are probably imitations struck by the Danes.

There are also a few pennies bearing the names of Lincoln and St Martin, which provoke many interesting questions. On the obverse of these pennies is a sword, a device which suggests a connection with the coins of Sihtric of Northumbria and a date of about 925,[2] or with the coinage of Eric Bloodaxe, one of the Norse kings who ruled in York in the middle years of the tenth century, or with the memorial coinage of St Peter of York.[3] On the reverse is a large open cross enclosing a small plain one: a cross similar in form appears in the inscription over the south door at Kirkdale Church in Yorkshire and on runic monuments in Scandinavia.[4] Only one type of the St Martin penny is recorded in the *British Museum Catalogue of Anglo-*

[1] The *Anglo-Saxon Chronicle* (R.S.), I, 274–5, describes them as the chief thegns belonging to the Seven Boroughs. The phrase certainly includes the Five Boroughs: Professor Stenton (op. cit. p. 383 n.) suggests that York and Torksey were the other two.

[2] See Mr Derek Allen's paper on 'Northumbrian Pennies of the Tenth Century' in *British Numismatic Journal*, XXII (1934–7; 3rd ser. ii), pp. 175 et seq. *Yorkshire Archaeological Journal*, IV, 78.

[3] Brooke, *English Coins* (1932), p. 37. Sir Charles Oman comments (*Coinage of England* (1931), p. 46) that the sword is rather inappropriate to St Martin, who, although a soldier in his youth, was not a martyr like St Peter. He thinks (p. 50) that the coin must be dated before 917, when Lincoln fell into English hands, as it would not have issued autonomous coins after that date.

[4] Baldwin Brown, *Arts in Early England*, I, 357; Hawkins, *Silver Coins of England* (ed. 1887), p. 102.

Saxon Coins,[1] and though there are three known varieties,[2] there is no indication that their issue continued long. It is natural to compare the St Martin penny with the St Peter penny of York and the memorial coinage of St Edmund in East Anglia. Yet there are two important distinctions to be drawn between these two types and the St Martin penny. In the first place there were many more varieties of St Peter and St Edmund; of the latter 68 moneyers are recorded,[3] and of the former 52 varieties.[4] Secondly, both of them commemorate saints who were clearly the patron saints of the places of origin of the coins. St Martin is not known to have been so established in Lincoln: the precedence of St Mary was established beyond question before the Norman Conquest,[5] after which St Martin's Church was secured by the bishop apparently by displacement of a private owner.[6] The facts suggest an attempt to establish a coinage under the patronage of St Martin; if so, the experiment was not successful, and it was not long maintained.

The earliest coins of regular issue bearing the mint name of Lincoln are those of the moneyer Ascman under Edgar. This bearer of an Old English name was not alone, however, for several moneyers who gave their mint town as Lincoln under Edward the Martyr (975–9) were already coining under Edgar. They were the Old English Eanulf and perhaps Old English Adelaver and the Scandinavian Grind. Others under Edward were Grim and Hafgrim (Sc.) and Leofwig (OE.).

Vast numbers of pennies have survived from the reign of Æthelred II. Many were used in payment of danegeld, bribes to the Scandinavian invaders to go away; and hoards of them have been found in Scandinavia and other parts of Europe.[7] Nevertheless, such vast issues of coin could not have been struck unless there was growing wealth in the country, and this points to increasing trade. For Lincoln alone there are 55 moneyers under Æthelred, and for the period from Æthelred to Harold II (979–1066) there are 95, compared with 141 for London, 91 for York, 75 for Winchester, 38 for Norwich, 29 for Oxford. For the other members of the

[1] I, 138. It is always possible that new finds may yield other types. Most of the St Edmund pennies came from the Cuerdale hoard.

[2] See Mr Derek Allen's paper. Maurice Johnson, 'Dissertation on the Mint at Lincoln' in *An Account of the Gentlemen's Society at Spalding* (1784), p. 59, mentions two; Lindsay, *View of the Coinage of the Heptarchy* (1842), p. 71, gives one type with three varieties of legend. Hawkins, op. cit. p. 101, mentions three. The specimen once in the Rashleigh and Grantley collections is now in the writer's possession. Nothing is known about the provenance of the coins.

[3] Brooke, op. cit. p. 32. 1,800 of the pennies were found at Cuerdale.

[4] *British Museum Catalogue of Anglo-Saxon Coins*, I, 239–44.

[5] Infra, pp. 67 et seq.

[6] Infra, p. 142.

[7] The National Collection at Stockholm has the richest collection of coins of the period.

Five Boroughs the numbers are: Stamford, 52; Nottingham, 13; Derby, 13; Leicester, 21.[1]

A like result is given by Mr Stainer's list of varieties recorded in Hildebrand's *Catalogue of the National Collection at Stockholm*; and though, as Dr Salter points out, the number of varieties issued does not of necessity indicate the relative amounts that were issued, yet probably a die was worn out with stamping neither more nor less quickly in one place than another, and when a new die was made, it was a new variety.[2] The varieties for the period from Æthelred II to Edward the Confessor as given by Mr Stainer are: London, 2,517; Lincoln, 1,045; York, 1,020; Winchester, 628; Stamford, 403. Among other mint towns are Norwich with 260 varieties, Oxford with 177, and Cambridge with 174.[3]

As in the reign of Edward the Martyr, so to the end of the period the Lincoln moneyers bear names both English and Scandinavian. The English are slightly the more numerous, and it is noteworthy that whilst under Æthelred the proportions are approximately equal, under the Confessor the English names are twice as numerous as the Scandinavian.[4] The English, who were probably always the greater part of the population of the city, were beginning to absorb their conquerors.

This great establishment of moneyers in Lincoln, approaching half of that for the city of London, and equalling that of York, is evidence of a substantial volume of trade. The commercial community engaged in it had long ceased to be able to live upon the produce of the town fields. It is true that the coinage of Æthelred may in part be due to the payment of bribes to the Danish raiders, but this explanation does not apply to the reign of the Confessor, and it may be noted that in proportion to the length of the two reigns the number of their moneyers in Lincoln is roughly the same.[5] Furthermore, the coins found in Scandinavia have been found

[1] These totals are taken from Brooke, op. cit. pp. 69–78.

[2] H. E. Salter, *Medieval Oxford* (1936), pp. 16–17.

[3] C. L. Stainer, *Oxford Silver Pennies* (1904), p. xi.

[4] Brooke gives the following moneyers for Æthelred II: Ælfsige, Æscman, Æthelbriht, Æthelmaer, Æthelnoth, Boga, Bruntat, Colgrim, Cytlbern, Dreng, Eadmund, Faerman, Faerthen, Garfin, Gife, Godinc, Godwine, Grim, Grind, Iustein, Leofman, Leofric, Leofwig, Leofwine, Lifinc, Mana, Osferth, Osfram, Osgot, Osmund, Othbern, Othgrim, Raeinold, Rafen, Rodberht, Snelinc, Stegenbit, Stegencil, Stircar, Sumerlede, Sunegod, Theodgeld, Theodred, Thurcetel, Thurstan, Ulf, Unbegen, Wulfbeorn, Wulfcetel, Wulfgaet, Wulfgar, Wulfgrim, Wulfmaer, Wulfric, Wulfwine. And for Edward the Confessor: Ælfgaet, Ælfnoth, Ælfwine, Agamund, Auti, Brihtric, Bruninc, Cillin, Colgrim, Eadmund, Eadric, Eadwine, Garfin, Gife, Godric, Leodmaer, Leofwine, Leofwold, Lifinc, Mana, Osferth, Oslac, Othbern, Othgrim, Sumerlede, Swafa, Swartinc, Thurgrim, Ulf, Walraeffen, Wineman, Wulfbeorn, Wulfgar, Wulfric.

[5] Æthelred reigned 37 years and had 55 Lincoln moneyers; Edward 24 years with 34 Lincoln moneyers.

mostly in Eastern Sweden, and on the islands of Oland and Gothland, which is not where the evidence of Viking raiders would be sought.[1] To this evidence can be added the interesting fact that from the reign of Magnus the Good, king of Norway (1035–47) there are coins bearing on the reverse the names of Lincoln and the moneyers Lefwine and Oindi (a form of Odin); they have been found in at least two different hoards deposited about 1050. The reason for the use of these Lincoln reverse stamps in Norway is unknown, but it is evidence of the close association of the city with the Scandinavian countries.[2] There cannot be any doubt that Lincoln was something much more than a fortified *burh* with a rural settlement around it: it was a commercial centre living an urban life.

Such a conclusion prompts the inquiry whether there is any topographical evidence of settlement beyond the walls of the city or of growing population within them. The most satisfactory evidence on the subject comes from Domesday Book, and will be examined later, but meanwhile it is useful to consider the evidence supplied by place-names within the city and environs. In using them it has to be remembered that though it is tempting to compile lists of street and place-names, label them English, Scandinavian or French, and date from them the districts to which they belong, such a method has its dangers. Dr Lindkvist argues that the extent of Danish settlement at York may be determined by the prevalence of Scandinavian names, particularly those ending in *-gate* with the meaning of street. Here Professor Stephenson enters a caveat. He points out that the word *gate*, though originally Danish, unquestionably became good English through a wide region, and is so cited by the *Oxford Dictionary* for so late a period as the sixteenth and seventeenth centuries. He adds that in many towns the usage became so common as not to be entirely primitive, and that in some cases the name proves that the street is a later creation.[3] He might have added a warning against modern imitation.

[1] *Cambridge Medieval History*, III, 333. With them are finds of Oriental coins, many minted at Samarcand and Bagdad, which reached Sweden overland through Russia. Cf. the Stora Sojdeby hoard: Schnittger's analysis in *Fornvännen* (Stockholm (1915), Parts 2 and 4). In this hoard the coins of Æthelred and Cnut are far more numerous than those of the Confessor. The figures for London are: Æthelred, 110; Cnut, 91; Edward, 4. For Lincoln: Æthelred, 34; Cnut, 27; Edward, 6. For York: Æthelred, 28; Cnut, 32; Edward, 4. The small number of Edward's coins in the hoard makes all the more striking the establishment of moneyers in his reign, and it points to an increase in the home trade.

[2] These pieces are in the Royal Collection at the National Museum at Copenhagen. The writer is indebted for this information to Mr Georg Galster, who adds that the Collection has the following coins from Lincoln: Æthelred II, 123; Cnut, 316; Harold I, 37; Harthacnut, 7; Edward the Confessor, 87; Harold II, 0; William I, 3; William II, 1.

[3] Lindkvist, 'A Study of Medieval York' in *Anglia* (1926), pp. 345 et seq. Stephenson, *Borough and Town* (1933), p. 190 n. *Gate* in the sense of 'street' appears as a dialect word in Scott and Burns.

In face of this caution it is well to examine the many Lincoln street names ending in *-gate* with care. A directory of 1842 mentions seventeen such names. Some of them are certainly not old. The small piece of road called Exchequergate, outside the surviving gatehouse of that name, has come to be so called by analogy; it used to be the Chequer. Priorygate for both road and gateway is an obvious fraud, and cannot be older than the attachment of the name of 'the Priory' to an old house to the east of the Minster: a name which was probably first adopted to give romance and dignity to a private school kept there. Langworthgate, being a Roman road, was generally called Langworth street. Michaelgate, its northern end near St Michael's church, looks like a conscious archaism for a street once Parchemingate, and later simply 'the back hill': it may have been suggested by the former Mikelgate, which was farther south. Bailgate cannot be older than the building of the castle, and it probably superseded 'the Bail' only in modern times. Further inquiry may well show that a public body, such as the Lighting and Paving Commissioners, or a road surveyor was tidying up street names in the nineteenth century. Broadgate has not been found before the sixteenth century;[1] formerly it was the king's ditch, the *werkdyke*, which must early have become a roadway.

There remains a large residue of medieval *gates*.[2] There are Eastgate and Westgate, beginning inside the Roman walls, the former extending beyond them. In the fields (or rather where the fields were) are Northgate and Greetwellgate still: there used also to be Nettlehamgate, Kirtongate, Burtongate, Cliffgate, Stowgate, whose names indicate their direction. St Giligate cannot be older than the foundation of St Giles' hospital, probably in the thirteenth century. Among the roads through the fields the Ermine Street (the modern Riseholme Road) enjoyed the greater dignity of a street: it was Humber Street.

Danesgate, which is in the lower city, denotes a settlement of Danes at a time when the Danes were in a minority. Pottergate stretched obliquely on the hillside east of the wall, from the Close as far south (until the easier gradient of Lindum Road was made in 1785) as Clasketgate. This latter street, whose earlier form is *Clachislide*, preserves the Scandinavian name Klakk, and is 'Klakk's door'. Hungate, Hundegate, was the street of the hounds. Saltergate and Flaxengate are survivors of a group of streets named from trades: there once were Baxtergate, the street of the baksters or bakers; Parchemingate, where the makers of parchment lived; and Walkergate, the home of the walkers or dyers. Sastangate or Sextonesgate, in Newport, was perhaps named from the Old English personal name

[1] C.C.M. 1564–99, f. 118b (1580).

[2] For the names that follow see Appendix I and Figure 17.

Seaxstān, and Skolegate records the site of a school, probably the Jewish *scola*. Brancegate probably preserves the Scandinavian personal name of *Brand*. The high street from St Martin's southwards was Mikelgate, the great street, until it narrowed into Briggate, just north of the Stonebow, leading to the High Bridge.

There are a few other Scandinavian place-names. Crackpole, now preserved only in the name of the cathedral prebend of St Mary Crackpole, which was endowed from the former parish church of the same name, is a corruption of *Krakepol*, from the Old Norse *kraka*, a crow or water-crake. It was a pool or creek between the river and the south wall of the city in the region of Newland. Several street names ended in *-stigh*, from the Old English or Old Norse *stig*, a path: Wainwellstigh survives in Winnowsty Lane; St Mary Stigh; Haraldstigh; Lefwinstigh, which can be dated with some probability to the twelfth century; and Hornesty.

Many of the lesser names in the fields are Scandinavian. There are several *holms*, or islands, in the lands near the river which flooded in winter: Carholme (Old Norse *kiarr*, marsh ground), the Holmes, Bager holme, Coltholme (corrupted into Coultham). Several meadows bore the name of *wong*: the Wong, St John's wong, and (in later days) Bagerholm wong. Many enclosures were called from the Old Norse *garth*: Vinegarth (which became Vinegar Lane, now the more elegant James Street), Boungarth, East garths, Hempgarth.

The Old Scandinavian *steinn*, a stone, appears in a few names. Stonebow, or Stanboge, is a stone arch; the church of St Peter which stood at the foot of the modern Michaelgate was St Peter Stanthaket, the stone-thatched church; and the word seems to appear again in the Stamp, the boundary stone, and the Stamp causeway in the Monks Liberty leading to the still familiar Stamp End.

Intermingled with these Scandinavian names is a large number of Old English ones. In the fields are the *leys* or pastures: the long leys, the short leys, the shooting leys, later the Monks leys. Among crofts or fields were Calfcroft, Tentercroft, where the weavers tented their cloth, and St Hugh croft, where St Hugh's fair was held. East Bight and West Bight contain the Old English *byht*, a loop, which suits their curving course.

The Greestone Stairs, for a time the Grecian Stairs, were once the *greesen*, Old English for steps. St Martin in the Dernstall stood in an enclosure, now St Martin's Lane, with a narrow entry from High Street: *Dernstall* seems to derive from the Old English *dierne*, hidden, *steall*, a place. Near the Minster was the stodfald (OE. *stōd*, stud), a fold for horses. At the junction of Great Gowts drain with the Sincil Dyke was Nicarpool, apparently named from the Old English *nicor*, or water monster, once deemed to haunt it.

All these names are further evidence of the mixture of races and tongues, but it is only when the names of the suburbs are examined that any hint is obtained of the periods when the various extramural settlements were made. The most important of them was Wigford, straggling from High Bridge southwards to the later Bargate. Apparently its name comes from the Old English *wic*, an early loan-word from the Latin *vicus*, and means a hamlet or street. This settlement by the ford lay to the east of Brayford whose early form of *Braythford*, associated with *Brademere*, points to the Old English *brād* or Old Norse *breit*, meaning broad: the broad ford, or the ford by the broad mere. The pool was much larger in the Middle Ages than it is now. There were Roman dwellings along the Ermine Street in Wigford: though outside the walls of the city, the suburb was protected by water, and there is evidence of its importance at the time of the Norman Conquest.

East of the lower walled city was another suburb, sometimes wrongly described in modern times as Butterwick. The early form of the name was *Butwerk*, from the Old English *but*, outside (as in 'but and ben') and *weorc*, a defensive work, meaning the settlement outside the wall and ditch. The ditch itself was called the *werkdyke*.

South of Butwerk and the river was Thorngate. It was approached from the city by the street still called Thorngate and the Thornbridge (probably named from the thorn bushes on the river bank). The name suggests that it cannot have been settled earlier than the Danes, and it may belong to the post-Conquest period.

On the hillside to the west of the city was a suburb known by the alternative names of Willingthorpe and Westgate; the latter no doubt because it was approached from above hill by the street of that name. The former name suggests an Old English settlement or *thorpe* of Willa's people. That it was in existence in 1066 is almost certain, because here was the little manor of Bishop Remigius.[1]

The northern suburb of Newport is probably of Norman origin, its French name meaning 'new town'. Beside it may be set Newland, the *nova terra* being recorded in the twelfth century.

Place-names, therefore, give ground for the conclusion that the city had overflowed its walls to the south of the river and on the eastern and western hillsides before 1066; and they throw their own light upon the mixture of races which has been referred to earlier. The names recorded in Appendix I are generally of Old or Middle English character.

[1] See infra, pp. 328–9.

Of course there are exceptions such as the very remarkable Clasketgate; and the use of *gata* for road, like the frequency of names showing *ei* instead of *a* or modern *o*, would even by itself prove that there had been a strong Scandinavian colony in the city. Even so, there is a real contrast between the general character of these names and the markedly Scandinavian colour of the earliest personal names shown on coins and in twelfth-century charters. More precisely, it is remarkable that there are so few clear parallels to the Scandinavian, and indeed the Norwegian, local names which abound in York.[1] The difference illustrates the extraordinary density of the Scandinavian colonisation of York in comparison with any settlement of the kind south of the Humber.[2]

The conclusion that the city had overflowed its walls before 1066 receives some support from a survey of church dedications. These are not very satisfactory as evidence, as the only certain limit of date is the death or the canonisation of the patron saint. Sometimes, however, there is special reason for the later popularity of the saint which suggests a later chronological limit. St Nicholas became popular after 1079, when a church was built at Bari to enshrine his remains; a conclusion which suits the date suggested above for Newport. In Wigford, the church of St Edward the King cannot be earlier than 978, when the king was murdered at Corfe Castle. In Butwerk the juxtaposition of St Bavon, the patron saint of Ghent, and St Rumbold, the patron saint of Malines, suggests Flemish post-Conquest piety; and there was a St Clement, a favourite Danish dedication, in the same suburb, and another in the north-west corner of the upper city. Apart from this intramural St Clement, there are only two churches inside the walls which clearly belong to the period after the Danish invasion. They are St Swithin, whose patron saint was a bishop of Winchester who died in 862; and St Edmund the King (of East Anglia) who was martyred by the Danes in 870. All the others *could* be pre-Danish in origin: a fact which calls for a review of the evidence of the reconversion of the Five Boroughs.

It is scanty. Sir Allen Mawer has pointed out that the *Anglo-Saxon Chronicle* poem on the redemption of the Five Boroughs shows that the Norwegians from York were still considered heathens in 942 when the Danes of the Boroughs were considered Christian.[3] Probably the submission of the Five Boroughs to Edward the Elder about 918 involved some official acceptance of Christianity: and the St Martin penny, which may well belong to the period between these dates, implies conversion. In Lincolnshire, as in the eastern counties, no Viking burials have been found,

[1] See A. H. Smith, *Place-Names of East Riding of Yorkshire and York* (English Place-Name Society), pp. 275–300.

[2] Professor Stenton's comment on the list of place-names in Appendix I.

[3] *E.H.R.* XXXVIII (1923), pp. 551 et seq. Supra, p. 27.

a fact which suggests that the Viking settlements lost their pagan customs rapidly.[1]

Professor Stenton has shown that there is no evidence that the Danes who settled in England were fiercely antagonistic to Christianity, which was not obliterated, though it was imperilled by the lack of clergy, and its estates were lost.[2] There may have been only two generations between the period of Danish settlement and the restoration of Christian forms, and even if the churches of Lincoln were all destroyed or abandoned, memory or tradition may have preserved a record of their sites and dedications. If St Mary and St Peter are of too general an appeal to be of any help in dating churches, the dedications of other churches upon central sites are of some help. A dedication to St Paul without St Peter is rarely found, and is evidence of early date: St Paul in London was founded by Ethelbert of Kent in the first days of Augustine's mission. St Martin at Canterbury was the first church to be founded by that mission in England; St Cuthbert was the great apostle of the north; and St Lawrence may commemorate either the Roman deacon whose relics were sent by the pope to Oswy of Northumbria in 667, or the archbishop of Canterbury who died in 619. There is nothing improbable, therefore, in the supposition that there was some continuity at least of tradition to carry the churches of the city from the age of English rule across the Scandinavian pagan period into the mixed society which accepted Christianity.

But if the religion of the English prevailed the Scandinavian conquerors imposed their own institutions. The evidence of these institutions from the Five Boroughs has been assembled by Sir Allen Mawer.[3] In the first place, instead of the English 'hundred' as the chief division of the county there is found the Danish 'wapentake'; to which it may be added that Lindsey, like Yorkshire, was divided into thrithings or ridings. Secondly, land was assessed by carucates in multiples and submultiples of twelve, as opposed to that by hides arranged on the decimal system.[4] Thirdly, there was the use of the ore of 16*d.*, instead of that of 20*d.*, in Derbyshire, Nottinghamshire and Lincolnshire. And fourthly, there was the use of the Danish 'long' hundred of 120, as when a fine of £8 (120 ores) was imposed for breaking the king's peace. It is clear that Edgar's express authority to the Danes to continue their own customs was no dead letter.

Perhaps the most interesting Danish institution in this region was that

[1] Miss Whitelock finds evidence of wide acceptance of Christianity in the Eastern Danelaw by the end of the ninth century. 'Conversion of the Eastern Danelaw' in *Saga Book*, XII, 175.

[2] *Anglo-Saxon England*, pp. 427–8.

[3] *Cambridge Medieval History*, III, 336.

[4] See also Stenton in *L.D.* pp. xi et seq.

of the lawmen. Generally, when the Vikings established permanent settlements,

hereditary kingship became common and royal houses bore sway in Dublin and other Irish towns: thence a hereditary line of kings was introduced into Northumbria. The rulership of Normandy was hereditary and so possibly was the kingship in East Anglia, but in the districts grouped round the Five Boroughs the organization was of a different kind, the chief authority resting with the Lawmen. We find frequent mention of these Lawmen both in Scandinavia itself and in those countries where Scandinavian influence prevailed. Originally men skilled in the law, who could state and interpret it when required, they often presided in the Thing or popular assembly and represented the local or provincial community as against the king or his officers, though they do not themselves seem to have exercised judicial functions. They are usually mentioned in the plural number and probably acted as a collective body. In England and the Western Isles they attained a position of yet greater importance. In Man and the Hebrides they became actual chieftains and are mentioned side by side with the kings, while it is probable that they were the chief judicial authorities in the aristocratic organisation of the Five Boroughs and other parts of the Danelaw. They were usually twelve in number, and their presence may be definitely traced in Cambridge, Stamford, Lincoln, York and Chester. Their office would seem as a rule to have been hereditary.[1]

The Lincoln lawmen are known only from Domesday Book, where the Domesday clerks describe them as men having sake and soke;[2] the clerks do not refer to their function as a panel of experts in law and custom. Similarly at Stamford the lawmen are said to have sake and soke within their own houses and over their own men, with certain exceptions.[3] There is no later trace of the lawmen in Lincoln, though at Stamford they still existed in 1275, when the Hundred Roll jurors could only say of them that their ancestors were of old time judges in the law holding of the king in chief, for further information referring to Domesday.[4] Perhaps as a bench or panel the lawmen had already dissolved in 1086, and had become simply individual magnates with privileges in common with other magnates and dignified by an hereditary title peculiar to themselves.

The names of this Scandinavian aristocracy in 1066 point to that blending of races which has been noticed earlier. Three of them, Brictric, Godric son of Eddeve, and Leuuine, are certainly English: Aluuold may be either English or Scandinavian; Suartin son of Grimbold had a Frankish father.[5] No doubt they came into office through intermarriage and hereditary succession; Hardecnut was succeeded by his son Suardinc; Sortebrand followed his father Ulf, son of another Sortebrand; Agemund

[1] *Cambridge Medieval History*, III, 333–4; and see Vinogradoff, *English Society in the Eleventh Century* (1908), pp. 5, 6.

[2] Appendix II.

[3] *L.D.* pp. 8, 9.

[4] *R.H.* I, 352, 354.

[5] Stenton in *L.D.* p. xxix.

his father Walraven; Godwin his father Brictric; Buruolt his father Lewin the priest, who had become a monk.

Of several of the pre-Conquest lawmen Domesday shows that they held land outside the city as well as within it. Sortebrand had his father Ulf's carucate in the Lincoln fields. In Burton by Lincoln he succeeded Ednod in three carucates, over which he had sake and soke: he had two teams in demesne and eight villeins and three bordars with a team, and four farmers rendering eight shillings. There were eight acres of meadow. In the time of the Confessor it was worth 21*s*.; in 1086 40*s*. He still held them about 1115.[1] In the adjoining parish of South Carlton he had six oxen in a team, and a man of his had one team, and eight sokemen and six villeins and four bordars with 2½ teams, and 30½ acres of meadow, and 100 acres of meadow in Nottinghamshire. It had been and still was worth 40*s*., and it paid tallage of 40*s*.[2] In Metheringham he had one team in demesne, and two sokemen and ten villeins and four bordars having four teams. There was a church there, and 100 acres of meadow, and eight acres of underwood. It had been and was still worth 40*s*.[3] Although Sortebrand and his father Ulf bore Scandinavian names, the son found favour with the Norman rulers, or at least was not in disfavour, for his holdings in Burton, South Carlton and Metheringham had all been acquired since the Conquest. He also had a claim to 140 acres at Canwick, and the wapentake upheld his claim on the ground that his father Ulf gave one mark of gold, receiving the land as a pledge.[4] This entry suggests that the other lands may have been acquired by purchase or other business operation. A Sortebrand also had land near the Lincolnshire coast in the wapentake of Candleshoe: at Candlesby half a carucate, at Bratoft two bovates, and at Friskney two bovates.[5]

The lawman Walraven was succeeded by his son Agemund. In Middle Carlton Agemund had two carucates and two bovates, being land for 18 oxen. Here he had pledged land to three burgesses of Lincoln, Gudret, Lewin and Siwin, which was later claimed by Gocelin son of Lambert, apparently in right of the mortgagees.[6] In Canwick Walraven had one carucate, being land for six oxen, and another two carucates and 1½ bovates.[7] Agemund held a carucate in Canwick.[8] As Norman Crassus supplanted both Agemund and Walraven, it seems likely that these two lawmen were the landholders of those names in Middle Carlton and Canwick. Godric (son of Eddeve) had two carucates at Burton by Lincoln[9] as well as a

[1] *L.D.* pp. 200 (1), 221 (1), 242.
[2] p. 200 (2).
[3] p. 200 (4).
[4] p. 227 (18).
[5] p. 201 (8, 9, 11).
[6] pp. 150 (1), 221 (3).
[7] pp. 53 (51), 150 (2).
[8] p. 200 (26).
[9] p. 189 (1).

carucate in the Lincoln fields. Of the three burgesses who were lending money on mortgage, Gudret may have been Guret the lawman and Lewin may have been the priest-lawman of that name.

Evidently these magnates had extended their sphere of activity beyond the bounds of the city and its lands. The population of Lincoln must have drawn on the countryside for its supplies, and the leading citizens might well find in the neighbouring manors a profitable means of supplying the market.

Another source of profit to these citizens is indicated by the number of names shared by the lawmen of 1066 and the Lincoln moneyers of Edward the Confessor. There are six names to be found in both lists: Suartin, Ulf, Walraven, Britric, Godric and Lefwine. Guret the lawman may be the same as Gire(t) the moneyer.[1] These similarities are too many to be dismissed as coincidences, and taken together with the foregoing evidence of landholding they point to a group of leading citizens strikingly like that found in the twelfth and thirteenth centuries.[2]

The names of a few other citizens of the pre-Conquest period have survived. Domesday Book has several references to Turgot lag', who held land at Ingleby near Lincoln of Robert de Todeni, and also held the manor of Greatford near Stamford and other lands.[3] In Yorkshire he held other manors of Robert de Todeni, and he also had lands in the counties of Nottingham and Oxford.[4] He has been claimed as a lawman of Lincoln,[5] and may have been so, but the *lag'* seems to be, not *lageman*, but *lagen*, meaning low or short in Old English.[6] Thurgod lagen witnesses the endowment of St Mary of Stow by Earl Leofric and Godgifu, in company with Siferth, Godric, Owine and Siric and the citizens of Lincoln. Godric was probably the lawman of that name, and the others named may all have belonged to the same class.[7] Siferth may have been the Siward the priest who was a lawman in 1066; and he and Siric may have been Siworth and Siric, the brothers of Brand, the post-Conquest abbot of Peterborough. These, with another brother Askil, gave lands in Scotter, Scotton, Northorpe, Riseholme, Messingham, Manton and many other places, including land in Lincoln worth 12*s.* a year, to Peterborough abbey.[8] Askil appears again as a witness to Edward the Confessor's grant of Fiskerton to the

[1] The similarities were pointed out by Andrews, *Numismatic History of the Reign of Henry I*, p. 265. The further comparison he makes between the lawmen of 1086 and the Conqueror's moneyers breaks down on examination.

[2] Infra, Appendix v.

[3] *L.D.* 18/1, 7, 13, 29.

[4] *V.C.H. Yorks*, II, 145–6.

[5] Farrer, *Early Yorkshire Charters*, I, 460.

[6] Tengvik, *Old English Names* (Uppsala, 1938), p. 320.

[7] Robertson, *Anglo-Saxon Charters*, pp. 214, 468; and see infra, pp. 51–2.

[8] Mellows, *Peterborough Chronicle of Hugh Candidus* (1941), p. 35.

abbot of Peterborough, in a charter whose witnesses include Queen Edith, Archbishop Stigand, Wulfwig bishop of Lincoln, the Dukes Harold and Tostig, Merleswein, perhaps then sheriff of Lincoln, Ulf of Lincoln, and Askyl Tokes son.[1] Wigod of Lincoln witnessed Edward's charter to Ramsey abbey, which confirms Johol of Lincoln's gift of Quarrington near Sleaford to that house.[2]

Besides these local magnates, some of the greatest men in the realm had houses in Lincoln.[3] The Earl Harold who had a messuage with sake and soke was certainly King Harold, who fell at Hastings, and whose title to the throne was not acknowledged by William the Conqueror. Earl Morcar also had a house with sake and soke: he was the son of Ælfgar and the grandson of Leofric, both earls of Mercia, and he became earl of Northumbria after the rising of the Northumbrians against Tostig, Harold's brother, who had been imposed upon them as earl. He had considerable holdings in Lincolnshire, including the third penny of all customs in Torksey.[4] It is curious that his brother Edwin, who was earl of Mercia, is returned in Domesday as owner of only one Lincolnshire estate, at Kirton in Lindsey. Merleswein, once a sheriff of the county, was a great landowner not only in Yorkshire and Lincolnshire but also in Devon and Somerset: he had a messuage in Lincoln quit of all custom. The Ulf who had a house in Lincoln was Ulf of Funen (*Fenisc*), one of the greatest landowners in the Danelaw, with estates in the counties of Lincoln, Nottingham, Derby, Huntingdon and Cambridge. His chief Lincolnshire estate was at Folkingham, where his manor extended into twenty-seven villages. Stori, who had a house in Lincoln, was lord of Belchford and Bolingbroke and Hough on the Hill. Within a few years all these great men had disappeared and their estates had gone as spoils to the Norman victors. The smaller men, the ordinary citizens of Lincoln, were not to fare so badly.

[1] Thorpe, *Diplomatarium Anglicum Ævi Saxonici*, pp. 386–7.

[2] Ibid. p. 385. *Cartularium Monasterii de Rameseia* (R.S.), II, 74, 78; III, 167.

[3] See *L.D.* index.

[4] For a possible connection of Earl Morcar with the church of St Peter of Lincoln, see infra, p. 130.

CHAPTER III

THE NORMAN CONQUEST

In the stormy last years of the Old English state the great earls died in succession. Earl Godwin of Wessex died in 1053, and was succeeded by his son Harold. When Siward of Northumbria died in 1055 his son Waltheof, probably a child, was set aside, and Harold's brother Tostig was imposed on the northern earldom. In 1057 Leofric of Mercia died. He was succeeded by his son Ælfgar, who probably died in 1062, and was in turn succeeded by his son Edwin. A revolt broke out in Northumbria in 1065 against Tostig. The rebels descended on York, proclaimed Tostig an outlaw, and invited Edwin's brother Morcar to be their earl. Morcar and the rebels marched into the midlands, gathered reinforcements from the Mercian shires of Lincoln, Nottingham and Derby, and occupied Northampton. Negotiations with the rebels, conducted by Earl Harold on behalf of Edward the Confessor, resulted in agreement upon the rebel claim that Morcar should be earl of Northumbria. Tostig fled overseas to Baldwin of Flanders.

Edward died on 5 January 1066, and the council chose Harold as his successor. He could hardly have succeeded at a more difficult moment, for his kingdom was menaced by the duke of Normandy, the king of Norway, and Tostig. In May Tostig appeared off the Isle of Wight; then, moving northwards up the east coast, disembarked on the south bank of the Humber, and ravaged the country. He was heavily defeated by Earl Edwin and the Lindsey militia, and moving north again was prevented from landing in Yorkshire by Earl Morcar and the Northumbrians, after which he went to Scotland, to concert plans with Harold Hardrada of Norway.

In September Harold Hardrada invaded England, and was joined by Tostig, apparently in the Tyne. His fleet entered the Humber and anchored in the Ouse 10 miles from York. The Norse army encountered Edwin and Morcar and their men, and defeated them, on 20 September, at Fulford. Five days later they were attacked by King Harold of England at Stamfordbridge, where the king of Norway and Tostig were killed and their forces overthrown. As Professor Stenton has pointed out, the losses of Edwin and Morcar at Fulford must have deprived them of any chance of effective action in the following weeks.

They have often been regarded as unpatriotic because they held aloof from the campaign of Hastings. It can at least be urged on their behalf that they had recently stood for the defence of the realm against the greatest northern warrior of the age, and that the battle of Hastings had been fought long before either of them could have replaced the men whom he had lost at Fulford.[1]

On 28 September the fleet of William of Normandy entered Pevensey Bay. Harold marched south by Bawtry, Littleborough, Lincoln and Huntingdon with all speed,[2] and without waiting for his army to assemble from the shires gave battle to William on 14 October at Hastings. In the battle that followed—the best-known event in English history—Harold was killed, and William laid the foundations of his English kingdom. The English leaders turned to Edgar the Ætheling, the grandson of Edmund Ironside, as Harold's successor, but they soon submitted to William, and Edwin and Morcar among them.

Among those who had been with the English army at Hastings was Leofric, the abbot of Peterborough, a nephew of Earl Leofric of Mercia, who combined that abbacy with those of Coventry, Burton on Trent, Crowland and Thorney. He died soon afterwards, on 1 November, and the monks of Peterborough chose as abbot the provost Brand, a man of Lincolnshire connections, 'because he was a very good man, and very wise, and sent him to Edgar Ætheling, because the people of the land weened that he should be king; and the Ætheling blithely assented thereto'. This miscalculation incurred the wrath of the Conqueror, who was only appeased by the mediation of good men and the payment of forty marks of gold.[3] At the same time, or soon afterwards, William granted a charter to the abbey, confirming, at the request of Abbot Brand, the privileges granted by Edgar and other kings, and all the lands held by the monks at the time of Edward the Confessor, including the gifts of Brand and his brothers.[4] The witnesses to the charter are a very interesting group. They are Ealdred, archbishop of York, who had just crowned the king; Wulfwig bishop of Lincoln; Merleswein the sheriff of Lincolnshire who had been King Harold's representative in the north at the time of the battle of Hastings; Ulf son of Tope, a kinsman of Abbot Brand; Earl William Fitz-Osbern of Hereford; William Malet, who had been lord of Alkborough before the Conquest, and who became the first Norman sheriff of York; and Ingelric the priest, who had been one of the Confessor's chaplains.[5] This combination of English and Norman magnates, the English being named first, illustrates, as does a number of other charters, William's desire to govern

[1] Stenton, *Anglo-Saxon England*, p. 582. The whole of the preceding passage is summarised from Professor Stenton.

[2] *V.C.H. Notts*, I, 239 n.

[3] *Anglo-Saxon Chronicle* (R.S.), I, 337.

[4] Supra, p. 40.

[5] Davis, *Regesta Regum Anglo-Normannorum*, I, no. 8; *Monasticon*, I, 383.

England through men who had held high office in King Edward's day.[1] It was perhaps as part of the same policy, or because William was only playing for time, that when Bishop Wulfwig died in 1067, and he appointed Remigius, the almoner of the abbey of Fécamp, in his place, the new bishop was allowed to go to the English Archbishop Stigand for consecration. It was not until 1070 that, on papal initiative, Stigand was deposed.

This attempt to govern through Englishmen was defeated by the series of risings that followed. Edgar the Ætheling and Merleswein and others took refuge in Scotland,[2] and Edwin and Morcar left the king's court for the north, joining rebel forces round York. William thereupon set out to subdue the north: he marched through Nottingham to York, where many of the Yorkshire magnates submitted, and he staved off a Scottish invasion by negotiations with the king of Scots, returning to London by way of Lincoln, Huntingdon and Cambridge. In all these county towns he ordered the building of castles, and made provision for their garrisons. Lincoln Castle will be dealt with in a later chapter.[3]

In 1069 a party of exiles descended from Scotland, headed by the Ætheling, and was admitted to York by the citizens. William at once bore down upon them and they were scattered. There followed a Danish invasion. The new invaders were joined by the Ætheling and his followers, and together they sailed up the Humber and entered York. The Ætheling set off on a plundering expedition in Lindsey, in the course of which he was unexpectedly attacked by the king's garrison from Lincoln, who took the whole party prisoner except the Ætheling and two others. The garrison also destroyed their ship, which was abandoned by its guards in alarm.[4]

William marched to the Humber, and to elude him the Danes crossed into the Isle of Axholme. The king followed them, but again they escaped. After visiting the west country to quell rebellion there, William heard that the Danes were moving towards York once more and he turned to attack them. They retired before him, and to ensure against further trouble in Yorkshire, the king visited it with the most terrible punishment, laying whole areas desolate.

In the spring of 1070 King Swein himself entered the Humber, and the country people made peace with him. Some of his men went to Ely, where they were joined by Englishmen from the fens. Led by the famous Hereward, a Lincolnshire thegn of moderate estate,[5] they raided and burnt Peterborough. Swein came to terms with William in the summer, and

[1] Stenton, *Anglo-Saxon England*, p. 615; *L.D.* p. xlii. For the will of Ulf son of Tope, see *Anglo-Saxon Wills* (ed. Dorothy Whitelock, 1930), no. XXXIX, pp. 94–7.

[2] *Anglo-Saxon Chronicle*, I, 341.

[3] Infra, Chapter V.

[4] Ordericus Vitalis, *Historia Ecclesiastica*, bk. IV, ch. V.

[5] Stenton, op. cit. p. 597.

withdrew his men, but Hereward continued the defence of the Isle of Ely, where he was joined by English leaders. Earl Edwin had been killed on his way to Scotland, but his brother Morcar came to Ely. William besieged the island and secured the surrender of most of the garrison, though Hereward and a few others escaped.

Happily Lincolnshire for the most part was not identified with rebellion, and so escaped the fate of Yorkshire, but the king took precautions. Hostages for all Lindsey were kept in the new castle at Lincoln.[1] Among the hostages was the young priest Turgot, who escaped to Grimsby, and lay hidden from the royal officers, who sought him, in a Norwegian ship lying in port there. He crossed to Norway, and was well received by King Olaf. Later he became prior of Durham, bishop of St Andrews, confessor to the famous Queen Margaret of Scotland, and almost certainly[2] her biographer.

Following soon upon these disturbances occurred the most important event of the reign in the history of Lincoln. In pursuance of the policy of transferring episcopal sees from villages to towns, the see of Dorchester, a combination of several ancient dioceses, including that of Lindsey, was moved to Lincoln: the transfer can be dated 1072–3.[3] The city became the capital of the largest of the English dioceses, reaching from the Humber to the Thames, and there resulted the building of the Minster which has ever since been Lincoln's greatest glory. The history of the bishop's church of St Mary and the transfer of the see is dealt with in another chapter.[4]

After the various risings with which he had to cope it became clear to William that he could not govern through Englishmen. The results of his change of policy appear in Domesday Book, which was compiled in 1086. With the rarest of exceptions the English magnates were deprived of their lands, and were succeeded by Norman lords or other adventurers who had invested in William's English enterprise. There are no details of the process of substitution, but it was complete or almost so by 1086. It is clearly illustrated by the Domesday account of Lincoln.[5]

The longest passage in this account relates to Tochi son of Outi. With small exceptions, all his lands in the counties of Lincoln, Northampton, Nottingham, Leicester, Derby and York passed to Geoffrey Alselin, whose chief seat at Laxton in Nottinghamshire (now best known because of the survival of open fields there)[6] later became the head of the Everingham

[1] Symeon of Durham, *Historia Regum* (R.S.), II, 202.

[2] Hume Brown, *History of Scotland* (1911), I, 49. See Knowles, *Monastic Order in England* (1941), pp. 167–8.

[3] Infra, p. 65.

[4] Infra, Chapter IV.

[5] See Appendix II.

[6] Described in Orwin, *The Open Fields* (1938).

barony. In Lincoln, Tochi had had his hall, 30 messuages and 2½ churches; these passed to Geoffrey. There were thirty other messuages of his which Bishop Remigius secured in right of the church of St Mary. There is some ground for thinking that one of Tochi's churches was St Peter at Arches, and that the houses that the bishop secured stood in St Mary Stigh, between the Stonebow and the river.[1]

Save for a few manors, the entire estate of the Sheriff Merleswein in Yorkshire, Lincolnshire, Northamptonshire, Gloucestershire, Somerset and Devon was granted to Ralph Paynel: he had had eight manors in Lincolnshire, including Irnham, Burton Stather, Roxby, Tealby and West Rasen, and he had a house in Lincoln. Besides this vast estate Ralph received Earl Morcar's manor at Burton Coggles, and manors or lands in Burton Stather, Scawby and Sturton which had belonged to Grinchel, a thegn who forfeited his manors for treason to King Edward, who had then granted them to Merleswein.[2] Ralph Paynel appears as sheriff of Yorkshire in 1088.

Earl Morcar's house in Lincoln went to Ernuin the priest who, according to another passage in Domesday, was a kinsman and apparently the heir of Godric the son of Gareuine. Perhaps he was the son of Gareuine and brother of Godric: for Ernui[n] and Godric jointly held a manor in Shippon and Streeton near Leeds. Godric had once owned the church of All Saints (in the Bail) in Lincoln with its lands, and when he became a monk of Peterborough both the abbot and Godric's kinsman Ernuin claimed the church. In King Edward's time Ernuin had had a large holding in Stamford—twenty-two houses, two churches, and land—which he lost; but he retained land at South Witham and secured some at Ingham. He may also have held land in other counties, and it seems likely that he was one of King Edward's priests, who had been presented to more than one church. It seems that he did not at first submit to William, for Domesday refers to the day 'Ernwin' the priest was taken; and though he lost heavily after the Conquest he received some small compensation from the new king, including Morcar's Lincoln house, perhaps to dissuade him from rebellion.[3]

A certain Ulf had a messuage in Lincoln, and the fact that he was supplanted by Gilbert de Gant shows that he was Ulf of Funen (*Fenisc*), one of the greatest landowners in the pre-Conquest Danelaw. Gilbert also secured a messuage in Lincoln formerly of Siward, who had had lands in West Ashby and Driby.[4] Gilbert, who took his name from Ghent, was the

[1] Infra, pp. 132–3.

[2] *V.C.H. Yorks*, II, 173. Ellis, 'Yorkshire Tenants in Domesday Book' in *Yorkshire Archaeological and Topographical Journal*, IV, 220.

[3] *D.B.* I, 347b; *L.D.* p. xxxii; *V.C.H. Lancs*, I, 275; *V.C.H. Derby*, I, 307; *V.C.H. Yorks*, II, 162; Ellis, op. cit. IV, 394.

[4] *L.D.* p. xxxi.

son of Ralf, count of Alost near Ghent, and a descendant of the ancient counts and one of the *grands seigneurs* of Flanders; he was descended also from Alfred the Great through his daughter Elfthryth, wife of Baldwin count of Flanders, and their granddaughter Leutgarde, who married Wichman, count of the castle of Ghent.[1] Gilbert was left in joint command at York in 1068 by the Conqueror. Folkingham was the head of his barony, as it had been of Ulf's; and he is now perhaps best remembered as the refounder of Bardney Abbey.

The Lincoln house of 'Earl', that is, King, Harold, like most of Harold's estates, went to Hugh of Avranches, son of Richard vicomte d'Avranches, and a kinsman of the Conqueror. He seems to have come to England as a young man a short time after Hastings, to help the new king. In 1071 he received the county palatine of Chester, and became one of the greatest magnates in the realm, having besides, lands and manors in seventeen counties.[2] Suen the son of Suave, who had a messuage in Lincoln and a manor at Greetwell, just outside the city boundary, lost both to Roger de Busli. Of Roger little is known, save that he became the greatest of Nottinghamshire landowners, lord of the castle of Tickhill, and founder of the priory of Blyth.[3]

The Countess Judith, who had come into possession of a messuage in Lincoln which had once belonged to Stori, was the widow of Earl Waltheof of Northumbria (who was executed for treason in 1076) and the niece of William the Conqueror. Her estates, which lay chiefly in Huntingdon, Cambridge, Bedford and Northampton, seem to have consisted partly of lands once her husband's, and partly of grants personal to herself.[4] Her Lincoln house was claimed by Ivo Taillebois, who had succeeded Stori as lord of Belchford and Bolingbroke. Judith had probably secured it because she had succeeded Stori in a manor at Hough on the Hill; apparently it was doubtful to which of these estates the Lincoln messuage belonged.

Domesday Book does not give a complete list of landholders: those it mentions are referred to for a particular reason. Generally it is that a certain holder of land has special rights of jurisdiction over his tenants, known as 'sake and soke', and that he is free from certain taxation, 'quit of all custom'. Those landholders who are not mentioned had presumably made or established no claim to special privileges when the Domesday inquiry was being held. A few others are mentioned because of their failure to pay the king's geld as they ought. The abbot of Peterborough

[1] *V.C.H. Yorks*, II, 174–5; Ellis, op. cit. pp. 230–3.
[2] *Complete Peerage* (2nd ed.), III, 165.
[3] *V.C.H. Notts*, I, 223; Ellis, op. cit. p. 142.
[4] *V.C.H. Northants*, I, 293; *V.C.H. Hunts*, I, 334; *V.C.H. Bedford*, I, 203–4.

had not paid geld for a house and three tofts of land. Earl Hugh of Chester had not paid it for any of his, nor had Geoffrey Alselin for two tofts. Another defaulter, Hugh son of Baldric, had been sheriff of York from 1069 to some time after 1078, and sheriff of Nottingham before 1086. His chief holdings of land were in Yorkshire and Lincolnshire.[1]

Most of the magnates who held lands and houses in Lincoln have no other place in the history of the city. They had much greater interests elsewhere. But there were a few tenants in chief whose local connections were much stronger. Among them was Colswein, one of the most interesting landholders mentioned in the Domesday account of Lincoln. It says of him:

> Colsuen has in the city of Lincoln 4 tofts of his *nepos* Cole's land; and outside the city he has 36 houses and 2 churches to which nothing belongs, which he built on the waste land that the king gave him, and that was never before built upon. Now the king has all the customs from them.

The tofts in the city he inherited; but the land outside the city he received by the king's favour, and he built houses and churches thereon, though he had not endowed the churches. The whereabouts of Colswein's extramural estate will be discussed later.[2] His name shows plainly that he is of native descent—the only one among William's tenants in chief in Lincolnshire and one of only two native holders of estates of baronial size in all England south of the Tees[3]—and yet it is significant that the Domesday account of his lands and manors does not show a single instance in which he held land at the time of the Conquest. He seems to have secured a large number of grants of the estates of small men, and built up his large fee upon their ruin. His descendants are found owing the duty of castle guard at Lincoln Castle, and he may also have owed it.[4] He must have been in high favour with William to receive such special treatment, and the fact that he bore a native name raises the unpleasant suspicion that he was a 'quisling'. His lands consisted chiefly of two groups, one to the north of the city, the other in east Kesteven. Fortunately, Domesday shows what lands were occupied by tenants, and what were 'in demesne', or kept in the lord's own hands, cultivated by his own servants, the produce of which was available for his own household. The accompanying map (p. 49) shows that Colswein had his own teams of oxen at work in a number of his manors to the north of Lincoln, at Sudbrook, Reepham, Riseholme, Scothern, Brattleby, all within a few miles of the city, and in others only

[1] *Calendar of Documents preserved in France*, p. 108; *V.C.H. Yorks*, II, 176–8.

[2] Infra, pp. 133–4.

[3] Stenton, *Anglo-Saxon England*, p. 618. Colswein, father of Picot, was a benefactor of Lincoln Minster, *L.C.S.* II, p. ccxxxv.

[4] Infra, Chapter V.

Fig. 4. Distribution of Colswein's lands in Domesday Book. Place-names in capitals indicate land in demesne: the number following shows the number of teams in demesne.

a little farther away. He had a smaller number of teams in the southern group, but none in his outlying manors. Apparently he made his home in Lincoln or its neighbourhood, perhaps on his extra-mural estate, perhaps in the castle.

Another tenant in chief, Alfred of Lincoln, had three tofts of land in the city, from which he received all customs except the geld in respect of minting. Domesday describes him as the *nepos* of Thorold, who was sometime sheriff of Lincoln; and Alan of Lincoln, who succeeded to Alfred's estates, was the uncle of the Countess Lucy.[1] The names of Alfred and Alan suggest their Breton origin:[2] there must have been many men from Brittany and Flanders and other lands round Normandy willing to join William in his English adventure. Alfred's lands became the barony of Bayeux: the barony had a free court in the city of Lincoln which was the court of the whole barony. It became the manor of Hungate or Beaumont Fee, the latter name being derived from the family into whose possession it came. In the hands of tenacious lords the barony was held together for a remarkable length of time: a suit roll of the manor drawn in 1708 includes a series of place-names every one of which appears among the holdings of Alfred of Lincoln in Domesday Book.[3]

At later dates several of the other great fees in the county were represented in the city, and they may already have been so represented in 1086. The bishop of Durham had land in the parish of All Saints in the Bail.[4] The abbot of Ramsey had a rent of 10*s.* in Lincoln in 1178,[5] and Roger of Poitou had a church there in 1094.[6] Roger was the son of Roger de Montgomery, earl of Shrewsbury, and brother of Robert de Belesme, count of Alençon. Through his marriage with the daughter of the count of la Marche he acquired his Poitou estates. In 1086 he had already lost a great estate between Ribble and Mersey, but kept others in Yorkshire, Lincolnshire, Essex and Suffolk, only to lose them by rebellion in 1101.[7]

Osbern the priest, one of the smaller tenants in chief, is the Osbert the sheriff who gave the church of St Margaret to St Mary of Lincoln.[8] Land was held in the city of the fee of Croun,[9] and at least one member of the

[1] Infra, p. 92.

[2] For Alfred, see Round, *Feudal England* (1909), p. 328.

[3] Hill, 'Manor of Hungate' in *A.A.S.R.* XXXVIII (1926), p. 202. For the holdings of Alfred, see *V.C.H. Bedford*, I, 211; *V.C.H. Rutland*, I, 131 n.

[4] D. & C., Dii, 77/3/68.

[5] *Cartularium Monasterii de Rameseia* (R.S.), II, 137.

[6] *Calendar of Documents preserved in France*, p. 237.

[7] Tait, *Mediaeval Manchester and the Beginnings of Lancashire* (1904), pp. 4, 6, and see index.

[8] *R.A.* I, 22; *E.H.R.* XXX (1915), pp. 279–80; infra, p. 142.

[9] *C. Chart. R.* IV, 46; D. & C., Dii, 81/2/9.

Malet family held land in the Bail.[1] The Aincurt fee was represented in the Bail[2] and in Hungate.[3] Walter de Aincurt was a kinsman of Remigius, with estates in the counties of Nottingham, Derby, Lincoln and York. His chief seat was at Branston, and the fact that his son founded the Augustinian priory of Thurgarton no doubt explains the considerable estate which that house acquired in Lincoln.[4]

Although Maitland's famous 'garrison theory' is no longer accepted, it is still of interest to inquire how far it could be applied to Lincoln. The theory was that the tenth-century *burh* was first and foremost a fortress garrisoned by the landowners of its district, who kept houses and warrior *burgware* in it for defence and wall repair.[5] In support of the theory Ballard tried to calculate the number of lords holding lands in the county or district who also held houses in the borough, and who were supposed to contribute to defence and wall repair.[6] There is no complete list of the tenants in chief holding houses in Lincoln, but taking the evidence so far as it is available, fourteen such tenants are mentioned in Domesday Book. To this total can be added perhaps six more from the later sources mentioned above. The fact that there are 65 tenants in chief in Lincolnshire mentioned in Domesday shows that the theory does not receive any impressive support from the Lincoln evidence. Probably convenience was the main reason why the county magnates should have a house or a henchman in the county town.

As has been noticed, the Norman settlement involved almost a clean sweep of the English magnates; but the smaller men were for the most part left alone. Even such local notables as the lawmen were not as a class disturbed: Ulf of Lincoln retained his manors of Burton and South Carlton. Of the lawmen of 1066, three were still living and in office in 1086; five had been succeeded by their sons. Two had been displaced by Frenchmen. Their successors in the lawmanry were the successors to their lands, and it is clear that the Normans were treating a title which they did not understand as annexed to and going with a particular landholding. Perhaps a modern parallel can be found in the practice of conveying the lordship of a manor with a manor house or a manor farm where the lordship has long ceased to have any meaning or value other than that of a pleasant historical association.

[1] D. & C., Dii, 81/2/10, 14; *Lincs N. & Q.* VIII, 58.
[2] Barlings Cartulary, f. 57d.
[3] *R.A.* III, 32.
[4] See *V.C.H. Notts*, I, 230. Perhaps he built the church tower at Branston: the arcade upon its west side shows the influence of Remigius' west front at Lincoln.
[5] Maitland, *Domesday Book and Beyond* (1897), section on the Boroughs.
[6] *Domesday Boroughs* (1904), ch. II.

Godric the son of Eddeve was succeeded by Peter de Valognes, both as lawman and in his carucate of land in the Lincoln fields and his carucates at Burton just outside the city. Peter's accessions in and near Lincoln formed but a tiny part of his barony, which extended over six counties in the east of England, and centred in Hertfordshire. He was sometime sheriff of Hertford and Essex, and he founded Binham Priory in Norfolk, which he later made a cell to St Albans.[1] He frequently appears as a witness to charters sealed in the king's court;[2] and when a dispute arose in 1106 between Osbert the sheriff of York and the archbishop concerning the rights of the church of York, the king sent a commission to inquire into the matter. Among the commissioners were Robert bishop of Lincoln, Ranulph le Meschin and Peter de Valognes.[3] So great a man as Peter, with his chief interests elsewhere, is not likely to have paid much regard to the fact that he held an obscure and almost unintelligible office like that of a lawman of Lincoln.

The other intruder upon the group of lawmen was Norman Crassus. He displaced Guret, or Godred,[4] in office, and he claimed a house which Godred had in mortgage, but this was also claimed by the abbot of Peterborough. The holdings described as Norman's in Domesday Book, two in number, at Middle Carlton and Canwick, formerly belonged respectively to Agemund and Walraven. They must be the Agemund who was a lawman in 1086, and his father Walraven, who was a lawman in 1066. Apparently Norman secured the estates of two lawmen, but he took the office of him whose Lincoln property he secured: which suggests that the lawmanry was regarded as annexed to a burgage holding in the city. There is no evidence that Norman was one of the greater tenants like Peter de Valognes, but he is found in attendance at the king's court on one occasion. When Ivo Taillebois, with the consent of the king, at Gloucester in 1085, gave the church of Spalding to the abbey of St Nicholas of Angers, the grant was witnessed by (among others) Remigius bishop of Lincoln and Norman Crassus.[5]

The moneyers as a class, like the lawmen, were not disturbed by the Conquest. At the end of Edward the Confessor's reign there were eight at work in Lincoln: at the beginning of William's there seem to be seven who continued from the Confessor or Harold. William not only retained these

[1] *V.C.H. Herts*, I, 273, 282–3; *V.C.H. Essex*, I, 349.

[2] Davis, *Regesta Regum Anglo-Normannorum*, see index.

[3] Leach, *Visitations and Memorials of Southwell Minster*, p. 191. Among the jurors impanelled at York was Ulvet son of Forno, by hereditary right lawman of York 'which in Latin may be translated lawgiver or judge' (p. 192).

[4] These are almost certainly different forms of the same name.

[5] Davis, op. cit. no. 288a.

men, 'but what is absolutely astounding, when these old men began to die out or retire, he supplied their places with other Englishmen'[1] or, at Lincoln, with other Scandinavians. To the Confessor's moneyers Agemund, Outhgrim and Ulf, and the English Ælfnot, William added the Scandinavian Siward, Thorstan and Unspac, and the English Garvin, Almaer, Sigwaword, Wulsi, Wihtric and Wulstan. Under William Rufus there appear the Scandinavian Ascil, the English Wulfwine and Lefwine, and Folcaerd, perhaps a German. Henry I added the Scandinavian Arnwi and the English Aslac, Godric, Leofric, Aelwi (Ælfwine), Bruman and Edmund. Under Stephen appear the first French names of Paen and Hugh; and the persistence of the old strains is illustrated by the names of the moneyers signing the Tealby pennies of Henry II: Andrew, Godric, Lanfram, Raven, Raulf Swein.[2]

It is convenient to discuss the erection of the castle in a later chapter;[3] but as the passage referring to the clearance of the site to make room for it has importance in other respects, it is quoted here with the other passages relating to the size of the city. They are as follows:

In the city of Lincoln there were in the time of King Edward 970 inhabited messuages. This number is reckoned according to the English method, 100 counting for 120.

Of the aforesaid messuages which were inhabited in the time of King Edward, there are now waste 200 by English reckoning, that is 240; and by the same reckoning 760 are now inhabited.

Of the aforesaid waste messuages, 166 were destroyed on account of the castle. The remaining 74 are waste outside the castle boundary, not because of the oppression of the sheriffs and officers but by reason of misfortune and poverty and the ravages of fires.

The habit of calculating in twelves and sixes seems to be confined to the district of the Five Boroughs and the ancient kingdom of York, that is to those parts of England settled by the Danes in 876 and 877.[4] The 'long

[1] Oman, *Coinage of England* (1931), p. 80; Brooke, *Catalogue of English Coins, Norman Kings* (1916), I, p. clxxiv.

[2] The Tealby pennies are so called because a hoard of over 6,000 was found on the estate of George Tennyson at Tealby on the Lincolnshire Wolds in 1807. 'A selection of the pieces has been deposited in the British Museum; others have gone to enrich private collections, particularly that of Sir Joseph Banks who undertook their arrangement; and the rest continue in Mr Tennyson's possession. The deposit was made in what but a few years since was a large and wild open field, on the highest part of the wolds; a road formerly ran near the spot, which is a rising ground, by some supposed to be a tumulus or barrow. The circumjacent land has been carefully dug over in the expectation of additional treasures, but without success.' *Lincoln, Rutland and Stamford Mercury*, 20 November 1807.

[3] Infra, Chapter v.

[4] Round, *Feudal England*, pp. 69–82; Stenton in *L.D.* p. xii.

hundred' of 120, though probably in common use in the northern Danelaw, is only used in Domesday Book in its account of Lincoln. It continued in popular use until much later times: in 1613 the common council of Lincoln ordered the city brickmaker to allow six score bricks to the hundred.[1]

Allowing 120 for every 100, according to 'the English method', the 970 houses inhabited in the time of Edward the Confessor become 1,150. It is by no means certain that every messuage (*mansio*) was occupied by only one burgess, as the tenement originally assessed for the land-toll penny (to be mentioned later) might have been divided into two or more holdings; but for the purposes of a rough calculation the equation *mansio* = *house* may be assumed, and if there is error it will be on the low side. In addition to 1,150 householders or burgesses paying the royal customs, there were about 120 paying custom to various lords. This gives a total of 1,270 households, and estimating on the usual basis of five persons to a house, there would be a population of 6,350 persons at the time of the Conquest. London and Winchester do not appear in the Domesday Survey, but of those towns that do appear, York was the largest with an estimated population of 8,000: Norwich seems to have been similar in size to Lincoln with 6,600, and is followed by Thetford with about 4,750 and Ipswich with over 3,000 burgess inhabitants.[2]

Between 1066 and 1086 there had been a decline in the population of Lincoln. In 1086, 240 houses (by English reckoning, 200) were lying waste, leaving 900 (by English reckoning, 760) occupied. The Domesday clerks had made a mistake in their arithmetic, for they here account for 1,140 houses, and the total given previously was 1,150. Clearly they were dealing in round figures. Of the 240 houses which had gone, 166 were destroyed to make room for the king's new castle. The remaining 74 were laid waste, not (as the jurors or the clerks thought might have been expected) on account of the oppression of the sheriffs, but by reason of poverty and fire.

The area of the castle can still be measured, and the reference to the 166 houses destroyed to make room for it therefore provides one of the few pieces of evidence of the density of population, or rather of housing, in the eleventh-century borough. Professor Carl Stephenson takes the view that there was little town life in England before the Norman Conquest, and he argues that with perhaps a few exceptions the urban population of a borough was accommodated within its Roman or Danish fortifications: that the Anglo-Saxon boroughs were in fact little more than the fortified *burhs* of the tenth century. Lincoln and York he admits as exceptions to his general view, and he agrees that their history turned upon the establishment of a Danish trading settlement. He does, however, argue from the

[1] C.C.M. 1599–1638, f. 99.

[2] Tait, *Medieval English Borough*, p. 76.

area of the castle and the number of houses cleared for it, that the mass of the inhabitants at the Conquest were living in the upper walled city:

> The actual area of the castle precinct is about one-sixth of the upper city,[1] but we should probably assume that a somewhat wider expanse was actually laid waste. By assigning eight acres to the 166 mansiones, we obtain an average of 20 to the acre; which would imply one house for every 250 square yards or so—that is to say, on a lot 30 by 75 feet. Thus, even if we decrease our average to 15 or 16 *mansiones* per acre, we still have to imagine three-fifths of Lincoln's population about 1066 crowded into the oldest enclosure, while the lower city in large part lay vacant. Perhaps there was a separate mercantile settlement by the river, but on this point Domesday, which provides much detail concerning the holdings of burgesses in the surrounding fields, has nothing to say.[2]

There is no doubt that (as he suggests) there was a mercantile settlement by the river, but Domesday has no separate name for it, and if it was not included in the account of the city then it was omitted from Domesday altogether.[3]

This difficulty is resolved by a re-examination of the calculation about the clearance of the castle site. It is true that the area enclosed by the walls is about 6¾ acres,[4] but this is not the area which had to be cleared. With the original ditches the area is 13¾ acres: levelling and building have obscured the limits of the ditches, but the older plans make them quite clear. Of this total area the ditches on the west and south sides were outside the upper city, but houses may have had to be pulled down to make them; and the area affected may have been greater than the area occupied, for the street called Westgate was pushed towards the north to make room for the defences, and houses on the north side of the street may well have been taken down and rebuilt farther back. All these possibilities make calculation a risky matter. Nevertheless, it is clear that Professor Stephenson underestimates the area affected by the castle works, and instead of it being about a fifth of the upper city which was affected (that is, 8 acres out of 41), it may well have been a third. Assuming this proportion, the number of houses in the upper city would be three times the number destroyed (166), or about 500, something between a third and a half of the Conquest total of 1,150 houses in the city.

There are other grounds for thinking that this view is nearer to the facts than that of Professor Stephenson. Although Lincoln has no detailed survey of burgess holdings as Cambridge has,[5] the continuity of the land-gable rents

[1] The upper city has an area of about 41 acres.

[2] *Borough and Town: a Study of Urban Origins in England* (1933), p. 193.

[3] The argument is of course that of Maitland, *Township and Borough*, p. 99.

[4] Mrs Armitage, *Early Norman Castles*, table to appendix, gives 5¾ acres.

[5] Maitland, op. cit. p. 142. Miss H. M. Cam, 'Origin of the Borough of Cambridge', *Cambridge Antiquarian Society*, xxxv, 48 (reprinted in *Liberties and Communities in Medieval England*, 1944, p. 14).

(to be discussed later) can be assumed, and two figures are available for comparison. The 900 houses of 1086 presumably paid 900 land-toll pence. A roll of the city revenues for one of the years between 1290 and 1300 (apparently 1292–3), when the city was in the king's hand, shows a return of 50*s.* for land-toll pence.[1] That means 600 houses. Why this drop of exactly one-third? Obviously the deduction is a conventional one. The answer is that the upper city has been detached from the rest of the city and has become the Bail, and a rough-and-ready assessment put it at a third of the whole city. Confirmation of this answer comes in the course of a dispute between the citizens and the constable of the castle in 1375. The citizens contended that the bailey was a part of the city, and indeed the third part of the whole.[2]

Such a conclusion implies a density of about 7½ tenements to the acre in the Bail. Another calculation can be made of the average size of tenements from the area cleared for the site of the bishop's palace, this time in the north-east corner of the lower walled city, the land being back land where building might be expected to be less dense than in areas adjoining main streets. About 1157 Henry II commanded the barons of the Exchequer to allow to the sheriff of Lincolnshire and the reeves of Lincoln in the king's farm of Lincoln 13 pence every year in respect of land-gable, for the land which the king gave to the church of Lincoln and Bishop Robert II and his successors for their buildings; and as the area so granted can be identified with reasonable confidence, it may be said that the ground affected, some 10,000 square yards, was occupied by 13 tenements.[3] This is 6¼ tenements to the acre: a conclusion which strengthens faith in the foregoing calculation.

It seems probable that within the city walls, and perhaps especially in the upper city, the population was denser, and the holdings smaller, than in the districts of later settlement. Domesday mentions that there were 36 crofts in Lincoln, and until modern times there were many large gardens within the old city bounds: these would reduce the average density of population, and they also constitute a warning against calculations of the average size of burgess holdings. Broadly, however, it appears that about a third of the citizens lived in the upper city, and that after allowing a handful of people to the suburbs on the hillside and above hill, the remainder lived in the lower walled city and the extra-mural settlement in Wigford.

There are several references to land-gable in Domesday. Tochi had formerly had a penny from each of his houses, namely land-gable. Geoffrey had a messuage outside the wall, from which, like Tochi, he received a

[1] P.R.O. Exchequer Accounts, 505/24.

[2] *C.C.R.* 1374–77, p. 262.

[3] *R.A.* I, 104, 270–2.

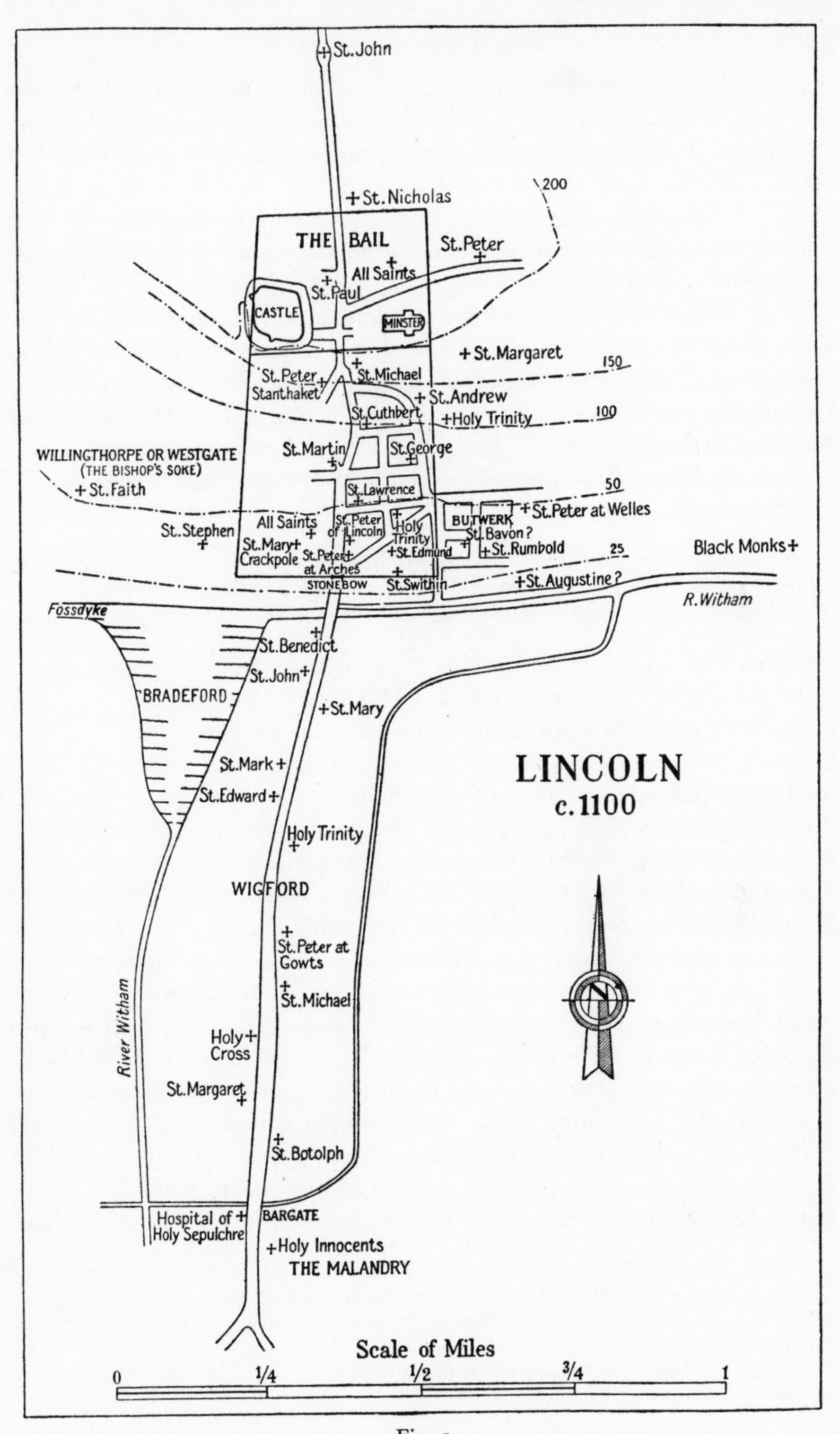
St. John
St. Nicholas
200
THE BAIL
St. Peter
All Saints
St. Paul
CASTLE
MINSTER
St. Margaret
150
St. Peter Stanthaket
St. Michael
St. Andrew
St. Cuthbert
Holy Trinity
100
St. Martin
St. George
WILLINGTHORPE OR WESTGATE
(THE BISHOP'S SOKE)
St. Faith
St. Lawrence
50
All Saints
St. Peter of Lincoln
Holy Trinity
BUTWERK
St. Peter at Welles
St. Stephen
St. Mary Crackpole
St. Bavon ?
St. Peter at Arches
St. Edmund
St. Rumbold
25
Black Monks
STONEBOW
St. Swithin
St. Augustine ?
Fossdyke
R. Witham
St. Benedict
St. John
BRADEFORD
St. Mary
St. Mark
LINCOLN
c. 1100
St. Edward
Holy Trinity
WIGFORD
St. Peter at Gowts
St. Michael
River Witham
Holy Cross
St. Margaret
St. Botolph
Hospital of Holy Sepulchre
BARGATE
Holy Innocents
THE MALANDRY
Scale of Miles
0
1/4
1/2
3/4
1

Fig. 5.

penny. Earl Hugh had land-gable from two messuages. These statements that certain landholders had land-gable, or customs, or sake and soke, were statements of exception from the general rule that such revenues belonged to the king. The king's reeve looked to the holder of each messuage to pay the usual dues; the onus of proof of privilege was on the claimant, and if he had not secured a record of his claim by the Domesday jurors his prospects of exemption were small.

Three conclusions emerge from the land-gable passages. In the first place there was a uniform rent or tax of one penny per messuage. It was known to that careful historian John Ross, who said that the tax was called the lantol-penny.[1] This statement aroused the scorn of Dr Hemmeon, the historian of burgage tenure: he agreed that the amount of the rent was correct, though as Ross gave no reference he assumed that it was a guess, and he continued,

> if the name for the burgage rent be as Mr Ross tells us, then Lincoln, where of all places one would expect to meet hawgable, must be placed in a class by itself in respect of a name for the rent of assise.[2]

Yet Ross was right. The land-toll penny recurs constantly in grants of land in Lincoln, and it appears in Edward IV's charter to the city.[3]

Secondly, there is a strong presumption that the land-gable rent was the same before the Conquest as after it. Its name, the land-toll, and its uniformity (taking no account of the varying size of holdings) indicate that it is in origin a tax rather than a rent. The penny rent appears in the oldest boroughs—Bristol, Carlisle, Colchester, Ipswich, London, Northampton, Winchester, York—though not always uniformly, whilst in the later boroughs the normal land-gable is frequently higher. Dr Hemmeon divides the older boroughs into two classes, one where the land-gable was about the same for each tenement, and the other where wide variations occur. In the first class he puts most of the boroughs of the Danelaw and the older boroughs of the shires, including London and Lincoln.[4] Who first imposed the land-toll and on what occasion remains to be discovered.

Thirdly, the uniformity of the land-gable in Lincoln both within and without the walls is illustrated by many land grants. It appears that at Oxford no houses outside the walls and not all those inside paid land-gable,[5] but in Lincoln instances occur of its payment in the suburbs of Wigford,

[1] *Civitas Lincolnia* (1870), p. 94.

[2] *Burgage Tenure in Medieval England* (Harvard, 1914), p. 67 n. 2.

[3] *L.D.* p. 3 n.; Birch, p. 143 (inspected in the charter of Richard III); *C.P.R.* 1358–61, p. 319; Gild Certificates (1389), no. 145b.

[4] Op. cit. p. 165. And see pp. 67–70 of his book.

[5] Salter, *Medieval Oxford* (1936), p. 27.

Butwerk, Newport, Pottergate and Eastgate.[1] Two general statements of liability have been noticed. In 1405 keepers were appointed of the chapel and lands of the Black Monks 'whereof with all its appurtenances one Rumfar of Lincoln was sometime seised in his demesne as of fee, holding it of the king in burgage as all the city of Lincoln is held, by service of one penny a year'.[2] And in 1589 the common council of Lincoln directed the chamberlains to gather land-toll pence yearly of the lands in their wards except the common chamber lands.[3]

The incidents of burgage tenure, the form of landholding peculiar to the boroughs, have been summarised by Professor Tait: the burgess tenement was heritable, it could be given or sold without royal licence, subject sometimes to the rights of the borough or the kin, and it could be mortgaged.[4] As to the power to mortgage, Domesday tells of a house in Lincoln, for which the abbot of Peterborough, according to the jurors, had not paid geld, which had been held in pledge by Godred for 3½ marks of silver. It is not stated to have been a burgess tenement but the uniformity noted above makes it likely that it was.

Burgage tenure was, indeed, similar to the modern freehold tenure, and much more so than the medieval free tenures outside the boroughs. Yet at the time of Domesday it had not fully escaped from the customary law by which the owner's kin were entitled to some say in the disposal of land. The Lincoln account has an interesting story of the claims of the kin. A carucate of land in the fields, with twelve tofts and four crofts, had belonged to the church of All Saints in the time of King Edward. Godric son of Gareuin had this church and the church's land and whatever belonged to it; but on his becoming a monk the abbot of Peterborough obtained it. 'But all the burgesses of Lincoln say that he has it unjustly, because neither Gareuine nor his son Godric nor anyone else could give it outside the city or outside their kindred, except by grant of the king. The church and what belongs thereto Ernuin the priest claims by inheritance from his kinsman Godric.' Thereafter there is no sign that All Saints belonged to the abbot of Peterborough, and it would seem that the custom of the borough was upheld.

A custom of this kind must have made it extremely difficult to buy a burgage tenement with any assurance that the title to it was and would

[1] *C.P.R.* 1367–70, p. 247 (Newport); 1348–50, p. 112 (Pottergate); D. & C., Dii, 71/1/2 (Butwerk); Dii, 76/3/12 (Wigford); Barlings Cartulary, f. 63d (Eastgate).

[2] *C.F.R.* XII, 307.

[3] C.C.M. 1564–99, f. 187b. When the extant rolls of the mayors and chamberlains begin in 1685 there is no trace of the land-toll pence.

[4] *Medieval English Borough*, pp. 101–2. As to borough customs, see Holdsworth, *History of English Law* (3rd ed.), III, 269–75.

remain a good title: that it would not be impeached by the burgesses or the heir or other of the vendor's kin. In a trading centre where new men were constantly coming to settle this was a matter of fundamental importance, and it is not surprising therefore that a limit was set to the period of challenge. In 1157 Henry II granted a charter to Lincoln providing that if anyone bought land in the city of the burgage of Lincoln, and should have held it for a year and a day without challenge, and could show that the challenger had been in the realm of England within the year and had not challenged, then the purchaser should thenceforth hold his land well and in peace and without plea.[1]

In spite of this provision it was in the thirteenth century the practice on a sale or gift of land in Lincoln expressly to declare that a man sold or gave his land with the consent of his wife and his sons and daughters. If they were not made parties to the deed they might be named as witnesses thereto, and frequently on the death of the grantor deeds of confirmation were obtained from the most likely claimants among the kin. Sometimes a vendor was expressed to sell 'in my great necessity', the phrase implying, perhaps, that it justified the alienation of land on the ground that it was involuntary.[2] Conveyancers are notoriously conservative and like to take the precaution of 'getting in' all outstanding interests; but the grantee would not habitually have gone to the expense of obtaining one or more confirmatory deeds without at least some reason.

Domesday describes various holders of land as having sake and soke and other private rights of jurisdiction; they were privileged persons with rights to hold courts for their tenants and men, or had other special powers over them, the exact nature of which is a matter for the legal rather than the local historian. These rights were the exceptions to the general rule that the burgesses attended the borough court and there sought the justice to which they were entitled. In Lincoln the court was called the *burwarmot*, the moot or assembly of the *burhwaras* or burgesses. Where was the burwarmot held? The place is suggested by the name of the church of St Peter *ad placita*, which stood to the north of St Peter at Arches. The church's name cannot be explained (as has sometimes been attempted) by its proximity to the gildhall over the Stonebow where the court was at a later time held, because the church was not so near to the gildhall as St Peter at Arches; nor is there any evidence that the burwarmot was held over

[1] Birch, p. 2.

[2] Compare the laws of the Saxons in Germany: 'No one may make a transfer of his inheritance except to the king or the church, and so disinherit his heir, unless he do it compelled by hunger, to be fed by the man to whom he transfers it.' Jenks, *Law and Politics in the Middle Ages* (1919 ed.), p. 213.

the Stonebow as early as the name of St Peter *ad placita* appears. The church was certainly known by that name in the later part of the twelfth century;[1] and it is known to have existed in 1094, when Earl Roger of Poitou gave St Peter of Lincoln to the abbey of St Martin of Sées,[2] and it is this St Peter which is found in the patronage of Sées in the time of Bishop Hugh de Welles.[3] The English form of the church's name has been found only in the cartulary of Thurgarton Priory in a fifteenth-century charter. The church is there described as St Peter *ad motston*.[4] The mootstone which marked the meeting place of the burwarmot may have stood in the churchyard or just outside it. Evidently it was an open-air court. At Leicester in the twelfth century the court was held in the churchyard, at Oxford in the churchyard of St Martin, at Norwich in Tombland near St Michael de Motstowe or *ad placita*, and at Ipswich in the thingstead.[5] It was no doubt at the mootstone by St Peter of Lincoln that the burgesses, in company with a great number of magnates, witnessed a gift by Earl Leofric of Mercia and his wife Godgifu for the endowment of the church of St Mary of Stow. This incident, which can be dated 1053–5, appears to afford the earliest reference to the burgesses acting collectively.[6]

The special privileges of some magnates, such as sake and soke, do not affect the nature of burgage tenure. Tochi had received land-gable from his messuages in Lincoln, though the king retained toll and forfeiture: evidently Tochi or his predecessor had either received a royal grant of the land-gable, or had successfully usurped it. Bishop Remigius had a little manor near the city free of custom save for danegeld, which his houses (that is, their occupants) paid with the burgesses. This little manor, as Canon Foster discovered,[7] was the manor of Westgate or Willingthorpe, and Professor Tait calls attention to its description as *burgum de Willingtorp*. The word *burgum* implies burgess tenure: and indeed, forty years later the bishop's court decided that four *mansiones* there were free of all service *preter burgagium*.[8] Some of them, therefore, were held by burgage rent, and perhaps all paid land-toll to the bishop, they being regarded as free as between bishop and king.[9]

Another point emerges from the Domesday account of the bishop's little manor: his men paid geld with the burgesses. This implies that they did not rank as burgesses. Domesday's business was the king's revenue: the

[1] D. & C., Dii, 80/3/29, 30.
[2] Round, *Calendar of Documents preserved in France*, p. 237.
[3] *Rotuli Hugonis de Welles* (L.R.S.), III, 115, 198.
[4] Thurgarton Cartulary, f. 157d.
[5] Tait, *Medieval English Borough*, p. 63 n.
[6] Infra, p. 75.
[7] *R.A.* I, 188 et seq. For Willingthorpe, see infra, p. 328.
[8] *D.C.* p. 343.
[9] Tait, op. cit. p. 93.

bishop's men do not contribute to the royal revenue from the borough, they do not pay the king's land-toll penny, and they are not royal burgesses. They are not 'in consuetudine regis'.[1]

In the bishop's manor was a carucate of land. Apart from this there were 12½ carucates in the city fields.[2] This is no more than many villages possessed, and if Lincoln had ever been self-supporting it must have been very small: by the time that it had grown to the population indicated by Domesday its boundaries had taken shape, and it had to be fed by the flow of produce to its market, and by the cultivation of land in the county by magnates and burgesses. Of these carucates three had been held by lawmen, one had belonged to the church of All Saints and the half carucate to St Mary of Lincoln, in which the bishop had placed his seat. The churches and burgesses also had 36 crofts. There remained eight carucates, which the king and the earl were said to have in demesne, with 231 acres of arable inland and 100 acres of meadow: at the time there was no earl, but the rights of any future holder of the office were being reserved. One of these carucates had been disposed of by the king, who sold it to a certain Ulchel in exchange for a ship. But the vendor of the ship was dead, and the carucate was back in the king's hand until he should re-grant it. Perhaps the process of disposing of all the lands forfeited by former owners had not proceeded as far in the Lincoln fields as it had elsewhere. If this is so, it implies a severance of land in the fields from particular burgage holdings in the city; certainly there are few if any indications of such links, nor is there any sign of land-gable being paid in respect of land in the fields. Professor Tait has argued that the statement that the churches and burgesses had 36 crofts, apart from (*exceptis*) the 12½ carucates, implies that the churches and burgesses had the use of the carucates; but this is difficult to reconcile with the statement that the king and the earl had them in demesne.

But he makes the attempt. He suggests that the king and the earl had released their custom over some of the arable to lawmen and churches, but retained it over the other two-thirds: which would mean that the king and the earl only had 'in demesne' certain profitable rights in the land. Professor Tait meets this further difficulty by saying that the conveyance of land when only profitable rights in it are transferred is a common enough feature of Anglo-Saxon practice. He acknowledges, however, that this interpretation raises another problem, namely how the king could exchange a carucate with Ulchel for a ship; and he has to explain this

[1] The account of the abbot of Peterborough's estates mentions under Scotton that there are three burgesses in Lincoln rendering 5*s*. *L.D.* 8/15.

[2] See infra, pp. 330–1.

passage in the same way, by saying that Ulchel only received the custom from his carucate, which was in the possession of churches and burgesses.[1] The theory is somewhat academic, and the more natural explanation of the deal with Ulchel, that he really did get the land, seems to be more satisfactory. This would mean that the king and the earl had the eight carucates at their disposal; the churches and the burgesses may have had some kind of tenancy of them. Whatever the explanation may be, it is clear that by the thirteenth century all the strips in the fields were or had been in individual possession. The arable plays a very small part in the history of the city, but the pasture continued until recent times to concern all residents, free and unfree, within the city proper and the suburbs north of the river.[2]

Perhaps the most direct effect of the Conquest upon the majority of the citizens, who were not disturbed in their property or livelihood, was the increase of taxation. In the time of the Confessor the city had to render to the king and the earl yearly the sum of £30. By 1086 the assessment was raised to £100, and the mint rendered £75: what the mint rendered in 1066 is not recorded. Perhaps its yield was included in the £30. The tax on Colchester was increased fivefold, Hereford threefold, and Norwich only slightly less. The increases were enormous, and must have been regarded as a very heavy burden. The former assessments may, however, have been old and traditional ones, not related to capacity to pay at the time of the Conquest. The new levies on the principal towns give an approximate idea of their relative importance. London and Winchester are not given in Domesday, though in the time of the Conqueror the farm of London was £300. Lincoln and York come next with £100 each. Norwich paid £90, with payments to the sheriff which brought it to much the same amount. Colchester paid £82 plus £5 to the sheriff; Chester and Thetford £76 each; Gloucester, Hereford and Oxford £60 each.[3] Lincoln was not to enjoy (or suffer) the same relative position very long.[4]

[1] Op. cit. pp. 115–16. Miss Cam prefers Tait's theory. The view stated above has the support of Professor Stenton.

[2] Infra, Chapter XVI.

[3] Tait, op. cit. pp. 154, 184.

[4] Infra, p. 183.

CHAPTER IV

THE OLD MINSTER AND THE NEW

THE death of Wulfwig bishop of Dorchester in 1067 gave the Conqueror his first opportunity of strengthening his hold on the Church, and at the same time enabled him to reward a follower, by appointing him to an English diocese. He chose Remigius, almoner of the abbey of Fécamp, a Norman house which already before the Conquest had enjoyed lands in England. Remigius had contributed a ship with twenty knights to William's expeditionary force.[1] His aid was given for a consideration. Eadmer roundly declares that Remigius made it a condition that if the invasion of England succeeded he should have a bishopric,[2] and he is followed by William of Malmesbury, who says that he received the see as the price of his help at Hastings.[3] Giraldus, who was writing to promote Remigius' claim to sanctity, does not mention the transaction, and Henry of Huntingdon, loyal to his own church of Lincoln, is silent too; but the Lincoln chronicler John de Schalby combines honesty with discretion by saying that the appointment was made for a certain reason (*ob certam causam*)[4]. Remigius was consecrated by Stigand, the schismatic archbishop of Canterbury, with whom William was not yet ready to quarrel; after Stigand's deprivation Remigius made his profession to the new archbishop Lanfranc, acknowledging that he ruled over a union of bishoprics by describing himself as bishop of Dorchester, Leicester and Lincoln and the other provinces of his predecessors.[5]

Remigius began to build a cathedral at Dorchester,[6] but soon there came a change of plan. Episcopal sees had hitherto been placed in the smaller towns, but in 1072 a council at Windsor decreed their removal to the larger towns. The decree was confirmed by a council in London in 1075. At the first of these councils Remigius was described as bishop of Dorchester, but at the second as bishop of Lincoln. The date of the transfer is fixed within narrower limits by a royal writ issued to T. the sheriff (perhaps Thorold, who is known to have been sheriff of Lincolnshire

[1] *Report of Commissioners on Public Records*, 1800–19, I, 488. Giraldus Cambrensis, whose evidence is not so good, says he brought ten knights. *Opera* (R.S.), VII, 14.

[2] *Historia Novorum* (R.S.), p. 11.

[3] *Gesta Pontificum* (R.S.), p. 312.

[4] Printed in Giraldus Cambrensis, *Opera* (R.S.), VII, 193.

[5] Ibid. p. 151. Mr Freeman comments (p. lxxiii) on the absence of Lindsey from this description, but there can be no doubt that 'Lincoln' was intended to include Lindsey.

[6] William of Malmesbury, *Gesta Pontificum* (R.S.), p. 312.

c. 1076–9 and perhaps earlier) and to all the sheriffs in the bishopric of Remigius telling them that by the authority and advice of Pope Alexander II and his legates and of Archbishop Lanfranc and other bishops of his realm, the king had transferred the see of Dorchester to Lincoln, and had given land there free from all customary payments for the building of the mother church of the whole diocese and the other buildings (*officinas*) thereof.[1] Pope Alexander died on 21 April 1073, to be succeeded by the famous Hildebrand, Pope Gregory VII; and the transfer of the see can therefore be dated 1072–3.[2]

Henry of Huntingdon says that it seemed inconvenient to Remigius that his see should be placed at the extreme end of the diocese; but the remark is not a happy one, for the bishop moved from its southern extremity, on the Thames, to a place near to its northern extremity, on the Humber, if indeed Lindsey rightfully belonged to the diocese at all. The question whether Lindsey belonged to the see of Dorchester or the see of York was far from settled; and there was to be much trouble before the claim of the see of York to Lindsey in right of its spiritual conquest by Paulinus of York was finally overruled. Henry does, however, illustrate the Norman policy by adding that a noble city like Lincoln was more worthy to be the episcopal seat than a poor town.[3]

Already Bishop Wulfwig had had to contend against Archbishop Ealdred of York, who had seized the diocese of Lindsey (*maxime parrochiam Lindisi*) and the church of Stow with Newark. Wulfwig appealed to Pope Nicholas II, who issued a bull in 1061 awarding the disputed territory to the diocese of Dorchester.[4] Remigius had to meet the claim again. Thomas archbishop of York claimed that the three sees of Dorchester, Lichfield and Worcester belonged to the province of York. The pope referred the claim to a council to be held in England, and in 1072 a council at Winchester ruled that the Humber was the boundary between the provinces of York and Canterbury. The York claim was silenced for the moment.

Remigius began to build his new church of Lincoln, and it was ready for consecration in 1092. A few days before the day appointed for the purpose Remigius was forbidden to proceed by Thomas of York on the ground that the church was in the latter's diocese. For a consideration Remigius secured the king's support, and a royal summons was sent to the bishops of England to assemble for the ceremony. Two days before the day appointed Remigius died.[5] When the king's chancellor Robert Bloet was elected to the see of

[1] Davis, *Regesta Regum Anglo-Normannorum*, I, no. 283; *R.A.* I, 3.
[2] *Handbook of British Chronology* (Royal Historical Society) adopts 1072.
[3] *Historia Anglorum* (R.S.), p. 212.
[4] *R.A.* I, 186–8.
[5] Florence of Worcester, *Chronicon ex Chronicis* (ed. Thorpe), II, 30.

Lincoln, Archbishop Thomas of York warned Anselm archbishop of Canterbury against consecrating him as bishop of Lincoln, claiming that the town of Lincoln, great part of the diocese of Lindsey, and the three vills of Stow, Louth and Newark belonged to St Peter of York.[1] Again the royal aid against York was procured. About 1093 William Rufus issued a charter declaring that he had from his own possessions bought out the claim which the church of York and Thomas its archbishop had upon Lincoln and Lindsey and the manors of Stow and Louth; and instead he had given to St Peter of York the abbey of St German of Selby and the church of St Oswald of Gloucester, in such wise that Archbishop Thomas and his successors should hold the abbey as the archbishop of Canterbury held the bishopric of Rochester. On his part Archbishop Thomas had with the consent of his clergy, in the presence of the king and the bishops and the magnates, abandoned his aforesaid claim to the king and Bishop Robert of Lincoln and his successors. The king, said the charter, had done this in favour of Bishop Robert because the bishop was his chancellor.[2] Clearly the redemption of the York claim was preceded by a bargain between the king and Bishop Robert. The statement that the king had settled the claim out of regard for his chancellor was 'a decent evasion of a somewhat unbecoming fact',[3] for according to Hugh the Chantor, the historian of the first Norman archbishops of York, the king enforced an agreement between these prelates, although the archbishop was very unwilling to lose his authority over Lindsey and his possessions of Stow, Louth and Newark: Hugh adds that all England knew that Bishop Robert gave the king three thousand pounds for this agreement.[4] This evidence might be criticised as coming from a prejudiced Yorkist source if it were not that Henry of Huntingdon, an adherent of Bishop Robert, says plainly that the price was five thousand pounds.[5] The settlement was confirmed by Pope Paschal II in 1106 and again by Pope Alexander III in 1177.[6]

So ended the dispute between the prelates, but the decree of William II embodied in his charter does not close the question in its historical aspect as it did in the sphere of law and politics. The two facts that the bishop of Lincoln had to pay a high price to the king for a favourable judgement, and that the king had to pay a high price to the unwilling archbishop to persuade him to forego his claim, indicate that the York claim was one of substance. Other hints point to the same conclusion. When William II

[1] Hugh the Chantor in Raine, *Historians of the Church of York and its Archbishops* (R.S.), II, 105.

[2] *R.A.* I, 11.

[3] Professor Stenton in *R.A.* I, 13.

[4] Raine, op. cit. II, 106.

[5] *Historia Anglorum* (R.S.), p. 216.

[6] Raine, op. cit. III, 28.

confirmed the gifts of Godgifu to St Mary of Stow he addressed his writ to Thomas archbishop of York;[1] and Giraldus and John de Schalby both look on Lindsey as a district won by Remigius for his diocese and the province of Canterbury.[2]

There is a reference to the transfer of the see from Dorchester to Lincoln in Domesday Book, but it could hardly be more casual. The account of the Lincoln fields states that 'St Mary of Lincoln, in which the bishopric now is, had' (in 1066) 'and has' (in 1086) half a carucate of land in the fields.[3] The Domesday clerks knew that the church in which Remigius placed his stool was a foundation existing before the transfer. They record that it already had some endowment, however small, and their reference to it as 'St Mary of Lincoln' shows that the church had some special precedence among churches, suggesting comparison with St Peter of York, St John of Beverley, or St Oswald of Gloucester.

Another Domesday passage supplies further evidence. The jurors of the wapentake of Louthesk in the south riding of Lindsey declare:

> Those lands which Alsi and Olgrim had in Lindsey they placed in the church of St Mary of Lincoln and at the discretion of Bishop Wulfwig; and therefore Bishop Remigius claims them because they (Alsi and Olgrim) had eight score pounds for these lands in the time of King Edward.[4]

The sale of these lands to St Mary of Lincoln had the effect of putting them into the hands of Bishop Wulfwig. Remigius was claiming that what belonged to St Mary and Bishop Wulfwig belonged to him; in short, that St Mary was the bishop's church. The Lindsey Survey indicates that the claim was successful, and that the land was in Louth, where, in 1115–18, the bishop of Lincoln had twelve carucates.[5] When therefore Remigius transferred the chief seat of the whole diocese to St Mary of Lincoln he came to a church which was already his own.

St Mary of Lincoln almost certainly enjoyed other endowments, as will later be noticed, but it is difficult to discern them because of the practice of referring to all the endowments of the diocese as those of St Mary of Lincoln. The bishop's chief endowment lay in Oxfordshire, where Dorchester, Thame, Great Milton, Banbury and Cropredy formed 'a great episcopal estate of immemorial antiquity';[6] yet Cropredy could be described

[1] *Cartulary of Eynsham*, I, 48. Davis, *Regesta Regum Anglo-Normannorum*, no. 266, marks the writ 'spurious?'.

[2] Giraldus Cambrensis, *Opera* (R.S.), VII, pp. lxxx, 6, 19, 194.

[3] *L.D.* pp. 4, 5. Infra, p. 370. See Appendix III for Schalby's statement that Remigius placed his seat in St Mary Magdalene.

[4] *L.D.* 69/5. *D.B.* f. 375a, Olgrim may be the Ougrim 'who gave his land to St Mary', and who appears as a benefactor in the Minster Obituary under 13 December. *L.C.S.* II, p. ccxlii.

[5] *L.D.* p. 259.

[6] Stenton, *Anglo-Saxon England*, p. 432.

as having been, in 1066, of St Mary of Lincoln.[1] In Leicestershire, among lands of the bishop of Lincoln, those in Leicester, Knighton and Leire were described as lands of St Mary of Lincoln;[2] they could have been appropriated to the canons of St Mary by 1086, but it would not be safe to assume that they were. The practice of using 'St Mary of Lincoln' as synonymous with the diocese or the bishop is illustrated by the return made by Bishop Robert II to the royal inquiry as to the enfeoffments of knights by the barons; the sixty knights which it was his duty to find for the feudal host were described in the bishop's *carta* as being of the fee of St Mary of Lincoln.[3]

The royal and papal confirmations of the estates and privileges of the church of Lincoln for the most part relate to grants made after the Conquest, and therefore they throw little light on the earlier history of St Mary of Lincoln. There is, however, an important clue in the bull which Pope Alexander III addressed in 1163 to the dean and canons, in which he confirmed 'the benefit which in Lincolnshire the parishioners of the same shire of old time granted and gave to the church of Lincoln, annually yielding from every ploughland, to wit, one thrave of corn, which is commonly called St Mary corn'.[4] *Thrave* is a word still in use in the north country for bundles of straw. The thrave of corn consisted apparently of two of the small stacks (or stooks) of sheaves made in the cornfield before the corn was carried away to the granaries.[5] It was a form of tithe ordained by one of the laws of Edgar (959–75): 'And all tithes shall be paid to the old minsters to which obedience is due; and payment shall be made both from the thegn's demesne land and the land held by his tenants—all that is under the plough.'[6]

The classic instance of the payment of thraves to an old minster comes from Beverley. The Beverley chapter acts constantly refer to them; and the chronicler of Meaux Abbey complained that four thraves were due to the provost of Beverley throughout the east riding of Yorkshire from every carucate or ploughland, that is, land under coulter and ploughshare.[7] These 'thraves of St John' of Beverley were presumably assigned from the church of York by the archbishop because elsewhere 'Peter corn' is declared to be due to the church of St Peter of York by every ploughland in Yorkshire.[8]

[1] *D.B.* I, 155.
[2] Ibid. f. 231.
[3] *Red Book of the Exchequer*, I, 374.
[4] *R.A.* I, 206.
[5] Leach, *Beverley Chapter Act Book* (Surtees Society), I, p. xcviii. Coulton, *Medieval Village*, p. 77 n. says a thrave was a score of sheaves.
[6] 2 Edgar, c. 1, 1. Robertson, *Laws of the Kings of England from Edmund to Henry I*, pp. 20, 21.
[7] *Chronica Monasterii de Melsa* (R.S.), II, 236.
[8] *Historians of the Church of York* (R.S.), III, 162.

Evidently a church that enjoyed thraves was the head church, or mother church, of a district, entitled to obedience from all within the district, and as its title of *old minster* in Edgar's law indicates, it was of earlier foundation than its subordinate churches. The special status of an old minster is further explained by the classification of churches contained in the laws of Æthelred II and Cnut. There was the head minster, the minster of medium rank, the smaller church with a graveyard, and the country chapel: for 'not all churches are to be regarded as possessing the same status in civil law, though from the side of religion they all possess the same sanctity'.[1] The head minster was the cathedral, in which the bishop had his seat. The medium or ordinary minster is the *old minster* of other laws, the *matrix ecclesia* of medieval documents. 'In many, perhaps in most cases, the lesser church arose within the original parish of the *matrix ecclesia*, and the memory of its origin was often preserved by a pension from its priest to the rector of the parish from which its territory had been withdrawn.'[2] *Minster* is the Anglo-Saxon form of *monasterium*, and the word was often used of a church, not monastic in the usual sense, but served by a group or college of clergy sharing a communal life. The name is still used at York, Southwell, and Beverley, in each of which there was a college of clergy; and its use at Lincoln (exemplified in Minster Yard) has the same reason.

The earliest English parishes were large districts served by such a group of clergy, stationed at a mother church, from which they went out as missionaries to teach the Christian faith to the inhabitants of their district or 'parish'. The bull of Pope Nicholas II mentions the *maxime parrochiam* of Lindsey;[3] Pope Honorius II refers to the episcopal parish of Lindsey in addition to Lincolnshire;[4] Innocent II confirms the liberty of the church of Lincoln with its parish, to wit Lincolnshire with all Lindsey.[5] It was the duty of the parishioners of each such parish to provide for the maintenance of their clergy, and one of the sources of maintenance was the thraves. The old minster of St Mary of Lincoln had (or ought to have had) its St Mary corn from all the ploughlands throughout its parish; and its parish was Lincolnshire.

A system whereby so large an area was administered from a single centre must have been highly unsatisfactory and appropriate only to the earliest missionary stage of evangelisation; and at a very early date it began to give way to the parish system, with the ideal of a church and a priest in every township. The law of Edgar, quoted above, goes on to contemplate

[1] 8 Æthelred II, c. 5, 1; 1 Cnut, c. 3, 3a. Robertson, op. cit. pp. 119, 157.

[2] Stenton, *Anglo-Saxon England*, pp. 148–9.

[3] *R.A.* I, 186.

[4] Ibid. p. 189.

[5] Ibid. p. 191. Thomas of York claimed that Lincoln Minster was built in his parish. Florence of Worcester, *Chronicon ex Chronicis* (ed. Thorpe), II, 30.

this development: 'If, however, there is a thegn who, on the land which he holds by title-deed, has a church to which is attached a graveyard, he shall pay the third part of his own tithes to his church.'[1] This diversion of a third of the tithe from the old minster to the new church built by the thegn upon his own land left the old minster in possession of two-thirds of his tithe; and a list of the parishes from which the old minster received such a fraction of the tithe from the lord's land might be regarded with some confidence as a list of the parishes in which churches were built within the original parish of the old minster during the period when the principle laid down by Edgar was being observed.

The bull of Pope Eugenius III (1146) mentions a few such parishes. Besides Kilsby (Northampton), Staughton (Huntingdon), and Greetwell, near Lincoln, all prebendal endowments, there were two parts of the tithe of a carucate once belonging to one Alfred in Scawby, which belonged to the common of the canons, that part of the chapter revenue not appropriated to particular prebends. Perhaps more interesting is the reference to Stow, where the prebendal income included the whole tithe of the lord bishop in Stow, and two parts of the tithe of the parishioners in the same township.[2] The bull of Alexander III (1163) adds two parts of the tithe of Walter de Amundaville in Kingerby and Elsham and two parts from Scothern.[3] About 1203 the abbot and convent of Barlings, who had acquired the church of Scothern, agreed with the dean and chapter of Lincoln that two parts of the tithes of sheaves at Scothern belonged of old to the prebend of All Saints Hungate in the church of Lincoln: and William the bishop confirmed the agreement.[4] A fourteenth-century account of the tithes in Fulbeck records that of old time the mother church of Lincoln had received two sheaves and the church of Fulbeck one;[5] and a terrier of tithes at Spridlington and Faldingworth shows that the dean and chapter received two sheaves and the rector one.[6] There is also a summary, in a hand which Canon Foster identified as that of John de Schalby, of portions of tithes in churches which did not belong to the dean and chapter; and in some of these 'alien' parishes, as at Fulbeck, Swallow and Riby, and parts of Great Gonerby, Belton and Scawby, the dean and chapter were entitled to two parts of the lord's tithe. At Canwick the prior of St Katharine of Lincoln paid 20*s*. for two parts of the tithe of the prebend of Canwick.[7]

This list of contributory parishes is a very short one, and could no doubt be greatly increased. For example, the *Valor Ecclesiasticus* of 1535

[1] 2 Edgar, c. 2. Robertson, op. cit. p. 21.
[2] *R.A.* I, 199, 200.
[3] Ibid. p. 206.
[4] Ibid. pp. 144–5.
[5] *R.A.* III, 377.
[6] Ibid. pp. 380–3.
[7] Ibid. pp. 376–7.

gives a list of portions of tithes belonging to the dean and chapter: the list mentions a number of the parishes already referred to, and adds Willoughby by Sleaford, Ingham and Cotes, Haydor, Barrow, Cuxwold, Grantham, Kirkby Laythorpe, and land in several other parishes.[1] An account of revenues of the dean and chapter compiled in 1668 concludes with a list of pensions due from parishes in Lincolnshire: these may have originated in various ways, among them being commutation of tithe, and as among the parishes mentioned are some already noted as paying a portion of tithe to the church of Lincoln, it is at least possible that the other parishes made contribution for the same reason.[2]

There are other hints of ancient connexion between parishes in the county and the mother church. The chapter acts of the sixteenth century contain a number of entries relating to probate before the dean and chapter of wills of persons who died on the Oldminster Fee. In 1521 Matthew Helwys of Grainthorpe died on the fee, and his will was proved in the chapter court; about the same time occur the wills of testators living at Asgarby, Searby, Scamblesby and Burgh le Marsh.[3] Asgarby, Searby and Scamblesby are among the parishes in which the dean and chapter had jurisdiction in probate before 1856;[4] and the prior and convent of Alvingham, which held the rectory of Grainthorpe, paid the dean and chapter two shillings yearly by way of pension for it.[5]

The phrase 'Oldminster Fee' has another import. The accounts of the chapter include an item 'Old Mynster Fee, rents of assise and at will' which in 1535 amounted to £21. 14*s*. 9½*d*. net. This was a small proportion of the total income of the chapter, which was given as £506. 13*s*. 4¾*d*. exclusive of fabric, chantry and prebendal revenues: yet it was carefully kept apart from other revenue, as is illustrated by the fact that in the accounts of the chapter for the manor of Navenby there is a deduction of 2*s*. 6*d*. to the chapter of Lincoln for the Oldminster Fee, and no doubt there was a corresponding entry on the credit side of the accounts of the fee.[6]

[1] IV, 9b. The list is printed in *Chapter Acts*, 1536–47 (L.R.S.), p. 170.

[2] D. & C., Bii, 2/1/f. 6d. The places mentioned are Spilsby, Fulstow and Louth Park, Helpringham, Grainthorpe, Wainfleet, Horncastle, Newsam, Legbourne, Stow in Lindsey, Owston and Haxey, Scamblesby, Brattleby, Willoughby by Sleaford, Spridlington, Faldingworth, Friesthorpe, Kirkby Laythorpe, Gonerby north and south. Stow paid 20*d*.

[3] *Chapter Acts*, 1520–36 (L.R.S.), pp. 19, 20, 23, 35, 62; and Chapter Acts, Liber VI (ii), f. 119 (1507) which also refers to Grainthorpe *super le olde mynster fee*.

[4] See Swan, *Practical Treatise on Jurisdiction of Ecclesiastical Courts relating to Probates and Administrations* (1830), p. 105. Several prebendaries had testamentary jurisdiction: the prebendary of Stow in Lindsey had it in the parish of Stow and the townships of Sturton and Normanby by Stow.

[5] *Valor Ecclesiasticus*, IV, 58; *Chapter Acts*, 1536–47 (L.R.S.), p. 169.

[6] *Valor Ecclesiasticus*, IV, 12; *Chapter Acts*, 1536–47 (L.R.S.), p. 173.

Canon Cole contents himself with referring to the Oldminster Fee as 'the ancient endowment of the cathedral',[1] a description which has the appearance of being correct. A surviving rental of the fee for the year 1672 shows that few of the rents exceed a pound, and many are only a few shillings.[2] They may well represent the small gifts made to the old minster of Lincoln before the transfer of the see from Dorchester, maintained by conservatism as a separate account through following centuries. If this is so it becomes of interest to inquire from what area the revenues of the fee are drawn. With the exceptions of Kelham and Newark all come from Lincolnshire, though the extreme north of Lindsey, south Kesteven and all Holland are unrepresented. In Kesteven the church of St Wulfram at Grantham enjoyed all the tithes and ecclesiastical customs from the king's sokes and inlands in the wapentakes of Winnibriggs and Threo;[3] but it may have been for this privilege that St Wulfram paid 10*s.* yearly to the church of Lincoln.[4] Farther south the old minster of Lincoln had to meet the competition of the abbeys of Peterborough and Ramsey; and in the north of the county the influence of Beverley may well have been strong.[5]

Whatever the precise value of some of these facts may be, it is clear that St Mary of Lincoln, to which Remigius transferred the see, was the old minster, the mother church of Lincolnshire, its clergy being entitled to receive tithes from all the parishes within the original 'parish' of Lincolnshire. When was the old minster established, or, at least when was it established as the mother church of this great area? It could not have been before the recovery of the Five Boroughs by Edward the Elder and his sister about 918, and was probably not before their second recovery by Edmund from the Norse rulers of York;[6] it was probably after the issue of the St Martin pennies, which held out St Martin as the patron saint of Lincoln;[7] but in 953 there appears a bishop of Lindsey, Leofwine. As Professor Darlington remarks:

> It is probably not by accident that the sees of Elmham and Lindsey re-appear when Oda was archbishop of Canterbury,[8] for there are other indications that his pontificate was a notable period in diocesan re-organization. Between 942 and 946 he promulgated a body of *constitutiones* or canons, ten in number, touching upon the immunity of the Church from secular burdens, the respect

[1] *Chapter Acts*, 1520–36 (L.R.S.), p. xix.
[2] D. & C., Bii, 3/9.
[3] *L.D.* 5/1–5, 72/24; *D.B.* ff. 343d, 377a.
[4] *Valor Ecclesiasticus*, IV, 9; *Chapter Acts*, 1536–47 (L.R.S.), p. 170.
[5] For the story of King Athelstan meeting no small concourse of people in the diocese of Lincoln who had come from Beverley, see Leach, *Beverley Chapter Act Book* (Surtees Society), I, xxii. For miracles wrought by St John of Beverley in Lincolnshire people, see *Historians of the Church of York*, I, 313–15.
[6] Supra, p. 27.
[7] Supra, pp. 29–30.
[8] *c.* 942–*c.* 958.

to be shown to prelates by laymen, the duties of bishops, who are ordered to make annual visitations of their bishoprics and preach sedulously to and watch over their flocks, the duties of priests who are commanded to set a good example to the people by their teaching and their manner of life, the duties of clerks who are likewise exhorted to live canonically and set a good example to the laity, the duties of monks, the avoidance by the laity of uncanonical marriages and of discords, the observance of fasts, the duty of almsgiving, and the rendering of tithes.[1]

Leofwine became also bishop of Dorchester in 958, and the sees were still being held together, but it is suggestive that the title of the most northern of his combined dioceses was occasionally used. The recovered Danish districts must have given him ample scope for his activities in the organisation of the church and the carrying out of Oda's canons.

Of Leofwine's successors in the diocese the barest facts are recorded. Ælfnoth (*c.* 965–*c.* 979) attested the charter of foundation of Ramsey Abbey by Edgar in 974.[2] Bishop Æscwig (*c.* 979–*c.* 1002) was an intimate friend of St Oswald of Worcester, who, with St Dunstan and Ethelwold of Winchester, was a pioneer of the monastic revival of the tenth century.[3] When the church of Ramsey was consecrated in 991, the great men of several counties were present, including the men of Kesteven, with the Bishop Æscwig of Dorchester, 'a man of great sanctity and authority'.[4] Bishop Ælfhelm, who was consecrated in 1002, was succeeded in 1006 by Eadnoth, the first abbot of Ramsey, who had been a monk at the old minster at Winchester, had known St Oswald, and who is identified as the founder of St Mary of Stow. After the murder of Archbishop Alphege by the Danes in 1012, Eadnoth was one of the bishops to receive the body and give it burial in St Paul's, London.[5] In 1016 he was killed at the battle of Ashingdon by the side of Edmund Ironside. The two succeeding bishops, Æthelric and Eadnoth II, also came from Ramsey Abbey.[6] On the death of the second Eadnoth in 1049 King Edward the Confessor gave the bishopric to Ulf, his priest, and one of his Norman favourites, and 'ill bestowed it' upon one who 'was afterwards driven out because he did nothing bishoplike there, so that it shames us to tell more now'.[7] Ulf narrowly escaped deposition by the pope; and when Earl Godwin and Harold returned in triumph from exile to England Ulf and other foreign favourites fled overseas. He was succeeded by the Saxon Wulfwig, who held the bishopric from 1053 until his death in 1067.

[1] *E.H.R.* LI (1936), p. 386.
[2] *Cartularium Monasterii de Rameseia* (R.S.), II, 58.
[3] *Historians of the Church of York* (R.S.), I, 463.
[4] *Chronicon Abbatiae Rameseiensis* (R.S.), p. 93.
[5] Ibid. p. 115.
[6] Ibid. p. 148.
[7] *Anglo-Saxon Chronicle* (R.S.), I, 307, 310.

There is no record of the number of parish churches built within the original parish of the mother church of Lincoln in the century between Bishop Leofwine and the Norman Conquest. Sir Henry Ellis estimated that 222 churches are mentioned in Domesday Book as existing in Lincolnshire in 1086.[1] Canon Foster's index to the Lincolnshire Domesday gives about 250; fractions of churches make an exact computation impossible.[2] The Domesday enumeration is certainly not complete: there must, for example, have been many more churches in Lincoln than the five mentioned therein.[3] Professor Baldwin Brown has recorded thirty-nine Lincolnshire churches where Saxon and Saxo-Norman work is still extant.[4] Of this total some may well belong to the period after 1086, but it is worthy of notice that seventeen of them are not represented in the Domesday list. The list of places in which are preserved pre-Conquest carved stones of the tenth and eleventh centuries recorded for Lincolnshire numbers forty-nine, only one of them—a cross-shaft with a runic inscription at Crowle—showing any trace of Scandinavian feeling.[5] Twenty-two of the stones are in parishes not represented by a church either in Domesday or in Baldwin Brown's list. It seems likely therefore that by (say) 1100 there were between 300 and 400 churches in Lincolnshire.

The bishops who presided over this vast building programme and all that it implies were for the most part products of the monastic revival, but it was only in this indirect way that the religious houses contributed to it. Though by the end of the tenth century there had come into being the fenland monasteries of Ely, Ramsey, Peterborough and Thorney, yet, as Professor Stenton has pointed out, the Anglo-Danish noblemen beyond the Welland seem to have ignored them. In 1066 the only monastery in the shires of Lincoln, Leicester, Nottingham, Derby and York was Crowland.[6] Perhaps it may be inferred that the impetus given to the building of churches in Lincolnshire by the bishops was given through the medium of the old minster at Lincoln.

It is only of one foundation in Lincolnshire that there is any documentary evidence. According to Florence of Worcester the church of Stow was built by Bishop Eadnoth,[7] and Ralph de Diceto gives Elnoth Lincolniensis as the founder.[8] It was assumed by Mr Freeman that it was the

[1] *Introduction to D.B.* I, 286. Compare Norfolk with 243, Suffolk with 364.

[2] *L.D.* index sub 'Churches'. Dr William Page says there is evidence of about 255 manorial churches in the county. *Archaeologia*, LXVI (1915), p. 92.

[3] Infra, Chapter VII.

[4] *Arts in Early England* (2nd ed.), II, ch. xiv.

[5] D. S. Davies, 'Pre-Conquest Carved Stones in Lincolnshire', with introduction by A. W. Clapham, *Arch. Journ.* LXXXIII (1926), pp. 1–20.

[6] *Anglo-Saxon England*, p. 450.

[7] *Chronicon ex Chronicis* (ed. Thorpe), I, 216.

[8] *Opera Historica* (R.S.), II, 211.

second Eadnoth (1034–49) who was the founder,[1] but, as Dr Salter has pointed out,[2] the charter of Leofric which mentions the food rent which Æthelric (1017–34) had enjoyed indicates that the founder must have been Eadnoth I (1006–16). According to a York chronicler Kensius (Cynesige) archbishop of York (1051–60) gave two great bells to Stow as well as to Beverley and Southwell,[3] a gift which suggests the recent building of a tower. He was claiming that Stow, like Beverley and Southwell, belonged to him.[4]

Apparently it was intended to place a small community at Stow, probably from Eynsham, though nothing more is known of it until the Anglo-Saxon record of its endowment by Earl Leofric and Godgifu his wife, which can be dated 1053–5, and which Miss Robertson translates as follows:

Here it is declared in this document how arrangements have been made between Bishop Wulfwig and Earl Leofric and Godgifu, the earl's wife, with regard to the monastery at Stow St Mary. In the first place they asked the bishop for permission to endow the monastery and assign lands to it with his full consent, and the bishop granted their request, and was very glad to have any assistance for that purpose. Now they have furnished it with priests and desire that divine service should be celebrated there as it is at St Paul's in London. And the lands which they assign to it shall provide food and clothing for the brethren who are therein. And the bishop shall have as food-rent for himself everything which Bishop Æthelric and Bishop Eadnoth had before him and which by rights belongs to his bishopric, namely two-thirds of everything that comes into the monastery, and the priests shall have the remaining third except at the two festivals. The bishop, however, shall have everything that accrues to it for eight days at the earlier festival of St Mary, and for eight days at the later festival of St Mary, except for food alone. The priests, however, shall have the third part of the food which accrues to it. And the lands which the bishop and the earl and Godgifu and good men grant to it shall remain for all time in the possession of the holy foundation for the needs of the brethren and the endowment of the monastery, so that no bishop who succeeds him shall demand any food-rent from it except what by rights belongs to his bishopric, as other bishops had before him.

This is done with King Edward's full consent and with his cognisance and that of his wife Eadgyth and of Archbishop Stigand and of Archbishop Cynesige and of Bishop Hereman and of Bishop Duduc and of Bishop Leofric and of Bishop Ealdred and of Bishop Heca and of Bishop Æthelmaer and of Bishop Ælfwold and of Bishop William and of Bishop Leofwine and of Earl Siweard and of Earl Harold and of Earl Raulf and of Earl Ælfgar and of Abbot Manni and of Abbot Ælfwine and of Abbot Leofsige and of Abbot Leofric and of the other Abbot Leofsige and of Abbot Brihtmaer and of Esgar the Staller and of Raulf

[1] *Norman Conquest*, II, 49 n.
[2] *Cartulary of Eynsham*, I, p. x.
[3] *Historians of the Church of York* (R.S.), II, 344.
[4] For the York claim see supra, pp. 65–7.

the Staller and of Lyfing the Staller and of all the king's household officers and chaplains and of Thurgod *lagen* and of Siferth and of Godric and of Owine and of Siric, and with the cognisance of all the citizens of Lincoln and of all the men who attend the yearly market at Stow. And if anyone increases (the property of) the community with benefactions, God Almighty shall increase the days of his life here in this life, and in the future he shall be allowed to have his dwelling with God's elect. And if anyone expels them and alienates the lands from the holy foundation, he shall be rejected by God and St Mary and all his saints on the great Judgement Day.

There are three of these documents. One is in the king's sanctuary, the second is in Earl Leofric's possession, and the third is in the possession of the bishop at the holy foundation.[1]

It will be noticed that two-thirds of the food-rent, or tithe, are reserved to the bishop, and a third to the priests of Stow. The bishop's two-thirds went to his minster in Lincoln, to which he also gave the whole tithe from his own lands in Stow.[2] The bishop could do what he liked with his own, but he was observing the rights of the mother church to her St Mary corn from the Stow endowment, in accordance with the principles laid down in the law of Edgar.

'A spurious but not necessarily untruthful deed' says that Leofric and Godgifu's endowment consisted of the manors of Newark and Fledborough in Nottinghamshire, and Brampton and Marton in Lincolnshire. According to this deed William I confirmed their gift of Newark and Fledborough and the wapentake of Well (in which Stow is situate) to St Mary of Stow, and, at the request of Remigius, added the church of Eynsham with its lands: an abbot was to be appointed, and the abbey was to be in the patronage of the king 'like the other abbeys throughout England', and instead of the portion of the oblations which was reserved to the bishop, the king granted him the manor of Sleaford.[3] The transaction referred to in the document cannot be later than 1086, as Sleaford and a two-thirds interest in Well wapentake were in the bishop's hands by that date.

The monastery was not founded at once. Domesday merely states that 'there is a church there and a priest'.[4] In the charter attributed to William II (1090) the king confirms the right of Remigius to appoint the abbot of St Mary of Stow, since it is in his episcopal manor, and grants to the monks the alms of Newark, Fledborough and Well wapentake except the third penny of the county.[5] The next year the bishop, with the king's approval, appointed Columbanus, already abbot of Eynsham, to be abbot

[1] *Anglo-Saxon Charters* (1939), p. 213; *Cartulary of Eynsham*, I, 28.
[2] Supra, p. 70.
[3] *Cartulary of Eynsham*, I, pp. x, 32; Davis, *Regesta Regum Anglo-Normannorum*, no. 266.
[4] *L.D.* 7/1.
[5] *R.A.* I, 5, 6.

of Stow; and he and his monks were transferred from Eynsham to Stow.[1] Dr Salter suggests that the delay in carrying out the foundation of the abbey at Stow is easy to understand, for though it was decided about 1072 to transfer the bishop's seat from Dorchester to Lincoln, the first part of the new cathedral was not ready for use until 1092; and the bishop would not move his monks from Eynsham until he was ready to move himself.[2]

Robert Bloet was consecrated bishop of Lincoln in December 1093, and he lost no time in moving the monks back to Eynsham, keeping Stow and its manors for himself, and making the monks other gifts in exchange.[3] It was convenient to the bishop to have Stow in his own hands, and the use made of the manor-house and the park by his successors (notably by St Hugh) justifies his policy. The transfer was made before the death of William Rufus in 1100, and may have been made in 1094.[4] Later, Henry II confirmed to Eynsham whatever Bishop Robert gave in exchange for Newark and Stow.[5] Though Stow remained an episcopal manor, and gave its name to an archdeaconry and prebend in the church of Lincoln, its subsequent ecclesiastical history was similar to that of any other parish. There is no evidence of the existence of a church at Stow before the time of Bishop Eadnoth I: it is only in comparatively modern times that it has been claimed that the church there is the 'mother church of Lincoln'.[6]

In Lincolnshire such a position clearly belonged to St Mary of Lincoln. Like many other old minsters in England, though it was not a cathedral in the modern sense, it was the mother church of its original parish. Such minsters were, as a rule, served by a college of clergy, and in so far as there was a general customary number of clergy or canons, it was seven. There were seven canons at York; this was the traditional number at Ripon, and it was probably the number at Southwell. At St Mary in the Castle at Leicester, at All Saints Derby, St John's Chester and St Mary's Shrewsbury, there were a dean and seven canons. The number suggests that in the earlier stages of their history these foundations had seven priests each, and that, as happened at York at the Conquest, a dean was added as the result of a Norman reorganisation of the chapter.[7]

How many canons there were at the old minster in Lincoln is not recorded. According to Giraldus and Schalby the establishment of Remigius comprised twenty-one canons, this high figure being doubled by Bloet and further augmented later.[8] In this number of twenty-one were included the

[1] *Cartulary of Eynsham*, I, 32, 33. [2] Ibid. p. xi.
[3] Ibid. p. 36. [4] Ibid. p. xi. [5] *R.A.* I, 83.
[6] For modern claims concerning Stow, see Appendix III.
[7] Hamilton Thompson, 'Notes on Colleges of Secular Canons in England' in *Arch. Journ.* LXXIV (1917), pp. 143–52.
[8] Giraldus Cambrensis, *Opera* (R.S.), VII, 19, 32, 195.

dignitaries who, after the bishop, were, according to the Black Book (*c.* 1236), the dean, precentor, chancellor, treasurer and subdean, with eight archdeacons—Lincoln, Northampton, Leicester, Buckingham, Bedford, Oxford, Huntingdon and Stow.[1] This would account for fourteen of the canons, and it is tempting to proceed by subtraction to an original pre-Norman chapter of seven canons. It is not certain, however, that the Norman dignitaries were as stated by the Black Book. When Henry of Huntingdon, himself archdeacon of Huntingdon, wrote his letter to Walter about 1135, he referred to the dean, the treasurer, the precentor; and he mentions other priests, some of whom may have filled the office of chancellor, though he does not say so. He adds that Remigius placed seven archdeacons over the seven provinces, and he mentions all those named above save Stow, adding that he passes over the rest of the clergy.[2] There certainly was a subdean about 1135,[3] and an archdeacon of Stow about 1150, and possibly earlier;[4] and both offices may have been instituted by Remigius. Yet in view of these doubts it cannot be said with confidence that the 'residuary' number of pre-Conquest canons was seven; but analogy suggests that the college of canons at the old minster of Lincoln was not very different in number from the number noted in like foundations elsewhere.

Of the old minster of Lincoln removed by Remigius nothing remains: there is no evidence that there had ever been a crypt. There are two carved pre-Conquest stones in the Minster cloisters: one is a tomb-slab about 5 ft. long by about 21 in. tapering to 19½ in., with a plain border and a Latin cross, with panels of interlacement between the arms. The other, possibly a headstone, is an oblong block, 3 ft. high by 23 in., and 10½ in. in thickness. It has a cable moulding round the top, continued halfway down the sides of the face. On the face are two plain incised crosses, one within the other, and there is a deeply cut hole about the middle of the stone for the insertion of a fastening.[5] This second stone was found in the morning chapel, at the north-west corner of the nave, in 1894, in what was presumably the graveyard of old St Mary's.

By comparison with the majestic new minster of the Normans, the old minster may well have been a humble structure; and the great establishment required for the mother church of a vast diocese no doubt made the Saxon foundation of perhaps seven canons with a meagre endowment seem a poor affair. Add to these considerations the contempt of the Norman conqueror for the conquered races, and there is perhaps sufficient

[1] *L.C.S.* I, 301–5.

[2] *Historia Anglorum* (R.S.), pp. 301–3. [3] *R.A.* II, 254.

[4] D. & C., Registrum, 1912; Dii, 78/2/62. Giraldus mentions the archdeacon of the west riding in his life of St Hugh, *Opera* (R.S.), VII, 147.

[5] See Davies in *Arch. Journ.* LXXXIII (1926), p. 16.

explanation of the lack of reference in post-Conquest documents to the old minster. Its existence was casually acknowledged by Domesday Book, and that is all. Yet it was probably in the mind of Henry of Huntingdon when he referred to the building of the new church (*ecclesia moderna*) of Lincoln.[1] Centuries later it seems to have been mentioned to Leland, and to have been in his mind when he wrote that where the dean's house was in the minster close there was a monastery of nuns before the time that Remigius began the new minster of Lincoln, and that certain tokens of the house yet remained.[2] The use of the term 'Oldminster Fee' in the seventeenth century has already been mentioned, and in colloquial usage the old name *minster* has held its ground in Lincoln as at York, Beverley, Ripon and Southwell.[3]

Though some memory of the old minster remained, it was completely ignored by later historians. Giraldus, who was promoting Remigius' claims to sanctity about 1200, proclaimed him founder of the cathedral and first bishop of Lincoln.[4] Schalby, either copying Giraldus or using the same common source, uses the same words;[5] and the biographer of St Hugh also refers to Remigius as founder.[6] Yet earlier evidences, while ignoring the old minster, do not claim Remigius as founder. The Minster Obituary, of date 1182–9, calls him, not *fundator*, but *stabilitor*.[7] A memorial tablet in the Minster Library commemorates William son of Walter Aiencurt, a kinsman of Remigius, 'who made this church'.[8] Though Henry of Huntingdon says in one passage that Remigius founded the church of Lincoln, yet he qualifies the statement in another by referring to him as author of the modern church of Lincoln.[9] William of Malmesbury, followed by Ralph de Diceto, says that Remigius transferred the see to the city of Lincoln, where he filled the church founded there (*fundatam ecclesiam*) with many canons; he refounded (*ex novo fecit*) the monastery of St Mary of Stow; and renewed the old house of Bardney by his favour:[10] he is here being presented as a renewer of old foundations. Giraldus himself records that he was buried, not before the high altar as a founder might have been, but before the altar of the Holy Cross.[11]

It would seem that St Mary of Lincoln had acquired its status as the mother church of Lindsey and Lincolnshire by the middle years of the

[1] *Historia Anglorum* (R.S.), p. 213. [2] *Itinerary* (ed. Toulmin Smith), v, 123.

[3] In the sixteenth century the Lincoln Common Council minutes generally refer to 'the minster'.

[4] *Opera* (R.S.), VII, 13, 19. [5] Ibid. pp. xvi, 194.

[6] *Magna Vita Sancti Hugonis* (R.S.), p. 189.

[7] Giraldus, *Opera* (R.S.), VII, 157; *L.C.S.* II, pp. ccxxxiv, ccxxxviii.

[8] *A.A.S.R.* IV (1857), p. 36; *Proceedings of the Archaeological Institute* (1848), pp. xliv, 248.

[9] Loc. cit. pp. 213, 301.

[10] *Gesta Pontificum* (R.S.), p. 312; Diceto, *Opera Historica* (R.S.), II, 201.

[11] *Opera* (R.S.), VII, 22, 26.

tenth century, and the St Martin penny, of slightly earlier date,[1] argues against St Mary having any special precedence before that time. There remains the question when St Mary was founded, and by whom. It seems likely that some tradition of sites and dedications survived the Danish settlement,[2] and the position of St Mary in the upper Roman city, combined with the fact that it was a bishop's church, points to an early foundation. One of the manuscripts of Ralph de Diceto makes a high claim. It appears in a list of pre-Conquest founders of churches, and so far as that list can readily be checked it seems to be reliable. It records that St Paul's, London, was founded by Æthelbert, Peterborough by Saxulf, Bath and St Albans by Offa, Glastonbury by Ine, Ramsey by Earl Ælfwine, Thorney by King Edgar, Crowland by Waltheof, Coventry by Earl Leofric and Godgifu, St Mary of Stow by Elnoth bishop of Lincoln. The foundation of St Mary of Lincoln is attributed to Paulinus, first archbishop of York.[3]

Such a statement tempts belief: yet on consideration doubts arise. A list of pre-Conquest founders necessarily relates mainly to the midlands, the south and west; and north of the fens only York and Lincoln (apart from Stow) appear, and they come together in the list. There is no Durham, or Ripon or Hexham. The reference to York as founded by Edwin 'rege Northanhymbrorum' suggests that the writer took his information from Bede, who records that Edwin was baptised in the church of St Peter at York, which he had built;[4] and Diceto may well have inferred that Paulinus' church in Lincoln had similarly become the minster. His uncertainty is shown in his list of the archbishops of Canterbury, in which he says that Honorius, the fifth archbishop, was consecrated by Paulinus in the town of Lincoln, in the church there called St Paul, but in the time of the English called St Paulinus.[5] This latter passage, it is true, does not say that St Paul's was the church founded by Paulinus, but there can be little doubt that this was what the writer meant.

The evidence of Diceto cannot be regarded as convincing. If, however, a choice had to be made between existing churches for the honour of being Paulinus' church, St Mary has one distinct advantage, for when it is first mentioned it is found to be a bishop's church, whilst St Paul and St Martin (other churches for which such a claim has been made) are both found in private ownership,[6] without any hint of distinguished origin. Furthermore, the omission of the earlier post-Conquest historians to mention any tradition of Pauline foundation might be explained by reference to the York claim,

[1] Supra, pp. 29–30.
[2] Supra, p. 37.
[3] *Opera Historica* (R.S.), II, 211.
[4] *Historia Ecclesiastica*, II, c. xiv.
[5] *Opera Historica* (R.S.), II, 196.
[6] For St Paul, see infra, p. 103; for St Martin, p. 142.

LINCOLN CASTLE. *From Buck's sketch book*

LINCOLN CASTLE IN 1726. *From an engraving by Buck*

[*See p.* 84

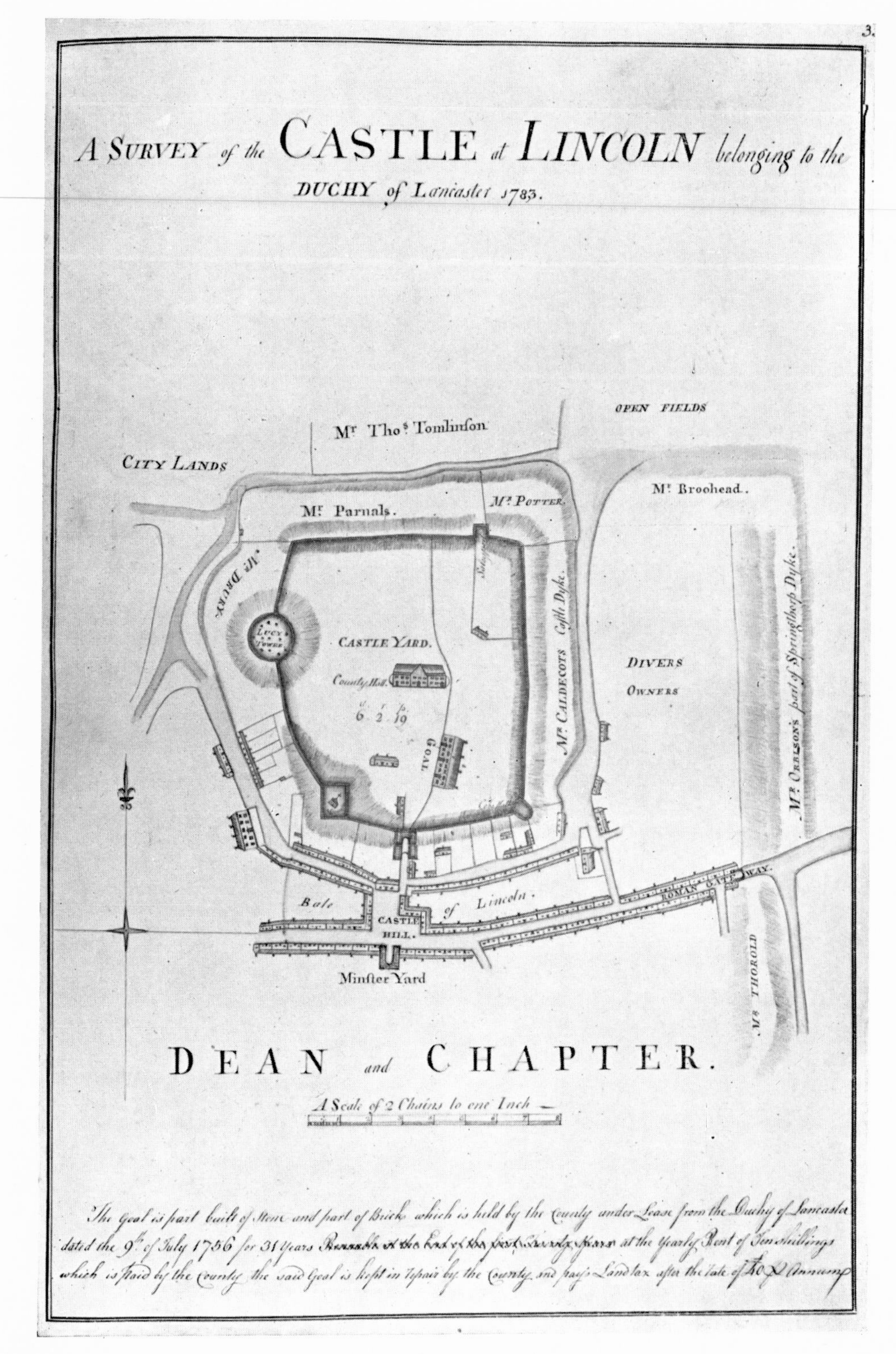

PLAN OF LINCOLN CASTLE IN 1783

See p. 100] *From a Survey of the Duchy of Lancaster.* (*The north point is, in fact, west*)

based on the spiritual conquest of Lindsey by Paulinus. Any acknowledgement of the foundation of the old minster by Paulinus would have strengthened the York case, and would not be likely to be made. On the other hand, though the York claim may have implied that St Mary was Paulinus' church the York chroniclers do not refer to any such tradition, and had they known of it they would surely have expressly declared it. The identification of Paulinus' church is not likely ever to be settled unless excavation should bring new evidence to light, and it has to be remembered that his stone church may have vanished without trace.

CHAPTER V

THE CASTLE AND THE BAIL

LINCOLN CASTLE consists of two fortified mounts with a large bailey annexed. It was placed in the south-west quarter of the upper Roman city, and the strategic advantages of the site are as evident to-day as they were to the builders. There were the Roman walls on the west and south, and to the north and east the Roman enclosure could be annexed as an outer bailey. Towards the south the defenders could command the steep ascent from the river and the lower city, and if necessary cut the communications between the two enclosures; and towards the west they could look out over the valley of the Trent (the river being only some ten miles away), and watch the highway by which invaders from overseas had had (and might again have) access to the heart of the country.

On the east, north and west sides ditches were dug and earthen banks thrown up within them. The banks are from 50 to 80 yards broad, and from 20 to 30 ft. high, and are externally steep and internally of easy slope. A bank was not raised on the south side, perhaps in order to accentuate the height of any mound thrown up there, but there was a well-defined ditch, depicted in one of the paintings of De Wint.

The banks are surmounted by stone walls, and Mr Willson, a learned architect and antiquary of the nineteenth century, inferred from their crooked and irregular lines that they were built in haste.[1] The view that the walls were built early is supported by the use of the word *murus* of the castle defences in 1115: it is a word which could 'hardly be applied to an earthwork or a palisade. The presence, too, of herring-bone coursing seems to point to a date not long after the Conquest for certain parts at least of the existing walls'.[2] The walls and their method of construction are described by Mr Willson:

> The masonry of the castle walls, wherever the original facing remains, is very rude, the stones being laid together in unhewn masses; but the whole was so well grouted and filled up with good mortar that the substance of the work is mostly sound and firm. In some parts, the walls were faced with thin stones, set diagonally, the courses leaning alternately to the right hand and to the left, in

[1] See his valuable paper 'Lincoln Castle' in the *Proceedings of the Archaeological Institute*, on the visit to Lincoln in 1848 (at p. 285). The architectural descriptions given here are borrowed from him and from G. T. Clark, *Medieval Military Architecture* (1884), II, 189 et seq. (reprinting an article in *A.A.S.R.* XIII (1876), p. 176).

[2] Canon Foster in *R.A.* I, 267.

what is called the *herring-bone* fashion. . . . The extensive repairs that were made in the walls and towers of Lincoln Castle, since it was purchased by the magistrates for the use of the county, brought to light some curious particulars of their ancient form and construction. The bottom courses of masonry were found to have been set upon frames of rough timber, in which three or four parallel lines of beams were laid upon the rubble on which the walls were to be raised, and these lines were crossed, at short distances, by other beams, to hold them in their right places. All this timber work had decayed and fallen to dust in those parts that were discovered, but the cavities in the walls showed plainly the forms and size of the beams.[1]

The castle has two principal gateways, one in the east wall, which is still in use, opening on to Castle Hill and facing the Minster; the other, now long disused, on the west, formerly giving access to open country. It would be important for the holder of the castle to have free ingress and egress independently of a perhaps adverse holder of the city. Both gates, once similar, consisted of a plain Norman arch placed in a rectangular recess in the wall. The bay may have been closed in the rear by a cross wall with a second archway. The east gate was probably damaged in the battle of Lincoln in 1217, for in 1227 the sheriff of Lincoln was ordered to survey the gates of the castle which, the king heard, were broken, and the tower of the great gate of the castle towards the church of St Mary, which tower was not then finished: and to cause the gates to be repaired and the tower completed.[2]

In the fourteenth century the Norman east gate was masked by a pointed arch springing from two angular corbels. Above, the outer angles were capped by two round turrets, and between them the curtain made to project at an obtuse angle. The gateway was no doubt considerably higher than it is now, and must have resembled Micklegate Bar and Monk Bar at York. Barbican walls and towers once projected in front of the gatehouse, but were for the most part taken down in 1791; the base of the southern barbican tower can still be seen.

The western gate has escaped alteration. Its portcullis groove can be seen and there is a rebate for the door. The upper floor has two small Norman windows in front, and a small door, flat headed, but with a round-headed arch of relief, opening upon the battlements of the barbican. This latter was composed of two flanking walls and an outer gate of which there remains the north wall and part of the south.

It was once supposed that the western gate of the castle was the Roman western gate, brought into service by the Normans. The discovery in 1836 of the Roman gate buried in the castle banks just to the north of the castle gate disposed of this theory. In 1782 Sir Henry Englefield had made a

[1] Op. cit. pp. 285–6.

[2] *Cal. Liberate Rolls*, 1226–40, pp. 36, 46.

careful examination of the gateway and discerned sufficient differences between it and the surviving Roman work to save him from this error; he concluded, however, that the gatehouse was there before the castle was built, and that the Normans turned it into a postern when they dug out the ditch and built a flight of steps to it.[1] He was writing by way of postscript to Edward King's 'Sequel to the Observations on Ancient Castles', from which paper it appears[2] that King's account of the castle's eastern gateway omits to notice the Norman arch concealed by the later pointed arch: he does not mention the western gateway at all, and only refers to information given him upon it by Englefield. Perhaps if they had realised how similar the two gateways once were they would have come to the view, taken later by Mr Willson and Mr Clark, that the western gateway is coeval with the castle.[3]

The most remarkable feature of the castle is that instead of having the single mound and keep usual in Norman castles it has two, like Lewes; but whilst at Lewes the two mounds are at each end of an oval bailey, at Lincoln both are in the south curtain wall, their bases being less than 200 ft. apart.[4] For reasons that will be mentioned below it seems likely that the western and larger mound and keep were added later, and that the one in the south-east corner is the original. This, indeed, is where the mound might be expected to be, if it is assumed that one of the purposes of the castle was to subdue the city: for there the tower commands as nearly as may be the steep approach from the lower city to the upper. Rather oddly, the tower is set back a little from the curtain instead of flanking it. The lower part of the tower is Norman, and is rectangular in shape, being 25 ft. by 40 ft. It is of two floors and contains a mural staircase. On the eastern side has been added a front, also of two storeys, flanked by square turrets, converting the tower into a 40 ft. square. A range of galleries, or narrow rooms, abutting on the curtain wall once connected the tower with the chambers over the eastern gateway of the castle. In the course of repairs a circular staircase was found which descended below the ground

[1] *Archaeologia*, VI (1782), pp. 379–80. [2] Ibid. pp. 264–5.

[3] Canon Foster, looking for a doorway licensed to be made in the castle wall for the convenience of the bishop's house (*R.A.* I, 20, 21; for the bishop's house, see infra, p. 127), thought he had found it in this western gateway (p. 268). But it seems hardly likely that a gatehouse of such impressive size would be built for the bishop's convenience: one would look rather for a small doorway such as was made in the Roman wall between the cathedral and the bishop's palace when the bishops moved their residence to the present palace site. There are two small doorways (both blocked) in the castle curtain; one on the south side, between the two mounds, the other on the north, a little to the west of Cobb Hall, now visible only from the outside of the wall. For a possible explanation of this latter doorway, see infra, p. 105.

[4] See Armitage, *Early Norman Castles* (1912), pp. 165–8.

floor and then entered a subterranean passage. This passage was traced a short distance to the west, where it was stopped by ruins. The tower is now called the Observatory Tower, from the little turret which was added to it by a modern governor of the gaol who was a student of astronomy.[1]

To the west of this tower, and near to the point at which the south-west corner of the castle joined the city wall, is the larger mound, crowned by a fine example of a shell keep. It is of late twelfth-century character, and replaces a predecessor which was probably damaged during the disorders of the Anarchy.[2] It measures 74 ft. from east to west and 64 ft. from north to south within the walls, which are 8 ft. thick. In shape it is an irregular polygon having twelve sides within and fifteen without, each angle being capped by a broad flat pilaster, all rising from a common plinth. The wall is 20 ft. high to the rampart walk but the parapet has gone. The keep has an entrance from the north-east, within the bailey, consisting of a full-centred arch of 7 ft. set in a broad projecting buttress. The arch of the actual doorway and of its inner recess is segmental. The door was defended by a stout wooden bar. Above the outer arch is a hood-moulding, said to be a restoration of the original Norman ornament.

On the south-west of the keep, opening on to the castle ditch, is another doorway, 5 ft. 6 in. wide. It is quite plain and the arches are segmental. There is no trace of any buildings within the keep, and it is evident that the quarters there must have consisted of timber structures built against the wall. At each point where it joins the keep, the curtain wall contains, at rampart level, a mural chamber: that to the west is a garde-robe. There was something more on the east side: Buck's engraving of 1726 (Plate 1) shows the remains of a building with two narrow windows at different levels.

When King described the keep in 1782 it was already approached by a steep flight of steps from the bailey, as it is to-day. He refers also to a drawbridge over a ditch. The ground has now been levelled inside the bailey, though the ditch of the keep is still discernible outside towards the south-west. In illustration of his point that the tower could be held either independently of the castle or with it, King described the strange manner in which it was connected with the rest of the defences. From the south-eastern tower, along the upper part of the curtain wall towards the keep, were the remains of a passage or covered way leading to a flight of steps

[1] 'Our governor was a genius in his way; he was not an educated man, but had the reputation of being an adept in astronomy. He had a handsome mounted telescope, and frequently spent whole nights in star-gazing—a very proper employment, I thought, for the governor of a prison. One or two desperate attempts at escape had been promptly foiled by his vigilance and that of his sub-officer.' Bamford, *Passages in the Life of a Radical* (ed. Dunckley), p. 313.

[2] See pp. 177–80.

on the side of the keep. These steps gave no immediate access to the keep, 'nor could there ever have been such; but they must clearly have ascended, with many windings, towards the top of this great tower, and must then have descended again, through a strong projecting and adjoining building ... before any entrance could be gained into it'.[1] This may be the building on the eastern face outside the curtain indicated by Buck. Unfortunately, the eastern bay of the keep has been rebuilt: Willson's plan of 1832 omits it.

The keep has traditionally been known as Lucy's Tower. It is so named in the plan of 1783 reproduced in Plate 2. Samuel Bamford, a political prisoner in Lincoln Castle in 1819 after the 'Peterloo Massacre', says that 'an ancient keep, called Lucy's Tower, in the rear of the jail—part of the original fortification—was not kept locked, and was tenanted only by owls, and an immense number of snail shells, which completely formed its floor'.[2] Mr Willson wrote that the name of Lucy Tower was formerly attached to the keep, and so continued down to a recent time (he was writing in 1848); and that it had been improperly transferred to a small round tower at the south end of the western city wall, on the north bank of Brayford Pool. He added that this error seemed to have originated in a statement of Stukeley who referred to this little tower as the Lucy Tower.[3] Stukeley is exonerated, however, by the discovery that in 1611 the Lincoln common council were granting a lease of 'Leucie tower at Braford side in the west ward'.[4] Perhaps there was a half-humorous copying of the name of the castle keep.

At the north-east corner of the bailey of the castle is a flanking tower of horse-shoe shape, known as Cobb Hall. It is an insertion, built probably in the thirteenth century, though whether it replaces an earlier tower is unknown.

The construction of the castle and the demolition of houses to make room for it have already been discussed.[5] The earliest piece of evidence concerning the guard of the castle has been brought to light by Canon Foster. In a writ which can be dated 1123–33, Henry I gave Bishop Alexander licence to assign the third part of the knights of the bishopric to the new castle which the bishop was building at Newark where one of the arms of the river Trent met the river Devon; and a bull of Pope Innocent II shows that it was at Lincoln that these knights had been accustomed to do service.[6] In 1166 the bishop had forty-five knights, of

[1] *Archaeologia*, VI (1782), p. 263. [2] Op. cit. p. 310.
[3] Willson, op. cit. p. 288; Stukeley, *Itinerarium Curiosum*, p. 84.
[4] Lincoln Corporation Muniments, vol. LVII, Entry of Leases.
[5] Supra, pp. 53–5. [6] *R.A.* I, 35, 191.

whom all save two had been enfeoffed before 1135, but in all the bishop owed service of sixty knights to the king,[1] and it appears therefore (though it cannot be said to be proved) that the bishop had owed service of twenty knights at Lincoln Castle.[2] The discovery of this association between the bishop and the castle in the city to which he had transferred his see lends force to Canon Foster's remark that the grant of so large a body of knights to the bishop 'indicates that it was part of William the Conqueror's policy that the bishop should have a large share in defending a part of the kingdom which was remote from the seat of government'.[3]

The association of the family of la Haye with the castle lasted very much longer. In 1155 Henry II granted to Richard de la Haye a charter confirming to him all the lands of his father Robert de la Haye in Lincolnshire and also the constableship of Lincoln Castle.[4] It is not surprising that Richard should make an early effort to obtain confirmation of his rights from the new king after the turbulence of Stephen's reign, when, it is likely, the la Hayes were dispossessed. The charter does not expressly say that Robert had held the constableship of Lincoln Castle, but it is evident that he did so: father and son appear together in a grant of land in the Bail which is witnessed by Robert the constable and Richard de Haia.[5] Robert is mentioned in the Lindsey Survey (1115–18) as holding the lands held in Domesday Book by Colswein.[6] It was formerly suggested that Robert la Haye's estates came to him by royal grant on the forfeiture of Picot son of Colswein,[7] but a charter of Henry I proves that Robert's estates came to him through his wife Muriel by inheritance.[8] Now Robert had a son Richard, who succeeded him, and a daughter Cecily, who carried part of his property, the honour of Halnaker, to the St Johns on her marriage to a member of that family. Moreover, Picot son of Colswein had a nephew Richard and a niece Cecily, both of whom are mentioned in his charter to Spalding Priory.[9] When it is added that Robert de la Haye came into possession of Colswein's estates and that he acquired them

[1] *Red Book of the Exchequer*, I, 374–6.

[2] See Round, 'Knight Service' in *Feudal England*, p. 225, and for la Haye, p. 242. There is no sign of any subsequent service owed by the bishop's tenants at Lincoln Castle. John de Rye was a tenant of the bishop, and he owed 5*s*. 5*d*. for guard at the castle, but this was in respect of a knight's fee held of the earl of Lincoln in right of the la Hayes. *Cal. Inq. p.m.* II, no. 371 (8 Edward I). See Stenton, *English Feudalism*, 1066–1166, p. 212.

[3] *R.A.* I, 267.

[4] Round, *Ancient Charters* (P.R.S.), p. 58.

[5] D. & C., Dii, 81/2/10. And see p. 88, n. 6.

[6] See index to *L.D.* (Robert de Haia).

[7] Chester Waters, *Survey of Lindsey*, pp. 8, 15.

[8] Round, *Calendar of Documents preserved in France*, no. 923, and see p. xlviii. The connecting link that follows was discovered by Dr Round.

[9] Dugdale, *Monasticon*, III, 218.

through his wife Muriel, it cannot be doubted that Robert's wife Muriel was the sister of Picot and the daughter of Colswein.

As will be seen, the family later held the constableship of the castle by service of castle guard. This system of castle guard arose in the time immediately following the Norman settlement,[1] and it is to be inferred therefore that the knight service owed by the la Hayes at the castle had been owed also by Picot and his father Colswein, at one time jointly with the bishop. The grouping of baronies for the provision of garrisons in royal castles existed elsewhere: four baronies were combined for the defence of Windsor Castle, and nine at Dover.[2] There may have been others so grouped at Lincoln, though if so no trace of them has been found apart from the claims to custody of one of the towers which will be mentioned later.

By comparison with the bishop's total service of sixty knights, the la Hayes had a modest establishment of knights. In 1166 Richard de la Haye returned eleven knights enfeoffed before 1135, four enfeoffed since that date, and five charged on his demesne: his fee was originally assessed at sixteen knights.[3] Robert de la Haye was certainly living in 1131, and probably in 1134,[4] and he seems therefore to have been the holder of the barony when the bishop was given leave to transfer his knights from Lincoln Castle. Perhaps he was made constable after the transfer: he was a Frenchman, with estates in Normandy, and would be more likely to be trusted with that office than his wife's brother Picot or her father Colswein, both of them natives. As will presently be noticed, Henry I had other reasons for placing the castle in the hands of a subject who was not overmighty.

Richard de la Haye died in the lifetime of Henry II leaving three daughters and co-heiresses. By family arrangement his Norman estates passed to the two younger daughters, whilst his English inheritance went to Nicholaa, the eldest,[5] who married Gerard de Camville. Henry II died in July 1189, and in August Nicholaa and Gerard obtained from Richard I at Barfleur, without waiting for him to cross to England to be crowned, a charter confirming to them their inheritance in England and Normandy, with the constableship of Lincoln Castle, as held by Nicholaa's father Richard and her grandfather Robert.[6] William of Newburgh implies that

[1] Stenton, *English Feudalism*, 1066–1166, p. 212. In support of the view that the quotas of knight service remained substantially unchanged between the Conquest and 1166, Dom David Knowles points out that no religious house founded after the Conquest appears in the list of tenants in chief owing knight service. *Monastic Order in England*, (1941), p. 609.

[2] Stenton, op. cit. pp. 210, 211.

[3] *Red Book of the Exchequer*, I, 390.

[4] Round, *Calendar of Documents preserved in France*, nos. 373, 375.

[5] *Bracton's Note Book*, II, 392.

[6] Round, *Ancient Charters* (P.R.S.), pp. 91, 92.

the shrievalty of the county was included in the grant.[1] It is not mentioned in the charter but shortly afterwards it is found in Gerard's hands, and the Pipe Roll of 1190 records that the price to Gerard of the shrievalty and the castle was 700 marks.[2]

The quarrel between Gerard de Camville and the chancellor Longchamp is mentioned later.[3] Gerard died before 15 January 1215; Richard de Camville, son of Gerard and Nicholaa, apparently died soon after February 1217, and Nicholaa, who finally resigned the charge of the castle in 1226, died before 20 November 1230.[4]

Nicholaa had been appointed joint sheriff with Philip Marc by King John the day before his death, and after being relieved of her charge had the castle, city and county restored to her.[5] Dr Round cites this case: he finds in a woman's right to hold the office of sheriff and to confer it on her husband strong evidence of the connection between an hereditary shrievalty and the constableship of the chief castle of the county; and he adds that 'it has always seemed to me that this connexion between the sheriff and the king's chief castle in a county is one of the principal distinctions introduced at the Conquest between the sheriff's office before and after that event. For the castle itself was a novelty introduced by the Normans'.[6] Though there is no earlier evidence of the shrievalty being in the hands of Nicholaa's family, there is no doubt at all of the closeness of the link between the shrievalty and Lincoln Castle. For example, when Henry I granted to Bishop Bloet licence to make a way of egress in the castle wall for the convenience of his house, the writ was addressed to Ranulph le Meschin, Osbert the sheriff, Picot son of Colswein, and all the king's barons of Lincoln:[7] to Ranulph by virtue of the hereditary claims of his wife Lucy which will be mentioned later; to the sheriff because the safety of the castle concerned him closely; and no doubt to Picot because he owed the king service of castle guard there.

Nicholaa's son Richard had married Eustachia, daughter and heiress of Gilbert Basset, and had by her a daughter Idonea, who married William Lungespee, son of William Lungespee earl of Salisbury. Idonea and William had a grand-daughter Margaret Lungespee, who brought the constableship of Lincoln Castle to the earldom of Lincoln by her marriage with the Earl Henry de Lacy.

The inquisition held on Lacy's death (he died on 5 February 1311) found that he held the constableship of Lincoln Castle to which belonged

[1] *Chronicles of Stephen* (R.S.), I, 337. [2] P.R. 2 *Richard I*, p. 89.
[3] Infra, p. 190. [4] Farrer, *Honors and Knights' Fees*, II, 221. [5] Infra, pp. 205–6.
[6] 'Early Sheriffs of Norfolk' in *E.H.R.* xxxv (1920), pp. 495–6, and references there cited. [7] *R.A.* I, 20, 21.

the keepership of the prison of the castle, together with wardships and all other profits issuing from the castle, and rents from tenants in the Bail and from foreign tenants in Kesteven and Lindsey for castle guard, held by the curtesy of England of the inheritance of Margaret, sometime his wife, of the king in chief by service of guarding the castle in fee.[1]

Alice de Lacy, daughter and heiress of Henry and Margaret, had married Thomas earl of Lancaster, who did fealty to the king for both the Lacy and Lungespee inheritances. When in February 1322 Thomas took arms against the king, Edward II ordered the sheriff of Lincoln to take the castle, then in the hands of the king's enemies, into safe keeping.[2] He was also to take Bolingbroke Castle: this he did, and put in it six men-at-arms and ten archers. He occupied Lincoln Castle, and maintained for some weeks a garrison there of 20 men-at-arms, 24 crossbowmen and 26 archers.[3] Thomas was taken at Pontefract in March and beheaded and his lands were forfeited. His widow Alice made a deal with Edward and his favourites the Despencers, as a result of which she surrendered her interest in Lincoln Castle and the court of the bailey and certain manors to the king, and he granted to her for life the court of the fee of La Haye, the bailey before the gate of Lincoln Castle and £20 for the third penny of the county. Though the grant does not expressly mention the castle, orders were given for it to be delivered to her with the court, the bailey and the £20.[4] Before 10 November 1324 Alice married Ebulo Lestrange, and in 1331 they obtained from Edward III confirmation of their tenure of Lincoln Castle, with the bailey and third penny of the county, and various other estates.[5] She married a third husband, Sir Hugh le Frene, before 23 March 1336. She died on 2 October 1348 and was buried at Barlings with her second husband.

Meanwhile Thomas of Lancaster had been posthumously rehabilitated by Parliament and his brother Henry of Lancaster was recognised as his

[1] *Cal. Inq. p.m.* v, no. 279; *C.P.R.* 1377–81, p. 82. The castle guard rents given in the inquisition *post mortem* are: freeholders in the Bail, £5; foreign tenants in Kesteven, £4. 5*s*. 0*d*.; foreign tenants in Lindsey, £2. 16*s*. 10*d*.; total, £12. 1*s*. 10*d*. In the early days of knight service the daily wage of a knight was 8*d*. At this rate of wage the castle guard rents would provide a knight for guard for 362¾ days in the year: not a bad result for the rough-and-ready methods of medieval arithmetic, especially when it is remembered that in 1311 the fixed rents were already more than a century old, and some of the rents may have been lost. The commutation of rents on the basis of the 8*d*. wage must have taken place before 1173, for in that year, when Henry II was faced with rebellion, there was a sudden demand for knights, and wages rose. Knights hired to defend Lincoln Castle in that year were paid a shilling a day. It may be doubted whether the freeholders in the Bail ever performed the duty of castle guard in kind: the round sum of £5 suggests that from the first they paid for the hire of knights. See Hill, 'Lincoln Castle: the Constables and the Guard' in *A.A.S.R.* XL (1930), pp. 1–14.

[2] *C.F.R.* 1319–27, p. 101.

[3] *C.C.R.* 1323–7, pp. 70, 71.

[4] *C.C.R.* 1318–23, pp. 575, 596.

[5] *C. Chart. R.* IV (1327–41), p. 213.

heir. He died in 1345 and was succeeded by his son Henry, who, at the termination of Alice's life interest, received livery of her lands. He obtained the castle and honour of Bolingbroke, the castle of Lincoln with the keep, and the manors of Waddington, Scartho and Saltfleetby, and as he was serving the king beyond the sea, his homage and fealty were respited.[1] Henry was created earl of Lincoln on 20 August 1349. He had previously maintained some association with the city and county. In 1344, at the request of certain people in the county, licence was granted for a tourney to be held at Lincoln every June, and Henry, then earl of Derby, was appointed captain of the jousting knights during his life. At Easter 1348 he held a tournament at Lincoln.[2]

Henry died on 24 March 1361. Blanche, his younger daughter and eventually his sole heiress, had married (19 May 1359) John of Gaunt, earl of Richmond, fourth son of Edward III. After Henry's death John of Gaunt styled himself earl of Richmond, Lancaster, Derby and Lincoln, and on 13 November 1362 he was created duke of Lancaster. 'Time-honoured Lancaster' died on 2 February 1399. His estates were seized by Richard II, but before the end of the year Gaunt's son Henry had landed in England, procured the abdication of Richard, and begun his reign as Henry IV. The duchy of Lancaster was united to the Crown, and with it the constableship of Lincoln Castle.

So much for the constableship of the castle from the time when it became hereditary in the family of la Haye. It is necessary now to consider the connection with the castle of a much greater family, the details of which are less distinct.

It has already been noticed[3] that the keep of Lincoln Castle is known as 'Lucy's Tower'. A charter granted by Stephen to Ranulph earl of Chester, to be quoted later, records that Ranulph's mother (the Countess Lucy) had fortified (*firmavit*) a tower of the castle; the Pipe Roll of 1200 refers to the repair of the new tower;[4] and in 1225 there is a reference to the repair of the tower 'de Luce'.[5] Dr Round formed a theory, based on evidence other than that of Lincoln, that the keep and the castle were elements different in origin, and, for a time, looked upon as distinct. The compound fortress could not long retain the compound name of castle and tower: the entire fortress must take the name of one or the other. The question which was to prevail would depend upon their relative age and importance. The Tower of London and the Tower of Rouen, for example, prevailed. Dr Round

[1] *C.F.R.* 1347–56, p. 97. The castle and keep were held by service of keeping the gaol; the reference to both is of interest in view of the subsequent narrative.

[2] *Chronicon Galfridi le Baker* (ed. Thompson), p. 97; *Complete Peerage* (2nd ed.), VII, 409–10.

[3] Supra, p. 86.
[4] P.R. 2 *John*, p. 64.
[5] *Rot. Lit. Claus.* II, 29.

adds that so important a fortress as Rochester was without a keep in the eleventh century, and well into the twelfth century other castles, probably Newcastle and certainly Exeter, must have been similarly destitute.[1] There is therefore nothing startling in the suggestion that the keep at Lincoln was built as an addition to the original fortress: without it the fortress would have a bailey and one mount, which was the usual Norman pattern. Nor is it any surprise that a tower was attached to a particular barony, and not in the hands of the constable.[2] It is of greater interest to inquire into the nature of the claims of Lucy's family upon the castle, though the question is not so easy to answer.

Lucy is a mysterious person. There may even have been two Lucys, though it is not necessary to suppose that there were.[3] All that can be said with certainty of her family connections is that she was the niece of Robert Malet of Eye and of Alan of Lincoln,[4] and that Thorold the sheriff was a kinsman. The Peterborough Chronicle and the pseudo-Ingulf of Crowland agree in saying that she was the daughter of Ælfgar earl of Mercia and niece or grandniece of Thorold. The link between Lucy and Ælfgar is the manor of Spalding which was held by Ælfgar before the Conquest and by Lucy's first husband Ivo Taillebois (in her right) at the time of Domesday Book. Yet no close connection between the two is mentioned in any contemporary document, and the only known children of Ælfgar are Edwin, Morcar and Ældgitha, wife of Harold. Possession of the manor is not enough to justify the inference of relationship.

Another theory is that Lucy was the daughter of Thorold the sheriff: it is based on the interpretation of statements in charters and the succession of lands. Thorold appears to have founded a cell at Spalding subject to Crowland Abbey. The manor came into the hands of Ivo Taillebois who gave lands in Spalding to the abbey of St Nicholas, Angers, for the souls of himself and Lucy his wife and of their ancestors, 'to wit, Thorold and his wife'. About 1135 Lucy gave the manor of Spalding to the church and monks of St Nicholas of Spalding (not Angers) as she held it 'in the times of Ivo de Thallebos and Roger Fitzgerold and earl Ranulph'—her three husbands—'in alms for my soul and for the redemption of the soul of my father and of my mother and of my husbands and kinsmen'.

It appears therefore that the manor of Spalding passed from Ælfgar through Thorold to Lucy and that Ivo held it in Domesday in right of his wife. Belchford, Stenigot, Tetney and Donington, other manors of

[1] *Geoffrey de Mandeville*, Appendix O, p. 333.

[2] Stenton, *English Feudalism*, 1066–1166, p. 241.

[3] The following account of Lucy is taken chiefly from *Complete Peerage* (2nd ed.), VII, 743–6.

[4] Farrer, *Lancashire Pipe Rolls*, p. 371.

Thorold, also passed to Lucy. She had held Alkborough which had belonged in the time of the Confessor to William Malet, father of Lucy's uncle Robert Malet of Eye. If Lucy's mother was William Malet's daughter this may have been her *maritagium*.

Lucy's first husband Ivo was probably sheriff of Lincoln,[1] and also of Bedford:[2] he probably died about 1094. By him Lucy had no issue. By her second husband Roger Fitzgerold, who died before 1100, she had a son William de Roumare. Her third husband was Ranulph le Meschin, hereditary vicomte de Bayeux and lord of the honour of Carlisle. When Ranulph's cousin Richard d'Avranches, earl of Chester, died in the White Ship, Henry I granted his earldom of Chester to Ranulph, though then or at some time later Ranulph lost Carlisle. Perhaps it was the price of the earldom. Lucy and Ranulph le Meschin had a son Ranulph les Gernons who became earl of Chester when his father died in 1129.

In the Pipe Roll of 1130 Lucy accounted for £266. 13*s*. 4*d*. for land of her father, having paid during the year all but £100 of this sum. She also owed 500 marks to be excused from marrying for five years, and 45 marks in addition to any whom the king might name, of which she had paid 20 marks to the queen. She also paid 100 marks for doing justice in her court between her own men, presumably of Bolingbroke or perhaps Spalding.[3] Ranulph le Meschin, her third husband, had been compelled to surrender many of Lucy's manors to the king on succeeding to the earldom of Chester. It has been suggested that the king probably allowed her a third part for life, with reversion to himself, and kept the remainder. This latter part, apparently, was restored to her son William de Roumare when he was reconciled to the king in 1127. The Pipe Roll of 1130 suggests that she was recovering the rest of her inheritance for her younger son Ranulph. If so, she was successful, for in 1165 the earl of Chester accounted for twenty knights' fees in Lincolnshire 'of the fee of Thorold the sheriff', while at the same time Richard de Camville, the custodian of the fees of William de Roumare (a minor, and son of William of the same name) accounted for £26. 13*s*. 4*d*., the sum due for forty knights' fees.[4]

Lucy's inheritance was thus divided and it is no surprise to find that Ranulph, though working in close co-operation with his half-brother William, stands out as the champion of Lucy's family claims in Lincolnshire. He had his own estate in the county and a house in Lincoln: thence he issued a charter, in almost royal style, addressed to his barons, sheriffs, ministers, bailiffs and all his men of Lincolnshire, French and English, in the presence of his barons, at Lincoln, in his house.[5] Though William

[1] *L.D.* 71/4. [2] *D.B.* I, 209 and b. [3] P.R. 31 *Henry I*, p. 110.
[4] P.R. 11 *Henry II*, pp. 37, 38. [5] *D.C.* p. 363; *C. Chart. R.* IV, 235.

de Roumare held his court at Bolingbroke, Ranulph also held court there.[1]

The designs of Ranulph upon Lincoln Castle are dealt with later.[2] To summarise the story, Ranulph seized the castle in 1140; Stephen was defeated and taken prisoner at the battle of Lincoln in 1141; but in 1146 he seized Ranulph and extorted from him the surrender of the castle. There followed the charter of 1149 which allowed the earl to 'fortify' one of his towers in the castle and hold it until the king gave him possession of Tickhill Castle. Then the tower and the city of Lincoln were to pass to the king, the earl retaining the tower his mother had fortified and the constableship of Lincoln and Lincolnshire. 'In view of the reference to the earl's other towers in the castle, it becomes probable that hereditary claims of which we know nothing really lay behind his action in 1140.'[3]

It is evident that there were such claims. Stephen's charter of 1149 distinguishes between what Ranulph might hold pending the return of Tickhill and what he might retain thereafter, namely, his mother's tower at Lincoln and the constableship of Lincoln and Lincolnshire. Ranulph's half-brother William de Roumare was created earl of Lincoln about 1141; and before Gilbert de Gant was given the same earldom in 1147–8 he had married Rohaise, daughter of Adeliza, sister of Ranulph les Gernons, so that the earldom was not given outside the family. Before the battle in Lincoln in 1141 Ranulph claimed (though without success) to lead Matilda's forces on the ground that the quarrel was his. When in 1217 (William de Roumare's grandson Earl William having died about 1198) the royalist army advanced to the relief of Lincoln, Ranulph les Gernons' grandson Ranulph de Blundeville earl of Chester insisted on leading the van, and after the battle his hereditary claim was acknowledged and he was created earl of Lincoln.[4]

[1] *D.C.* p. 370. [2] Infra, pp. 177 et seq.

[3] Stenton, *English Feudalism*, 1066–1166, p. 241.

[4] On the same day the sheriff was ordered to pay the third penny of the county due to him as heir of his father R. (*Rot. Lit. Claus.* I, 308). His father was Hugh earl of Chester, though his grandfather was Ranulph. His right seems to have been questioned (idem, pp. 351, 355), and in October 1220 an inquiry was ordered. The editor of *Complete Peerage* (2nd ed.) adds (VII, 675 n.): 'Ranulph may have considered himself heir to William de Roumare's Earldom of Lincoln, being heir to his lands in the county. Further, the belief that his great-grandmother Lucy the countess had been Countess of Lincoln may have obtained ground already, being associated with the lordship of Bolingbroke.' Stubbs, *Constitutional History* (4th ed.), I, 391–2, suggested that the earldom of Lincoln was possibly connected with an hereditary sheriffdom; and he pointed out that the earls of Salisbury were hereditary sheriffs of Wilts, and that the Beauchamp earldom of Warwick was founded on an hereditary sheriffdom held almost from the Conquest. G.E.C. *Complete Peerage* (1st ed.) bears this out for the Salisbury line; and it certainly shows that the first earl of Warwick was constable of Warwick Castle. For other earldoms derived from hereditary or near hereditary sheriffdoms—like those of the Mandevilles in Essex and the Bigods in Norfolk—see Morris, *Medieval English Sheriff* (1927), p. 48.

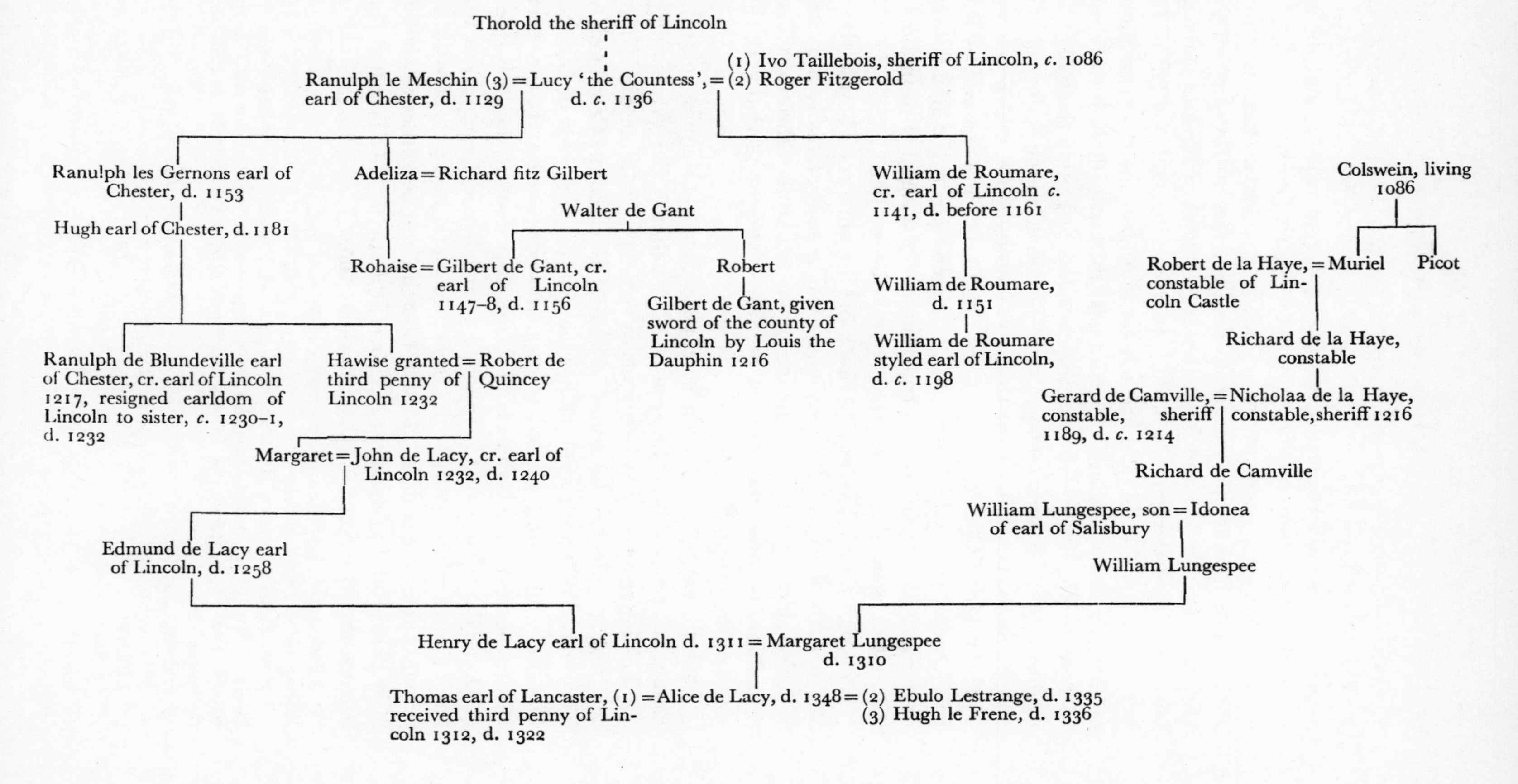

TABLE SHOWING SUCCESSIVE CREATIONS OF THE EARLDOM OF LINCOLN WITH THE DESCENT OF THE CONSTABLESHIP OF LINCOLN CASTLE
Thorold the sheriff of Lincoln
(1) Ivo Taillebois, sheriff of Lincoln, c. 1086
Ranulph le Meschin (3) = Lucy 'the Countess', = (2) Roger Fitzgerold
earl of Chester, d. 1129
d. c. 1136
Ranulph les Gernons earl of Chester, d. 1153
Adeliza = Richard fitz Gilbert
William de Roumare, cr. earl of Lincoln c. 1141, d. before 1161
Colswein, living 1086
Walter de Gant
Hugh earl of Chester, d. 1181
Rohaise = Gilbert de Gant, cr. earl of Lincoln 1147–8, d. 1156
Robert
William de Roumare, d. 1151
Robert de la Haye, = Muriel
Picot
constable of Lincoln Castle
Gilbert de Gant, given sword of the county of Lincoln by Louis the Dauphin 1216
William de Roumare styled earl of Lincoln, d. c. 1198
Richard de la Haye, constable
Ranulph de Blundeville earl of Chester, cr. earl of Lincoln 1217, resigned earldom of Lincoln to sister, c. 1230–1, d. 1232
Hawise granted = Robert de Quincey
third penny of Lincoln 1232
Gerard de Camville, = Nicholaa de la Haye,
constable, sheriff 1189, d. c. 1214
constable, sheriff 1216
Margaret = John de Lacy, cr. earl of Lincoln 1232, d. 1240
Richard de Camville
William Lungespee, son = Idonea
of earl of Salisbury
Edmund de Lacy earl of Lincoln, d. 1258
William Lungespee
Henry de Lacy earl of Lincoln d. 1311 = Margaret Lungespee
d. 1310
Thomas earl of Lancaster, (1) = Alice de Lacy, d. 1348 = (2) Ebulo Lestrange, d. 1335
received third penny of Lincoln 1312, d. 1322
(3) Hugh le Frene, d. 1336

Even the Gilbert de Gant who was given the sword of the county of Lincoln by Louis the Dauphin in 1216, and so styled earl of Lincoln, was a nephew of the Gilbert created earl by Stephen in 1147–8; and the nephew could therefore claim a connection with Lucy's family.

There are other indications of family interest in the city. In 1181 Ranulph de Blundeville granted to the burgesses of Coventry all the laws and customs, the best and freest that the citizens of Lincoln had; and the king confirmed the grant in 1186.[1] It was presumably by gift of Lucy or her family that the abbot of St Nicholas of Angers and the prior and monks of Spalding had a lodging in Lincoln near the castle ditch: it was confirmed to them by Richard I.[2] In 1241 the church of St Paul in the Bail of Lincoln belonged to the Augustinian priory of Trentham in the county of Stafford: and it cannot be an accident that this remote house, which was founded by Hugh earl of Chester between 1087 and 1100, and restored by Ranulph les Gernons, is found in possession of the church in the Bail.[3] Trentham Priory also had an interest in the churches of a number of manors which had once belonged to Lucy and Thorold before her.

Lucy was the descendant, perhaps the daughter, of Thorold the sheriff, and her first husband Ivo Taillebois was almost certainly also sheriff of Lincoln. Here surely is evidence of an hereditary shrievalty, and the probability becomes the stronger because of the connection with the chief castle of the county.[4]

Thorold was not, as was once supposed, a pre-Conquest sheriff, for, as Round has pointed out,[5] he appears as *Lincoliensis Turoldus*, taking part in a judicial eyre at Bury St Edmunds in 1076–9.[6] In Domesday Thorold the sheriff is recorded as the donor of land at Bucknall to Crowland Abbey.[7] The writ of William I announcing the transfer of the see of Dorchester to Lincoln, which can be dated 1072–3, was addressed to T. the sheriff and all the sheriffs in the bishopric of Remigius.[8] Ivo the sheriff is referred to in Domesday: Norman Crassus had pledged land to him in Scampton.[9] He is addressed, together with Osbert the clerk, in a writ of William II in favour of the canons of St Mary of Lincoln, and he witnesses another writ of William Rufus addressed to O[sbert] the sheriff.[10] Osbert had therefore become sheriff before Ivo died, in about 1094.

[1] *B.B.C.* (1), p. 27. Ranulph's charter is printed in Cunningham, *Growth of English Industry and Commerce*, I, 616.

[2] *C. Chart. R.* IV, 163.

[3] *Rotuli Roberti Grosseteste* (L.R.S.), p. 60; and see Parker, 'Chartulary of the "Austin" Priory of Trentham' in *Historical Collections of Staffordshire* (William Salt Arch. Society), XI, 295–6. The Veres, tenants of Lucy's family, owned St Bartholomew's church west of the castle. Infra, p. 145.

[4] See supra, pp. 89, 94.

[5] *Feudal England*, p. 329.

[6] *Memorials of St Edmunds Abbey* (R.S.), I, 63–4.

[7] *L.D.* 11/9.

[8] *R.A.* I, 2–4.

[9] *L.D.* 71/4.

[10] *R.A.* I, 16, 17.

PLATE 3

THE WORKS CHANTRY, which formerly stood to the west of the Deanery

From a drawing in the Willson Collection in the Cathedral Library

[*See p.* 112

POTTERGATE

From Buck's sketch book

THE 'EAST GATE'

probably of the Bail or upper city, removed in the eighteenth century

From Buck's sketch book

[*See p.* 116

Osbert, variously described as 'the priest', 'the clerk', Osbert of Humber, and Osbern the priest, was sheriff of Lincoln from 1093 and sheriff of York, perhaps from the same period and certainly from the beginning of the reign of Henry I, until some time before 1114. As Osbern the priest he appears in Domesday Book as tenant in chief of manors in Faldingworth and Binbrook and elsewhere in Lincolnshire.[1] He was ancestor of the family of Chamberlain whose estates lay in Duffield (Yorks) and Wickenby (Lincs): and it is evident from the very considerable estate which Osbert amassed and left to his sons Richard of Lincoln and William Turniant that he stood high in favour with Henry I.[2]

Osbert was succeeded as sheriff of Lincoln by Wigot of Lincoln, who held land in Broxholme.[3] He gave land in Ousegate, York, to St Mary of York, and his son Alan was a benefactor of the same house.[4] A few other names of sheriffs of the period survive.

At the Conquest the office of sheriff had fallen into the hands of the barons and by 1100 it was threatening in places to become hereditary: several families were holding in the second generation sheriffdoms granted by the Conqueror. It was the interest of the Crown to curb the power of the barons, and the substitution of lesser men in the shrievalties of the counties was part of the royal policy. It would seem that it was in pursuance of this policy, and an early example of it, that Osbert became sheriff of Lincoln in place of Ivo.[5]

If there had continued a succession of strong kings like Henry I nothing might ever have been heard again of the claims of Lucy's family in Lincoln: but the accession of Stephen and his struggle with Matilda gave the feudal magnates their opportunity. Ranulph earl of Chester, like Geoffrey de Mandeville, was willing to sell his support 'in turn to the two contending factions, in the well-grounded hope that they would outbid each other'. Besides his own earldom of Chester, Ranulph had in Lincolnshire the great fiefs of his own father Earl Ranulph, and of his father's kinsman and predecessor Earl Richard; and his half-brother William de Roumare held the great estate of their mother Lucy.[6] His hereditary claims to the castle and the shrievalty, whatever they really amounted to, were a useful weapon, good enough for the purpose. There was certainly a family interest

[1] *L.D.* nos. 53 and 54.

[2] Farrer, 'Sheriffs of Lincolnshire and Yorkshire' in *E.H.R.* xxx (1915), pp. 277–85, and also in *Early Yorkshire Charters*, I, 119, 355; II, p. vi. For writs addressed to Osbert, see *R.A.* I, index.

[3] Lindsey Survey in *L.D.* p. 241.

[4] *Early Yorkshire Charters*, I, 274–5.

[5] See Jolliffe, *Constitutional History of Medieval England*, p. 197, for a statement of the royal policy.

[6] Round, 'King Stephen and the Earl of Chester' in *E.H.R.* x (1895), p. 87.

in the castle and certainly some show of claim to the office of sheriff. A castle, especially the chief castle of the county, was often held with the shrievalty.[1] The Norman *vicomte* was the keeper of the king's castles and the earlier sheriffs of the Conqueror often appear in this capacity. William Malet, sheriff of York, held the castle at York. At Exeter the custody of the castle became hereditary in the family of Baldwin, the sheriff who erected it. The constableship of Gloucester was attached to the shrievalty at least as early as Walter of Gloucester and in the reign of Henry I his son Miles held it in right of his father.[2]

To sum up: it seems probable that Lucy's family claims were based on an hereditary shrievalty, held first by Thorold, her ancestor, and perhaps her father, and then probably by Ivo her husband: it was an office which involved the closest association with the chief castle of the county. Thorold was probably sheriff when the site was cleared and the castle built: Lucy herself built a tower there. Their hold on the office of sheriff was lost before the death of Ivo, and smaller men took their place. Under Henry I Robert de la Haye, also a smaller man, who owed service of castle guard there, appears as constable of the castle. The anarchy of Stephen gave Ranulph his chance and he found to his hand an excuse for seizing the castle. His success was short-lived and after the accession of Henry II there was less prospect of a successful claim to an hereditary shrievalty in England.[3] It does seem likely, however, that that claim lay behind the later claim of Ranulph de Blundeville earl of Chester to the earldom of Lincoln; and it may even be that when still later the constableship of the la Hayes passed by marriage to the earldom the alliance was regarded as a satisfactory merger of the ancient claims of the two families.

The names of a number of persons described as constables and seneschals of the castle are preserved in the witness clauses of charters and elsewhere, but they appear to be persons holding on behalf of the hereditary constables; and some, such as William de Ingleby, were probably tenants of the la Hayes.[4] After the second battle of Lincoln in 1217, the castle of Lincoln played no further part in medieval military history; and indeed,

[1] Morris, *Medieval English Sheriff* (1927), p. 51.

[2] Ibid. pp. 51–60. And see Round, 'Early Sheriffs of Norfolk' in *E.H.R.* xxxv (1920), pp. 481 et seq. In 1729 the hereditary shrievalty of Westmorland was said still to descend with the castle and manor of Appleby. Monson Papers and Correspondence at Burton Hall, xv.

[3] The Longsword law-suit in the reign of Henry III established the position of the Crown in this respect. *Bracton's Note Book*, no. 1235. Pollock and Maitland, *History of English Law*, I, 534.

[4] William de Engleby witnessed as constable *c.* 1250. D. & C., Dii, 77/3/1. William de Newton signed as constable *c.* 1215–21, Dii, 76/2/22, 80/2/6, 81/2/12. Roger de Campville was constable *c.* 1210, 81/2/44. Joselin de Engleby and Reginald de Newton were among the knights of Richard de la Haye in 1166. *Red Book of the Exchequer*, I, 12, 13, 390.

apart from a brief half hour in which it was stormed in 1644 by Lord Manchester and Cromwell, its military history was ended. It long continued, however, to house the county gaol and the shire hall there housed the courts of assize, the county court, and provided headquarters for the county administration.

A survey made under the orders of Parliament in 1652 describes the house in the bailey adjoining the gaol. It consisted of a cellar, a hall, and parlour below stairs, a kitchen, a buttery, a large dining-room with four chambers and four garrets over the same, with a brewhouse and buttery, and two small gardens adjoining walled about with high stone walls, and a small hay house. There was also the shire hall but unfortunately this was not described, as it was assumed to be outside the Act for the sale of the king's lands.[1] Whether it was the great hall mentioned in 1335[2] or its successor is unknown.

The ditches of course belonged to the castle and were an integral part of its defences. A survey of 1608 shows that they and adjoining patches of land were being let at rents: there were the north dyke and the west dyke, the north knowle, a garden called Magdalen dunghill, the south dyke and south knowle, the towers adjoining the castle gate, and near by were Hangman's dyke and the battle place.[3] At that time the ditches were held by copy of court roll, of a copyhold court of the duchy of Lancaster. All trace of copyhold tenure in the Bail has long since disappeared, and the reason given in a report made to the duchy in 1815, when the state of the ditches was causing alarm, was that the ditches were granted away at rents of assize by Charles I.[4] Financial stringency was no doubt his excuse, but his action was to cause trouble later, for the impossibility of preventing building in the alienated ditches gave anxiety to the county justices, who foresaw that roofs near to the castle wall would invite the escape of prisoners. Counsel, indeed, advised that as it had been long held that a man might justify digging in the land of another to raise a bulwark against the king's enemies, because it was done for the safety of the public, so he thought that by analogy an entry on adjacent land for repair of the walls might be

[1] P.R.O. Lists and Indexes, XIV, 38 (Duchy of Lancaster).

[2] *C.C.R.* 1333–7, p. 389. In 1669 the judges of assize ordered the Lincolnshire justices to raise £100 towards the repair of the middle part of the shire hall house in the castle: Lindsey was to pay half. *V.C.H. Lincs*, II, 338. And see Peyton, *Kesteven Quarter Sessions Minutes* (L.R.S.), I, 28, 99.

[3] Duchy of Lancaster: Surveys of Estates in Lincolnshire, James I, f. 142. Hangman's dyke was the piece of land on the north-west of the junction of Westgate and Burton Road, where executions took place. The battle place is now occupied by the Burton Road Hospital, and is shown on the plan of 1783 (Plate 2), as occupied by Mr Tomlinson.

[4] Report of R. S. Harper by virtue of a commission under the Duchy seal, 1815. (Papers in possession of Major G. R. Sills, Steward of the Bail, who kindly allowed the writer to examine them.)

justified: and he suggested that buildings recently erected near the walls so as to render the prison insecure should be prosecuted as a public nuisance.[1]

It does not appear that any action was taken on this opinion. The Act of 1831 empowering the justices of the three divisions of the county to purchase the castle recited that encroachments on or near the castle wall were endangering the security of the prison, and it empowered the justices to acquire houses and lands near the walls or bulwarks of the castle. The provision was a dead letter and building in the ditches continued until the castle was obscured and disfigured on all sides.[2] The progress of slum clearance has made it possible to remove the buildings near Cobb Hall, and the removal of a house on Castle Hill by the Lincoln Corporation has improved the view of the castle gateway and east wall and uncovered the base of the southern barbican tower. It may be hoped that in future there will be other opportunities of undoing the mischief set in train by the unwitting Charles I.

A meeting of magistrates had been held at the castle in 1775 at which it was resolved to petition Parliament for an Act to empower trustees to purchase the perpetuity of the castle yard for the use of the county for ever.[3] The gaol was reported to be in a ruinous condition. A new county hall was built in 1776 but in 1822 it was pronounced insecure, and an Act obtained for its rebuilding. It was not until 1831 that the Act was passed for purchase of the castle and for maintenance and support of the judges' house, the county hall and courts of assize. The purchase from the duchy was completed in that year, the price being £2,000. The prison, or part of it, had already been built in 1787 and the assize courts in 1826.

When the era of reform was introduced by the struggle for the Reform Bill, commissioners were appointed to report on the proposed division of counties and the boundaries of boroughs.[4] The report found that in Lincoln there were three divisions, the City, the Bail and Close, and the County of the City, comprising four parishes outside the city. It recommended

[1] Opinion of William Walton, 4 March 1816 (Steward of the Bail's papers). For a dispute about the land at the south-west corner of the castle, where Hilton House, the former home of De Wint and his brother-in-law William Hilton, R.A., now stands, see *Lincolnshire Magazine*, III (1936–8), p. 235.

[2] 'It is much to be lamented that the *mounds* and *dykes* on the outside of the walls have not been made public property as well as the castle itself. Had this been done a few years since, before the ditches were encroached upon and filled up, Lincoln Castle would have presented a grand and picturesque specimen of the ancient fortress; but now its stately walls are closely surrounded by masses of mean and vulgar buildings, whilst every year brings an increase of this intolerable nuisance so that the "castle dykes" are become a reproach to the city.' Willson in the *Proceedings of Archaeological Institute* (1848), p. 292.

[3] *Lincoln, Rutland and Stamford Mercury*, 15 December 1775.

[4] *Reports from Commissioners on Proposed Division of Counties and Boundaries of Boroughs* (*Accounts and Papers*, 1831–2, XXXIX).

that the future city should include the city as it then was, the Bail, the Close, and Canwick Common (as to which there was doubt whether it was within the city or not); the four outlying parishes were to be restored to Kesteven, and extra-parochial portions, the Monks Liberty and the Liberty of Beaumont Fee, were included in the city. The Parliamentary Boundary Act carried these recommendations into effect, expressly including 'all extra-parochial places, if any, which are surrounded by the old city of Lincoln, the Bail and Close, and the said Common, and any or either of them or by the boundaries or boundary of any or either of them'.[1]

The Municipal Corporations Act of 1835 provided that the metes and bounds of certain boroughs, including Lincoln, should remain as they were then taken to be; and added that every place and precinct which should be included within the metes and bounds of any borough before referred to should be part of such borough. The intention clearly was that any liberties surrounded by a borough should be merged therein. There is a proviso that every county gaol, court of justice or judge's lodging which at the time of the passing of the Act was taken for any purpose to be within a county, should still, for all such purposes, be taken to be within such county.[2]

In accordance with the Act the revising barristers divided the new city into two wards, the Minster Ward and the Bridge Ward, the former including the parishes of St Paul, St Mary Magdalene, and St Margaret with the palace precinct; that is to say, including the Bail and Close. Although that division was disapproved by Order in Council, it continued to be used for purposes of municipal elections, as the Act directed, until another division into three wards was substituted in 1845; of these three, the Upper, the Middle and the Lower, the Upper included the parishes of the Bail and Close.[3]

This legislation did not affect other rights of the duchy of Lancaster. A market was held on Castle Hill on Saturday evenings; the parishes of St Margaret, St Peter in Eastgate and St Mary Magdalene paid a fixed sum annually to the duchy for free stallage to all who chose to use it. The duchy abandoned the market tolls in 1847, though the steward of the Bail continued to hold his court until 1861.[4]

[1] 2 and 3 William IV, c. 64, s. 37 and Schedule O, no. 21.

[2] 5 and 6 William IV, c. 76, ss. 7, 8.

[3] Council Minute Book commencing 1 January 1836, pp. 1, 5, 6, 542, 544, 548, 573, 580–1, 606.

[4] The charge to the leet jury then in use related to the attendance of all who owed suit and service; encroachments on the lord's lands or highways; nuisances; weights and measures; the assize of bread and ale; price of meat and grain; whether bailiff or constable had pursued hue and cry according to law; treasure trove; goods or cattle which had been within the liberty for a year and a day, thereby belonging to the lord; forestalling and regrating; repair of highways, footpaths, and maintenance of hedges and ditches.

From time to time there has been doubt whether the castle and judges' lodgings are situate within the city or the county of Lincoln. Such doubt may be due to the proviso in the Municipal Corporations Act about courts of justice, and to a like provision in the Act of 1831 for purchase of the castle. This convenient fiction adopted for judicial purposes has no bearing on the general question; and the confusion of thought might have been resolved earlier but for the statutory rule that courts of justice are exempt from rating. The question was examined by the Local Government Act Committee of the Lindsey County Council in 1896, when they reached the conclusion that the castle and the judges' lodgings are within the city. Their report was approved by the County Council and accepted by the Local Government Board.[1] No evidence has ever been adduced to support the contrary view which is a picturesque survival illustrating the strength of a medieval tradition.

[1] The uncertainty which had long prevailed is illustrated by the report of the County Council Committee, which is as follows:

The Committee considered correspondence between the Local Government Board, the Clerk of the County Council and the Deputy Town Clerk of Lincoln, relative to the Castle of Lincoln, the County Hall and the Judges' Lodgings; and it appeared that in the last census tables those had been returned as not forming any part of the County Borough of Lincoln, but as being situate in the County, and the Ordnance Survey shows both the Castle and Judges' Lodgings as not within the municipal boundary of the City of Lincoln. The Committee find that for many years past they have been treated for all purposes as not being situate within the County Borough of Lincoln, but on the contrary have been deemed to be situate in the County; but the area seems to have been treated as extra-parochial, and the keeper of the Castle and the caretaker at the Judges' Lodgings are not registered as electors either for the county or city, and they are not rated and pay no rates whatever to any authority. Under the Act passed in 1831, relating to the Gaol Sessions for the three Divisions of Lindsey, Kesteven and Holland, it is provided that the Judges' Lodgings shall for all purposes relative to jurisdiction of Justices of the Peace for Lindsey, Kesteven and Holland be deemed to be within each of such Divisions, and it is probable that this may have given rise to the assumption that the Judges' Lodgings, and also the Castle, are locally situate not in any City Parish but in the County; and the concluding portion of section 8 of the Municipal Corporations Act, 1835, which provides that every County Gaol, Court of Justice or Judges' Lodging, which was then taken to be for any purpose within any County should still for all such purposes be taken to be within such County, has probably been taken as giving foundation to the mistaken belief that the Castle and Judges' Lodgings are situate in the County; and this assumption has probably been strengthened by the fact that under old Acts of Parliament relating to the Castle, it has been there described as situate within the Bail of Lincoln, in the Parts or Division of Lindsey, and that in the Lincoln Waterworks Act, 1846, the Bail of Lincoln is described as being in the Parts of Lindsey. The Committee are satisfied that these assumptions are not correct, and upon full consideration of all the circumstances, and the various Acts of Parliament bearing upon the question, the Committee are of opinion that under section 27 of the Poor Law Amendment Act, 1868, the Castle and the Judges' Lodgings which had heretofore been an extra-parochial place, became from and after the 25th December 1868, for all civil and parochial purposes annexed to and incorporated with the Parish of Saint Mary Magdalene, being the next adjoining parish with which they had then the longest common boundary; and that, since the Municipal Corporations Act, 1835, the Castle and Judges' House have under that Act formed part of and been included in the Municipal Borough of Lincoln, and the Committee consider that full effect ought to be given to this view. The adoption thereof will not abrogate or in any way lessen the effect of the Gaol Sessions Acts before referred to, and for all judicial purposes the Castle and Judges' Lodgings will still remain within each of the three County Divisions of Lindsey, Kesteven and Holland.

For the general question of the relation between castle and castle fee and the borough in which it is situate, see Round, 'Shire House and Castle Yard' in *E.H.R.* XXXVI (1921), pp. 210–14.

It is convenient here to add a few notes about the churches in the Bail. The church of St Paul stands at the junction of Bailgate and Westgate at the centre of the Bail; and Speed's map of 1610 indicates that its churchyard formerly covered the whole area bounded by Bailgate, Westgate and Gordon Street, most of which is now built over. Before the church passed into the hands of Trentham Priory it belonged to a member of one of the principal Lincoln families. In an interesting charter of *c.* 1200 William son of Warner of Hungate gave to Robert the baker and Beatrice his wife the house in which Herbert the Poitevin lived, which he held of William in the lifetime of the latter's father Warner, near the cemetery of St Paul towards the north, holding of the said church, and yielding to William while he should be rector of the church, and after his death to his successors, a yearly rent of 5*s.* and a cock and two hens at Christmas.[1]

There can be little doubt that the church was founded at an early date. It is only in early foundations that St Paul occurs as sole patron of a church: he is more usually joined with St Peter. Ralph de Diceto, who became dean of St Paul's in 1180, said that in this church Paulinus consecrated Honorius archbishop of Canterbury, and that in the time of the English it was called St Paulinus,[2] thereby implying that this was Paulinus' own stone church. This identification was popularised by Stukeley, who wrote in 1735:

In July last I went to Lincoln, for curiosity onely: I examined with particular care the old church above hill, in the center of the Roman city, called S. Paul's. This has commonly been thought the church built by Paulinus, when he converted Blecca, the governor, to the Christian faith. I am of opinion the truth is so. I see in many parts of it, that there have been more than one rebuildings of the church upon the old foundation, and I seem to discern part of the very church built by Paulinus, which Bede saw in ruins, particularly at the north door, where you descend into the church by 6 steps on the outside. The capitals and nailwork without is of the style of those times, thus: Above it the nail work was originally continued round the arch, now a modern one, though yett very ancient; and this seems to have been the door by which Paulinus himself, and Blecca, used to enter the church, for opposite to it is that famous fragment of a very great Roman building, probably the remains of the palace, and where Blecca resided.... Within the church are many very ancient inscriptions on tombstones of black marble, in the Norman character. I observed that the older part of the walls on the outside is made of very old cutt stones, and of an old sort of stones, most likely the ruins of the first church. At the south-east corner of the church, and on the outside, I saw a springer of an arch, low in the ground, perhaps one of the original church. It is not difficult to think how the church came in latter times to be called S. Paul's corruptly for St Paullinus's.[3]

[1] D. & C., Dii, 80/2/17. The church is described as a *monasterium* in a charter of R. de Haye and Maud his wife. *C. Chart. R.* III, 363.

[2] *Opera Historica* (R.S.), II, 196.

[3] Stukeley, *Diaries and Letters* (Surtees Society), II, 273–4.

Stukeley's claim has become the 'traditional' one. It was pleasant to find Paulinus' church at the very centre of the Roman city on the ruins of a great Roman building. Freeman accepted the identification[1] and Professor Baldwin Brown pointed out that the church of St Paul's Cray, in Kent, which stands on the site of a Roman basilica, was sometimes called St Paulinus.[2]

Yet the evidence is against the theory. Stukeley's own editor remarks that Stukeley's knowledge of architecture was of that kind which supposed

Fig. 6. St Paul's church, taken down in 1786. From a drawing in the possession of the rector and churchwardens.

Norman work to be Saxon and that the 'capitals and nail work', of which he gave a sketch, were of early Norman character.[3] Buck's sketch, made a few years before Stukeley's visit, shows a tower with two-light openings but no midwall shaft, and the rest of the church of considerably later date. This is consistent with the letters mandatory issued for the rebuilding of the church by Bishop Dalderby in 1302, when, he said, nearly the whole of the church had fallen to the ground.[4] There may well have been signs of the Norman church, and perhaps a Saxon predecessor, but these would not be enough to establish the high claim that Stukeley makes. The chief objection to his theory is that it requires two changes of dedication: first, the aban-

[1] *Norman Conquest*, IV, 212. Venables was cautious. *A.A.S.R.* XIII (1876), p. 209.
[2] *Arts in Early England*, I, 168.
[3] Op. cit. II, 274 n.
[4] *A.A.S.R.* XIX (1888), p. 342.

donment of the original one in favour of the famous and saintly founder; and secondly, an abridgment of the founder's name to that of St Paul. This second change would imply that the origins of the church had been forgotten. But this would also mean that the story told by Bede of Paulinus' stone church had been forgotten also, and this is hardly possible. Bede's history was widely known. Over 133 manuscript copies of it are recorded and it was translated into English.[1] Unlike St Mary of Lincoln, St Paul, when first heard of, is in private hands, without hint of distinguished origin. The theory is probably no more than a guess, even though it was first made by Diceto in the twelfth century, based on the resemblance between the names of Paul and Paulinus.

The parish now includes the whole north-west quarter of the Bail, extending along Bailgate a little south of Gordon Street and it embraces a small area east of Bailgate near Newport Arch. In some part of the north-west quarter were once the church and parish of St Clement in West Bight. Of the church itself nothing is known; probably the churchyard in West Bight which now belongs to St Mary Magdalene formerly belonged to St Clement and it may mark the site of St Clement's church. The parish was cut off from Bailgate by St Paul's parish, but Westgate formed its southern boundary, and it touched the new western gateway of the Bail (made when the castle works covered the old gate) which was known as the west postern. The parish seems to have been specially associated with the castle, as if the knights owing castle guard and other feudal services there wished to have a house at hand but outside the fortress itself. A small doorway in the north wall of the castle may have been for their use.

Robert Bardolf, who held land in St Clement,[2] had associations with both the great castle families. In 1212 he held half a knight's fee of the earl of Chester at Waddington, and two knights' fees of Gerard de Camville at Scothern and Riseholme. The Bardolfs gave their name to the house in which the constables of the castle held court for their tenants. The inquisition *post mortem* of Henry de Lacy, earl of Lincoln, tells of foreign tenants who owe suit at the free court of la Haye at Bardolfhalle in the town of Lincoln,[3] and the whereabouts of the hall is indicated by the record of a charter which was exhibited in court in the parish of St Clement before John de Esseby the seneschal and William de Neville the constable.[4] Hugh Malet of Irby had a fee near the king's postern:[5] he may have been the

[1] C. E. Whiting in *Bede, His Life, Times and Writings* (ed. Hamilton Thompson, 1935), p. 37.

[2] D. & C., Dii, 81/2/9.

[3] *Cal. Inq. p.m.* v, no. 279.

[4] D. & C., Dii, 76/2/22.

[5] D. & C., Dii, 81/2/10.

Hugh Malet who held a knight's fee in Gringlethorpe of the honour of Lancaster.[1] Guy de Creon had land in the parish,[2] and in St Paul's Richard of Croxton had held of Robert de la Haye: he owed two knights to Richard de la Haye in 1166,[3] and a later Richard had land in Reepham of the earl of Salisbury, who held the Haye fee.

The Bail was still called 'Old Lincoln' in the time of Gough;[4] a name which may be due to surviving architectural remains, though it may also preserve some memory of the ancient origin of this part of the city.

[1] *Red Book of the Exchequer*, II, 589. [2] D. & C., Dii, 81/2/9.
[3] D. & C., Dii, 80/2/13.
[4] Camden, *Britannia* (Gough's ed. 1806), II, 363.

CHAPTER VI

THE MINSTER AND THE CLOSE

THE constitution which Remigius adopted for the cathedral church of his whole diocese—said, like the constitutions of York and Salisbury, to derive from Bayeux[1]—required an establishment of clergy[2] far beyond the resources of the old minster of Lincoln, and indeed of the bishopric itself. The new charges on revenue could not have been supported unless the bishop had procured extensive grants of land from William the Conqueror; and already by 1086, and before the new minster was complete, he had appropriated some of the new endowments for the support of some of the canons.

The Lincolnshire Domesday illustrates the process. William I had given the manor of Welton *in prebendam* to St Mary, and the gift was confirmed by Henry I.[3] In 1086 five teamlands in Welton belonged to six canons; they had become the *prebenda* or provision of six canonries. Five of these canonries were still in being in 1535, their names being Welton Beckhall, Welton Brinkhall, Welton Paynshall, Welton Rivall, and Welton Westhall with Gorehall.[4] The Lindsey Survey notes that the canons of St Mary had in Welton, Riseholme and Cherry Willingham fourteen carucates and two bovates.[5]

Domesday Book also records that at Redbourne Bishop Remigius and the canons of St Mary had two villeins ploughing with three oxen and 24 acres of meadow:[6] the land is attributed to St Mary by the Lindsey Survey, which also mentions several other holdings by the canons: Hugh the canon had six bovates in Well wapentake, probably at Stow; Jordan the canon had a bovate at Fulstow; Ralf the canon, brother of Osbert the sheriff, had two carucates five bovates in Dunholme; Robert de Grenville, the canon, had three carucates in Bolingbroke wapentake; and St Mary of Lincoln had two carucates one bovate in Friesthorpe which Nigel held.[7]

Whilst some of the canons had lands or revenues allotted to them, those who had not had to be provided for by the bishop, or out of the income of the chapter held in common. The accounts of the bishop are not forthcoming, but some indication of the charges borne by the bishop's revenues for the support of the canons not specifically provided for is given by the

[1] Mr Lewis C. Loyd, in an unpublished paper which he has kindly allowed the writer to see, has given reasons for doubt.

[2] Supra, p. 77.

[3] *R.A.* I, 25.

[4] *L.D.* 7/8; Bacon, *Liber Regis*, p. 395.

[5] *L.D.* p. 240.

[6] *L.D.* 7/57.

[7] *L.D.* pp. 237, 241, 243, 247, 252.

Pipe Rolls for the period when the see was vacant and its estates in the hands of the king. In 1167–8 (Bishop Chesney having died in December 1166) the keepers of the see paid the following prebendal salaries: Herbert of Ivelchester £10, Gervase Pullus 100*s.*, Ilbert the canon 100*s.*, the chancellor of the church 100*s.*, Roger of Worcester £10, William son of Gunter 110*s.*, Hervey the canon 19*s.* 4*d.*, Gerard the canon 30*s.*, and Roger the little 8*s.*, making a total of £43. 7*s.* 4*d.*[1]

The king's son Geoffrey Plantagenet was given the bishopric in 1172: although he was not a priest he could enjoy the revenues. These were again in the king's hands in the last quarter of 1180–1, during which a payment was made to the chancellor of 66*s.* 8*d.* for his maintenance by the king's writ.[2] The following year a payment of £31. 12*s.* 8*d.* was made from the episcopal manors to 73 prebendaries, a modest charge upon the total revenues of the see, which amounted to £1,290. 4*s.* 11*d.* Bread for them at Christmas cost 79*s.* 1*d.* and the burial of eight of them cost 4*s.*[3] In the first half of 1182–3 there were similar charges, but on the income side there was £45. 4*s.* 8*d.* from the deanery and prebends which were vacant.[4] Here the Pipe Rolls cease to record the accounts of the bishopric, for Walter of Coutances became bishop in 1183, and when next the see was vacant similar details were not recorded.[5]

By that time the cathedral church built by Remigius was in ruins. It had conformed closely to the type being built in Normandy; so closely that Mr Bilson found it possible to recover its main lines with comparatively little excavation. It 'consisted of a choir of three bays, terminating eastward in an apse, and flanked by aisles which extended eastward as far as the springing of the great apse; a transept, each arm of which consisted of two bays, one of which was opposite the aisles of the choir and nave, and the other, beyond to the north and south, had an eastern aisle of a single bay; a nave of ten bays in length, with north and south aisles; and two western towers at the ends of the aisles, with the nave extended an additional bay between them'. The church so closely resembled the Conqueror's own church of Saint Étienne at Caen, which was founded in 1064, as to suggest that Remigius' master of the works must have been employed on the Conqueror's own church before he began work at Lincoln.

Mr Bilson sums up his conclusions as follows:

The plan of Bishop Remi's church, as worked out from the remains which have been found, is an admirable illustration of the logical precision, clearly

[1] P.R. 14 *Henry II*, p. 77.

[2] P.R. 27 *Henry II*, p. 64.

[3] P.R. 28 *Henry II*, p. 59. This number of prebendaries, in excess of the establishment of 54, is as yet unexplained.

[4] P.R. 29 *Henry II*, p. 33.

[5] Since this was written a *compotus* for 9 *John* has been published by the Pipe Roll Society.

defined structural organization, and feeling for monumental form which characterize the best work of the Norman school. It conforms very closely to the 'type' of the contemporary works of the continental school of Normandy, much more closely than do most of the great churches built in England after the Norman Conquest. It shows some indications, though as yet but slight, of the great expansion of scale which is illustrated in the nearly contemporary church of Winchester, and it is an important landmark between the plans of the earlier Norman churches and such a completely developed plan as that of Durham. And its western work stands almost alone as a magnificently original piece of monumental building, a speaking witness of the powerful architectural expression of a masterful race.[1]

The great new church of Lincoln extended from the present west front to a point about 12 or 15 yards from the Roman wall. It was complete in 1092. The building was badly damaged by fire shortly before 1146: according to Giraldus and Schalby, the third bishop, Alexander the Magnificent (1123–48), set about replacing the wooden roof of the nave by a stone vault.[2] Mr Bilson points out that the detail in the chancel of Stow church so closely resembles Alexander's work at Lincoln as to prove that it was executed by the same school of masons, and he points to the vault at Stow to show what the vault at Lincoln was like.[3] Henry of Huntingdon, who does not mention the vault, says that the bishop restored the church with such subtle workmanship that it came forth more beautiful than it was before, and second to none in the kingdom.[4] To his work of enrichment belong the highly decorated Norman doorways of the west front and the lower part of the western towers.[5]

On 15 April 1185 the church was split from top to bottom, the calamity being attributed to a great earthquake.[6] Howden says that the earthquake was 'heard' throughout all England, and was such as had not been heard in the land since the beginning of the world; that rocks were split asunder and stone houses fell.[7] It may be noted, however, that the only damage specifically recorded is that suffered by the church of Lincoln, and it may

[1] Bilson, 'Plan of the First Cathedral Church of Lincoln' in *Archaeologia*, LXII (1911), pp. 553–4, 564.

[2] Giraldus Cambrensis, *Opera* (R.S.), VII, 33, 198. The *Anglo-Saxon Chronicle* (sub 1123) mentions a most destructive fire in Lincoln, but does not mention damage to the cathedral. The Margam Annals expressly except the minster and bishop's house when they say that the city was consumed by fire. *Annales Monastici* (R.S.), I, 11.

[3] Bilson, 'The Beginnings of Gothic Architecture' in *Journal of R.I.B.A.* 3rd series, VI (25 March 1899), pp. 316–17. He seems not to have known that the present vault in the chancel at Stow was wholly built *c.* 1850.

[4] *Historia Anglorum* (R.S.), pp. 278–9.

[5] In 1167–8 there was a payment of 118*s.* to masons and carpenters of the church of Lincoln; P.R. 14 *Henry II*, p. 77: in the following year £10. 6*s.* 2*d*; P.R. 15 *Henry II*, p. 45.

[6] Benedict Abbas, *Gesta Regis Henrici Secundi* (R.S.), I, 337.

[7] Roger Hoveden, *Chronica* (R.S.), II, 302.

be that to the damage done by the earth tremors Alexander's bold experiment of a stone vault was a contributory cause.

In the following year St Hugh became bishop of Lincoln, and in the words of John de Schalby 'he constituted anew the fabric of the mother church from the foundation'.[1] Hugh was a Carthusian monk who had been prior of Henry II's foundation of Witham in Somerset, and who had accepted election as bishop with reluctance. After his death he was canonised and the miracle stories about him are evidence of the love and veneration in which he was held. He was a man of simple tastes, and good to the poor and the oppressed, among whom were the Jews, who wept for him at his funeral. But there was another side to his character. He was a strong-minded man of great courage, and knew how to withstand the waywardness of Angevin kings and the arrogance of their officials. Mr Coulton says of him that he was one of the holiest of medieval saints and one of the keenest psychologists and a most determined business man.

> This man [he says] was one of those knights of the Holy Ghost who can dare, and carry off successfully, what no ordinary man would dream of; the man who faced and tamed Henry II, and treated Richard like a naughty child in the presence of two archbishops and four bishops, and within the walls of the royal chapel.[2]

The building of the new cathedral began in 1192,[3] and was carried out in the new style of pointed architecture. It seems to be generally agreed that when St Hugh died in 1200 the choir with its apsidal ending, with the eastern transepts, was complete, and perhaps the first bays north and south of the crossing in the great transepts. His work belongs to the experimental stage of Early English architecture, and, if the design of the choir and particularly of its vault is open to criticism, it has all the interest of an experiment and its builder is entitled to the credit due to the pioneer. The progress of the work in the new century first in the great transept and later in the nave shows that 'the versatility of the craftsmen and their growing skill and mastery of their material had produced a building, which in its rich variety and wealth of sculptured ornament, makes it one of the most splendid examples of Early English Gothic art'.[4]

[1] Giraldus Cambrensis, *Opera* (R.S.), VII, 200.

[2] *Five Centuries of Religion* (1936), III, 119. The most recent serious biography is that of Woolley, *St Hugh of Lincoln* (1927); and see *The Life of St Hugh of Lincoln*, translated from the French Carthusian *Life* and edited with large additions by Father Thurston, S.J. (1898).

[3] Dimock in Giraldus Cambrensis, *Opera* (R.S.), VII, p. xl n. Hugh's *constructor* of the cathedral was Geoffrey de Noiers. *Magna Vita S. Hugonis* (R.S.), p. 336.

[4] J. H. Srawley, *The Story of Lincoln Minster* (1933), p. 27.

The building included a tower which fell in 1237, on account, according to Abbot John of Peterborough, of the badness of construction.[1] The fall damaged the western bay of the choir, which still shows signs of the efforts made to provide support for a central tower. Building continued westwards, and the nave was completed by 1250, incorporating in the new west front the front of the Norman minster.

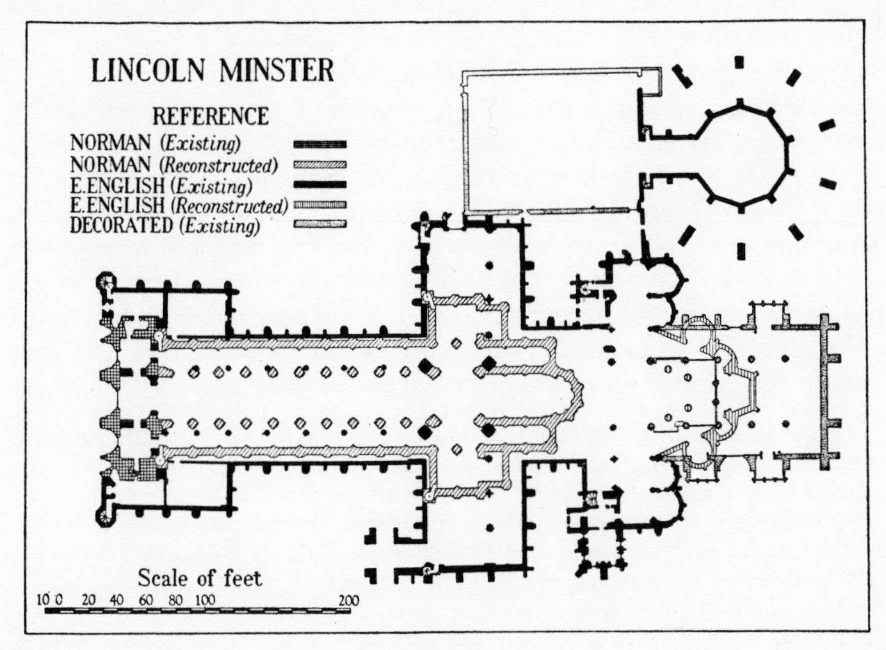

Fig. 7.

As the new church owed its erection to St Hugh in his life, so the new square east end in place of his apse owed its building to his reputation for sanctity after his death. Evidence of the miracles performed at his tomb accumulated, and among the witnesses were some Lincoln citizens who can be identified. A dumb boy of Wigford who recovered his speech was a pensioner of Adam the mayor and Reimbald the rich. A dumb boy of Pottergate and a mad girl of Wigford were cured. The wife of William son of Lamfram (who had a house in the parish of St Andrew on the Mount,

[1] Sparke, *Scriptores Varii*, *Chronicon Johannis Abbatis de St Petro de Burgo*, p. 107: 'Ruinae ecclesiae Lincolniensis propter artificii insolentiam.' And see *Annales Monastici* (Dunstable Annals), III, 149. Matthew Paris adorns the tale by saying that one of the canons, whilst preaching to the people in church and complaining of the tyranny of the bishop (Grosseteste) exclaimed: 'If we should hold our peace, the very stones would cry out'; whereupon a large portion of the church broke away and fell down. *Chronica Majora* (R.S.), III, 529.

which he gave to Welbeck Abbey)[1] was cured of dropsy.[2] Hugh was canonised in 1220 by Pope Honorius III, who decreed that the body should be removed to a more honourable place. The noble Angel Choir was the result. It was begun in 1255, and it was sufficiently far advanced in 1280 to be consecrated in the presence of Edward I and his queen Eleanor.[3] The great central tower was complete by 1311; and the small Norman west towers were crowned by perpendicular additions towards the end of the fourteenth century.

The vast operations, begun by St Hugh in 1192 and carried on for more than a century, obviously called for a tremendous financial effort.[4] Hugh wrote to his archdeacons to encourage regular offerings to the mother church, and he and others granted indulgences to contributors to the fabric fund.[5] He instituted a gild, the members of which undertook to contribute to the fabric according to an assessment. The gild revenue was about 1000 marks a year.[6] By his will, dated 1233, Bishop Hugh de Welles bequeathed to the Fabric 100 marks and all the cut timber on his estates, although his successor might redeem the timber for 50 marks.[7] The most interesting source of all is thus described by Canon Foster:

> The archives of this Church prove that if kings and feudal magnates endowed the Church with rich gifts of land in the first sixty years of its existence, the end of the 12th century was specially the day of smaller men. On either side of the year 1200 there is a truly astonishing number of grants of land, often of very small pieces of land, to God and St Mary and the Church of Lincoln. A charter will state that a peasant has placed upon the altar of St Mary half an acre of land—no doubt by laying there a sod or some other sacramental token. In some charters God is cited as the first of the witnesses. Frequently these grants are the gifts of very humble people, peasants whose names prove them to be descendants of the Danish army which resettled this county in 879. Such a phenomenon was possible only in Lincolnshire and to a lesser extent in a few neighbouring counties of the Northern Danelaw, for there alone in England was there a large body of free peasant men, that is, with personal liberty, and having

[1] Welbeck Cartulary, f. 105b. Her name was Gunnilda.

[2] The published miracle stories are collected by Canon Woolley, *St Hugh of Lincoln* (1927), ch. xiv. There is a roll of miracles, B.M. Cottonian Roll, xiii, 27.

[3] Eleanor died at Harby in 1290. Her *viscera* were buried in the Minster at the altar of St John; the first of the Eleanor Crosses, marking the stages of her last journey, being erected without Bargate. A chantry for her soul, founded at Harby, was transferred to the Minster in 1311. Chapter Acts, Liber 1, f. 32v.

[4] The sum of 11,000 silver marks in the hands of the precentor, Geoffrey of Deeping, and destined for the building of the nave, was looted after the death of King John and the battle of Lincoln. *Liber Antiquus Hugonis Welles* (ed. Gibbons), p. vii.

[5] Giraldus Cambrensis, *Opera* (R.S.), vii, 200, 217.

[6] Coggeshall, *Chronicon Anglicanum* (R.S.), p. 111. *Rot. Lit. Pat.* p. 57. The new work is referred to in another letter of John in 1209, p. 88b.

[7] Giraldus Cambrensis, *Opera* (R.S.), vii, 226.

EASTERN EXCHEQUER GATE

From a drawing in the Willson Collection in the Cathedral Library

WESTERN EXCHEQUER GATE (taken down *c.* 1800)

From a drawing in the Willson Collection in the Cathedral Library

[*See p.* 120

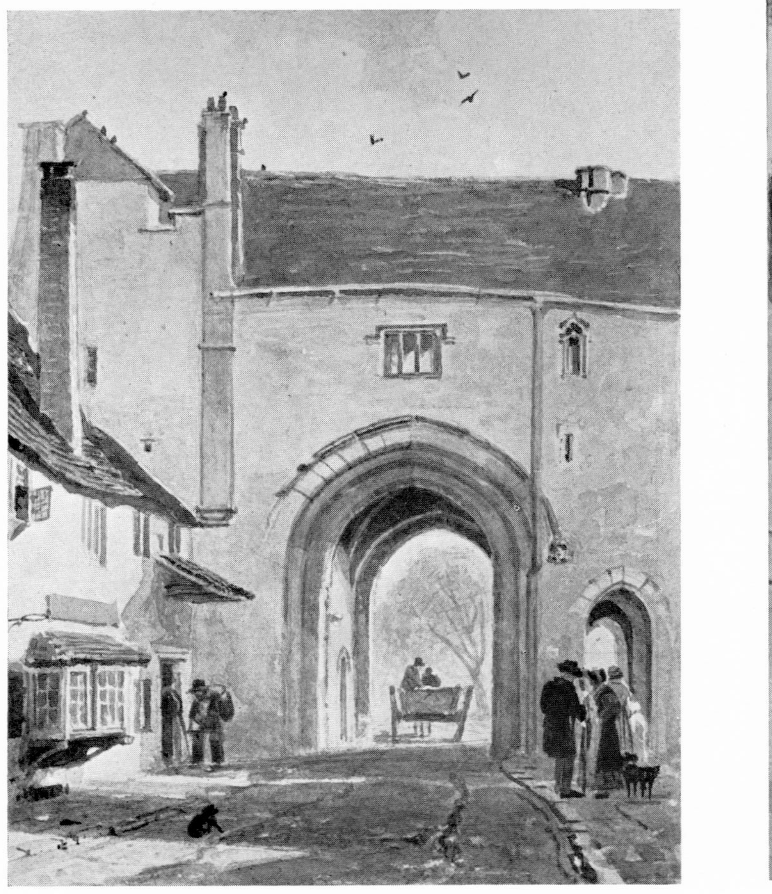

NORTH GATE OF THE CLOSE (now taken down)
From a sepia drawing by Peter de Wint in the Usher Art Gallery

THE BAIL GATE AT THE WEST END OF EAST-GATE AND ONE OF THE CLOSE GATES (both taken down)

From a sepia drawing by Peter de Wint in the Usher Art Gallery

See p. 128]

the power to do what they liked with their land. These gifts are often made for the maintenance of the canons, but not a few are for the fabric of the Church.[1]

For the encouragement of giving, the Works Chantry was founded for the benefit of the souls of benefactors of the fabric. It was founded either by St Hugh's predecessor, Walter of Coutances (1183–5), or by St Hugh's successor, William of Blois (1203–6): Mr Dimock thought the latter, and as it appears that the Chantry chapel was the northernmost of the chapels in the great south transept, the later date seems the more likely, for this was the point which the new building is thought to have reached when William of Blois succeeded to the see. The present stone screen of the chapel has the inscription 'Orate pro benefactoribus istius ecclesie' and on each side effigies of chantry priests kneeling.[2] Associated with the chantry were the two keepers of the fabric; and Miss Major has called attention to the very interesting fact that sometimes these keepers were both canons, and sometimes one was a canon and one a citizen. In one year Master Robert of Brinkhill served with Peter of the Bail; in another, Peter, then described as mayor, served with William of Winchecumbe; and in a third with Canon Robert de Gravele. Walter Brand, a leading citizen, held the office with William of Ingham, a canon; another time with John son of Martin, and once with John of Louth, who was mayor in 1263.[3] The name of Brand was commemorated in another place. On the vaulted roof of the nave was painted a number of names, of which these are recorded: Helias Pictor, Walterus Brand, Wilhelmus Baldwin, Ricardus de Ponte, Wilhelmus Paris, Robertus Saris.[4] Helias, being a painter, may have commemorated himself; Richard de Ponte and William de Paris both held the mayoralty in the middle years of the thirteenth century, and may well have been associated with the building of the nave.

The names of a few master masons have also been preserved. Master Richard the mason was holding land near the gate leading to Nettleham in the later part of the twelfth century.[5] Master Michael, master of the works, held land in the parish of St Michael on the Mount of Newhouse Abbey: he had a charter from the abbey which he lost during the war.[6]

[1] 'A wise Master Builder': a sermon preached on St Hugh's Day, 17 November 1932. *Lincoln Diocesan Magazine*, Dec. 1932.

[2] Giraldus Cambrensis *Opera* (R.S.), VII, 217 n., 219; Wordsworth, *Medieval Services* (1898), p. 302.

[3] *R.A.* IV, pp. viii, 95, 99, 100, 102; D. & C., Dii, 77/2/10, 80/1/141.

[4] Brooke, *Lincoln Cathedral*, p. 91, quoting Mr Sympson's notes. Brooke says that since Sympson's time the names may have been effaced, but that the name of Paris was perceptible in the centre vault of the nave not far from the great tower.

[5] D. & C., Dii, 79/2/16.

[6] Harl. Cart. 53 D43. The war must have been that between John and the barons, and the second charter can be dated *c.* 1230.

Master Alexander the mason, and master of the works, appears about 1235, and presumably had a share in the building of the nave. Cerlo the mason, whose name is a late survival of the Old English *ceorl*, a churl, appears about 1248,[1] though he is not described as master of the works. Master Simon de Tresk, or Thersk, seems to have held that office for some time prior to 1275, and he was still witnessing with Adam de Thresk in 1290.[2] With him in later years witnessed Richard de Stow, mason.[3] In due time Richard de Stow became master mason himself, and, according to Precentor Venables, in 1306 the chapter entered into a contract with Richard de Stow, or Gainsborough, *cementarius*, for the new work, the plain work to be done by measure (that is, piecework) and the carved work and sculpture by the day (or timework).[4] In the cathedral cloisters are the remains of a tomb-slab of Richard of Gainsborough, *olym cementarius istius eclesie*, who died in 1300, though the date is not beyond doubt. Venables describes him as 'certainly the builder and probably the designer of much of the Central Tower and the "Angel Choir" of the Cathedral, and of the

Fig. 8. Tomb-slab of Richard of Gainsborough, *cementarius*, in the cloisters of Lincoln Cathedral. From a drawing by M. S. Briggs, published in *The Architect in History* (Oxford University Press).

[1] *R.A.* IV, 97. D. & C., Dii, 81/1/34.

[2] D. & C., Dii, 78/1/130, 80/1/141. He held houses in the Bail of Barlings Abbey. Barlings Cartulary, f. 57d. Symon de Beverley, *cementarius*, occurs in a charter witnessed by him, *c.* 1270, Dii, 80/1/138.

[3] D. & C., Dii, 77/2/10, 77/3/57. Richard of Stow was one of the jury of *secondarii* in the Hundred Rolls inquiry. See Appendix VI and pp. 296–7.

[4] *Arch. Journ.* L (1893), p. 42. It is not clear whether the identification of Richard of Stow and Richard of Gainsborough is based on evidence or is a guess.

first of the series of Eleanor Crosses once standing outside the south gate of Lincoln';[1] but so far as concerns the central tower this seems to be going beyond the evidence. The contract of 1306 evidently related to the building of this tower, for on 14 March 1307 the chapter directed that the masons should begin work on the tower as soon as the time was suitable. On 8 April 1307 Robert de Bokinghale was appointed carpenter of the church for life, at a salary of nine silver marks a year: he took the oath as master carpenter in 1308.[2]

The cathedral clergy made their homes round the Minster. It was told that a young man cured of paralysis at the tomb of St Hugh had subsisted as a beggar in a hut in the churchyard of St Mary in front of the precentor's door: the miracle must be attributed to the period 1208–13.[3] Geoffrey de Thame, who became precentor about 1263, built houses upon the town wall, probably in the place still occupied by the precentory: the citizens complained that he and Canon Adam de Bukefeld, who had done the same thing, had rendered the defence of the wall impossible in case of necessity.[4] Already about 1160 the subdean lived somewhere to the south of the cathedral.[5]

On the north side of Eastgate, between the present James Street and East Bight, stood the endowed church of All Saints. In the time of the Confessor there belonged to it one carucate of land in the Lincoln fields, and twelve tofts and four crofts. It had belonged to Godric, and when he became a monk it was claimed by the abbot of Peterborough. The claim was denied by the citizens on the ground that none could give it outside the city or the kin except by grant of the king. Godric's kinsman Ernuin the priest claimed it on this principle.[6] By the time of Bishop Alexander it belonged to the church of Lincoln, for he gave half a carucate of its land

[1] *A.A.S.R.* XXI (1892), p. 191. The will of a Richard de Gaynesburgh, painter, was proved in the burwarmote in 1351. B.B. f. 213v.

[2] Chapter Acts, Liber I, ff. 5, 6v., 11. There was a dispute in September 1307 between the masters of the works and the servants of the chapter about the annual rent of 2*s*. for houses in St John in Newport, and of 8*s*. in St Augustine, and of 12*d*. for houses formerly of Master Nassington, and of 10*s*. in the churchyard, and it was decided by the chapter that all the rents contained in the old rental should stand. This seems to refer to houses provided for the craftsmen working in the town, who apparently thought the rents their employers were charging them were too high. Ibid. f. 7v. For John Porter, the mason who lived at Lincoln, was sent for by the dean and chapter of York, returned to Lincoln, and then became master mason at York, 1456, see *Fabric Rolls of York Minster* (Surtees Society), p. 650, index. Philip de Lincoln was master carpenter at York in the fourteenth century.

[3] Giraldus Cambrensis, *Opera* (R.S.), VII, 144; Woolley, *St Hugh of Lincoln*, pp. 172, 174.

[4] *R.H.* I, 311. The encroachment on the wall between the upper city (the Bail) and the lower one cannot have been a very serious matter from the point of view of defence.

[5] *R.A.* II, 22.

[6] Appendix II. See supra, p. 59.

to Humphrey *in prebendam*.[1] By about 1160 the church of All Saints had been appropriated to the chancellor.[2] In its churchyard were houses of an early dean of Lincoln. About 1169–76 Geoffrey the dean granted to his nephews Hugh and Geoffrey his houses in the cemetery of All Saints: he had built them himself.[3]

The chapter declared that the dean's nephew Geoffrey the chaplain held his house, situate between the minster (*monasterium*) of All Saints and two royal streets, of Hamo the chancellor.[4] Later the houses passed into the hands of William Lupus, archdeacon of Lincoln, who left them by will to his brother Richard Lupus, who sold them to Roger de Fuldon, archdeacon of Lincoln, about 1258, for 110 marks. About 1280 Roger's executors sold them to William de la Gare, archdeacon of Lincoln, for 130 marks. Perhaps because another home had by then been found for the archdeacon of Lincoln the executor of de la Gare, who died in 1290, sold the houses to Richard de St Frideswide, archdeacon of Buckingham; and in 1299 the latter's executors sold to Roger de Mortivall, archdeacon of Leicester.[5] The archdeacons of Northampton were for some time established in houses on the east side of the chancel of All Saints;[6] and a charter endorsement indicates that other houses near All Saints were appropriated to the archdeacon of Huntingdon,[7] one holder of which office was charged with blocking a path in All Saints churchyard.[8] Many charters illustrate the gradual acquisition of the land north of All Saints up the East Bight. Geoffrey Scot, one of the canons, bought the great garden in the Bight from Peter of the Bail; this passed into the hands of John de North Leverton, rector of St Mary Magdalene.[9]

In 1191–3 the bishop-elect of Worcester (Robert fitz Ralph) granted to Roger de Rolveston, archdeacon of Leicester and soon to be dean of Lincoln, houses in the churchyard of the church of Lincoln which were formerly of Robert the constable.[10] This was probably part of the present deanery site: certainly by 1208 the dean had part of the present site.[11] The buildings spread eastwards towards the wall of the Bail: about 1220 Osbert de Middelenton gave to God and St Mary and William the dean and his successors land which Robert Lightfoot once held of Nicholaa de la Haye in the Bail between the gate of Eastgate and the dean's house.[12] In 1226–8

[1] *R.A.* II, 20.
[2] *L.C.S.* I, 310. D. & C., Dii, 77/3/72–5.
[3] D. & C., Dii, 77/3/23, 24.
[4] D. & C., Dii, 77/3/25.
[5] D. & C., Dii, 77/3/13, 14, 15, 21.
[6] D. & C., Dii, 77/3/50, 57.
[7] D. & C., Dii, 77/3/73.
[8] *R.H.* I, 310b.
[9] D. & C., Dii, 77/3/5, 34 (and see endorsement).
[10] D. & C., Dii, 81/2/29.
[11] *Final Concords* (L.R.S.), II, 332.
[12] D. & C., Dii, 81/2/32.

William the dean was assessed at 6*d.* yearly for an encroachment at the gate of the Bail.[1] It appears therefore that the western part of the present deanery stands within the old churchyard of St Mary, and the eastern part, being near the wall of the Bail, had at one time been in the hands of the constables of the castle.[2]

This expanding ecclesiastical settlement was a serious encroachment upon the area of the Bail. Almost the whole of the south-east quarter of this area was occupied, as well as nearly all the back land, the land behind the houses fronting to Bailgate, in the north-east quarter. Yet the area available was not enough, and the clerical population early expanded beyond the walls of the Bail. Outside its eastern gateway was Eastgate, and running southwards from Eastgate was Pottergate, which ran obliquely down the hill to Clasketgate. By 1163 there were houses in Eastgate belonging to the church of Lincoln,[3] and in the thirteenth century grantors of land acknowledged that they held land in or near Eastgate of the chancellor. Beatrix daughter of Ralf the villein granted to Roger son of Silvester land *retro subtus terram cancellarii*, in which Sigward Saxe lived.[4] About 1212 Robert Falconer, son of Ivo, with the consent of Basillida his wife and John his son and his daughters, granted to Canon Hugh of St Edward land in Eastgate which he held of the chancery, and which lay between land late of Hugh the Norwegian and land of Gilbert Chay. The grant was made before the chancellor.[5] Over half a century later (*c.* 1275) John, son of Joan daughter of Robert Falconer, granted to Simon de Barton, archdeacon of Stow, all his interest in land in Eastgate which his ancestors held of the chancery, and which Simon had bought from the executors of Ralf, the late treasurer.[6] About 1240 Ralf de Leicester, the treasurer, had bought from the executors of Walter de St Edmund, a former treasurer, houses in Eastgate, which Walter had bought of Robert de Hayles, then archdeacon of Lincoln, and land in Pottergate, which he had bought of Walter de Chamville, for 100 marks.[7] On its purchase by Walter de St Edmund the Pottergate land was described as adjoining the court of the treasurer and a house formerly of William de Dratton, archdeacon of Leicester.[8] Evidently the treasurer lived in Pottergate,[9] and his garden may have stretched up to

[1] *Book of Fees*, I, 363.

[2] Leland says that where the dean's house is in the Minster Close and thereabout was a 'monastery of nuns' before the time that Remigius began the new minster of Lincoln, and that of this house there yet remained certain tokens of it. *Itinerary* (ed. Toulmin Smith), v, 123. There is no other evidence of the existence of this house.

[3] *R.A.* I, 205.

[4] D. & C., Dii, 79/2/11.

[5] D. & C., Dii, 79/2/26, 28.

[6] D. & C., Dii, 79/3/60.

[7] D. & C., Dii, 79/2/27.

[8] D. & C., Dii, 79/2/29.

[9] Pottergate seems to have included the old line of Lindum Road and the road through Minster Yard to Priory Gate.

or nearly to Eastgate: there is little doubt that his house stood on the site of the misnamed 'Priory'.[1]

Simon de Barton, the archdeacon of Stow, as has been said, bought land in Eastgate from the executors of Ralf the treasurer, the land being held of the chancery.[2] In 1259 P[eter] de Audeham, the precentor, presumably as rector of St Peter in Eastgate (which church belonged to the precentory), licensed Simon's erection of an oratory with an altar, and the celebration of divine service there: so also did the bishop.[3]

The charters of St Margaret's parish illustrate the building up of chapter lands west of the present Pottergate. About 1270 Richard de Ingham granted to Jordan de Ingham his houses with a courtyard in the parish of St Margaret on the hill bounded by the lane of *la boune* leading towards the friars preachers on the west, the houses of Master William de Blaby, east, St Margaret's cemetery, north, and a toft of John de Stradcote, south. A later endorsement on another charter confirms the identification of Boun Lane with the present Greestone Stairs by calling it the lane that leads towards the postern in the Close.[4]

Another settlement was made between Boun Lane and the bishop's palace (to be mentioned later). Bishop Oliver Sutton (who died in 1300) ordered that a court be built near the palace, where the vicars might dwell together in common. By 1309, a hall, kitchen and certain chambers were finished, enough, it would seem, for the senior vicars; for in 1305 the chapter ordered that none was to be admitted as vicar unless he should first swear to dwell with the other vicars in the new houses, and to have commons with them at table, except for some reasonable cause. The vicars of the second form, who were not priests, were provided for in 1328,

[1] Chapter Acts, Liber II, f. 8.

[2] D. & C., Dii, 78/2/3, 79/3/58, 60.

[3] According to Precentor Venables (who quotes Thomas Sympson), Antony Bek, chancellor of the cathedral and afterwards bishop of Norwich, moved his residence from the site of the Works Chantry—west of the deanery—to the present Chancery site: and he links the move with the licence of 1315 to divert a lane from Eastgate to Pottergate (see p. 121), the purpose being to enlarge the garden of the Chancery. On 9 May 1321, says Sympson, 'a house and two cottages in All Saints parish belonging to the chancellor were settled on the Fabrick; and the present Chancery belonging to the Fabrick was assigned to Antony Beke and his successors reserving 10*s*. a year to the Fabrick'. *A.A.S.R.* XIX (1887), pp. 47, 67. The authority for this statement may well be found in the chapter archives. It is clear, however, that the chancellor's interest in the land without the walls of the Bail did not begin with the exchange with the Works Chantry. It may be noted that in 1535 the chancellor paid an annual rent of 10*s*. to the Fabric and received from the Fabric 8*s*. 4½*d*. and from the Works Chantry 16*d*. *Valor Ecclesiasticus*, IV, 15, 17; Cole, *Chapter Acts*, 1536–47 (L.R.S.), p. 184.

[4] D. & C., Dii, 78/3/76, 77. To the west of Boun Lane was the home of the vicars, the present Vicars Court. This was enclosed by the Close wall, though the bishop's palace, to the west of it, was not.

when the dean and chapter granted to them a piece of ground within the close of the priest vicars in which they might live and build new houses, so that all the vicars might live in an enclosure according to Sutton's ordinance.[1]

Several charters mention 'Stothfald' or 'Stodfald'. About 1150, in the chapter, David archdeacon of Buckingham with the consent of the chapter granted to Martell, clerk of Humfrey the subdean, a waste and empty croft on the south part of the church of St Margaret in Eastgate, which had Stothfald on one of its boundaries.[2] In *c.* 1210 William Martell granted his buildings and garden called 'Stodfaldes' to Robert de Camville: he held it of the prebend of Robert Bardolf, and had bought his interest from the abbot and convent of Bruerne (Oxford). He reserved a rent of 4*s.*[3] Soon afterwards William granted his reversion in Stodfaldes, subject to Camville's interest, to the dean and chapter to provide a chaplain at the altar of St Denis in the great church.[4] On 29 April 1221, in the presence of Bishop Hugh de Welles, Peter de Ponte the mayor, and others, Robert Camville surrendered to the dean and chapter all his interest in Stodfald to the use of the chaplain at St Denis' altar. The chapter then regranted the land to Robert's son Alexander for life at a rent of 4*s.*, and because Alexander was a minor his father placed his seal on the deed.[5] Where was Stodfald? The name suggests a paddock, and references to it suggest a central position. As it lay to the south of St Margaret's church, it seems probable that it was part of the space between the modern Pottergate and the modern Greestone Stairs.

The early clerical settlement was within the Bail, and accordingly one of the earliest royal writs issued to protect the rights of the canons was addressed to Ivo Taillebois (the husband of the Countess Lucy) and Osbert the clerk, who was probably sheriff: it commands that the canons of St Mary of Lincoln shall have their tithes and customary dues as they had them in the time of William I: another writ grants that their lands shall be quit of all customary dues.[6] In 1110 Henry I commanded that the canons of St Mary of Lincoln should be quit of the aid which he had received for his daughter's business.[7] A writ of Henry II directed that the bishop should hold his tenements within and without the borough as freely as any of his predecessors in the time of the king's grandfather; and that the clerks and servants of St Mary of Lincoln should have the lands, customs and fran-

[1] Maddison, *Vicars Choral of Lincoln Cathedral* (1878), p. 8. Chapter Acts, Liber I, f. 1; Liber II, f. 9. The *Deknehouses* at the south-east corner of the Bail are mentioned in 1390. *C.P.R.* 1389–92, p. 220.

[2] D. & C., Dii, 78/2/63.

[3] D. & C., Dii, 78/2/59.

[4] D. & C., Dii, 78/2/50, 61.

[5] D. & C., Dii, 78/2/53, 58.

[6] *R.A.* I, 16.

[7] Ibid. p. 26.

chises which they were wont to have at that time; and that no new customs should be demanded from the bishop or his men.[1] The suggestion that the canons must be protected from the officers of the city appears in another writ of Henry II. It commanded the bailiffs (*prepositis*) of Lincoln to cause an acknowledgement to be made by the oaths of the most ancient and lawful men of that city, before the sheriff of Lincolnshire, of the franchises which the bishops had in their land at Lincoln and in burgage in the time of Henry I, and of what franchises the clerks of the city had at the same time; and in accordance with the finding to cause the bishop and his men and the clerks of the city to have those franchises, and to demand no new customs from them. The bishop was to have his tenements in the city as his predecessors did in the time of Henry I.[2] What the franchises of the bishop and the clergy were emerges more clearly later.[3]

The Norman church of Lincoln stood wholly within the walls of the Bail. It is clear, however, that when (about 1192) St Hugh built his choir and apse he must have removed the wall and built across the city ditch, for the foundations of the Roman wall run under the lesser transepts before the high altar.[4] So far no record has been found of the removal of the wall, nor of the building of a new wall farther eastwards, nor of the line that such wall followed. Yet the proceedings taken when the church was again to be extended eastwards show that such a wall was built, though the area incorporated was not sufficient to permit the addition of the present east end. On 5 November 1255 the king issued a commission to Henry de Bathonia to inquire touching a petition of the dean and canons of the church of Lincoln for licence to lengthen their church towards the east by removal of the east wall of the city, which was opposite to the church, whether it would be to the damage of the king or the city or anyone, and if not, by what places and what bounds it could be done. He was to make his inquiry in the presence of the mayor, bailiffs and other citizens, and report to the king: the sheriff was to provide a jury. On 19 July 1256, Henry III issued letters patent recording his approval of the enclosure and extension of the walls round the church, which had been made with the king's licence and the consent of the citizens.[5]

The result was that the Minster and the clergy who had lived within the Bail no longer enjoyed the protection of the old town wall. There

[1] *R.A.* I, 66, and see ibid. p. 98. [2] *R.A.* I, 110. [3] Infra, pp. 124–7, 264–7.

[4] That part of the Minster within the boundaries of the Bail is in St Mary Magdalene's parish; and the eastern part outside the Bail is in St Margaret's. When marriages are celebrated in the Minster they are registered in St Mary Magdalene, and the bride and groom must stand a little distance to the west of the altar rails in order to ensure that the marriage is solemnised in that parish.

[5] *C.P.R.* 1247–58, p. 506. *R.A.* I, 184–5.

began a movement for a new enclosure for the Minster and the clergy and their servants. In 1285, very soon after the new east end was completed, the dean and chapter complained that they could not pass from their houses to their church without being attacked: and the king gave them licence to enclose the precinct of their church with a wall, 12 ft. high, in suitable places, at Pottergate Street and at the street leading from the high road of the Bail to the Eastgate with the two adjoining lanes on the north side (doubtless the present James Street was one, but the other has vanished; East Bight is outside the Close); the said wall to be provided with sufficient gates with locks, to the custody of which they and their successors should appoint one of their body to close them at dusk and open them again before sunrise.[1] It was the north, east and south-east sides of the precinct that needed protection. Perhaps there was some delay in building—the central tower and the Vicars Court were occupying attention—or perhaps the ideas of the canons developed both as to the degree of protection to be secured and as to the area to be enclosed, for several other grants followed. On 1 September 1315 a confirmation of the grant of 1285 and of various charters of land was obtained, the reason given for the grant being the homicides and other crimes committed at night by thieves and others wandering through the streets and lanes around the precinct and in it, and for the security of the canons and other ministers of the church passing by night between their lodgings and the church through the streets and lanes for celebration of the various services.[2] On 21 February 1316 the dean and chapter were licensed to enclose a lane in the suburb of Lincoln, adjoining the dwelling-places of certain canons, leading from the way of Eastgate to Pottergate towards the south, that is, from the southern part of another lane leading towards Wayneswelle to Pottergate, for the enlargement of the said dwelling-places and the security of them and of other ministers of the church.[3] This seems to indicate that a lane was pushed eastwards to the present Winnowsty Lane to provide a larger garden for the Chancery and adjoining houses. Licence to crenellate the wall was also granted in 1316,[4] and in 1318 the chapter were empowered to raise the wall beyond the height of 12 ft., and build turrets and crenellate the wall so raised.[5] The wall was built by 1327.[6] As to part of the circuit the dean and chapter had relied on the wall of the Bail and the city, though they had no right therein. In the same year (1327) the king appointed

[1] *C.P.R.* 1281–92, p. 161. They had licence to enclose a lane in 1280–1. *Inq. A.Q.D.* (P.R.O. Lists and Indexes), p. 10.

[2] *C.P.R.* 1313–17, p. 361.

[3] Ibid. p. 435.

[4] Ibid. p. 436.

[5] *C.P.R.* 1317–21, p. 257.

[6] Thomas de Luda, the treasurer, lent the dean and chapter £20 sterling in 1326 in aid of the works of the Close.

a commission to survey the wall, and to inquire whether it would be to the king's detriment to grant to the dean and chapter the wall of the bailey of Lincoln Castle which joined the precinct on the south, east and north, namely by a circuit from the south gate of the bailey towards Eastgate, and thence northwards and to the western part of the precinct, which wall was

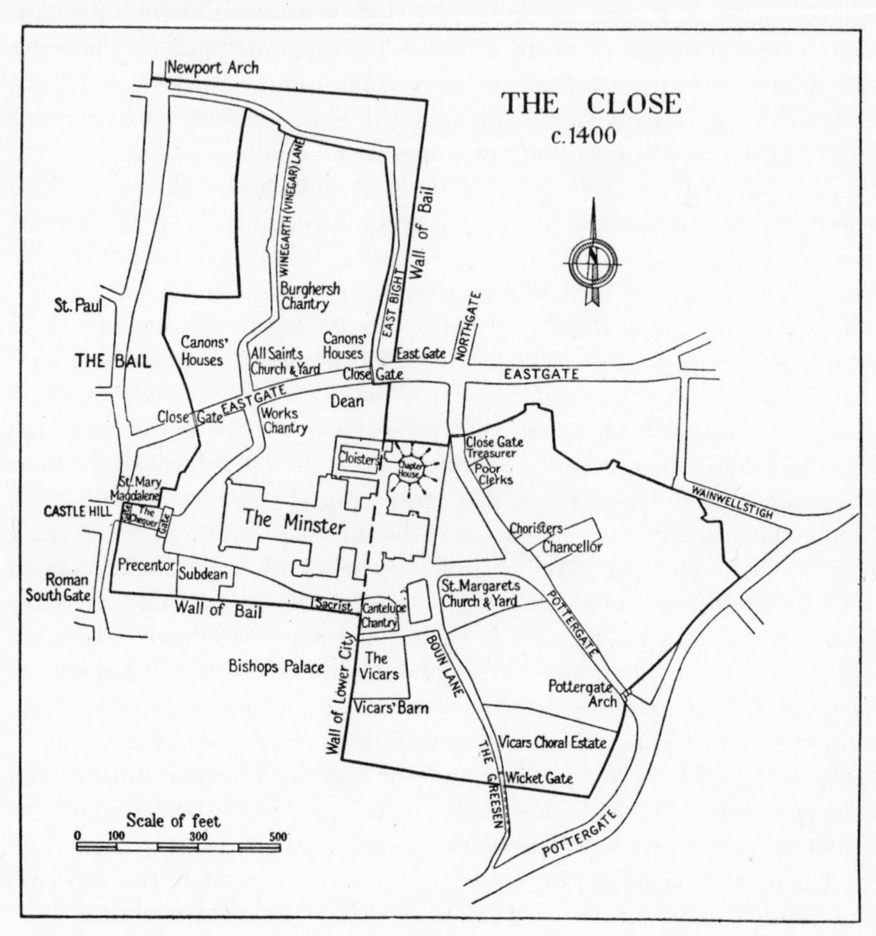

Fig. 9.

in several places ruinous and destroyed; and also to grant to them the part of the city wall which joined the precinct on the south of the church from the bailey wall to the south end of the vicars' garden, so that they should repair, crenellate and turrellate the walls, and build in and on them and on the south and east gates of the bailey, and extend the precinct so as to include the wall of the bailey.[1] The general result of this provision

[1] *C.P.R.* 1327–30, p. 219.

is clear. The Roman wall almost from the south gate of the upper town (on the Steep Hill) to the south-east corner, and thence southwards along the east wall of the lower town to the south-west corner of the Vicars Court, was adopted by the dean and chapter and became part of the Close wall. It was probably many years before the walls, surviving gates, and the gates of which there is pictorial record, were complete. Leland said that the principal gate was the Escheker Gate.[1] The remaining gatehouse at the west front is the inner member of a double gate, the outer member having been built level with the west end of St Mary Magdalene's church. A much restored Pottergate Arch to the south-east has survived,[2] and so also has a rebuilt wicket gate in the *greesen*, or Greestone Stairs. The modern and misnamed Priory Gate stands on the site of a medieval gatehouse and there were two gates astride Eastgate, record of one of which is preserved in a drawing by De Wint.[3] The east gate of the Bail was left outside the enclosure.

Of all the land within the Close the dean and chapter, and the vicars and the chantries, were in some sense collectively or individually the owners, though out of various plots rents were payable to a great variety of persons, representing the holders from whom the land had been originally acquired. A list of rents payable out of chapter lands in 1535 does not distinguish between lands in the Close and lands in the city, where the chapter were large landowners, but it does illustrate the extraordinary network of rents created by successive grants of land in a comparatively small area. Rents were paid by the chapter to the king for a garden in 'lee Est Bight', to the bishop, several churches in the city, the chancellor, several prebendaries, the prior of St Katharine's, the lepers without Lincoln, the vicars of the cathedral, the abbot of Bardney, the prioress of Fosse, the bishop of Durham, the hospitallers of Willoughton, the prior of Sixhill, the cathedral Fabric, the prior of Thurgarton, the abbot of Crowland, the Black Monks without Lincoln, Fitzmartin's Chantry, the prior of Drax, the prior of

[1] *Itinerary* (ed. Toulmin Smith), v, 123.

[2] It has been restored in accordance with Buck's sketch. When De Wint painted the arch it had a tiled roof.

[3] One of them adjoined the corner of the walls enclosing the deanery garden; the inner gate crossed the street a little farther towards the west, so that the end of Turnabout Lane (James Street) was enclosed between the two gates.

The date when the two gates were taken down has not been discovered, but there can be little doubt that De Wint's sepia sketch, now in the Usher Art Gallery collection, and reproduced in Plate 6, shows one of them. De Wint first came to Lincoln in 1805, and he married William Hilton's sister in 1810. He bought the house now known as Hilton House in Drury Lane (at the south-west corner of the castle) in 1814, and sold it in 1846. (From deeds kindly lent by Mr C. Reynolds Scorer.) Here lived the Hilton family, and it was during this period that De Wint on his visits to them painted his many pictures of Lincoln.

Hartsholme, the prior of Bullington, the precentor, the heirs of John Blake, and the duke of Lancaster for the enlargement of the Close and 'lee Angel' Inn in the Bail.[1]

The jurisdiction of the dean and chapter within the Close continued undisturbed until the Civil War. During the interregnum the common council of the city claimed jurisdiction within the Close as a matter of right.[2] At the Restoration, however, the dean and chapter vigorously reasserted their ancient privileges: owing to 'the licenciousness of the late times of usurpation, when all things were laid in common, and the rights of the church were violated', the sergeants of the city sheriffs were forced to humble themselves before Dean Honywood and the chapter, and acknowledge that the sheriffs and their officers 'did take upon themselves to execute writs and other process within the Close of Lincoln (your own proper Franchise in right of the Cathedral Church of Lincoln)', and that they themselves had 'for a little lucre and contrary to our knowledge, continued the said violation and intromission by arresting one Mr Browne, a clergyman, within the said Close of Lincoln'. The sergeants were amerced by the leet jury of the Galilee Court the sum of 50*s*. apiece, and they acknowledged the justice of the fine. In 1669 John Hall of Lincoln appeared before the dean and acknowledged that in ignorance he illegally arrested a man within the Close without the consent of the dean and chapter first had and obtained, and he made his submission.[3]

In the first years of the eighteenth century these matters were again to the fore, and the dean and chapter submitted to counsel 'the Case of the Close of Lincoln and the Liberties of the Dean and Chapter'. It set out that at the time of the Conquest the city had neither mayor nor bailiffs, but only provosts appointed by the king to gather the Crown rents: it recited the royal authority to Remigius to remove his see to Lincoln, the release of lands within the Close from all secular powers, the licence to enclose the precincts and later to enlarge them; and the plea of the dean and chapter before the justices itinerant in 1219:

The dean and chapter of Lincoln, by their attorney, have come before the Justices and sought the liberties and rights of their church of Lincoln. For they say that all pleas as well of the crown as other pleas of assizes and other writs belonging to the lord king which have arisen touching the prebends of the canons of Welton [by Lincoln] with appurtenances and touching the village of Friesthorpe which belongs to the common of the canons of Lincoln ought to be held at the door of the great church of Lincoln, so nevertheless that the Justices

[1] *Valor Ecclesiasticus*, IV, 12; Cole, *Chapter Acts*, 1536–47 (L.R.S.), pp. 175–6.

[2] C.C.M. 1653, p. 2; 1655–1710, f. 63. They also claimed jurisdiction in Beaumont Fee, C.C.M. 1655–1710, p. 67.

[3] Brooke, *Additions on the Cathedral*, pp. vii, viii.

shall send there a certain discreet knight on behalf of the lord king who shall be present there and hear that those pleas shall be reasonably treated and brought to a due end. Moreover, the shire, asked about this, records in common that in the times of all the Justices whose eyres they remember the canons had those liberties, so that some of the knights of the shire were present who say that by the command of the Justices they were present at those pleas, namely, at the door of the church. Therefore let them have the aforesaid liberties.[1]

The case continued that in 1375–6 a writ of 'Quo Warranto' was brought against the dean and chapter by the mayor and commonalty of the city to show by what authority they challenged felons' goods and return of writs, appointed their own coroner, and took stallage and amercements of the inhabitants of the Close; and it was held that they had enjoyed the same privileges since the Conquest. After referring to charters of the city which reserved the rights of the cathedral church, the case continued:

And agreeable to these charters it has been the practice when any writ against any inhabitant of the Close has been issued whether directed to the sheriff of the county at large or to the county of the city, their bailiffs applied themselves to the Dean and Chapter, and upon their granting leave the steward of the Close made out a warrant to the constable thereof, and the writ was executed by the constable and bailiffs in what part soever thereof the party lived and to whomsoever the said writ was directed.

But within twelve or fourteen years last all causes under a limited sum were begun and determined in the Court of the said Dean and Chapter; by a warrant from their steward the debtor was arrested by their constable, and if no bail was given carried to the prison of the Dean and Chapter.

As to the Leet all the inhabitants of the Close being Tenants to the Dean and Chapter have constantly done suit and service thereto and were never summoned to any court or sessions of the city.

The steward of the Dean and Chapter is also in the same patent made their coroner and executes the office thereof as occasion requires. The constable is an office by patent and usually for life.

About February or March 1701/2 an arrest was made in the Close by the officers of the city of Lincoln, without any leave of the Dean and Chapter, and tho' that was the first attempt of that kind yet 'tis said the city will justify them therein, and two or three times within a few years the juries of the city have come to the Close and pretended to amerce for defects in payments.

And ever since the great rebellion the Justices of the city have granted licences to such alehouse keepers as live in that part of the Close which was anciently within the liberty of the said city, and under that pretence have of late pretended to require them to bring in their measures to their sessions, tho' the steward of the Dean and Chapter be also their Clerk of their Markets, and appoints an aletaster, takes cognizance of weights and measures, and weighs the bread of the bakers who sell in the Close.

[1] See Mrs D. M. Stenton, *Rolls of the Justices in Eyre in Lincolnshire and Worcestershire* (Selden Society), no. 577, whence this translation is taken.

Upon the case so presented, counsel advised that the Close not being within the county of the city, the sheriffs or justices of the city had no power to arrest, or quarter soldiers, or license alehouses within the Close; that against any such action the dean and chapter could proceed by 'Quo Warranto', or, more easily and speedily, by an action of trespass or false imprisonment. To the question who could license alehouses in the Close, counsel implied that only justices of the peace for the Close could do so; and when he was asked where (the chapter having long disused the trial of felons) felons within the Close should be tried, he replied that felons must be tried in the county at large.[1]

In August 1704 the common council was preparing to defend an action at the next assizes brought by the dean and chapter. Apparently the defence failed, for the only other entry in the council minutes referred to 'the special verdict in the cause against Mr Hooton and Eure relating to the Dean and Chapter' and to the payment of counsel.[2] Hooton and Eure were the sheriffs of the city in the year 1701–2. The chapter resumed the holding of their 'View of Frankpledge and Court of Galilee', but evidently they did so more as a matter of principle and by way of preserving their rights than for practical purposes, for the record ceases in 1729.[3]

Independence had its disadvantages, however, and when there was an outbreak of burglaries the inhabitants of the Bail and Close had to organise a night watch, the Bail providing two watchmen, and the Close entering into a liberal subscription to establish the same in the Close.[4] In consequence of such practical difficulties the Bail and Close were brought within the Act for lighting, watching and paving the city in 1828. The Close was assimilated to the Bail, and when a county rate was charged upon it the dean and chapter deemed it expedient to submit.[5] The two areas formed a single petty sessional division of Lindsey. Like the Bail, the Close was brought into the parliamentary constituency of Lincoln in 1832, and into the municipal borough in 1836.[6]

When in 1866 an inspector of the Local Government Board held an inquiry upon a petition from the Lincoln Local Government Board for the repeal of parts of the Act of 1828, Mr Swan fought a gallant rearguard action on behalf of the dean and chapter. He said that the whole of the Close belonged to the chapter, and that there was no thoroughfare through

[1] D. & C., Bii/3/15. Lincoln Corporation, Miscellaneous Papers.
[2] C.C.M. 1655–1710, pp. 598, 615. [3] D. & C., Bii/3/15.
[4] *Lincoln Gazetteer*, 13 and 20 May 1785.
[5] *Reports from Commissioners on Proposed Division of Counties and Boundaries of Boroughs* (*Accounts and Papers*, 1831–2, XXXIX).
[6] Supra, p. 101.

it until about one hundred years earlier,[1] when it was thrown open to the public for general traffic. Before that, it was enclosed, and there were gates at each entrance. The Close consisted entirely of the cathedral and private residence houses, footways across, and public highways as well. Mr Hebb, for the Lincoln Board, said the Close was a thoroughfare, and some of the approaches were very inconvenient. It was used for bringing wool and corn into the city, and was a great nuisance to the inhabitants. One of the approaches, Pottergate, was very dangerous. The Board only wished for power to regulate the paving round the Minster, to put lamps in the Minster Yard, and to have control over the highways. Mr Swan claimed for the chapter the power of preventing lamps being placed in the Close without their consent, or of altering roads and footways. Mr Hebb agreed to a clause excluding the right to place lamp-posts on the walls of the cathedral or the rails surrounding the same.[2]

Like the Bail, the Close is now part of the city for all purposes, and perhaps the last survivor of the temporal jurisdiction of the dean and chapter is the cathedral constable.

Although the Bishop's Palace is not situate within the Close, it is convenient to deal with the subject of the bishop's successive dwelling-places in Lincoln here.[3] The present palace site is not the first to be mentioned. Henry I granted to Bishop Bloet licence to make a way of egress in the wall of the king's castle of Lincoln for the convenience of the bishop's house, provided that the wall was not thereby weakened.[4] This provision calls to mind the bishop's soke, the little manor of Willingthorpe on the western hillside,[5] where there may have been a manor-house: a piece of land there called the bishop's garden is mentioned about 1300.[6] Whether the doorway was really made in the castle wall by the bishop is unknown.[7] There is no evidence of it in the present western wall, but it is possible that extensive repairs in the south-west corner of the castle may have obliterated all trace of it.

In 1130–3 Henry I gave to Bishop Alexander the gate of Eastgate with the tower over it, in order that he might use it as a lodging for himself.[8] This was the eastern gate of the Bail, and could only have provided very close quarters for the bishop. It was, however, near to the Minster, and

[1] Apparently the dean and chapter abandoned their rights in this respect about the time of the first Turnpike Act in 1756.

[2] MS. Report of Local Government Inquiry, 1866, in Lincoln Public Library.

[3] Upon the whole matter, see App. I to *R.A.* I, which is summarised here. The writer has not been able to adopt all Canon Foster's views.

[4] *R.A.* I, 20, 21.

[5] See p. 328.

[6] *R.A.* III, 376–7.

[7] Supra, p. 84 n.

[8] *R.A.* I, 34, 269.

would be a convenient town lodging if the bishop were living at Nettleham or Stow or one of his other manors.

The record in the Margam Annals that in 1122 the city was consumed by fire with the exception of the Minster and the bishop's house suggests that the two may have been close together;[1] but the first evidence of the bishop's association with the present palace site appears in a charter of Stephen, dated 1135–8, granting to Bishop Alexander land for a dwelling-house for himself between St Michael's church and the city ditch, with adjoining land and the ditch and wall themselves through which to make a way of ingress.[2] In the troublous times that followed Alexander may not have taken any action on the grant; but whether for this reason or because Stephen's grant was invalid in the eyes of his successor, Bishop Chesney obtained from Henry II (1155–8) a grant of all the land with the ditch from the wall of the king's bailey, on the east side, round the church of St Michael to the cemetery of St Andrew's church, and thence to the city wall to the east, free of land-gable and other outgoings: with leave to pierce the wall of the bailey for the purpose of making a gate for coming and going towards the church.[3] The land referred to in both grants appears to be the same: but the earlier one includes a gift of a piece of the city wall, whilst the later confers a right to pierce the wall of the Bail. The difference in phraseology suggests that Alexander contemplated piercing the east wall of the city, where the main entrance to the palace now is, but that Chesney chose the direct route to the cathedral through the south wall of the Bail. In his plan of Lincoln[4] Stukeley seems to show a door in this wall with a turret at each side, but the very steep gradient from the level of the palace up to the Minster makes it difficult to believe that this was the main entrance to the palace, or indeed that there was ever more than the footway which has lately been reopened in the wall of the Bail through an ancient doorway which is probably work of Chesney's own time.[5] Probably the chief way of access in early times was through St Michael's churchyard. An account of the translation of St Hugh in 1280 refers to conduits of wine outside the west door of the bishop's manor.[6] A carriage way existed on this side until it was closed some years before 1850.[7]

According to Giraldus, Chesney began to build, and his statement is borne out by the reference in the papal bull of 1163 to the bishop's house

[1] *Annales Monastici* (R.S.), I, 11. This is presumably the fire mentioned in the *Anglo-Saxon Chronicle* sub 1123. [2] *R.A.* I, 54–5. [3] Ibid. pp. 86–7.

[4] *Itinerarium Curiosum*, p. 83. He may have intended the turrets to represent the palace itself.

[5] It has been opened since Canon Foster wrote.

[6] Giraldus Cambrensis, *Opera* (R.S.), VII, 220.

[7] Brooke, *Survey of the Antiquities of the City of Lincoln*, p. 32.

PRE-CONQUEST CARVED STONE BUILT INTO THE TOWER ARCH OF ST MARY LE WIGFORD CHURCH

[*See p.* 138

ST BENEDICT'S CHURCH

From a drawing in the Willson Collection in the Cathedral Library

[*See p.* 134

ST MARY LE WIGFORD CHURCH

From Buck's sketch book

See p. 136]

near the Bail to the south.[1] Schalby's first reference to building attributes the beginning to St Hugh, who, he says, began to build a splendid episcopal hall, which, with the kitchen, was finished by Bishop Hugh of Wells.[2] The latter was still building in 1223, when Henry III directed the mayor and bailiffs of Lincoln to allow the bishop to dig and take stone in the ditch of the city, near his house, for building his house at Lincoln, if stone could there be taken without damage to the city;[3] and in 1224 the bishop was to have forty trees from the king's forest of Sherwood to make beams and joists for his hall.[4] The hall measured 85 ft. in length from north to south, and 58 ft. in width, and its roof was supported by two arcades with pillars of Purbeck marble.

In 1329 Bishop Henry Burghersh, the king's chancellor, obtained royal licence to repair, raise, crenellate and turrellate the walls of the palace (then partly enclosed with a stone wall, crenellated and turrellated), with a grant in frankalmoign of the old wall to the east. The whole palace precinct was to have the same immunity as the church itself, offenders within it being held violators of the liberties of Holy Church.[5]

Presumably either Burghersh or one of his successors made the approach to the palace by way of Minster Yard which is now in use. The outer gateway bears the arms of Bishop William Smith (1496–1514), and Bishop William Alnwick (1436–49) built a new chapel and the entrance tower at the north-east corner of the great hall.[6]

The palace was burned by the Royalists in the Civil War, and thereafter the bishops of Lincoln had no residence in Lincoln or its vicinity until Riseholme, two miles to the north, was bought in 1841, at the time when the counties of Bedford, Buckingham, Leicester, Huntingdon, and Hertford were severed from the diocese. When Edward King became bishop in 1885 Riseholme was sold and the Old Palace at Lincoln restored to use.[7]

[1] *R.A.* I, 203.
[2] Giraldus Cambrensis *Opera* (R.S.), VII, 35, 41, 200, 204.
[3] *Rot. Lit. Claus.* I, 580.
[4] Ibid. p. 595.
[5] *C.P.R.* 1327–30, p. 453.
[6] *R.A.* I, 275. For the later history of the palace see references cited by Canon Foster.
[7] Buckden (Hunts), on the Great North Road, was for several centuries the chief residence of the bishops. Stow was alienated by Bishop Holbeach (1547–52); the house at Nettleham was demolished about 1630, after it had 'for three score years and more been deserted and not habitable'. *Cal. State Papers Domestic*, 1629–31, pp. 166, 190.

CHAPTER VII

PARISH CHURCHES AND RELIGIOUS HOUSES

DOMESDAY BOOK makes no attempt to record the names of all the churches in the city. It mentions five. One, St Lawrence, is referred to casually in order to identify a piece of land belonging to the bishop.[1] The others are mentioned because of their own landholdings. St Mary of Lincoln and All Saints have already been discussed.[2] St Michael (presumably of Lincoln) is recorded because it had land at Riseholme. Agemund the priest, who evidently ranked as a thegn had half a carucate of land there, enough for four oxen. He was still in possession in 1086: 'The same man himself has one team there [in demesne]. This belongs to the church of St Michael. In the time of King Edward it was worth ten shillings; now twenty shillings.'[3]

The fifth church which Domesday Book mentions by name is St Peter:

In Wellingore earl Morcar had 18 carucates of land [assessed] to the geld. There is land for as many teams. Now the king has two teams there [in demesne], and 7 villeins and 7 bordars with one team, and 28 sokemen with 7 teams. There is a church there and a priest, having 2 carucates and 2 bovates of the same land. And the said church belongs to the church of St Peter in Lincoln. There are 129 acres of meadow there, and [other] 14 acres belonging to the church. In the time of King Edward it was worth £30; now £15 by weight.[4]

Presently Earl Roger of Poitou[5] is found in possession both of Wellingore church and of St Peter of Lincoln. As he is known to have succeeded Morcar in Wellingore church, and he became the owner of St Peter of Lincoln, to which Wellingore had belonged, it seems probable that his predecessor in St Peter also was Morcar.

The document which shows Roger in possession of St Peter also makes it possible to say which of the several churches of that dedication in the city is the one referred to in Domesday. In 1094 Roger gave St Peter of Lincoln and the churches of Wellingore, Navenby and Boothby with other endowments to the abbey of St Martin of Sées in Normandy;[6] and in the episcopate of Hugh de Welles the abbot and convent of Sées presented to St Peter at Pleas.[7]

[1] *L.D.* p. 6. [2] Supra, pp. 67, 115. [3] *L.D.* p. 204.
[4] Ibid. pp. 15, 16. [5] Supra, p. 50.
[6] Round, *Calendar of Documents preserved in France*, p. 237.
[7] *Rotuli Hugonis de Welles* (L.R.S.), III, 115, 198. Mr William Page mistakenly assumed that this was St Peter at Gowts church, remarking that Saxon remains still exist. 'Some Remarks on the Churches of Domesday Book' in *Archaeologia*, LXVI (1915), p. 89.

The reference to this church as St Peter of Lincoln implies some precedence at a time when there were several churches of St Peter in the city, and it is interesting to find that this important and endowed church, probably once the property of Earl Morcar (and perhaps inherited by him from the great Earl Leofric of Mercia), is the church situate at the moot-stone.[1] Though it is impossible to say whether the church or the court held there was the older, their juxtaposition implies an early foundation of the church. The church stood on the east side of the High Street, or Mikelgate, at the point where the street narrowed southwards into Briggate. It was immediately to the north of St Peter at Arches, and to distinguish it from the latter was called in deeds St Peter *superior* (being higher up the hill), or *in magno vico*. The parish was united to St Peter at Arches in 1549 and there is no surviving description of the church.

Though no other churches are mentioned by name in Domesday several people are mentioned as owning churches. St Peter at Arches may well be one of these churches. References to the church, *ad arcus*, or *in Briggate*, appear in deeds of the late twelfth century,[2] and in the Pipe Roll of 1182–3 Henry de Archis and his father Gerbert de Arches are mentioned.[3] Bishop Hugh de Welles collated the church to Walter of Louth by authority of the Council.[4] Later in the same episcopate Roger de Faversham, clerk, was presented to the church by the prior and convent of Shelford in Nottinghamshire.[5] This was a house of Austin canons, founded by Ralf Haunselin in the time of Henry II. According to the ministers' accounts at the time of the dissolution of religious houses, it had rents of 9*s*. in the city of Lincoln, and drew a pension of 10*s*. 8*d*. from St Peter's church.[6] In a deed probably of the middle of the thirteenth century, Gocelin, rector of St Peter *ad arcus*, was granting land between land of St Mary on one side and land of William Barber on the other, in Walkergate in the parish of St Peter, at a rent for the betterment of his church.[7]

Another Ralf Haunselin or Alselin (i.e. son of Elsi or Ælfsige), appears in the Domesday account of Lincoln. He was the nephew of Geoffrey Alselin, who succeeded to part of the Lincoln estates of Tochi son of Outi,[8] and to estates of Tochi at Laxton in Nottinghamshire and elsewhere.[9] Tochi had in Lincoln 30 messuages besides his hall and 2½ churches: the bishop had secured the 30 messuages for his church of St Mary, but Geoffrey had succeeded to the hall and apparently to the churches. The

[1] Supra, p. 61.
[2] D. & C., Dii, 80/3/48, and endorsement.
[3] P.R. 29 *Henry II*, p. 66.
[4] *Rotuli Hugonis de Welles* (L.R.S.), I, 101.
[5] Ibid. III, 139, and see *Rotuli Roberti Grosseteste* (L.R.S.), p. 4.
[6] *Monasticon*, VI, 578.
[7] D. & C., Dii, 80/3/17.
[8] *L.D.* p. 3. See Appendix II.
[9] Supra, p. 45.

association of Shelford with Ralf Alselin the younger, and the Shelford rights in St Peter at Arches, suggest that this was one of Tochi's churches (or perhaps the church in which he had a half share). Other evidence points to the same conclusion. In 1257–8 there was a dispute between William Bardolf and Adam de Everingham for the patronage of Shelford Priory. Bardolf claimed that his ancestor Ralf Haunselin was the founder; Adam made a like claim for his ancestor Robert de Cauz (who married a daughter of Geoffrey Alselin). The jury found that Ralf was the founder of the priory and William was its patron.[1] This account does not mention St Peter at Arches, but the church does appear in an account of another dispute relating to the same matter. In 1263 the prior of Shelford claimed land in Shelford and elsewhere, advowsons of churches, and the moiety of advowsons of other churches including St Peter at Arches, against Adam de Everingham. Agreement was reached between the parties, the moieties going to the priory.[2]

It seems likely therefore that St Peter's church or a moiety of it was part of Tochi's estate. It cannot of course be proved that the church was standing in 1086, but when the eighteenth-century successor of the old church was taken down in 1933 fragments of twelfth-century work were found in the foundations.[3]

To digress for a moment, it is a point of interest in the Domesday account of Tochi's estate that his normal successor did not secure the whole of it. The thirty messuages were secured by the bishop in respect of the church of St Mary, Geoffrey Alselin having nothing by way of exchange or otherwise. Did the Minster hold land in that part of the united parish of St Peter at Arches and St Peter at Pleas (that is, the southern part) which presumably had belonged to the Arches church? The old parish no doubt included a small area north of the Stonebow and that part of the modern parish outside the wall and to the north of the river.

The Minster did own such a piece of land. Several deeds refer to land in *semita Sanctae Mariae* or St Mary Stigh in the parish of St Peter *ad archus*,[4] and the White Book mentions St Mary Stigh in Briggate in 1616.[5] The lane is precisely identified by a Corporation lease (dated 1748) of the Reindeer Inn abutting south upon a lane formerly called St Mary Stigh but then known as 'Mutch Lane'. The Reindeer Inn has been succeeded by the Midland Bank, at the junction of High Street and Guildhall Street, but Much Lane (its entry from High Street now narrowed to a passage)

[1] *Monasticon*, VI, 578. [2] *Final Concords* (L.R.S.), II, 289.

[3] Some of them are depicted in *The Story of a Great Adventure*, an appeal for funds for the new church of St Giles.

[4] D. & C., Dii, 80/3/41, 50, 51. [5] f. 213.

remains. Here on this valuable commercial site, between the city wall and the river wharves, were, it would seem, the houses which the bishop secured for his church. A series of leases of the thirteenth century relating to the houses and land in the Stigh has survived among the dean and chapter's muniments. Though the chapter had many other pieces of property in the city, there is no other record of any considerable number of houses grouped together which could be identified as Tochi's former estate. A difficult passage in Domesday Book refers to 'other thirty messuages he (Tochi) had by way of letting (*locationem*)'.[1] Whether these were booths adjoining the other thirty is not clear, but it is clear that St Mary Stigh was in an excellent position for visiting merchants who did not wish to buy a freehold or burgage tenement, but would be glad to take a shop or warehouse at a rental. Land tenure had already taken on a commercial aspect.

To attempt to identify Tochi's other churches would be mere guesswork. Domesday says that two churches belonged to the bishop, but it will be more convenient to discuss these elsewhere;[2] and it mentions the two built by Colswein, an interesting figure who has been discussed before.[3] Professor Freeman had no hesitation in placing Colswein's new colony in Wigford, and he declared that the Domesday passage concerning it made it absolutely certain that the towers of St Mary le Wigford and St Peter at Gowts were built by Colswein between the years 1066 and 1086. Elsewhere he writes that without the aid of Domesday 'we could never have fixed a landmark so precious alike in the local history of his own city and in the history of English, and even of European art'.[4] To-day Freeman's certainty has gone: there are reasons for thinking the settlement in Wigford of earlier date, and the one clear piece of evidence points to a different site for Colswein's estate.

In a general confirmation granted by Henry II to the abbey of St Mary of York in 1156–7 are these passages relating to gifts:

> Picotus in Lincolnia ecclesiam Sancti Petri.
> Picotus filius Colsuani Lincolnie ii mansuras terre et quatuor acras in campis et le Hevedland.[5]

In the absence of evidence to the contrary it is reasonable to assume that Picot was parting with a portion of his inheritance from his father Colswein, and that where this church of St Peter is found there also is Colswein's estate. Picot's St Peter is identified as St Peter *ad fontem*, or 'in Bagger-

[1] Appendix II. [2] Infra, pp. 328–50. [3] Supra, p. 48.
[4] *Norman Conquest* (1876), IV, 219 n.; V, 38. And see his *English Towns and Districts* (1883), pp. 210–13.
[5] *Monasticon*, III, 549; Farrer, *Early Yorkshire Charters*, I, 274–5.

holme', or 'atte welles' by the fact that St Mary of York presented to this church.[1] It probably stood on the hillside to the east of the city, south of Monks Road, east of Rosemary Lane: perhaps in St Hugh Croft, which was certainly in St Peter's parish. Such a site is near the western boundary of the liberty of the Black Monks, which extended thence to the bounds of Greetwell. It is just beyond the built-up eastern suburb of the city as it continued to exist until a century ago. Colswein built on land which had never been built on before, but it would be to his advantage to secure his land as nearly as possible to the already occupied area, where the potential value of the waste would be the highest. If it may be assumed that Colswein's new colony has been located, perhaps it may also be assumed that there was already at the Conquest an eastern suburb.[2] There is no evidence to show which was Colswein's other church, but it may have been St Augustine, near the north bank of the river and not far from Rosemary Lane end: this would put it in a similar longitude to St Peter. The other churches of the suburb of Butwerk seem to have stood farther west.

The three surviving medieval parish churches of Lincoln are all situate south of the river in the suburb of Wigford. On the west side of High Street, near the High Bridge, is St Benedict. The earliest documentary evidence of the church's existence is a writ of Henry I granting to St Mary of Lincoln and Bishop Robert I and his successors the church of St Benedict of Wicheford at the request of Roger Bigod, who gave it in alms to St Mary. As Bigod died in 1107 the writ can be dated 1100–7.[3] Bigod is not returned in Domesday Book as holding any land in the county, and the manner of his acquisition of the church is unknown. He shared in land forfeited by Ralf de Gael, son of Ralf the Staller, who held lands in Norfolk, Suffolk and Lincolnshire and an estate in Cornwall; but as Ralf forfeited his Lincolnshire estates before 1086 this may not account for Bigod's ownership of St Benedict.

The church tower is attributed by Professor Baldwin Brown to the period of the Confessor and after: he describes it as a tower of the 'Lincolnshire' type with midwall work but no caps, and adds that 'there are no other signs of Saxon features or technique in the very picturesque old building'. Unlike the tall narrow towers of St Mary and St Peter, St Benedict is squat, and 'more of the type of Harpswell and other examples that affect a Norman rather than a Saxon seeming'.[4]

But conclusions are not to be drawn from the present proportions of the tower, for it has been rebuilt. There now remain of the church only the

[1] *Rotuli Hugonis de Welles* (L.R.S.), III, 212.
[2] Infra, p. 161.
[3] *R.A.* I, 27.
[4] *Arts in Early England* (2nd ed. 1925), II, 466, 468.

chancel and side-chapel and the tower: the nave either perished in the Civil War or suffered so severely that it was demolished thereafter. The parish accounts tell of repairs to the church walls between 1655 and 1667, and extensive building activity was going on about 1701. An account of the Lincoln churches of about 1674 notes that the steeple fell down and was lately rebuilt.[1] The tower now stands across the chancel arch. The rebuilders inserted the double belfry openings with the midwall shafts, but the absence of other Saxon features proves nothing about its predecessor. The rebuilders had before them not only the lofty towers of St Mary and St Peter but also the squat tower of St Margaret;[2] they may have chosen the latter form on grounds of economy rather than for the sake of reproducing the original. The chancel is Early English in character: a fine window with curvilinear tracery has been inserted in the east end, and a north aisle added of perpendicular style.[3] The church was appropriated to the cathedral prebend of North Kelsey, the prebendary being patron.

The two churches of St Mary le Wigford and St Peter at Gowts have generally been considered together. They are both situate on the east side of Ermine Street in the suburb of Wigford and are only about 700 yards apart; their towers are similar in style; and they were assumed by Freeman to have had a common founder in Colswein.[4] For the reasons stated above this account of their origin has been abandoned, and there are differences in the two towers which make it desirable to consider them separately as well as together.

Both are tall and narrow—Baldwin Brown speaks of their gaunt and vigorous leanness[5]—and both have the double belfry openings with mid-wall shafts which are one of the common characteristics of the Saxon style. Neither, however, has long and short quoins, pilaster strips or double splayed windows, which are the decisive evidence of pre-Conquest origin.

[1] Ross, Scrap Books at Burton Hall, quoting MSS. Willis, 27, 40.

[2] See Plate 11.

[3] Between the years 1927 and 1929 a struggle was carried on to preserve this church. The Ecclesiastical Commissioners had entered into a provisional contract for the sale of its site and that of St Peter at Arches to the Lincoln Corporation. It was due mainly to the efforts of the Lincoln Churches Defence Committee that the church of St Benedict was saved and a fund provided for its maintenance. The fight to save St Peter's church was carried to the Judicial Committee of the Privy Council. Although the appeal was lost the Lord Chancellor (Lord Sankey) elicited from the Commissioners (25 June 1931) an undertaking to carry out to the utmost a suggestion to use the materials of the church in the new church to be built in the suburbs of the city. After a period of uncertainty whether the pledge would be honoured or not, Dr Nugent Hicks succeeded to the bishopric. The facts were laid before him, and after inquiry he ruled that the undertaking must be honoured. The result is the noble building erected under the care of Mr W. G. Watkins, incorporating the design and the furnishings of the old church.

[4] Supra, p. 133.

[5] *Arts in Early England* (2nd ed. 1925), II, 468.

Because of the presence of the one set of characteristics and the absence of the other they have been attributed to the period of the Saxo-Norman overlap, the period following the Norman Conquest before Saxon building fashions fully gave way to the Norman.

Fig. 10. Western face of church towers: (1) St Mary le Wigford, (2) St Peter at Gowts.

Yet in St Mary's there is no evidence of Norman influence. The doorway is plain, and the capitals of the midwall shafts unadorned: they 'represent somewhat crude methods of getting down from the square of the top of the cap to the octagon or circle of the summit of the shaft'.[1]

In addition to these features bearing upon the date of the tower, there is one especially interesting piece of evidence. Built into the tower, on the south side of the west door, is a Roman tombstone, consisting of a panel recessed for an inscription and a gabled top. The builder of the tower may well have found the stone on the site: Stukeley noted that many funeral

[1] Baldwin Brown, *Arts in Early England* (2nd ed. 1925), II, 410, and figure 192 (1).

monuments of the Romans had been found on both sides of the Roman road.[1] The trouble involved in incorporating this stone in the tower was not taken without reason, for in the triangle formed by the gabled top is a second inscription in Anglo-Saxon. Stukeley mentions an obscure Christian inscription;[2] and it was figured by Gough.[3] It was examined again by Canon John Wordsworth, later bishop of Salisbury, in 1879, and he published a drawing based on a photograph.[4] It is hopeless to-day to expect to get a better record of the inscription than that of Wordsworth. He and Professor Bruce Dickins are agreed that it must be read upwards from the bottom line, and it is as follows:

MARIE
OFE 7 SCE
NCRISTE TO L
AN 7 FIOS GODIA
Ƿ EIRTIG ME LET WIRCE

(Eirtig had me built and endowed to the glory of Christ and S. Mary.[5])

The reading is not altogether free from doubt, and in particular it is curious that the name 'Eirtig', if that is the correct reading, seems not to be recorded anywhere else. The ending *-ig*, as in Tostig and Ranig, is presumably the Scandinavian *-i*, the nominatival inflection of the weak noun.[6] Eirtig was apparently therefore a Dane, but no evidence has been found to identify him, or to date his work, as Mr Bilson has identified Herbert the chamberlain as the founder of Weaverthorpe church in the East Riding of Yorkshire.[7] Weaverthorpe is thus shown, in spite of its Saxon air, to belong to the early twelfth century, and as might be expected, the inscription recording the name of its founder is in Latin. The Lincoln inscription suggests comparison rather with that of Kirkdale in Yorkshire, which is in Anglo-Saxon, and from its mention of Edward the Confessor and Tostig the earl can be dated between 1055 and 1065.[8] The fact that the inscription at St Mary's is in Anglo-Saxon and not in Latin in itself suggests a pre-Conquest date; and though the argument from silence is a dangerous one, it does seem probable that after the Conquest any man great and wealthy enough to build St Mary's tower would have left some other record of his existence, perhaps in Domesday or the Obituary of the

[1] *Itinerarium Curiosum*, p. 85. [2] Ibid. p. 86.
[3] In his edition of Camden's *Britannia* (1806), II, plate vii.
[4] *A.A.S.R.* XV (1879), p. 16. There is another drawing in Smith, *Roman Inscribed Stones found in the City of Lincoln*, p. 9.
[5] Baldwin Brown, op. cit. II, 467.
[6] The writer is indebted to Professor Bruce Dickins for this comment.
[7] *Archaeologia*, LXXII (1922), pp. 51–70.
[8] Baldwin Brown, op. cit. I, 355–7.

dean and chapter, or in a charter. Furthermore, after the Conquest, magnates with Danish names became a very rare species. These considerations, coupled with the absence of Norman characteristics in the tower, seem to warrant the conclusion that it was built before the Conquest.

The fact that the tower is not bonded into the nave of the church shows that the tower was built independently, and implies that the original church was older than the tower, not as at Winterton, where church and tower were built together.[1] Some confirmation of this view is found in a

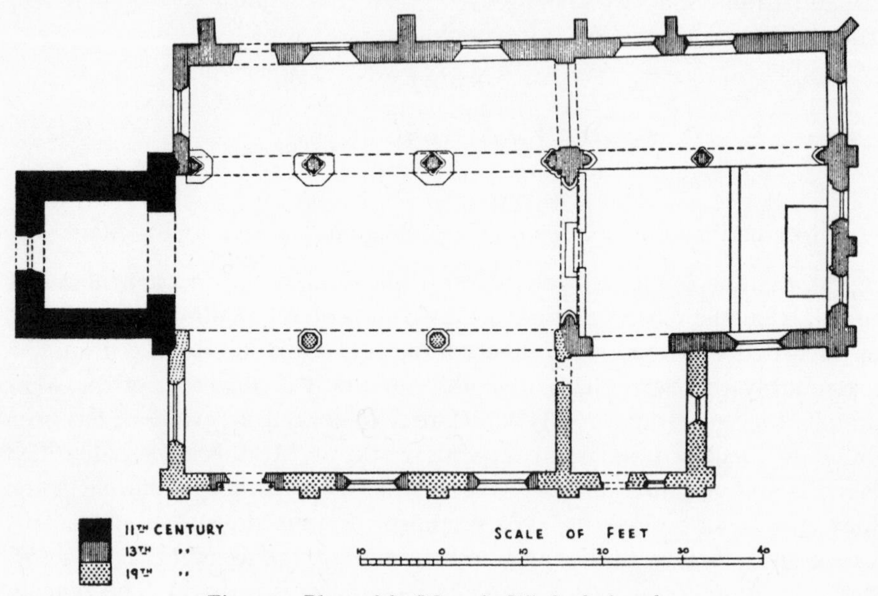

Fig. 11. Plan of St Mary le Wigford church.

carved stone built into the south jamb of the tower arch a little above ground-level. Its interlacing design of the later Saxon period indicates the existence of a building on the site of a date earlier than the tower.[2]

By 1163 the church had come into the hands of the dean and chapter, to whom it was confirmed by Pope Alexander III.[3] It was appropriated to the prebend of Gretton. By 1263 it had been united with the churches of St Faith and St Andrew under the palace, and Bishop Gravesend ordained a vicarage, reserving to the rector of the prebendal church of Gretton, who was the prebendary, seven marks annually from the endowment. At that time the rector, Roger de Fuldon, was archdeacon of Lincoln; the arch-

[1] Hamilton Thompson, in *Memorials of Old Lincolnshire*, p. 76.

[2] This stone is not recorded in Davies, 'Pre-Conquest Carved Stones in Lincolnshire' in *Arch. Journ.* LXXXIII (1926), pp. 1–20. It is reproduced in Plate 7.

[3] *R.A.* I, 205.

deaconry and the rectory went together.[1] The existing nave, chancel, and north aisle are Early English in style, and may have been built in Gravesend's time. The south aisle and arcade were added in the nineteenth century, the old south windows and south door being inserted in the new south wall.[2]

Of St Peter at Gowts' tower Baldwin Brown says that it offers the characteristics of the Lincolnshire group of towers in an epitome. It is tall and narrow and though the walls are in the main vertical, they draw in a little in a curious fashion just under the string course.[3] Below the string course and immediately above the single-light window on the west face of the tower is a carved stone depicting a figure variously said to be St Peter or Jupiter. A recent photograph shows that although it is very much worn

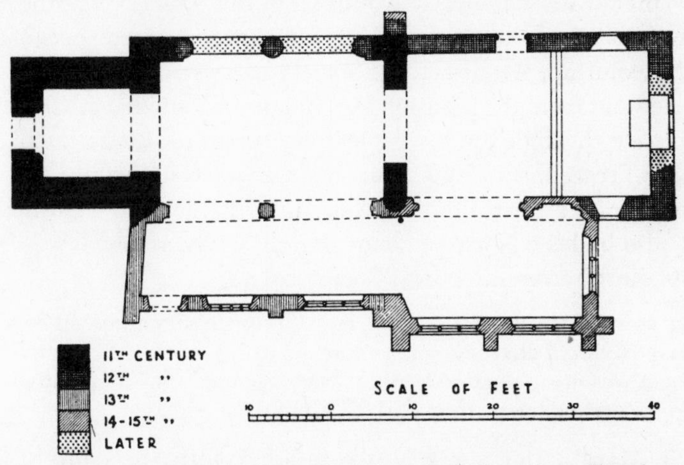

Fig. 12. Plan of St Peter at Gowts church before alteration. Based on a plan (*c.* 1840–50) in the possession of the Society of Antiquaries.

it is still possible to discern a seated figure, and it seems likely that it depicts Christ in majesty. Of the capitals of the midwall shafts, the eastern one has a bulbous shape, which is found in both Saxon and Norman period buildings;[4] those on the south and west are ornamented with volutes and upright leaves and have 'considerable elegance of design and sharp and delicate cutting'.[5] It has been possible to secure a photograph of the western capital: 'it is very definitely un-Norman, and whatever its date is in the Saxon tradition.'[6]

[1] *Rotuli Ricardi Gravesend* (L.R.S.), pp. 15, 279.
[2] Buck's sketch shows the south windows and door in their old positions.
[3] Baldwin Brown, op. cit. II, 386–90, 466.
[4] Clapham, *English Romanesque Architecture before the Conquest* (1930), p. 124.
[5] Baldwin Brown, op. cit. II, 413.
[6] Sir Alfred Clapham's comment in a letter to the writer. The carving and this capital are shown in Plate 9.

The jambs of the west door consist of stone slabs laid flat and set up on end alternately. The doorway has a tympanum filled in with decorative stonework, which Baldwin Brown describes as a Norman feature.[1] A close inspection of the doorway, with its sharp outlines showing no signs of wear, raises suspicions of its date, which are fully confirmed by De Wint's painting of the church. This shows the whole doorway to be blocked with masonry, and jambs, arch and tympanum to be later insertions: so also is the single round-headed window above. These insertions must have been part of one of the 'restorations' of the nineteenth century which have gone far to destroy the architectural interest of the church.

Buck's sketch of St Peter's shows a porch before the south door, as also does De Wint's water colour. It would seem that before 1852 the doorway in the tower had been opened and the south door closed, because in that year the Lincolnshire Architectural Society expressed regret that the work being carried out from the plans of Mr Nicholson provided for the retention of the entrance through the tower, leaving the south door closed.

When Mr Freeman first saw Lincoln in 1847, traces could still be seen of the Romanesque north aisle of the church: they had vanished before 1866.[2] So also had the Norman chancel arch, whose removal was censured by the Lincolnshire Architectural Society:

> We have to regret the, as it seemed to us, unnecessary removal of a chancel arch of Early Norman character; the more so, as the advice the committee gave on the subject was misunderstood, and it was supposed that they had given their sanction to an arrangement they had all along opposed.[3]

As at St Mary's, the tower is not bonded with the church, and the inference that there was a church earlier in date than the tower is confirmed by the fact that the quoins of the nave, unlike those of the tower itself, have long and short work. A plan made before the alterations of 1850 shows that, as is usual in pre-Conquest architecture,[4] the nave approximated to rather less than two squares. In the twelfth century were added a north aisle and arcade of two bays and a chancel slightly longer than the nave. A south aisle was added, probably in the thirteenth century, and the chapel of a chantry founded by Ralph Jolyff in 1347 to the east of it: these have survived. The present north aisle and arcade are of nineteenth-century date: the chancel has been twice enlarged.

The date of the tower cannot be settled with certainty. There is no sign that it was influenced by the new Norman minster on the hill, which is

[1] Op. cit. II, 389, 468.

[2] *Norman Conquest*, IV, 219 n. The north arcade is depicted in Parker, *Introduction to Gothic Architecture* (9th ed. 1891), p. 36.

[3] *A.A.S.R.* II (1852), p. xxviii.

[4] Clapham, op. cit. p. 103.

evidently the source of the arcade on the west side of the tower at Branston. Now that it is known that the doorway and tympanum are not to be relied on as evidence of date, there are no clear indications of post-Conquest work in the tower, and two of the capitals of the midwall shafts are certainly of Saxon character. Its similarity to the tower of St Mary at least suggests that St Peter's tower also may have been built before the Conquest.

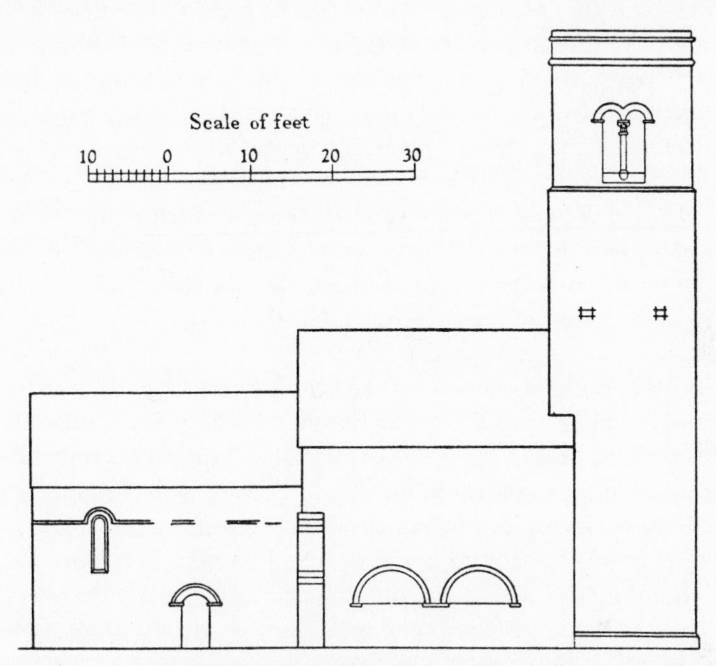

Fig. 13. St Peter at Gowts church, *c.* 1840–50. From a drawing in the possession of the Society of Antiquaries.

The church differs from St Mary's in that there is nothing to show who built it. It is first mentioned with other churches in 1147–8, when it is found in the hands of the bishop.[1] Its proximity to St Mary's Guildhall, round which, in the twelfth century, were grouped some of the great merchant houses of Lincoln, suggests that perhaps already in the eleventh century there were well-to-do citizens in the parish who combined to adorn the existing church with a stately tower, and that a later generation added a Norman chancel and north aisle.

It has already been noticed that one of the urgent problems facing the first Norman bishop was to provide maintenance for the canons serving the Minster.[2] A charter of William the Conqueror granted to Remigius

[1] *R.A.* I, 262.

[2] Supra, p. 107.

the churches of St Lawrence and St Martin in Lincoln:[1] and as this is only the first of a series of such grants it is interesting to find another writ giving a glimpse of a dispossessed owner seeking compensation. The writ gives to the church of Lincoln and the bishop the church of St Martin and its appurtenances, and commands that if 'Norman' shall justly claim any compensation the bishop shall pay it.[2] Who Norman was (perhaps he was Norman Crassus the lawman), what claim he had, whether he pursued it, and whether the bishop was the judge in his own cause, is unknown. The bishop gathered up most of the churches of the city into his own hands too quickly for the preservation of much information about magnates or citizens who had owned them. As has been noted,[3] St Lawrence, which stood on the site of the Theatre Royal in Clasketgate, is mentioned in Domesday Book. The name of St Martin on Lincoln coins of the first half of the tenth century, with the suggestion that the saint was once regarded as patron of the city,[4] implies an early foundation of the church of that dedication, which stood in the present St Martin's Lane.

The church that existed in the nineteenth century consisted of a nave and north aisle, divided by two rather broad Early English arches, with a chancel and north aisle, and a tower rebuilt in 1740.[5] Over the south door of the church was, or had been, an ample square rag-stone, much defaced, and bearing a sculpture shown in Figure 14: it was copied and recorded by Maurice Johnson in his account of the Lincoln mint, who was at pains to claim it as referring to the mint, and as being Roman in origin. He found in it the emperor with a nimbus, the imperial eagle, the mint master, and the square box used to receive newly coined money from the mint.[6] Johnson's identification is not to be taken seriously, though credit is due to him for recording the carving at all. It is certainly Norman in character, and seems to depict the baptism of Christ, though there are some features which are puzzling, and it bears little resemblance to the usual representations of the subject.

In 1115 Henry I confirmed to the church of Lincoln the churches of St Margaret in Lincoln and Haceby in the county, which Osbert the sheriff had given.[7] St Margaret stood on the green to the south-east of the

[1] *R.A.* I, 3. [2] Ibid. p. 15. [3] Supra, p. 130.

[4] Supra, p. 30. It was claimed by Maurice Johnson that St Martin was Paulinus' church (see note (6) below). [5] *A.A.S.R.* XIII (1876), p. 215.

[6] 'Dissertation on the Mint at Lincoln' in *Account of the Gentlemen's Society at Spalding* (1784), pp. 61–2. The appropriate comment has been made by Ruding (*Annals of the Coinage of Britain*, III, 68): 'He who would find all these things in the engraving of this stone must

'purge with Euphrasie and Rue
The Visual nerve, for he has much to see.'

[7] *R.A.* I, 22.

cathedral: it was within the Close, but in the twelfth century it stood outside the city wall, and was often known as St Margaret in Pottergate. Extant drawings of the church show a squat tower with double belfry openings but no midwall shaft, evidently of Norman date: the east end had an Early English window and a *vesica piscis*. In 1847 there was found in a stone coffin in this part of the Close a cruciform leaden plate bearing the following inscription: 'Corpvs Sifordi Presbiteri Sce Elene et Sce Margarete

Fig. 14. Carved stone formerly over the south door of old St Martin's church. From a drawing by Maurice Johnson (see p. 142).

titvlatvs hic jacet.'[1] No other evidence has been found of a dedication to St Helen. If, as has been suggested, the plate belongs to the eleventh century, it would be tempting to identify in Siford the Siward the priest who was a lawman in 1066.

Roger Bigod's gift of St Benedict has already been mentioned.[2] The death of Osbert the sheriff brought another acquisition. Henry I committed to Bishop Robert I the church of All Saints [in Hungate] and whatever belonged to it within the borough and without, and the churches

[1] *Proceedings of the Archaeological Institute* (1848), p. xliv. For St Margaret, see Plate 11.

[2] Supra, p. 134.

of Grimsby, as Osbert had them on the day that he was alive and dead, and the king commanded Wigot, then sheriff, to put the bishop in seisin thereof (1114–16).[1] Pope Honorius II confirmed the church to Bishop Alexander in 1126.[2] It is believed to have stood on the east side of and near the southern end of Hungate. It became a prebendal church giving its name of All Saints to the prebend. In the early fifteenth century it ceased to be parochial, and the parish was united to St Martin.

Between the years 1123 and 1148 Bishop Alexander granted to Humphrey *in prebendam* the church of St John in Newport, half a carucate of land which was Aye the priest's, half a carucate which was of All Saints [in the Bail], half the church of Holy Trinity in Wigford, and land in Dunholme and elsewhere. This charter effected the endowment of the prebend of Newport and Dunham.[3]

Already before these churches had been secured Bishop Robert had obtained from Henry I a very important writ by which Henry gave to God and the church of St Mary of Lincoln and Bishop Robert all the churches in the borough of Lincoln, within and without, which their priests held of the king, any customary payments belonging to the king being reserved (1100–7).[4] The effect of this grant presumably was that if it could be proved that the priest held of an individual lord then the lord's rights in the church were undisturbed, but if not, then the priest was deemed to hold of the king and under the royal grant the church passed to the bishop. The onus of proof shifted from the bishop to the former owner, and it can be imagined that there were many cases where either the title to a church was difficult to prove, or the citizens who had built the churches or their descendants thought it imprudent to challenge a powerful bishop who had the support of the king.

Henry's gift was confirmed by King Stephen,[5] and in 1146 Pope Eugenius III confirmed to the canons of Lincoln the churches of St Martin and St Lawrence and the other churches of Lincoln in the king's fee, All Saints in Lincoln with its lands and tithes, and St John in Newport.[6] Bishop Alexander, still engaged in making provision for the canons of his church, notified Adelmus, the dean, and the chapter that he had given the dignity of the office of precentor to their canon, Roger de Almaria, and had appropriated to this dignity all the churches in the borough of Lincoln of the demesne and gift of King Henry I which had not yet been confirmed to a particular prebend (*in prebendam*) or to the common of canons. He also confirmed to Roger the school of song. The churches so appropriated were St Michael near the gate, St Peter in Parchemingate, St George, Holy

[1] *R.A.* I, 43. [2] Ibid. p. 188. [3] *R.A.* II, 20.
[4] *R.A.* I, 33. [5] Ibid. p. 48. [6] Ibid. p. 198.

PLATE 9

CARVED STONE ABOVE THE SINGLE LIGHT WINDOW ON THE WEST FACE OF ST PETER AT GOWTS CHURCH TOWER

CAPITAL OF THE MIDWALL SHAFT ON THE WEST FACE OF ST PETER AT GOWTS CHURCH TOWER

[*See pp.* 138–9

PLATE 10

ST PETER AT GOWTS CHURCH

From a painting by Peter de Wint, by permission of the Museum and Art Gallery Committee of the Corporation of Birmingham

[*See p.* 140

Trinity, St Edmund and St Swithin; and outside the walls Holy Trinity, St Rumold, St Bavon, St Augustine; in Eastgate St Peter; in Wigford, St John, Holy Trinity, St Michael, St Margaret, St Mark. The appropriation was confirmed by Theobald, archbishop of Canterbury.[1]

The process of gathering up the churches as opportunity offered was made possible by the general grant of Henry I. Many years later this process was recalled by a jury which presented a return to the justices in eyre who sat at Lincoln in 1226–7. The return is inaccurate in detail as is natural after the lapse of time, but it may give the essential truth. The jury said that in the time of King Henry, the king's grandfather (or in another version King Richard), the citizens of Lincoln held many churches and there were many parsons of them. Then the king summoned the citizens to answer for the advowsons of their churches; and because they did not come, the advowsons were taken into the king's hand, and the king gave them to the bishop (or in the other version the dean), who gave them to the precentor.[2]

Some further acquisitions are mentioned in a bull of confirmation granted by Pope Alexander III to the dean and canons in 1163. They were St Mary le Wigford, St Stephen, St Faith in the bishop's soke, St John in Newport and St Leonard as belonging to particular prebends, and also St Nicholas in Newport and St Giles.[3]

At a later date the dean and chapter secured the church of St Bartholomew to the west of the castle. It is first mentioned in a charter (*c.* 1189) by which Guy de Vere gave the church with other endowments to the abbey of Selby, for an obit for his brother Gilbert de Vere, a former abbot of that house.[4] The Veres, which may be a corruption of Vermis, were tenants of the Countess Lucy's family. Two acres in Scotton which Guy de Vermis held of Ranulf le Meschin in 1115–18[5] are no doubt part of the knight's fee in that place which Walter de Ver held of the earl of Chester in 1212.[6] A Guy de Ver held a knight's fee of William de Roumare in 1166.[7]

In 1275 the abbot and convent of Selby sent letters to Bishop Gravesend presenting William son of Gernagan, clerk, to the church of St Bartholomew, vacant by the resignation of Master William of Foston.[8] During William Gernagan's tenure of the rectory he entered into treaty with the dean and chapter, and on account of the straitness of the cemetery of the church of Lincoln, gave leave to them and to the constable of the castle to

[1] Ibid. pp. 262–3.
[2] *Book of Fees*, I, 363–4.
[3] *R.A.* I, 205, 207.
[4] Fowler, *Coucher Book of Selby* (Yorkshire Archaeological and Topographical Association), II, 297.
[5] *L.D.* p. 243.
[6] *Book of Fees*, I, 191.
[7] *Red Book of the Exchequer*, I, 376.
[8] *R.A.* II, 169.

bury their dead in the cemetery of St Bartholomew (1295).[1] There followed negotiations for the acquisition of the advowson,[2] and on 3 May 1295 the abbot and convent formally granted the church and the adjoining glebe to the dean and chapter. William then resigned the rectory.[3] In 1297 Bishop Sutton assigned the church, already in the patronage of the dean and chapter, on the death or cession of the then rector, to the canons of Lincoln as a burial place, their own burial ground being unsuitable on account of the nearness of the public street and the trampling of the place, and it might be unhealthy for the canons and other inhabitants; for a long time, he declared, the church of St Bartholomew had had no parishioner and was for the most part extremely ruinous. The fruits of the church were to augment the maintenance of the choir boys, reserving sufficient for the fabric of the church.[4] The site of the church is now in the grounds of the Lawn Hospital. According to Venables the steeple of the church fell in 1468, and out of the fragments the chapter built a little chapel of ease. St Barth's chapel is mentioned in the common council minutes in 1562.[5]

In a list of prebends contained in the Black Book of the Minster, of date *c.* 1305, are three which take their names from city churches not hitherto mentioned: St Botolph, Holy Cross, and St Mary Crackpole.[6] As those churches which had not passed into the hands of religious houses had either been secured early by the bishop and allotted to prebends, or obtained under the general grant of Henry I and allotted in the 'residue' to the precentor, it seems highly probable that these prebendal churches were in being in the eleventh century or at the latest in the first half of the twelfth: the dedication of St Botolph also points to early foundation. Remigius' constitution of the cathedral church provided for twenty-one canons, Bishop Robert I doubled the number, Bishop Alexander added a few more, and by the time of St Hugh the number had reached fifty-four.[7] There is a probability, therefore, that churches giving their names to prebends can be dated to the earliest two or three episcopates.

The long tale of parish churches is not yet complete. Charters tell of St Cuthbert in the corn market, on the Steep Hill facing the Jews Court.[8] St Andrew under the palace, so far mentioned only as being united to St Mary le Wigford, was in Danesgate: it is found in the late twelfth century.[9] Bardney Abbey had land in the parish of St John the Poor, under the castle[10] and in St Clement in Butwerk, where Barlings Abbey also had

[1] *R.A.* II, 170.
[2] Ibid. p. 171.
[3] Ibid. pp. 165, 167, 169.
[4] Ibid. p. 167.
[5] C.C.M. 1541–64, f. 175b.
[6] *L.C.S.* I, 301–5.
[7] Supra, p. 77.
[8] E.g. D. & C., Dii, 74/3/14.
[9] D. & C., Dii, 74/3/25.
[10] Bardney Cartulary, f. 245; *R.A.* II, 117.

land.[1] In Wigford St Edward is mentioned in the cartulary of Thurgarton Priory.[2]

The late Precentor Venables collected a great deal of information about the parish churches of Lincoln,[3] and before him John Ross had printed a list compiled by Thomas Sympson.[4] This list gave a total of fifty-two, a total to which Sympson was committed by Leland.[5] Venables reduces this number to forty-nine by pointing out that two of Ross' numbers are identical, that St Thomas of Canterbury (which must be mentioned later) was not a parish church but a bridge chapel, and that St Giles (also to be mentioned later) was the chapel of a hospital apparently without parochial rights.[6] From this reduced total must be deducted St Denis, which disappears altogether on a close scrutiny. It was supposed to have stood in Thorngate, but there is no evidence of either church or parish, and there can be little doubt that the altar of St Denis in the Minster was mistakenly identified as a parish church.[7] St Gregory and All Hallows in the fish market must also rest under suspicion, as evidence of their existence is not forthcoming: the former may have been a misreading of St George, which stood to the north of the supposed site of St Gregory.

It is not easy in all cases to say with certainty whether a church was strictly a parish church, but it would appear that the total number was forty-six. Out of this number it may be said with confidence that forty-three of them were in being by the middle years of the twelfth century. There can be no such confidence as to the number at any earlier date, though the guess may be hazarded that not fewer than thirty-five of them were founded by 1100.

It is obvious that the parishes must for the most part have been small and the churches poor. There were fifteen in the walled city (outside the Bail) alone, and some of these intra-mural parishes cannot have comprised more than a cluster of houses. In Wigford the ribbon of houses straggled southwards from the High Bridge for about a mile to Bargate, growing sparse beyond Gowts Bridge: on the east side of the road were five churches, on the west, seven. The Taxation of Pope Nicholas, made in 1291, gives small values for the churches named.[8] When the Act of Union

[1] Bardney Cartulary, f. 253; Barlings Cartulary, f. 59d.

[2] f. 155d.

[3] *A.A.S.R.* XIX (1888), p. 326.

[4] *Civitas Lincolnia* (1870), p. 97.

[5] *Itinerary* (ed. Toulmin Smith), I, 30.

[6] It is true that a papal relaxation of 1453 refers to the parish church of St Giles (infra, p. 286), but there is no evidence of any parochial rights.

[7] Ross, p. 97. Canon Foster was much impressed by Ross' work, and was inclined to accept St Denis on his authority. *R.A.* I, 281.

[8] *Taxatio Ecclesiastica P. Nicholai* (R.C.), p. 76. St Peter *ad placita* is valued at £3. 6*s*. 8*d*., St Peter *ad fontem* at £2. 13*s*. 4*d*., St Paul at £3. 6*s*. 8*d*., All Saints in the Bail at £2, St Peter in Wigford at £2. 6*s*. 8*d*., and St Bartholomew at £1. 6*s*. 8*d*. The prebendal churches are valued with the prebends; the prebend of Thorngate was worth only £2. 10*s*., whilst that

of parishes was passed in 1549 it declared that divers of the benefices were not above the clear yearly value of 30*s.* and it authorised the union of livings so that each new living should not exceed £14 in value. The parishes of St Botolph, St Margaret and Holy Cross, with the Malandry and St Katharine, combined with lands and tithes, were brought up to £8. 13*s.* 4*d.*; and after deducting 20*s.* for the prebendary of St Botolph, and 3*s.* 4*d.* for the precentor there was a clear £7. 10*s.* for the curate. A similar total was aimed at in the other parishes: St Peter at Arches and St Peter at Pleas, totalling £6, had income from land added to bring them up to £8. 5*s.* 4*d.*, and after several deductions there remained £7. 5*s.* 4*d.* St Swithin, which had already embraced several of the Butwerk parishes with lands and tithes, could only muster £6 with certainty.[1]

A perusal of the parish terriers, which survive from the seventeenth century, indicates that the principal item of these revenues is the tithe of houses, lands and orchards of the parishioners, the amount of which was fixed by ancient custom and did not vary: it is variously described as house tithe, or yearly due by house-row. Sometimes the parish enjoyed property, and in some instances houses and shops had been built in the churchyard, the tenants paying rent therefor. The average area of the remaining churchyard seems to have been half an acre.[2]

In 1549 the parishes were reduced to nine in number, not including those in the Bail and Close and the uphill suburbs. The common council exercised the right to dispose of the fabrics of the disused churches, apparently invoking the doctrine of escheat. Many of the churches that survived were not impressive; Defoe, who saw them after the depredations of time and the Civil War, described them as 'the meanest to look on that are anywhere to be seen'.[3] This severe judgement may mitigate the disappointment caused by the small number of survivors of the medieval churches. Of these three, St Benedict is but a fragment, and St Peter at Gowts has been mutilated by repeated 'restorations'. Only St Mary le Wigford remains in substantially its medieval form.

of North Kelsey, comprising the church of North Kelsey with the churches of St Cuthbert and St Benedict, Lincoln, was worth £44. The church of St Botolph was apparently the sole endowment of its prebend, and worth £3. 6*s.* 8*d.*, and similarly St Martin, £6. 13*s.* 4*d.* The precentor, who enjoyed the income from many of the city churches, was assessed at £13. 6*s.* 8*d.*, so that his endowment was not excessive, when compared with the treasurer's £20, or the subdean's £40. The chancellor had a mere £4. *Taxatio Ecclesiastica P. Nicholai* (R.C.), p. 56.

[1] C.C.M. 1541–64, ff. 98, 104. Venables printed the award of the commissioners in *A.A.S.R.* XIX (1888), p. 350, from an eighteenth-century copy which is inaccurate in some details.

[2] See terriers of city churches in Lincoln Diocesan Record Office.

[3] *Tour* (Everyman Edition), II, 91.

Apart from the parish churches there were several other religious foundations in the city. The chapel of St Thomas of Canterbury upon the High Bridge can be dated within fairly narrow limits. Thomas Becket was murdered in 1170 and canonised in 1173. In 1200 King John granted to Peter de Paris the advowson of the chapel.[1] The church of St Giles occurs in the papal bull of 1163;[2] between 1275 and 1280 Oliver Sutton, then dean of Lincoln, assigned the house and its revenues to the vicars choral of the cathedral. To the condition that they should sing masses for benefactors of the house was added the proviso that weak and infirm vicars might live there.[3] The house stood on the Wragby Road, where a fragment of the ruins still stood until a few years ago.

There were several other hospitals in the city, including St Leonard and St Bartholomew without the castle, and that of St Mary Magdalene, which are only known by casual references, and play no part in the history of the city.[4]

With the Gilbertine priory of St Katharine, the Malandry and the cell of the Black Monks it will be more convenient to deal in another chapter.[5] The friars followed them in the thirteenth century. The Franciscans were apparently the first to arrive in the city. Before 7 February 1231 William de Beningworth, subdean of Lincoln, had given them land, for on that date the citizens of Lincoln, with the consent of the king, allotted adjoining land near their gildhall for the use of the friars.[6] In 1237, at the request of Henry III, the citizens gave the site of the gildhall itself to the friars.[7] The quarters they thus procured were in the south-east corner of the lower city, and their boundaries then or later were Silver Street to the north, Free School Lane to the west and the city wall down the west side of Broadgate and along the south side of the modern St Swithin's church on the east and south. In 1258 they were licensed to block a postern in the wall and to enclose a lane.[8] A royal gift of ten oaks from Sherwood Forest in 1268 for the fabric of their church[9] shows that building operations were in hand, and like gifts in 1280 and 1284[10] that work was still proceeding.

The surviving building of the Grey Friars is of two storeys, the lower having a vaulted undercroft. Mr A. R. Martin points out that the sills of

[1] *Cartae Antiquae* (P.R.S.), no. 144. For the Paris family, see Appendix v.

[2] *R.A.* I, 207.

[3] Maddison, *Vicars Choral of Lincoln Cathedral* (1878), p. 12. For the confirmation charter of the house, see *C. Chart. R.* III, 363.

[4] *V.C.H. Lincs*, II, 233–4. The leper hospital near St Bartholomew's church is mentioned in D. & C., Dii, 74/2/48.

[5] Infra, Chapter XVI.

[6] *C.P.R.* 1225–32, pp. 422–3.

[7] *C.C.R.* 1234–7, pp. 495, 500.

[8] *C.P.R.* 1247–58, p. 652.

[9] Close Roll, 52 Henry III, m. 3, quoted by A. R. Martin, 'The Greyfriars of Lincoln' in *Arch. Journ.* XCII (1935), p. 44.

[10] *C.C.R.* 1279–88, pp. 35, 251.

the original lancet windows on the north side, and of the triple lancets in the east wall, are some 4 ft. below the level of the upper floor, and can be partially seen in the undercroft below; and he infers that the building was originally of one storey only, and that the vaulting is a later insertion. When it was inserted the ground-level inside was lowered. The building has been much altered from time to time.[1] After the suppression of the house in 1539 it was occupied by the grammar school (or part of it) from 1568 to 1900; and it now serves as the City and County Museum.

The Black Friars settled on the hillside to the east of the city. In 1238 Henry III gave them thirty trees for their building works.[2] In 1260 they obtained leave to make a conduit of water along the high road from Greetwell to Lincoln, and carry it along the road to their house and to repair it when necessary.[3]

Towards the end of the century they were building again; in 1284 Edward I gave them twelve oaks to make shingles,[4] and in 1290 another four for the work of their church.[5] In 1284–5 they obtained licence to enclose a piece of land; in 1291–2 a lane in the parish of Holy Trinity under the hill.[6] The church and churchyard, with the altars in the chapel of the Virgin Mary, were consecrated in 1311.[7] When the house was surrendered, its lands had grown to ten acres.[8]

The construction of the present Lindum Road has made it difficult to recover the old boundaries. The Greestone Stairs used to continue southwards in a lane called Holgate to Monks Road. This lane seems to have been the western boundary of the friars: in modern times their land has been divided into four closes, which now contain the City School, the Technical College, and the cattle market. During the building of the college in 1931 the foundations of an apsidal building were discovered which may have been part of the friary chapel.[9]

The Lincoln House of the Carmelite Friars was founded by 1269,[10] and in 1280 Edward I authorised them to receive lands adjoining their house for the enlargement of their area.[11] Their buildings, which have vanished,

[1] 'The Greyfriars of Lincoln', in *Arch. Journ.* XCII (1935), pp. 50–3.

[2] *Close Rolls*, 1237–42, p. 61.

[3] *C.P.R.* 1258–66, p. 67.

[4] *C.C.R.* 1279–88, p. 253.

[5] *C.C.R.* 1288–96, p. 78.

[6] *Inq. A.Q.D.* (P.R.O. Lists and Indexes), pp. 13, 770.

[7] Linc. Episc. Reg. Memo. Dalderby, f. 191 b.

[8] *V.C.H. Lincs*, II, 222.

[9] When the Sessions House was built, gravestones and capitals were found. Ross (Scrap Books, Lincoln I) thought the friars were here: but it may be the site of St Clement.

[10] *C.P.R.* 1266–72, p. 400.

[11] *C.C.R.* 1279–88, p. 35. About 1490 their buildings were struck by lightning, and the tower, dormitory and great part of the books burnt. *York Fabric Rolls* (Surtees Society), p. 241.

stood on the site of the London, Midland and Scottish Railway station; a close to the west of it continued to be known as Friarholme until a century ago. The Austin Friars settled in Newport about the same time; they were receiving oaks in 1280.[1] The Friars of the Sack (the Penance of Jesus Christ) settled in Thorngate on a site south of St Hugh Croft and west of Stamp Causeway before 1266: in that year they procured from the commonalty of the city a vacant place, part of the common pasture,[2] and the king confirmed it to them for the enlargement of their oratory.[3] They had ceased to occupy the house in 1307, when the abbot of Barlings tried to acquire the site. The jury to whom the question was referred declared that it would be to the serious injury of the city if the abbot and canons obtained the site, for they intended to pull down the church and set up warehouses in which to store their tanned hides, wool, corn and other products until they could sell them at a profit like common merchants.[4] The abbot did not obtain the site, though a meeting of the abbots of the Premonstratensian Order in England was held in the church in 1310.[5] In 1313 inquiry was made whether the site should be granted to Philip of Kyme, and the jurors returned a favourable answer;[6] and in 1358 Joan, the wife first of William of Kyme and then of Nicholas de Cantilupe, had leave to found a chantry of five chaplains in honour of St Peter in the suburb of Lincoln, in the place where the Friars of the Sack formerly dwelt, to celebrate divine service in the chapel there for the souls of Nicholas and Joan, and to assign to them in mortmain the said place and a house and two perches of land, held of the king in free burgage, for their habitation.[7]

This is only one of a very large number of licences for the alienation of land in mortmain. The Statute of Mortmain, which was enacted in 1279, provided that if any person either sold or gave land to any religious body, the land should be forfeited. The pious founder could, however, obtain a royal dispensation from the operation of the statute; with the result that it did not prevent, or perhaps even lessen, acquisitions of land by the church, but it secured to the crown some control over the grants and an opportunity of obtaining some profit from them.[8] The issue of licences has the advantage to the historian that it has preserved records of a vast number of pious benefactions of which without such records little would be known. The

[1] *C.C.R.* 1279–88, p. 35.
[2] *Inq. A.Q.D.* (P.R.O. Lists and Indexes), p. 99.
[3] *C.P.R.* 1258–66, p. 608.
[4] *Inq. A.Q.D.* (P.R.O. Lists and Indexes), p. 99.
[5] Ed. Gasquet, *Collectanea Anglo-Premonstratensia*, I, 7, 14.
[6] *Inq. A.Q.D.* (P.R.O. Lists and Indexes), p. 135.
[7] *C.P.R.* 1358–61, p. 92. For the charter, see *Lincs N. & Q.* II, 74. A house called the Sekfreres was devised by the will of John of Blyton, 1323, B.B. f. 93.
[8] K. Wood-Legh, *Church Life under Edward III* (1934), p. 69.

beginnings of the chantry of Nicholas and Joan de Cantilupe have already been mentioned;[1] in 1374 the dean and chapter as patrons of the chantry of five chaplains had licence to transfer it to the altar of St Nicholas in the cathedral church;[2] beside it may be set the Burghersh Chantry, whose founders directed among other things that six poor boys professing the art of grammar should be maintained at school, between the ages of seven and sixteen.[3]

Only a few of such foundations by wealthy citizens can be mentioned. Robert Dalderby founded a chantry in the church of St Benedict, entering into an arrangement with the prior and convent of Thurgarton that in exchange for a lump sum payment of 300 pounds of silver, the convent would pay to two chaplains celebrating at St Benedict a yearly rent of 10 pounds of silver. Alexander son of John son of Martin founded a chantry in St Lawrence's church, endowing it with lands and rents in Lincoln, vesting the patronage in the commonalty of the city of Lincoln. Another was founded by John of Blyton in St Margaret in Wigford. These three founders were leading citizens in the fourteenth century:[4] the process had begun earlier, for in the thirteenth century Roger son of Benedict had founded a chantry in St Peter in Eastgate.[5] Gifts to the cathedral continued, as also did gifts to religious houses outside the city. The list of inquisitions taken between 1280 and 1350 suggests that Barlings Abbey was among the most popular, but twelve other houses, mostly in Lincolnshire, appear among those receiving lands in the city.

It is clear that by the end of the Middle Ages a considerable proportion of the soil of the city was vested in religious corporations. The Taxation of Pope Nicholas, made in 1291, mentions 55 religious houses holding land in the deanery of Lincoln. Apart of course from the Minster, the highest in assessment is Bardney with a total of over £12; the Black Monks of Lincoln follow with £10, and their parent house of St Mary of York with £8. Kirkstead, Revesby, Kyme, Barlings, Worksop, Stainfield, are all over £4. St Katharine's, surprisingly, is only assessed at £2. 8*s*. 8*d*.[6]

[1] Supra, p. 151.
[2] *C.P.R.* 1370–4, p. 444.
[3] See 'Chantry Certificates of Lincoln and Lincolnshire' ed. Foster and Thompson in *A.A.S.R.* XXXVI (1922), p. 207.
[4] Ibid. pp. 199, 201, 204.
[5] *Inq. A.Q.D.* (P.R.O. Lists and Indexes), pp. 12, 16, 32.
[6] *Taxatio Ecclesiastica P. Nicholai* (R.C.), pp. 67–74.

CHAPTER VIII

THE MEDIEVAL CITY

When the upper Roman enclosure became the Bail, the lower Roman enclosure became the medieval city proper. It covered a modest 56 acres, all of it upon the hillside. The altitude at the centre of the Bail is about 220 ft. above sea-level; at the south Bail gate it has dropped to about 190 ft.; at the Dernstall, or lower end of the Strait, to 65 ft.; and at the Stonebow to 25 ft. This drop of 165 ft. from the south Bail gate is accomplished in a distance of about 670 yards, an average gradient of 1 in 12; the gradient in its steepest part is 1 in 4.

Domesday Book clearly recognises the distinction between the city itself and the settlements 'without the city' which became its suburbs and liberties. The bishop's little manor is *near* the city; the fields are *outside* the city; Colswein had his tofts *in* the city, and his house and churches *outside* the city.[1] There is no reason to suppose that the distinction had any legal significance, for the citizens dwelling without the walls took their customs and privileges with them. The distinction is merely geographical; the city is the walled area.

The city is bisected by the Ermine Street, which runs northwards from the Stonebow. To-day it bears the dull modern names of the Steep Hill, the Strait, and High Street; and it is to be deplored that unlike York, Lincoln has abandoned many of its interesting medieval street names. Just below the site of the south Bail gate is an open space between the Bishop's Hostel and Christ's Hospital Terrace: it is all that remains of the old fish market, or high market.[2] The stalls of the fishmongers had of course to be kept within the city, so that the rents and other dues could be collected by the bailiffs in aid of the farm of the city, but it may be supposed that the fishmongers sought to be as near as possible to their ecclesiastical patrons dwelling round the Minster. Lower down the hill, at the junction of the Steep Hill and the Strait, the roadway widens again. Here was the corn market, and the church of St Cuthbert *ad forum bladi*[3] stood on the east side

[1] *L.D.* pp. 4–7. Infra, Appendix II.

[2] D. & C., Dii, 76/2/4. Hereabouts, to the west, stood the church of St John (the Poor) in the Fishmarket.

[3] D. & C., Dii, 74/3/14. No evidence has been found to support the theory that this was the Bullring. The present Danes Terrace is called Bullring Lane by Gough in his edition of Camden's *Britannia* (1806), II, 373, following Thomas Sympson who said he saw the stone in the middle of the street. Adversaria, p. 309. Newspaper references to bull-baiting do not mention the Bullring.

of it. In 1572 the common council ordered that the stones of the cross in the late parish of St Cuthbert, then lately taken down, should be gathered up.[1] This was probably the corn-market cross. Between the fish market and the corn market (that is, on the present Steep Hill) was the poultry market, *pultria* or *le pultri* in the fourteenth,[2] *Polther hill* or *the Pultry* in the sixteenth and seventeenth centuries.[3] Below the corn market was Mikelgate, extending nearly to the Stonebow but narrowing just north of it into Briggate, which led through the arch to the great bridge. In later times the butcher market occupied the part of Mikelgate from the Dernstall to the end of Clasketgate (the old St Lawrence Lane), but whether it did so in the thirteenth century is uncertain: in 1201 there is a complaint that the burgesses have removed the shambles (*bucheria*) to a less central place, which the burgesses deny.[4]

To the west of Poultry another road led downhill from the high market, and an open space at the junction of this road (the modern Michaelgate) and Spring Hill can be identified as the skin market. St Peter *attechinmarkethe*[5] (*ad forum pellium*) or St Peter Stanthaket stood in the angle formed by these two roads. Michaelgate itself was Parchemingate, the street of the parchment-makers.[6] Skinnergate was evidently somewhere near, in the parish of St Martin.[7] Between Poultry and Parchemingate was and still is the Drapery; here was the cloth market, the *forum draperie* or *Parmentaria*.[8] The Hundred Rolls (1275) record that John de Keleby had a house in the market where they used to sell cloth in the parish of St Michael on the Mount 30 years before.[9] Several of these market places were identified by Thomas Sympson, who records (*c.* 1738) that a street with a few poor cottages running from the top of the hill westwards was called the old fish market, and he adds that the removal of this and other markets into the great street below the hill had contributed not a little to the decay of the places where they were anciently kept.[10] At one time the markets had been held in the churchyards; in 1223 it was ordered that they be held in the streets, at places which were most convenient.[11]

Mikelgate seems to have been the principal shopping area. Some of the Jews lived there. Ivo the goldsmith and Andrew and Thomas the goldsmiths are mentioned in deeds of the later twelfth and early thirteenth

[1] *H.M.C. Lincoln*, p. 66.
[2] B.B. ff. 171, 198.
[3] White Book, f. 196b. Corporation leases, 1769, 1799.
[4] *C.R. Rolls*, II, 20.
[5] D. & C., Dii, 80/3/38.
[6] *C.R. Rolls*, VI, 67; Welbeck Cartulary, f. 106; *C.A.D.* I, 164.
[7] B.B. f. 198.
[8] *C. Chart. R.* I, 467; *R.H.* I, 322b; *Book of Fees*, I, 365.
[9] *R.H.* I, 311a.
[10] Adversaria, pp. 311–12.
[11] *Rot. Lit. Claus.* I, 547.

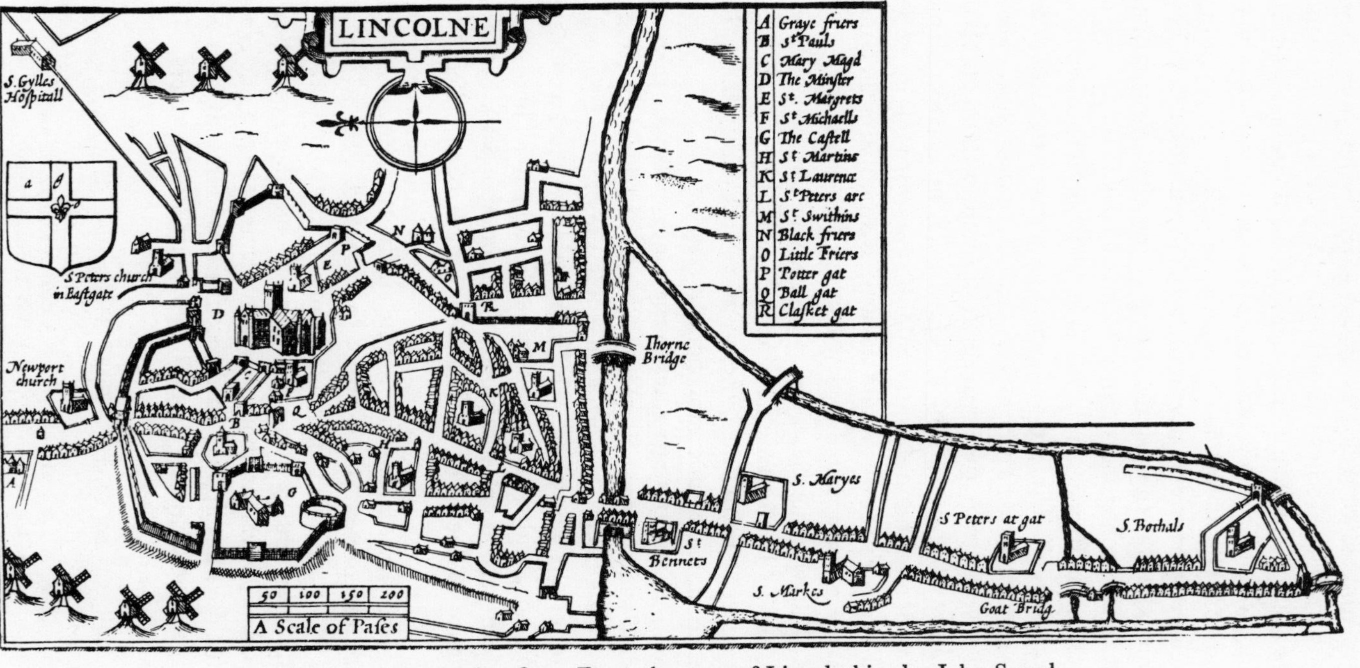

Fig. 15. Lincoln in 1610. From the map of Lincolnshire by John Speed.

centuries relating to St Peter at Pleas' parish,[1] and John the sealsmith occurs in St Peter at Arches.[2] Several of the principal merchant families had houses there.[3] The district just north of the Stonebow had the advantage of being within the walls and yet near to the river, facts which account for the presence of the mootstone by St Peter of Lincoln:[4] the gildhall was in the south-east corner of the city until it was given up to the Grey Friars.[5]

The Stonebow was the principal gate of the city. Excavations suggest that the Roman arch stood slightly to the north of the present arch, but whether it was the Roman arch or a successor that was taken down before 1390 is not known.[6] The other main gateway was the Claxledegate, or Clasketgate, which stood at the eastern end of the street now called by that name, and gave access to the predecessor of Lindum Road, to Monks Lane, and the suburb of Butwerk. Buck's drawing of the gateway depicts a low gatehouse with a round arch in the middle, and slits high up on each side. At the end of the gatehouse, inside the wall, is an apparently pointed arch. The gatehouse is surmounted by battlements (see Plate 13).

It is not clear whether there was a gateway in the west wall of the city, corresponding to Clasketgate. There was probably a lane through the fields leading to St Faith, but if there was a street within the walls leading in that direction, it was not an important one.

There were several postern gates in the south wall, and there may have been others of which there is no record. The Grey Friars blocked a postern.[7] There must have been a postern connecting the present Free School Lane with the important Thorngate, which, though now short and insignificant, then led to Thornbridge and the suburb of Thorngate. There was probably also a postern gate at the south end of the present Bank Street: the lane leading thence to the river bank seems to have been called Watergangstigh.[8]

To the west of the Stonebow a gate in the south wall probably gave access from the present Park Street to Newland: this is the district of Krakepol, which gave its name to the church of St Mary Crackpole. Mint Street at its lower end is a modern creation, but there may have been a gateway in the city wall at about this point, facing the present Water Lane: such a name does not appear until recent times, and may be a corruption of Walkergate or Walker's Lane,[9] the home of the dyers, which was certainly hereabouts.

[1] D. & C., Dii, 80/3/20, 29, 32
[2] Thurgarton Cartulary, f. 156, no. 1042.
[3] See Appendix v.
[4] Supra, p. 61.
[5] Supra, p. 149.
[6] *C.C.R.* 1389–92, p. 135.
[7] *R.H.* I, 311a, 319a.
[8] B.B. f. 108b (1328).
[9] D. & C., Dii, 75/1/17; 80/3/17: Walker's Lane, leading down to Brayford Head, 1693. C.C.M. 1655–1710, p. 486.

The space between the south wall and the river must have been occupied early. The lane running west from Briggate (High Street), and known as St Mary Stigh (now Much Lane), may well have existed at the Conquest.[1] Farther west, the New Land (*nova terra*), occupied perhaps as the water receded, is mentioned in the middle years of the twelfth century, and soon afterwards it was becoming a surname.[2] Between St Mary Stigh and the wall was Baxtergate, the street of the bakers, apparently where Guildhall Street now is: Robert the miller is mentioned (*c.* 1250) in St Mary Stigh near by, with an oven there.[3] Ralf, son of Lefwine, and Ivetta, the widow of Richard the villein, were involved in a dispute with the canons of Thurgarton Priory about an oven in Saper Lane.[4] This lane seems to have been part of the modern Saltergate, to the east of the Stonebow.[5] Saltergate, another part of the modern street of that name, is described as being in St Swithin's parish.[6] This river-side strip, besides being the home of the soapmakers and the salters, also held the malt market.[7]

Edward III's charter to Lincoln of 1327 mentions that the citizens' ancestors had built houses on a wall of the city which ran from Newland gate as far as the house of the Friars Minor, in various places near Walkergate and Soper Lane, but the houses being for the improvement and security of the city, they were allowed to remain.[8] Newland gate appears also in the Hundred Rolls (1275): encroachments from the gate of Newland to St Swithin's church are reported.[9] By this date therefore the west wall of the city had been extended southwards beyond the south wall to Brayford Pool. The gate stood in the modern Newland at a point between the Park and Lucy Tower Street, down the east side of which street the new wall continued, ending in a round tower on Brayford bank. The gateway was still standing in 1773; Buck's sketch of it depicts a pointed archway surmounted by a steep gable (see Plate 13). To the round tower at the water's edge became attached the name of Lucy Tower.[10]

At the eastern end of the riverside strip was a corresponding wall, though here, it would seem, the gate did not stand, as might have been expected, at the junction of the modern St Swithin's Square with the modern Broadgate. It stood on the river bank. In 1383 the mayor and citizens granted to John Norman a lease of their common tower with a like plot east of it,

[1] Supra, pp. 132–3.

[2] *D.C.* p. 343 (1163–6); Mrs D. M. Stenton, *Earliest Lincolnshire Assize Rolls* (L.R.S.), pp. 167 (1202), 261. Constancius de Neweland is mentioned.

[3] D. & C., Dii, 80/3/13, 15, 23, 41.

[4] Thurgarton Cartulary, f. 158b, no. 1066.

[5] B.B. ff. 108b, 190.

[6] D. & C., Dii, 76/1/32 (*c.* 1260); B.B. f. 176b.

[7] B.B. ff. 165, 206b.

[8] Birch, pp. 55, 57.

[9] *R.H.* I, 318b.

[10] As to this, see p. 86.

lying in Butwerk in the parish of St Bavon, 72 ells long from the city gate by the river bank northwards by the city wall, and 8½ ells wide, with power to build and enclose without interference by the city, unless *ryderwak* intervened, as in time of war or siege of the city.[1] Here the citizens were leasing a tower, corresponding in some way to the so-called Lucy Tower, and part of the city ditch, reserving the right of re-entry whenever the city's safety required. The tower was still standing in 1728, when the Corporation granted a lease of it with the Tower Garth. It stood in the yard of the Green Dragon hotel, and must therefore have been very close to the gateway on the river bank.

The street called Thorngate led to the river at a point immediately within this wall. Here stood the Thornbridge, slightly to the west of the modern bridge, which is in line with the city ditch, now become Broadgate. The bridge is described as *pons de Thorn'* in a charter of *c.* 1240.[2] A road following the north bank of the river eastwards from the bridge seems to have been called Thornbridgegate;[3] the Barlings Cartulary mentions a house in Thorngate in the parish of St Augustine.[4] South of the river and east of Thornbridge was another area forming part of the district of Thorngate: it occupied the loop between the Witham and Sincil Dyke, extending eastwards to their former junction at Stamp End.[5] There was a road along the south bank of the river, and many charters show that individual holdings of land extended from this road southwards to Sincil Dyke: they are described as reaching from water to water, or sometimes from the king's highway on the north to the water on the south.[6] In the thirteenth century leading merchants had property there. Robert son of Peter de Ponte[7] had a hall there, and the abbot and convent of Bardney made him a grant of land to the east of it, adjoining land held of the abbey by William son of John son of Gamel the archer.[8] James Brand had land in St Swithin's parish which can be identified as being in this area.[9]

The local historian John Ross thought that Thorngate extended west of Thornbridge south of the river as well as to the north of it, but no evidence has been found to support this view. His attempt to identify the several parishes in the area was influenced by his belief in the existence of a church

[1] *C.P.R.* 1381–5, p. 302.

[2] D. & C., D ii, 76/1/26. And see *R.A.* I, App. II.

[3] *Inq. A.Q.D.* (P.R.O. Lists and Indexes), p. 135.

[4] f. 64.

[5] It was only after 1812 that the Sincil Dyke was carried down to Bardney as part of a drainage scheme.

[6] Bardney Cartulary, ff. 257b, 259, 259b.

[7] See p. 395.

[8] Bardney Cartulary, f. 259b.

[9] D. & C., Dii, 76/1/24.

and parish of St Denis:[1] apparently he placed them in this district because he thought that their endowments were appropriated to the prebend of Thorngate. But there is no evidence that such a church existed, and the endowments of the prebend of Thorngate near the High Bridge do not help at all.[2]

When the area south-east of Thornbridge was first settled it is impossible to say. It is low-lying, and was until recent times very liable to flood; commercial convenience was, however, some compensation and it is clear that it was occupied in the early years of the thirteenth century. Whether there was any building south-west of Thornbridge until modern times may be doubted.

The *castellum de Torngat* which Alice de Condet pledged, along with land in several counties, to King Stephen, who granted the pledge to Bishop Alexander (probably in 1141), was identified by Canon Foster as standing in Thorngate.[3] This may well be so, though no other express reference has been found to it.

When the Hundred Roll jurors were asked in 1275 about military fees in Lincoln given or sold to religious persons or bodies, they replied that Philip de Kyme had a manor house in the parish of St Swithin.[4] This can be located approximately by a charter (*c.* 1240), by which Ivo son of Fulk gave to the church of St Oswald of Bardney a house on the Witham between land belonging to Robert son of Giles and land belonging to Margery the widow of Richard son of James,[5] and abutting towards the north on land of the lord Philip de Kyme.[6] Clearly this is north of the river, and being in St Swithin's parish is west of Thornbridge, in the strip, that is to say, between the present Saltergate and St Swithin's Square on the north and the Waterside North on the south, where in recent years the foundations of many substantial stone buildings have been uncovered.

When a later Philip de Kyme died in 1322 he was found to be possessed of a messuage in Lincoln worth £4 a year, with the manors of Kyme, Sotby, Croft, Goltho, Muckton, Immingham and others.[7] Sir Walter

[1] Supra, p. 147. [2] *R.A.* I, 277–80. [3] Ibid. pp. 61, 282.

[4] *R.H.* I, 312b. There is an inquisition *ad quod damnum*, 6 Edward II, for Philip de Kyme to have a grant of a messuage in Thornbridge gate, formerly inhabited by the brethren of the Penance of Jesus Christ (the Sack Friars). It was 540 ft. by 420 ft. *Inq. A.Q.D.* (P.R.O. Lists and Indexes), p. 135. This, however, stood east of Thornbridge on the north of the river. In 1360 Lady Joan Cantilupe gave a certain place where the friars of the Sack formerly dwelt, with a house and land, as endowment for the Cantilupe chantry in the cathedral. *C.P.R.* 1358–61, p. 92; *Lincs N. & Q.* II, 74, 75 (Charter at Gunby Hall). See supra, p. 151.

[5] See Appendix v.

[6] Bardney Cartulary, f. 260. [7] *Cal. Inq. p.m.* (R.C.), I, 305.

Tailboys succeeded to the Kyme patrimony, and about 1391 he sold the family residence by Thornbridge gate, commonly called Kyme Hall.[1]

Kyme Hall may well have been the castle of Thorngate mentioned above. As has been noted, the Hundred Rolls mention the Kyme house under the heading of military fees in the hands of the religious; and the Kymes may have obtained the house from the bishop of Lincoln and held it of him. They were a great family, who besides being tenants in chief of the king, were mesne tenants of a number of other tenants in chief: in 1166 a Philip de Kyme held two knights' fees of the bishop of Lincoln, one and a half of William de Roumare of the honour of Bolingbroke, one fee (jointly with another knight) of Walter de Ainecurt, three fees of the old feoffment with one fee of increase, and half a fee of the new feoffment of Earl Simon, two fees (jointly with another knight) of Richard de la Haye, and three of the bishop of Durham, in addition to what he held of the king in chief and of the honours of Peverel and Chester.[2] If Kyme Hall is not the *castellum*, then it is not likely ever to be identified.

At Thornbridge, probably just within the extended city wall and the gate on the river bank, was the 'Staple place where the staple of wools, hides, woolfells and lead is held'.[3] This was a centre of commercial activity, and as has been noticed, leading merchant families had their houses along the northern river bank.

There is no evidence of any churches having been built in the river strip from Newland gate to Thornbridge, or in the suburb of Thorngate south of the river. The area was appropriated to churches within the walls: to St Mary Crackpole, St Peter at Arches, St Edmund and St Swithin, which last parish embraced Thorngate south of the river. It would seem that when this area developed the time for building parish churches had gone by. Those in existence had probably established their boundaries and rights to revenue, and there was no room and certainly no need for any more.

In the eastern suburb of Butwerk the position was quite different. It occupied the area bounded on the west by the Werkdyke or city ditch (now become Broadgate) and on the east by a line running roughly from the foot of the Greesen (Greestone Stairs) to Rosemary Lane and thence southwards to the Witham. The whole appearance of the area has been altered by the removal of the city wall and the Clasketgate, the levelling of the ditch, and the making, about 1785, of Lindum Road. Before that

[1] Trollope, *Sleaford and the Wapentakes of Flaxwell and Aswardhurn* (1872), p. 252. For the Kyme family, see Farrer, *Honors and Knights' Fees* (1924), II, 118–25.

[2] *Red Book of the Exchequer*, passim.

[3] *C.P.R.* 1354–8, p. 8; 'Stapleplace in the parish of St Swithin' (1437), *L.C.S.* III, 408.

ST MARGARET'S CHURCH, taken down *c.* 1780

From a painting by Moses Griffith in the Usher Art Gallery

[*See p.* 142

PLATE 12

ST PETER IN EASTGATE CHURCH, ruined in the Civil War, taken down *c.* 1780

From Buck's sketch book

THE GREYFRIARS IN 1784, showing the remains of St Swithin's Church on the left

See pp. 149–50] *From a drawing by S. H. Grimm in the British Museum*

relatively easy gradient was provided, access to the Close was much more difficult:

> the traveller descending the hill in those days, after passing Pottergate Arch turned sharply to the right hand for a few yards, as far as to the foot of a high garden wall, visible from the present road, being the ancient wall of the Close, which was an extensive circumvallation, still traceable.... Of the steepness of the original Pottergate road, traditions were current in the last generation, describing its difficulties as such that market carriers from the lower town, whose work required them to ascend the hill, spent a full half of the day in making the ascent. The descent was, of course, correspondingly difficult; and was avoided by the carriages of the gentry when possible. From this cause more first class inns were required in the upper town than is the case in our day.[1]

This account comes from the middle years of the nineteenth century, but it gives some idea of the difficulties of the medieval citizens.

There were six churches in Butwerk: four of them, Holy Trinity at the Stairs, St Rumbold, St Bavon and St Augustine, were assigned by the bishop to the precentor in 1147–8, the bishop having acquired them by the gift of Henry I (1100–7).[2] Of the others St Peter *ad fontem* is probably one of the two Domesday churches of Colswein; it was given by his son Picot to the black monks of St Mary of York.[3] St Clement is not likely to have been later in date than the others; it bore a favourite Danish dedication, and apparently it stood nearest of the six to the gate of Claxlede. Evidently it was principally from this gate, and not from the riverside, that this suburb with an Old English name was approached in early days: as late as *c.* 1233 St Rumbold, which stood nearer to the river than to the gate, was described as St Rumwold *extra clachislide*.[4]

There can be little, if any, doubt that Butwerk was a pre-Conquest suburb. To-day the wide thoroughfare of Broadgate gives a misleading impression, for this was the Werkdyke, whereas the main street running north and south in Butwerk was probably Friars Lane, so named from its proximity to the Black Friars. There is no sign here of rich merchants; rather it was a poor suburb of small people. There was land in St Rumbold's parish which once belonged to Matilda Drincalhut, whose name suggests a street cry and its appropriate trade. Here too were Henry the illuminator and Ralf the tailor.[5] Peter son of John the fisherman had land in Butwerk.[6]

The evidence of place-names and churches for an early occupation of Wigford has already been discussed,[7] and the rights of common enjoyed by the men of Wigford over the southern waste suggest that they were in

[1] Papers of William Brooke, from scrap-book of the late Precentor Venables.
[2] *R.A.* I, 262, 263.
[3] Supra, pp. 133–4.
[4] D. & C., Dii, 74/2/17.
[5] D. & C., Dii, 74/2/3; 74/1/21.
[6] D. & C., Dii, 76/1/53.
[7] Supra, pp. 35–6.

possession before the foundation of religious houses there.[1] At the end of the twelfth century the king's bar (*barra regis*) appears in a grant of land near it to Bullington Priory, and it is known that the priory had land in Holy Trinity parish in Wigford.[2] The king's bar is, no doubt, Bargate. Buck's sketches show a Great Bargate—which stood on High Street to the north of the Bargate bridge—with a pointed arch and a gabled roof, but this must be a rebuilding and not the original gate, for the Little Bargate to the east of it (leading to Canwick) is shown by Buck to have a Norman arch flanked by round towers. These two gates, and the short piece of wall between them, are the only known defences of Wigford other than the waterways;[3] in 1228 there is an allowance to the men of Lincoln in their tallage due to the king of £20 that they had expended by his order on the walls and turrets (*turellis*) of Vicford towards St Katharine's Hospital.[4] Perhaps repairs were needed after the battle of Lincoln in 1217. The cartulary of Thurgarton Priory records a grant of land in St Botolph's parish bounded by the wall of the city, and another of a toft in Lincoln town near to the east Bargate.[5]

Apart from the churches the only medieval building that survives in Wigford is St Mary's Guildhall, still sometimes known as John of Gaunt's stables. It stands on the east side of High Street a little to the north of St Peter at Gowts church. The entrance range has been variously dated from about 1160 to 1180–90, and it

includes an elaborate gateway and string course. The doorway has mutilated heads of bishops on the stopchamfer of the jambs; there is a slightly pointed arch but the outer rings to it are round headed; these include a hood with rosette ornament, and beneath a line of dog-tooth in hollow chamfer, two rings of roll moulding cut with a hollow on the under side somewhat akin to the quirked ogee. Above are two projecting heads resting on an ornate string-course carved with scrolls, acanthus and fantastic creatures. The wall is 4 feet 7 inches in thickness, built in large blocks of ashlar oolite, nicely squared and coursed; the flat buttresses flanking the gate and north of it are original. Inside are remnants of arcading on the north wall at first floor level; the halves of two wide semi-circular arches remain supported by an extremely lovely capital of wing or acanthus design. It was hidden behind a modern wall till just recently, hence the excellent state of preservation. Near it is a smaller capital, also beautifully

[1] See Chapter XVI.

[2] *D.C.* pp. 47, 51.

[3] There is no evidence for the wall along the western bank of Sincil Dyke shown in Marrat's map. The Little Bargate is figured in a painting by De Wint now at the Usher Art Gallery, Lincoln, reproduced in Plate 22.

[4] *Cal. Liberate Rolls*, 1226–40, I, 63.

[5] Thurgarton Cartulary, nos. 1085, 1093. For the blocking of the king's road called East Bargate leading to Canwick by the mayor and bailiffs in 1375, see Flower, *Public Works in Medieval Law* (Selden Society, 1915), I, 276.

carved, and a doorway. There are traces of an internal string on the west wall and the bases of window shafts, but the upper storey has mostly gone. It was apparently a first floor hall over a basement.[1]

Another building to the south once spanned the end of the present Sibthorp Street. An eighteenth-century drawing shows that this building contained later but still medieval work.

Inside the courtyard facing south, and at right angles to the entrance range, is another building which has the appearance of a Norman house. The south wall of the upper storey has two windows, each containing two round-headed lights, and between them, outside the fireplace on the upper floor, is 'a thick buttress-like projection' continuing to the ground, indicating another fireplace on the ground floor. Professor Hamilton Thompson has remarked that 'the whole building follows the conventional lines of the early mediaeval dwelling-house, such as are indicated by the representation of Harold's manor-house at Bosham in the Bayeux tapestry', and resembles the houses at Boothby Pagnell and elsewhere.[2] Yet in spite of this resemblance the building seems not to be genuine in its present form. The north wall is admitted to be twelfth century, but the south wall is much thinner, and 'built up with Norman stones, two-shafted windows and a buttress'. It has been suggested[3] that it may have been built in the seventeenth century, a suggestion which receives some support from a resolution of the common council in 1664 that Mary Hall should be leased to Edward Fawkes, 'it being much in decay'.[4]

Various theories have been advanced as to the original use of the gildhall. Professor Hamilton Thompson thought it had been a private dwelling-house; Mr Watkins that it had been a training school for masons; Miss Wood thought this possible, and added that the proximity of John of Gaunt's palace made it possible that the building, then old and decayed, might have been used as stables as the popular name suggests. The history of 'John of Gaunt's palace' will be discussed later. Here it may be noted that there is no evidence at all to suggest the existence of a training

[1] Margaret A. Wood, 'Norman Domestic Architecture' in *Arch. Journ.* XCII (1935), p. 193.

[2] *St Mary's Guildhall, Lincoln* (1935), specially written by Professor Hamilton Thompson for a committee formed to acquire the building for the public. The purchase price was found partly by subscription and partly by the Lincoln Corporation, and the property was vested in the Corporation, which entered into a deed of covenant with the National Trust for its maintenance.

[3] By Miss Wood, op. cit. p. 191. Mr William Watkins had pointed out that the south wall was only 20 in. thick, whilst the north wall is 3 ft. 6 in. *Journal of R.I.B.A.* 3rd ser. XX (11 Jan. 1913), p. 160.

[4] C.C.M. 1655–1710, p. 142. It is a point of interest that at about the same time the tower of St Benedict's church was being rebuilt.

school for masons, and indeed it is difficult to see why the hall should not from its foundation have been the hall of St Mary's Gild, as it clearly was in the thirteenth century. The elaborate gateway seems more appropriate to such a gildhall than to a private house.

There are a few charter references to the gild and to its hall and adjoining property. In 1250 Henry III confirmed to Michael de la Burne his butler a messuage in the city of Lincoln which Warner Engayne held for his life of the king's bailey, at a yearly rent of a pound of cummin.[1] Michael then granted to the graceman and brethren of the great gild of St Mary, land and buildings in the parish of St Andrew in Wigford, which he had of the gift of Henry III: they lay between land of Adam del Howme to the north and land of Thomas de Bawfowe to the south, and stretched from the king's highway on the west to the water on the east. A rent of pepper was reserved. This charter was witnessed by Gilbert de Keal, sheriff of Lincolnshire, and a group of leading citizens, William de Paris, Adam de Howme, John de Luda, Alan de Gayton, Osbert son of Giles and Jordan his brother, William Brand and others, most of whose names appear in the list of civic officers, and who were probably members of the great gild themselves.[2] This gift adjoined land of Adam de Holm, which itself adjoined St Mary's Guildhall. In a charter which can be dated *c.* 1284 Peter de Holm, son of Adam de Holm, heir of Adam the first mayor and descendant of Adam's sister Matilda,[3] sold the house of his ancestors to Peter de Goxhill. This house is described as being in Wigford, and extending in length from the king's highway to the water called the dyke (*fossatum*) and in width from the hall of the great gild of St Mary in Wigford to the house formerly of Jordan the clerk of Lincoln.[4] It is tempting to surmise that among the ancestors of Peter and Adam de Holm who had lived in the house next to the gildhall had been Eilsi of Wigford and Reginald, grandfather and father of the first mayor, in the days when the hall was being built; also perhaps Adam himself when he reigned as alderman of the gild merchant and mayor of the city and St Hugh healed the dumb boy brought up in the great houses of Wigford.[5] Among the boy's patrons had been, besides Adam, Reimbald the rich, who had a toft in the parish of St Peter in Wigford.[6]

In 1304–5 the warden, brethren and sisters of the gild had licence to found a hospital in the suburbs of the city.[7] In 1309–10 Nicholas the

[1] Gild Certificates, no. 145c. *C. Chart. R.* I, 349.

[2] Gild Certificates, no. 145c.

[3] See Appendix v.

[4] Goxhill Leiger, no. 298. Ralph de Goxhill was found to have held a house of the heirs of Peter de Holm by service of 1*d.* in 1293–4. *Cal. Inq. p.m.* III, no. 209.

[5] See Woolley, *St Hugh of Lincoln* (1927), p. 170.

[6] *Sempringham Charters*, no. 7.

[7] *Inq. A.Q.D.* (P.R.O. Lists and Indexes), p. 80; and see *Cal. Inq. p.m.* (R.C.), I, 204, for a house in the suburb of Lincoln and 43*s.* 3*d.* paid for building a hospital there.

chandler had licence to grant land in Lincoln to Alexander son of John son of Martin, master of the great gild, and the brethren of the same.[1] In 1348 Robert Dalderby and John Outhorpe had licence to alienate four messuages, two shops and 50*s*. rent in Lincoln and the suburb to two chaplains in St Andrew's church to celebrate for the graceman, brothers and sisters of the ancient gild of St Mary, and for the soul of King Henry III, a former brother of the gild.[2] In 1363 Peter Belassise and John Blyth of Lincoln had licence to alienate a messuage in Lincoln to two chaplains as before.[3] William son of John de Blyton the elder had leave to grant rent to the gild.[4]

In the gild return made in 1389 Ralf de Scremby, master and warden of 'the old great gild in honour of God and St Mary', referred to some of the grants mentioned above.[5]

Near the gildhall, perhaps opposite, in St Andrew's parish, was the hall which Walter Brand, a mayor and a wealthy citizen, granted to Sir Philip Marmion.[6] The mention of Marmion is interesting. He served with Henry III against France in 1253, and for several years in Henry's Welsh campaigns. In the struggle with Simon de Montfort he was loyal to the king. He took part in the siege of Kenilworth Castle, and after its surrender became its constable. It was found later by inquisition that Sir Philip and his men took 280 pieces of lead belonging to a burgess of Nottingham from Boston to Lincoln, disposing of them partly to the Carmelites there (they lived near his house in Wigford) and to others, and left the rest in Sir Philip's name with the brethren of the Hospital of Lincoln.[7] His chief lordship was at Tamworth, but he also held Scrivelsby in Lincolnshire; he died in 1291, and having only daughters he was the last of the elder line of Marmions. The inquisition taken on his death sets out his Lincolnshire estates as Scrivelsby and Langton held by barony, and Winteringham, Willingham near Lincoln, Kisby, Fulstow and other holdings of land. A link with a citizen family is provided by Thomas de Faxefleete, described as the heir of Peter de Holm, who had a messuage and two carucates of land in South Langton by tenure of half a fee as a member of the manor of

[1] *Inq. A.Q.D.* (P.R.O. Lists and Indexes), p. 115. Alexander son of Martin was mayor in 1306 and 1311.

[2] *C.P.R.* 1348–50, p. 12; *Inq. A.Q.D.* (P.R.O. Lists and Indexes), p. 434.

[3] *C.P.R.* 1361–64, p. 332; *Inq. A.Q.D.* (P.R.O. Lists and Indexes), p. 536; Gild Certificates, no. 145b.

[4] *Inq. A.Q.D.* (P.R.O. Lists and Indexes), p. 536.

[5] Gild Certificates, no. 145a. Scremby was bailiff of the city in 1386–7, when Richard II granted to the mayor the right to have a sword carried before him. Infra, p. 258. For the later history of the gildhall see Hill, 'Three Lists' in *A.A.S.R.* XXXVIII (1929), p. 221.

[6] D. & C., Dii, 74/3/27–30.

[7] *Cal. Inq. Misc.* I, no. 500.

Scrivelsby.[1] In Lincoln Marmion held a messuage of the king valued at 8*s.* yearly; and another messuage held of the church of St Andrew in Wigford, of no value because it was fallen.[2] These were probably the hall bought from Walter Brand and an adjoining house bought from the same vendor for six marks: one of them paid a rent to St Andrew's church.

These houses may have occupied the same site as a later house of which much has been heard. Leland says that 'a very goodly house longging to Sutton is hard on the north syde of S. Anne's chirch yarde'.[3] There was no church of St Anne, but the gild of St Anne had a chapel in the church of St Andrew in Wigford. The Suttons were one of the greatest Lincoln families in the fourteenth and fifteenth centuries. John de Sutton, by his will dated 1391, provided for the repair of his father's tomb in Holy Trinity in Wigford, and for his mother's in St Mary's Nottingham. He left 13*s.* 4*d.* to Isabella, the recluse in St Andrew in Wigford. He himself was to be buried in the priory church of St Katharine without Lincoln.[4] Perhaps he had begun the family connection with St Andrew's parish. In 1381–2 Robert Sutton his son sought leave to grant a house and land in the parishes of St Mark and St Mary Magdalene to a chaplain in St Andrew in Wigford.[5] By his will, proved in 1414, Robert directed that he be buried in the churchyard of St Andrew. He left legacies to the great gild of St Mary, St Katharine's Priory, the provincial of the Carmelites (the White Friars), all neighbours, and 100*s.* for the repair of bridges and roads if his executors should think fit.[6] When at the Reformation the common council obtained an act of Parliament for the union of parishes it was claimed (in 1550) on behalf of the Sutton family

that the church of St Andrew in Wigford was no parish church and that the predecessors of the late Suttons in Lincoln builded the same for a church for the only commodity and ease of themselves wherefore they claimed a property in the same for the use of the said Suttons and as in the mere right of the said predecessors of the said Suttons.

The common council declared that the church and parish had ever been a parish church and a parish of itself, and ordered a search of the cathedral and city records. The next year it was ordered that the church should be taken down and sold by the mayor:[7] it had been adjudged a parish church.

[1] See Appendix v.

[2] See Palmer, *History of the Baronial Family of Marmion* (Tamworth, 1875).

[3] *Itinerary* (ed. Toulmin Smith), I, 30.

[4] Gibbons, *Early Lincoln Wills* (1888), p. 76.

[5] *Inq. A.Q.D.* (P.R.O. Lists and Indexes), p. 624. In 1389–90 Agnes widow of William de Spaigne of Boston was given leave to grant a messuage in Holy Trinity in Wigford to chaplains of Robert de Sutton's chantry. *Inq. A.Q.D.* (P.R.O. Lists and Indexes), p. 647, and see p. 656.

[6] Gibbons, op. cit. p. 139.

[7] C.C.M. 1541–64, ff. 75b, 82b.

The house on the north side of 'St Anne's' churchyard was the house engraved by Buck in 1726. According to his engraving, the northern portion, with some decorated work in the windows, had under a gable in the middle of the building a shield bearing the arms of John of Gaunt,[1] surmounted by his helm and mantling. The southern part of the house was of perpendicular style, as is shown by a plate by Grimm, showing two-light square-headed windows, a plain buttress and a battlemented cornice. The decorated oriel window shown in the south wall in Buck's print was moved to the castle gateway in the nineteenth century. The only other feature surviving to-day is a perpendicular window in the rear of the modern buildings.[2] The house is described by Buck as 'John of Gaunt's Palace', with the inscription:

the Castle was his: but standing much exposed to cold winds, and a place of office for the public service, and frequently garrison'd, that prince probably built this below the hill for warmth, and for the use of his family and domesticks, whilst he resided in this most ancient city, where and at Bolingbrook, a castle of his Highnesses in this County, he spent great part of his later days, having marry'd the lady Kath: Swynford, widow of a Lincolnshire knight.

For this identification of the house and the account of Gaunt's reasons for building it there seems to be no evidence other than the shield of arms in the gable. Gaunt dated a few letters from Lincoln, perhaps from the castle, and a few from Bolingbroke, and he dated some from Kettlethorpe, the home of Katharine Swynford; but there is no trace in his register of a house in Wigford,[3] nor has any evidence of it been found elsewhere. When Katharine died in 1403 she had been living in a house belonging to the dean and chapter and usually occupied by one of the canons.[4] Buck's story was unknown to Leland, who was quoted by Camden. Stukeley, writing about 1724, mentions that a stone building of ancient model in the lower city was said to be the palace of John of Gaunt and that his arms were carved there.[5] Gough refers to this, adding that opposite 'is another ancient building called *John of Gaunt's Stables*, but more likely to have been his palace than the other'.[6] Drawings made by Grimm, the Swiss artist, in 1784, bear inscriptions referring to 'the pretended house of John of Gaunt at Lincoln', and to the old house 'pretended by some to have been the

[1] France and England quarterly, with a label of three points ermine.

[2] Sympson, *Lincoln* (1906), p. 392.

[3] *John of Gaunt's Register* has been published in four volumes of the Camden Series of the Royal Historical Society.

[4] Chapter Acts, Liber VI (i), ff. 2, 3. Gaunt died in 1399.

[5] *Itinerarium Curiosum*, p. 85. This was about the same time as Buck published his print.

[6] Camden's *Britannia* (Gough's ed. 1806), II, 265. Byng noted in 1791 'the remains of the palace of John of Gaunt', part having fallen down, and the stables being pulled down: 'what remains is in horrid decay.' *Torrington Diaries* (1935), II, 344.

stables of John of Gaunt, by some a religious house, and by others the old Town Hall and a prison'.[1] As Grimm was brought to Lincoln by and worked for Sir Richard Kaye, who was dean of Lincoln from 1783 to 1809, and a noted antiquary, the inscriptions no doubt emanate from the dean. Evidently there was a local belief, recorded without acceptance by Stukeley and rejected by Grimm or Dean Kaye, but elaborated by Buck, which has since been followed without question in spite of the knowledge that the greater part of the house belonged to a period later than that of Gaunt.

But if the house was not John of Gaunt's, why were his arms on the gable? The explanation is suggested by a letter in Gaunt's register, dated from Lincoln in 1374, to William de Spaigne, the duke's feodor in Lincolnshire, for the homage of John de Sutton for certain lands in the county of Lincoln.[2] The duke was Sutton's feudal lord and perhaps his patron. If John de Sutton began the building of the family mansion, as he may have done, he may also have sought and obtained leave to place his lord's arms upon his house. Camden says that gentlemen beginning to bear arms borrowed those of their lords of whom they held in fee, or to whom they were most devoted.[3] As all the evidence, with the exception of the shield of arms, points to the ownership of Sutton to the exclusion of Gaunt, it seems probable that it was the shield alone which gave rise to the error propagated by Buck.[4]

Other great families of citizens were associated with other Wigford parishes, as is shown by the foundation of chantries, like those of John de Blyton in St Margaret, and Robert Dalderby and Roger Tateshall in St Benedict;[5] but enough has been written to show the great importance

[1] B.M. Add. MSS. 15542.

[2] *John of Gaunt's Register*, 1372–6, no. 135. In 1387 John de Severby of Lincoln granted to Katharine Swynford rent in Kettlethorpe and elsewhere: the first witness was John de Sutton, citizen of Lincoln. *Arch. Journ.* XXI (1864), p. 256. Thomas de Sutton, clerk, was godfather to Katharine's son, Sir Thomas Swynford. Canon Cole in *A.A.S.R.* XXXI (1911), pp. 56, 58.

[3] Camden, *Remains concerning Britain* (1870 ed.), p. 231.

[4] Deeds kindly given to the writer by Messrs West indicate that in the eighteenth century the mansion (divided into three tenements) was known as Broxholme's great house. Part of the property passed into the hands of the Bromhead family. For the Broxholmes, see Dudding, *Parish Register of St Peter at Gowts*, 1538–1837 (L.R.S.), p. xi. The *Lincoln, Rutland and Stamford Mercury* records (30 March 1849) that the palace of John of Gaunt in Lincoln had been sold by auction, and that it was reported that the building was to be pulled down and the materials sold. On 30 November 1849 the newspaper noted that the beautiful oriel window, which had been advertised for sale, had been sold to the Earl Brownlow, who presented it to the county magistrates with a view to its being preserved in the castle. The front of the 'Palace' had been entirely pulled down and rebuilt, and deprived of its ancient character and ornament.

[5] Foster and Thompson, 'Chantry Certificates for Lincoln and Lincolnshire' in *A.A.S.R.* XXXVI (1922), nos. 1, 2, and 4.

of Wigford at an early date. Perhaps the leading citizens were glad to escape from the crowded and insanitary walled city into the wider spaces and relatively rural surroundings of the suburb. Speed's map of 1610 shows a ribbon of houses on both sides of the High Street, and many documents prove that the gardens and closes belonging to the houses stretched from the houses themselves to the Witham or the Sincil Dyke. It was only in the nineteenth century that the side streets began to appear.

With the district of Newland it is more convenient to deal elsewhere,[1] but there is one other suburb that calls for notice. Newport is the name of the district extending northwards from Newport Arch along each side of the Ermine Street to a point marked by traces of earthworks in the garden of the Diocesan Training College, a distance of 450 yards from north to south. Leland assumed that this was a British settlement, and Camden followed him;[2] and so, long after, did Professor Freeman.[3] Mr G. T. Clark, noting its geometrical relation to the Ermine Street, which bisects it, pointed out that it must be post-Roman, and proposed a Romano-British origin.[4] There can be little doubt, however, that Newport is a post-Conquest settlement, 'port' having come to mean a town and especially a market town.[5] In spite of Stukeley's map, which shows a wall on the west, north and east sides, with towers at the two northern corners,[6] there is no clear evidence that the suburb was ever walled with stone. It was surrounded by a ditch.[7]

Newport was certainly an established suburb in the middle years of the twelfth century. The two churches of St John and St Nicholas are mentioned in the papal bull of 1146;[8] and a charter addressed to Richard de la Haye, who died before 1189, refers to a house in *Newportia*, and is witnessed by William the clerk of Newport.[9] The suburb, like Wigford, furnished an example of ribbon building; houses stretched along the Ermine Street, and their gardens extended east and west to the ditches of the suburb. One other street in Newport is mentioned: Sastangate or Sextonesgate in the

[1] Infra, pp. 329–30.

[2] *Itinerary* (ed. Toulmin Smith), I, 30–1; Gibson's edition of Camden's *Britannia* (1695), col. 468.

[3] *English Towns and Districts* (1883), p. 196.

[4] 'Lincoln Castle' in *A.A.S.R.* XIII (1876), p. 177, and *Medieval Military Architecture* (1884), II, 191.

[5] Excavation carried out in 1937 in the north ditch of Newport failed to show any pottery of earlier than fourteenth century date, this being found in such a position as to imply that the earthwork was made earlier. Stanwell and Baker, 'The Newport Earthwork, Lincoln', in *Lincolnshire Magazine*, III (1936–8), pp. 255–61.

[6] *Itinerarium Curiosum*, opposite p. 83. Stukeley is followed by Marrat in his map of 1817.

[7] D. & C., Dii, 77/2/8, refers to the *fossatum* on the west side. There is mention, however, of *murum domini regis* in the parish of St John in Newport, Dii, 77/2/26.

[8] *R.A.* I, 198–9.

[9] D. & C., Dii, 77/2/40.

parish of St Nicholas,[1] which ran east and west and may now be represented by Rasen Lane. The Augustinian friary stood in Newport, but the suburb contained no other building of note, and it seems not to have been of much importance. The inhabitants were mostly farmers and their servants, engaged in the city fields. In the autumn, in harvest time, hiring of reapers and servants took place at Newport Cross only.[2]

There was, however, one aspect in which Newport mattered to the city. With the Bail and Close under separate jurisdictions Newport was the chief inhabited area uphill ruled by the citizens. Difficulties of communication between the lower city and the upper made it desirable that country folk coming to market with their goods should be able to sell them above hill; and the dwellers in the Bail and Close provided, or should have provided, a considerable number of customers. It is not surprising therefore to hear of a market and market cross in Newport: the cross stood in the middle of the street by St John's church.

In the fourteenth century Newport also had a fair. In the course of a dispute with the constable of the Bail the citizens complained that they had a royal grant of a fair to be holden in Newport from St Botolph's Day to that of SS. Peter and Paul (17 to 29 June), and that the constables had encroached on the city's rights by drawing stallage within the Bail and outside the bounds of the fair.[3] That a fair existed before the royal grant of 1327, however, is made evident by the city accounts at the end of the preceding century, which show the revenue from the fair to have been considerable.[4]

To return to the walled city. Of the Norman houses still surviving the Jews' House and its neighbour the Jews' Court are dealt with elsewhere.[5] The house which has been identified in modern times as Aaron's house, though mistakenly,[6] can best be mentioned here. It stands at the corner of Steep Hill and Christ's Hospital Terrace in the parish of St Michael on the Mount and belongs, apparently, to the second half of the twelfth century. In the middle of the front, facing west, is an entrance arch with terminal grotesques to the hood, and originally there was a fireplace buttress above it. A restored Norman window, said to have been found in pieces in a ground floor recess, has been inserted in the front of the house. The south wall has been partially faced with brick, but it retains fragments of a string course. In a semi-underground cellar there is a good barrel vault

[1] *Book of Fees*, I, 364; *Cal. Inq. Misc.* I, no. 1939.

[2] *C.C.R.* 1374–7, p. 262.

[3] Ibid. The grant of confirmation of the fair was made by Edward III in 1327; it does not mention where the fair was held, but apparently the citizens had allocated it to Newport. Birch, pp. 54, 56.

[4] Infra, p. 215.
[5] Infra, pp. 234–7.
[6] Infra, pp. 221–3.

and aumbry.[1] The house is now divided into four tenements, and when an investigation of the interior becomes possible it may yield interesting results.

The ownership of this house in the middle of the thirteenth century is made plain by deeds of land adjoining on the north and east. About 1240 Peter of Legbourne, with the consent of his wife Joan, granted to Thorald the cooper part of his land touching the wall of the Bail on the south side, at a rent of 8*s*. Later, Joan of Legbourne, in her widowhood, confirmed to Thorald the land (16 ells in length and 11 in width) between her great house called the hall on the south side and the wall of the Bail on the north. Still later (*c*. 1270) Thorald's son Warin granted it to Master William de Roveston the doctor (*medicus*),[2] who seems to have given it to the dean and chapter as part of the endowment of his chantry, known later as the Ruffus Chantry.[3] This is clearly the house to the north of the hall and to the south of the Bail wall.

Other deeds relate to the land adjoining the hall to the east. Peter, son of Robert of Legbourne, with his wife Joan's consent, granted to Thorald the fruiterer land formerly of William de Tillebroc, situate between the land of John the baker near the gate of the cemetery (of St Michael) and Peter's house called the hall, at a rent of 4*s*. Joan, when a widow, confirmed the grant to Thorald's nephew John. By his will, made in 1280, John directed that his executors should sell the land and buildings, which he had bought from the Lady Joan, to pay his debts, and accordingly they sold it to William de Roveston the doctor (*phisicus*). This property also passed to the Ruffus Chantry.[4]

Who was Peter of Legbourne who held the hall? As his name suggests, and to judge by his holdings of land, he seems to have belonged to the Louth district. He held of Earl Ferrers in Raithby, Tathwell and elsewhere; through a mesne tenant of William de Percy in Louthesk; of William de Cantilupe in Saltfleetby and Somercotes; and in Trusthorpe of the honour of Bolingbroke.[5] John, son of Richard of Rippingale, held land of him in Rippingale and Ringsdon by service of a quarter of a knight's fee: Peter held of Robert de Ros, who held of the king in chief.[6] He was descended from Robert of Ropsley,[7] but there is nothing to show how Peter became possessed of his hall in Lincoln: it may have come to him through his wife Joan, as her concurrence is expressed in his grants, and

[1] Miss Wood's article, *Arch. Journ.* XCII (1935), p. 197.

[2] D. & C., Dii, 76/2/18, 24, 27, 31. *R.H.* I, 311a.

[3] *L.C.S.* III, 897.

[4] D. & C., Dii, 76/2/23, 26, 29, 30.

[5] *Book of Fees*, II, 1002, 1053–5, 1058.

[6] *R.H.* I, 253b.

[7] *Lincs N. & Q.* VIII, 249–50; *A.A.S.R.* XXVI (1902), p. 325; Farrer, *Honors and Knights' Fees* (1924), II, 106–9; *R.A.* V, see index.

she confirmed them (not merely releasing her dower) after his death. It remains to be discovered, however, who Joan was.

Lincoln is fortunate in its remaining Norman houses, but there must have been many others which long survived, as an eighteenth-century observer testifies:

> The original magnificence of this city may easily be conceived from a circumstance almost peculiar to it of all the cities of England; which is, the vast number of beautiful Saxon and Norman doorways, constructed in the most finished manner, and to be met with in every part of the streets; and in the walls of what are now the most private houses.[1]

[1] King, 'Sequel to Observations on Ancient Castles', in *Archaeologia*, VI (1782), p. 261. Defoe remarked on the great number of Gothic remains, though he put the matter differently: 'Lincoln is an antient, ragged, decay'd, and still decaying city; it is so full of the ruins of monasteries and religious houses, that, in short, the very barns, stables, out-houses, and as they shew'd me, some of the very hog-styes, were built church-fashion; that is to say, with stone walls and arch'd windows and doors.' *Tour* (Everyman Edition), II, 91.

CHAPTER IX

THE TWELFTH CENTURY

RECORDS of the early years of the twelfth century are scanty. There is no Domesday Book to throw light upon the period, and the surviving Pipe Rolls (with a solitary exception) do not begin until the second half of the century. The *Anglo-Saxon Chronicle* records that almost the whole city was burnt in 1123, and 'so much harm was there done as no man could describe to another'.[1] Fires must have been common in towns built of wood; no doubt the damage was quickly repaired, and the statements recorded in the annals of a distant monastic house are not always to be taken as literally true.[2] Symeon of Durham mentions a much more interesting fact: that in 1121 the Fossdyke was opened for traffic.[3] How long it had been obstructed is not recorded, but it may be that its obstruction had something to do with the apparent setback in the fortunes of the city after the Conquest. Nevertheless, about the same time William of Malmesbury, echoing Bede's reference to London, could describe the city as one of the most populous in England, and the market of men coming by land and sea.[4] The evidence of the Pipe Roll of 1130 it will be more convenient to consider later.

The reticence of the chroniclers must be regarded as satisfactory in so far as it implies absence of fire, earthquake, rebellion or civil war. Armed resistance to the Norman conquerors had ceased, but the ties of blood between the people of the Danelaw and the Scandinavian countries were not to be severed as easily as the political links; and it was only gradually that the districts of Danish settlement came to look towards France and Flanders rather than Norway and Denmark. Scandinavian personal names continued in common use until the end of the century, and there are several striking pieces of evidence of the closeness of the ties between Lincolnshire and Scandinavia.

The historian Orderic has a remarkable story of Magnus Barefoot, king of Norway. When about 1103 he sailed on an expedition to Ireland, he left his treasure with a rich citizen of Lincoln, who acted as his agent and supplied him with arms, plate, ornaments, furniture and whatever the royal service required. Magnus lost his life in an ambush. On hearing of

[1] (R.S.), I, 375.

[2] The Winchester Annals say that London and Lincoln were burnt in 1105, and that in 1113 there was a fire at Worcester, and the castle at Devizes, and London and Lincoln were burnt. *Annales Monastici* (R.S.), II, 42, 44.

[3] (R.S.), II, 260.

[4] *Gesta Pontificum Anglorum* (R.S.), p. 312. Cf. Bede, *Historia Ecclesiastica*, bk. II, ch. iii.

his death the agent hurriedly returned to Lincoln, and soon amassed vast wealth by trading with the king's treasure. Trading implies some lapse of time, but presently Henry I of England, who had heard with satisfaction of Magnus' death, called on the Lincoln citizen to surrender the treasure: this may have been on the occasion of Henry's visit to Lincoln in 1108–9.[1] The citizen first denied possession, but Henry having convicted him of falsehood, suddenly arrested him, and, it was said, extorted from him more than 20,000 pounds of silver.[2] King Magnus had clearly acted with imprudence, but his action in leaving his treasure in Lincoln indicates that he hardly regarded Lincoln as part of a foreign land.[3]

Half a century later Henry II acknowledged the existence and importance of the Norwegian trade in Lincolnshire. He addressed a writ to all the men of Norway who came to the port of Grimsby, or other Lincolnshire ports, commanding them to yield to the king's bailiffs of Lincoln all the rights and customs which they had been wont so to yield, with a penalty for the withholding of toll.[4] The Norwegians' exports were probably furs, horses, wool and flesh, and their imports articles of luxury.[5] Norway hawks were in great demand in England. The king's falconer went to Boston to buy birds, and an Iceland girfalcon is also mentioned.[6] In Lincolnshire these hawks seem to have been treated almost as currency:[7] Everwine of Lincoln owed two Norway hawks for having his plea against William of Paris and his sons-in-law John and Walter about scarlet cloth before the justices:[8] John son of Ordgar owed one Norway hawk for having the king's writ to the king of Norway concerning his claim to the chattels of his brother Godard;[9] and Outi the chaplain owed one hawk for the right to

[1] Round, *Calendar of Documents preserved in France*, p. 504.

[2] Ordericus Vitalis, *Historia Ecclesiastica*, bk. IX, ch. viii.

[3] Andrews, *Numismatic History of the Reign of Henry I*, pp. 260–1, adds that this account is peculiarly interesting in view of certain coins of Magnus the Good, and Norse kings of the period, perhaps of Magnus Barefoot, which bear on the reverse the name of Lincoln, with the moneyers' names Osgar, Steinbit, Lefwine and Arcil. He points out that a Lefwine coined in Lincoln for Rufus, and Arcil for Henry I, and suggests that the latter might even have been the 'rich citizen' of the Magnus Barefoot story. Inquiry has failed to locate any such coins of later date than Magnus the Good (1035–47); they are unknown at the British Museum, or in Oslo, Stockholm or Copenhagen. For coins of Magnus the Good bearing the names of Lincoln with Lefwine and Oindi, see supra, p. 32. The Arcil penny of Magnus may have been struck at Lund in Sweden.

[4] *B.B.C.* (1), p. 178; Birch, p. 18. One of the other ports was doubtless Boston: somewhere off the mouth of the Witham was a place called *Normandepe*. *Placita de Quo Warranto*, p. 427; Thompson, *Boston*, p. 332.

[5] *Cambridge Medieval History*, III, 332.

[6] P.R. 22 *Henry II*, pp. 77, 79.

[7] Ibid. p. xxv.

[8] P.R. 31 *Henry II*, p. 84. William of Paris accounted for 2 marks for inquiry into the truth of John the Norwegian's appeal against him. Ibid. p. 89.

[9] Ibid. p. 90.

recover four hawks and four falcons against Godwin the rich and William son of Engelbert, but Outi was in Norway.[1] In the roll of 1162–3 the Lincoln city account bore a payment of £14 to the messengers of the king of Norway, by writ of the earl of Leicester.[2]

The Scandinavian origin of Grimsby is indicated by its name, and legends of its foundation current in the twelfth century have this much of truth in them. One story was that the founder was Grim, a Norwegian pirate of vast stature;[3] and the thirteenth-century seal of the borough bears one large and two small figures whose relative size may have some reference to the story. The more famous legend, however, is of Grim, Havelok and Goldborough, all of whose names appear on the seal. The tale, 'in which there exists primarily the viking atmosphere of tenth-century England',[4] tells how a Danish prince and an English princess came into their own. The hero, son of a Danish king, was handed over by his wicked guardian Godard to a fisherman, Grim, to be drowned. A mystic light, however, revealed Havelok's royal birth to the simple Grim, who saved the situation by crossing to England. They landed at Grimsby, where Grim tried to support his household by fishing. He hawked his catches in the towns and granges round about; and when he caught great lampreys, he took them to Lincoln, 'the good borough', and went through and through it until he had sold them all. Then he bought wastels and simnels (cakes), filled his pokes with meal and corn, flesh of neats, sheep and pigs, took hemp for his lines, and went home again. When Havelok grew up he also took to fishing, and in a famine year Grim sent him to Lincoln. During his first two days there he went fasting. The third day he heard the earl's cook call for porters. In his hurry to get work he shoved down nine or ten men, took the meat which the cook had bought at the bridge, and bore it to the castle, where he was given a farthing cake for his trouble. The next day he looked out for the earl's cook till he saw him on the bridge, with the many fish he had bought lying beside him. When the cook had also bought the earl's meat, he called for porters. Havelok again secured work, and took up a cartload of cuttle-fish, salmon, broad plaice, great lampreys and eels to the castle. The cook gave him work. When the earl's men came together at Lincoln for the games, Havelok, who towered above them all, put a heavy stone farther than anyone else.[5] All the knights in the castle, up in the hall,

[1] Ibid. p. 91.
[2] P.R. 9 *Henry II*, p. 68.
[3] Holles, *Church Notes* (L.R.S.), p. 4.
[4] *Cambridge History of English Literature*, I, 303, from which this summary of the tale is in part taken.
[5] Robert Mannyng of Bourne translated Peter Langtoft's chronicle about 1338, and in an interpolated passage says that the stone that Havelok threw was said still to lie in Lincoln Castle. See *The Lay of Havelok the Dane* (ed. Skeat, revised by K. Sisam), p. xvi.

heard of the feat, and Havelok's master Godrich forcibly married the Princess Goldborough to his 'cook's knave' in the hope of keeping to himself her inheritance. Havelok took Goldborough to Denmark, where he recovered his inheritance, and then returned to England to recover hers. Godrich was taken in battle, carried in fetters to the queen at Lincoln, where he was taken to a green and burnt.

In this romantic tale there must have been much which its hearers in the twelfth century and after recognised as true to life: the fishermen going from Grimsby to Lincoln; the fish and meat sold on the High Bridge in the city; the porters waiting there to be hired, as they still were in the eighteenth century; the servants of the great men uphill coming down to buy; the annual games for retainers; the intimate association of England in men's minds with Scandinavia.

Another example of this association comes from one of the Icelandic sagas. It is told that at the age of fifteen the boy Kali fared west with chapmen to England, with good wares for sale. They came to Grimsby: 'thither came a very great crowd of men both from Norway, the Orkneys, and from Scotland, and also from the Southern isles'. There Kali met Gillichrist, who asked much about Norway, and they became great friends. Gillichrist told Kali as a secret that he was a son of King Magnus Barefoot, but that his mother's stock was in the southern isles, and some of them in Ireland.[1]

A few links between the north countries and Grimsby continued long after the twelfth century. Holles recorded the great privileges and immunities that the town enjoyed in Denmark above any other in England, such as freedom from toll.[2] It is elsewhere mentioned that the burgesses of Grimsby were free from toll at the port of Elsinore in Denmark:[3] here merchants from all parts assembled at the annual fair, booths were erected along the shore, and foreign wares were bartered for fish, hides and valuable furs, whilst various games and all sorts of merry-making took place.[4]

Some hints survive of ties between the churchmen in Lincolnshire and Norway. The Cistercian house of Hovedo in Norway was settled about 1147 by monks from Kirkstead Abbey, and Laurence, who was abbot of

[1] *Icelandic Sagas* (R.S.), III, 97–8 (*c.* 1116). The local colour provided by Kali's song carries conviction:

> Weeks of grimmest walking five,
> We have waded through the mud;
> In mid Grimsby where we were,
> Was no want of mud and mire.

[2] *Church Notes* (L.R.S.), p. 3.

[3] Oliver, *Monumental Antiquities of Great Grimsby* (1825), p. 15.

[4] Worsaae, *Danes and Norwegians in England* (1852), p. 100.

CLASKET GATE (taken down in the eighteenth century)

From Buck's sketch book

NEWLAND GATE (taken down in the eighteenth century)

From Buck's sketch book [*See p.* 156

PLATE 14

LITTLE OR EAST BARGATE, probably taken down *c.* 1828

From Buck's sketch book

GREAT OR WEST BARGATE (taken down by 1759)

See p. 162] *From Buck's sketch book*

Hovedo in the thirteenth century, became abbot of Kirkstead. The Augustinian abbey of Wellow at Grimsby was founded by Henry I and dedicated to St Augustine and the Norwegian royal saint Olave, to whom the little Wold church of Ruckland near Louth is also dedicated.[1] In 1165–6 the Lincolnshire account at the Exchequer was credited with 66*s*. 8*d*. laid out by the king's writ in gifts to a Norwegian bishop;[2] and the previous year a Norwegian archdeacon and his companion received £6. 13*s*. 4*d*. on the Lincoln city account by royal writ.[3]

It has been noted earlier[4] that traders travelled from Sweden across Russia to the Eastern Empire, and some may have gone by sea to the same parts. One citizen of Lincoln is heard of there, though what his original mission was is not recorded. The Emperor Alexius Comnenus, wishing to send letters and gifts to King Henry I of England and his queen, Matilda, chose as his messenger Wulfric, an Englishman and a native of the town of Lincoln. The mission was performed with great pomp; and among the gifts were relics of St John Chrysostom, which were entrusted to the abbey of Abingdon.[5]

Of individual citizens of Lincoln in the earlier half of the century practically nothing is known. A few benefactors of the Minster and the Black Monks[6] are recorded, and there are several persons of note described as 'of Lincoln'. Yet these are not necessarily citizens; they are rather county magnates, even though they may have lived in or near the city: and indeed, the designation points to tenure of the shrievalty.[7] Wigot of Lincoln was sheriff of the county about 1114–16,[8] and Richard of Lincoln, son of Osbert the sheriff, held land in Elsham, Benniworth and elsewhere in Lindsey about 1115.[9] The hints of developing civic life are more conveniently discussed later.[10]

In the anarchy of Stephen's reign the city was closely linked with the fortunes and activities of Ranulf earl of Chester, and it suffered much in consequence. The Empress Matilda and her brother Robert earl of Gloucester landed in England in the autumn of 1140, bringing 140 knights with them. At some time before Christmas she seized Lincoln city and castle, but Stephen recovered them, and Matilda escaped. About Christmas-

[1] Dickins, 'The Cult of St Olave in the British Isles' in *Saga Book*, XII, 54, 59–60. The abbot of Grimsby visited Norway in 1163.

[2] P.R. 12 *Henry II*, p. 3, and see Bishop Stubbs' comment on pp. xi–xii.

[3] P.R. 11 *Henry II*, p. 39.

[4] Supra, p. 32 n.

[5] *Chronicon Monasterii de Abingdon* (R.S.), II, 46–7.

[6] As to the latter, see pp. 133, 339.

[7] Round, 'Early Sheriffs of Norfolk' in *E.H.R.* XXXV (1920), p. 490.

[8] *R.A.* I, 43: he held land in Broxholme and Ingleby. *L.D.* Lindsey Survey, 3/16.

[9] *L.D.* see index.

[10] Infra, pp. 183 et seq.

time the keep, then in Stephen's hands, was seized by Ranulph and his half-brother William de Roumare. The story of their stratagem is told by Orderic:

> They craftily chose a time when the garrison of the tower (*turrenses*) were dispersed abroad and engaged in sports, and then they sent their wives to the citadel (*ad arcem*) as though for the sake of pastime. And so, while the two countesses continued their visit, playing and chatting with the wife of the knight whose duty it was to defend the tower, the earl of Chester came unarmed and without his coat of mail, as if to fetch his wife away, followed by three knights, nobody suspecting any harm. Having thus entered they suddenly seized crowbars and arms that lay near, and violently ejected the king's guards. Then William, and armed knights with him, arrived as had previously been arranged, and so the two brothers subdued the tower (*turrim*) with the whole city to themselves.[1]

The action of the earls was reported to Stephen by Bishop Alexander, who had himself been imprisoned by the king, but was now released.[2] The citizens of Lincoln also reported the earls' action to him, being no doubt influenced by the heavy demands that Ranulph and William were making of them, probably by requisitions for victualling and arming the castle.[3] Stephen at once set out for Lincoln. Evidently he arrived before he was expected, for he seized some men-at-arms lying in the city who had not had time to retire to the castle.

The castle was invested on all sides, but Ranulph succeeded in escaping, and he sought the aid of the empress' brother Earl Robert. Together they marched from Gloucester; and when they reached the Trent they found it could not be forded, so the whole party swam across the river.[4] They advanced by the Fosse Way, and crossed a marsh which was almost impassable.[5] The *Gesta Stephani* says that the king sent a detachment to oppose the passage of a ford,[6] and Miss Norgate suggests that the earls advanced almost up to the High Bridge over the Witham and used the ford between the bridge and Brayford Head.[7] The suggestion takes no account of the existence of the suburb of Wigford, which the earls would have had to pass through first in order to reach a ford commanded by the south wall of the city itself. Moreover, the theory ignores the mention of

[1] *Historia Ecclesiastica*, bk. XIII, ch. xliii. Mr Nichols gives the passage in his article on the earldom of Lincoln in the *Proceedings of the Archaeological Institute* (1848), p. 260, but he translates *turris* as *castle*, and the distinction between keep and castle is lost. The keep is Lucy's Tower (see pp. 85, 91) and the only part of the castle which was separately defensible.

[2] Ralph de Diceto, *Opera Historica* (R.S.), I, 252.

[3] *Gesta Stephani* in *Chronicles of Stephen* (R.S.), III, 69.

[4] William of Malmesbury, *Gesta Regum*, II, 571. Apparently there was still no bridge at Newark, although Bishop Alexander had lately obtained from Henry I licence to build such a bridge to his castle of Newark, provided it was of no harm to the king's city of Lincoln or to his borough of Nottingham (1129–33). *R.A.* I, 38.

[5] Henry of Huntingdon, *Historia Anglorum* (R.S.), p. 268.

[6] p. 377.

[7] Norgate, *England under the Angevin Kings* (1887), I, 345.

the almost impassable marsh, and the more generally accepted view, that the earls crossed the Fossdyke west of Brayford, where there was certainly a marsh and may also have been a ford, is the more probable one.[1]

The king drew his troops out of the city to meet the attack. The site of the battle which followed is in doubt. Miss Norgate proposed a piece of ground on the south-west side of the hill, on or near the west common, discarding a 'tradition' which said that the battle was fought to the north of the city. Sir James Ramsay also mentions the 'tradition', but it is unknown to local historians. The battle has sometimes been put to the west of the castle, no doubt because an adjoining piece of land was known as the 'battle-place', but according to the jurors in the Hundred Rolls it was so called because it had been set apart for trials by battle.[2] The truth is that there is no satisfactory evidence upon which to decide the question. If the battle were fought on the hillside, Stephen, holding the higher ground, would have the advantage; and it could not have been fought on the hilltop unless Stephen had first allowed his foes to take that advantage from him. Further speculation is unprofitable.

Wherever the site may have been, Stephen resolved to give battle at once. Apparently the leaders of both sides made speeches before going into action, each side claiming justice for its own and blaming the other. In the speech attributed to Robert of Gloucester, he referred to the citizens of Lincoln, standing in array nearest to their walls, and he prophesied that they would yield before the onslaught upon them and seek refuge in their homes.[3]

In the battle that ensued most of Stephen's army was quickly driven off the field. Stephen himself, surrounded by his infantry, made a desperate stand, fighting first with his sword and then with a Danish battle-axe, put into his hand by a citizen of Lincoln.[4] At last he was seized, and he surrendered to Robert of Gloucester.

Many of the citizens, warned of the victory of the earls, fled to the river, intending to escape by water; but the overcrowded boats were swamped, and most of those aboard were drowned. Those who remained behind were slaughtered without mercy, and the city was sacked.[5]

The king was imprisoned at Bristol. By the following September Robert of Gloucester had been captured by the king's party, and an exchange of Stephen and Robert was arranged, Robert stipulating that his friends

[1] Oman, *History of the Art of War in the Middle Ages* (1898 ed.), pp. 392–3; Ramsay, *Foundations of England*, II, 398.

[2] *R.H.* I, 312a, 398b. See Appendix I.

[3] Henry of Huntingdon, *Historia Anglorum* (R.S.), p. 269.

[4] Symeon of Durham, *Historia Regum* (R.S.), II, 308.

[5] Ordericus Vitalis, *Historia Ecclesiastica*, bk. XIII, ch. xliii.

should keep all castles and lands acquired by them since the battle of Lincoln.[1]

In the spring of 1142 Stephen met Ranulph and William de Roumare at Stamford and came to terms with them. William received a grant of Kirton-in-Lindsey and a confirmation of the right to hold Gainsborough Castle and the Trent Bridge, 'with all rights enjoyed by any English earl in respect of his castles'.[2] The treaty did not last long. In 1144 Stephen made another attack on Lincoln Castle, and he constructed a *munitio* against it. It is generally said that this fortification survived in three sides of a square earthwork which are clearly marked in early nineteenth-century maps within the grounds of the Lawn Hospital, opposite the western gateway of the castle. The earthwork can now be seen only with the eye of faith. While the works were being thrown up, some eighty of Stephen's men were cut off by the enemy, and Stephen abandoned his attack.[3]

The fortunes of war inclined in Stephen's favour in 1146, and Ranulph came over to the winning side, taking Bedford on the king's behalf. He did not, however, offer to surrender Lincoln Castle, and his refusal to do so led to his seizure by the king at Northampton. His castles were extorted from him and he was released. Stephen presently went to Lincoln to take possession, and he celebrated Christmas there. Several of the chroniclers mention a superstition which forbade a king to wear his crown in the city. Stephen, however, wore his crown in state, to show how little importance he attached to such superstition.[4]

After his departure Ranulph revolted and attacked Lincoln. His commander was slain at the north gate of the city, and after losing many men he was forced to retire. The citizens gave thanks for their successful defence to their patron and protectress, the Blessed Virgin Mary, an interesting early reference to the patron saint of the city.

In 1149 Matilda's son, Henry of Anjou, landed in England, and Stephen was in need of support. It is probably to this occasion that must be attributed a charter granted by Stephen to Earl Ranulph.[5] Among many other gifts Stephen granted to him the castle and city of Lincoln as a pledge until Stephen should restore to him his lands and castles in Normandy.

[1] William of Malmesbury, *Gesta Regum* (R.S.), II, 589.

[2] Round, *Geoffrey de Mandeville* (1892), p. 159.

[3] Henry of Huntingdon, *Historia Anglorum* (R.S.), p. 277.

[4] Ibid. p. 279; William of Newburgh in *Chronicles of Stephen* (R.S.), I, 57, and see p. 118, where he says he believes Henry II was crowned *in vico suburbano* because of the old superstition. *Annales Monastici* (R.S.), II, 232 (Waverley Annals).

[5] The text of the memorandum giving all that is known of the charter is printed by Canon Foster in *R.A.* I, 287–8. See Stenton, *First Century of English Feudalism* (1932), p. 240.

The king also allowed him to fortify one of his towers in the castle and hold it until the king had delivered Tickhill Castle to him. On that event, the tower and the city of Lincoln were to revert to the king, whilst the earl was to retain the tower which his mother (the Countess Lucy) had fortified, and the constableship of Lincoln and Lincolnshire. The precise effect of the grant is not clear. The earl was to retain his mother's tower, no doubt the keep, permanently; which fact suggests that the tower he was to fortify and hold pending the delivery of Tickhill was the tower on the eastern mound (the present Observatory Tower). The constableship of the castle was claimed apart from Lucy's Tower.[1]

Henry paid another visit to England in 1153, and this time it was he who bought Ranulph's support by making him grants greater even than those of Stephen. Lincoln is not specifically mentioned in Henry's charter; probably, like Stephen, he was not willing to part with the permanent possession of the city and castle. In the same year Stephen and Henry of Anjou came to terms. Stephen was to be recognised as king during his life, and Henry was to succeed to the throne at Stephen's death. The treaty of pacification included a clause directing that Lincoln Castle should be delivered to Jordan de Bussey, who was to swear that at Stephen's death he would yield it up to Henry.[2]

The rivals having come to terms, they were no longer concerned to buy Ranulph's support, and they no doubt welcomed the chance of dispossessing him of the castle. Ranulph died in 1153 and Stephen in 1154, and the advantages that Ranulph had gained by his treaties with Stephen and Henry did not survive him. The royal demesne which he held reverted to the Crown.[3] The claims of Lucy's family on the castle were ignored; and in 1155 Richard de la Haye (whose family was, it appears, dispossessed during the anarchy) obtained a grant from Henry II confirming him in the constableship of Lincoln Castle as his father Robert had held it in the time of Henry I.[4]

Henry II at once took steps to restore order. He expelled Flemish mercenaries from the country, ordered the demolition of 'adulterine' or unauthorised castles, and resumed the grants made by Stephen. After these initial measures he started for the north and passed through Oxford, Northampton and Peterborough to Lincoln, which he reached about January 1155. Probably Bishop Robert II took this opportunity of securing

[1] For the association of Lucy and her family with the castle see pp. 91 et seq.

[2] Rymer, *Foedera*, I, 18.

[3] Farrer, *Honors and Knights' Fees* (1924), II, 7.

[4] Round, *Ancient Charters*, p. 58. On the whole question of Ranulph's relations with Stephen and Lincoln Castle, see Round, 'King Stephen and the Earl of Chester' in *E.H.R.* x (1895), p. 87, and Cronne, 'Ranulf de Gernons, Earl of Chester, 1129–1153' in *Trans. Royal Hist. Soc.* 4th ser. xx, 103.

confirmation of some of his existing rights, including a writ confirming to the church of Lincoln the franchises and gifts granted by William the Conqueror; and also a confirmation of Henry I's gift of the churches in Lincoln which their priests held of the king.[1]

Having visited York and Scarborough, Henry moved to Nottingham, and it is likely that on this occasion he issued two more writs which are probably the results of representations made to him at Lincoln. One, the confirmation of the constableship of the castle to Richard de la Haye, has already been mentioned.[2] The other is a grant to the city of Lincoln, the oldest surviving document in the city muniment room:[3] this will be mentioned again.

In 1157, after conducting a campaign against the Welsh, Henry returned to Lincoln to keep Christmas. It is a tribute to the position of the city in national affairs that he caused himself to be crowned a second time while in Lincoln. He wore his crown in Wigford, outside the walls of the city,[4] in deference, it has been suggested, to the local superstition which Stephen had rashly defied. So strong-minded a king was hardly likely to be much influenced by such a tale, but he may have thought it wise to make a concession to local feeling. On the other hand the reason may have been merely a practical one: perhaps his house was in Wigford.[5]

The expenses of the celebrations give some idea of their scale. The following Michaelmas the sheriffs of Nottingham and Derby, Worcester, Essex and Hertford, and Warwick, when accounting at the Exchequer, were allowed their expenses in sending venison to Lincoln. The sheriffs of London despatched 20 tuns of wine, 100 wooden cups, 1,000 pounds of wax, 60 pounds of pepper and a great number of scullions. The sheriff of Lincoln had to repair the king's house (*hospicium*) in Lincoln, to find quarters for the royal huntsmen and squires, and pay other expenses of the king's sojourn in the city.[6]

Henry's acknowledgement of the high position of the city in the kingdom finds confirmation in the records. The relative importance of the

[1] *R.A.* I, 90, 101. It seems that the archbishop of Canterbury and the Master of the Temple were with Henry at Lincoln. Lees, *Records of Templars in England in the Twelfth Century*, pp. 241–2.

[2] Supra, p. 181.

[3] Birch, p. 1, following Macray, dated this charter 1157, pointing out that Henry was at Nottingham in that year. The fact that the writ is attested by Ernulph bishop of Lisieux points to 1155. Round, *Ancient Charters*, p. 57. Eyton, *Itinerary of Henry II*, pp. 4, 6, agrees.

[4] Roger Hoveden, *Chronica* (R.S.), I, 216.

[5] In 1228 King Henry III bought a house (formerly of John de Holm) in Wigford for 60 marks, and the next year wine was ordered to be delivered to his cellar there from Boston. *Cal. Liberate Rolls*, 1226–40, pp. 79, 135.

[6] P.R. 2, 3 and 4 *Henry II*, pp. 113, 132, 136, 153, 155, 184.

boroughs is shown, broadly, by the taxation imposed on them. The aids charged on the principal towns in 1130 and 1156 were as follows: London £120, Winchester (1130 only) £80, Lincoln £60, York £40, Norwich £30 and £33. 6*s*. 8*d*.[1] Perhaps these financial assessments were in need of revision, for the average of aids under Henry II, worked out by Professor Stephenson, yields a somewhat different result: London 997 marks, York 334, Norwich 264, Lincoln 246, Northampton 210. Winchester drops to eighth place with 124 marks.[2] The lists must be received with caution, for some towns, such as Bristol, Leicester and Chester, were not in the king's hands and did not pay aids. By either test, however, it is evident that under Henry II Lincoln found a place in the first half dozen boroughs of England. It made a quick recovery from the period of anarchy and plunder under Stephen, and visible evidence remains to-day of its prosperity in St Mary's Guildhall, the houses associated with the Jews, and the High Bridge. No other part of the Middle Ages is represented to-day by such a wealth of secular building in Lincoln.

It is no surprise therefore to find the city making advances towards self-government. A comparison with the royal system of administration in the Domesday period brings this out. In the eleventh century the oppression of the sheriff was a common theme: it has been noted that the Domesday clerks thought it well to record that the wastage of houses in Lincoln was not due to such a cause.[3] As the sheriff had power to vary the sum raised in revenue from a borough, it was one of the first objects of a growing community to escape from his financial grip.

The sheriff must generally have collected the revenues of his shire through undersheriffs or agents, and he sometimes farmed out part of his revenue. Domesday Book shows that the burgesses of Northampton were farming their town from the sheriff. They were, however, still in his hands, for the sheriff alone was accountable to the king.[4]

The next available evidence is the Pipe Roll of 1130, which a happy chance has preserved. This record of the Exchequer accounts shows a few boroughs—Winchester, Southampton, Malmesbury, Dover, Canterbury, Wallingford, Colchester and Northampton—being farmed separately from their counties: the amounts of the farms had varied since 1086, some having risen, some fallen.[5] There were no doubt special reasons for this method of accounting, as at Colchester and Northampton which had escheated to the Crown. But the burgesses of those boroughs derived no benefit from

[1] Maitland, *Domesday Book and Beyond*, p. 175.

[2] *Borough and Town*, p. 225. Grimsby averaged 47 marks, Nottingham 40.

[3] Supra, p. 53.

[4] Tait, *Medieval English Borough*, p. 140.

[5] Ibid. p. 156.

the separate account. The cities of London and Lincoln carried matters a stage farther. The men of London proffered 100 marks to be allowed to elect their own sheriffs.[1] Their sheriffs had already been citizens, but now they were chosen by the citizens themselves and not by the king or his servants. Lincoln had hitherto been farmed by sheriffs who were external officials, and the citizens had more to gain by a change. They offered 200 marks of silver and 4 marks of gold that they might hold the city of the king in chief.[2] The fact that they paid a higher price than the Londoners suggests that their concession may have been the greater, and it is at least possible that whilst London was paying only for temporary possession of the farm, Lincoln was securing the farm in fee (*feodi firma*), which—at least in theory—was a perpetual grant. Certainly Lincoln fared better than London in this respect during the struggle between Stephen and Matilda, for both the rival rulers granted the shrievalty of London to Geoffrey de Mandeville, and ignored a charter which Henry I had granted to the capital.[3] On the other hand, there is no indication that Lincoln lost its farm during the war: Stephen gave a tithe of it, £14, to the church of Lincoln, showing that the farm was then £140.[4] At Michaelmas 1155 Aubrey the reeve accounted for a whole year of the farm, including the last weeks of Stephen's reign, the sum being credited to the sheriff in the county farm.[5]

It must have been at the beginning of his reign, perhaps on his first visit to Lincoln, that Henry II granted the city a charter declaring that he had delivered the city to the citizens at that farm at which it was wont to be in the time of King Henry his grandfather, with all liberties pertaining to the city within and without.[6] By Michaelmas 1156 the farm had been raised from £140 to £180,[7] and at that figure it remained. For a time the method of accounting was irregular: two years later it was transferred to the new sheriff, though it was not in arrears.[8] It was still regarded as a separate item, though it went through the sheriff's hands. Although the citizens were accounting for £180, the sheriff continued to be allowed the old farm of £140, thereby keeping on record the fact that the citizens were paying the price of a measure of fiscal independence. Their new liberty was precarious. Whatever the precise meaning of the city's privilege under Henry I, his grandson's grant was a concession which he might revoke at his own whim.

Some other boroughs secured the farm under Henry II, only to lose it again, and among them was Grimsby. By the end of the reign only Lincoln,

[1] P.R. 31 *Henry I*, p. 148.
[2] Ibid. p. 114.
[3] Tait, op. cit. p. 157.
[4] *R.A.* I, 55.
[5] *Red Book of the Exchequer*, II, 656–7.
[6] *B.B.C.* (1), p. 221.
[7] P.R. 2, 3 *and* 4 *Henry II*, p. 28.
[8] Ibid. p. 136. Tait, op. cit. pp. 162–3.

Cambridge, Northampton, Shrewsbury and Bridgnorth were clearly being farmed by the burgesses, the first three by charter. London was not yet to recover its farm: Henry's charter omitted reference to the farm, and to the right to elect the sheriffs and justices. Henry's restrictive policy for the time being prevented further progress towards municipal self-government.[1]

When the citizens of Lincoln secured the farm of the city, the grant included all the royal revenues collected within the city and its liberties. Now (as will be noted later), for ease of collection of tolls, the rule was certainly established as early as Henry I that foreign merchants trading to Lincolnshire must go to Lincoln and pay tolls. It followed that if a Lincolnshire merchant wanted to trade with a foreigner he too must go to Lincoln. But he could not expect to enjoy the advantages of foreign trade in the same way as Lincoln merchants unless he paid the same taxes as Lincoln merchants. When the tolls and taxes were farmed by the sheriff the only interest the citizens had in them was that the presence of the tolbooth made Lincoln a busy centre of trade; but when the citizens took a lease of the royal revenues those tolls and taxes went to the credit of the city's account. The monopoly of foreign trade within the county became a principal source of the revenue which the city farmed. The annual farm of £180 must be paid to the Exchequer whether trade was good or bad, and the citizens must show constant vigilance if they were to protect their revenues, or rather those royal revenues of which they were in possession.

Several grants of Henry II illustrate the vigilance of the citizens; they did not fail to point out that they were the king's agents, protecting his rights and collecting his revenue. Henry II issued a writ to the sheriffs of Lincolnshire commanding them to cause the foreign merchants to come to Lincoln and there deal with their merchandise as reasonably and justly as they were wont to do in the time of Henry I, lest the king's bailiffs of Lincoln should lose the royal customs:[2] and he also addressed a writ to all the men of Norway who came to the port of Grimsby or other Lincolnshire ports, commanding them to yield to the king's bailiffs of Lincoln all the rights and customs which they had been wont so to yield, there being a penalty of ten pounds for the withholding of toll.[3]

So the foreign merchants trading to Lincolnshire were compelled to come to Lincoln. The corollary that those who sought to trade with them must also come to Lincoln, and do business on the same footing as the Lincoln merchants, is dealt with in other writs. Henry laid it down that those merchants who came to market in Lincoln must pay the same gelds and assizes (that is, taxes) as the citizens;[4] and again, that merchant

[1] Tait, op. cit. pp. 163, 173–6.

[2] *B.B.C.* (1), p. 168; Birch, p. 14.

[3] *B.B.C.* (1), p. 178; Birch, p. 18.

[4] *B.B.C.* (1), p. 108; Birch, p. 20.

strangers trading in Lincoln must be in the gild and rated to all the customs of the town.[1] Another writ confirmed to the citizens of Lincoln the gild merchant of the men of the city and of the other merchants of the county;[2] which is to say that the county merchants are in gild membership, with its right to trade with foreigners and its duty of paying the city taxes, but nevertheless the gild 'belongs' to the citizens. The king regarded the gild as an instrument for the collection of his revenues; when those revenues were farmed by the citizens the gild passed, as it were, under new management. It 'belonged' to the citizens. Before they acquired the farm the position was comparable to that in Cambridgeshire. Henry I issued a writ to the bishop of Ely and the barons of Cambridgeshire which had the object of making the borough of Cambridge the one 'port' in the shire. 'Indubitably', wrote Maitland, 'if all traffic by water were thus banned to the hithes of the county town, that town would be a gainer. Still it was toll that the king wanted, and that toll would be paid to the king's officers for the king's use. It is therefore only by a stretch of words that we can give this remarkable writ a place among the borough's Charters of Liberties.'[3] But when the Cambridge burgesses acquired the farm of the borough in 1185 they no doubt changed their view of Henry's writ, and thought it worthy of a high place among their liberties.

In his *Gild Merchant*, Dr Gross lays it down that the history of the Gild Merchant begins with the Norman Conquest.[4] As a broad generalisation this may be correct, but it must be noted that one of Henry II's writs expressly states that the Lincoln gild had existed in the times of Edward and William and Henry, kings of England.[5] The statement may be nothing more than a rhetorical way of saying that it had existed for a long time, so long that its origin was uncertain, but the assertion is not to be lightly dismissed. It receives some support from the Domesday evidence that Torksey and the neighbouring village of Hardwick rendered in Lincoln the fifth penny of the city's geld.[6] The traders of Torksey (which is described as a *suburbium*, evidently of Lincoln) were taxed with the traders of Lincoln, perhaps through the medium of a gild of which they were members, 'the gild merchant of the men of the city and of the other merchants of the county'.

Lincoln being the largest place in the county, the city merchants must always have dominated the gild. When the citizens began to farm the king's revenues, they, as citizens, acquired a direct financial interest in a concern which they (or much the same people) as merchants, already controlled.

[1] *B.B.C.* (1), p. 210; Birch, p. 19.
[2] *B.B.C.* (1), p. 204; Birch, p. 1.
[3] *Cambridge Borough Charters*, p. xiii.
[4] Vol. 1, p. 2.
[5] Birch, p. 1. Gross notes this at op. cit. 1, 13 n.
[6] *L.D.* p. 12.

It comes, therefore, as no surprise to find that presently the two bodies were so closely linked as to become different aspects of the same thing. There were merchants of the county who were not citizens, but who paid city gelds in order to enjoy city privileges; and there were no doubt citizens who, not being merchants, were not members of the gild. The same people were, however, the leading spirits in both gild and city, and the old court of burwarmote, which had met at the mootstone by St Peter of Lincoln, was transferred to the more modern gildhall, a transfer symbolic of the close association of the court and the gild. Probably the merchants had attained to power in the court by various processes such as intermarriage, the purchase of burgages, payment of taxes, and service in office. By 1237 Henry III was asking the good men of Lincoln to give to the friars minor 'the place where their pleas were held, that used to be their gildhall'.[1] In the later years of the thirteenth century the gild merchant was, it appears, only a name for the monopoly of foreign trade within the county which the city was struggling to enforce; the court of burwarmote, in a new setting, with new civic officers, was to last for centuries.

As was almost inevitable in a community of perhaps 7,000 persons, the real control was in the hands of a small wealthy group, the 'caucus in the gildhall',[2] and their names can be gathered from the recorded names of the bailiffs who accounted at the Exchequer for the farm of the city.[3] In twenty-five years, twenty-three persons held the office, two each year. Several of them, Warner, James of Holm, Robert son of Martin and perhaps William of Paris, belonged to families which were to hold their places in the select group of magnates for a century to come.[4] Ralf the villein, who served for four years, recalls the provision in a writ of Henry II that if anyone should dwell in the city for a year and a day without challenge and should pay the customs of the city, and the citizens could show that the challenger was in the realm without making challenge, he should remain in peace in the city as a citizen without plea.[5] Ralf's name implies that he had begun life as a villein attached to a manor: the rule of a year and a day must have been one of the most cherished of the city's liberties, and an important way of recruiting the ranks of the citizens. Little is known of some others who served the office of bailiff. Ailwin Net held land at Ingham.[6] Hugh Fleming took part in an assault on the Jews in 1191, and his fine of 20 marks places him in the ranks of the wealthy: John son of Suave was fortunate enough to escape with a fine of two marks.[7]

[1] *C.C.R.* 1234–7, p. 495.
[2] Stephenson, *Borough and Town*, p. 172.
[3] See Appendix IV.
[4] See Appendix V.
[5] *B.B.C.* (1), p. 104; Birch, p. 2.
[6] *D.C.* pp. 7, 15.
[7] P.R. 3 *and* 4 *Richard I*, II, 15–16.

The list of citizens fined for taking part in the assault on the Jews is an interesting one. The names that the Normans brought have prevailed, sometimes in the last generation: William son of Ougrim, Walter son of Wulmer, William son of Brictive (OE. Beorhtgifu), Roger and Alan sons of Brand, Robert son of Suartebrand, Robert son of Goscelin, Nicholas son of Gunnild (ON. Gunnhildr), Martin son of Ædric, Peter son-in-law of Leofric, William son of Gladewin, Thomas son of Goda, Robert son of Gamel (ON. Gamall). Others clung to the old names; Wiger the palmer, Gundred the tanner, Godwin the rich, Wigot son of Wigot, old Gamel, Ulf of Hundesgate, Osbert son of Turgar, Leofwin the moneyer. These latter were, however, in a dwindling minority, and it would presently become a noticeable eccentricity to use an English or Scandinavian name. Those in the list are, it seems, a representative cross-section of the community. Several of the notables appear in it, and with them are five tailors, four tanners, three weavers, a dyer, a porter, a mercer, a draper, a moneyer, a boatman, and the son of a smith. The fines range from £100 to half a mark.[1]

There were in the city two groups of men who though they dwelt in it were yet not of it. Of one group, the Jews, something is said elsewhere.[2] The other class consisted of the weavers and fullers. In 1130 the Lincoln weavers paid a gold mark (six pounds) for their gild, and two hunters to have their customs as the king had commanded by his writ.[3] In the same year there were gilds of weavers in London and Oxford (paying £16 and a gold mark respectively), and in the early years of Henry II's reign there were such gilds also at York, Winchester, Huntingdon and Nottingham. There seems to have been a special conflict of interest between the weavers and fullers and the other trades. The monopoly of their own craft secured for the weavers by their gild caused resentment. In 1200 the citizens of London, for a payment to the Exchequer, secured the abolition of the London weavers' gild, though it was restored within a few years. The laws of Winchester, Oxford, Beverley and Marlborough concerning weavers and fullers drew a distinction between the craftsman and the freeman of the borough. If a craftsman became rich and wished to be a freeman, he must first forswear his craft and get rid of his tools from his house. No weaver or fuller must go outside his town to sell his own cloth, nor must he sell to any save a merchant of the town.[4] The Lincoln weavers were in the same position as their brethren in other towns. Their names appear in lists of persons fined for assaulting Jews, and they become pledges for other

[1] P.R. 3 *and* 4 *Richard I*, II, 15–16.

[2] See Chapter XI.

[3] P.R. 31 *Henry I*, pp. 109, 114.

[4] Ashley, *Economic History*, I, i, 81–3.

people, but they are not found among any groups of citizens. They are not free of the city.

It happens that there is a little more evidence in Lincoln about the allied trades of fullers and dyers. In 1200 the men of these trades complained in the king's court that the alderman and bailiffs of Lincoln seized and detained their cloth, and they claimed the right of dyeing as free citizens, as they had it in the time of Henry I and Henry II; and they pleaded the king's charter which granted to the citizens of Lincoln their liberties according to the liberty of London and the laws of the city of Lincoln. In defence the alderman and bailiffs roundly declared that the fullers had no law or fellowship with free citizens, and that the dyers dyed contrary to the law and custom of the city. As the claimants could produce nothing save the general words of the charter, it was decreed that they were at the mercy of the court.[1] The following year, however, a like dispute between the dyers and the citizens went in favour of the dyers by default, as the citizens did not come to the court, and excused themselves from showing their liberties. The court ordered that the dyers should continue their office, and that the bailiffs should restore their chattels.[2]

In the first of these cases it was only of the fullers that the alderman and bailiffs said that they had no law or fellowship with free citizens; of the dyers it was only said that they dyed contrary to custom, a much vaguer phrase, and when the dyers returned to the attack the citizens did not resist them. It is clear, therefore, that (as in other towns) the fullers were grouped with the weavers in their exclusion from the liberties of the city, but that the dyers were free citizens.

Henry II, under whom the city had prospered greatly, died on 6 July 1189, and his son Richard I hurried to England to prepare for his crusade to the Holy Land. In a number of places the fervour aroused by these preparations served to cloak an attack upon the Jews. At Lynn and Norwich, and above all at York, Jews were plundered and slain. Stamford was invaded by bands of crusaders, and, though most of the Jews escaped to the castle, their houses were sacked.[3] It was afterwards complained that Gerard de Camville was implicated in the Stamford raid.[4] At Lincoln also an attack was prepared, but the Jews were warned in time, and took refuge in the castle.[5]

As a result of the Lincoln outbreak, fines were imposed on nearly 100

[1] *C.R. Rolls*, I, 259–60. *Abbreviatio Placitorum*, p. 65.

[2] *C.R. Rolls*, II, 20. And see *Cal. Inq. Misc.* I, no. 1202.

[3] William of Newburgh, *Chronicles of Stephen* (R.S.), I, 310, 311. Ralph de Diceto, *Opera Historica* (R.S.), II, 75.

[4] Roger Hoveden, *Chronica* (R.S.), III, 242.

[5] William of Newburgh, *Chronicles of Stephen* (R.S.), I, 312.

citizens and others,[1] and the citizens lost their farm of the city. They had continued to farm it on Richard's accession, but for the second half of the fiscal year 1189–90 the city was in the hands of Hugh Bardolf, a royal official.[2] Bardolf also accounted for the first part of the next year, whereafter the city was farmed by Gerard de Camville, who was sheriff.[3]

Hostilities soon broke out between Richard's chancellor Longchamp, who was left in charge of the realm when the king went on his crusade, and the king's brother John. Gerard de Camville, declaring that he was John's man, refused to be answerable to Longchamp. As soon as he was able, Longchamp marched to Lincoln, besieged the castle, deprived Gerard of the shrievalty, and summoned him to answer before the justiciars for having made his castle a hold of robbers and bandits. Presently, however, Gerard and Longchamp came to terms, and Gerard was restored to the shrievalty[4] and confirmed in the constableship of Lincoln Castle. Soon afterwards the sum of £82 was spent in strengthening the bailey of the castle, work made necessary, perhaps, by the chancellor's siege. There is no indication that Camville took part in John's rebellion in 1193.

Richard I returned to England in 1194, and dealt promptly with John's supporters. Camville was charged at Nottingham with harbouring the robbers of merchants who were going to Stamford fair, and deprived of both the castle and the shire. The king put up the shires of Lincoln and York to auction. Longchamp made a bid for Yorkshire, but was outbidden by Geoffrey, archbishop of York. Simon of Kyme secured Lincolnshire.[5] Camville recovered his estates by a payment of 2,000 marks,[6] but the castle and the shrievalty were lost to him for the remainder of the reign: the castle he regained on the accession of John.[7] The Pipe Roll for 1195 records a payment to two knights to keep the peace in the city of Lincoln (appointed no doubt in pursuance of the general edict of the peace of 1194), and two clerks for the same time, and two sergeants to attach and summon pleas:[8] this temporary establishment suggests that its business was to carry on the civic administration during the suspension of the city's farm.

During his brief stay in England, Richard I was engaged in raising money for his crusade, and he was willing to sell charters to boroughs, and,

[1] P.R. 3 *and* 4 *Richard I*, pp. 15, 16, 242. Supra, p. 188.

[2] P.R. 2 *Richard I*, p. 76. Tait, op. cit. p. 180.

[3] P.R. 3 *and* 4 *Richard I*, pp. 2, 232.

[4] Mrs D. M. Stenton, Introduction to P.R. 3 *and* 4 *Richard I*, p. xvi, and references there cited.

[5] P.R. 6 *Richard I*, pp. xvii–xix, 102.

[6] Ibid. p. 118.

[7] P.R. 1 *John*, p. xxi.

[8] P.R. 7 *Richard I*, p. 159. The knights' wages work out at approximately a shilling a day.

indeed, to almost all comers. In 1194 the citizens of Lincoln bought a charter from him for the sum of 500 marks. The transaction was strictly for cash.[1] It was issued at Winchester on 23 April by the hand of the Chancellor Longchamp, and was witnessed by Archbishop Hubert Walter, William Marshal, Geoffrey son of John, and Hugh Bardolf.[2]

The Pipe Roll says that the citizens were granted the customs of Northampton, but the charter specifies the customs of London, and it was London that was always cited in support of claims to liberties in Lincoln. In the first place it granted that the citizens other than the king's moneyers and servants need not plead outside the city in any matter except concerning land outside of it. Whether this is a new grant is uncertain: London had such a privilege in 1131 and had it confirmed in 1194. In any case it was a much-valued privilege, and it was important to have it properly granted and recorded. Then the citizens were exempted from the fine for murder; duelling was forbidden; in pleas of the Crown they might defend themselves according to the customs of London; billeting by the marshal was forbidden.

Exemption from toll and lastage throughout the kingdom and in the seaports was granted; miskenning, or the dismissal of a suit for some technical rule of pleading, was forbidden; the court of burwarmote was to be held only once weekly. It was also provided that if anyone in England took toll or custom from the men of Lincoln without making redress, the bailiff of Lincoln was to take distress therefor at Lincoln: he would retaliate by distraining upon the goods of merchants coming from the town where the toll was taken. Exemption from several old payments, bridgetoll, childwite, year's gift and scotale, was also granted.

The most interesting provision comes last: the farm of the city is restored to the citizens at the former rent of £180, and the citizens were authorised to choose a bailiff from among themselves who should be suitable to the king and to themselves. The two parts of this provision go together, because it was the bailiff's chief duty to collect and account for the annual farm. The following year the citizens rendered their own account at the Exchequer,[3] though, unfortunately, the clerks did not return to their practice under Henry II of recording the names of the accounting persons.

The grant was stated to be made to the citizens that they and their heirs might have and hold these things by inheritance of the king and his heirs. The words, taken at their face-value, imply a freehold, a perpetual right, though theory must take account of the fact that the privileges were enjoyed only at the pleasure of the king, to be forfeited or re-bought and

[1] P.R. 6 *Richard I*, p. 118.
[2] Birch, pp. 3–5.
[3] P.R. 7 *Richard I*, p. 152.

confirmed at his will. Even so, they were not likely to be forfeited without some cause, and when they were re-bought the transaction was decently presented in the guise of a confirmation. Between 1189 and 1216 eighteen towns were granted the *firma burgi*, and such an innovation, once made, could not be lightly revoked. As Professor Tait says, the change 'must have played no inconsiderable part in the decline of the power of the sheriff and in the evolution of that nice balance of attraction and repulsion between county and borough which resulted in the House of Commons. Henry I had laid the train, and Henry II's restrictive policy could not have been permanently maintained'.[1]

[1] *Medieval English Borough*, p. 179.

ST MARY'S GUILDHALL

From a drawing in the Ross Collection at Burton Hall

HOUSE IN THE COURTYARD OF ST MARY'S GUILDHALL

From a drawing in the Ross Collection at Burton Hall [*See p.* 164

PLATE 16

HIGH BRIDGE

From a painting by Peter de Wint, by permission of Miss Helen Barlow

[See pp. 182-3

CHAPTER X

THE THIRTEENTH CENTURY

RICHARD I died on 6 April 1199 of a wound received at the siege of Chalus in the Limousin, and his brother John was crowned king on 27 May. That autumn the citizens of Lincoln, perhaps not without an indication of the alternative before them, sought a new charter from him. Apparently it cost 300 marks, half of that sum being paid at the Exchequer in cash and the other half left owing.[1] It was issued on 23 April 1200.

The charter resembles that of Richard in most respects,[2] though it may be noted that the right of retaliation for toll wrongly taken was abolished, and a £10 penalty substituted. The charter also directs the election of four of the more lawful and discreet citizens to keep the pleas of the Crown and protect other royal rights, and to see that the bailiffs treat both rich and poor justly and lawfully. These are the coroners, and their number remained unchanged until 1835. Their duties were not confined to cases of sudden death, but at first extended to many criminal and even to some civil matters; and the royal permission to appoint such officers for the city as distinct from the county of Lincoln marks a stage in Lincoln's growing self-government.

It is also provided by the charter that the citizens taking counsel together may elect two of the more lawful and discreet citizens and present them to the chief justice at Westminster. These two are well and faithfully to keep the office of provost or bailiff (*prepositus*), holding office during good conduct unless removed by the citizens in common counsel together. Richard's charter had provided for one bailiff: there is no indication of any special significance in the change, which may well have been made in order to conform with existing practice.

The king's grant was no protection against the king's rapacity. John spent more time in Lincolnshire in 1200–1 than was pleasant. In November 1200 he met the king of Scots, William the Lion, at Lincoln, receiving his homage without the walls; and he assisted at the burial of St Hugh. Most of his other recorded activities were concerned with extortion. The unfortunate citizens, who had just bought a charter, found themselves owing 700 marks and 7 palfreys for having their liberties which the king confirmed to them, and that they might be quit of Martin Martel's appeal touching the breaking of the king's peace.[3] So was justice bought and sold. In 1202

[1] P.R. 1 *John*, p. 151.
[2] Birch, p. 6.
[3] P.R. 3 *John*, pp. xiii–xiv, 18.

there were several impositions. The men of Lincoln made fine in 40 marks in order that they might buy and sell dyed cloth as in the time of King Henry; that is, that they might be free from an assize of Richard I imposing a standard width and quality on manufacturers in the interest of buyers. The citizens were fined £160. 4*s*. by way of a gift assessed by the king's justices on individual men. The weavers, besides paying the usual £6 for their gild, were fined 56*s*. 8*d*. In the general tallage of the same year two citizens, Reimbald the rich, and Richard of Newport, were tallaged 20 marks and £6 respectively; the city owed 100 marks for respite of pleas; there followed another tallage of a large number of named citizens, the tax varying from 5 marks downwards. The city in its corporate capacity (*communa*) owed £89. 15*s*. 4*d*. There follows a list of fines.[1] Tallage was the accepted tax upon the boroughs: its imposition by the king was entirely arbitrary, and it was greatly dreaded by townsmen.

There was emerging a new aspect of city life. Bailiffs chosen by the citizens, or at least from among the citizens, there had been since the early days of Henry II: but the bailiffs were royal officers, collecting the royal revenues, even though by royal grace the revenues were farmed. The bailiffs' collection belonged to the king, though when the citizens had the farm of the city there might be a surplus which belonged to the citizens collectively, forming the nucleus of a common purse or a common chest. As has been noticed above, the *city*, as distinct from the citizens, paid money to the king. The *communa* had money of its own. Used in this context, *communa* had no special legal significance; Lincoln and Grimsby had a *communa*, but so also had Torksey and Clee.[2] The word merely recorded a fact, namely that there was a common purse, supplied by the citizens among themselves, or recruited from sources to which they were collectively entitled. Yet the idea of the commune, which came from France, had great social and political significance: under its influence 'the burgesses were organising themselves as sworn associations and in the more advanced towns were symbolising their new unity of administration by setting up an entirely new officer, the mayor, with a council of twelve or twenty-four to act with him on behalf of the community'.[3]

The development of communal activity into the later idea of a legal corporation was marked by the appearance of a new civic officer. The alderman has already been found in conjunction with the bailiffs;[4] in 1206 there occurs the earliest reference so far noticed to the mayor.[5] The alder-

[1] P.R. 4 *John*, pp. xx, 219, 239, 240–3.
[2] Ibid. p. 237.
[3] Tait, *Medieval English Borough* (1936), p. 234. For the twenty-four of Lincoln, see pp. 294 et seq.
[4] Supra, p. 189.
[5] Mrs D. M. Stenton, *Earliest Lincolnshire Assize Rolls* (L.R.S.), no. 1448.

man of 1200 was probably Adam son of Reginald son of Eilsi (OE. Ælfsige). In 1201 Adam witnesses as alderman, with John the Fleming and Richard son of James (his nephew and brother-in-law respectively) as bailiffs.[1] In other charters (probably of 1202) he is found witnessing with Thomas of the Bail and Hamo of Wigford as bailiffs.[2] Probably he was the mayor of 1206; certainly he held the new office in 1210, when the citizens paid £100 to the Exchequer that they might have Adam as mayor so long as he should please the king and serve him well.[3] He still held office in 1212, when his bailiffs were Thomas of Paris and Ralf son of Lefwine;[4] and in 1214, his bailiffs being Roger and Robert.[5] Several other charters name him as mayor, two pairs of bailiffs being mentioned with him, Walter Cause and Nicholas son of Gunnilda, and Hugh of Marston and James son of Brand.[6] As will be noted later, Adam was still mayor in 1216.

Dr Tait marshals evidence from a number of towns to show that the alderman was the head of the gild merchant, and that as the French conception of the commune took hold he assumed the new French name of 'the mayor'. At Oxford the citizens in their double capacity as members of the commune and of the gild speak of 'our alderman', and with his help transact town business which has nothing to do with trade. At Southampton the alderman is described as 'the head of the town and the gild'. The alderman of the gild merchant of Leicester about 1226 is called 'the alderman of Leicester', and he continued as chief officer of the town until his title was changed to that of mayor. The Southampton gild succeeded in suppressing the mayoralty when it was created, and finally invested its alderman with the title of mayor. It seems that there was a tradition or belief at Chester and Lynn that, before they had a mayor, the warden or alderman of the gild merchant was their civic head.[7]

As Dr Tait also points out, the action of the alderman and bailiffs of Lincoln in 1200 had a gild aspect: it was against the fullers and dyers. The scanty Lincoln evidence certainly conforms with his explanation of the transition from alderman to mayor, and ample evidence shows that Adam was a member of a wealthy merchant family and a man who might be expected to hold high office in the gild merchant.[8] This office of alderman is heard of only once more. Adam was deprived of the mayoralty in 1216: on 3 November 1217 a writ was issued to the bailiffs of Lincoln ordering them to give such seisin of the aldermanry of Lincoln and its appurtenances

[1] D. & C., Dii, 76/3/9. See Appendix v.

[2] D. & C., Dii, 77/1/3, 8. See Mrs D. M. Stenton, op. cit. no. 1012.

[3] Madox, *History and Antiquities of the Exchequer*, p. 352.

[4] Madox, *Firma Burgi*, p. 182, n. (b).

[5] D. & C., Dii, 80/3/7.

[6] D. & C., Dii, 79/1/107; 80/3/11.

[7] Tait, op. cit. pp. 226–32.

[8] Infra, Appendix v.

to John de Holm as his uncle Adam had on the day when he quitted the mayoralty (*die quo se dimisit de majoritate*).[1] The writ implies that the offices were still distinct, and indeed they must have been, for on 6 October 1217 William nephew of Warner was confirmed as mayor.[2] The writ is perhaps hardly sufficient to establish the theory that the aldermanry was hereditary; Adam was almost certainly not dead at the time, though John de Holm seems to have become his heir. Perhaps the writ was a bid after King John's death to placate a powerful mercantile interest in the city which was offended by Adam's deprivation. As far as is known, John had no successors in the separate office of alderman.[3]

Casual references show that by this time there was a large civic establishment. In 1202, besides the two bailiffs and the four coroners there were four bedells of the city.[4] No doubt then, as later, their duties were to attend upon the mayor and the court of burwarmote, to keep the peace and to execute legal processes. There were also two clerks of the city, or notaries, whose duty it was to draw up deeds, to keep such records as the court had and to conduct official correspondence: in the first days of the mayoralty the clerks were John son of Adam and John de Brancegath, who may also have been called John of Bristowe.[5]

About the same time the cities and boroughs were beginning to use common seals to authenticate their common or corporate acts. The citizens of Oxford and York were using one about 1191, and the burgesses of Ipswich in 1200. It happens that the common seal of London is not mentioned until 1219, though this omission must be accidental.[6] The earliest reference yet found to the common seal of Lincoln occurs in the Barlings Cartulary, in a document which can perhaps be dated 1220–30. The cartulary registers an agreement between Peter de Paris, chaplain, and Thomas son of Raimbald of Lincoln: Thomas built a mill near stone houses of Peter in Sapergate contrary to the custom of the city; and he agreed to indemnify Peter against damage caused to his houses in tile, timber or wall by the mill. In the event of damage the matter was to be referred to the mayor and two other lawful citizens whom the mayor should appoint with him. The parties attached their seals, and for better security the mayor and

[1] *Rot. Lit. Claus.* I, 340b; Madox, *Firma Burgi*, p. 14.

[2] *Patent Rolls*, 1216–25, p. 100.

[3] This office of alderman had of course no connection with the twelve aldermen who appear later. Mrs Green (*Town Life in the Fifteenth Century*, II, 279 n.) says that in London, Canterbury and Lincoln the aldermen were the hereditary owners of the various wards. It seems that as to Lincoln she confused the gild alderman with a ward alderman, and probably relied on the writ of 1217 for the view that the aldermanry was hereditary.

[4] *Earliest Lincolnshire Assize Rolls* (L.R.S.), no. 1012.

[5] D. & C., Dii, 75/1/39, 75/2/5, 79/1/140.

[6] Tait, op. cit. p. 236.

citizens attached their common seal.[1] Another reference to the Lincoln common seal belongs to 1263, when the mayor and commonalty made an agreement with the dean and chapter about the rights of the cathedral church, both bodies affixing their seals.[2] Analogy makes it likely that a seal was in use by the commonalty at the beginning of the century. No common seal earlier than the fifteenth century has survived, but the matrix of a mayoralty seal attributed to the thirteenth century was presented to the British Museum in 1850 by Lady Fellows. It is described in the Museum's *Catalogue of Seals* as follows:

> The Virgin standing on a carved corbel under a trefoiled arch, crocketed and supported on architectural piers, with crown, the Child with nimbus, on the left arm, in the right hand a ball. In the field on each side a lion passant guardant of England. SIGILL' MAIORITATIS LINCOLNIE. Beaded borders.[3]

'The seal of the mayoralty made of silver in a purse with four keys' is mentioned in the inventory of effects delivered by the mayor to his successor in 1514.[4] How it came to be lost is unknown. On the initiative of Colonel Williams, who was mayor of Lincoln in 1899, the design of the seal is now used as a badge by the mayors of Lincoln, reminding them of the long succession in which they stand.

Such refinements were, however, remote from realities in the turbulent days of King John and the first mayor. In 1207 Pope Innocent III chose Stephen Langton, a cardinal whose family came from the village of Langton by Wragby near Lincoln, to be archbishop of Canterbury. The king refused to accept him, and the following year the pope laid England under an interdict. A number of bishoprics had fallen vacant, including Lincoln, which had been so since the death of William of Blois in 1206. In 1209 John nominated Hugh, archdeacon of Wells, to the see of Lincoln. The new bishop was bidden to go to France to seek consecration at the hands of the archbishop of Rouen. Hugh instead secured consecration from Langton. John, in consequence of this act of defiance, dismissed Hugh from his office.[5]

In 1212 John moved north on one of his progresses, which, whether undertaken from policy or restlessness, had the advantage of impressing

[1] Barlings Cartulary, f. 65d (and see f. 64d). The seal is mentioned *c.* 1237 in P.R.O. Lists, 15, *Ancient Correspondence*, IV, no. 11.

[2] *R.A.* III, 300–4.

[3] British Museum, *Catalogue of Seals*, II, 5064. And see Williams in *Lincs N. & Q.* VI, 101. The mayoralty seal and the common seal of 1445 are reproduced in Plate 21.

[4] C.C.M. 1511–41, f. 166. The mayor's seal and the common seal were both fixed to a chantry presentation in 1344, the latter by order of the citizens present. Chapter Acts, Liber III, f. 15.

[5] Roger of Wendover, *Chronica* (R.S.), II, 54.

people with a sense of his omnipresence.[1] He visited Lincolnshire, and apparently Lincoln, for Adam the mayor had to buy his goodwill with a fine of 500 marks. The whole city was mainprised to pay this enormous exaction. The sum of £219 was paid into the Treasury, and Thomas of Paris and Ralf son of Lefwine the bailiffs became pledges for payment of the balance.[2]

The king submitted to the papacy in 1213, and the interdict was raised. His German allies were defeated at Bouvines in Flanders by the French in 1214, and at home he was confronted by a band of discontented barons. At Easter the barons assembled at Stamford: one of their forces captured London, and in Whitsun week another party established itself in Lincoln.[3] Meanwhile the barons' main body had marched south and been admitted to London. John met them at Staines, and on 15 June 1215 Magna Carta was sealed at Runnymede. Among the bishops present on that famous day was the bishop of Lincoln, Hugh of Wells, and to him were issued two writs for the execution of the charter, one for Oxford and one for Bedford. He received them on 24 June.[4] The usual practice was to direct the sheriff to proclaim the charter throughout his shire: and it has been suggested that the reason why the task of publishing the charter in the counties of Oxford and Bedford (both within his diocese) was given to the bishop of Lincoln may have been that the sheriff of Bedford had been displaced, and the sheriff of Oxford was, it appears, one of John's foreign mercenaries.[5] It was, however, customary to deposit in the cathedral church of any diocese the charters issued by kings in special circumstances.[6] Whatever the reason for its deposit in Lincoln, one of the four surviving original copies is the most cherished possession of the library of the dean and chapter.[7]

John had no intention of observing the charter. He appealed to Pope Innocent III, who declared it void, and issued a bull of excommunication against the disturbers of the country. Both parties prepared for war, and the barons offered the crown of England to Louis the dauphin of France.

After ravaging the midlands and the north the king entered Lincolnshire. He was at Lincoln from 23 to 27 February 1216.[8] There he imposed

[1] Ramsey, *Angevin Empire* (1903), p. 433.

[2] Madox, *Firma Burgi*, p. 182.

[3] Walter of Coventry, *Memoriale* (R.S.), II, 221.

[4] *Rot. Lit. Pat.* p. 180b.

[5] F. W. Brooks, 'The Provenance of the Lincoln Magna Carta' in *Lincs N. & Q.* XVIII, 100–3.

[6] R. L. Poole, in *E.H.R.* XXVIII (1913), pp. 444–53; Kathleen Major in *Lincolnshire Magazine*, IV (1939), p. 110. Apparently the existence of the Lincoln copy was unknown until it was discovered by the Record Commissioners in 1810.

[7] The word 'Lincolnia' is endorsed in two places on folds of the parchment, though McKechnie (*Magna Carta* (2nd ed. 1914), p. 167) says these endorsements are in a later hand.

[8] Itinerary in *Rot. Lit. Pat.*

on the unhappy citizens the enormous penalty of £1,000; on the 28th, at Stamford, he acknowledged the receipt in his chamber by the hands of Peter of the Bail, clerk, and William of Paris of the sum of £50 in money and plate on account of the fine.[1] The utter unpreparedness of the city for this exaction is indicated by the size of the payment made, even that being partly in kind. To make it clear that he would not be trifled with, the king took hostages for payment of the balance. On 5 March he ordered the constable of Oxford to receive Reimbald the rich and Peter Bridge (*de ponte*), burgesses of Lincoln, and to keep them in Oxford with honour until further orders.[2] Two others, Alan Braund and Richard son of Duve, were sent to Nottingham to be held there by Philip Marc, the sheriff: and on 5 April the king told Philip that if the citizens paid him the two hostages were to be released.[3] On 20 April Reimbald and Peter were ordered to be sent from Oxford to Nottingham,[4] and on 15 May Philip Marc was authorised to release the citizens of Lincoln in his custody.[5]

It is either to John's February visit to Lincoln or to one made later in the year that there must be attributed the story about John and the lady Nicholaa de la Haye, the constable of the castle. Her husband, Gerard de Camville, was dead. The story was told by the jurors, whose evidence is given in the Hundred Rolls 60 years later. They said that when John came to Lincoln, the Lady Nicholaa went out of the eastern gate of the castle to meet the king carrying the castle keys in her hands. She offered the keys to him as her lord, saying that she was a woman of great age, and unable to bear the burden of office any longer. Whereupon the king besought her, saying: 'My beloved Nicholaa, I will that you keep the castle as hitherto, until I shall order otherwise.' The jurors added that she retained it as long as John lived, and that after his death she kept it under King Henry III.[6] Nicholaa resigned in 1226, and died before 20 November 1230.[7]

The papal bull against the leaders of the baronial party arrived in England about the time of John's visit to Lincoln, and shortly afterwards the papal commissioners excommunicated thirty lesser offenders, among them Adam of Lincoln. The city of London alone treated the bull with contempt.[8]

There can be no doubt that Adam of Lincoln was Adam the mayor. It is significant that his name does not appear among those who accounted for part of the £1,000 fine or who were held as hostages for its payment,

[1] Ibid. p. 167b. [2] Ibid. p. 168b. [3] Ibid. p. 174b.
[4] Ibid. p. 178. [5] Ibid. p. 180. [6] *R.H.* I, 309, 315.
[7] Farrer, *Honors and Knights' Fees* (1924), II, 221.
[8] Roger of Wendover, *Chronica* (R.S.), II, 170–1.

and he is not likely to have been anathematised among quite a select company unless he had taken an active part in the baronial campaign. Presumably he was absent on service with the barons during John's February visit to Lincoln. His inclusion by name in the bull is an acknowledgement that he was a person of some note in national as well as local affairs, and it explains his later removal from office.

Louis of France landed in England in May in response to the baronial invitation, and received the adhesion of the malcontents. He occupied London and Winchester, and a party of his troops under Gilbert de Gant and Robert de Ropsley took the city of Lincoln, though the castle withstood them; and they laid a tax on the whole of Lindsey. In August Gant was reinforced by a party from the north, but Nicholaa de la Haye, the constable of the castle, bought them off.[1] In September King John entered the eastern counties, and Gant, who had remained in Lincoln, fled. The king entered Lincoln on the 22nd, visited Scotter and Stow for three days, and returned to the city on the 28th, remaining there until 2 October. Then he went to Grimsby and south to Louth, Boston, Spalding and King's Lynn, burning and sacking all that lay in his path. At Lynn he fell ill, and moving thence by Swineshead and Sleaford, died at Newark on the night of 18–19 October.

As has been noticed, Michaelmas (29 September) was spent by John at Lincoln. At that season of the year the general court leet was held, and the bailiffs were appointed. There were few, if any, precedents governing the election of a mayor, and in consequence of the disgrace of Adam the device was adopted of attaching the office to that of the senior bailiff. On 30 December 1216 letters patent were issued to the honest men of Lincoln telling them that the king had appointed William nephew of Warner and Peter of the Bail to be bailiffs of the city as long as it should please the king;[2] and on 6 October following further letters were issued to the citizens confirming William nephew of Warner as mayor, as he was in the time of John.[3] He was to be 'your mayor' and 'our bailiff', thereby making it clear that the mayor was a popular and civic official, but the bailiff was a royal servant, though himself a citizen. In 1218 the citizens, having by common consent elected Peter Bridge to be their mayor, cautiously sought and obtained royal confirmation of the election. Peter, like his predecessor, was both mayor and bailiff.[4] This early combination of the two offices is illustrated by a case in *Bracton's Note Book*. The bailiffs of Lincoln were summoned to court to answer the burgesses of Beverley: the bailiffs who appeared were 'the mayor of Lincoln and Robert son of

[1] Walter of Coventry, *Memoriale* (R.S.), II, 230.
[2] *Rot. Lit. Pat.* p. 162.
[3] *Patent Rolls*, 1216–25, p. 100.
[4] Ibid. p. 160.

Eudo the bailiffs'.[1] The practice of combining the offices cannot however have lasted long, for deeds of land show that quite early in the reign of Henry III the mayor and two bailiffs acted as witnesses.

It seems probable that the choice of new civic officers was dictated by John at Michaelmas 1216: and the royal acknowledgement of the mayoralty in 1217 is of interest because earlier royal letters had reserved the title of mayor to two cities, as for example, in a letter of 1214 to the mayor and barons of London, the mayor and good men of Winchester, and the good men of Northampton, Lincoln, York, and other towns.[2] The office and title were of popular creation, and only gradually established themselves beyond dispute.

After John's death Gilbert de Gant, created earl of Lincoln by Louis, returned to the city and resumed the siege of the castle. Louis followed him, but all his efforts to induce Nicholaa to yield the castle failed. He then returned to London, and sent Hugh the castellan of Arras to take up his quarters at Lincoln. Hugh persuaded the baronial army to join him in the siege, declaring that the castle was about to fall. The whole force was quartered in and around the city.

The forces defending the cause of the infant King Henry III were commanded by William the Marshal, who summoned all loyal knights and castellans to muster at Newark on Whit Monday, 15 May. After his submission to the papacy John had received the support of the pope, and Louis had been excommunicated and his invasion of England denounced. Now the papal legate excommunicated Louis again, with all his accomplices and abettors, especially those who were besieging Lincoln Castle, 'together with the city of Lincoln and all its contents'; and he granted plenary absolution to all who, having made a truthful confession, supported the king's arms.

The most direct route from Newark to Lincoln was by the Fosse Way, but the disadvantage of this route was that it would have brought the attackers to the wrong end of the city, and have made it necessary for them to fight their way through Wigford and the walled city to the castle; it was probably to avoid this that before the first battle of Lincoln the earls of Gloucester and Chester had forded the Fossdyke to the west of the city.[3] Accordingly, the royal army marched north-westward to Torksey and Stow, and thence reached the high ground: they were thereby able to approach the castle from the west, from which direction alone had they any chance of getting into touch with the defenders without entering the city.

[1] Ed. Maitland, *Bracton's Note Book*, II, 121. And see Round, 'Origin of the Mayoralty of London' in *Arch. Journ.* L (1893), pp. 254–5.

[2] *Rot. Lit. Pat.* p. 111b, and see p. 84b.

[3] Supra, p. 179.

The royal army advanced on the city in four 'battles', the first led by the earl of Chester, the second by the Marshal himself and his sons, the third by William Lungespee earl of Salisbury, and the fourth by Peter des Roches, bishop of Winchester. The Marshal's choice of leaders is interesting. Chester was the grandson of Ranulph les Gernons, and there seems to be little doubt that he had in mind hereditary claims on the castle: not only did he insist on being allowed to lead the van, but after the battle he was created earl of Lincoln. William Lungespee's son was later to marry Idonea de Camville, Nicholaa's granddaughter, and thereby secure the hereditary constableship of the castle. Peter des Roches was the master mind behind the attack, and he was specially equipped for the task, for not only was he a warrior, but he had been precentor of Lincoln Minster before he became a bishop, and no doubt knew the lie of the land more intimately than his colleagues.

The details of the battle have been examined with care by a number of historians, and they need only be summarised here.[1] When Louis' leaders heard of the approach of the royalists they sent out a reconnoitring party, who reported that the royalists were weaker than themselves. The comte du Perche, who commanded the French troops, insisted on making his own inspection, and was deceived by the royalist baggage guard into thinking the attackers stronger than the besiegers. He therefore insisted on keeping his forces on the defensive within the city walls. It is tempting to try to identify the gate by which these scouting parties went out, but there is no evidence on the point, and indeed there is no evidence that Newland gate, marked on Oman's map, was standing at the time of the battle.[2]

As the Marshal approached the city he paused to allow his nephew John Marshal, with a small party, to enter the castle by its postern gate. Presumably this was the castle west gate, which gave direct access to open country. The simplest story, that of Roger of Wendover, who was prior of Belvoir at the time, is that Falkes de Breauté and his crossbowmen then entered the castle, mounted the ramparts, and sent a hail of arrows down upon the besiegers within the city. Meanwhile, the rest of the royal army forced the city north gate, the Newport Arch, and as they advanced upon the enemy (along Bailgate) Falkes made a sally from the castle. He was taken prisoner and rescued, and in the ensuing struggle Perche was killed.[3] Thereupon the Frenchmen took to flight and fled downhill to the south

[1] Oman, *Art of War in the Middle Ages* (1st ed. 1898), pp. 407–13; Norgate, *Minority of Henry III* (1912), pp. 34–5 and n. ii; Ramsay, *Dawn of the Constitution* (1907), pp. 9–11; *Collected Papers of T. F. Tout*, II, 191–220, reprinted from *E.H.R.* XVIII (1903), pp. 240–65; Brooks and Oakley, 'Campaign and Battle of Lincoln, 1217' in *A.A.S.R.* XXXVI (1922), pp. 295–312.

[2] See supra, p. 157.

[3] He is commemorated by a window in Chartres Cathedral.

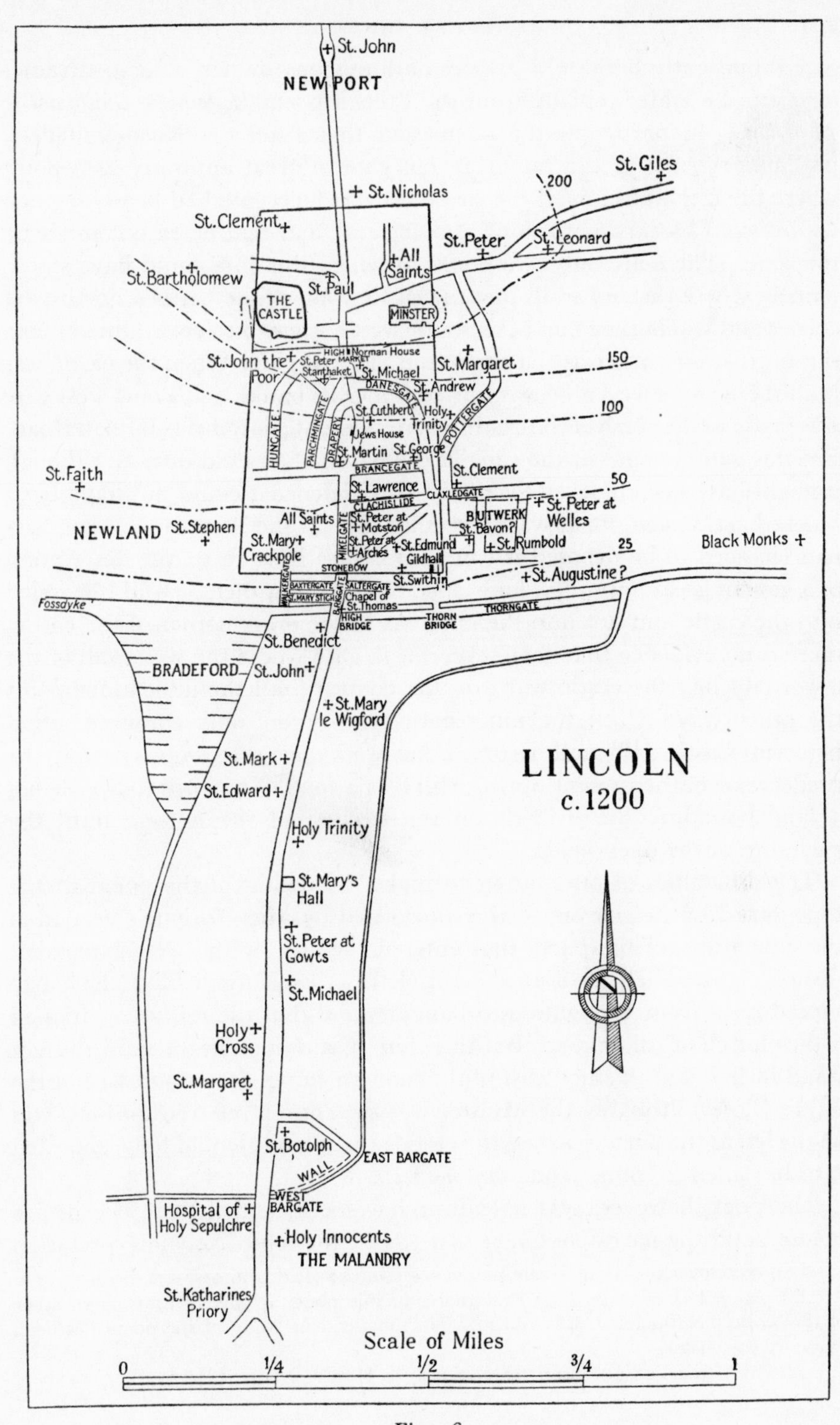

St. John
NEW PORT
St. Giles
200
St. Nicholas
St. Clement
St. Peter
St. Leonard
All Saints
St. Bartholomew
St. Paul
THE CASTLE
MINSTER
HIGH MARKET
Norman House
St. John the Poor
St. Peter Stanthaket
St. Michael
St. Margaret
150
DANESGATE
St. Andrew
St. Cuthbert
Holy Trinity
100
HUNGATE
PARCHMINGATE
DRAPERY
POTTERGATE
Jews House
St. Martin
St. George
BRANCEGATE
St. Clement
St. Faith
St. Lawrence
50
CLACHISLIDE
CLAXLEDGATE
St. Peter at Welles
All Saints
St. Peter at Motston
BUTWERK
NEWLAND
St. Stephen
St. Bavon?
St. Mary Crackpole
MIKELGATE
St. Peter at Arches
St. Edmund
St. Rumbold
25
Black Monks
Gildhall
STONEBOW
St. Swithin
St. Augustine?
BAXTERGATE
SALTERGATE
WALKERGATE
ST. MARY STIGH
BRIGGATE
Chapel of St. Thomas
Fossdyke
THORNGATE
HIGH BRIDGE
THORN BRIDGE
St. Benedict
BRADEFORD
St. John
St. Mary le Wigford
LINCOLN
c. 1200
St. Mark
St. Edward
Holy Trinity
St. Mary's Hall
St. Peter at Gowts
St. Michael
Holy Cross
St. Margaret
St. Botolph
EAST BARGATE
WALL
WEST BARGATE
Hospital of Holy Sepulchre
Holy Innocents
THE MALANDRY
St. Katharines Priory
Scale of Miles
0
1/4
1/2
3/4
1

Fig. 16.

gate (apparently Bargate).[1] To this outline many details, some contradictory, can be added, chiefly from the French poem *Histoire de Guillaume le Maréchal*.[2] In particular the poem says that Peter des Roches made a preliminary survey, and found an old gate of great antiquity at a point where the city walls joined the castle walls, which gate had been long ago (*ancïenement*) blocked with stone and cement; and that entry was made by this gate. There are only two points at which this gate could have stood, namely where the city walls met the castle walls at the castle's north-west corner and where they met at its south-west corner. Professor Oman chose the north-west corner as the site of the blocked gate. When the castle was built the Roman west gate was buried under its banks, and a new west gate was made to the north of the castle where Westgate now meets Burton Road. But this gate was not at the time of the battle a very old one, and though it might have been blocked for purposes of defence it could not have been blocked *ancïenement*, for it was in regular use. If the Roman west gateway had chanced to be exposed it would of course have fitted the description of a gate of great antiquity, long since blocked, but then it would have led into the castle and not into the city. As to the other corner of the castle, there is no evidence that there ever was a gate where the west wall of the lower city met the castle wall: on the contrary, all the indications point the other way. Until the nineteenth century the only communication between Castle Hill and Drury Lane was a narrow footway, and the predecessor of the present Spring Hill was a road of no importance, being a lane bounding waste lands on the steepest of the hillside until the enclosure of the open fields.

The difficulties of attempting to make the details of the poem fit the topography of the city are further illustrated by Miss Norgate's version of the adventures of the party that entered the city by the west gate; as it turned right, it left *un mostier* on its left. Miss Norgate says the party turned right from Westgate into Bailgate, and that the *mostier* mentioned is the church of All Saints.[3] But this church (although in the Bail) did not stand in Bailgate: it stood east of the modern James Street and within the future Close. Probably the Minster was the church referred to, for it was on the left as the party reached the castle; though one would have expected it to be called *le* (rather than *un*) *mostier*.

The poet, however, was not an archaeologist, and if these details are ignored and the narrative taken as a whole, the most likely interpretation

[1] For Wendover's account of the battle, see *Chronica* (R.S.), II, 215–17.

[2] Ed. Michel (Paris, 1894). All references to this poem are taken from one or other of the works mentioned in n. 1, p. 202. No independent study of the poem has been made by the writer.

[3] All Saints is called a minster (*monasterium*) in D. & C., Dii, 77/3/25.

is that a royalist party entered the western gate of the Bail, passed along Westgate, turned right at St Paul's and so reached the eastern gate of the castle. It is not inconsistent with Wendover's suggestion of an entry by Newport Arch and a sally from the castle.

The results of the battle were more important to Lincoln than the battle itself. The citizens had the misfortune to be committed to the side which lost, and the royalists not only seized the baggage and valuables of the rebel barons and the French nobles, but they also 'despoiled the whole city, even to the uttermost farthing'. On the strength of the papal legate's exhortation to treat the canons of the cathedral as excommunicate (they too having been against King John), they pillaged the churches, broke open chests and store rooms, and seized and carried off gold and silver, jewellery and vestments. The precentor, Geoffrey of Deeping, lost eleven thousand marks of silver which were in his custody.[1] Many of the women took to small boats with their children and their goods, but the boats, being overloaded and ill-handled, capsized and their occupants perished.[2] In derision of Louis and the barons the battle was known as 'The Fair': a reference also perhaps to the rich plunder gained by the victors.[3]

After the battle the rebels came to terms with the king's party and Louis returned to France. The Marshal at once took steps to consolidate his position. On 18 October 1216, a few hours before his death, King John had appointed Nicholaa de la Haye and Philip Marc to be joint sheriffs of Lincolnshire,[4] no doubt thinking thereby to strengthen Nicholaa's hands. On John's death Philip disappeared from the joint shrievalty, Geoffrey de Serland being appointed 'bailiff' with Nicholaa. William nephew of Warner, mayor of Lincoln, and the other true men of the city were ordered to be obedient to them.[5] On 24 May 1217 (three days after the battle) the city and county of Lincoln (including, it appears, the castle) were committed to William Lungespee, earl of Salisbury, who was the young king's uncle.[6] Evidently Nicholaa, in spite of her age, was not pleased to be relieved of her burden of office as castellan, for she visited the court in London and sought to recover her castle, recalling her services to the king's father. She obtained letters patent ordering Salisbury to restore

[1] Supra, p. 112 n.

[2] Roger of Wendover, *Chronica* (R.S.), II, 218. According to the Tewkesbury Annals about 40 magnates, over 300 knights, and an unknown number of servants were taken prisoner. *Annales Monastici* (R.S.), I, 63. One royalist knight was killed; he belonged to the family of Earl Ferrers. Burton Annals in ibid. I, 224.

[3] Professor Tout thought (op. cit. II, 209) that Lincoln was probably almost an open town, but he did not know that the medieval city had inherited Roman walls. His arguments are fully dealt with by Messrs Brooks and Oakley, op. cit. p. 299.

[4] *Rot. Lit. Pat.* p. 199b.

[5] *Patent Rolls*, 1216–25, p. 20.

[6] Ibid. p. 65.

the castle, city and county to her, and the mayor and citizens were notified of her appointment.[1] A few months later Salisbury was again appointed 'bailiff' of the county, Nicholaa retaining city and castle.[2] After the Marshal's death Nicholaa again sought the aid of the court against Salisbury, and Falkes de Breauté was assigned to aid her in the defence of the castle.[3] She resigned in 1226.

After their bitter experience in the civil war and the battle, the citizens were not likely to venture upon action without official sanction. As has been noted, on 29 June 1218 the king (or his ministers in his name) confirmed the election of Peter Bridge as mayor. Like his predecessor William nephew of Warner, he was to be 'your mayor' and 'our bailiff'.[4] Again in 1225 the citizens obtained the royal permission to elect a mayor,[5] and in 1227 the king confirmed the election of John of Paris, 'our citizen of Lincoln', to the mayoralty.[6]

The havoc wrought by the battle received one piece of official recognition. In 1225 licence was granted for the levying of tolls on goods brought into the city for three days for the purpose of repairing the walls. There is no record of the yield of the tolls, but the tariff gives an interesting list of the various forms of transport: from every cartload ½*d.* or 1*d.*; every pack-horse load ¼*d.*; every horse or head of cattle ½*d.*; every large ship 8*d.*; every middle-sized ship 4*d.*; every boat 2*d.*[7]

The declaration that the young King Henry III was of age led to a general renewal of borough charters, most of the new grants being confirmations of liberties granted by the king's predecessors, and in particular by John. The new Lincoln charter of 20 April 1227 followed the charter of John, with two additional clauses. The first directed that if anyone in England should take toll or custom from the men of Lincoln the bailiff of Lincoln should take distress at Lincoln. This was the old rule of retaliation, for which a fine had been substituted in John's charter in 1200: apparently the fine had not been effective, and the old practice of civic self-help was restored. The second addition summarised valued privileges already enjoyed by the citizens: the grant of the gild merchant of the city and of other merchants of the county, as they had it in the time of the king's grandfather Henry II; the grant that those who dwelt within the four boundaries of the city and carried on trade should be at the same gelds, customs and assizes as under Henry II; and the rule that a bondman

[1] *Patent Rolls*, 1216–25, pp. 117, 118.
[2] Ibid. p. 130.
[3] Ibid. p. 201. And see *Royal Letters of Henry III* (R.S.), I, 73.
[4] Supra, p. 200.
[5] *Rot. Lit. Claus.* p. 19.
[6] *C.P.R.* 1225–32, p. 171.
[7] *Patent Rolls*, 1216–25, p. 518.

living in the city for a year and a day without claim might abide there as the king's citizen. These were among the most cherished of the city's privileges and could not be asserted and confirmed too often.[1]

It was about this time that the new orders of friars were beginning to arrive in the city. The Franciscans are mentioned first; and William of Benniworth, the subdean, was either the founder or an early benefactor of their friary. He granted to the citizens a place near the gildhall to house the friars minor, and the citizens then granted to the friars part of the land on which the gildhall stood, the grant being confirmed by the king on 7 February 1231.[2] A few years later (17 September 1237) Henry III asked the men of Lincoln to give 'the place where their pleas are held', which used to be the gildhall, to the friars minor, and he promised the citizens another place in the town. The old gildhall was thereupon assigned to the friars by the mayor and bailiffs.[3]

The Dominicans had settled on the hillside to the east of the city before 1238, and were followed some years later by the White Friars (apparently 1269), the Friars of the Sack (before 1266) and the Austin Friars (about 1269).[4]

A great friend of the friars, Robert Grosseteste, was consecrated bishop of Lincoln in June 1235. That great scholar and statesman not only sought to visit and reform the chapter of his cathedral church, but knew how to withstand both king and pope. In 1244 he was one of a committee of twelve chosen from the king's council to draw up articles to regulate the conduct of the king and to force him to appoint responsible ministers. The king had become extremely unpopular. He had brought in greedy foreign favourites, some of them relatives of his queen Eleanor, daughter of Count Raymond of Provence; he was reckless in expenditure, and he was subservient to the papacy. The king had been withstood in his evil ways by Edmund Rich, archbishop of Canterbury and a friend of Grosseteste. Rich gave up his duties in despair, and retired to Pontigny, where he died in 1240. A few years later he was canonised. It is significant of the friendship of Rich and Grosseteste, and also of sympathy with Rich in his struggle with Henry and his foreign friends, that in Lincoln was founded (in

[1] *C. Chart. R.* I, 33, which gives 30 April; Birch, p. 9; *B.B.C.* (2), p. liv.

[2] *C.P.R.* 1225–32, pp. 422–3.

[3] *Close Rolls*, 1234–7, pp. 495, 500. Where did the citizens hold their pleas after giving up the gildhall to the friars minor? A charter of 1317 enrolled in the Burwarmote Book refers to premises in St Peter at Arches parish bounded by the plea hall on the south. B.B. f. 81. The hall in use was called both the plea hall and the gildhall. P.R.O. Assize Roll 523. Probably they moved to the Stonebow, which the king could hand over to them without cost to himself. They were there shortly before 1390. Infra, p. 254.

[4] See pp. 150–1; and *V.C.H. Lincs*, II, 219–25.

1276) the only gild dedicated to St Edmund of Pontigny of which there is record.[1]

Lincoln was given direct and practical ground for dislike of the queen's family. The earldom of Richmond, which had been in the king's hands since 1235, was conferred upon the queen's uncle, Peter of Savoy, with the wardenship of the Cinque Ports, in 1241, and other honours followed. The town of Boston formed part of the honour of Richmond, and the citizens had occasion to complain loudly of Peter's extortions in his strategic position at the mouth of the river Witham.[2]

Dissension between the king and the barons came to a head when the king's council met in April 1258. The barons' original demand for a confirmation of Magna Carta gave way to a new measure of reform in the appointment of a committee of twenty-four, half of the royal and half of the baronial party, to prepare a plan of government. The result was the Provisions of Oxford, the details of which do not specially concern Lincoln.

One of the measures adopted was to send the Justiciar Hugh Bigod out into the counties to hear complaints. He was at Lincoln, accompanied, apparently, by the king, in August and September 1258. There he heard a complaint against the sheriff of Lincolnshire, John of Cockerington, for refusing to proceed upon a writ which was brought to him by a certain plaintiff, and the sheriff, having no defence to make of this denial of justice, was in the mercy of the court.[3] That autumn the barons appointed their own sheriffs, who took the oath to avoid extortion, and to act as keepers, not being allowed to farm out the hundreds or wapentakes to others.

In 1261 the Provisions were denounced by the pope, and the king made a bid for his freedom. He appointed his own sheriffs: the council appointed theirs, and a committee of six was set up to arrange a compromise, one of the baronial representatives being Robert Marsh, dean of Lincoln.[4] During this period before the outbreak of fighting, the citizens of Lincoln, who were having difficulty in protecting their rights in foreign trade against the interference of Peter of Savoy's servants at Boston, took the opportunity of obtaining from the king at Windsor a confirmation (dated 7 March 1262) of one of the grants of Henry II, directing that foreign merchants should come to Lincoln to trade lest the king's bailiffs of Lincoln should lose the royal customs; and the new grant, directed to the king's sheriffs and ministers of the county of Lincoln, ordered that the

[1] Gild Certificates, no. 140; Westlake, *Parish Gilds of Medieval England* (1919), pp. 17, 169. Relics of St Edmund the archbishop were preserved in the cathedral. Dugdale, *Monasticon*, VI, 1279. Grosseteste died in 1253; by 1255 the miracles of St Robert were being reported. *Annales Monastici*, I, 336.

[2] See pp. 318–20.

[3] Jacob, *Studies in the Period of Baronial Reform and Rebellion*, 1258–67 (1925), pp. 41 n., 49.

[4] Ibid. p. 74 n.

same practice should be continued, as it had been until the king's first passage over the sea into Brittany;[1] that is, until 1230, before the era of misgovernment began.

After some fighting between king and barons their dispute was referred to the arbitration of Louis IX of France. His award, which was wholly in favour of Henry, was not accepted by the barons, and war was resumed. In April 1264 the king stormed Northampton and occupied Leicester and Nottingham, and ordered the constable of Lincoln Castle, Alexander de Montfort, to deliver the castle to William de Gray.[2] The war having come unpleasantly near to their walls, the citizens of Lincoln discreetly obtained a letter of protection from Henry III.[3] On 14 May Henry met the baronial army under Simon de Montfort at Lewes, and was overthrown, he and his son Prince Edward being taken prisoners. For the moment de Montfort was supreme. Evidently an invasion of the eastern counties in aid of the prisoner-king was expected, for after Lewes a considerable proportion of the able-bodied population had to guard the coast, and at de Montfort's command, no pleas were held in Lincolnshire, Norfolk and Suffolk until September.[4] On 14 December de Montfort called the Parliament for which he is now chiefly remembered. The citizens of York, the citizens of Lincoln, and other towns of England were bidden to send to it two of their discreet, loyal and honest citizens or burgesses: this was a precedent of great importance for the future.

The civil war provided an opportunity for a new attack on the Jews, who were massacred in London and Canterbury, and were certainly attacked in Lincoln, where the chirograph chest was burned to destroy the evidence of debts owing to the Jews.[5] After the event, on 6 May 1265, a letter was sent in the king's name to twenty-four named citizens of Lincoln ordering them to protect the Jews of Lincoln in person and goods, as after the late disturbance in the realm the king took the Jews of England, by counsel of the barons, under his special protection.[6] On 18 July 1266 Henry III wrote from Kenilworth, which he was besieging, to the sheriffs and keepers of the peace in the counties of Lincoln, Nottingham and York, that he had granted to Benedict and Hagin and other Lincoln Jews, in compensation for the losses they had suffered at the hands of the king's enemies in the conflict at Lincoln during the disturbance of the realm, that their pledges named in the chirographs made between them and their debtors, in whosesoever hands the pledges might be, should be seized by

[1] Birch, p. 14.

[2] *C.P.R.* 1258–66, p. 313. Alexander was seneschal of Henry de Lacy. D. & C., Dii, 80/2/25, 40.

[3] *C.P.R.* 1258–66, p. 312.

[4] Jacob, op. cit. p. 272.

[5] *Select Pleas of the Jewish Exchequer* (Selden Society), p. 41.

[6] *C.P.R.* 1258–66, p. 421.

them according to the law and custom of the king's Jewry, until the debts were paid.[1]

Meanwhile Henry's son Edward had escaped from Simon's custody, and at Evesham on 4 August 1265 the baronial party was overthrown and Simon was killed. Five days later the citizens obtained from the victorious king another letter of protection.[2] They had reason for their apprehension. In his triumph the king seized the liberties of London, and there followed wholesale confiscations of estates. His severity provoked another rising. The younger Simon de Montfort occupied the isle of Axholme, and John d'Eyville and Baldwin Wake sacked Lincoln and assaulted the castle.[3] In 1266 Edward was sent to expel them.

The confiscation of rebel lands in Lincolnshire was entrusted to Antony Bek and Alexander de Montfort, who seems to have been faithful to the king. Baldwin Wake's lands in Skellingthorpe, Hykeham, Waddington and elsewhere were seized. John of Bracebridge, who held a knight's fee in Bracebridge of Baldwin Wake, and who was at Northampton, lost his lands. John de la Haye lost his manor of Burwell, and Peter de Montfort the younger his lands at Harlaxton and elsewhere.[4]

The city of Lincoln did not escape. The king imposed a fine of 1,000 marks on it; and because the fine was not paid by the appointed day he seized the city into his hands, suspending its liberties and issuing, on 22 January 1267, letters patent reciting that whereas the citizens had lately made fine to have the king's grace, though they had often been written to they had not troubled to observe the terms of payment. The king had therefore committed the town during his pleasure to John de Limar', who was to answer for its revenues at the king's mandate.[5] This drastic measure roused the citizens to the need for instant action, and within three weeks they had sought and obtained (10 February) the king's pardon for all the trespasses and forfeitures which they were said to have committed against the king in the time of the disturbance of the realm: the king, added the letters, being unwilling that they should be molested in their persons, lands, possessions, or liberties, they were admitted (to pardon), provided that they were of good behaviour and stood to the settlement of the realm known as the award of Kenilworth. The price of the royal pardon was fixed at the enormous sum of £1,000.[6] In July £300 of the fine was still unpaid, and the king again took the city into his hand. Royal commissioners were ordered to impanel a jury and to inquire who were the persons in the city

[1] *C.P.R.* 1258–66, p. 617; and 1266–72, p. 95. [2] *C.P.R.* 1258–66, p. 437.

[3] *Cal. Inq. Misc.* I, no. 313; Waverley Annals in *Annales Monastici* (R.S.), II, 368.

[4] *Cal. Inq. Misc.* I, nos. 785–803.

[5] *C.P.R.* 1266–72, p. 28. For the amount of the fine see below, p. 211.

[6] Ibid. p. 34.

who were against the king during the disturbance; how much of the £1,000 was actually raised; and if more than £1,000 was raised, how much more, who received it, and whether any citizens were aggrieved by unfair assessment.[1]

This inquiry apparently brought to light certain grievances, for on 4 November a commission of oyer and terminer was issued on complaint of some of the citizens. It was alleged that although the city charters granted that all who stayed in the city for a year and a day without challenge from anyone, and had been at scot and lot during that time, should henceforth become free citizens, yet mayors and others in times past had by the most grievous distraints forced men so living in the city to pay for the liberties to which they had become entitled; that though the city pleas were to be held weekly on Mondays and the fines imposed were to be paid to the bailiffs towards the farm of the city, the persons appointed to hold pleas deferred them, sometimes from month to month, sometimes so that they were held scarcely twice or thrice in the year; that out of the tronage of Lincoln collected at Boston fair, to which the commonalty of the city were entitled, mayors and others had, without the commonalty being summoned or giving consent, granted under the seal of the commonalty to Peter count of Savoy and his heirs the sum of £10 a year; that they misappropriated the rent of stalls near the bridge of Lincoln which should have gone towards the farm; that they levied taxes and failed to account for them; that many had refused to contribute towards the fine imposed by the king, with the result that the king had twice taken the city into his hand; and that during the late disturbances many of them had borne themselves against the king in ways that they should not have done.[2]

By way of supplement to these grave charges may be added a plea from an assize roll of the city, in which Thomas de Beaufou claimed from William de Holgate, mayor, and others, the sum of £110, stating that when the commonalty of the city fined with 1,000 marks for their trespasses in the time of disturbance of the kingdom, Thomas, being then mayor, paid £110 for the citizens. The defendants replied that they having complained before the justices that Thomas, when mayor, made many extortions and took fines, toll and murage which he did not place to the profit of the city, it had been agreed that the one claim should be taken as settling the other.[3]

To these internal disputes it will be necessary to return, but meanwhile it may be noted that the suspension of civic liberties did not last long. William de Holgate was mayor about 1267 and in the years following;[4]

[1] *C.P.R.* 1266–72, p. 152.
[2] Ibid. p. 270.
[3] *V.C.H. Lincs*, II, 313.
[4] D. & C., Dii, 80/3/21. See Appendix IV.

and also in 1270, when the king granted, for a fine of 200 marks made by William, that the citizens should be quit of the twentieth to be levied in aid of the Holy Land, provided the money was paid by a certain date, failing which the mayor and those whom he should appoint were to assess the twentieth in the same way as in other places.[1] On 12 February 1272 the king granted the city a charter confirming his own grant of 1227. That grant had provided that the citizens (except moneyers and royal servants) should not be called upon to plead outside the city save in respect of land outside it. The new grant added that all city pleas and no others should be held in the plea hall of the city called the gildhall, and not elsewhere against the will of the citizens, with the exceptions aforesaid.[2] This provision seems to hint that there had been irregularities in the place of holding the court of burwarmote.

The complaints of the citizens—through the mouths of a jury of great men—against the ruling junta are heard again in the Hundred Rolls in 1275. It was declared that William son of Giles, then mayor, by the counsel of Jordan son of Giles, Walter Brand, Thomas son of Robert, Thomas de Beaufou and Alexander son of Giles, without the consent of the other citizens came to terms with the bailiffs of Peter of Savoy at Boston, and entered into a composition granting to Peter a farm of £10 a year, out of money which the king ought to receive from the farm of Lincoln. When they were attached by their fellow-citizens in the city court for this unauthorised deal, the mayor's brother Jordan implied that the Lincoln men's participation in Boston fair was at stake. He declared that he would rather have given £10 out of his own property than lose his Boston fair.[3] It is clear that the principal Lincoln merchants were determined at whatever cost to retain their footing at Boston, and they no doubt argued that, however irregular the method of effecting the deal, it was in the city's interest to make a settlement with Peter's bailiffs on unfavourable terms rather than not make a settlement at all. It is significant that William de Holgate, described by the jurors as 'a great lord and power in Lincoln'[4] was charged with taking stone out of the king's quarry at Lincoln and sending it, when squared by the stonemasons, to Boston to build houses there.[5]

It was not only in respect of the Boston trade that the chief citizens were charged with selfish and high-handed action. The burgesses of Beverley had been refusing to pay toll in Lincoln ever since the mayoralty of Peter of Paris, 'a great man of his time', who was said to have given this freedom

[1] *C.P.R.* 1266–72, p. 422.
[2] *B.B.C.* (2), p. 154; Birch, p. 16.
[3] *R.H.* I, 313b, 320a.
[4] Ibid. p. 322b.
[5] Ibid. pp. 315a, 322b, 399a.

from toll as a marriage portion with his daughter to a certain Robert Ingelberd of Beverley.[1]

These internal grievances must have simmered for a long time. At last they came to a head. In 1290 some of the rich citizens were indicted by a jury of twenty-four for divers offences. They were charged with selling the tronage of the city without the consent of the poor; with distraining the poor for 200 marks paid to the king as the value of concealed goods of Jews who had been condemned; and with unfairly assessing and collecting tallages from the poor; and there were other grievances. On 16 July the king issued a commission of oyer and terminer to appease the discords between rich and poor, and a second commission was issued on 23 November at Harby, five days before the death there of Edward's beloved Queen Eleanor.[2] According to Ross the city was seized into the king's hand on 16 May 1290, though he does not give his authority for the statement.[3] The city's liberties certainly were forfeited, and the city, first put into the hands of the earl of Lincoln, was delivered to Robert le Venour as keeper of the city at Easter 1291.[4]

Robert le Venour seems to have been a royal official though he was probably a local man, as he was returned in 1298 among those having £40 worth of land in Lincolnshire. He had houses in Lincoln to the south of the castle.[5] He was sheriff of the county from October 1293 to April 1297, and keeper of the city until Michaelmas 1297. It is especially interesting to note that during 1290–2 he paid out of the issues of the city to the master of the works of the cathedral the sum of £20 'to do that which for Eleanor, sometime queen of England...was enjoined by Robert bishop of Bath and Wells and Robert de Tybetot, on behalf of the king...'. In 1295 he began to be in difficulties; he was severely reprimanded for being in arrears at the Exchequer in accounting for taxes. By 1297 he was delivered to the Marshalsea for various debts owing on his account, including the sum of £34. 11*s*. 2*d*. of arrears on his account as keeper of the city. In 1299 the sheriff was ordered to imprison him and seize his possessions until further orders.

He was succeeded as keeper of the city by William Cause, a leading citizen of Lincoln, who first accounted at the Exchequer at Easter 1298.

[1] *R.H.* pp. 309b, 316a. Philip Ingelberd, son of Peter's daughter Alice and Robert Ingelberd, gave an endowment to a hall at Oxford, apparently Balliol, consisting of lands (now mostly under the Humber) at Paull and Keyingham, Yorkshire. Poulson, *Beverlac* (1829), p. 452 n. Licence was given for alienation on 17 February 1317.

[2] *C.P.R.* 1281–92, pp. 404, 451.

[3] *Civitas Lincolnia*, p. 11.

[4] For this date, and subsequent references to Robert le Venour, see Sinclair Thomson, *A Lincolnshire Assize Roll for* 1298 (L.R.S.), Biographical Index.

[5] In the parish of St John the Poor: they had belonged to a Jew, Benedict the Count. Birch, pp. 140–1.

His appointment may have been the first step towards the restoration of the city's liberties. He is found witnessing as keeper with two sets of bailiffs, and thereafter as mayor with two sets. He was the first mayor to hold office after the grant of a new charter by Edward I in 1301.[1] During the suspension of the liberties the office of bailiff continued to be served by citizens, but instead of their accounting at the Exchequer for the fixed annual farm of £180, the keeper accounted, it seems, for his actual receipts.

The accounts for two years of the suspension, one of Robert le Venour's years and one of William Cause's, have survived.[2] They show that the king was a loser by the suspension of the liberties, and justify at least to some extent the complaints of the citizens about the burden of the fee farm rent. The jurors themselves said in 1275 that they who had been bailiffs of Lincoln could scarcely rise from poverty and misery.[3] It is to be expected that complaints of the burden of taxation should always tend to exaggeration, but the surviving accounts do show a deficiency, and for the balance of the fee farm rent the bailiffs were (when they were farming the city) personally liable. A century later the number of bailiffs was increased to three, and still later to four, for the purpose of distributing the annual burden over more shoulders. For Robert le Venour's year (apparently 1292–3) the revenue collected came to approximately £176; for William Cause's year to approximately £158.[4] Perhaps William Cause, being a citizen, showed less zeal in collecting the royal revenues from his fellow townsmen, and it may be that falling revenue was an encouragement to the king to restore to the citizens their liberties and so to secure the full farm of £180 again.

It is worth while to examine Robert le Venour's figures in more detail. The largest item consists of the weekly receipts in the tolbooth: they totalled £71. This high figure explains why the boroughs attached so much importance to payment of toll by others, and to the freedom from toll claimed for their own burgesses: perhaps, as Maitland said, the burgesses regarded freedom from toll as the most vital of all their rights.[5]

The city kept a firm hand on the victualling trades, both by taxing them and enforcing the assize of bread and ale. Ale-toll, apparently a payment

[1] He appears regularly as a member of the council of twenty-four until *c.* 1315. An inquisition held on his death revealed (1326) that he had 5 acres of meadow and 40*s.* rent at South Clifton (Notts), £4. 6*s.* 8*d.* rent at Laceby, a toft, 120 acres of land, 3 acres of meadow, a water mill, 40*s.* rent, and a bovate of land at Alesby, and in Lincoln suburb 1 messuage, 2 bovates in the fields there, and 4 bovates of land and a windmill. *Cal. Inq. p.m.* VI, no. 736.

[2] P.R.O. Exchequer Accounts, 505/24, 28.

[3] *R.H.* I, 317a.

[4] The totals are given as approximate because figures in the accounts cannot all be read with certainty.

[5] Pollock and Maitland, *History of English Law* (2nd ed.), I, 650.

made by the brewer for the right to brew, was paid in the Martinmas term by 133 persons, including many women, the standard rate of toll being 12*d.*: at Easter 119 persons paid 8*d.* each. In Newport, 21 people each paid 4*d.* Fines imposed on brewers range from 12*d.* to 5*s.* 4*d.* and they brought in £29. 7*s.* 10*d.* during the year. Baxtergeld was collected at Martinmas, and 31 persons paid 25*s.* in sums of either 6*d.* or 8*d.* Bakers' fines totalled £6. 3*s.* 6*d.*

The perquisites of the city court amounted to £13. 16*s.* 1*d.* and at Newport £1. 16*s.* 4*d.* Windowtoll brought in £1. 6*s.* 8*d.*; 'wakebreste' £1. 13*s.* 0*d.*: fines for pigs (probably for roaming the streets) 10*s.*; fines for tolls (probably for non-payment thereof) £6. 13*s.* 9*d.*

A list of rents certain, amounting to £9. 11*s.* 0*d.*, is of particular interest. It means that pieces of waste land were being let by the city to individual citizens for the benefit of the city farm. Charter authority for such letting was to follow in 1316,[1] perhaps because title to these rents was in question, but their significance is that they imply that, in the absence of any other owner, land within the city and suburbs belonged to the citizens collectively, and they go some way towards establishing the civic body as a lord of the manor.

A list of tolls calls for reproduction in full:

	£	*s.*	*d.*
From Dockdyke	4	0	0
From Bracebridge		6	0
From Engelby	1	2	0
From le Barregate		5	0
From le Loufe Market		11	0
From stallage in High Market		11	0
From measure of honey		10	0
From salmon and fish	2	10	0
From Newport at the time of the fair and stallage	6	15	0
From stallage of the whole city		11	1
From landtoll pennies	2	10	0
From salt toll	1	1	0
From booths at the time of Newport fair		5	0
From bread baskets (*corbellis*) and charcoal measures (*vannis*)		1	8
	£20	18	9

Dockdyke, or Dogdyke, is the point on the river Witham at which the river is joined by the Bain (from Horncastle) and the Slea, or Kyme Eau (from Sleaford). Here was a tolbooth at which were collected dues on

[1] Infra, p. 242. A yearly rent to the commonalty for a piece of land under the king's wall in Walkergate is mentioned *c.* 1290. D. & C., Dii, 75/1/15.

merchandise, which were among those sources of royal revenue farmed out to the citizens. These dues continued to be collected long after the city's monopoly of foreign trade within the county had ceased to be enforceable. There is entered upon the city court roll in 1339 a power of attorney by the bailiffs to two deputies 'to collect the tolls of the king and the bailiffs at Docdyke pertaining to the king's farm of the said city', with power to distrain for payment where necessary.[1] Still later, when the rights of the city were being reviewed, a like authority for the year 1461 was copied into the city records.[2] Ingleby is in the parish of Saxilby, and was evidently the point on the Fossdyke at which toll was taken. There are small receipts from Bargate and Bracebridge: the reason for the latter is not obvious, as it was outside the city, but it may be that then, as later, the city was responsible for maintenance of part of the bridge over the Witham there, and that the toll was a bridge toll.[3] The revenue from fairs and markets was considerable; and the proximity to the Bail of Newport on the north and the high market on the south becomes significant when disputes with the constable of the castle and the dean and chapter on the question of stallage in the Bail and Close break out later.

William Cause's account includes a heading 'of fines for having the freedom': some fifteen persons were admitted freemen of the city on payment of sums ranging from 11*d.* to a mark, the usual fee being half a mark.

[1] B.B. f. 141 v.

[2] Birch, *Catalogue of Royal Charters and Documents*, List of Books, no. 1 (9), among papers relating to privileges of the castle and Bail.

[3] See pp. 357–8.

CHAPTER XI

THE JEWS

THE earliest known reference to the Jews in Lincolnshire occurs in 1159, when the sheriff accounted for £40 for them: they appear in other places about the same time.[1] Unlike the Frenchmen who had come to England with the Conqueror, they did not merge with the race in possession. By blood and religion they remained distinct. They did not acquire citizenship, they were not admitted to gilds, and could not carry on trade. The only scope for their talents was in finance, and in that profitable field of activity they were (at least in theory) protected from competition by the canonical prohibition of usury which debarred Christians from taking interest on loans. They themselves and all their chattels were regarded as the property of the king, who might, and sometimes did, seize the goods of a Jew on his death. The king could thus, at second hand, secure a share of the profits of usury without infringing the letter of the canon law.

Lincoln soon had one of the largest and richest Jewries in England. When the Jews were called upon in 1194 to contribute towards the ransom of Richard I, taken prisoner by Leopold duke of Austria on his way home from the crusades, the Lincoln community ranked second only to the London community in the amount of its contribution, whilst the number of its contributors exceeded the London number. York did not appear in the list, no doubt because of the massacre there at the time of Richard's coronation. When the Jews had to contribute to an 'aid' for the marriage of the king's sister Joan to Alexander II of Scotland in 1221, the York total was twice as large as that of London; Winchester came third, only slightly exceeding Lincoln, which was fourth.[2]

Little is known of the individual Jews who settled in Lincoln under Henry II, with one conspicuous exception. Aaron of Lincoln was the most famous Jewish financier of his time in England. He was in full activity from 1166 until his death about 1185. Of the man himself, and whence he came, nothing is known. He is known only by his widespread financial operations.

[1] P.R. 5 *Henry II*, p. 65; Jacobs, *Jews of Angevin England*, p. 28.

[2] Towards the *donum* of 1194 London contributed £486, Lincoln £287, Canterbury £241, Northampton £165, Norwich £88, Winchester £43. According to Jacobs, 29 London and 40 Lincoln Jews paid. See *Jewish Historical Society Miscellanies*, I, pp. lix–lxxiv; Jacobs, op. cit. pp. 162, 381. For the aid to marry, see Miss H. M. Chew, 'A Jewish Aid to Marry, 1221', in *Trans. of the Jewish Hist. Soc. of England*, XI (1924–7), pp. 92–111. Among the totals were, York £164, London £80, Winchester £53, Lincoln £52, Northampton £47, Stamford £37, Norwich £28, Nottingham £6.

In 1165–6 the king was indebted to Aaron for the sum of £29. 8*s*. 10*d*., which he paid by a draft on the sheriff: but the Pipe Roll shows the king directing the sheriffs of nine counties to pay sums out of their farms to Aaron, the total authorised payment to him being £616. 12*s*. 8*d*. As the king's whole income did not exceed £35,000, it will be seen that Aaron had advanced about one-fiftieth of it. He did not need to visit the other counties to collect his money from the sheriffs, for he had agents to act for him. The Jews of Warwick received money from the sheriff of Leicester as his attorneys, and another Jew collected money at York for him.[1]

Aaron lived in a time of great monastic building activity, and when the religious communities built beyond the gifts of the faithful they resorted to borrowing. After Aaron's death it was found that nine Cistercian abbeys, all of them built between 1140 and 1152, owed money to him, totalling 6,400 marks and more. They were Rievaulx, Newminster, Kirkstead, Louth Park, Revesby, Rufford, Kirkstall, Roche and Biddlesden. Their vast debt having vested in the king, Richard I settled it for 1,000 marks, released the debts, and returned the bonds acknowledging them.[2] The chronicler of St Albans tells that when Abbot Simon died he left his abbey in debt for more than 600 marks to the Jews besides other debts of 200 marks and more. 'Whereupon Aaron the Jew who held us in his debt coming to the house of St Alban in great pride and boasting, with threats kept on boasting that it was he who made the window for our St Alban, and that he had prepared for the saint a home when he was without one.'[3] Giraldus Cambrensis recorded in his life of Remigius that Bishop Chesney of Lincoln (1148–66), being in serious financial difficulties, had pawned the ornaments of his church to Aaron, and that one of the very first acts of his successor was to redeem them.[4]

When Aaron died[5] his property passed to the king, and so there is on the Pipe Rolls a list of his debtors. It is an astonishing list. Besides a great number of small people, William the Lion, king of Scotland, the earls of Northampton, Leicester, Arundel, Aumale, and Chester, the abbot of Westminster and the prior of the Hospitallers, the bishops of Lincoln and Bangor, the archdeacons of Colchester and Carlisle, the towns of Winchester and Southampton, and the sheriff of Norfolk, were all on Aaron's

[1] Jacobs, 'Aaron of Lincoln' in *Trans. of the Jewish Hist. Soc. of England*, 1896–8, pp. 157 et seq.

[2] *Memorials of Fountains Abbey* (Surtees Society), II, 18; Jacobs, *Jews of Angevin England*, p. 108. Meaux was in debt to Aaron in 1176. P.R. 9 *Richard I*, 62. *Chronica Monasterii de Melsa* (R.S.), I, 173–4.

[3] *Gesta Sancti Albani* (ed. Riley), p. 193; Jacobs, *Jews of Angevin England*, p. 79.

[4] *Opera* (R.S.), VII, 36; Jacobs, *Jews of Angevin England*, p. 57.

[5] He is mentioned as dead in P.R. 32 *Henry II* (1185–6), p. 195.

books. Baldwin archbishop of Canterbury owed 100 marks on land in Kent.[1]

The list of Lincoln debts gives a striking picture of Aaron's grip on merchant and churchman in his headquarter city. To mention only a few of his customers, William son of Fulk, founder of a chantry in the cathedral, owed £68. 1*s.* 4*d.* secured on his mill at Washingborough, his stalls at Stow, and his land in the parish of St Peter Stanthaket; Thomas son of Godwin owed £7 by deed on his land and houses in Lincoln, Ralf of Colchester being pledge, and 40 marks on his land in the churchyard of St Peter Stanthaket, and another bond charged his land in Parcheminstreet; Ralf son of Fulk owed £7. 9*s.* 6*d.* by deed, and 20 marks on his house in Hungate by another deed; Saulf of Wigford owed 50*s.* for John the mercer; Robert the constable owed 2 marks as pledge for his brother William; Osbert the Long of Butwerk owed £9. 4*s.* 0*d.* by pledge of Brian son of Askell; James Fleming, brother-in-law of Adam the first mayor, owed 25 marks; John son of August owed 2½ marks on land and houses in the high market; Warin the draper owed 63*s.* by pledge of Godwin the rich and Gamel, Warin's brother; Elwin Net, several times bailiff of Lincoln, owed 29 marks by pledge of Gilbert his brother and Robert Cause; Reinbald son of Ralf owed 50*s.* 6*d.* on his lands in Bakestergate.

Among the clergy, John the priest of St Margaret owed 4*s.*, Gregory the priest of St Faith owed 16*s.* 4*d.* by deed, and Outi the clerk of Eastgate owed 10*s.* on his house and orchard in the parish of Holy Trinity. The sacrist of the cathedral and five of the canons were among the debtors.

Aaron also dealt in chattels. Roger de Estreby, a knight of Lincoln, pawned his coat of mail to Aaron, and had it miraculously returned to him. He was told in a vision that it was at the foot of his bed, and so it was.[2] Other types of transaction appear from a few promissory notes that have survived. One declares that the debtor owes Aaron 25 soams of hay, Stamford measure, every two loads to make one great bundle, Lincoln measure, and that he will render it within 15 days on demand; and a surety binds himself for 40 soams of hay. Another note acknowledges a debt, and

[1] See appendix to Mr Jacobs' article on Aaron. The debts are grouped by counties in P.R. 3 *Richard I.* The greater part of lands in mortgage is in Lincolnshire and Yorkshire, but they extend as far as Shropshire and Southampton. See also Roth, *History of the Jews in England* (1941), p. 16. The king of Scotland owed Aaron £2,776 by ten deeds, his brother Earl David being surety, Laurie, *Annals of Malcolm and William, Kings of Scotland, 1153–1214* (1910), p. 358.

[2] Jacobs, *Jews of Angevin England*, p. 272. Roger de Esterbi is witness to a Saltfleetby charter, late Henry II, *D.C.* p. 391. See also Lees, *Records of Templars in England in the Twelfth Century*, p. 107, nn. 5 and 7.

promises interest at the rate of 2*d.* per pound per week, which is 43 %; land is given as security and there is a guarantor. A third provides for interest if there is delay in payment, this, by a fiction, being regarded not as usury but as a penalty.[1] The first of these notes is interesting in view of many later references to debts of corn and wool due to Jews: whether they really traded or lent on bills of sale is not clear. It must of course be remembered when rates of interest are being considered that the risks run by the Jewish financiers were enormous. The difficulties of the Exchequer in getting in Aaron's debts after his death give some idea of the difficulties Aaron himself must have had.

In his lifetime Aaron was a source of revenue to the Exchequer. The Pipe Roll of 1190 notes, under the Surrey forest pleas, that he owes £36 for 6 gold marks, and under London and Middlesex that he owes 500 marks imposed by Henry II, adding 'but he is dead, and the king has his goods'.[2] Henry II was in France early in 1187, and a great part of his retinue and of Aaron's treasure was lost at sea between Shoreham and Dieppe.[3] Richard Fitz Nigel, the treasurer, described the loss as a grave misfortune. To collect his debts a special branch of the Exchequer was set up, with two treasurers and two clerks. According to Mr Jacobs the debts entered upon the Pipe Rolls were 430 in number and amounted to £15,000. By 1201 there was still about £12,000 outstanding, and like modern collectors of doubtful debts the king's clerks were taking any offers they could get. The king, however, had the incidental advantage that the debts gave him a hold on magnates and gentry.[4]

Where did Aaron live? According to a list of escheats, taken in 1226–8, the house (*domus*) of Aaron the Jew in the Bail was worth 6*s.* yearly; it had escheated to the king and was held by Nicholaa de Haya the constable for the purposes of the castle (*occasione castri*).[5] This modest annual value does not point to a large house, and indeed *domus* may mean only an office or room. There are several references to Aaron in the Hundred Rolls. One says that Aaron the Jew encroached on the king's wall; another that land formerly of Aaron the rich on the west side of the gate of the Bail had escheated and was worth 40*s.* yearly; and a third that all the houses situate within the old gate of the Bail on the west side had escheated from Aaron the rich to the king, extending from opposite the castle gate to the castle

[1] Jacobs, *Jews of Angevin England*, p. 66.
[2] P.R. 2 *Richard I*, pp. 153, 157.
[3] *Gesta Henrici* (ed. Stubbs), (R.S.), II, 5. Jacobs, op. cit. p. 91.
[4] Jacobs, op. cit. pp. 142–3. And see his paper, 'Aaron of Lincoln', p. 168.
[5] *Book of Fees*, I, 365. The Pipe Roll for 1230 records a payment by Robert son of Ywein of 10*s.* for a house which was Aaron's, and for 2½ years' arrears at the same rate (P.R. 14 *Henry III*, p. 302), but it appears that the house had been taken by Aaron under a mortgage. *Book of Fees*, I, 364.

ditch.[1] It is evident from his constant description as 'of Lincoln', and from the fact that a large part of his business was in Lincolnshire, that Lincoln was regarded as his headquarters, but it may be that in his later years he found it necessary to spend much of his time in London. The heavy fine imposed on him in the London and Middlesex Exchequer accounts points to this conclusion and it is to be noted that he had a house in Lothbury, near Walbrook.[2]

After some space of time Aaron seems to have been forgotten. He is not enshrined in any ballad literature, nor is he mentioned by antiquaries like Leland or Camden. The local histories of the early nineteenth century, beginning with that of Adam Stark in 1810, do not know him. Although he appears in the Hundred Rolls, published in 1812, his importance seems not to have been rediscovered until the publication in 1844 of the Pipe Roll of 1 Richard I (1189–90) by the Rev. Joseph Hunter for the Record Commission. The 1842 edition of White's *Gazetteer* of the county does not mention him, but the edition of 1856 says:

> the State Records mention seventeen or eighteen persons who were immensely rich; the chief of whom was Aaron, commonly called by our historians *Aaron of York*, but he resided above hill in a house and premises extending from Bailgate beyond the gate of the castle westward to the castle ditch.[3]

Up to this date there is no trace of the 'tradition' that Aaron lived in the stone house on the east side of the Steep Hill at the corner of Christ's Hospital Terrace now associated with his name. Thomas Sympson, writing about 1737, refers to this house, following the cathedral charters, as the great hall which once belonged to Peter de Lekeburn and Joan his wife.[4] A pamphlet published in Lincoln in 1850 merely refers to it as 'the other Norman house... higher up the hill, on the right hand side, near the County Hospital' (now the Bishop's Hostel) and adds 'at present it is occupied as a butcher's shop'.[5]

[1] *R.H.* I, 318b, 321a, 322b. The second and third of these references relate to the same land, and perhaps the first does also. Davis, 'The Medieval Jews of Lincoln' in *Arch. Journ.* XXXVIII (1881), p. 187.

[2] Davis, op. cit. p. 187. In 1185–6 Aaron's rents are dealt with in the Exchequer on the Essex and Hertford roll, the cost of bringing in his deeds (*cartae*) and the hutches containing them is charged in London and Middlesex, money is mentioned on the Notts and Derby roll, and his death is recorded among the forest fines of Surrey. P.R. 32 *Henry II*, p. xxx, and references there cited. Aaron's family, his brother Benedict, his sons Abraham, Vives, Benedict and Elias, Jacob his sister's son (*sororius*), and Benedict his nephew, were still active in Lincoln. Ibid. pp. 80–1. *Jewish Historical Society Miscellanies*, I, pp. lxvii–lxx.

[3] p. 70. The reference to his houses clearly comes from the Hundred Rolls. For Aaron of York, with whom he is confused, see Adler, *Jews of Medieval England* (1939), pp. 127–73.

[4] Adversaria, p. 312. Supra, p. 171.

[5] *Survey of Antiquities of the City of Lincoln*, published by W. and B. Brooke, p. 25.

Professor Freeman seems to have been the first to pronounce that this house was Aaron's. In his *Norman Conquest* (1876) he refers generally to houses of the Jews at Lincoln and Bury St Edmunds. In his Introduction to the works of Giraldus Cambrensis (1877), however, he remarks that Aaron's house was still shown near the south gate of Lindum.[1] Miss Kate Norgate accepted the identification. In her *England under the Angevin Kings*, published in 1887, she writes:

> His house, as it stands at the head of the 'Steep Hill' of Lincoln to this day, is one of the best examples of a mode of domestic architecture to which Christian townsfolk had scarcely yet begun to aspire, but which was already growing common among those of his race: a house built entirely of stone, in place of the wooden or rubble walls and thatched roofs, which, even after Fitz-Aylwine's Assize, still formed the majority of dwellings in the capital itself.

Her preface mentions that in her references to Lincoln she was assisted by the local knowledge of Precentor Venables,[2] who was also friendly with Freeman, and who repeated the identification in his *Walks through the Streets of Lincoln* in 1888.[3]

Then came the historian of the Jews. Mr Jacobs accepted the house without question as Aaron's, reproduced a picture of it, and compared it with 'the other' Jews' House. This was in 1893.[4] In 1897–8 he delivered his presidential address to the Jewish Historical Society of England on 'Aaron of Lincoln', and declared for the 'traditional' identification of the house:

> On the steep hill of that town, on the right-hand side as you go up to the cathedral, there is a house which tradition has always associated with Aaron of Lincoln, and which antiquaries are united in dating in the twelfth century, so that there is every likelihood that the tradition is founded on fact, especially as no one, for the last six hundred years at least, has known of the importance of Aaron of Lincoln.[5]

Dr Mansel Sympson copied Jacobs in his *Lincoln*,[6] and the claim is made again in the *Jewish Encyclopaedia*.[7]

[1] *Norman Conquest* (1876), v, 819; Giraldus Cambrensis, *Opera* (R.S.), VII, p. lxxxvii. In his *English Towns and Districts* (1883), p. 215, he says that 'in the local history he [Aaron] bears a name as the reputed builder, not of the famous Jews' house, but of the other house of the same style higher up the hill'.

[2] II, 487, and preface to vol. I.

[3] For a letter from Freeman to Venables, suggesting subjects for the chapter house windows, see Stephens, *Life and Letters of Edward A. Freeman*, II, 68.

[4] Jacobs, *Jews of Angevin England*, p. 91.

[5] *Trans. of the Jewish Hist. Soc. of England*, 1896–8, p. 172. In the same volume Mr Frank Haes gives an architectural account of the house in a survey of the Jews' houses in Lincoln, pp. 181–2.

[6] (1906), pp. 89–91.

[7] See article on Aaron of Lincoln. Dr Roth also accepts the identification, *History of the Jews in England* (1941), p. 15.

Jacobs knew that for some six hundred years nobody had known of the importance of Aaron, and, hearing of 'Aaron's house', no doubt concluded that the identification was a traditional one. Yet there is no evidence that when he wrote the identification was more than about twenty years old. Such evidence as is available shows that Aaron lived in the Bail; and although in the Hundred Rolls, compiled nearly a century after his death, land is described as having formerly belonged to him, yet by 1240 the house lately attributed to him is found in other hands without any hint that it had ever belonged to Aaron or had escheated to the king.[1] So much for local 'tradition'.

The best days of English Jewry came to an end on the death of Henry II, and as if to symbolise this fact there was an anti-Jewish riot in London at the coronation of Richard I. In spite of a royal proclamation for protection of the Jews, the fanaticism aroused by the impending crusade led to a series of attacks on the Jews at Lynn, Norwich, Stamford and other places. 'The men of Lincoln', says William of Newburgh,

> hearing of what was being done to the Jews, seizing the opportunity and encouraged by these examples, thought that something should be attempted, and gathering in a mob broke out into a sudden rising against their Jewish fellow-citizens. But they, rendered more cautious by knowing the fate or the terror of their fellows in various places, had betaken themselves betimes with their money to the fortified part of the town. And so nothing much being done, though much investigation was carried on by the royal officials, that vain rising quickly subsided.[2]

The Jews were less fortunate in York, where there was fearful slaughter, and it is significant that one of the leaders of the attack, Richard de Malebys, was, or had been, deeply in debt to Aaron of Lincoln.[3]

'The fortified part of the town' of Lincoln evidently means the Bail; within that sanctuary the Jews would be safe from the fury of the crowd of citizens, consisting of wealthy merchants like Godwin the rich, Reimbald of Wigford and William son of Warner, as well as craftsmen and small men, whose names, with the penalties imposed upon them, are recorded on the Pipe Roll for 1191.[4]

In the thirteenth century there were periodic outbreaks of anti-Jewish feeling. In 1202 the discovery of a child's body outside the walls of Lincoln aroused suspicion against the Jews.[5] In 1220 the men of Walter de Evermeu slew Moses of Lincoln, and the sheriff was ordered to bring them

[1] See supra, p. 171.

[2] I, 312. Jacobs, *Jews of Angevin England*, p. 117.

[3] Davis, 'Hebrew Deeds of English Jews before 1290' in *Anglo-Jewish Historical Exhibition Papers* (1887), II, no. 147. Jacobs, op. cit. p. 77.

[4] P.R. 3 *Richard I*, pp. 15, 16.

[5] Mrs D. M. Stenton, *Earliest Lincolnshire Assize Rolls* (L.R.S.), no. 996.

before the justices; and he was further ordered to bid the mayor of Lincoln have before the justices at the same term the Christians that slew Deulecresse and Sarra his wife.[1]

Two instances show the king and his officers protecting the Jews against clerical intolerance. In 1223 the archbishop of Canterbury and the bishop of Lincoln ordered that none in their diocese should sell victuals to the Jews or have any communication with them. The king intervened, and sent letters to the sheriffs ordering that victuals and other necessaries should be sold to them. In 1234, Jacob, a Lincoln Jew, was said to have been murdered by Alexander of Lincoln, a clerk, who was arrested for the crime by the sheriff.[2]

There followed in 1255 the most famous (or infamous) incident in the history of Lincoln Jewry. The charge of ritual murder so often made against the Jews appeared first in the story of William of Norwich in 1144; there the suggestion that a Christian child had been crucified was made by an apostate Jew. The story appears again at Gloucester in 1168 and at Bury St Edmunds in 1181. After Lincoln follows London in 1257; and abroad the story appears at Blois in 1171, Paris in 1180, and elsewhere.

The classic English case is that of Little St Hugh of Lincoln. The story is told by Matthew Paris. In 1255,

> about the feast of the apostles Peter and Paul, the Jews of Lincoln stole a boy called Hugh, who was about eight years old. After shutting him up in a secret chamber where they fed him on milk and other childish food, they sent to almost all the cities of England in which there were Jews, and summoned some of their sect from each city to be present at a sacrifice to take place at Lincoln in contumely and insult of Jesus Christ. For, as they said, they had a boy concealed for the purpose of being crucified; so a great number of them assembled at Lincoln, and then they appointed a Jew of Lincoln as judge to take the place of Pilate, by whose sentence and with the concurrence of all, the boy was subjected to various tortures. They scourged him till the blood flowed, they crowned him with thorns, mocked him and spat upon him, each of them also pierced him with a knife, and they made him drink gall, and scoffed at him with blasphemous insults, and kept gnashing their teeth and calling him Jesus, the false prophet. And after tormenting him in divers ways they crucified him, and pierced him to the heart with a spear. When the boy was dead, they took the body down from the cross, and for some reason disembowelled it; it is said for the purpose of their magic arts. The boy's mother, when her son had been missing several days, sought for him diligently, and the neighbours told her that they had last seen him playing with some Jewish boys of his own age, and going into the house of a Jew. So the mother entered the house suddenly and saw the boy's body lying in

[1] Rigg, *Exchequer of Jews*, I, 31.

[2] *C.C.R.* 1231–4, p. 571. Rye, 'Persecutions of Jews' in *Anglo-Jewish Historical Exhibition Papers* (1887), I, 152, 156 (where the accused man's name is given as Abraham, and it is suggested that he was a convert).

a well; the bailiffs of the city were then cautiously summoned, and the body was found and drawn up. It was a remarkable sight which then presented itself to the people; the mother's cries and lamentations provoked all the citizens assembled there to tears. There was present John of Lexington, a man of learning, wise and prudent, who said 'We have heard sometimes the Jews have dared to attempt such things in insult of our crucified Lord Jesus Christ'; and then addressing the Jew whose house the boy had entered whilst at play, and who, as being for that reason a greater object of suspicion, had been arrested, 'Wretched man, dost thou not know that a speedy end awaits thee? All the gold in England will not suffice to ransom or save thee. Yet unworthy though thou art, I will tell thee how thou canst save thy life and limb from destruction. Both these will I save thee, if without fear or falsehood, thou wilt expose to me all that has been done in this matter.' Then the Jew, whose name was Copin, thinking that he had found a way of escape, answered, 'My lord John, if thou wilt repay my words with deeds, I will show wondrous things unto thee.' Then when John zealously urged and encouraged him, the Jew continued: 'What the Christians say is true. Almost every year the Jews crucify one boy in injury and insult to Jesus. But one is not found every year, for they do this privately, and in remote and secret places. This boy whom they call Hugh, our Jews crucified without mercy; and after he was dead, and they wished to hide his corpse, they could not bury or conceal it. (This they wished to do, as the body of an innocent boy was considered useless for augury, which was the reason for disembowelling it.) In the morning when they thought it was hidden away, the earth vomited and cast it forth, and there it lay unburied on the ground to the horror of the Jews. At length they threw it into a well, but still they could not hide it, for the mother never wearied in her search, and finding the body informed the bailiffs.' The Jew was kept in chains, and the body given to the canons of Lincoln, who had asked for it, and who, after displaying it to an immense number of people, buried it honourably in the church of Lincoln, as if it had been that of a precious martyr. The king, when he heard what had happened, was angry with John for having promised life and limb to such a wicked being, which he had no right to do; for a blasphemer and murderer such as that man deserved to die many times over. Then the guilty man said, 'My death is imminent, nor can John give me any assistance. I will tell the truth to you all. Nearly all the Jews in England agreed to the death of this boy, and from nearly every English city where Jews live, some were chosen to be present at this sacrifice as a Paschal offering.' Then he was tied to a horse's tail and dragged to the gallows, where he was delivered body and soul to the devils of the air. The other Jews who shared in the guilt, to the number of 994 were taken to London and imprisoned there; and if any Christians pitied them, they were only dry tears which their rivals the Caursines shed.

The Franciscans intervened on behalf of the imprisoned Jews, who, after being kept in the Tower as criminals, bound hand and foot, were set free on 12 March 1256. Matthew Paris repeats that they were found guilty on the assertion of a Jew who had been hanged at Lincoln.[1]

[1] Matthew Paris, *Historia Majora* (R.S.), v, 516–18, 522, 546, 552. The translation is taken from Hutton, *Simon de Montfort and his Cause*, 1251–66, pp. 55–8. The story is fully discussed in Jacobs, 'Little St Hugh of Lincoln' in *Jewish Ideals and other Essays* (1896).

The story, even as told by a chronicler hostile to the Jews, is unconvincing. The child was kept for ten days, according to Paris; Jews from other towns could not well have been assembled in a shorter time. The mother did not begin her search for several days, and her negligence is the more surprising in view of the fact that the boy had been seen playing with Jewish children and entering the house of a Jew. It is clear that the charges rested upon the evidence of the Jew Copin, and that his evidence was extorted from him under promise of his life by John of Lexington: John almost put the evidence into his mouth. Then when he found that John's promise would be broken he made a desperate bid to save himself by incriminating the whole of the Jews in England. It is no wonder that Matthew Paris refers to his *deliramenta*.

Another version of the story is given in the annals of the abbey of Burton on Trent. The boy was kept alive for twenty-six days instead of ten, and he was starved instead of being fed. His death was decreed by a council of Jews, who cut off his nose and crucified him. A large number of Jews had assembled in Lincoln for a wedding. Suspicion being aroused against them, the mother set off to Scotland to petition the king for an inquisition. The Jews then threw the body into a well. When it was drawn up a blind woman rubbed her eyes with the moisture of the body and recovered her sight. The parish priest wished to keep the rich prize of a boy martyr for his own church, but notwithstanding his protests the corpse was taken to the Minster. The king then arrived, investigated the charges, and ordered the arrest of the Jews. Thereupon a riot occurred and the Jews' houses were stormed. Copin confessed in reliance on John of Lexington's promise, but failed to save his life. Eighteen others were hanged in London, though in this version it was the Dominicans who tried to save them. Seventy-one others, the richest Jews in the land, were saved by the king's brother Richard of Cornwall.[1]

Although the evidence in support of Copin's story is lacking, there is confirmation of the reports of the proceedings that followed. On 14 October 1255 the constable of Lincoln Castle was ordered to deliver the Jews accused of the crucifixion to the sheriff of Lincoln, who was to bring them to Westminster; the sheriffs of Huntingdon and Hertford were bidden to help him on his way through their counties.[2] On 22 November ninety-two Jews, then imprisoned in the Tower, were brought before the king, and eighteen of them refused to submit themselves to the verdict of a jury unless there were Jews on it. Thereupon they were indicted, condemned and executed the same day, refusal to plead being regarded as a confession of guilt.[3]

[1] *Annales Monastici* (R.S.), I, 340–8.
[2] *Close Rolls*, 1254–6, p. 145.
[3] *Liber de Antiquis Legibus* (Camden Society), p. 23.

With this warning before them the other Jews were prepared to submit to trial, even in the county of Lincoln, where feeling against them might be expected to be strongest, for on 7 January 1256 the king wrote to the sheriff of Lincoln that a certain number of Jews had thrown themselves on the county to take their trial for the alleged murder of Hugh son of Beatrice.[1] Mr Jacobs could find no record of proceedings taken either in London or in Lincoln, but according to Matthew Paris they were released. Some Lincoln Jews seem to have been in prison in 1257, 'touching Hagin of Lincoln'; whether this was connected with the ritual murder charge is not stated.[2]

Normally the king would have benefited by the forfeiture of the property of the condemned men. He had, however, sold all his rights in the Jews to his brother Richard of Cornwall in February 1255. In pursuance of this deal the king appointed commissioners on 26 November to have a jury value the houses of the Lincoln Jews who fled or were hanged or detained in prison for the death of the boy, and to seize their chattels and take account of the debts due to them; for the king had granted these to his brother in payment of his debts. The constable and the mayor, bailiffs, and the chirographers of the Lincoln Jews were ordered to give their aid. The Jews of Lincoln, however, owed the queen £172. 8*s*. 2*d*. for her gold, and this debt was to have priority.[3]

Four months later (27 March 1256) another commission was issued to inquire into the murder; and in particular to inquire who were of the synagogue (*scola*) of Peytevin the Great who fled on account of the boy's death. The sheriff of Lincoln was ordered to impanel a county jury and a city jury to inquire with the mayor, bailiffs and coroners of Lincoln and the coroners of the county. All Jews and Jewesses who had been attendant on any of the Lincoln Jews during the last two years must be present. On 20 August the Jews' houses were ordered to be sold, and another effort made at collecting all their chattels.[4] The spoils of the affair, as they came into possession, were being turned into money. In consideration of a fine paid to the king, Hagin of Lincoln, a Jew, son of Master Moses, obtained a grant of all the houses, lands and rents late of Jacob son of Leo, a Lincoln Jew hanged for the boy said to be crucified at Lincoln: there were three houses lying between land of Henna, a Jewess, towards the south, and the land of Robert the turner towards the north; one in the parish of St Cuthbert; one, in which Jacob had dwelt, in the parish of St Michael on the hill,

[1] Shirley, *Royal Letters of Henry III* (R.S.), II, 110.

[2] *Close Rolls*, 1256–9, p. 23.

[3] *C.P.R.* 1247–58, pp. 451–2. The king's acknowledgement of his brother's rights disposes of Mr Jacobs' suggestion that he was evading his grant to Richard and taking forfeitures under the ordinary law. *Jewish Ideals and other Essays*, pp. 206–7.

[4] *C.P.R.* 1247–58, pp. 493, 510.

of the fee of the abbot of Newsum (*sic*); and one in the same parish of Robert the turner's fee; a house in the parish of St Andrew in the corner opposite to the house in which Jacob had lived, which was of the fee of the Hospitallers of Lincoln; a house in St Michael's parish between Robert the turner's land to the south and the high market to the north, and a house in Parchemingate in the same parish, sometime of Beatrice Paynel, by the land of Godred the chaplain of Magdalen; and half a mark of rent from land of Martin the cordwainer, formerly of Richard Wlberne (*sic*) in the parish of St Edmund. Hagin also obtained a house late of Vives of Northampton, a Jew hanged for the said boy, which lay in Brancegate in St George's parish between the land of Samuel, son-in-law of Leo, on the east and the land of Vives of Norwich on the west; and a house which Isaac, son of Elias Martrin, a Jew, held in St Cuthbert's parish, between the land of the mother church of Lincoln on the south and land of Henna, a Jewess, on the north.[1] Walter de Kivelingho[lm] paid a gold mark to the king's use for a house which Vives of Norwich, 'a Jew hanged for the crucifixion of a boy as it is said', held in Brancegate in St Martin's parish.[2]

The master and brethren of the Knights Templars obtained from the king with the assent of Herman de Budbergh, king's yeoman, houses in the parish of St Martin in the cloth market, late of Leo son of Salomon, a Lincoln Jew hanged for the death of the boy crucified at Lincoln, whereby the houses escheated to the king, who gave them to Herman.[3]

Hatred, hysteria and self-interest stand out as the governing forces behind the anti-Jewish outburst, and, as the charge of ritual murder spread over Europe, it is worthy of note that in one exalted quarter credulity was resisted. Popes Innocent IV and Gregory X both denounced stories like that of Little St Hugh of Lincoln. In a bull issued in 1272 the latter decreed that in these cases the Christian charges against the Jews were not to be listened to, and all Jews imprisoned without serious cause were to be released.[4]

Whatever the manner in which the child Hugh met his death, the body was secured by the cathedral clergy and added to their collection of relics. Little St Hugh appears in the calendar of the Lincoln Use, his day being 27 August. His tomb seems to have been a popular one in its early days. It was one of the five in the Minster to which offerings were made in the name of Edward I in 1299–1300.[5] In 1363 a gild was formed by certain

[1] *C. Chart. R.* I, 460 (6 Jan. 1257). [2] *Excerpta e Rotulis Finium* (R.C.), II, 255.

[3] *C. Chart. R.* I, 467. For purchases by Thomas de Beaufou and John le Long, see *Close Rolls*, 1256–9, p. 236.

[4] See Vacandard, 'La Question du Meurtre Rituel chez les Juifs', in *Études du Critique et d'Histoire*, vol. III.

[5] *Liber Quotidianus Contrarotulatoris Garderobae* (1787), p. 37.

parishioners of St Cuthbert and St Andrew on the hill in Lincoln in honour of Our Lord, St Mary and All Saints, and especially in honour of St Mary 'who stands by the tomb of St Hugh Junior'.[1] The popularity of the tomb declined, however, as the Jews became a memory, and in the accounts for 1420–1 the offerings made there were only 10½*d.*[2]

The tomb stands in the passage behind the south wall of the choir. After the upheavals of the Reformation and the Civil War it seems to have been all but forgotten, and the shrine was depicted by Stukeley as that of St Hugh the Bishop.[3] The error was noticed by Smart Lethieullier, who visited Lincoln in 1736, and who writes:

> Upon a strict enquiry, I was informed by one of the minor canons (a gentleman who has a taste for these studies), that there was an old tradition among the members of the church, that this was the tomb of the crucified child; and as a farther proof, the verger showed me a statue of a boy made of free-stone painted, about twenty inches high, which by tradition they affirm was removed from the said tomb or shrine. I have inclosed a slight sketch of it, by which you will observe the marks of crucifixion in the hands and feet, and the wound made on the right side, from whence blood is painted on the original as issuing; the left hand is on the breast, but the right held up, with the two fingers extended in the usual posture of benediction; which attitude, I apprehend, denotes his being a saint, as the wounds do his being a martyr.

The head was broken off. Lethieullier thought, no doubt rightly, that Stukeley took his drawing of the shrine from the book of drawings of cathedral monuments made for Dugdale before the Civil War; and he suggested that the statue of the boy escaped transference to the Exchequer under Henry VIII because it was only of stone.[4]

The tomb was opened in 1791 by Dean Kaye and Sir Joseph Banks, who found the complete skeleton of a boy 3 ft. 3 in. long: one account says that the body was in a leaden cerecloth in a kind of pickle, which Sir Joseph, with a curiosity proper to a President of the Royal Society, is said to have tasted.[5]

The Lincoln story was still remembered a century after Hugh's death, as witness Chaucer's oft-quoted lines in the *Prioresse's Tale*:

> O yonge Hugh of Lincoln, sleyn also
> With cursed Jewes, as it is notable
> For it nis but a litel whyle ago.

[1] Gild Certificates, no. 140 (b).

[2] Wordsworth, *Notes on Medieval Services in England* (1898), p. 109.

[3] *Itinerarium Curiosum*, plate 29.

[4] *Archaeologia*, I (1770), pp. 28–9. The drawing of the headless statue is reproduced by Sir Charles Anderson, *Lincoln Pocket Guide* (3rd ed. 1892), plate iv. Henry Best once broke the toe off a foot that stood out beyond the wrappers in which an embalmed body was involved: he believed it to be that of Little St Hugh. *Personal and Literary Memorials* (1829), p. 244.

[5] Anderson, op. cit. p. 117. Brooke, *Notes on Lincoln Cathedral*, p. xvii.

It caught the popular imagination, and took form as a ballad, of which there are said to be six versions:

> they concur in representing that a schoolboy of tender years was induced, by means of an apple, to enter the house of a Jew; that the Jew's daughter who enticed him put him to death in a secret apartment, and afterwards threw the body into a draw-well. They all represent the anxiety of the mother in seeking for her son; and the miraculous circumstance of his detailing the fact and manner of his murder from the bottom of the well. In all the copies the conversation is carried on in the most natural manner: the mother expects, as a matter of course, that her dead son can and will reply to her inquiry.[1]

As might be expected, there are many differences between the versions; but perhaps the most notable fact is that these ballads contain no reference to Matthew Paris' charge of ritual murder, nor indeed any charge against the Jews as a community. A child certainly died. He may have been murdered: he may have been murdered by a Jewess. It is, after all, possible that the ballad contains, in its own romantic form, something nearer to the real truth than the solemn record of the chronicler.

There also survives a much more elaborate ballad in old French, which appears to be contemporary or nearly so. It gives a full account of the crucifixion and murder, the concealment and discovery of the body, its removal and burial in the mother church, and the capture, confession, trial and execution of the Jews, prefixing an appeal by the anguished mother to the king for aid. Its author was clearly one with some information about local topography:

> Ore oez un bel chançon
> Des Jues de Nichole, qui par tréison
> Firent la cruel occision
> De un enfant que Huchon out non.
>
> En Nichole, la riche citié,
> Dreit en Dernestal, l'enfant fui néé;
> De Peitevin le Ju fu emblé
> A la gule de aust, en un vespré.

He knew Nichole was the French name of Lincoln, and he knew also the Dernstall, the area in which St Martin's church stood, and in which Hugh was born. After the murder the body was taken to a well

> Derere le chastel del cité

and plunged in. After the trial Copin (or Jopin) was dragged by horses to the gibbet outside the town:

[1] Abraham Hume, *Sir Hugh of Lincoln* (1849), p. 32. He gives four versions of the ballad in parallel columns.

A coste de Canevic, sur halt mont
U la gent pendu sunt
Que larcin ni treson funt:
Mult urent Jus à lur hont.[1]

The ballad puts the well to the west of (or behind) the castle. Long afterwards Stukeley was told that it was called Grantham's well, and was in Newport.[2] Thomas Sympson noted the tradition that it was in one of the houses in St Martin's parish (he refers to the Jews' houses) in the Strait that the Child Hugh was crucified.[3] These vague references have been elaborated by some later writers. Dr Mansel Sympson says:

> In the front room of the ground floor of the house just north of the entry to the 'Jews' Court', on the Steep Hill, is a well traditionally considered to be the well in which the boy's corpse was put; another tradition places the well in the middle of Newport, just outside Newport Arch, which had the name of Grantham's well. The front room on the first floor of the house in 'Jews' Court' is traditionally said to have been the Synagogue.[4]

He wrote in 1906. In 1911 the Jews' Court passed into new ownership, and about that time there appeared a brochure entitled *Jew's Court and the Legend of Little St Hugh of Lincoln* by Thomas R. Howitt, Lincoln. This production declares that the chief interest of the building centres in the right-hand room in the basement, 'for in the corner of this room, at the left-hand side of the fireplace, is the veritable well into which the body of little Hugh was thrown after his crucifixion'. The well, it goes on,

> which has recently been uncovered and restored, is not, as the poetic licence of the ballad has it, 'full fifty fathoms deep', but is large enough and deep enough to play the grim part assigned to it in the tragedy. It is a cavity some three feet deep and some three feet square, sunk in the foundations of the building, and lined with rough stonework,

and it adds that the same spring still supplies it that bubbled forth in Little St Hugh's day. After quoting Matthew Paris and the ballad, it cites the authority of Pugin in support of the ritual murder charge against the Jews. It adds a picture of 'St Hugh's Well', giving it a cavernous appearance

[1] Ibid. pp. 43, 48, 54. The city gallows stood on Canwick Hill at its junction with the Heighington lane. About 1846, in face of the new railway competition, the Lincolnshire horse-breeders (with a view to keeping the stage-coaches on the road) persuaded the authorities to make a deep cutting near the top of the hill to ease the gradient. The Heighington lane had to be cut down to the new level and the mound at the foot of the gallows was cut away for the purpose. The cutting was believed to be haunted by a ghost, and travellers after dark would avoid it by using lanes through Canwick village. In 1894 a new parsonage house was built on the site of the gallows, and thereafter the ghost was seen no more. This story was told by the late vicar of Canwick, the Rev. H. J. Watney, quoting a former parish clerk, Richard Henry Ellis.

[2] *Itinerarium Curiosum*, p. 85.

[3] Adversaria, p. 296.

[4] *Lincoln*, p. 87.

which bears no resemblance to the neat stone basin 'uncovered and restored' about that time.[1]

In 1923 the Lincoln Corporation made an order under the Housing Acts for the rehousing of the tenants of certain houses, including the Jews' Court, and the acquisition and demolition of the houses. At that time the Jews' Court was divided into seven tenements. The owner contended that the compensation to be paid to him should take into account the antiquarian value of the building, but his claim could not be maintained. On 5 June 1928 the City Council resolved to demolish the house but to preserve the well associated with the legend. This announcement aroused a great deal of discussion, in the course of which a workman came forward to declare that he had been employed to make the well some years before. It would seem therefore that the 'uncovering and restoring' of the pamphlet is an understatement. So perished the widely accepted belief in the authenticity of 'St Hugh's Well'.[2]

It is pleasant to record that after lengthy negotiations the Lincoln Corporation sold the Jews' Court to the Lincolnshire Architectural and Archaeological Society, which has carefully restored it. It is now occupied by the Lincoln Diocesan Trust and Board of Finance. The question of the house's association with the Jewish community must be mentioned later.

Though the events surrounding the story of Little St Hugh constitute by far the best-known incident in the history of Lincoln Jewry, it cannot be said that the executions and forfeitures that followed it were the worst blow suffered by the community. The civil war between Henry III and Simon de Montfort provided the opportunity for another onslaught, during which the chirograph chest containing the evidence of debts due to the Jews

[1] Howitt was sanitary inspector to a rural district council. He was killed in the War of 1914–18.

[2] The workman said he was told to excavate in places where he thought the well might be situated, and with a labourer, searched the whole of the ground at the back of the court, but although they dug for a depth of 3 ft. they found no trace of a well. On being told this the purchaser of the premises gave instructions for a well to be built. His instructions were carried out and a well was dug in a dark corner of the room facing the Strait. Over the cavity made there was some boarding which looked like a cupboard. The well was made about 3 ft. deep and about 3 ft. square, and it was paved with ancient looking stones found in the vicinity. In front of the excavation was placed a board which prevented anyone from putting a stick or an umbrella into the hole to see how deep it was, and also to prevent people from falling in. The well was filled with buckets of water, and it was further filled with water which ran down the hill in wet weather. The owner of the property then issued a notice outside the building inviting people to inspect the famous well where Little St Hugh was drowned. Threepence admission was charged. The builder stated that there was a hole in the room where the present well was situate, and which might have been the remains of the well of legend fame. In accordance with instructions the walls of the hole or well were built up to a depth of 3 ft. and a concrete bed was put in. *Lincolnshire Echo*, 15 June 1928.

was burnt, and the king took the Jews under his protection.[1] They must have been greatly impoverished during their remaining years in England: but even so they were not left in peace, for in 1278 a charge of clipping coin was brought against all the Jews in England, and many of them were hanged.

The Dernstall has already been mentioned.[2] It adjoined the north end of High Street and the south end of the Strait. In the course of time the name corrupted into 'Danstallak', 'Darnstan lock', 'Dunstan lock'; and this corruption, combined with the facts that at its south end the Strait is very narrow, and that the historic Jews' House stands near by, has given rise to a popular belief that there was a ghetto here. Sir Charles Anderson refers to St Dunstan's lock, and says:

> The lock possibly refers to a barrier placed across the entrance of the Strait, and secured at night. It might be to shut in the Jews; as in Rome, till lately, the Jews' quarter, called the 'Ghetto', was locked up.[3]

He is followed by subsequent writers. A glance at the map shows that the Strait is part of the main highway from the upper city to the lower, and it would be ridiculous to suppose that it could be barred at night; furthermore, the documents make it plain that the Jews lived on both sides of this imaginary barrier. They lived on or near to the main street, in which most of the markets were held. In this respect the Lincoln Jews were no exception to the general practice of their community in England. As Mr Jacobs, writing of the London Jews, says:

> The position of the Jewry near the chief market seems so natural as scarcely to need explanation, and almost all the English Jewries are so situated. In York, it was near the Guildhall, as in London, for the mayor was the natural protector in both cases. In Lincoln the synagogue adjoined the market; at Oxford the Jewry was just in the centre of the town at Carfax (or *Quatre voies*); at Cambridge, at first near the castle, but afterwards near the market; and the same holds good of Warwick, Gloucester and Winchester; and if at Bristol and Southampton the Jewries were by the chief quays, it was for the same reason. The only exceptions to their being near the market are at Canterbury and Leicester.[4]

Mr Davis thought that the Lincoln Jews gathered in the Bail under the protection of the constable of the castle, but though some may have done so, the local evidence points to a different conclusion.[5]

The cathedral charters and monastic cartularies show that Mr Jacobs' conclusion applies to Lincoln. Several Jews were gathered near the high

[1] See p. 209. [2] Supra, pp. 34, 230.

[3] *Lincoln Pocket Guide* (1892 ed.), p. 169.

[4] 'London Jewry, 1290', in *Anglo-Jewish Historical Exhibition Papers* (1887), I, 37.

[5] 'Medieval Jews of Lincoln' in *Arch. Journ.* XXXVIII (1881), pp. 178, 179.

market in St Michael's parish. A house just outside the south gate of the Bail belonged to Ursell the Jew. Near by, Moses son of Benedict owned land. Jacob (probably the son of Leon) bought a piece from Robert son of Alan the turner. Vives the Jew had land near St John the Poor and Jacob son of Leon and Benedict son of Moses of London held a toft in St John's parish of Bardney Abbey for 5*s.* yearly. Leon held land in the parish of St Peter Stanthaket.[1] In St Martin's parish Moses the Jew appears again. Abraham son of Aaron held land of Lincoln Hospital, and Hagin also was there. After the expulsion King Edward I granted to William de Tame, cordwainer, houses in St Martin's parish which had belonged to Floria of London, a Lincoln Jewess.[2]

The list of escheats given in the *Book of Fees* contains some properties which might perhaps be identified with some of those mentioned above. It adds others. Elias the fat held a house in Brancegate of Peter of the Bail for 10*s.* The house which Jacob and Samuel, sons of Vives, held in Brancegate, had escheated: it owed to John the clerk, the chief lord, 20*s.* a year. There was a group of Jews living in Brancegate, which was the medieval name of the present Grantham Street.[3]

Deulecres held in St Peter at Pleas' parish.[4] Though, as might be expected, most of the Jews lived within the city wall, a few either lived or owned property in Wigford. Ursell Levy the Jew of Wigford had houses in St Mark's parish. Jacob Levi had houses in St Benedict.[5]

The Jews' House, popularly so called, has long been identified with one referred to in the cathedral charters: a stone house, situate in St Cuthbert's parish, on the west side of Steep Hill, given by William de Thornton to the dean and chapter. There can be little doubt that the identification is correct. The house is of the right date; it is in the right position in the modern parish of St Michael (by succession to St Cuthbert) and near to the boundary of St Martin; and it belongs to the dean and chapter.

The relevant deeds may be summarised as follows. At the expulsion Belaset daughter of Solomon of Wallingford was recorded to have owned £4. 13*s.* 4*d.* in money and a house of the yearly value of 19*s.* 6*d.*[6] On 20 March 1291, at Welbeck, Edward I granted to Walter le Foure of Fulletby those houses in Lincoln which had belonged to Belaset of Wallingford, who had been hanged for clipping the king's coin and whose houses had so been forfeited to the king. They had been valued at 19*s.* 6*d.*, and

[1] D. & C., Dii, 76/2/21, 22, 53. Bardney Cartulary, ff. 245, 245d; D. & C. Dii, 80/3/1.
[2] D. & C., Dii, 75/2/15, 27, 34, 35, 36, 39.
[3] *Book of Fees*, I, 364–5.
[4] D. & C., Dii, 80/3/25.
[5] Birch, pp. 136–42.
[6] Abrahams, 'Condition of the Jews in England in 1290', in *Trans. of the Jewish Hist. Soc. of England*, 1894–5, pp. 94–5.

were to be held by Walter and his heirs according to the custom of the city of Lincoln, yielding to the king *2d.* yearly (evidently the landtoll on two burgages) at the hands of the bailiffs of Lincoln.[1]

In 1309 Walter de Fulletby, who was a smith, granted to Roger le bower of Newcastle who lived in Lincoln, two stalls in St Cuthbert's parish in the corn market between the entry to Walter's hall on the north, and John le furbur of St Martin's parish on the south, having a frontage of 6½ ells 4 in., and a length from the gable of Walter's stone house to the king's highway, 5½ ells more or less. Roger sold the stalls to William de Thornton, a canon of Lincoln.[2]

Walter died almost immediately, for in 1310 his brother and heir William de Fulletby granted to Thornton the tenement in St Cuthbert's parish late of his brother. It was bounded by land of Henry Breyhaldon on the north and land of William de Lounesdale and formerly of Adam Acke on the south, by the king's highway on the east, and by the Drapery on the west. In 1311 Walter's widow Lecia released to Thornton any claim she might have in the property in right of dower or otherwise, doing so in the presence of the mayor and bailiffs.[3]

Thornton's purpose in acquiring this and other property was to provide endowment for a chantry; in 1311 he obtained the king's licence for alienation in mortmain, and in the same year granted this and other property to the dean and chapter, to maintain a chaplain to celebrate for the souls of William de la Gare, late archdeacon of Lincoln, and Thornton himself, their ancestors and all the faithful departed.[4]

There is a later reference to the same house in a charter granted by Edward IV to the city (now preserved only in an inspeximus charter of Richard III) in which the king, for the relief of the city's fee farm rent, released a large number of small payments due from the bailiffs to the Exchequer. Among them there are two sums, one of *2d.* due from houses formerly of Belaset the Jewess and later of Walter de Foure of Fulletby and his heirs, and one of 19*s.* 6*d.* yearly out of houses which had belonged to Belaset of Wallingford, the Jewess who was condemned, and which were the king's escheats owing to her felony.[5] It is difficult to see why the Exchequer was still receiving 19*s.* 6*d.* yearly after Edward I's grant to Walter in 1291.

This Belaset is not to be confused with another Belaset, the wife of Hagin of Lincoln and daughter of Benedict son of Moses. Moses was a

[1] Lib. Cant. f. 107, no. 290.
[2] D. & C., Dii, 74/3/13, 14. Lib. Cant. ff. 281, 284.
[3] D. & C., Dii, 74/3/12, 15.
[4] Lib. Cant. f. 192.
[5] Birch, pp. 137–9.

rabbi and a notable authority on Jewish law: Benedict also was a rabbi. He had a house in St Benedict's parish which he sold to his son Hagin for £60.[1]

The marriage contract by which this Belaset or Bellassez undertook to marry her daughter Judith to Aaron son of Benjamin is of such interest that the details must be quoted. In 1271 Judah son of Rabbi Meir, Abraham Hayim, Rabbi, son of Rabbi Joseph, and Joseph son of Rabbi Joshua having received a blessing from a 'minyan' of ten (no important religious task was performed without the presence of ten male adults) undertook the functions of a Bethdin—a tribunal of three—to arrange the following transaction between Benjamin son of Joseph Jechiel on the one part and Bellassez daughter of Rabbi Benedict on the other part. This Benedict is Master Benedict son of Master Moses.

Bellassez undertook to marry her daughter Judith to Aaron son of Benjamin, giving as a wedding gift to the young bridegroom 20 marks sterling and the 24 books of the Hebrew Bible, written on calfskin, properly provided with punctuation, Targum, Haphtaroth and Masora. Further details of this book were appended. The young folks being too youthful to marry yet, the father of the bridegroom undertook to take charge of the book and to keep it for the use of the young couple. Bellassez also delivered into the hands of the father these 20 marks sterling, to be lent out at interest to Gentiles, until Aaron be grown up. In lieu of this, at the period of Aaron's marriage with Judith, Benjamin undertook to give them 20 pounds sterling, and more if more had accrued out of the original 20 marks by way of interest in the meanwhile. Out of this sum also he was to provide both bride and bridegroom with wedding apparel befitting their station, both Sabbath and weekday clothing, and to make the wedding feast. He was to put forth no further claim on Bellassez, the mother.

The wedding was arranged to take place in the month of Adar (end of February) 1275, four years later, unless some impediment arose. If such difficulty occurred, the nuptials were to take place within one month after the lapse of such impediment. Benjamin mortgaged all his chattels and property, real and personal, as a guarantee that he would perform his part of the covenant. Should the affair not go well, Benjamin refusing at a later date to marry his son, he must either restore the volume or retain it at his pleasure, giving 6 marks for it in exchange. As to the 20 marks, Benjamin was to be believed on oath as to what he might have gained by them in the course of time, and undertook to refund one half of the amount, reserving the other half to himself. The parties then entered into

[1] Davis, 'Hebrew Deeds of English Jews before 1290' in *Anglo-Jewish Historical Exhibition Papers* (1887), II, no. 154. Rigg, *Exchequer of Jews*, II, 163, 173.

a solemn compact, holding a sacred emblem in their hands, and swore to perform their respective shares of the covenant. They thereupon placed a deposit or fine in the hands of the Bethdin, amounting to 100*s*. sterling, with the following undertaking. Should Aaron ever refuse to marry Judith and settle on her £100 'as is the custom of the isle', or should the father refuse his consent to the match, the deposit was to go absolutely to the mother of the jilted bride, or *vice versa*.[1]

Where was the synagogue in which sat the Bethdin? Dr Mansel Sympson refers to the tradition which places it on the first floor of the Jews' Court, the building north of the Jews' House, and although tradition must be received with caution it is not necessarily wrong. Dr Roth in a recent paper accepts the identification. He thinks that the front door of the Court, being a mere hole in the wall, is a later insertion, and that the room was approached from the back by an external ramp: and he sees in a recess in the eastern (or front) wall of the room the niche in which the scrolls of the law were kept.[2]

Dr Roth's claim receives some support from a deed of 1344 by which Peter le quilter granted to Roger le bower a plot of land with buildings in the parish of St Cuthbert in the corn market, in which plot the Jews' School used to stand.[3] Though this deed fixes the site within fairly narrow limits it does not identify the building, and the claim of the Jews' Court, while not improbable, cannot be regarded as proved. It is to be noted that there was a street called Scolegate, not in St Cuthbert's parish, but in that of St George. The Jews' burial ground is mentioned once, but without any reference to its site.[4]

When the Jews were expelled from England in 1290 they were a community impoverished by persecution and the anti-usury legislation of Edward I. There is no evidence of the numbers of the Lincoln Jews, for there must have been a considerable proportion with nothing to lend, and of whom there are no records. Of those who were in business or had property a list of 66 persons has been compiled by Sir Lionel Abrahams. Sums of money owing to them ranged from £196. 13*s*. 4*d*. due to Hagin son of Benedict, and £80 due to Jacob son of Hagin, to a few pounds: corn owing to them reached a total value of £601. 9*s*. 4*d*., and wool a value of £1,595. 6*s*. 0*d*. How they dealt in these commodities is not clear,

[1] Davis, op. cit. no. 156. Adler, *Jews of Medieval England* (1939), p. 43.

[2] See his 'Medieval Lincoln Jewry, and its Synagogue' (Jewish Historical Society), a paper read to the Society during its visit to Lincoln in 1934, in the room said to be the synagogue. See also Helen Rosenau, 'Note on the Relationship of Jews' Court and the Lincoln Synagogue' in *Arch. Journ.* XCIII (1936), pp. 51 et seq.

[3] B.B. f. 168 v.

[4] Birch, p. 142.

but the corn and wool certainly had to do with some form of money lending.[1]

What was the effect of the expulsion of the Jews from the city it is difficult to say. Merchants may have groaned about the hard bargains driven with them by the Jews, but the sudden disappearance of this source of credit must have had a disturbing effect on wholesale trade; and retailers could not fail to miss substantial people who lived near the markets. Years after, when the citizens were crying out to Richard III for relief from their burdens, they recalled that the Jews used once to bring much trade to the city.[2]

[1] Abrahams, op. cit. pp. 94, 95.

[2] *H.M.C. Lincoln*, p. 263.

CHAPTER XII

THE FOURTEENTH CENTURY

EDWARD I summoned his Parliament to meet at Lincoln on 20 January 1301. He was engrossed in his Scottish campaign, and had just been confronted by a papal claim to the overlordship of Scotland. There was a great gathering of notables, for the meeting was an important one:

> The date a thousand was and three hundred even,
> At Lincoln the parlement was in Lyndesay and Kesteven,
> At the Pask afterward, his parlement set he,
> The gode king Edward, at Lyncoln his cite.
> At Sant Katerine hous the erle Marschalle lay
> In the brode gate lay the Brus, erle was he that day.
> The kyng lay at Netilham, it is bisshope's toun,
> And other lordes there cam in the cuntre up and doun.[1]

The king was the guest of the bishop, John Dalderby, at the manor house of Nettleham until 12 February, when he moved into the city, and stayed there until 4 March.

The task of catering for so large and distinguished an assembly was a difficult one, and provisions poured into Lincoln. On 28 October 1300 a writ was addressed from Dumfries to the sheriff of Lincoln ordering him to provide 400 quarters of corn, 1,000 quarters of oats, hay enough for 400 horses for a month, 100 cows and oxen, 100 pigs and 300 sheep, for the meeting of Parliament. On 9 November, another writ, from Carlisle, called for 400 quarters of corn, 100 beeves, 60 live pigs and 400 sheep for the use of the royal household: the beeves and sheep were to be well salted and placed in the larder at Lincoln. Between 19 February and 1 March 3,121 gallons of ale, at a penny a gallon, were consumed. Stephen de Stanham, one of the principal citizens and a merchant of Lincoln, supplied sugar, figs and other goods amounting in value to £96. 14*s*. 5*d*.; fish to the cook's office for £54. 10*s*. 0*d*.; and herrings and stockfish to the king's son Edward for £6. 16*s*. 0*d*.[2] This was a very important aspect of Parliament to the city in which it met.

[1] *Peter Langtoft's Chronicle* (ed. Hearne), II, 312. The earl marshal was Roger Bigod, earl of Norfolk, and 'the Brus' was the father of Robert Bruce, king of Scotland. It may have been at the Grey Friary in Broadgate that he stayed.

[2] For these details see *Proceedings of the Archaeological Institute* (1848), pp. 28–9. *V.C.H. Lincs*, II, 263. Sixty dozen of good parchment were also required, followed by fourscore dozen more.

The royal sojourn had a special significance for the city of Lincoln. Opportunity was taken to lay before the king a plea for the restoration of the liberties granted by the king's ancestors, and forfeited in 1290. The application was successful, and on 25 February the king granted letters patent inspecting and confirming previous grants; with the additional provision that none of the liberties should be lost by non-user, and a quittance from murage, pavage, pontage, wharfage, stallage and terrage through all the king's realm, land and power.[1] This meant that the citizens should not be liable to payment of any taxes levied elsewhere in the kingdom, for the maintenance of walls, roads, bridges, wharves, or payment for stalls and like dues. The guess may be hazarded that Bishop Dalderby helped the citizens to get the charter. He did not become bishop until 1300, but previously he had been chancellor of the cathedral, and he must have been familiar with local conditions. He was one of the witnesses of the charter. The next day, on 26 February, the king granted to the mayor, bailiffs and good men of the city the right to levy taxes for repair of the roads (that is, pavage) for six years.[2]

Perhaps it was in appreciation of the king's new grant, or perhaps only in fulfilment of a condition made when the charter was granted, that the mayor (then restored) and the good men and the whole commonalty of the city paid £400 into the Exchequer during the year. Parliament had granted the king a fifteenth of movables, and in August Edward, then in Glasgow on his Scottish campaign, discharged the citizens of the tax in consideration of the cash payment, adding that if the £400 exceeded the city's assessment to the tax, the city should have credit for the balance, or, if the fifteenth were not paid at all, should have credit for the whole.[3]

The king died in 1307, on the eve of another Scottish campaign. One of the early incidents of the new reign affecting Lincoln was the suppression of the order of Knights Templars at the instigation of the pope and the king of France. Some of the knights were imprisoned in the Claxlede (or Clasket) gate—one of the few early references to this gatehouse—and the knights from seven counties were sent to Lincoln and tried in the chapter house of the Minster. The king's hopes of a substantial windfall from their forfeited goods were baulked by the Council of Vienne, which awarded their goods to the Knights Hospitallers.

One of the king's ways of raising money was to borrow from Italian bankers, and in particular from the Frescobaldi of Florence. By way of security he granted to Emery de Frescobald a number of manors in Lincoln-

[1] *C. Chart. R.* III, 7; Birch, pp. 18–27. For the *Provisions* for the government of the city which belong to this period, see infra, Appendix VII.

[2] *C.P.R.* 1292–1301, p. 576.

[3] Ibid. p. 605.

NORMAN HOUSE ON STEEP HILL, latterly attributed to Aaron the Jew

From a drawing (made c. 1800) *in the Banks Collection in Lincoln Public Library*

JEWS' HOUSE

From a drawing (made c. 1800) *in the Banks Collection in Lincoln Public Library*

[*See p.* 234

shire and a free court in the city of Lincoln, with the saving of the rights of the lawful owners of a moiety, who were out of possession.[1] Emery did not long enjoy his security, for the barons, with a list of grievances to redress, forced the king to accept the Ordinances of 1311. They disliked foreign moneylenders, and ordered the Frescobaldi to account by a certain day; meanwhile the foreigners were to be arrested and their lands and goods seized. If Emery himself did not come by the appointed time he was to be banished and held as an enemy.[2]

The Ordinances contained other provisions which were to affect this free court in Lincoln. Two of the royal favourites of whom the barons were determined to be rid were Henry de Beaumont and his sister Isabella de Vescy. The Ordinances directed that both should be removed from the royal court, and Isabella was to give up the royal castle of Bamburgh. In spite of the Ordinances, in 1312 the king granted Isabella a life interest in the estates which Emery had held as security; and in 1318 the reversion in the estates was granted to her brother Henry and his wife Alice and the heirs of his body. This grant spurred Peter de Rabayn, the rightful claimant to a moiety of the estates, into activity. He petitioned Parliament, and in the result the estates were divided, the free court in Lincoln being allotted to Isabella for life and after her to Henry in fee tail.[3] This free court, the manor of Hungate, thus acquired the name of Beaumont Fee, a name still preserved in a street name. The Beaumont family held the fee (except during the vicissitudes of the Wars of the Roses) until 1507.[4]

The Scottish war dragged on, and in 1314 the king began to prepare another expedition in the hope of saving Stirling from Robert Bruce. The army was ordered to assemble at Wark on Tweed on 10 June. A fortnight later the English army met with crushing defeat at Bannockburn, and returned to England.

The Parliament of 1315 met in no friendly mood, and Edward resorted to private borrowing again. On 1 November he promised repayment in the next Parliament of 900 marks borrowed from the bishop, dean and chapter of Lincoln, who were secured by recognisance of twelve leading citizens of Lincoln; the money was borrowed for defence of the realm against the Scots. The citizens were given an indemnity against loss.[5]

Parliament met in Lincoln on 28 January 1316, when Thomas earl of

[1] *C.P.R.* 1307–13, pp. 84, 152. For the Frescobaldi, see Rhodes, 'Italian Bankers in England' in *Owens College Historical Essays* (1902), pp. 145 et seq.

[2] Ordinance 21. Conway Davies, *Baronial Opposition to Edward II* (1918), pp. 370, 371.

[3] For these dealings see *C.F.R.* 1307–19, p. 131; *C.P.R.* 1307–13, p. 460; 1313–17, p. 29; 1317–21, pp. 71, 351; *C.C.R.* 1318–23, p. 174.

[4] See Hill, 'The Manor of Hungate' in *A.A.S.R.* XXXVIII (1927), pp. 175–208.

[5] *C.P.R.* 1313–17, pp. 189, 369.

Lancaster (who had succeeded to the earldoms of Lincoln and Salisbury in right of his wife Alice de Lacy on the death of Henry de Lacy in 1311), virtually took control of the country's affairs. The prelates, earls and others met in a chamber in the house of the dean of Lincoln. A 'full' Parliament met in the dean's hall on 12 February, and further meetings were held in the chapter house of the cathedral and at the convent of the Carmelites.[1] During his visit the king founded a chantry in the cathedral, endowing it with an income of £2 a year from the farm of the city, which sum was to be paid to a priest whom the king and his successors should nominate, to celebrate divine service daily for the good estate of the king, his queen Isabella, their first-born son, and for the souls of the king's ancestors and heirs and all Christians.[2]

Probably the citizens obtained the promise of a new charter during this royal visit, though the charter itself is dated 15 June. It confirms earlier grants, and recites that the citizens had hitherto had the tronage of wools and the pesage of other merchandise in aid of the farm of the city, but their rights had been impeached in the court of the king and his predecessors on the ground that they had no royal charter thereof; that the citizens in the king's absence had the assize of bread and ale and the custody and trial of weights and measures and other things belonging to the office of the market; and that the citizens had been granted the liberties of London, which had the aforesaid rights in the king's presence, so that the king's clerk or minister of the market did not enter the city of London to discharge his office. The charter then formally grants the tronage and pesage of wool and other goods, the assize of bread and ale and trial of weights and measures, to the exclusion of the king's clerk of the market or other servants, the profits from these rights going to the citizens in aid of their farm. There was a proviso that if the mayor, bailiffs or keepers of the city were charged with neglect in these matters, the king's chancellor or his deputy might investigate complaints and punish the civic officers.

There was also a grant of 'all the king's empty and waste places' in the city and suburb, to be held by the citizens for their profit as they thought fit, provided that there was no damage to the cathedral church of St Mary, or to the free tenement of any person, and that the streets were not excessively narrowed thereby.

The fine paid for the charter was £300.[3] As has been noticed above,[4]

[1] Conway Davies, op. cit. pp. 408–11.

[2] *C.P.R.* 1313–17, p. 398. Foster and Thompson, 'Chantry Certificates for Lincoln and Lincolnshire' in *A.A.S.R.* XXXVI (1922), p. 237.

[3] *C. Chart. R.* III, 312. The original charter is lost, but its provisions are contained in an inspeximus of Edward III. Birch, pp. 48–52.

[4] Supra, pp. 214–15.

most of these sources of revenue were already being tapped in aid of the farm, but the absence of express charter authority caused difficulty, and the new grant was secured for the removal of doubts and the avoidance of litigation.

Parliament met again in Lincoln in July 1316. A papal attempt to impose a truce in the Scottish war failed; and as part of his plan for the defence of the Border Edward took the castle of Wark on Tweed from William de Roos of Helmsley, one of his household, and gave him in exchange 400 marks a year out of the farms of the cities of York and Lincoln until the king should make other provision for him. The amount to be paid from the Lincoln farm was £146. 13*s.* 4*d.*[1] Other provision for William de Roos was never made. So began a connection between the Roos family (whose rights were later to pass to the earls of Rutland) and the city which gave trouble from time to time until the redemption of the farm in the sixteenth century.

The remainder of the farm was soon to be alienated by the Crown and to pass into the hands of the dean and chapter,[2] and though the city found its new financial relationships irksome and sometimes unpleasant, the alienation of the Exchequer revenues had one important result. The Crown was treating the fee farm as a rent charge, and to the Roos family it was nothing more than a rent charge. Originally the citizens were merely the agents of the Exchequer for the collection of revenue, and the king could seize the city into his hand if the farm were not regularly paid. After the alienation of the fee farm rent the king could still seize the city if he wished, but he was not likely to do so for non-payment, because he was not interested: if the city defaulted the Roos family and the chapter must seek their own remedy. They could not seize the city, and they could not even distrain for non-payment as a landlord could for his rent. All they could do was to sue for a debt. There was no feudal relationship; and when in 1553 the earl of Rutland claimed that the city should furnish him with a horseman for service under the queen, the common council repudiated the suggestion that he was entitled to service as lord of the city. 'You are misinformed', they wrote, 'in saying that we are your fermors. Although the Queen's progenitors granted to your ancestors a part of the rent of the fee farm of this city, more than it has been able to pay for a long time by reason of its decay, we are not tenants to you, the said rent having ever been a

[1] *C.P.R.* 1317–21, p. 29. The king's bargain was a bad one, for Wark fell to the Scots in 1318. In 1383 Thomas de Roos obtained licence to settle the fee farm rent upon himself and his wife in tail, with remainder to his right heirs. *C.P.R.* 1381–5, p. 236.

[2] Edward III granted £60 yearly in fee out of the farm of the city to Bartholomew Burghersh (brother of Henry Burghersh, bishop of Lincoln), who granted it to the chapter as part of the endowment of the Burghersh chantry. *C.P.R.* 1343–5, p. 381; 1345–8, p. 141; *A.A.S.R.* XXXVI (1922), pp. 210 et seq.

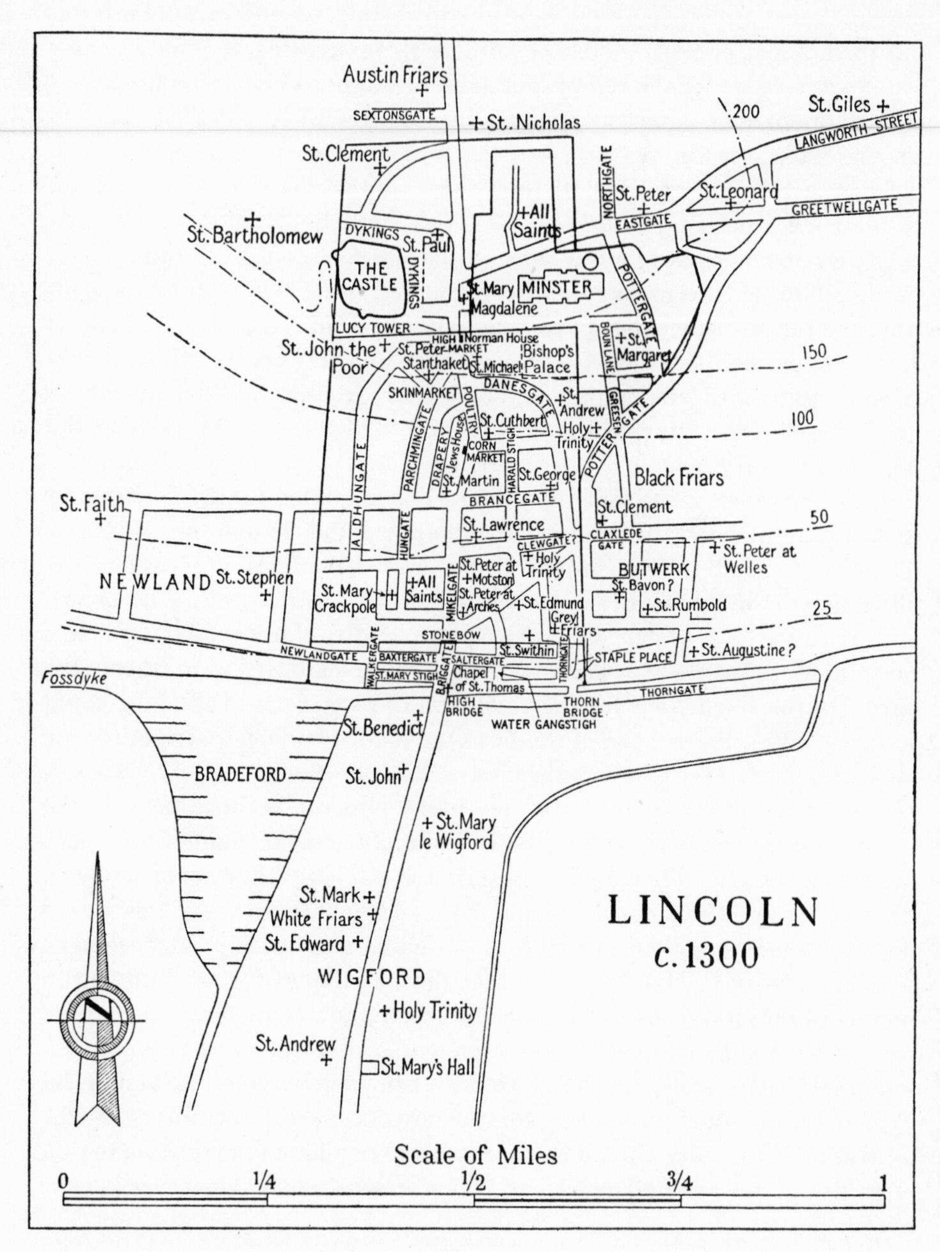
Austin Friars
SEXTONSGATE
St. Nicholas
St. Giles
200
LANGWORTH STREET
St. Clement
NORTHGATE
St. Peter
St. Leonard
GREETWELLGATE
EASTGATE
St. Bartholomew
DYKINGS
St. Paul
All Saints
THE CASTLE
DYKINGS
St. Mary Magdalene
MINSTER
POTTERGATE
LUCY TOWER
HIGH MARKET
Norman House
Bishop's Palace
BOUN LANE
St. Margaret
St. John the Poor
St. Peter Stanthaket
St. Michael
150
SKINMARKET
POULTRY
DANESGATE
St. Andrew
Holy Trinity
GREESEN
POTTERGATE
100
St. Cuthbert
DRAPERY
Jews House
CORN MARKET
HARALD STIGH
PARCHMINGATE
ALDHUNGATE
St. Martin
St. George
Black Friars
St. Faith
BRANCEGATE
St. Clement
St. Lawrence
50
HUNGATE
CLAXLEDE GATE
CLEWGATE?
Holy Trinity
St. Peter at Welles
St. Peter at Motston
BUTWERK
NEWLAND
St. Stephen
St. Mary Crackpole
All Saints
MIKELGATE
St. Peter at Arches
St. Edmund
St. Bavon?
St. Rumbold
Grey Friars
25
STONEBOW
NEWLANDGATE
WALKERGATE
BAXTERGATE
SALTERGATE
St. Swithin
THORNGATE
STAPLE PLACE
St. Augustine?
Fossdyke
ST. MARY STIGH
B. RIGGATE
Chapel of St. Thomas
THORNGATE
HIGH BRIDGE
THORN BRIDGE
WATER GANGSTIGH
St. Benedict
BRADEFORD
St. John
St. Mary le Wigford
St. Mark
White Friars
St. Edward
LINCOLN
c. 1300
WIGFORD
Holy Trinity
St. Andrew
St. Mary's Hall
N
Scale of Miles
0
1/4
1/2
3/4
1

Fig. 17.

rent seck.'[1] Slowly it was becoming possible to say that the mayor and citizens were the lords of the manor of the city of Lincoln.

Edward II was deposed on 20 January 1327 and his son Edward III crowned on 1 February. In September Parliament sat at Lincoln, and during its sessions the ex-king was murdered at Berkeley Castle. The counties and boroughs granted a twentieth for the expenses of the Scottish war. The mayor and citizens took the opportunity of seeking confirmation of their liberties, and on 7 October their new charter was sealed at Nottingham.[2]

After confirming a number of earlier grants, it refers to a writ of Henry II granting the citizens the farm of the city as in the time of Henry I, and recites that it had been found by inquisition that the mayor and citizens, by virtue of that charter, had from time immemorial had the tronage of wools and pesage of other merchandise in aid of the farm, and had been quit of tronage and pesage in other places within the king's realm and power; that the citizens had the return of writs; that they had three weekly markets on Mondays, Wednesdays and Fridays, and a yearly fair from St Botolph's Day (17 June) to St Peter and St Paul (29 June); that their ancestors had set up buildings on a wall from Newland gate to the house of the friars minor, that is, in places near Walkergate and Soper Lane, and that such buildings were an improvement to the city; that they had infangthief and outfangthief and the chattels of felons and fugitives from time immemorial; that no citizen had been wont to be convicted by any foreigner (that is, outsider) for any matter arising within the city or suburb unless it touched the community; and that the citizens had the keeping of the peace in the city and suburb, and had arrayed themselves for the keeping of the peace and the defence of the realm. The charter went on to say that it was not to the damage of the king that he should specify and grant these existing liberties, and that he therefore did so, save in cases of neglect by the citizens or their bailiffs; and that as Henry's charter had not mentioned the mayor (for the obvious reason that he did not exist) or the amount of the farm, the mayor and citizens should hold the city by rendering £180 yearly at the Exchequer. It directed that the burghmanmot should be held once a week in the gildhall on Mondays by the mayor and bailiffs, and that citizens should plead or be impleaded there upon any matter arising within the city or suburb (unless it touched the king or his heirs or the community of the city) before the mayor and bailiffs, whether in the king's presence or absence, without impediment: excepting pleas of trespass,

[1] *H.M.C. 12th Rep.* App. Part IV, p. 60.

[2] *C. Chart. R.* IV, 55; Birch, pp. 38–60. Among the witnesses is John de Ros, steward of the royal household.

agreements and contracts made in the king's household in his presence, and touching the king or any of his household. Lastly it was granted that no citizen, while resident in the city or suburb, should be put by the sheriff or other minister of the Crown upon assizes, juries or legal process outside the city merely by reason of his outside lands and tenements. For these valuable declarations of right the citizens paid the relatively moderate fine of £20.

On 22 February 1330, at Windsor, Edward confirmed his own charter, adding that all pleas of land situate within the city and suburb should be heard in the burghmanmot in the gildhall before the mayor and bailiffs, except pleas touching the king or the community of the city: this right, like those in an earlier charter, was already claimed by the citizens, who had found themselves in difficulties because it was not specified in their charters, and they wished to avoid a continuance of the frequent challenges of their jurisdiction.[1]

Of the manner in which the mayor and his brethren carried out their duties in these years there is no evidence save such as appears in the national records when they were suspected of neglecting their duties. The various inquiries that were held throw some light on those duties and the manner of their performance. For example, in 1331 a panel of jurors reported on the working of the assize of bread and ale in the city:

> The mayor, bailiffs and citizens of Lincoln do not make assay of the assize of bread and ale as often as is necessary, and when they do make it, they do not punish trespassers by the ordinary punishments, but by ransoms and amercements, which they levy to their own use; before now they have levied from Roger de Laghton for breach of the assize of bread and ale for a first offence 12d and for a second 18d; from John de Hole for a similar breach for a first offence 6d and for a second offence 12d; the said John was convicted a third time and deserved the pillory, which punishment he redeemed for an unknown sum of money; they levied from John de Scotre, baker, for default in the assize of bread, for which he deserved the pillory, a ransom of 10s; and from John de Sancto Ivone, for default in the weight of bread, for which he deserved the pillory, a ransom of 10s; Roger de Walkeryngham, John de Parys, and Emma de More, brewers, brew at their will without any assize of their ale, for a fine to be given to the bailiffs, and strangers commonly brew for sale without any assize, for a fine without punishment. The jurors have no knowledge of the weights and measures unless they were proved by the standard, but believe that they are not good.[2]

It was a natural consequence of a system in which fines were urgently needed to help to make up the city's farm that cash payments should be

[1] *C. Chart. R.* IV, 160; Birch, p. 60; *H.M.C. Lincoln*, p. 8. The witnesses include Bishop Burghersh of Lincoln who was the king's chancellor, and the queen-mother's paramour Roger Mortimer. Within the year Mortimer was hanged.

[2] *Cal. Inq. Misc.* II, no. 1201.

imposed in preference to the pillory; evidently, however, the fines had not the same deterrent effect, and the consumers of bread and ale were the losers. If the mayor and bailiffs maintained that justice was not bought and sold, the onlooker might be excused for sometimes thinking otherwise.

The taxes of pavage and murage, for the repair of roads and the city walls, could not be levied without royal licence. It was almost usual that some years after such a levy questions arose whether the proceeds of the tax had been properly applied. In 1301 Edward I, when he was at Lincoln, made a grant of pavage (to be levied on all wares brought for sale into the city) for six years to the mayor, bailiffs and good men of the city: in 1313 a commission was issued to Edmund de Eyncurt, Adam de Middelton and John of Blyton to audit the accounts of the pavage, the king having been told that the collectors had not carried out the road work, but had converted to their own uses a great sum of money accruing therefrom, to the city's great loss.[1] On further grants, the citizens who were to be responsible were appointed by name. In 1314 the duty of collection of a seven years' grant was laid on John of Blyton, Simon of Edlington, Henry de Outhorpe and Gilbert de Atherby, who were to be answerable for their agents.[2] In 1328 a five years' grant was made to the mayor, bailiffs and good men, to be collected by William of Blyton, Hugh of Edlington the elder, William of Hackthorn and William of Snarford or their deputies.[3]

A grant of murage for three years, made in 1322, was followed in 1325 by a commission to survey the walls of the city, to inquire the names of the collectors, to audit their accounts, and to compel them by distraint or otherwise to apply moneys received to their proper purpose.[4] A four years' grant was made in 1337, and another for seven years in 1345, when the king's clerk Henry de Edenstowe, John de Donham and Walter de Kelby were appointed to supervise the spending of the money.[5] The city was the king's city, and if he let it to the citizens at a rent, they must keep it in repair. The maintenance of the walls was especially important, for the city must be protected against the king's enemies. If the king was not concerned with the morals of the collectors he was much interested in the efficiency of the municipal administration in so far as it touched the safety and good order of the city.[6]

The maintenance of good order was in issue in 1322, when the king wrote to the mayor and good men of Lincoln, saying that he understood

[1] *C.P.R.* 1292–1301, p. 576; 1313–17, p. 63.

[2] *C.P.R.* 1313–17, p. 188.

[3] *C.P.R.* 1327–30, p. 321.

[4] *C.P.R.* 1321–4, p. 50; 1324–7, p. 236.

[5] *C.P.R.* 1334–8, p. 529; 1343–5, pp. 553, 590.

[6] For similar difficulty in ensuring the proper application of moneys collected for cleansing the Fossdyke, see p. 312.

that many persons resorted thither who did not obey the mayor in matters touching the safe keeping of the town, and ordering that an oath or other sufficient security for obedience should be taken from all persons staying there, and that any who were found contrary or rebellious should be imprisoned.[1] In 1330, when the king was faced with rebellion, he issued commissions to London and Lincoln and many other towns to array the knights and other men capable of bearing arms assembled by proclamation within those cities to resist the rebels against the king.[2] And on 1 August 1338 an order was issued to the mayor and bailiffs of Lincoln

to show such diligence in the safeguarding of that city and its suburbs, and the preservation of the peace there, that no harm may come for lack of such custody, for if it does the king will cause the city and suburbs and the liberties granted there to be seized into his hands, and will punish the mayor and bailiffs severely; as among other liberties, the king granted them that none of his ministers should intermeddle with the custody of the city, and now he has learned that the city and suburbs lack secure custody, because the king is now in parts beyond the sea, and because certain malefactors assemble in divers parts of the realm to do what harm they can.[3]

On 22 July Edward III had landed at Antwerp, and war with France had begun. His absence from home gave Philip of France an opportunity of invading England, and throughout the winter there was fear of invasion. The dire threat to seize the liberties of Lincoln was perhaps effective in inspiring vigilance, for it was not carried out. There is no record of such a threat being repeated thereafter.

The city's monopoly of foreign trade within the county, described above,[4] had become increasingly difficult to enforce as the thirteenth century drew to its close.[5] It was, however, followed by another system which was for a time to secure to Lincoln greater advantages. In the thirteenth century the greater part of the foreign trade was still in the hands of foreigners. Of 201 shipments of wool from Hull in 1275 only 13 can with safety be ascribed to Englishmen, though some English merchants, like William Feresseved of Lincoln,[6] were acting as agents for foreigners. Edward I drove the foreign trade in certain channels by a customs system at specified foreign ports. Later came the project of a home staple, its objects being to give the king an ally in the lesser merchants, to avoid mercantile losses, and to provide a diplomatic weapon. Hence the Ordinance of Kenilworth in

[1] *C.P.R.* 1321–4, p. 71.
[2] *C.P.R.* 1327–30, p. 572.
[3] *C.C.R.* 1337–9, p. 453.
[4] See pp. 185–6.
[5] See pp. 318–22.
[6] *C.F.R.* 1272–1307, p. 25. The mayor and bailiffs of Lincoln were ordered to seize his wool and chattels forfeited for trafficking with and going into partnership with men of Flanders contrary to the king's prohibition.

1326.[1] The staple towns established in England were Newcastle, York, Lincoln, Norwich, London, Winchester, Exeter, and Bristol; through these towns all wool, hides, skins, tin, and perhaps timber, had to pass.[2] From 1341 to 1353 the staple was transferred to Bruges, but in the latter year it was brought home again, and the Ordinance of the Staple directed that there should be a mayor of the staple in each staple town.

The list of mayors of the Lincoln staple makes interesting reading.[3] From 1353 to 1369 the office was held by only three men. In 1353 William de Spaigne was elected; the following year the election of Walter de Kelby was disputed and he was displaced by Spaigne. The next year William de Spaigne was again elected and he held the office until Robert of Dalderby secured election in 1359. Dalderby held it for two years, then Spaigne for two years, to be followed by Walter de Kelby, who was mayor of the staple until 1369.

Walter de Kelby was a merchant of Lincoln. He was a bailiff of the city in 1348,[4] and mayor in 1351. He represented the city in Parliament in 1348 and thereafter frequently until 1372. He appears with Dalderby among the Lincoln merchants to whom the collectors of customs at Lincoln were ordered to make allowances in 1349.[5] In 1357 the king commissioned him to investigate from time to time all ships and barges laden with wool and other merchandise liable to custom on export to foreign ports, in all ports and places along the Lincolnshire coast; to arrest any such found not customed or cocketed, or any corn or other victuals put in them contrary to the king's prohibition, as well as the ships and their masters and mariners; and to report to the king.[6] Again with Dalderby and others, he lent money to the Exchequer in 1359.[7] He also served the king as escheator in the county of Lincoln,[8] commissioner of array,[9] and was on the commission to keep the ordinance and statute of labourers and servants in the city and suburbs in 1356.[10] In 1392 Robert de Sutton and three others, apparently Kelby's executors, obtained licence for the alienation in mortmain of three houses, five shops and a toft of land in the parishes of St Peter at Arches, St Martin in le Dernestall and St Cross, Lincoln, held of the king in burgage, to the prior and convent of St Katharine's without Lincoln, for divine service for Kelby's soul.[11]

[1] See E. E. Rich, *Staple Court Books of Bristol* (Bristol Record Society), pp. 5–20, and his article 'Mayors of the Staples' in *Cambridge Historical Journal*, IV (1933), no. 2.

[2] Birch, p. 28. *H.M.C. Lincoln*, p. 6, dates the Ordinance 1291.

[3] The writer is much indebted to Mr Rich for a list of the mayors of the staple of Lincoln and Boston.

[4] *Cal. Inq. Misc.* II, no. 2074.

[5] *C.C.R.* 1349–54, p. 7.

[6] *C.P.R.* 1354–8, p. 653.

[7] *C.P.R.* 1358–61, p. 260.

[8] *C.P.R.* 1364–7, p. 384.

[9] Ibid. p. 432; 1374–7, p. 501.

[10] *C.P.R.* 1354–8, p. 392.

[11] *C.P.R.* 1391–6, p. 105.

Dalderby was an older man, and he seems not to have served the central government to the extent that Kelby did, but confined himself more to business. He was bailiff of Lincoln in 1339 and 1342 and a justice of labourers in 1356. In 1338 he is described as one of William de la Pole's merchants,[1] perhaps the Lincoln agent of that great merchant prince of Hull. In the following year, in satisfaction of £180 paid by him for wool bought for the king's use in Dordrecht, and of 100 marks lent to the royal household, and out of gratitude, the king granted him £60 yearly 'at the usual terms' out of the farm of the city of Lincoln for six years.[2] In 1352 he founded the Dalderby chantry in St Benedict's church.[3] His will was proved in 1363, and it shows that he owned a great deal of property in Lincoln, including 66 acres in the common fields.[4]

If William de Spaigne was ever a Lincoln man at all it must have been early in his career. His family was chiefly associated with Boston, where its memory is preserved in Spain Lane. Several members of his family appear in the rolls of the Corpus Christi Gild at Boston. There was a William de Spayne who was alderman of the gild in 1376 and 1377, during which time William de Spayne of Lincoln was admitted to the gild: perhaps he was the alderman's son, representing the firm in Lincoln. A William de Spayne was bailiff of Lincoln in 1362. William de Spayne of Lincoln received royal letters of protection in 1369 for a year when he went to join the Black Prince in Gascony.[5] A William de Spaigne was knight of the shire in 1380 and 1382, and feodary for the duke of Lancaster in Nottinghamshire in 1371 and Lincolnshire in 1372.[6] The family was allied to the gentry: when John de Multun, sometime lord of Frampton, died in 1368, his daughter and heiress Maud was married to William son of William de Spayne of Boston.[7]

Spayne's position in the Lincoln staple is significant. Boston, near the mouth of the Witham, had steadily waxed as Lincoln waned, and the influence of its merchants must have been constantly exerted to secure the transfer of the staple from Lincoln to Boston. The transfer was achieved in 1369. This was a severe blow to Lincoln, and every effort was made to recover the staple for the city. In 1376 the counties of Lincoln, Nottingham, Leicester and Derby petitioned that it might be restored to Lincoln, but they were told that it should continue at Boston during the king's pleasure.[8]

The Lincoln merchants were able to secure election as mayors of the staple at Boston occasionally. In 1375 John de Sutton was elected; in 1377

[1] *Cal. Inq. Misc.* II, no. 1628.
[2] *C.P.R.* 1338–40, p. 253.
[3] *A.A.S.R.* XXXVI (1922), p. 199.
[4] B.B. f. 255 v.
[5] Ibid. f. 267.
[6] *John of Gaunt's Register*, 1379–83, I, 25.
[7] *The Ancestor*, II, 206.
[8] *Rot. Parl.* II, 332 b.

John Norman; in 1379 Robert de Sutton; in 1381 William Snelleston; in 1384 John de Sutton; in 1389 William de Dalderby; in 1390 Robert de Ledes; in 1404 Peter de Saltby, while he was mayor of Lincoln; in 1419 and 1420 William Kirkeby; in 1432 and 1433 Roger Knight; in 1441 and 1442 John Huddleston. Immediately after the transfer the Lincoln merchants secured the mayoralty every second year; thereafter their tenure became less frequent and ceased in 1442, though the list of mayors of the Boston staple continues until 1461, the last mayor in the list being Robert de Sutton of, not Lincoln, as his name might suggest,[1] but Boston.

Before the removal of the staple in 1369 the city had suffered another disaster in the Black Death in 1349. Though this visitation affected the whole country it is clear that it fell heavily on Lincoln, which had not the same powers of recovery which prosperous places might have. The bishop of Lincoln sent a general power to regular and secular priests in his diocese to hear confessions and to absolve with full and entire episcopal power, except only in cases of debt. In such cases, the penitent, if able, was himself to make satisfaction whilst he lived, or at least others should do so with his property after his death. The pope granted an indult to the clergy and people of the city and diocese of Lincoln to choose confessors who should give them plenary remission at the time of death, by reason of the pestilence which 'by the hidden judgment of God has visited them'.[2]

It is possible to get some idea of the effect of the plague from statistics provided by the bishops' registers. Judging from records of presentations to benefices, mortality in and around Lincoln was far higher than in other parts of the diocese, and in Lincoln itself (the deanery of Christianity) reached 60 per cent.[3] It may well be that the clergy suffered more severely from the plague than some other classes, but even a smaller percentage would still imply a fearful calamity. There is, moreover, other evidence pointing to a high rate of mortality.

Mr Brooks has made an analysis of the Burwarmote Book preserved in the cathedral library. It covers the period from 1315 to 1376, apart from eight years which are missing. Thus it deals with 54 years, and during that time 295 wills disposing of burgage tenements were enrolled. Of that

[1] For the Suttons of Lincoln, see supra, p. 166.

[2] *Calendar of Papal Registers, Papal Letters*, III, 1342–62, p. 289. Gasquet, *The Great Pestilence* (1893), pp. 139, 149.

[3] Hamilton Thompson, 'Registers of John Gynewell, Bishop of Lincoln' in *Arch. Journ.* LXVIII (1911), pp. 325–6, 334. Professor Hamilton Thompson thought that the mortality round Lincoln was higher than that of any part of the East and West Ridings of Yorkshire and Nottinghamshire. The *Chronicle of Louth Park* (Lincolnshire Record Society, 1891), pp. 38–9, says that in many places the pestilence did not leave a fifth of the people alive; but this would seem to be an exaggeration.

number 105 were enrolled in 1349, leaving 190 for the other 53 years. About a third, therefore, belong to the plague year, the enrolments of that year being equal to those of thirty normal years. The confusion of the entries in the register itself illustrates the condition of the time, but so far as can be ascertained the numbers of wills for the material months are: May, 9; June, 44; July, 32; August, 3; September, 6.[1] Heavy mortality was concentrated in a period of about two months, and in placing these figures it has to be remembered that there was a time lag of a few weeks between the date of death and the date of probate of the will.

The mayor, John de Fenton, died in the plague period, but it is noticeable that not a great number of the leading citizens, who would almost certainly hold burgage tenements involving probate in the burwarmote, have their wills on the court book during the plague time. Among those of ex-mayors, the wills of Robert Quarrell (mayor 1336) and Robert de Huddlestone (mayor 1341) appear in June. Only two former bailiffs have been identified. Unfortunately, the Blickling Homilies[2] have not so far yielded a list of the mayor's council of twenty-four between 1335 and 1349, and in that interval a good many members might have died, from causes other than plague, or retired; but of the council of 1335 only five appear in September 1349, including Robert of Dalderby and William of Blyton, both leading merchants. This evidence is, therefore, indecisive, but it would seem that the richer citizens were able to escape more lightly than the rest of the citizens.

In a few instances two wills relating to the same property were proved on the same day; there was a great increase in the number of direct bequests to the Church, perhaps in default of near relatives, perhaps because the horrors of the time made the ghostly services of the clergy more than ever to be desired; and the litigation which normally occupied a large part of the court's time was at a standstill.[3] The whole dread experience was summed up by the city's common clerk, who wrote in the Blickling Homilies 'that in 1349 there was that great pestilence in Lincoln which spread over all parts of the world beginning on Palm Sunday in the year aforesaid until the Feast of the Nativity of St John the Baptist (24 June) next following, when it ceased, God be praised who reigns for ever and ever, Amen'.[4]

[1] The writer is indebted to Mr F. W. Brooks for his permission to use an unpublished paper on the Burwarmote Book.

[2] See p. 291.

[3] Mr Brooks' paper.

[4] p. 254. The words cannot all be deciphered, but the meaning is quite clear. In March 1350 the canons in chapter assembled were complaining that because of the scarcity of servants their parishioners' lands and the lands they kept in hand could not be tilled; and in December the rents of several of the chapter's manors, including

There can be no mistaking the signs of neglect and decay in Lincoln in the second half of the century. In 1365 the king issued letters patent to the mayor, bailiffs and whole commonalty of the city declaring that

it has lately come to the king's ears that by default of good rule in their city, to which merchants, alien and denizen, and others of the vicinage are wont to come at this time with merchandise, such merchants on account of the deep mud and the dung and filth thrown in the streets and lanes, and other loathsome things lying about and heaped up there, come but seldom, and thereby the evil name of them and their city grows worse and worse. He, therefore, enjoins on them to have the streets and lanes of the city cleansed at once and kept clean, and everyone having dwellings or domiciles in the city charged, and, if need be, compelled by grievous methods to pave before their dwellings, under a heavy penalty to be paid to the king and to the city, sparing neither poor nor rich, that within a year the city may be completely paved and brought into a state of cleanliness and the king be not by their default troubled further in the matter, whereby he would have to lay his hand more heavily upon them.[1]

It is to be noted that this threatening letter preceded by several years the removal of the staple to Boston, and may point to one of the reasons for its removal. Successive letters show that there was much difficulty in getting anything done. In 1371 the mayor and bailiffs were bidden to distrain all owners of lands or rents in the city, and all carrying on trade there, to contribute according to their means to the repair of the walls and towers, and the paving of the city. They were to take carpenters, masons and other workmen and put them to work at the cost of the commonalty, and to arrest all who were contrariant and commit them to prison until further order.[2]

On 14 February 1377 the citizens secured a grant of pavage for three years,[3] but the grant was followed on 26 March by a commission of inquiry, issued on information that collectors of a previous pavage had received money paid on goods coming to the city, and had converted it to their own use: the commissioners were to find out who collected it, for how long, how much they gathered, what they spent on paving and what they kept in their own hands, to hear and determine their accounts, and generally to probe a municipal scandal.[4] Another grant of pavage in 1381[5] was followed by another commission to audit the accounts in 1383.[6] Pavage was granted again in 1384[7] and 1387,[8] and still the work was not

Nettleham, Newport, and Glentham, were reduced. Excessive wage rates were also complained of. Two of the canons, Ralph Ergom and Richard de Whitewell, alone were in residence during the plague, in consideration whereof additional estates were granted to them. Chapter Acts, Liber IV, ff. 4 v., 7 v.

[1] *C.P.R.* 1364–7, p. 89.
[2] *C.P.R.* 1370–4, p. 47.
[3] *C.P.R.* 1374–7, p. 431.
[4] Ibid. p. 493.
[5] *C.P.R.* 1377–81, p. 585.
[6] *C.P.R.* 1381–5, p. 356.
[7] Ibid. p. 386.
[8] *C.P.R.* 1385–9, p. 356.

complete, for further grants, each for three years, were made in 1397[1] and 1401.[2]

Another cause of complaint appears in 1390. The king wrote to the mayor and bailiffs that he was informed that a hall called the 'Gildehalle', situate of old time athwart the street which leads through the middle of the city, and appointed for holding pleas and for assembly of the citizens for matters concerning the common weal, was by common assent of the citizens pulled down, because of the weakness thereof, and because the ground floor (*area*) thereof was low and very inconvenient and a nuisance to great number of strangers coming to the city with their victuals; and that though by common assent and will of the commonalty another hall was begun, loftier and more convenient, certain citizens,

> recking naught of honesty and advantage to the city, but with evil mind cleaving rather to their own will are refusing to contribute to the building thereof, whereof prayer is made to the king for a helping hand: and the king is aware that the hall is begun for the advantage and credit of the city, and may not be finished without great cost.

The mayor and bailiffs were therefore ordered to compel the citizens, by distress or otherwise, to contribute towards the building, sparing not; and the king's writ was not to be taken as an excuse for levying money for the building from strangers coming to the city with victuals and other wares.[3] Three years later Sir John Bussy, the mayor and others were directed to inquire what had happened to the great sums collected for paving the city and building the gildhall (which had been long pulled down), and to see that it was properly applied.[4] These peremptory orders do not seem to have had much effect upon the rebuilding of the gildhall, for the new hall was still in process of building in the early years of the sixteenth century.[5]

Loss of trade meant a fall in the revenue collected by the bailiffs for the payment of the city's fee farm rent, and as the bailiffs were personally liable for the rent the burden of office became more onerous. To distribute the burden a little more widely, there were in 1378, for the first time, three bailiffs instead of two,[6] and after a year or two the increased number became usual. Other towns had a like problem. Cambridge from the first had four bailiffs, each raising as best he could a certain sum from the

[1] *C.P.R.* 1396–9, p. 137.
[2] *C.P.R.* 1399–1401, p. 396.
[3] *C.C.R.* 1389–92, p. 135. In 1395–6 the Court of King's Bench visited Lincoln, and sat at Mary Hall, no doubt because the Stonebow and gildhall had been demolished. Hill, 'Three Lists' in *A.A.S.R.* XXXIX (1929), p. 231.
[4] *C.P.R.* 1391–6, p. 296.
[5] *H.M.C. Lincoln*, pp. 25, 27. A record at the cathedral notes that in 1520 the south part of the gildhall was 'new bylded'. *H.M.C.* 12*th Rep.* App. Part IX, p. 575. Hill, 'Three Lists' in *A.A.S.R.* XXXIX (1929), p. 242.
[6] Ibid. pp. 229, 232.

revenue assigned to him, and Gloucester complained in 1447 that as their revenue fell short by £20 of their fee farm rent, 'in time the town will be without bailiffs'.[1] Even with this much relief, the Lincoln bailiffs were soon asking for more. In 1401, the Blickling Homilies record, two bailiffs were elected and sworn on Holy Cross day; the third bailiff, who perhaps was not then present, was sworn the Monday following. The three then asked that by reason of their heavy burden they might have a fourth colleague assigned to them, to which the whole commonalty unanimously assented.

Whilst the burden of office was being spread the leading citizens were showing eagerness to pay for their exemption from office, and the reigning mayor was able to help himself by selling such exemptions. The government strongly disapproved of this practice, which had the effect of putting into office some of the less 'discreet' and 'worthy' men, and measures were taken to stop it. In September 1382 orders were issued to the mayor to revoke letters patent under the common seal of the city, made by his own authority, 'against the will of the major part of the city, to any of the more sufficient and discreet men thereof, discharging them in the future of the offices of mayor and bailiff'.[2] This was not enough. In the following May, letters were sent to the sheriff of the county, ordering him, despite the liberties of the city, to enter the same, and to levy sums sufficient to repay certain citizens the sums paid by them for exemption from office. It appeared that Hugh Garwell, who was mayor in 1374, had taken from William Snelleston 40 marks, and from John Norman 40 marks, each to be discharged from the mayoralty for life, and from Robert Messingham and Alexander Herle £20 each to be excused from the office of bailiff for life: the consideration had failed, for they had since been put into office. Hugh acknowledged receipt of the money, and averred that it had been applied for the public weal. The king's council found that no mayor had power to grant such exemptions, and ordered that restitution be made of the sums paid.[3] In July Snelleston, then mayor, was ordered to have Simon de Messingham before the king and his council, he having by his own authority when mayor discharged divers citizens from office.[4] The award of John of Gaunt, mentioned below,[5] contemplated and provided against another method of escaping civic office, that of flight into the Close.

Little is known of the effect of the Hundred Years' War with France upon the city, but there can be no doubt that high taxation, which weighs more heavily upon depressed than upon prosperous places, accelerated its

[1] Maitland, *Township and Borough*, p. 78.
[2] *C.C.R.* 1381–5, p. 159.
[3] Ibid. p. 268.
[4] Ibid. p. 391.
[5] Infra, p. 266.

decay. An example of the kind of burden placed upon the citizens in addition to ordinary taxation is recorded in the Patent Rolls. In 1373 the towns of Salisbury, Boston, Lincoln and Hull were bidden each to provide a barge, and commissioners were appointed to distrain all the citizens for the purpose. A few days later Roger de Tirington of Lincoln, Nicholas de Cameryngham, William Warde of Saltfleet haven and Thomas Baxter of Wainfleet were ordered

> to arrest timber, boards, pitch and all other things required for the making of a barge which the king has commanded to be made by the men of the city of Lincoln; also mariners and navigators, cables, cords and other instruments for the barge, as many as shall be necessary for the safe conduct thereof, to the place where the king has appointed it to be brought; and to imprison any found contrariant or rebellious in this, until the king give order for their deliverance.

The citizens were to pay a reasonable price for the timber and other goods and reasonable wages to the mariners and navigators.[1] Some incidents in the history of the barge are recorded in the rolls of the justices of the peace. John de Outhorpe of Lincoln had a royal warrant to attach seamen in the county for the keeping and defence of the Lincoln barge, and when he came to Saltfleet haven and was about to attach several men in pursuance of his duty he was assaulted by others who rescued one of the men. Another presentation said that when he came to array the ship to go to sea for the defence of the realm, several persons assaulted him and chased him to a house where they besieged him; and that he dared not come out for a long time, until he was rescued by the good men of the town.[2] The activities of the press gang were no more popular then than they were in Napoleonic days.

The later years of the fourteenth century in England were marked by a series of disturbances which indicated widespread social discontent, the causes of which are outside the scope of this book. It may have been no more than a matter of routine that on 4 March 1377 a commission was issued to the mayor and bailiffs to inquire in the city and suburbs touching all felonies and oppressions perpetrated there. On 16 June another commission was issued to the mayor and four named citizens, reciting the king's grant that his ministers should not intermeddle with the keeping of the peace in the city and suburbs, except through default of the citizens or

[1] *C.P.R.* 1370–4, pp. 245, 247. They were to take carpenters and smiths from Yorkshire and Lincolnshire. Richard 'of the Mylne' of Grimsby was to be surveyor, p. 233.

[2] Sillem, *Some Sessions of the Peace in Lincolnshire* (L.R.S.), pp. 43, 66. William Warde was indicted in the King's Bench at Lincoln for taking 6*s*. 8*d*. by extortion from Richard Haugham to exonerate him from serving in connection with the Lincoln barge, ibid. p. 43. The mayor and bailiffs were ordered to repair the barge and have it ready to sail with the king's fleet for defence of the realm by 1 March 1378. *C.C.R.* 1377–81, pp. 51, 182.

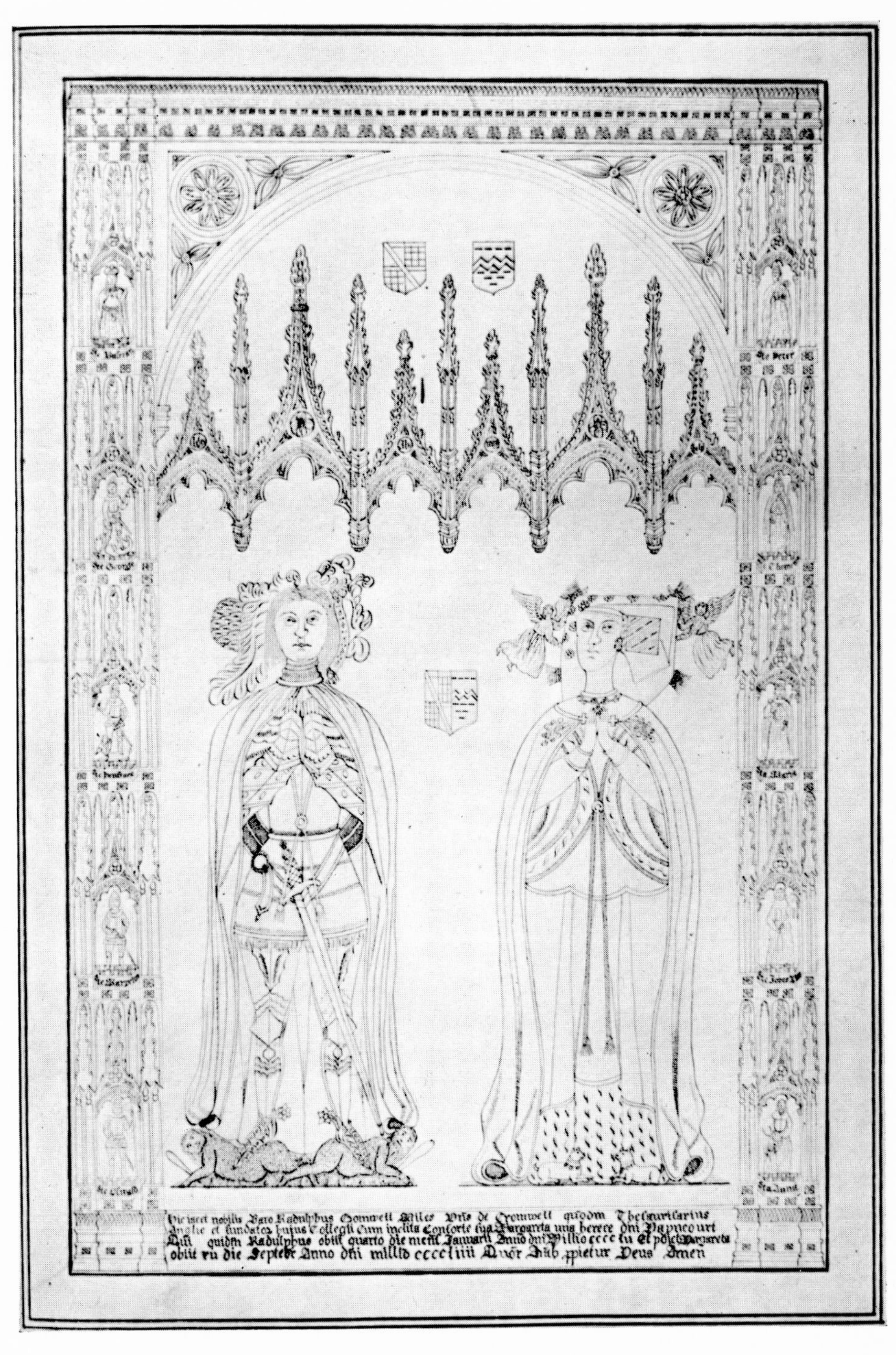

MEMORIAL BRASS OF RALPH LORD CROMWELL AND MARGARET HIS WIFE IN TATTERSHALL CHURCH

From a drawing in the Banks Collection in Lincoln Public Library

[*See p.* 280

PLATE 19

SIR THOMAS LOVELL

From a plaster cast in the National Portrait Gallery of the bronze medallion in Westminster Abbey

See p. 286]

through the king's wish to provide for the city's safety; and providing that for safety against hostile attacks they should array all defensible men in the city and suburbs, have them furnished with arms according to their estate and faculties, keep them in array to resist the malice of the king's enemies, and arrest and imprison all whom they found contrariant or rebellious.[1] The commission of array was renewed on 16 July in the name of the new king Richard II.[2]

The Peasants' Revolt broke out in May 1381. It soon spread northwards into Lincolnshire and Yorkshire. The only evidence of the rising in Lincolnshire consists of the measures taken by the government for its suppression. On 23 June letters were sent out to a number of counties, including Lincolnshire, directing a proclamation concerning the recent murder, under pretext of the royal authority, of Archbishop Sudbury, Chief Justice Cavendish, the prior of the Hospital of St John of Jerusalem and others by the rebels, and ordering that the rebels should be arrested and punished.[3] One of the objects of the revolt is suggested by an order dated 30 June 1381, addressed to William Bardolf, John Bussy, William Spaigne and others, directing them to proclaim in all parts of Lincolnshire that tenants must render the same services and rents as before the revolt.[4] Grievances against John of Gaunt, the young king's uncle, are indicated by writs of aid, directed to all the king's ministers and subjects, denying the insurgents' infamatory reports against Gaunt, who was by the king's command coming to him in haste with armed power.[5] A commission of array for Lincolnshire was issued on 10 July for the assembling and array of the king's lieges in the county to resist the insurgents. Among the commissioners were the nobility and gentry and William Spaigne: no citizen of Lincoln is to be identified in the list.[6] Apparently there was special trouble on the estates of the Hospital of St John of Jerusalem, for the Hospital tenants in Lincolnshire were to be ordered by proclamation to do their accustomed services to the keepers or governors of the Hospital, and the disobedient punished.[7] By 5 September the keepers of the peace were being bidden to remit the evidence against the rebels to the chancery, and to guard the prisoners.[8] On 9 December, in response to a petition in Parliament, the appointment of the keepers of the peace in Ripon, Beverley, York, Hull, Lincoln, Norwich, Yarmouth, Cambridge, Oxford, Coventry and Hertford, was revoked;[9] and new commissions were appointed for Lincolnshire and

[1] *C.P.R.* 1374–7, pp. 489, 501.
[2] *C.P.R.* 1377–81, p. 43.
[3] *C.P.R.* 1381–5, pp. 69–70.
[4] *C.C.R.* 1381–5, p. 74.
[5] *C.P.R.* 1381–5, pp. 25, 30.
[6] Ibid. p. 74.
[7] Ibid. p. 75.
[8] *C.C.R.* 1381–5, p. 7.
[9] Ibid. p. 104.

several other counties.[1] It would seem that the towns were not to be trusted, for there were no new town commissions: the county justices were to keep an eye on the towns.

The only citizen of Lincoln named as an insurgent was Hugh de Garwell, who has already been mentioned. On 20 May 1382, at the request of the queen, a pardon was granted to him for 'all treasons and felonies committed by him in the late insurrection between 1 May 1381 and All Saints next following, provided that he did not kill Simon archbishop of Canterbury, Robert Hales or John de Cavendish'. The pardon was granted by king and council in Parliament, and by a fine of £10 paid in the hanaper.[2] Garwell was apparently a member of the twenty-four of Lincoln in 1366; he was mayor in 1374; and a commissioner to assess the subsidy in 1377, and he and others had advanced money on behalf of the citizens to pay for the making of a balinger and the confirmation of the city's charter in 1378.[3] It is perhaps more to the present point that he was sent by the citizens to Parliament in 1378, and while there he may have joined the opposition, and later shared the sympathies and perhaps the activities of some of his former colleagues.

In 1386 Richard II was engaged in a struggle with the Lancastrian faction, and his enemies having installed themselves in London, he and his friends went on tour in the country in the hope of rallying support. On 27 March 1387, in the Lincoln chapter house, Richard and his Queen Anne were admitted by the bishop and the chapter as brother and sister 'of the same Church of Lincoln, with due solemnity according to the custom hitherto observed in the same Church, with many other noble men and women'.[4] During the same visit to the city, in the mayoralty of John Sutton, Richard granted to the mayor the right of having a sword carried before him. This single fact is recorded in a roll of mayors, but there is no indication in the record that the king gave a sword to accompany the right.[5] There is, however, some ground for thinking that the oldest of the

[1] *C.P.R.* 1381–5, pp. 84, 86. [2] Ibid. p. 119.

[3] *C.F.R.* VIII, 389. *C.P.R.* 1377–81, p. 628.

[4] Chapter Acts, Liber V, f. 24 v. For the medieval confraternity of the cathedral church, see Dr J. H. Srawley's article in *Lincoln Diocesan Magazine*, November, 1936. Henry Percy (Shakespeare's Hotspur) was admitted in 1386; and in the same year, in the presence of John of Gaunt, Gaunt's son Henry earl of Derby (later Henry IV), Thomas, son of Katharine Swynford, and Philippa Chaucer, apparently the sister of Katharine Swynford and wife of Geoffrey Chaucer. The visit to Lincoln of Richard II in 1387 adds a new date to Tout's itinerary; Richard was at Royston near Barnsley on 25 March, and at Nottingham Castle by 3 April. *Chapters in Medieval Administrative History* (1928), III, 420 n. In 1412 Bishop Repingdon appointed Thomas Chaucer, believed to have been the poet's son, constable and seneschal of the castle and town of Banbury for life. Chapter Acts, Liber VI (ii), f. 4 v. For the Chaucer family, see Skeat, *Complete Works of Geoffrey Chaucer*, I, pp. xlviii–li.

[5] Hill, 'Three Lists' in *A.A.S.R.* XXXIX (1929), p. 230.

existing state swords of the Corporation may have been presented by Richard on this occasion. In the first place, the sword is a 'splendid specimen of an actual 14th century fighting sword';[1] secondly, the arms of Edward III, which were borne by Richard, are engraved on the pommel; and thirdly, Richard is said to have given swords to York and Chester, both of which he visited in his tour of 1386.[2] Richard's canvassing of popular support did not prevent a violent outburst in Parliament against his ministers.

In September 1384 there is a hint of the unpopularity of John of Gaunt in a commission issued on a complaint by Katharine Swynford, his mistress and future wife, that a number of named persons, including Robert de Saltby, mayor, and the bailiffs broke her close at Lincoln, took away her goods, and assaulted her servants.[3]

The closing years of the century were marked by bitter quarrels between the 'more worthy citizens' and the commonalty touching the election of the mayor and bailiffs and the rights and privileges of the two parties. The fact that the dean and chapter took the side of the commonalty no doubt heightened bad feeling, because the authorities of the Bail and Close were pursuing their own quarrels with the mayor and his brethren. When the civic dispute was first referred to the king, he, at the suit of the commonalty, verbally appointed his chancellor Thomas Arundel, archbishop of York, to hear and determine the dispute. Arundel was prevented by affairs of state from making more than a partial examination in person, and he by consent of both parties referred the matter to Sir John Bussy, Sir Philip Tilney, Sir Walter Tailboys and John Rocheford, all Lincolnshire gentry. These commissioners all cautiously declared that before acting in so ambiguous and perilous a question they must have a special mandate from

[1] Jewitt and Hope, *Corporation Plate and Insignia of Office*, I (1895), p. lxxiv.

[2] The late Colonel J. G. Williams devoted much study to the Lincoln insignia, and the suggestion contained in the text is his. *Lincs N. & Q.* VII, 67–71; *Journal of the British Archaeological Association*, 1921, p. 181. According to Raine, *York* (1893), p. 77, and Benson, *Later Medieval York* (1919), p. 96, Richard presented his sword to the mayor of York in 1389, to be borne before him and his successors. Benson says that Richard empowered the mayor to have the sword carried before him with the point erect, except in the king's presence, within the liberties for ever; but this seems to be a quotation from Richard's charter of 18 May 1396. *Catalogue of Charters etc. belonging to the Corporation of York*, p. 13. Was Richard in York between 1387 and 1396? (See Tout, op. cit. IV, 222.) The York sword disappeared in 1795. Morris, *Chester in the Plantagenet and Tudor Reigns*, p. 31, says that the state sword was presented by the king to that city in 1394. For charter references to swords see Weinbaum, *British Borough Charters*, 1307–1660: Newcastle, 1391; York, 1396; Norwich, 1404; Chester, 1506. In the last three of these charters the charter raises the city into a county of itself. At Newcastle this follows in 1400.

[3] *C.P.R.* 1381–5, p. 504. Some of the same citizens journeyed to Grantham and broke her close there, p. 501. There is a like complaint by Roger Langford that his close in Lincoln was broken (p. 503).

the king, which was accordingly issued;[1] though a few days later it was partially revoked.[2] No more is heard of that commission, but on 6 September 1393 orders were issued to Bussy to take security of four named persons

that they shall make no unlawful assemblies within the city of Lincoln or the liberty thereof, henceforward making or procuring no attempt whereby the peace may be broken or the people disturbed, but shall stand to right, and abide the customs and honest ordinances of the city under governance of the mayor and other their superiors for the time being, and to give command to the now mayor and bailiffs to admit them to the city, altogether restoring them to their own therein, and honourably entreating them as other the citizens their fellows, and order to certify in chancery under his seal the security so taken; as the said knight is not ignorant how that by hateful incitement of the cunning enemy strife and controversy have arisen between the high and mighty persons of the city and the king's middling subjects thereof, whence were likely to happen many things not to be borne, and perhaps the ruin of the city, but for the intervention of grace from on high and wiser counsels, and how that the said four men of his middling subjects, appearing among others before the king at Westminster at his command, were after by report of the now mayor committed to the Flete prison, and at their suit were at last set free, under condition that they should not approach the bounds or liberty of the city until they had made agreement or unity with those high and mighty persons, or until other order should be taken by advice of the council; but after full ventilation of the whole matter before him, John duke of Aquitaine and Lancaster on his journey to the king's presence has made a concord between the parties, whereat the king is no little pleased, and those high and mighty ones have before him given their free assent that the said men be restored to the city, there to dwell in their first estate, finding security for their good behaviour.[3]

Holy Cross Day, when the citizens were wont to elect their mayor, was approaching, and the day before it (13 September) letters patent were issued at Grantham appointing Bussy to be personally present at the election of the mayor and bailiffs of Lincoln,

where the citizens are of contrary opinions in certain matters and affairs affecting the liberty of the city on account of fraudulent claims of liberties not hitherto enjoyed, or verbal traditions (*oracula*) not founded on the solid base of clear conscience (*super clare consciencie soliditatem fundata*), and so to direct the citizens that the election by his good counsel and guidance, with due information from all who have knowledge how the election has been from old time held, may be made pleasing to God and good for the king and the whole commonalty of the city, with power to imprison contrariants.[4]

The terms of the commission make it clear that Bussy's influence was to be used to support the ruling group of high and mighty citizens against the claims of the wider circle, the commonalty, the middling citizens. The

[1] *C.P.R.* 1391–6, p. 240 (5 March 1393).
[2] *C.C.R.* 1392–6, p. 133.
[3] Ibid. p. 162.
[4] *C.P.R.* 1391–6, p. 355.

result of the election suggests that Bussy was successful, for the new mayor was Robert Hairworth, who had served the office of bailiff, represented the city in three Parliaments, and who is mentioned with a group of leading merchants in a pardon for dealing with wool contrary to statute.[1]

An earlier result of the intervention of Bussy and his colleagues is recited in a subsequent act of the commonalty of Lincoln recorded in the White Book: on the Wednesday next before the feast of St Simon and St Jude (28 October) 1392, by the special authority of the commissioners appointed for the good of the city, and with the consent of the new mayor and the whole commonalty, it was ordained that the common seal should only be used for sealing in the presence of the mayor, twelve of his peers and twelve of the next worthiest citizens, or sixteen at least of the said twenty-four, with the four coroners and four treasurers, and ten citizens at least annually elected for the purpose by all the other citizens; and that any sealing contrary to the form of the ordinance should be void.[2] Here was an attempt to associate in the executive acts of the city all three classes; the high and mighty men who were the mayor's peers, the middling men, and the ordinary folk.

Bussy was a Lincolnshire knight, one of the Bussys of Hougham, of which family Leland was told that in the time of Richard II they had £1,000 a year in land, and that they had a great piece of the vale between Huntingdon and Lincoln, and two castles of which one was Folkingham.[3] He was sheriff of Lincolnshire in 1393, and sat in every Parliament from 1386 to 1398 except the Merciless Parliament. He was chosen Speaker of the House of Commons in 1394 and 1397, and probably also in 1395. When Henry of Bolingbroke landed at Ravenspur, Bussy, with other of Richard II's ministers, took possession of Bristol Castle. Shakespeare (who spells his name 'Bushy') makes Bolingbroke call him, Bagot and their accomplices

> The caterpillars of the commonwealth,
> Which I have sworn to weed and pluck away.

On the surrender of Bristol Bussy was executed without trial.

The disputes between the city of Lincoln and the constables of the castle and the dean and chapter were concerned chiefly with jurisdiction and its profits. They were of long standing but became more serious as the city's trade declined and the pressure of the fee farm rent became more burden-

[1] Robert Hairworth alias Robert Fuyster. *C.P.R.* 1391–6, p. 626. Hill, 'Three Lists' in *A.A.S.R.* XXXIX (1929), p. 231.

[2] White Book, f. 2b.

[3] *Itinerary* (ed. Toulmin Smith), v, 223. Tout, *Chapters in Medieval Administrative History*, IV, 11–13; Steel, *Richard II* (1941), pp. 221–2. For the Bussy family, and the Bussy Psalter, see Trollope, *Sleaford and the Wapentakes of Flaxwell and Aswardhurn* (1872), pp. 377–80, and *Lincs N. & Q.* II, 1.

some. In the thirteenth century there were small boundary grievances and some issues of jurisdiction emerged;[1] but the latter emerged more clearly in 1322. The bailiffs of the city maintained that they ought to have cognisance of pleas of lands and tenements within the city and suburbs, and also of trespasses and contracts made there, and amends of breaches of the assize of bread and ale, gabel, toll, and other customs, services and fines arising there in aid of the farm of the city; and they complained that when they in their official capacity came to a place within the city called 'Le Bayl' to perform the duties of their office, some of the inhabitants resisted them. A commission of oyer and terminer was issued on behalf of them and four of their predecessors.[2]

The other side of the dispute is given in letters close issued in 1331 to the mayor and bailiffs ordering them to permit Ebulo Lestrange and his wife Alice (daughter of Henry de Lacy earl of Lincoln), to whom Edward II had granted custody and ward of the castle with the bailey, to have the bailey by the prescribed metes and bounds, to have their court there, and the assay of weights and measures and other profits. Their predecessors had held their court within the bailey at the castle gate every Tuesday for all pleas that could be pleaded in court baron; and the profits of the bailey were the vacant plots and ditches, including the plot called Battleplace, taking rent for the herbage thereof a mark yearly, more or less, and stallage in the vacant plots in times of fairs and markets, and also window toll and ale-toll.[3]

In 1375 the quarrel was proceeding on similar lines. The citizens declared that they had in aid of their farm the return of all writs and Exchequer summonses of green wax, with their chartered liberties, namely, that pleas of land should be held in the gildhall, also infangthief, outfangthief, the chattels of felons and fugitives, the assize of bread and ale, the trial of weights and measures, and all other things pertaining to the office of the market and the profits thereof within the city and suburbs. Their specific complaint was that Oliver de Barton, the constable, who held the castle on behalf of John of Gaunt, and his ministers had for 26 years usurped all these powers of the citizens, save only the return of writs, levies of green wax, pleas of land, assizes of fresh force, writs of right, and proof of wills of land within the bailey. They added in particular that the constable used of old time to hold only a court baron once in three weeks, taking cognisance of debts not exceeding 40*s*., and that only of men living within the bailey, and without attaching any man by his body or exercising

[1] *R.H.* I, 309, 316. The citizens complained that William Lungespee the younger had deprived them of the assize of bread and ale within the Bail.

[2] *C.P.R.* 1321–4, p. 150.

[3] *C.C.R.* 1330–3, p. 255.

power of imprisonment; whereas Oliver and his predecessor held court every eight days, usurped pleas of debts of whatsoever sum of men without as well as within the bailey, took defendants by their bodies in pleas of trespass, and deprived the citizens of fines pertaining to the office of the market, chattels of felons and fugitives and all other profits which the citizens used to take within the bailey. The citizens asserted that the bailey was a part of the city, and indeed that it was a third part of the whole. Another grievance related to the fair holden by them in Newport from the feast of St Botolph to that of St Peter and St Paul (17–29 June) and for 13 days following: for 16 years the constables had appropriated part of the revenues of the fair by drawing stallage within the bailey, which was without the bounds of the fair. Furthermore, although on Sundays and feast days no market used to be held in any part of the city or suburb in the autumn season, and no hiring of reapers or servants save only at Newport Cross, Oliver and his ministers all the autumn season drew to themselves in the bailey such markets and hirings of servants, taking stallage and other profits thereof. Not only were these profits lost to the citizens, but reapers, workmen and servants were more dearly hired because the mayor and bailiffs were hindered by the constable from chastising them.

The proceedings against the constable were, however, stayed, because Oliver held the constableship on behalf of John of Gaunt, who was overseas upon the king's business, and in Gaunt's absence the memoranda and evidences relating to his rights were shut up in his treasury and inaccessible to his attorneys.[1]

During the suspension of proceedings the citizens continued to assert their rights; and in 1390 a commission was issued on complaint by John of Gaunt against the mayor and bailiffs, four former mayors and nine former bailiffs, and two of their late servants. It charged the defendants with entering the Bail, breaking and pulling up the stalls and stakes fixed within it for the sale of merchants' wares, and preventing the merchants from selling the same, building houses in the castle dykes within the Bail, and taking rents from them. The duke further complained that they had compelled tenants and residents in the Bail to come to the city court and be fined for breaches of the assize of bread and ale and other matters belonging to the duke's court, so that some of his tenants had left and he had lost the profits of the Bail and the court. When the letters patent were vacated in order to make some corrections, the amended letters stated that the loss suffered by the duke amounted to £1,000.[2] This sum must probably be regarded as a claim for damages rather than an estimate of loss suffered.

[1] *C.C.R.* 1374–7, p. 261.

[2] *C.P.R.* 1388–92, p. 270.

Against so powerful an enemy the citizens could not hope to prevail. It is not now worth while to inquire into the precise rights of the parties. It was agreed between them that the constable's jurisdiction in the Bail was not exclusive, and that the citizens had a voice in some matters there; and that being so, disputes were almost inevitable, especially in such matters as the holding of markets and fairs. What is of special interest is that the citizens grew bolder as they grew more desperate in their attempts to make ends meet.

The city's dispute with the dean and chapter proceeded on similar lines. In 1375, in a dispute in the king's court, a jury found that the dean and chapter and all their predecessors from the time of William the Conqueror, time out of mind, had had stalls for the sale of merchandise within the Close, the stallage rents being agreed between the merchants and the clerk of the fabric of the church. On 6 May 1382, a letter close was addressed to the sheriff of the county ordering him to suffer the dean and chapter to have their stalls within the Close, hindering no merchant or others who would come there, nor troubling them in aught.[1]

A month later a letter close was issued to the mayor, bailiffs and others, strictly ordering them to be in person in chancery on a day appointed to answer matters to be laid against them; the king reminded them of his order not to interfere with stalls within the Close, he having learned that the mayor and others, assembling great number of evildoers, and taking upon them royal power like the insurgents in the late devilish insurrection, had by their own authority made a proclamation in divers places of the city that no merchant or other should hold fair or market within the Close, nor sell goods there under pain of forfeiture thereof; they had by force of arms hindered the dean and chapter from having stalls and selds there, and prevented merchants from coming thither as they used to do from fixing pales and selds, setting up stalls for their own merchandise and having their easements, compelling some merchants who did set up stalls to withdraw, grieving them and others who would sell goods there by undue and vexatious summonses and extortions of money, and laying upon the dean and chapter threats and fear of death for certain of the said merchants if they should attempt aught contrary to the said proclamation, and committing other grievous wrongs in contempt of the king's command. The damage was estimated at £100.[2]

This was the case for the chapter. There was also a case for the city. A letter close issued to the dean and chapter on 27 July 1386, ordered

[1] *C.C.R.* 1381–5, pp. 56, 57. The walled Close did not exist until long after the time of William the Conqueror, but it may be that stalls were set up in the Minster Yard then as they were in the fourteenth century.

[2] *C.C.R.* 1381–5, p. 62.

them in person or by counsel to be before the king and council, bringing with them their charters concerning the liberties of their church, and meanwhile allowing nothing to be done in their name which might tend to the prejudice of the citizens and lieges of the city or to breach of the peace: as lately the king had appointed Henry de Percy earl of Northumberland and others to inquire by men of Lincolnshire into all dissensions and grievances between the dean and chapter and the citizens. The commission to Percy and his colleagues said that the king had been informed by credible persons of the danger of ruin to the citizens contrary to justice and without fault of their own: the citizens having offered at any time on reasonable warning to answer the dean and chapter or any other complainants.[1]

In 1387 Richard II and his queen visited Lincoln, and became members of the fraternity of the cathedral church,[2] and it may have been a result of this visit that a royal commission was issued to inquire into the losses and injuries suffered by the church of Lincoln.[3]

The struggle dragged on. On 3 March 1390 the mayor and bailiffs were ordered under penalty of £1,000 for particular causes laid before the king in Parliament to take security of Robert de Sutton, citizen of Lincoln, under pain of 500 marks, and of the whole community of Lincoln, under pain of 20,000 marks, that they should make no riots or unlawful assemblies, and make or procure no attempts which might tend to disturbance of the people, and especially of the bishop, the canons, officers, ministers, men servants and household of the cathedral church, and should by their friends, allies, men servants or others do no hurt or harm to the bishop and canons. The mayor and bailiffs were ordered to certify in chancery under the common seal of the city that the security was so taken. The mainprise was made by the mayor, bailiffs and others in chancery on the same day.[4]

In the following May a letter was sent to the sheriff of Lincolnshire enclosing an order to be delivered to the mayor and bailiffs again demanding that, for particular causes laid before the king in his last Parliament, they should take of the whole commonalty of the city security under a pain of 10,000 marks that they should make no riots or unlawful assemblies.[5]

The quarrel has left its mark on the statute book. The statute 13 Richard II (1389) c. 18 recites that the mayor and bailiffs had been summoned before the king and his council in Parliament with full power under the city's common seal to answer upon the things contained in the petition of the bishop and the dean and chapter. The mayor and bailiffs

[1] *C.C.R.* 1385–9, pp. 160, 161.
[2] Supra, p. 258.
[3] *H.M.C.* 12*th Rep.* App. Part IX, p. 563.
[4] *C.C.R.* 1389–92, pp. 123, 164, 165.
[5] Ibid. p. 135.

had appeared at the appointed time, but failed to bring sufficient warrant from the commonalty of the city, and therefore by their default the king, with the assent of the prelates and other lords in the same Parliament, had proceeded to examine the petition. The statute further recited that there had been a common clamour that many of the king's lieges had often suffered divers injuries in the city, because in respect of freeholds in the city, trespasses, contracts and other things arising within the city, triable by assize, jury or inquest, such matters had been tried by the people of the same city, who were so favourable to one another that they did not scruple to make false oaths; and in this they were encouraged, forasmuch as they had not been before that time convicted by foreigners by reason of their franchise. The statute provided, for the quietness of the church of Lincoln, and full right to be done to the bishop, dean and chapter and their successors, that in assizes, juries and all other inquests that should be taken between party and party before the mayor and bailiffs, if any party felt himself aggrieved by any false oath made by such assize, jury or inquest, the attaint should be granted to him, and the record sent by writ into king's bench or common pleas; and that the sheriff should impanel the jury of attaint of foreigners of the county (that is, county men) without sending to the franchise of the city (for citizens), and that the justices should accept the county jury, notwithstanding any franchise granted to the city or other usage to the contrary.[1]

This complaint about the perjury of city juries to the advantage of citizens and the detriment of the chapter is a new one, and as the mayor and bailiffs were regarded as having let the petition go by default, their answer is unknown.

The disputes as to local jurisdiction were referred to the arbitration of John of Gaunt, a choice ominous to the citizens because he himself had been engaged in similar controversy with them about his rights in the Bail. The award gave the dean and chapter complete immunity on certain terms, and agreement was reached on it, though there is nothing to show whether the agreement was made willingly or not. Gaunt awarded that the Close was to be free from all manner of profit, summons, attachment, distress or execution, and any demand whatsoever on the part of the mayor and citizens. The dean and chapter were to enjoy all their franchises, liberties and profits, and their coroners were to determine all cases within the church and Close which to their office did belong; and the mayor and citizens were by deed under their common seal to release all right within church and Close. If any citizen were impleaded in the gildhall or elsewhere in the city outside the Close, and got his chattels into the Close by

[1] *Statutes at Large*, II, 322.

fraud in order to secure illegal immunity, to oust or delay the plaintiff of his recovery, the mayor and bailiffs were to certify the dean and chapter, whose officers should make due execution. If any citizen were indicted for felony, and illegally took his goods and chattels to the Close, the dean and chapter on being certified and given security against damages, should deliver them up. If any tallage were granted to the king by the commons of the realm, the lay people living in the Close who had goods within it taxable amongst laymen should be taxed by the officers of the Close, and the tax delivered by them to the city collectors for the time being. After making provision concerning citizens who, having been elected mayor or bailiff, fled into the Close to escape service, the award made financial compensation to the mayor and citizens for the surrender of their claims. Certain tenements called Burton Rents in the parish of St Peter at Arches in the city were held by feoffees to the use of the dean and chapter, and these not being in mortmain were to be given by the feoffees to the mayor and bailiffs and commonalty in aid of their farm for ever. The dean and chapter were to pay 9*s*. 5*d*. yearly for their tenements in the city and the church and Close, and the citizens were to continue to pay to the dean and chapter the £80 of their farm which had been granted to the chapter. The question of the return of writs touching parties or things within the Close was reserved to the king's council.[1]

The award makes no reference at all to the vexed question of merchants setting up their stalls in the Close and so evading the city's claim to stallage and other control in time of market or fair. Nor is it possible to assess the value of the compensation paid to the citizens for the surrender of their claims. Many of the questions in issue arose almost inevitably from the juxtaposition of three separate jurisdictions in a community which economically was one. No doubt each of them did what it could to draw to itself trade and jurisdiction, with the resultant profits, and it may be that as the city's revenues declined the charges imposed on merchants were increased, thereby giving them an additional incentive to take shelter within Bail or Close.

It may have been in reference to the disorders arising from the quarrels between city, Bail and Close that on 20 October 1392 letters patent were issued, with the assent of the king's council, to the citizens and commonalty of Lincoln, granting a general pardon in respect of all insurrections, trespasses and other offences between Midsummer 1391 and the quinzaine

[1] The award was confirmed by letters patent. *C.P.R.* 1388–92, p. 309. If, as seems probable, the 9*s*. 5*d*. to be paid to the city was for land-toll pence, this would give a total of 113 burgage tenements within Close and city belonging to the dean and chapter. This does not necessarily mean 113 houses: more than one house might have been built on a single burgage holding.

of Michaelmas 1392, and of all forfeitures and fines, such pardon to operate in favour of each individual citizen as if especially granted to him.[1] If so, it was premature, for disturbances continued. On 8 January 1394, a commission was issued to inquire what evildoers lately leagued together and came to the cathedral church of St Mary of Lincoln, assaulted and maimed several clerks and ministers of the church, besides servants of the canons and other lieges, in the church and its cemetery and in the city, and so polluted both church and cemetery that divine service that Christmas ceased, and still continued unperformed. The perpetrators of these evil deeds were to be arrested and brought before the king and council.[2] It appears, however, that the evildoers were not all citizens, for in the May following Robert Pakynton, esquire and servant of John Shepey the dean, five menial servants of the dean, a chaplain, seven clerks and five other menials were pardoned of all trespasses, misprisions and contempts perpetrated by them as well at the cathedral church as in the city.[3]

[1] *C.P.R.* 1391–6, p. 216. [2] Ibid. p. 429. [3] Ibid. p. 410.

CHAPTER XIII

THE FIFTEENTH CENTURY

IN 1399 Henry of Bolingbroke, the son of John of Gaunt, landed at Ravenspur, near Spurn Point. His plans had evidently been concerted with the earl of Northumberland and the Lincolnshire magnates who met him there:

> In Holdernesse he landed with fourty menne
> Wher the lordes of Lyncolnshire hym mette;
> Bothe Wyloughby Roos and Darcy then.
> And Beaumont also with penouns proudly bette,
> By ordinance of Henry Percy sette
> Erle of Northumberland and Sir Henry
> His soone, wardeyns of the Marche severally.[1]

Henry claimed that he had come only to seek his own inheritance and to reform the government of Richard II. Adherents came in, and among them the duke of York, who was regent. After marching through the Midlands and receiving the surrender of Bristol, Henry came up with Richard at Flint, and took him to Chester and then to London. Writs were sent out to summon a Parliament at Westminster on 30 September. The day before it met a deputation visited Richard in the Tower and procured his abdication. Parliament then solemnly deposed him and assented to Henry's claim to the throne. Richard was imprisoned at Pontefract, and was dead by 14 February 1400. Adam of Usk says that the chief agent in his death was 'N. Swynford'. Sir Thomas Swynford, the son of Sir Hugh Swynford and Duchess Katharine, was at Pontefract at the time,[2] and he may be the 'chief agent' mentioned.

The Lincolnshire lords were loyal to the house of Lancaster. When in 1404 Henry IV published the names of his ministers it was found that William Lord Roos was treasurer, and William Lord Willoughby was in the list. Robert Lord Willoughby sailed with Henry V to France in 1417, was at the siege of Rouen in 1419, and distinguished himself at Cravant in 1423. John Lord Roos was also at Rouen, being killed at Baugé in 1421. Another Roos was at the siege of Orleans in 1428. Henry VI went to France in 1430 accompanied by a Roos, Lovell, Beaumont and Welles. Roos entered Paris, which he administered for a brief two days, but later was drowned in the Marne. Willoughby campaigned for several years; in

[1] J. Harding, *Chronicle*, p. 349, quoted by Ramsay, *Genesis of Lancaster*, II, 351.
[2] *Chronicon Adae de Usk*, 1377–1421 (ed. Thompson), p. 199.

1435 he took charge of Paris, but in the following year Charles VII of France recovered his capital and the English were compelled to retire.

The Parliament produced a crop of petitions, and among them one from the hopeful but hard hit city of Lincoln. Presumably it was presented by the city's burgesses in Parliament, Robert de Sutton, who had sat in many previous Parliaments and who belonged to a family closely associated with the king's father John of Gaunt,[1] and William de Blyton, like Sutton a member of a leading merchant family. The petition declared that by reason of pestilence and other unbearable burdens a great part of the farm could not be levied, and that citizens were leaving the city in order to escape from the outrageous and unbearable charge of the fee farm rent; that in the Parliament of 1396 the matter had been referred to the archbishop of Canterbury and others, but nothing had been done. It besought the king to grant relief and so save the city from destruction. The petition was referred to a committee.[2]

It was not until 1409 that the city obtained any result from the foregoing and no doubt other petitions. The letter patent then granted (21 November) is one of the most important in the civic series. It first confirmed Richard II's grant of confirmation in 1378, and then came to the central question of the fee farm rent, declaring that the lands, rents, franchises, liberties and profits out of which it was payable were so greatly wasted and reduced that the fee farm could not be raised within the city. After expressly reserving the rights of the dukes of Lancaster in the castle and Bail, the charter granted in relief of the city that henceforth in the place of bailiffs the city might elect two sheriffs, and the city be called the county of the city of Lincoln. The mayor was to be the king's escheator, and the sheriffs were to be sworn before the mayor and commonalty in the gildhall, and were to hold their county courts every six weeks as in the county of Lincoln. The old city courts were to continue. The commonalty were to elect four justices of the peace and of labourers and artificers. The chattels of outlaws, felons and fugitives among residents were to belong to the city, and so also were fines for all trespasses and offences whatsoever, with other profits of jurisdiction. There was a grant of a new fair to begin 15 days before the feast of the burial of St Hugh (17 November) and to continue 15 days thereafter. Furthermore, the annual farm of £6 paid direct to the Exchequer by the Lincoln weavers was to be paid to the city in aid of the farm. The rights of the dean and chapter were reserved, and the award of John of Gaunt[3] confirmed. The rights of Henry Beaumont in the Beaumont

[1] See supra, p. 168.
[2] P.R.O. Ancient Petitions, file 121/6033; *Rot. Parl.* III, 438a.
[3] See supra, pp. 266–7.

fee[1] were also reserved. The grant was sealed at Westminster on payment of a fee of 50 marks.[2]

It is by virtue of this grant that the city of Lincoln is still a county of itself, with its own sheriff (reduced from two to one in number by the Municipal Corporations Act of 1835), and its own assize. What the new county jurisdiction within the same bounds as those of the city court was worth in money it is impossible to say: it may be suspected that its profits were small. Yet the new winter fair, St Hugh's Fair, held in later days in St Hugh's Croft, to which it no doubt gave its name, must have been worth something, and there was the weavers' £6. Subsequent events indicate that the citizens did not think highly of the relief they had received.

The dean and chapter soon found that the citizens had seized upon the city's new status as a county as an argument for evading their liability to the chapter, for on 11 September 1410 they procured royal letters to the sheriffs of Lincoln notifying them that neither the change of their name from bailiffs to sheriffs nor any clause or word in the king's writ lately addressed to them should affect their payment of £80 (part of the fee farm rent) to the dean and chapter; the sheriffs having declared that they would not pay the £80 granted in almoign to the dean and chapter, the king's will was that the said sum granted as parcel of the endowment of the cathedral church should not be restricted in his time other than it was in the times of his predecessors.[3] The chapter also obtained confirmation by Parliament of the statute of Richard II concerning juries of attaint, lest some loophole should be found in the statute by the citizens.[4]

The citizens continued to cry out for aid, and when Parliament met the young King Henry V in 1414, and war with France was announced, there was a new flood of petitions, the royal need of money being always the popular opportunity. Apparently there was one from Lincoln, for Henry granted the city an *inspeximus* on 15 December.[5] It merely confirmed existing rights without adding to them. In 1421 the coronation of Queen Catherine was followed by a royal progress. On 15 April the king and queen visited Lincoln, but so far from this being an occasion for obtaining concessions, the citizens were no doubt mulcted in a wedding present and the cost of hospitality. A new confirmation was granted by Henry VI in 1424,[6] and in 1438 the citizens procured a letter from the king to the justices of assize in the county of Lincoln upholding the city's claim to the return of writs and to the weekly court of burhmanmote held before the mayor and bailiffs (the letter mentions bailiffs and not sheriffs, perhaps in error,

[1] See supra, p. 241.

[2] *C. Chart. R.* v, 442; Birch, pp. 74–87.

[3] *C.C.R.* 1409–13, p. 44.

[4] 3 Henry V, c. 5; *Statutes at Large*, III, 43.

[5] *C. Chart. R.* v, 474; Birch, p. 88.

[6] Birch, p. 93.

perhaps because it was referring to the old court long held before the mayor and bailiffs), and warning the judges not to encroach.[1] This was an important matter: not only were the profits of the court material, but its jurisdiction was one of the city's most cherished privileges.

At a time when most of the corporate towns were declining and asking for relief the special treatment accorded to Lincoln in relief from taxation puts beyond doubt the city's serious plight. The Lincoln laity were relieved of half the tax imposed in 1434 and 1436, and in 1437 Lincoln and Andover were totally exempt. In 1440 total exemption was granted to Lincoln and some Cambridgeshire towns or villages. In 1441 total exemption was granted to Lincoln, relief from half the tax to Cheltenham, Alresford and Andover (Southampton), Scarborough (York) and Headington (Oxford). In 1445 Lincoln was totally exempt, half relief was given to the same towns as before, and one-quarter relief given to Yarmouth. In 1446, twice in 1449, and in 1453, total exemption was granted to Lincoln and Yarmouth.[2] Lincoln was entirely relieved again in 1465 and 1472.[3] Such extraordinary treatment at a time of heavy taxation caused by the Hundred Years' War would not have been accorded without good cause.

Henry VI visited Lincoln in 1445–6, when it was ordered by the common council that the mayor, aldermen and sheriffs, with 80 or 100 of the more respectable and better-dressed persons, should ride to meet the king, as many others of the commons as possible going on foot, at the cross on the cliff, and there kneeling should reverently offer to the king, for the good relief which he had beforetime afforded them, £100 in gold.[4] This handsome gift was not made in vain, for in 1447 letters patent were issued in reply to a petition from the mayor and citizens. It declared that the citizens, in addition to the fee farm, paid £100 whenever a tenth and a fifteenth was granted, and that although the king by authority of Parliament had granted certain remissions, nevertheless the city was much impoverished by the withdrawal of merchants, a long-continued pestilence, and other troubles of the world, there being scarcely 200 citizens left. By way of relief they were authorised (notwithstanding the statute of mortmain) to acquire lands to the annual value of £120, and, perhaps more

[1] Birch, p. 90.

[2] *C.F.R.* XVI, 189, 281, 350; XVII, 139, 213, 324; XVIII, 31, 123, 129; XIX, 42.

[3] Cunningham, *Growth of English Industry and Commerce* (5th ed. 1915), I, 454–5. See infra, pp. 286–8. A levy of archers made in 1457 called for 46 from Lincoln, compared with Nottingham 30, Newcastle 53, Bristol 91, York 152, Norwich 121, Hull 50, Southampton 46, Coventry 76. *C.P.R.* 1452–61, p. 410.

[4] C.C.M. 1511–41, f. 267b; *H.M.C. Lincoln*, p. 35. There are notes of gifts presented on the occasion of several royal visits. These entries must have been copied from an earlier register, now lost.

important, they were granted remission from all tenths and fifteenths for 40 years.[1] In 1456, in pursuance of this licence, the citizens bought the manor of Canwick, on the southern boundary of the liberties, and with it 2*s.* worth of annual rent in the adjoining parish of Branston; a house, four tofts, 90 acres of land, 16 acres of meadow and 100 acres of pasture in Canwick, the whole whereof had been valued at 33*s.* 4*d.* yearly. The king expressly authorised the purchase, which was to rank as worth 40*s.* yearly on account of the licensed value of £120:[2] but it would be more accurate to say that such authority was issued in the king's name, for the king was a prisoner and the Wars of the Roses had begun.

In addition to remissions of direct taxation and licence to hold property, there was another way in which relief could be granted to distressed towns; namely that of partial remission of taxes on exports. In 1439 Parliament granted the king a three-years' subsidy of 53*s.* 4*d.* on each sack of wool and 33*s.* 4*d.* on every 240 woolfells of native merchants; but allowed the mayor and citizens of Lincoln to ship 60 sacks in each of the three years at Hull or Boston and carry them to the staple at Calais without payment of subsidy. In the two following years the wool was not dispatched, and the king authorised them to carry forward the arrears of privileged export without prejudice to their 60 sacks in the third year.[3] In 1441 a new licence permitting export to Calais of 60 sacks of wool yearly for three years free from the subsidy newly granted by Parliament was issued to the city.[4] A like authority for a like period was granted in 1449,[5] and in 1454 a like authority for five years: but the wool must not be from Cumberland or Westmorland.[6] Apparently some advantage was taken of these concessions, for in 1458 the citizens asked that as there had been no shipping of wool to Calais in the third year they might still ship the same amount for the year.[7]

One of the striking features of the period was the prevalence of lawlessness, disorder and violence. Several notable examples affecting Lincoln and the district can be given. A dispute broke out between William de Roos and Robert Tyrwhit, one of the justices of the court of king's bench, about rights of pasture at Wrawby near Brigg, and cognate matters. It came before Chief Justice Gascoigne, who directed the parties to attend a loveday, each accompanied by two friends and the usual attendants. Roos duly appeared, and so also did Justice Tyrwhit accompanied by about 500 men, armed and arrayed against the peace, to lie in wait for Roos.

[1] *C.P.R.* 1446–52, p. 80; Birch, p. 98.
[2] Birch, pp. 102–4; *Inq. A.Q.D.* II, 757.
[3] *C.P.R.* 1441–6, p. 148.
[4] White Book, ff. 11b, 12.
[5] *C.P.R.* 1446–52, p. 280.
[6] *C.P.R.* 1452–61, p. 199.
[7] Ibid. p. 428.

The latter appealed to Parliament which commanded Tyrwhit to make formal apology and amends.[1]

Another incident affected Lincoln more closely. Sir Walter Tailboys took a party of 160 armed men to Lincoln to beat or kill Sir Thomas Chaworth, who had gone there for his own amusement and was ignorant of Tailboys' malice. The sheriffs of the city feared a riot, and called on Tailboys and his men to find security to keep the peace. Tailboys and his party refused, assaulted the sheriffs and others, killed two citizens and wounded many others. Thereafter, with the assent of his friends and kin and especially of Geoffrey Lutterell, he often lay in ambush in divers places in the county and wounded certain citizens. The result was that the citizens were afraid to go to Hull and Boston to ship their wools, to their own great loss, to the damage of the king's customs, and to the delay in payment of the king's fee farm rent. They petitioned for relief, and a royal commission was issued to William de Roos and Henry de Beaumont, keepers of the peace in Lincolnshire, to cause Walter and Geoffrey to come before them to find sureties in the sum of £3,000 that they would not harm the mayor and citizens or other lieges of the king, and, if they refused, to arrest and imprison them, and to certify thereon to the king in chancery.[2]

The dean and chapter of Lincoln were not immune from the prevailing turbulence. John Macworth, who was dean from 1412 until his death in 1451, was involved in constant disputes with the chapter, whom he treated (as Canon Wordsworth points out) very much as in later days Dr Bentley treated the bishop of Ely and the Cambridge University authorities. He neglected to reside and did not provide a vicar in his place; he received rents without fulfilling the obligations for which the endowments had been provided; he neglected the obits of kings and bishops. He would not entertain the ministers of the cathedral upon double feasts, as the statutes required him to do. He summoned persons to attend him at distant and unstatutable places, and told scandalous stories about the canons to personages in high station. When he came to Lincoln he made the ringers stop the bells before the canon on duty could arrive at the church, and he sent word to the choir to wait for him to come to Mass long after the

[1] *Rot. Parl.* III, 649; Foss, *Judges of England*, sub Tirwhit; *Notices of the Family of Tyrwhitt*, pp. 9–13.

[2] *C.P.R.* 1408–13, p. 317 (1 May 1411). Tailboys had succeeded to the Kyme property: see supra, pp. 159–60. Another Lincolnshire notable, Lord Bardolf, joined the rebel earl of Northumberland in a raid southwards from Scotland. The earl died on the field of Bramham Moor (1408). Bardolf died of wounds. His body was quartered: his head was sent to Lincoln to be placed over a city gate, and his quarters to London, Lynn, Shrewsbury and York. Two months later his widow was granted the head and body for burial. *C.P.R.* 1405–8, p. 488; *Chronicon de Adae de Usk*, 1377–1421, p. 283.

celebrant had gone to the altar. He claimed to say Mass in place of the regular celebrant at a moment's notice. He introduced into the chapter house armed men to overawe the chapter, and a clerk to tell the secrets of their deliberations. His servants kept the Close gates open at improper hours, and interfered with the porter in the performance of his duty. He also took away the Black Book, the book of customs of the church, which might at any time be needed for reference or as evidence. These dissensions led to the *laudum* or award of Bishop Alnwick in 1439.[1]

Two incidents which have been recorded relate to citizens. It was charged against John Akewra and John Laverok that they of malice aforethought lay in ambush within the city armed with breastplates, palets, swords, daggers and a 'gundax' to kill Robert Athern and other lieges of the king. Akewra killed him with a 'gundax', and Laverok struck him in the breast with a sword, and would have killed him if he had not been dead already. Both men were servants of Robert de Sutton, a leading merchant, who procured a pardon for them.[2]

In 1422 William Athern the younger, a citizen of Lincoln, charged John Bigge, the recorder of the city and its burgess in four Parliaments, before the mayor, sheriffs and the other justices in the gildhall. The charges were that he had broken into Athern's house and raped his wife Jane, and stolen goods to the value of 40 marks; that he and others lay in wait for Athern, with swords, spears, bows and arrows, with intent to kill him, and the same day assaulted Athern's wife for refusing to take poison he offered her; and that he stole Athern's signet ring and forged six blank charters therewith. It was charged that on another occasion he stole cups, jewels, gold rings and linen and woollen cloths to the value of 100 marks. The indictment was brought into the king's court, and after many delays a jury found Bigge not guilty, and he was dismissed. Whether he lost his recordership is not known, but the city did not return him to Parliament again. It is difficult to know how much to believe of these sensational charges. The learned editor of *Year Books* suspects that 'the real root of the matter lay in what Bigge did with those blank charters, and all the rest of the case against him mattered very little. But the difficulty of knowing where to draw the line in separating facts from fiction must make the cautious reader very shy of using material to be found in accusations on the plea rolls as evidence of the life of the times'.[3]

The award made by Sir John Bussy in 1392 governing the use of the

[1] *The Laudum of Bishop Alnwick*, A.D. 1439, edited by R. M. Woolley, with an introduction by Christopher Wordsworth, 1913. The charges against Macworth are summarised from the Introduction at p. 16.

[2] *C.P.R.* 1408–13, p. 471.

[3] *Year Books of Henry VI*, ed. C. H. Williams (Selden Society), pp. xxxv, 1–10.

city's common seal[1] had not had the desired effect of preventing abuses. Matters came to a head in 1421. In that year the mayor, John Sparrow, summoned the whole commonalty to meet him at the gildhall, and there they solemnly confirmed the order of 1392 'in communi plena congregacione tocius communitatis', and by way of committing the individual citizens to observance of the order their names were enrolled as witnesses. There were present the mayor, the two sheriffs, 240 named citizens, Robert Shirwood the common clerk and 'other citizens of the same city'. It was then ordered that all writings sealed contrary to the order should be given up for cancellation. The example of surrender was set by a number of leading citizens, whose names and offices show how serious and widespread were the abuses to prevent which a new attempt was being made. In the list are William Kirkby and Walter Faldingworth, both past mayors, Robert Feriby and Agnes his wife, formerly wife of Seman Laxfeld, once mayor, two former bailiffs and a former sheriff, of whom two were to hold office as mayor in the future; and many other citizens, the total not being given.[2]

During the same mayoralty the wider question how to ascertain the will of the whole commonalty of the city was undertaken, and for the first time, so far as is known, a constitution was laid down for the common council. The earlier rules governing the common seal had in part provided an answer, but there was business to be done which did not end in the affixing of the seal, and an attempt was made to avoid uncertainty and disorder by laying down rules for the conduct of city affairs. The White Book records that on the Tuesday before the feast of St George the Martyr (23 April) 1422 a common congregation of the whole commonalty was held in the gildhall at the special request of all the citizens to make ordinances for the general good, there being present 200 citizens whose names are given. It was resolved that whenever the mayor should propose anything for the good of the commonalty, twelve of his peers, twenty-four of the more worthy men, and forty other citizens, ten from each ward, specially nominated every year for this purpose, were to be summoned, and the articles laid before them in the gildhall and not elsewhere. They were given the right of arguing and objecting, the decision, apparently, being in the hands of the mayor and his peers. The forty must elect a spokesman who alone might reply upon the articles on their behalf: if any other of them dared to speak he might be imprisoned and fined at the will of the mayor and his council. All the aforementioned citizens were allowed one privilege, that they should not, in any process, be liable to be arrested and imprisoned by the sheriffs if they could produce sureties.[3]

[1] Supra, p. 261. [2] White Book, ff. 2b–3. [3] Ibid. f. 3b.

The overhaul of the civic machinery was not complete. The extravagant habits of previous mayors were, by implication, rebuked in an order that no mayor should have more than two servants at the public expense, namely, the common sergeant at mace and the common clerk. The expenditure upon the livery of the minstrels was not to exceed 8*s*. for each of them, or 24*s*. in all; and another 8*s*. was allowed for a beadle.[1]

In the following year, 1423, another common congregation assembled in the gildhall, there being in attendance upon the mayor sixty citizens whose names are recorded, with the common clerk and other citizens there present. It may be supposed that this was really a meeting of the common council of the twelve, the twenty-four and the forty, or such of them whose attendance could be secured. It was, however, a common congregation, for the forty represented and spoke by their spokesman for the whole commonalty. There it was determined, for the healing of discord, that on the election of a mayor the outgoing mayor and his peers should prepare a calendar of four names of peers, according to seniority and wisdom, and present it to the commonalty, who after consultation should choose two of them, out of whom the mayor with the advice of his peers should select one to succeed to the mayoralty.[2]

It is clear that executive control was really vested in the mayor and his council of twelve, the commonalty having in general the right only to argue and object, and in the choice of mayor having only a veto on two out of the four names submitted to them. Even so, the commonalty had among them the twenty-four 'worthier' men who no doubt correspond to the middling citizens, the *secondarii* of the thirteenth century:[3] if this is so their sympathy would tend to be with the twelve, to whose ranks they might reasonably hope to climb with the advance of years and wealth. The representatives of the ordinary folk certainly had very little voice in affairs.

Nevertheless the government of Henry VI was concerned by the institution of rules too democratic for its taste, which taken in conjunction with a practice of exempting some of the chief citizens from civic office,[4] might have the effect of installing some of the less reputable and responsible citizens in office. For similar reasons Parliament had enacted in 1430 that no man should vote at the election of a knight of the shire unless he possessed a freehold tenement of the clear yearly value of 40*s*. In 1438

[1] Ibid. ff. 4, 4b. [2] Ibid. ff. 5, 5b. [3] Infra, pp. 296–8.

[4] In 1398 the mayor assessed fines upon four citizens for exemption from the office of mayor. Three were imprisoned for non-payment, and the other fled. *C.C.R.* 1396–9, p. 348. In 1429 Hamo Sutton, for benefits received by the city, was granted exemption from civic office under the common seal of the city. Sutton took the precaution of getting royal confirmation of the deed. *C.P.R.* 1429–36, p. 26.

royal letters patent were directed to the mayor, aldermen, sheriffs, good and true men and the whole commonalty of Lincoln, and were laid before a common congregation on the Sunday before Holy Cross Day, there being present the mayor, 96 named citizens and many others. The letters ran as follows:

Whereas we are credibly informed that divers persons before these times bearing the office of the mayoralty in the city aforesaid against the power form and effect of the liberties and franchises granted to you and, as is alleged, by us confirmed, have granted to some persons of the more worthy, more powerful, more good and true, more discreet, more influential and more sufficient and more befitting to occupy and exercise the office of mayor or sheriffs therein under the common seal of the city aforesaid without the will or assent of those whose interest in that behalf was lawfully requisite, but solely in accordance with their own private benefit, that those persons and any one of them should be totally exempt from bearing, exercising or occupying offices of such kind in the city aforesaid; on account whereof middling (*mediocres*) persons of the same city (not only clearly considering that matter but sufficiently recognising the burden of the mayor and sheriffs) have chosen that they would rather abide in their country than in the city, and have withdrawn themselves: and thus it would happen in process of time, if the foregoing were tolerated, some would be chosen to bear or occupy some such office therein who were not worthy, which we hope may not so happen to our heavy damage and prejudice, and would result in undoubted desolation of that city for ever. We, willing at this most opportune moment to provide remedy in this behalf as we are bound to do, command you to elect and take to you those who have been more worthy, more good and true, and more discreet and powerful, and more suitable for occupying and exercising such offices, and more fitting and not otherwise in any way whatever, notwithstanding any such manner of letters made to any such person of the city aforesaid up to the present time, which we will shall be of no strength or virtue. And this ye are in no wise to omit if ye wish to avoid and be relieved from our anger in this behalf, and to give us your affection; certifying us in our chancery of such elections when they have been thus made from time to time under the common seal of the city aforesaid.

Whereupon it was agreed by all present that the resolution of 1423 governing the election of mayor be rescinded; and the common congregation proceeded to elect John Rous (who had already been mayor twice and was burgess in Parliament in 1432) as mayor, and Edward Burton and John Tonard sheriffs.[1] It is not clear that the method of election laid down in 1423 was inconsistent with the king's letter: but it appears to have been thought that it might result in the choice of one of the less worthy candidates.

[1] White Book, ff. 8b–10. Birch, pp. 95–7, prints the king's letter. The injunction not to exempt citizens from office was not binding on the king himself: in 1441 Walter Lyndewode was so excused for life (*C.P.R.* 1436–41, p. 561), and in 1446 Seman Grantham was granted a life exemption (*C.P.R.* 1441–6, p. 442).

A new common seal was required in 1449, and a design for it was specified by the common congregation. It was to depict a castle with five towers and gate with portcullis; in the middle of the castle the arms of the city, and on each side of it a fleur-de-lys, with the inscription round it 'sigillum commune civitatis Lincoln'. The following year the rules for the common seal were revised. The rules of 1421 had already been modified, because the paucity of inhabitants had made it difficult to secure the presence of the specified number of persons. The amended rule had required the presence of the mayor, eight aldermen, the sheriffs, chamberlains, the mayor's clerk and the sheriffs' clerk, and twenty of the commons according to the mayor's choice. Even this modification involved delay in getting documents sealed: and so it was provided that if one, two, three or four aldermen were not present the number of eight aldermen might be made up by the mayor from amongst past sheriffs; and that the four chamberlains might appear by sufficient deputies. An exception was made of the sealing of letters of attorney for the annual accounts of the mayor, escheator and sheriffs at the Exchequer.[1]

After the city had been created a county of itself by Henry IV in 1409, parliamentary elections took place 'in the full county court of the city, held in the gildhall'. The electors were the mayor and about twenty-five of the more substantial citizens 'with the consent of other worthy citizens then being present'.[2] In the fourteenth century it had been the unvarying custom to return two citizens to Parliament, and in the fifteenth this was still often done. Hamo Sutton, a wealthy merchant and stapler of Calais, sat in seven Parliaments for the city and three for the shire, his son Hamo the younger in three, and his brother-in-law John Vavasour in one. Other citizens each sat in several. But a new class of representative was beginning to appear. Vavasour was a lawyer and clerk of estreats in the common bench. William Stanlowe of Silk Willoughby sat for the city in 1442: he acted as attorney for Sir Robert Cromwell in 1433, he appears in Cromwell family deeds and he witnessed the will of Ralph, Lord Cromwell in 1455. John Leynton sat in 1450–1; he was Lord Cromwell's servant, and executor of his will. John Saynton, a Lincoln lawyer, and officer of the duchy of

[1] White Book, ff. 15, 15b.

[2] McKisack, *Parliamentary Representation of English Boroughs during the Middle Ages* (1932), p. 53, citing P.R.O., C. 219, Bundles 11–16. The attitude of the elected representative is illustrated by the fact that in 1322 the mayor and community of Lincoln informed the master of the rolls that their fellow citizen, elected to represent them in Parliament, 'would not go for anything that they could do', and that they had had to elect another to 'act and assent on behalf of the city'. Pasquet, *Essay on the Origins of the House of Commons*, trans. Laffan (1925), quoting Brady, *Historical Treatise of Cities and Boroughs* (ed. 1777), p. 154.

Lancaster, sat in 1467–8 and 1472–5 for Lincoln, and in 1485–6 and 1487 for Grimsby. Sir Thomas Fitzwilliam of Louth and Mablethorpe, a lawyer of the Middle Temple and sometime recorder of London, sat for Lincoln in 1459.[1]

No doubt there was increasing difficulty in persuading citizens to undertake the unwelcome duty of attending Parliament, but an additional reason is suggested by the appearance of Lord Cromwell's servants. The magnates were beginning to find it worth while to have their nominees in the Commons. Lord Cromwell had estates in Lincolnshire and other counties, and notably at Tattershall, where he rebuilt the castle at a cost of 4,000 marks; his noble brick tower and gatehouse still stand, having been bought and restored by the late Lord Curzon and by him given by will to the National Trust. The 'divers baggs or purses cutt in the stonework' of the vast fireplaces there recall the fact that Cromwell served Henry VI as Lord High Treasurer from 1433 to 1443.[2] It may be surmised that the substantial remissions of taxation granted to Lincoln during his regime were largely due to his influence: there survives a petition to the king for relief which is marked 'per dominum de Crumwell'.[3] But if he became something like a patron of the city his position was a personal one and did not survive him.

The Wars of the Roses began in 1455. In 1460 the duke of York's party captured Henry VI at Northampton, but York himself fell at Wakefield. The victorious Lancastrians thence marched south along the great north road. Grantham, Stamford, Peterborough, Huntingdon and all the towns on the way to St Albans were sacked, and for once Lincoln might congratulate itself on being off the main road. The battle of Towton gave the crown to York's son, the earl of March, who became Edward IV.

The towns took little part in the dynastic struggle. Lincoln certainly had Lancastrian associations, but there is nothing to suggest that the citizens felt the slightest difficulty in accepting a Yorkist king and such favours as he had to bestow. Edward had an early opportunity of serving the city in two ways. Under letters patent of 1447 authorising the purchase of lands, property in Ingham and Cotes had been acquired from John Helwell late of Gunby: of this land the citizens had been deprived by William Lord Tailboys, the baron of Kyme, a staunch Lancastrian. Tailboys died on the

[1] See *History of Parliament*, 1439–1509; and for Stanlowe and Leynton, *H.M.C., MSS. of Lord De L'Isle and Dudley*, I (index).

[2] *Complete Peerage* (2nd ed.), III, 552–3. The same device of the purse was used in the building of his mansion at Colly Weston, Northants. See also Curzon and Tipping, *Tattershall Castle* (1929). For the brass of Cromwell and his wife, now sadly mutilated, see *Lincs N. & Q.* III, 193. It is reproduced in Plate 18.

[3] P.R.O. Ancient Petitions, file 121/6024.

scaffold in 1461, and his lands were forfeited to the Crown. The then owner of part of the city's fee farm rent, Thomas de Roos, was also on the losing side: he was attainted in 1461, and beheaded after the battle of Hexham in 1464. Edward passed through Lincoln on his way to Towton on 13 March 1461, and the city presented him with twelve pike, twelve tench and twelve bream.[1] This may have been the occasion on which the citizens petitioned for relief. Edward soon found himself able to favour a city of Lancastrian associations at no cost to himself. On 17 January 1462 he released to the mayor and citizens the fee farm rent of £100 which Roos had forfeited by the act of attainder, the reasons given being the impoverishment of the city owing to the heavy farm, the removal of the staple to Boston, and other losses. The king also restored lands at Ingham and Cotes seized by Lord Tailboys.[2]

This valuable aid was followed in 1463 by a confirmation of the grant made by Henry VI—lately king 'de facto et non de jure'—of licence to acquire lands;[3] and in 1466 another confirmation made important new concessions. It declared that on account of the desolation and decay of the city, and the ruin of houses, and the poverty and paucity of the inhabitants, the king granted to the mayor, sheriffs and commonalty and their successors for ever that the towns and townships of Branston, Waddington, Bracebridge and Canwick should be severed from the county of Lincoln and annexed to the county of the city; and the sheriffs, justices of the peace, coroners and escheators of the county of the city were given jurisdiction therein to the exclusion of the like officers of the county of Lincoln. The residents in the 'four towns' must contribute to scot and lot and all the other burdens of the city according to the discretion of the mayor, sheriffs and other civic officers, and they were to be liable to serve in the civic offices. The grant went on to remit a large number of payments due to be made yearly at the Exchequer by the bailiffs (as the letters patent call them) and to give to the citizens a number of messuages (one described as weak and ruinous) in Lincoln which were in the king's hands; and to hand over the right to forfeitures, treasure trove, waif and estray, and some other legal privileges and perquisites.[4]

In 1464 pardons were being granted to the mayor of the staple of Calais and other staple merchants, probably as a device for raising money from the merchant community. Several citizens of Lincoln were included in the

[1] C.C.M. 1511–41, f. 267b; *H.M.C. Lincoln*, p. 35.

[2] *C.P.R.* 1461–7, p. 115. The grant is inspected in the letter patent of Henry VIII in 1515. Birch, p. 158.

[3] *C.P.R.* 1461–7, p. 291; Birch, p. 105.

[4] *C.P.R.* 1461–7, p. 499. The letters patent were inspected by Richard III in 1484. Birch, pp. 131 et seq.

pardon.[1] The first was John Williamson, described as a citizen and merchant of Lincoln, a former mayor of Lincoln, and merchant of the Calais staple. He was mayor in 1458; and he may be the John Williamson who was charged with piracy in 1462.[2] If so, the pardon was more than formal. In 1464–5 Williamson and his wife acquired a house in Lincoln for 40 marks.[3] He was the benefactor of a window in St Mary le Wigford's church.[4]

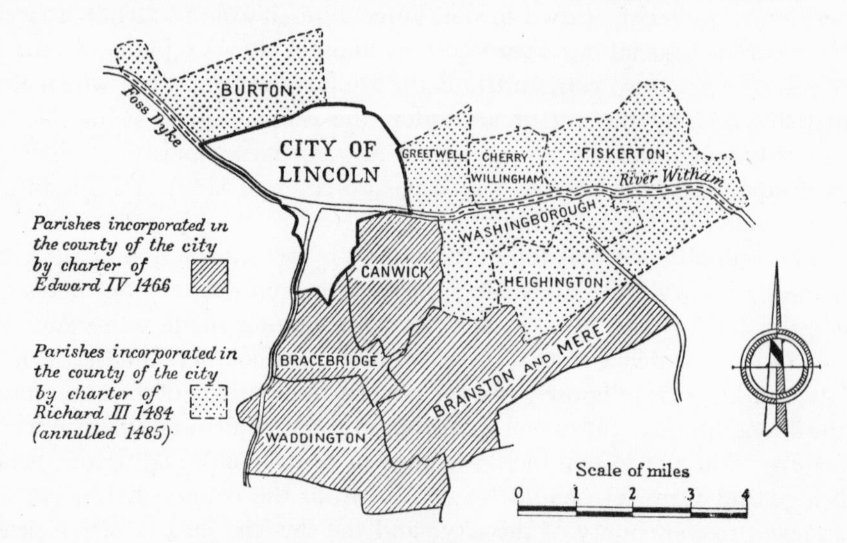

Fig. 18. The county of the city of Lincoln.

Another to be pardoned was John Caldebeke, described as a citizen and grocer of London, a merchant of the Calais staple, formerly a sheriff of the city of Lincoln, it being added, perhaps because of his peculiar name, that he was an Englishman. He had certainly been a sheriff of Lincoln: perhaps he was one of those driven away by the decay of the city's trade to make his fortune elsewhere. There was also Richard Cotes, another Lincoln merchant and Calais stapler, and Thomas Grantham who must be mentioned again.[5]

The civil war broke out again in 1469. Warwick the king-maker

[1] *C.P.R.* 1461–7, p. 351.

[2] Ibid. p. 202. A merchant of Middelburg had freighted a ship *le Pynke* with salt fish, linen cloth and white salt beyond the seas, and brought it to Eastness without Colnewater, when Richard King, of Sandwich, master of a vessel called *Groundhale* alias *Crakebote* (of which James Furness of Sandwich was owner) and John Williamson and William Costryne, with other pirates, asserting themselves to be servants of the king's kinsman Richard earl of Warwick, seized the ship on Midsummer Eve, and despoiled it of the merchandise and rigging, contrary to the ancient friendship between the king and the men of Seland.

[3] *Lincs N. & Q.* III, 182.

[4] Holles, *Church Notes* (L.R.S.), p. 55.

[5] Infra, p. 302.

deserted Edward IV and went over to the deposed Henry VI. One of the incidents in the renewed struggle was a rising in Lincolnshire. It seems to have arisen out of a private quarrel between Richard Lord Willoughby, who had become Lord Welles, and Sir Thomas de Burgh of Gainsborough. Burgh belonged to Edward's household, and Welles was upheld by the duke of Clarence, Warwick and others; and so the quarrel became a part of the civil war. The Yorkist *Chronicle of the Rebellion in Lincolnshire* records that Edward heard, on 7 March 1470, at Waltham, that Robert Welles (Lord Welles' son), calling himself a great captain of Lincolnshire, had proclamations made in all the churches of the shire, in the names of the king (Henry), Clarence, Warwick and himself, commanding every man to meet him at Ranby Hawe, on pain of death, to resist the king (Edward), who was coming to destroy the commons of Lincolnshire.[1] Thereupon Edward sent to London for Welles and his brother-in-law Sir Thomas Dymoke, who, according to another source, came under promise of safety.[2] Edward himself marched northwards; on the 8th a letter from Lord Cromwell's steward at Tattershall confirmed reports of the rising; and the same day, at Royston, Edward received a letter from Clarence offering to bring in Warwick to support him. Edward accepted the offer, and issued commissions to Clarence and Warwick to array the people of diverse shires and bring them to the king. But Clarence's letter was 'false dissimulation, as by the works after it appeared', for while he was at Lincoln Sir Robert Welles received a letter from Clarence, confirming the rumours of the king's intentions.

At Huntingdon, on the way northwards with the king, Lord Welles and Dymoke admitted their complicity in the rising, and Edward ordered Welles to send to his son requiring his submission on pain of death for both of them. At Fotheringhay the king heard that the rebels had passed Grantham and were marching to Leicester, where Clarence and Warwick had promised to meet them. Fortunately for the king, the younger Welles abandoned this project, and marched upon the royal forces at Stamford, without waiting for his allies, in order to rescue his father. Edward at once had the elder Welles and Dymoke executed, and marched out to meet the rebels. They met near Stamford, and the rebels were routed. Sir Robert Welles escaped from the field, but was brought in at Grantham and executed a few days later.[3] On 11 July 1470 Edward issued a commission of oyer and terminer to a number of nobles and the mayor of

[1] Sir R. Welles' confession says that noise was raised that the king was coming to hang and draw great numbers of the commons.

[2] Ramsay, *Lancaster and York*, II, 347, quoting Warkworth.

[3] See 'Chronicle of the Rebellion in Lincolnshire' in *Camden Miscellany*, I. Lord de Welles had a house and garden and four cottages in the parish of St Augustine in Lincoln. *Cal. Inq. p.m.* IV, 311.

Lincoln (Richard Crabden) in the county and city of Lincoln.[1] Two of the surviving rolls of mayors have notes that probably refer to this rising. One unfinished note mentions a rising that year, and the other records that the whole commonalty made a great insurrection upon Richard Bolton and others.[2] Richard Bolton was a former mayor of Lincoln and member of Parliament for the city; he had been pardoned in 1468 as 'late mayor of Lincoln, justice of the peace for Lincoln, one of the filacers of the Common Bench in Lincoln, gentleman, alias merchant, late of London'.[3] This entry may relate to the year before the rising, as it is noted as happening in the mayoralty of Richard Cotes, who preceded Crabden. There is, however, some doubt about the dating of the years of office of the mayors; and there is nothing to show what enterprise Bolton had been engaged upon to incur the wrath of the commonalty.

In the autumn of 1470 the fortune of war turned against Edward IV. He fled into Lincolnshire, crossed the Wash, secured shipping at Lynn, and sailed to the Low Countries. He soon returned, however, and defeated his enemies at Barnet and Tewkesbury (1471). The Exchequer being empty, he had to resort to compulsory 'gifts' and 'loans', and pardons were probably a further source of income. The merchants of the Calais staple received a collective pardon, and so also did a number of them individually, including Thomas Beseby 'late of Stowe by Lincoln, merchant, alias late mayor of Lincoln and escheator in that city, alias of Stowe St Mary, late one of the collectors of the first of the two-fifteenths and tenths granted to the king by the laity in 1468 in the parts of Lindsey, of all offences before 13 January 1472, and all arrears due to the king before 29 September 1469'.[4] Here was another citizen who had one foot inside the city and the other elsewhere.

Edward died in April 1483; his son Edward V was deposed in June, and he and his brother were murdered in the Tower in August by their uncle the duke of Gloucester, who became Richard III.[5] On 11 October Richard was at Lincoln, whence he wrote to his friends at York to say that the duke of Buckingham had turned traitor, and to call for the dispatch of mounted men to Leicester. The same day Lord Lovell, who was with the king at Lincoln, wrote to Sir William Stonor for help.[6] Buckingham's rising was

[1] *C.P.R.* 1467–77, p. 221. [2] Hill, 'Three Lists' in *A.A.S.R.* XXXIX (1929), p. 237.

[3] *History of Parliament*, 1439–1509, sub Bolton.

[4] *C.P.R.* 1467–77, p. 315 (18 January 1472).

[5] A list of mayors notes: 'This yere the kynge sons were put to silence'. *A.A.S.R.* XXXIX (1929), p. 238.

[6] P.R.O. Lists, 15, Ancient Correspondence, XLVI, 102. Kingsford, *English Historical Literature in the Fifteenth Century* (1913), p. 209. *H.M.C.* 11*th Rep.* App. Part III (Southampton MSS.), p. 103. Lovell was the nephew of Viscount Beaumont, and if he had been living and not attainted when Beaumont died in 1507, would have inherited the Beaumont fee in Lincoln. See Hill, 'The Manor of Hungate' in *A.A.S.R.* XXXVIII (1927), p. 182.

quickly suppressed: by 2 November he was caught and beheaded at Salisbury.

Richard's reign was short and stormy, but he made one interesting though abortive grant to Lincoln. On 30 November 1484 he inspected and confirmed Edward IV's letters patent;[1] and on 2 December he granted to the citizens, 'in consideration of the speedy remedy that their city then stood in need of to prevent its utter ruin, a circumstance that had caused him much grief', the right to add to the county of the city the villages and hamlets of Washingborough and Heighington in the parts of Kesteven, and Fiskerton, Greetwell, Burton and Cherry Willingham in the parts of Lindsey; with a new fair for 14 days from the Monday next after Quadragesima Sunday, with its fair court, the court of piepowder. They were also given the subsidy and ulnage of all saleable cloths within the city, suburbs and county of the city, for which the citizens were to pay the king 20*s.* per year. All fees on the rendering of accounts at the Exchequer were remitted, except 40*s.* for the fees of the clerks and other officers.[2] This grant seems not to have taken effect, for after the overthrow and death of Richard at the hands of Henry Tudor at the battle of Bosworth in 1485 Richard was proclaimed a usurper and his acts were annulled.

By an English convention the death of Richard and the accession of Henry VII are regarded as marking the end of the Middle Ages, though at the time the change to the house of Lancaster was in no way more remarkable than the triumph of York in the person of Edward IV had been. But for the city of Lincoln it was a disaster. One of Edward's grants had released the city from the fee farm rent payable to the attainted Lord Roos. In 1485 Roos' son Edmund obtained the reversal of his father's attainder, and this seems to have carried with it the restoration of his revenues, including the fee farm rent. In 1492, by an act of Parliament, 'the guiding and governance of this Edmund, Lord Roos, and his estates, the said Edmund not being of sufficient discretion to guide himself and his livelihood' was vested in Sir Thomas Lovell, who had married one of his sisters.[3] So far as the fee farm was concerned it appears that Lovell had a life interest in it. He had recognised the sorry plight of the city by accepting an annual payment of twenty marks in place of the £100 to which he was entitled. In 1520 the common council, foreseeing a return to the larger burden on their benefactor's death, instructed the recorder to seek Lovell's aid and influence in dealing with the then Lord Roos.[4] Four years later

[1] Birch, pp. 107–56.

[2] Ross, *Civitas Lincolnia* (1870), pp. 27–8. The document was missing in 1895. *H.M.C. Lincoln*, p. 14. On 24 December 1484 the city was granted exemption from tenths, fifteenths and other taxes and tallages for 60 years. *C.P.R.* 1476–85, p. 521.

[3] G.E.C. *Complete Peerage* (1st ed.), VI, 403.

[4] C.C.M. 1511–41, f. 122b.

Lovell died, and application was made to Roos for remission.[1] Sir George Manners had succeeded to the title of Roos: in 1525 his son Thomas was created earl of Rutland. The dispute between the Rutland family and the city about the fee farm rent continued until it was finally redeemed by the citizens half a century later.

Much of the evidence of the decay of the city so far reviewed comes from pleas for remission of taxation and the response thereto: and although the response itself gives some ground for assuming that there must have been need of it, there is always a suspicion of exaggeration about complaints of taxation. Yet ample confirmation of the city's decline is forthcoming from other sources. A list of mayors records the fact that in 1457 there was a time of great mortality among men and women, enough to recall that visitations of the plague were not confined to the Black Death.[2] The decline in numbers and wealth of the citizens made it difficult to maintain the parish churches. Several papal indulgences to this end were obtained. In 1392 a relaxation was granted to those who visited and gave alms to St Peter at Pleas; in 1395 to St Andrew on the Hill; and in 1396 to the chapel of St Mary and St Anne by the church of St Andrew in Wigford.[3] In 1411 Robert Cornubii, the rector of the church of St Peter at wells, value not exceeding 6 marks yearly, was given papal licence to hold also a chantry at the altar of St Nicholas in the church of Lincoln, value not exceeding 8 marks, notwithstanding the statutes of the church of Lincoln requiring personal residence.[4] Later, in 1453, a relaxation was granted to penitents who visited and gave alms towards the furnishing and maintenance in books, chalices and other ornaments of the parish church of St Giles without the walls.[5]

There was a notable shrinkage in the number of parish churches. It has been estimated that the highest total reached in Lincoln was 46;[6] deducting those in the Bail, the Close, Newport and Eastgate, but including St Leonard and St Bartholomew as they are included in the figures that follow, there were thirty-eight which the common council regarded as coming within their purview.[7] Of that number, nine remained after the union of parishes in 1549;[8] the order for the union mentions ten others which were merged

[1] C.C.M. 1511–41, f. 166b.

[2] Hill, 'Three Lists', op. cit. p. 236. It also records (1475) great trouble between the Close and the city (p. 238), probably due to financial difficulties again.

[3] *Cal. Papal Registers, Papal Letters*, IV, 451, 500, 545.

[4] Ibid. VI, 293.

[5] Ibid. X, 572.

[6] Supra, p. 147.

[7] It is worth noting that Leland was shown a roll of thirty-eight parish churches, though there is nothing to show how his list was made up. *Itinerary* (ed. Toulmin Smith), I, 30.

[8] SS. Botolph, Peter at Gowts, Mark, Mary le Wigford, Benedict, Peter at Arches, Swithin, Martin, Michael.

in the nine;[1] seven were taken down by order of the common council about 1533,[2] leaving twelve unaccounted for. Of these St Peter Stanthaket was certainly one, for a lease of the churchyard of this destroyed church was granted by the precentor in 1461.[3] In the suburb of Butwerk, St Rumbold, St Bavon, St Clement and St Peter at wells[4] have dropped out; and in addition Holy Innocents on the green south of Bargate, and some churches within the walls, St Edmund, St George, St Andrew on the Hill, St John the Poor. The position of St Faith and St Stephen in Newland is not clear: they may have been regarded as outside the purview of the common council because they were in the bishop's soke. They are, however, included in the thirty-eight mentioned above.

Yet the provision of parish churches was never related to the needs of the population in the modern sense, and the decline in their number might be due to decline in piety or change in point of view rather than to fall in population. An account of the collectors of a subsidy in 1428 is in this respect better evidence. The collectors returned that there were no inhabitants in St Clement in the city (meaning presumably St Clement in Butwerk, as the other St Clement was in the Bail), St Peter at Bakkarholm (*ad fontem*), in the eastern part of Butwerk, or St Bartholomew, to the west of the castle. Seventeen parishes were returned as not having more than ten inhabitants. In the walled city were All Saints (Hungate), Holy Trinity near the friars minor, St George, St Andrew (on the hill), St Peter at the skin market (Stanthaket), St John the Poor, St Edmund; in Wigford, St Michael and St Andrew, and beyond Bargate, Holy Innocents; in Butwerk, Holy Trinity near the stairs, St Rumbold, St Bavon; in the western suburb, St Faith; and above hill both churches in Newport, St John the Baptist and St Nicholas, and also St Leonard.[5] From this evidence, as from that of the churches themselves, it is clear that the suburbs were shrinking, and so also were the back streets of the city itself; and apart from the Bail and Close, Lincoln, always long and narrow in shape, had virtually become the single-street city depicted by Buck in the eighteenth century. So it remained until the industrial expansion of recent times.

[1] SS. Margaret, Holy Cross, Holy Trinity, Edward, Andrew, John (all in Wigford), Peter at Pleas, Lawrence, Mary Crackpole, Cuthbert.

[2] Holy Trinity at the Gresefoot, All Hallows, St Augustine, St Bartholomew, Holy Trinity at Greyfriars, St Michael at Gowts, St Leonard. C.C.M. 1511–41, ff. 228–48.

[3] White Book, f. 20. The parish was united to St Michael.

[4] St Peter *ad fontem* was united to the cell of St Mary Magdalene on account of the falling of the church to the ground and there being no parishioners to build it up. *V.C.H. Lincs*, II, 39, quoting Bishop Chedworth's Register.

[5] *Feudal Aids*, III, 339. The account was cancelled, but there is no reason to doubt the correctness of this part of the return.

Frequent reference is made to houses in ruins. In 1376 the king committed to Walter de Askeby the keeping of a garden and two ruinous plots in St Michael on the Mount and a ruinous plot in St Bavon;[1] and an inquisition taken on the death of Walter de Poynton of Canwick in 1367 recorded that in addition to Canwick manor he owned twelve messuages worth 100*s.* a year and no more because four of them had stood empty and without a tenant for the last three years, a cottage, four small shops, two plots and a garden, which were worth nothing because they were empty and unenclosed.[2] Here is evidence of depopulation going back almost to the days of the Black Death.

The earliest surviving minute book of the common council (which begins in 1511) shows that anxious attention was being paid to the same matter. In 1515 an attempt was made to arrest the demolition of houses. The chief constables of wards were ordered, on pain of 20*s.*, to allow no house or tenement to be taken down; if they failed to secure compliance they were to report to the mayor, who, if he failed, was to be fined 40*s.* for every house demolished. A house might be taken down for the purpose of rebuilding, or a licence might be obtained from the mayor and council if it were likely to fall.[3] To the same end the sale of tiles, stone and timber out of the city was forbidden.[4]

In 1584 William Lambarde, in words which for the most part would have applied a century earlier, described the economic position of the city as follows:

> Touching the present estate of Lincolne, I thinke it pietyfull; for albeit theare was hope, that after the making the statute 32 H. 8 for the re-edifienge of that, and other decaied townes, the ragged partes thereof should have been renewed; yet for as much as it hath neither the helpe of traffique by water, nor anie handycrafte, or arte by land, the condicion thearof is little better then of a commune market towne: and if a man should judge of the inner wealthe by the outward viewe, he might well think that the verie ruine thearof neare at hand, if some politique devise be not ministred in time to staie and uphold it.[5]

[1] *C.F.R.* VIII, 359.
[2] *Cal. Inq. p.m.* XII, no. 164.
[3] C.C.M. 1511–41, f. 48.
[4] Ibid. f. 96b.
[5] *H.M.C. 6th Rep.* App. Part I, p. 453a. (F. B. Frank Collection.) On the sale of the collection the volume containing Lambarde's account was bought by the Bodleian Library.

PLATE 20

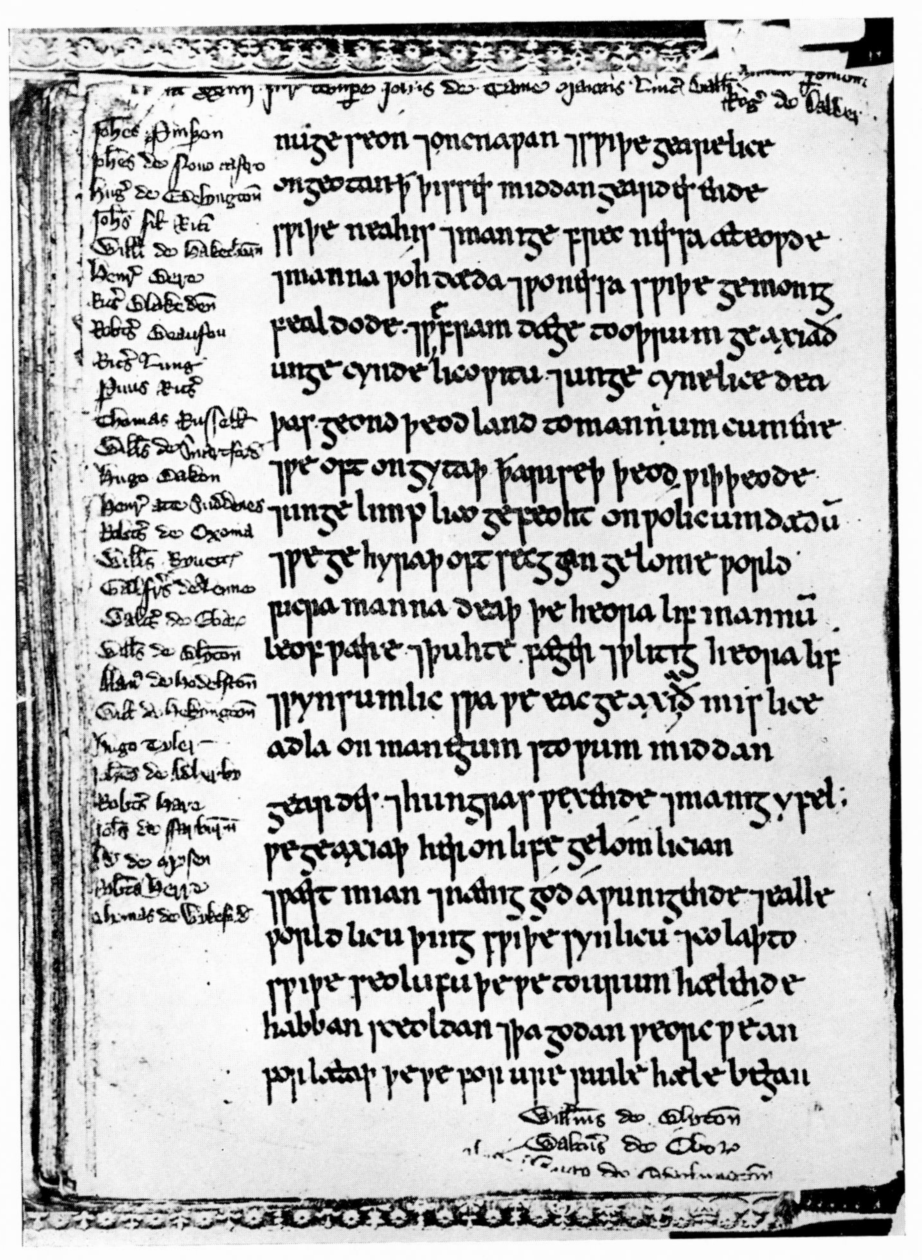

A PAGE FROM THE BLICKLING HOMILIES,

recording in the margin the names of the 'twenty-four', in the mayoralty of John de Tame (1322)

[*See p.* 292

COMMON SEAL OF THE CITY, 1449

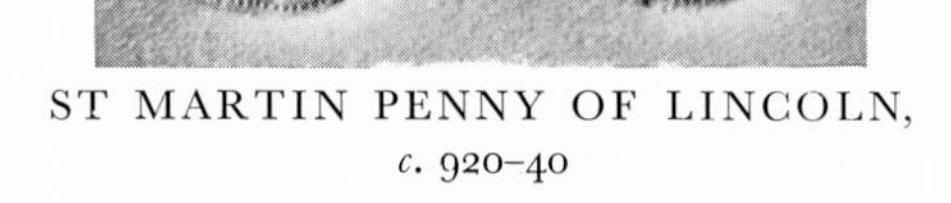

ST MARTIN PENNY OF LINCOLN, *c.* 920–40

MAYORALTY SEAL
thirteenth century (enlarged)

VIKING PENNY
with moneyer's name Heribert and Lincolla in monogram

See p. 302]

CHAPTER XIV

THE MAYOR AND COMMONALTY

EARLIER chapters have recorded the last years of a body of lawmen whose function it once had been to declare and interpret custom; the existence of the court of burwarmote, meeting in the open air at the mootstone, hearing pleas between the citizens; the appearance of citizens holding the office of bailiff and farming the king's revenues within the city and its liberties; the rise of the gild merchant and its virtual merger with the civic government, symbolised by the transfer of the burwarmote to the gildhall; the emergence of a new civic head, the mayor, chosen by the citizens from amongst themselves; the use of a common seal by which the citizens could bind the city in its corporate capacity; and the gradual increase of the civic liberties by charter and custom.[1]

Little help is to be gained from the records in the city archives in amplifying the history of the civic institutions. The surviving minutes of the common council begin in 1511. The only volume of earlier date to be found in the archives is the White Book, a volume of miscellaneous records which begins in 1421. In it are the several fifteenth-century passages which have been dealt with in Chapter XIII, and the custumal translated from French into English in 1483 which is to be mentioned later.[2] Apart from the charters, and a few other papers of which some account has been or will be given, no earlier documents remain in official custody.

Fortunately there are compensations to be found in other quarters. In the first place there are the rich store of original charters and the great registers of the dean and chapter of the church of Lincoln, now being published in the monumental edition planned and edited for the Lincoln Record Society by Canon Foster, and continued since his death in 1935 by Miss Kathleen Major.[3] The charters of land in Lincoln and its suburbs have not yet been printed, but there are several hundreds of them, some of the twelfth and many of the thirteenth century. These documents are the foundation of modern knowledge of the citizens of the thirteenth century, their families, their public offices, their property and their benefactions. They are supplemented by the cartularies of religious houses having a claim upon the devotion of the medieval citizens, such as Bardney, Barlings, Kirkstead and Thurgarton.

[1] See index.

[2] *H.M.C. Lincoln*, pp. 2 et seq.

[3] See introduction to *R.A.* I.

Secondly there is a translation of a document, in modern times called the *Provisions*, which can be dated *c.* 1300, and is in the nature of a civic constitution: indeed, an entry in the Blickling Homilies (to be mentioned shortly) under 1365 shows that it was called the *Constitutions*. It is described by John Ross in his *Civitas Lincolnia*:

These Provisions [says Ross] written in large and beautiful text on a vellum membrane, but without rubricks, are said to be only a portion of the original number agreed upon for the municipal regimen, but as the Great Seal was once appended to it, the fact of there being another membrane is not probable, because such appendage was generally attached to the last, and not to the first membrane of such instruments. The document seems to have been much consulted, and has several marginal alterations, but so faded as to be illegible. It is evident that it was in accordance with these provisional statutes that all succeeding Mayors, Aldermen, Bailiffs, Chamberlains, Constables (no other officers being, as yet, named) were required to discharge their respective duties till circumstances and political casualties gave rise to necessities and wants, which at that period of the city's annals were unknown and unthought of. This statutory instrument, which has long ceased to be of use for consultation, had the Great Seal attached to it to give it validity and force in case of dispute. It is not rolled but folded up, and is endorsed with the following writing in the modern character: 'No date of Seal: But supposed to be wrote towards the latter end of the Reign of Edward I or beginning of Reign of Edward II.' As a relic preserving a vivid memory of the incipient state of a subsequently flourishing Municipality, it possesses an interest which will well recommend it as an object especially worthy of protection, and will rescue it from a fate that has befallen many other contemporaneous and posterior documents of a like kind.[1]

Ross thought that the document was contemporary with the charter of Edward I (1301), following the ten years' suspension of the civic liberties, and suggested that 'the citizens, on recovering their Mayor, were resolved to prevent the recurrence of what had deprived them of him, and to provide for the time to come, certain regulations by which to be guided in the election of municipal or civic magistrates'.

There is irony in his remark that the interest of the document would recommend it as an object especially worthy of protection, for when the Reverend W. D. Macray examined the Lincoln records for the Historical Manuscripts Commission, he reported (1895) that the *Provisions* were missing.[2]

Ross refers to another opinion that there was a second membrane, and it is evident that he was familiar with a manuscript account of the Lincoln

[1] (1870), pp. 12–13.

[2] *H.M.C. Lincoln*, p. 14. No trace has since been found of the original document. There are no originals in the Ross Collection at Burton Hall.

charters written by Samuel Lyon, who was town clerk, in 1785. This account is still in the city muniment room, and happily it includes what seems to be a full translation of the missing *Provisions*. Lyon there says that there appears to have been a second skin, with the city seal annexed to the whole. As to the date of the *Provisions*, the two witnesses are in substantial agreement, for Lyon says that he compared the writing with a specimen given by Mr Astle in his publication upon the *Origin and Progress of Writing*, and found that in character and style it nearly resembled a record written in 1280.[1] Ross' suggestion of the Great Seal must be an error, since this was not attached to documents drawn up outside the chancery at this date, and it cannot have been a chancery document, for it has no dating clause.

In the third place, there is in the Lincoln Cathedral Library a volume of the proceedings of the court of burwarmote for the period from 1308 to 1376. How it reached its present home is unknown. It is bound with a collection of statutes and other documents, and it consists chiefly of enrolments of grants of land, pleas heard in the court, and wills of land in the city and liberties held by burgage tenure and therefore devisable by will, the wills being proved in the city court. This record is of special value upon matters of borough custom, though it also throws light upon topography and family history, and it gives the names of many holders of civic office.[2]

Fourthly, there is in the Lincoln Diocesan Registry a list of civic officers of Lincoln: the list of mayors begins in 1313 and that of bailiffs in 1360. The roll appears to have been written about 1532, and afterwards continued to 1599. The earlier part of the lists may have been compiled from the Burwarmote Book mentioned above; to it have been added entries of events of national or local importance, some of which are of value. It is to be regretted that the compiler of this incipient chronicle did not attempt something on a more ambitious scale.[3]

The fifth and last of these sources consists of entries written upon margins and blank spaces of the Blickling Homilies an Anglo-Saxon manuscript of the tenth century. The manuscript was sold by auction in New York in 1932 at the sale of the late Lord Lothian's library, and was resold at the

[1] Lyon's translation was printed by the writer in *Lincs N. & Q.* XX, 25–30. For convenience of reference it is reprinted in Appendix VII.

[2] See Woolley, *Catalogue of the Manuscripts of the Lincoln Cathedral Chapter Library* (1927), no. 169 (8). The volume has been calendared by Mr F. W. Brooks, who has kindly allowed the writer the use of his calendar and introduction.

[3] The roll is briefly described in *H.M.C. 12th Rep.* App. Part IX, pp. 574–5. Two other lists of mayors in the possession of the dean and chapter are mentioned on p. 563 of the same volume. For these see Hill, 'Three Lists' in *A.A.S.R.* XXXIX (1929), p. 217.

Courtlandt F. Bishop sale in 1938 to its present owner Mr John H. Scheide. The Lothian catalogue comments that

> for several hundred years this wonderful manuscript, one of the few Anglo-Saxon manuscripts existing in private hands, belonged to the city of Lincoln: from the xiii century to the year 1609, the margins contain notations by various mayors and sheriffs of Lincoln, recording their nomination or election.
>
> These historical records of the great English city, although they are of considerable local importance, seem to have escaped the attention of all British historians, and have remained unnoticed and unpublished.

The catalogue adds that from the Lincoln corporation the Blickling Homilies passed into the library of Sir Richard Ellys at Nocton in Lincolnshire, and thence into the Hobart family and to Blickling Hall, Norfolk.[1]

At the Lothian sale a 'Psalter in Latin, according to the Roman version, with occasional Gallican readings, viii century', was sold to the Pierpont Morgan Library. This psalter, known as the Blickling Psalter, has written upon various pages the names of members of the Lincoln corporation and their officials from 1505 to 1635, with a few other entries, but their local interest is slight. Apparently this volume accompanied the Homilies upon its travels until the Lothian sale.[2]

Sir Richard Ellys, who became the owner of the Blickling manuscripts, was a theologian and politician of sufficient note to find a place in the *Dictionary of National Biography*. He collected libraries at his London house and at Nocton. He was a member of the Gentlemen's Society at Spalding and to him Horsley dedicated his *Britannia Romana*. No doubt he made his greatest finds among the books and papers of the Lincoln corporation. On his death in 1742 his widow sent off his theological and antiquarian books to his second cousin and residuary legatee, Lord Hobart, at Blickling.[3]

From these varied sources and from scattered references it is possible to gather a good deal of information about the government of medieval Lincoln.

[1] *Illuminated MSS., Incunabula and Americana from the famous Libraries of the Most Hon. the Marquess of Lothian, C.H.* 1932.

[2] *Census of Medieval and Renaissance MSS. in U.S.A. and Canada*, by S. de Ricci, New York, 1937, Pierpont Morgan Library, p. 1502, no. 776. The Pierpont Morgan Library furnished the writer with photographs of the Lincoln entries. Both manuscripts were edited for the Early English Text Society in 1880. Mr Neil Ker suggests that the Homilies and the Psalter were used as oath-books, because both contain a calendar and the passages from the four gospels known as the *cursus*. Other MSS. which contain calendar and *cursus* are B.M. Royal 9 A. vii, B.M. Royal 9 A. xii (oath-book for a custom house), the Bridport oath-book, *H.M.C. 6th Rep.* p. 476, and the Fordwich oath-book, *H.M.C. 5th Rep.* p. 607.

[3] For Ellys, see Norgate and Footman, 'Some Notes for a History of Nocton', in *A.A.S.R.* XXIV (1898), pp. 365–6.

Any survey must begin with the oldest of the civic institutions, the court of burwarmote. In this court, presided over by the reeve or bailiff, first of the royal and then of the popular choice, the customs of the city were declared and applied. When in 1194 the charter of Richard I granted to the citizens the liberties and free customs of the citizens of London, it used the formula which became common form, 'according to the liberties of London and the laws of the city of Lincoln'.[1] This did not mean that the citizens of Lincoln were under any obligation to abrogate any of their own customs which did not conform with those of London: it meant that the citizens were free to adopt such of the customs of London as they thought fit. It was a convenient form of legislation by reference. That many of the London rules, both of substance and of procedure, were adopted is shown by an examination of the custumal translated into English in 1483. This custumal was described by Miss Bateson as consisting largely of a translation of the London rules in the *Liber Albus* of 1419.[2] No study of the customs of the city is attempted in this book, but examples may be given from sources outside the custumal of matters governed by local custom. It appears that Lincoln, alone of the Danish Five Boroughs, had the custom of primogeniture, inheritance of land by the eldest son, which became the rule of the common law: the other four, Derby, Stamford, Leicester and Nottingham, had the custom of Borough English, or ultimogeniture, inheritance by the youngest son.[3] A custom peculiar to Lincoln is mentioned by Mr Bolland: when a man had had two wives the issue of the first wife took three-quarters of his estate of inheritance, and the issue of the second took the other quarter.[4] In a *Year Book* of 1338–9 is an example of a rule of procedure: in a plea of trespass heard before the mayor and bailiffs of Lincoln one of the parties was taken and detained. The court agreed that in London and Lincoln trespass could warrant attachment of the body if the party had nothing whereof to be attached.[5]

In the early years of the thirteenth century there was in Lincoln as in other boroughs rapid institutional development. The mayor and the common seal both made their appearance,[6] and about the same time there came into being a council whose function it was to consult with the mayor. Whether that body was a native growth, gradually developing from the burwarmote, whether it took shape in the caucus of merchants in the gildhall, or whether it was due to conscious copying of the foreign com-

[1] Birch, p. 5.

[2] *Borough Customs* (Selden Society), I, p. xxxvii.

[3] Elton, *Origins of English History* (1882), p. 188; Bateson, *Records of Leicester*, I, p. xvi; *Records of Nottingham*, I, 172.

[4] *Manual of Year Book Studies* (1925), p. 16.

[5] *Year Book* 12 *and* 13 *Edward III* (R.S.), p. 78.

[6] Supra, pp. 194–7.

munes, is a question not to be settled by the evidence of a single borough. The example of London was probably enough for the citizens of Lincoln.[1]

The existence of this council is first mentioned in the most casual way. The Rolls of the Justices in Eyre for 1219 record that William son of Richard of Lincoln, one of the twenty-four of Lincoln, is in mercy because he contradicted the other twenty-three and was convicted of it.[2] The twenty-four were clearly an established body whose existence and identity did not need to be explained. Though no earlier express reference to the twenty-four has been found, its existence seems to be implied by an entry upon the assize roll for 1206. The judges were tallaging the boroughs and manors in the king's hand, and the principal citizens undertook with the judges that the city should provide £400 by two instalments. The mayor had the agreement in writing. There were present in court ten citizens, who are named, and who swore before the justices to observe the agreement: later fourteen other named citizens swore to the like effect.[3] It is of course possible that these twenty-four citizens were an *ad hoc* committee and not a standing twenty-four of the city. It would be a curious accident, however, if the same number were chosen for a different body, and it seems likely that the citizens who were parties to the agreement with the justices, and were acting on behalf of the whole city, were the standing council of the time. The list certainly included many of the leading citizens.[4]

Such a council already existed in London. There in 1193 the commune bound its members 'to be obedient to the mayor of the city of London and to the skivins (*skivini*) of the said commune...and to follow and maintain the decisions of the mayor and skivins and other good men (*probi homines*) who shall be associated with them':[5] in 1200–1 twenty-five of the more discreet citizens were elected and sworn 'pro consulendo civitatem una cum Maiore';[6] and in 1206 King John wrote to the barons of London ordering that for the avoidance of dissension, they should have elected by their common counsel, twenty-four of the more lawful, wise and discreet of their fellow citizens, 'who best know how and are willing to consult your [our?] rights and honour and the amendment of your city in administering its laws'.[7] The precise meaning for the history of London of these passages

[1] Pollock and Maitland, *History of English Law* (2nd ed.), I, 659; Round, *Commune of London*, ch. xi; Stephenson, *Borough and Town*, pp. 183–5; Tait, *Medieval English Borough*, pp. 285–301.

[2] Mrs D. M. Stenton, *Rolls of Justices in Eyre for Lincolnshire and Worcestershire* (Selden Society), no. 875. William son of Richard was no doubt the nephew of Adam the mayor, son of Adam's sister Margery and Richard son of James. See Appendix v.

[3] Mrs D. M. Stenton, *Earliest Lincolnshire Assize Rolls* (L.R.S.), no. 1448.

[4] See Appendix VI.

[5] Round, *Commune of London*, pp. 235–6.

[6] *Liber de Antiquis Legibus* (Camden Society), p. 2.

[7] *Rot. Lit. Claus.* I, 64a.

has been closely examined by Dr Round[1] and Professor Tait,[2] but it is sufficient for the present purpose to note that London provided a precedent for Lincoln in the constitution of a body of twenty-five or twenty-four to consult with the mayor. In the course of the thirteenth century, Winchester, Dublin, Berwick, Leicester and Exeter had councils of twenty-four, and the Northampton council of twelve was afterwards doubled. Ipswich and York and a number of other towns had twelve.[3]

The list of twenty-four citizens of 1206 is worth examining. Of a few of them nothing is known: they include a tailor and a carpenter. But of the majority it is possible to say with certainty that they are substantial citizens, owning property or belonging to families known to hold property, some of them serving as mayor or bailiff and some paying considerable fines for their part in the assault on the Jews in 1191. Beside this list may be set another list. In 1265 letters patent were issued to twenty-four named citizens of Lincoln ordering them to protect the Jews of the city in persons and goods.[4] Here again there is no certainty that this group of citizens is more than a body chosen for one specific purpose, but the number suggests as before that the whole council of twenty-four was chosen for the purpose of fixing the commonalty with responsibility. Of these men more is known than of their predecessors of 1206. Probably nine of them held the office of mayor; at least four others served the office of bailiff; eight of them belonged to the small group of ruling families described in Appendix v. Only two are described as craftsmen. The great majority were substantial men with money in land or in trade or both; and among them, there can be little doubt, are the *majores*, the group of ruling citizens.

There is no need to suppose that there was equality among the twenty-four. Some might never attain to civic office; others might become bailiffs, whose office, though of great importance, was unpopular because of the personal liability of the bailiffs for the farm of the city during their year of office: but the mayoralty was mostly the preserve of a more select group, many of them members of a few families. Their business dealings and pious benefactions have recorded a good deal of information about them.[5] Of the family to which the two Williams, the son and the nephew of Warner, belonged, Warner himself had been bailiff, apparently, six times in the reign of Henry II; William the nephew, who had been bailiff twice, was mayor on the deprivation of Adam; John, son of Warner's brother Osbert, was mayor, and his brother Giles bailiff. Of Giles' sons, William was

[1] Op. cit. pp. 235 et seq. [2] Op. cit. pp. 265–70.

[3] The Lincoln twenty-four was unknown to Professor Tait, who relied (p. 279) on the *Provisions* with their reference to the twelve judges.

[4] *C.P.R.* 1258–66, p. 421. [5] See Appendix v.

mayor for at least two years, Osbert for one year, and Jordan was bailiff. Of the family (if they were all related) bearing the name of Paris, William was bailiff for several years between 1164 and 1170, John of Paris was mayor for at least five years, and his nephew William of Paris and a Peter of Paris appear later. Of another family, part of which acquired the name of Bridge (*de ponte* or Attebrig), Peter was mayor for four or five years, and his son Richard was certainly mayor once. It is likely that James Bridge and Thomas son of Robert belonged to the same family.

In the half century following the fall of Adam, out of twenty-one known holders of the mayoralty, it seems as though ten of them belonged to three families. Of the others, Thomas of Beaufou held the office at least five years, and a later holder, Richard of Beaufou, was his son.[1] Peter of the Bail held office in two spells for a considerable number of years. The others seem only to have held office for one year each. Beyond this half century Roger son of Benedict was mayor for at least six years; he was gathering lands in the Lincoln fields to endow his chantry in St Peter in Eastgate church.

When, therefore, the complaint is heard that the citizens are being oppressed by the civic magnates, there can be no doubt where to look for the accused. They were entrenched in the twenty-four, and formed within it a smaller body wielding the substance of power. The formal existence of such a small and select body will be noticed later.

The inquiry recorded in the Hundred Rolls was conducted in Lincoln by means of three juries, the great men (*magni*), the second or middling men (*secondarii*), and the lesser men (*minores*).[2] At Norwich there were the greater, the middle and the poor citizens, and there was a similar division at York and Bristol; and at King's Lynn the greater men levied taxes on the poor and middle men of the town. The names of the great and the middling jurymen of Lincoln have been recorded.[3] Among the *magni* are two bailiffs, Adam of the hospital and Ralf of Gayton, and perhaps others with slightly varying surnames. Another of them, Walter of Crowland, was one of the twenty-four of 1265. Roger Gupil may have been a relative of a mayor, Henry Gopyl. But the greater mayoral families do not seem to be represented, for the reason, no doubt, that it was their deeds or misdeeds into which it was the jury's task to inquire.

The second jury is more interesting. The list is headed by William Cause. A William Cause, perhaps his son, later became a great man, the king's *custos* or keeper of the city during the suspension of the civic liberties, and mayor when they were restored. John Cotti was one of the twenty-four of 1265. William of Borton was a bailiff. Richard *medicus*, who enjoyed the

[1] *R.H.* I, 314b. [2] Ibid. pp. 309, 315, 322. [3] See Appendix VI.

title of *magister*, must have been a man of standing. Richard of Stow was a mason, and later in life became master mason of the Minster.[1]

When the replies of the juries to the questions put to them are compared, it is evident that the great men give the longest and fullest answers; the answers of the second men are similar, though there are many discrepancies, and it is clear that the statements of damages inflicted by divers wrongdoers are mere guesses, expressive of the strength of feeling of the jurors; the lesser men pretend to little knowledge, for when they give a figure they frequently add 'and more', and many of their estimates are obviously wrong.

There is no ground for supposing that the three juries represent a caste system, each man being confined for ever to his own class. On the contrary, the two jury lists indicate that the same kind of people are on both juries, and that men who will later rise to civic office and men of professional standing are among the *secondarii*. The dividing line between them must be arbitrary, and there can be little doubt that the divisions were made according to property and for purposes of assessment in payment of tallages and other taxes.[2] How much truth there was in specific complaints against the great men by their fellow-citizens it is of course impossible to say, though it is easy to imagine that there were grounds for complaints of inequality of assessment, with suspicion of favouritism. It is equally easy to surmise that the reply of the magnates, beyond a general denial, was that they really bore the greatest burden (especially in the office of bailiff), and that as they had to pay the piper they ought to be allowed to call the tune.

According to Lyon's translation it was laid down in the *Provisions* (or *Constitutions*) that the commonalty should with the advice of the mayor choose twelve fit and discreet men to be judges of the city. They must pay taxes like other people.[3] The number implies that these men were the aldermen: but the word *judges* is puzzling, and arouses regret that the original document is lost. Ross, in his account of it, mentions twelve 'judicial arbitrators or magistrates', as if the correct translation was not quite so simple; and it may be that the word in the original was not *judices* but *juratores* or some less familiar one. It may even have been *lagemanni*; the lawmen of Chester are described as *judices* in Domesday Book.

There is reason for thinking that the twelve existed within the twenty-four. That the larger body continued in the fourteenth century is proved by the Blickling Homilies, and the twelve aldermen survived until 1835. It

[1] See p. 114.

[2] Jacob, *Studies in the Period of Baronial Reform and Rebellion*, 1258–67 (1925), p. 119 n. Unwin, *History*, IX, no. 35, p. 234.

[3] See Appendix VII.

would not be difficult to choose from lists of the twenty-four those who might be expected from their prominence and length of service to belong to the more select body. Some confirmation of this view comes from the Patent Roll for 1314, where it is recorded that twelve named citizens had bound themselves at the king's request to the bishop, dean and chapter of Lincoln in the sum of 900 marks, which the king had borrowed from them in order to defend the realm against the Scots.[1] These twelve were certainly members of the twenty-four, and eight or ten of them could from other evidence have been pointed out with confidence as probable members of the twelve.

Further support comes from the ordinance of 1392 for the control of the common seal. The seal was to be used for sealing only in the presence of the mayor, twelve of his peers, and twelve of the next worthiest citizens, or sixteen at least of the said twenty-four, with the four coroners and four treasurers, and ten citizens at least elected by all the other citizens.[2] It would seem that the inferior half of the twenty-four were representatives of the middling citizens, a kind of second estate, and that the ten additional citizens spoke for the *minores*.

The middling citizens spoke for themselves in their foundation of the gild of Corpus Christi in the parish of St Michael on the hill in 1350:

> And whereas this gild was founded by folks of common and middling rank, it is ordained that no one of the rank of mayor or bailiff shall become a brother of the gild, unless he is found of humble good and honest conversation, and is admitted by the choice and common assent of the bretheren and sisteren of the gild. And none such shall meddle in any matter, unless specially summoned; nor shall such a one take on himself any office in the gild. He shall, on his admission, be sworn before the bretheren and sisteren to maintain and to keep the ordinances of the gild. And no one shall have any claim to office in this gild on account of the honour and dignity of his personal rank.[3]

Resentment of arrogance on the part of the greater men breathes through the ordinance. It is significant, however, that persons of the rank of mayor or bailiff are not excluded from membership. They are merely told that they must not assert themselves or, to use a modern colloquialism, they must not throw their weight about: which fact suggests that a member of this gild of middling citizens might rise to civic heights after his admission to membership.[4]

[1] *C.P.R.* 1313–17, p. 189.

[2] See p. 261.

[3] Gild Certificates, no. 135; Toulmin Smith, *English Gilds* (1870), p. 178.

[4] William de Belay, who was mayor in 1372 and M.P. in 1375, remembered the gild in his will; apparently Peter Dalton, canon and treasurer of Lincoln Cathedral, whose will was proved in 1402, was a brother of the gild, with a mayor and another canon. Gibbons, *Early Lincoln Wills* (1888), pp. 32, 97; Wordsworth, *Medieval Services in England*, p. 150. There were, however, other gilds of Corpus Christi in Lincoln.

Between the years 1303 and 1371 entries of the names of the twenty-four were made in the margins of the Blickling Homilies. 'The names of the xxiiii sworn to the mayor's council' is a typical heading. Some of the lists are indecipherable, but for the period 1303–22 (the date of the list is not always given, though it is easy to fix within narrow limits) twelve lists are available.[1] They show that some of the members held office continuously throughout the period or nearly so: generally these were the men who reached the mayoralty, and whom other evidence suggests to have been the leading men of the time. Others served on the twenty-four for a few years and then dropped out: a few occur only once. Later lists yield a like result. How the council was recruited is not stated, though new appointments seem to have been made in small batches, as if single vacancies were ignored. Nor was the number limited to twenty-four. That name had become a title: the numbers varied between 18 and 30. Perhaps when the numbers fell towards the lower figure the mayor made nominations to bring the number up to the official figure or beyond. It was all very much like a modern committee not unduly fettered by a constitution, finding people willing to serve and dropping those who were not.

Already in the reign of John there was a large civic establishment. There were the mayor, two bailiffs, four coroners and two city clerks.[2] There were also four beadles who were probably sergeants at mace attendant on the mayor.[3] The names of some of these officers appear as witnesses to charters, some of which were made or acknowledged in the burwarmote and written by the city clerks. No formal records of the court have survived from the thirteenth century. That some civic record was made is indicated by a charter stated to be made in the fifty-third year of King Henry (1268–9) in the second roll of the mayoralty of William of Holgate.[4] All the other indications, however, suggest that such record did not really amount to much, and that it disappeared at an early date. When the practice of making entries in the Blickling Homilies began about 1303 the agreement of 1263 with the dean and chapter was entered upon one of the flyleaves, clearly for the purpose of preserving a record of it. It is the only thirteenth-century document which has been noticed in the Homilies, and it is in a fourteenth-century hand. Furthermore, when the roll of mayors mentioned above[5] was made in the sixteenth century no names were recorded earlier than 1314. Presumably no rolls for an earlier date were available, though the space left at the beginning of the list shows that the compiler knew that

[1] Some of these are given in Appendix VI.

[2] See p. 196.

[3] Mrs D. M. Stenton, *Earliest Lincolnshire Assize Rolls* (L.R.S.), no. 1012.

[4] D. & C., Dii, 80/3/21.

[5] Supra, p. 291.

the mayoralty did not begin then, and left room for any earlier names that might be recovered.

It has been noticed above that the later years of the thirteenth century were marked by serious class quarrels culminating in the suspension of the civic liberties.[1] The lesson of the ten years 1290–1300 was not lost. The *Provisions* were almost certainly the result. About the same time the entries in the Blickling Homilies began, and within a few years the surviving Burwarmote Book was begun also. There was no return to the practice of the previous century whereby a citizen might hold office as mayor for several years together. There was a regular succession after William Cause, who, after serving as the king's *custos*, became mayor on the granting of the charter of Edward I. It need not be supposed that all the mayors were of equal authority, but at least the office did go round, and if the leading families wished to get their way they must resort to influence instead of to direct control.

The *Provisions* (or *Constitutions*) represent an attempt to introduce order into the city government. How far they formalise the pre-1290 practice or theory and how far they are new it is impossible to say. They direct that the commonalty every year shall elect a mayor, who must be assessed to the public taxes with other citizens, and therefore be a citizen himself; during his mayoralty he is to be exempt from all taxes, dues and tallages, and to be entitled to take his hansels, or customary presents from strangers, but not from the citizens and their sons and those who pay scot and lot in the city, and not from those within the county who ought not to be expected to pay (no doubt referring to the county merchants who were members of the gild merchant).[2]

The first hint of the method of election of the mayor comes from the Blickling Homilies. In 1361 a panel of seven names was prepared and submitted to the commonalty, from which they made their choice. The procedure of 1392 has already been quoted;[3] in the custumal it is set out more elaborately. On Holy Cross Day (14 September) all freemen must by use and custom assemble at the gildhall. Those who had been mayor sat 'opon the bynke', and those who had been sheriff sat 'within the chekyr'. The mayor and his brethren on the bench (the ex-mayors) made a calendar of four names of sufficient and discreet men of whom none had been mayor for seven years. The common clerk delivered the names written in a bill to all the other freemen: they chose two in writing, and of the two so chosen the mayor and his brethren made the final choice. If the mayor so chosen were present he took the oath at once or gave surety to take it: but if he refused to bear office he was committed to prison for a whole year,

[1] Supra, pp. 211–13. [2] Infra, Appendix VII; supra, p. 186. [3] Supra, pp. 261, 298.

his lands and goods seized for the king to the profit of the commonalty for a year, and half his goods were for ever forfeit at the year's end, and he was abjured for ever out of the city.[1]

Whether this rather elaborate procedure was adhered to may be doubted. In 1512 a calendar of four was voted on directly, the total votes polled being 90;[2] the following year there was voting on a panel of two, 46 votes being polled.[3] These variations did not, however, make much practical difference, the essential point being that the mayor and his brethren of the secret council prepared the panel from which the commonalty might choose.[4] There was no difficulty in making other departures: in 1520 the then mayor was entreated to continue in office by reason of the scarceness of corn.[5]

The *Provisions* further directed that the bailiffs should be chosen by the commonalty. It was their duty to discharge the fee farm rent each year, and the mayor and commonalty might distrain on their lands and chattels if they failed to do so, and make good out of their chattels any damage suffered by the city through their default in payment of the fee farm rent. This was the whole basis of the city's liberties, and could not be imperilled by any man with impunity. The bailiffs were allowed two clerks and four sergeants, to be presented to the mayor and commonalty at Michaelmas.

There were also to be elected, under the *Provisions*, a weigher of goods; four men of trust to keep the city's accounts, later to be called the chamberlains and allotted one to each ward, and they were to have one chest and four keys; and two parish constables for every parish. The other sections of the *Provisions* relate for the most part to the regulation of trade.[6]

It is perhaps significant that the lists of the twenty-four in the Blickling Homilies cease, so far as can be ascertained, in 1371. The real power was in the twelve or part of it, and after the Black Death it may have been difficult to maintain the number. The rules of 1392 for government of the common seal are the last occasion on which reference is made to the twelve mayor's peers and twelve of the next worthiest citizens, making together the twenty-four. In 1422 the whole commonalty assembled in common congregation decreed a change in the civic body. When the mayor proposed aught for the good of the commonalty he was to summon twelve of his peers, twenty-four of the next worthiest citizens, and forty other citizens, ten from each ward.[7] This was probably quite impracticable, and in 1449 the quorum necessary for the affixing of the common seal was reduced.[8] The difficulty of securing attendance continued to increase, and in 1511 it was ordered

[1] White Book, f. 47.
[2] C.C.M. 1511–41, f. 7.
[3] Ibid. f. 19b.
[4] Ibid. ff. 28b, 199b.
[5] Ibid. f. 121b.
[6] Infra, Appendix VII.
[7] Supra, p. 276.
[8] Supra, p. 279.

that for all acts to be made in the common council twenty-four persons should be chosen by common assent with the twelve aldermen to have full authority to make ordinances for the common weal of the city. The number varied: in 1514, twenty-two 'and no more' were sworn of the common council, and in 1520, fifteen.[1]

The custumal of 1483 was 'drawn out of French' into English by Thomas Grantham 'that hath been mayr of the same cite and mayr of the stapul at Cales...at the costys and labur and wryting of the sayd Thomas', and by the whole commonalty agreed to be perpetual. The rules for the election of mayor, quoted above,[2] point to a new classification of citizens. It was not the aldermen who sat upon the bench, but those who had been mayor, and not the middling citizens within the *chekyr*, but past sheriffs; and presently in 1524 it was ordered at the Michaelmas leet that Mr Mayor and the aldermen and sheriffs' peers and such of the chamberlains' peers as Mr Mayor and his brethren should assign and elect should have authority to keep the common council and to assemble together and to make such acts as should be for the common profit of the city and might stand with the common law.[3] In 1530 there was a slight variation: Mr Mayor should take and elect by his denomination to the twelve aldermen, twenty-four of the most discreet and able sheriff peers and chamberlain peers and no more to be of the common council.[4] These distinctions of rank were marked in the minutes by placing the names of persons present at the meetings in three groups: aldermen, past or present sheriffs, past or present chamberlains.

Probably then, as later, the chamberlains were nominated by the mayor; of the sheriffs, the custumal provided that one was to be chosen by the new mayor, and if he failed to choose, both were to be chosen by the freemen out of a calendar of six; vacancies on the aldermanic bench were sometimes filled by the common council, sometimes by the leet;[5] the common council was chosen by the mayor and aldermen, the right of nomination being in the mayor. The four justices of the peace were elected at the leet from a panel prepared by the mayor.[6]

The oligarchic character of the corporation was firmly established by the end of the medieval period; it was stereotyped by the charter of Charles I; and in its essentials remained the same until 1835. Only one aspect of the unreformed corporation denounced by the nineteenth-century reformers remained to be developed.

Who were the citizens, the men who were free of the city? Probably the earliest qualification for citizenship was the ownership of land or houses in

[1] C.C.M. 1511–41, ff. 4, 35, 121b.
[2] Supra, p. 300.
[3] C.C.M. 1511–41, f. 175.
[4] Ibid. f. 218b.
[5] Ibid. ff. 17b, 210, 284b.
[6] Ibid. f. 154.

the city.[1] An important clause in a writ of Henry II acknowledged another way of acquiring the freedom of the city. It provides:

> I confirm also to them that if any remain in my city of Lincoln for a year and a day without challenge from any claimant and pay the customs of the city, and the citizens can show according to the laws and customs of the city that a claimant was living in England and did not challenge him, thenceforward as heretofore, he shall remain peacefully in the city of Lincoln as my citizen.[2]

Such a provision let in the member of the gild merchant.

It must always have been the rule that the son of a freeman was entitled to the freedom. By the time that the Lincoln records begin it had been established that the freedom was in the control of the common council, and four avenues were recognised: first, patrimony; secondly, apprenticeship to a freeman for seven years; thirdly, purchase at a price in the control of the council; fourthly, gift, as where it was desired to encourage particular craftsmen to settle in the city. The old association with tenure of land had disappeared, and so also had the old rule about residence for a year and a day. Towards the end of the eighteenth century the seven-year apprenticeship was beginning to die out; sale of the freedom was virtually restricted to parliamentary candidates, who could not represent the city in the House of Commons unless they were freemen; gift of the freedom was rare; and for practical purposes admission by patrimony alone remained. The number of residents who were not free steadily increased, for the companies, successors of the gilds, had failed to preserve their monopolies of trade. Great numbers of non-residents took up the freedom solely for the purpose of claiming and selling their parliamentary votes, to which freemen alone were entitled. The corporation was ripe for reform.

[1] Tait, op. cit. p. 249.

[2] *B.B.C.* (i), p. 104; Birch, p. 2.

CHAPTER XV

COMMUNICATIONS AND TRADE

THE special position of four great English roads, two of which were the Ermine Street and the Fosse Way, in the eleventh century has already been mentioned.[1] Lincoln might then claim to be on the main road from north to south: in 1066 Harold, and in 1068 William, marched south through Bawtry, Littleborough, Lincoln and Huntingdon.[2] By the fourteenth century the Ermine Street had been superseded by the Old North Road, whose main points from London were Waltham Cross, Ware, Royston, Huntingdon, Wansford Bridge over the Nene, Stamford, Grantham, Newark and so north to Doncaster.[3] The Gough map in the Bodleian Library does not show many connecting roads to Lincoln, but it shows a road to Sleaford, and though it only marks Bourne, the Roman King Street ran through it, rejoining Ermine Street at Castor. There must have been a road from Grantham to Lincoln, and from Newark there was still the Fosse Way.[4] The traveller from London to Lincoln could therefore make his choice of the point at which to leave the main road and take to the lesser roads. When Henry VIII was making arrangements for the suppression of the Lincolnshire rising in 1536 letters were sent to the mayors and head officers of Waltham Cross, Ware, Royston, Huntingdon, Stilton, Stamford, Sleaford and Lincoln, ordering them to appoint horsemen to carry the king's letters from post to post.[5]

The Gough map also shows a road running north from Lincoln to the Humber, which it meets at Barton. It follows the Ermine Street to Spital on the Street, but leaves it to pass through Kirton Lindsey and Glandford Bridge (now called Brigg), where it crosses the Ancholme. The Barton ferry is recorded in Domesday Book.[6] In 1299 and 1300 the king's great barge appointed for the ferry and the smaller barge were ordered to be

[1] Supra, p. 10.

[2] Stenton in *V.C.H. Notts*, I, 238–9.

[3] As indicated by the Gough map, published by the Ordnance Survey. For this map and the subject generally see Stenton, 'Road System of Medieval England' in *Economic History Review*, VII (1936), no. 1, on which the writer has chiefly relied; and *Historical Geography of England before* 1800 (ed. Darby, 1936), pp. 260–5.

[4] Henry I gave Bishop Alexander licence to cause a bridge to be built over the Trent to his castle of Newark, provided it were of no harm to the king's city of Lincoln or his borough of Nottingham (1129–33). *R.A.* I, 38. In 1168–9 work was being carried out on the bridge. P.R. 15 *Henry II*, p. 45.

[5] C.C.M. 1511–41, f. 258.

[6] *L.D.* 24/13. Domesday records other ferries on the Humber at Grimsby and South Ferriby (at each of which there were two) and Winteringham.

LINCOLN FROM THE SOUTH, showing Little Bargate in the foreground

From a painting by Peter de Wint in the Usher Art Gallery

[*See p.* 352

repaired,[1] and in April 1300 the king crossed from Barton to Hessle on his way to Scotland. The passage of his retinue is said to have taken two days and required eleven barges and boats.[2]

Professor Stenton has adduced examples of routes taken by cross-country travellers and their rate of progress. In the winter of 1324–5, Robert of Nottingham was directed to superintend the purchase of wheat for the

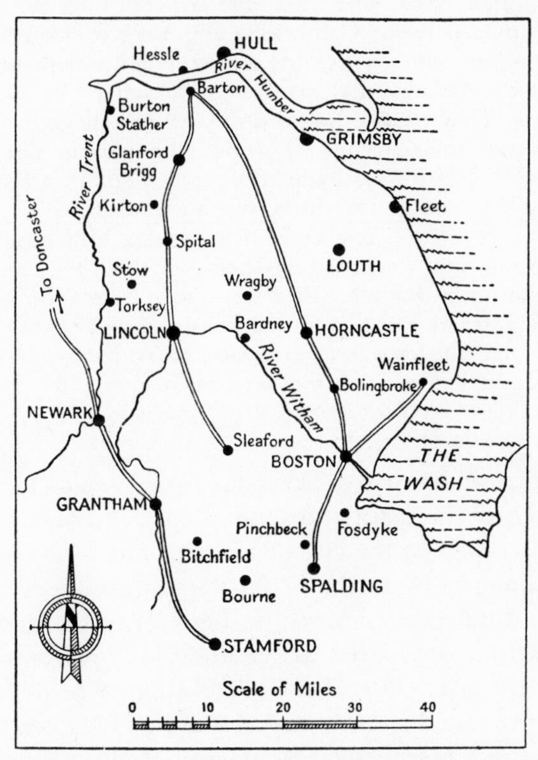

Fig. 19. Diagram of the Lincolnshire section of the Gough map.

king and its dispatch to Gascony from the ports of Grimsby and Boston. Starting from Nottingham he travelled on the first day to Southwell, a distance of 14 modern miles which he calls 10 *leucae*; then to Lincoln, 23 miles (16 *leucae*). After publishing his commission he rode to Burton Stather, 33 miles (30 *leucae*); thence by water to Howden (12 *leucae*), and next day to York (16 *leucae*). On his return he went by Doncaster, thence following the Roman road, which crosses the river Idle at Bawtry and the

[1] *C.C.R.* 1296–1302, pp. 232, 336.

[2] *Liber Quotidianus Contrarotulatoris Garderobae*, pp. xvii, 61. Prince Edward apparently went to Torksey, p. 39. Frost, *Notices of the Early History of Hull* (1827), pp. 60–1 and note; Poulson, *Beverlac* (1829), p. 84. For the ferries, see Barley, 'Lincolnshire Rivers in the Middle Ages' in *L.A.S.R.* (n.s.), I, 4–7.

Trent at Littleborough, on the way to Lincoln. The journey from Doncaster to Lincoln took two days, the first being the feast of Epiphany on which he travelled only 14 miles.[1]

Another example illustrates the combination of road and waterway in an itinerary:

In 1319 Edward II invited the scholars of King's Hall, Cambridge, to spend Christmas with him at York. The elder scholars, travelling by road, covered the distance of 151 miles between Cambridge and York on hackneys in five days. The younger scholars, who presumably were thought unequal to the hardships of the road, left Cambridge on December 20 by water. In two days they had reached Spalding. They passed the third day on horseback, travelling between Spalding and Boston, their luggage following them in carts. The fourth and fifth days were passed in a great boat, which brought them from Boston to Lincoln. The sixth, being the feast of Christmas, was spent at Lincoln. On the seventh day they passed through the Foss Dyke in two boats from Lincoln to Torksey, where another great boat was hired for them, in which they reached York two days later, on the ninth day after their departure from Cambridge, and three days late for the entertainment promised them by the king. The diary of their journey suggests that the voyage from Boston to York can rarely, if ever, have taken less than four full days, and it might well take more. In 1322 the Exchequer, moving by water between Torksey and York, was held up for a day and a night by storms at Burton on Stather.[2]

The perils of travel by road are recalled by the report to the Exchequer of the chief taxers of the tenth and sixth of 1322 in Lindsey that they had £600 of this tax stored in the city of Lincoln, but were unable to send it because of the dangers of the road.[3] In 1345 measures were authorised to stop the felonies and robberies on the Fosse Way between Newark and Lincoln, which were attributed to the absence of any town or any men dwelling there: the prior of the Hospital of St John of Jerusalem in England was given leave to found anew a chapel and build a town and houses on his own ground in a place called Swinderby Moor at his manor of Eagle (*Aycle*); the houses were to be let to men ready to inhabit them for the entertainment of travellers on the road; and the town was to have a weekly market and two yearly fairs.[4]

For purposes of trade the waterways were more important than the roads and, as Mrs Stenton has pointed out, the wealth of Lincoln was largely

[1] Stenton in *Economic History Review*, VII (1936), pp. 13–14, quoting Exch. Acct. Misc. 309/29.

[2] Ibid. p. 20, quoting Exch. Acct. Misc. 552/10, and Broome, 'Exchequer Migrations to York' in *Essays presented to T. F. Tout*, p. 296. In 1200–1 the king's venison was carried from Burton Stather to Lincoln probably by Trent and Fossdyke, and thence to London by road. P.R. 3 *John*, pp. xiv, 2.

[3] Willard, *Parliamentary Taxes on Personal Property*, 1290–1334 (1934), p. 194, quoting Lord Treasurer's Remembrancer's Memoranda Roll, no. 94, m. 167d.

[4] *C. Chart. R.* v, 40.

due to its twofold access to the sea. The returns of a tax on merchants for the period 1202–4 not only point to the importance of water transport, but show what a high relative position the two towns on the Witham had in the national scale. London paid £836. 12*s.* 10*d.* and was followed by Boston with £780. 15*s.* 3*d.* and Southampton with £712. 3*s.* 7*d.* Lincoln came fourth with £656. 12*s.* 2*d.* King's Lynn was only slightly less. The Humber ports were Hull (£344. 14*s.* 4½*d.*), Grimsby (£91. 15*s.* 0½*d.*), Hedon (£60. 8*s.* 4*d.*), Barton-on-Humber (£33. 11*s.* 9*d.*) and Immingham (£18. 15*s.* 10½*d.*). The Humber and the Wash were the two main routes of entry for the Baltic trade. Taking its five ports (Boston, Lincoln, Grimsby, Barton and Immingham) together Lincolnshire led every county in England.[1]

On Lincoln's system of waterways Torksey occupied a key position at the junction of the Fossdyke with the Trent. Its close association with Lincoln has already been noticed.[2] Apparently the earliest known reference to it is in 873, when the Danish host, after ravaging Northumbria, came under their king, Halfdene, to Lindsey, and wintered there at a place called Turcesige.[3] There was a moneyer at work there in the time of Æthelred II (978–1016) whose name, Thorcetel, is significant of this connection with the Danes: he was still at work under Cnut (1016–35). When Sweyn entered England by way of the Humber and the Trent in 1013 he dominated Torksey and Lincoln from his camp at Gainsborough.[4]

Domesday Book places Torksey as a borough next after Lincoln and Stamford. It states that in the time of King Edward there were 213 burgesses of the town, though in 1086 the number had fallen to 102, 111 messuages being waste.[5] In spite of this decline its yearly tax, or farm, had been increased from £18 to £30. The burgesses had the same customs as the people of Lincoln, and

> this in addition, that whoever of them had a messuage in the same vill used to give neither toll nor custom either coming in or going out. This, however, was their duty, that if the king's messengers should come thither the men of the same town should conduct them to York with their ships and their means of navigation, and the sheriff should find the messengers' and sailors' food out of his farm.

[1] P.R. 6 *John*, pp. xliv, 218.

[2] Supra, p. 186.

[3] *Anglo-Saxon Chronicle* (R.S.), I, 142–3. It is followed by Henry of Huntingdon and other chroniclers.

[4] A thirteenth-century jury declared that Torksey was the key of Lindsey as Dover was of England, and that ground in it was set apart wherein tents might be pitched by the levies who assembled for its defence. Cole, 'Royal Burgh of Torksey, its Churches, Monasteries and Castle', in *A.A.S.R.* XXVIII (1906), p. 473.

[5] The relative position of Torksey and other towns on the Trent is suggested by the fact that in 1086 Nottingham had 173 burgesses. At Newark the bishop of Lincoln had 56 burgesses, 42 villeins and 4 bordars.

But if any of the burgesses should wish to go elsewhere, and to sell [his] house which was in the same vill, he could do it, if he wished, without the knowledge [and licence] of the reeve.

This important service of carrying the king's messengers to York, with freedom from toll and the liberty of alienation of land all have a highly urban sound.[1] The decline of the town, to which Domesday refers, may have been due to the obstruction of the Fossdyke: in 1121 it was reopened for traffic.[2]

There were three parish churches in Torksey, All Saints, St Peter and St Mary, all of which came into the hands of the priory of St Leonard, an Augustinian house founded in the reign of Henry II, possibly by the king himself.[3] A small Cistercian house of nuns was founded at the southern end of the town, by the side of Fossdyke; and, being appropriately dedicated to St Nicholas, the patron saint of sailors, it became known as the priory of St Nicholas de Fossa, or the Fosse Nunnery.[4]

The surviving village of Torksey lies some 700 yards north of the Fossdyke, the intermediate area being already waste in the time of Leland:

The olde buildinges of Torkesey wer on the south of the new toune, but there now is litle seene of olde buildinges, more then a chapelle, wher men say was the paroch chirch of old Torkesey, and on Trent side the yerth so balkith up that it shewith that there be likelihod hath beene sum waulle; and by it is a hille of yerth cast up: they caulle it the Wynde Mille Hille, but I thinke the dungeon of sum olde castelle was there.

By olde Torkesey standith southely the ruines of Fosse Nunnery, hard by the stone bridge over Fosse Dik; and there Fosse Dike hath his entering ynto Trente.[5]

Canon Cole adds that in this space between Fossdyke and the present village foundations have been turned up, showing that the old town extended over it more or less continuously, yet so thickly that fifty-seven of its houses did not seem too large a proportion to assign to the two convents.[6] In 1535 the churches of St Mary and St Peter were both in being, but All Saints, which Leland was told was the parish church of old Torksey, is

[1] *L.D.* pp. xxxv, 12–13. Professor Stenton mentions that in the twelfth century its court, like that of Lincoln, was known as the burewarmot. Apparently it had also, like Lincoln, the penny burgage rent. Infra, p. 310, n. 2.

[2] Symeon of Durham, *Historia Regum* (R.S.), II, 260, who says the canal was cut by Henry I.

[3] A confirmation charter of John dated 1200 says that the house was 'of our alms and under our custody and protection', and alludes to letters of 'Henry our father' conferring privileges. *V.C.H. Lincs*, II, 170. In 1270–1 the prior and convent of Torksey were to have the men of Torksey in frankalmoign, free of all tallages and exactions. *Inq. A.Q.D.* (P.R.O. Lists and Indexes), p. 6.

[4] *V.C.H. Lincs*, II, 157. For Torksey generally, see Cole, 'Royal Burgh of Torksey, its Churches, Monasteries and Castle' in *A.A.S.R.* XXVIII (1906), pp. 452–530.

[5] Leland, *Itinerary* (ed. Toulmin Smith), I, 32.

[6] Op. cit. p. 464.

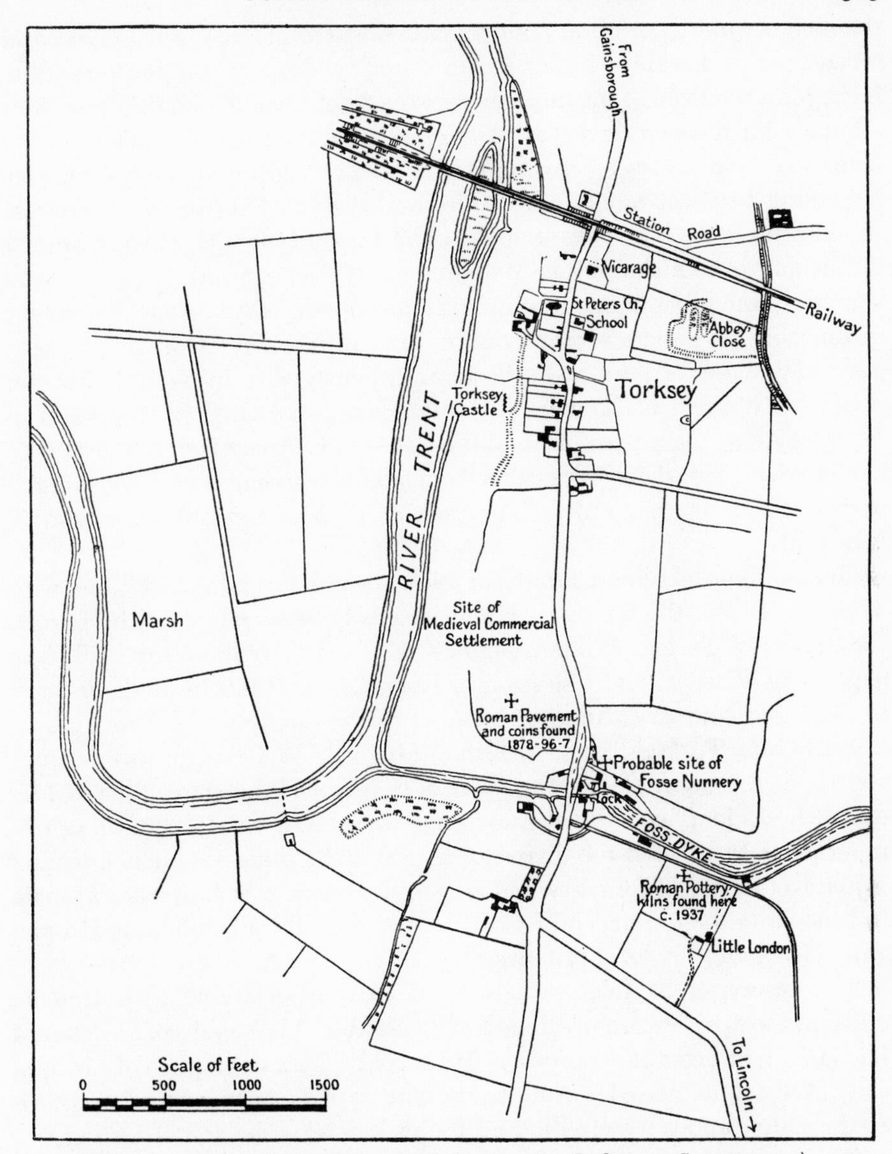

Fig. 20. Torksey (based by permission on the Ordnance Survey map).

described as 'another church there in ruins'.[1] When he was suppressing religious houses, Dr London mentioned the Fosse Nunnery contemptuously as 'a beggerly power ruynose howse'.[2]

The proximity of the house to the Fossdyke made it the object of the benevolence of the trading community. It was founded by the townspeople

[1] *Valor Ecclesiasticus*, IV, 131.

[2] Wright, *Letters relating to the Suppression of the Monasteries* (Camden Society, 1848), p. 214.

themselves, and its original endowment consisted of 124 acres of land and seven tofts in Torksey; by a charter dated at Stow on 14 January 1201 King John remitted to the nuns the two marks of silver which they paid him annually for their land; in 1237 Henry III granted them a charter of confirmation; and in 1331 Edward III, at Lincoln, granted them a charter inspecting between ninety and a hundred deeds.[1] The special interest of this charter is that it shows that the chief Lincoln merchants were among the benefactors of the house. William son of Richard son of James (who was one of the Lincoln twenty-four and the nephew of Adam the first mayor of Lincoln) gave them a rent from his land in Torksey; Godwin the rich gave 2½ bovates of land at Fulbeck, and, jointly with his wife, half a toft in the great street of Lincoln, his wife Alice also giving six tenements in Walkergate in the parish of St Mary Crackpole. Apart from citizens who can be identified, there were other benefactors whose names imply contact with Lincoln; for example, Henry son of John of Lincoln gave land in Newton.[2]

One leading merchant family of Lincoln had special associations with Torksey. It was the family of Hundegate.[3] Four members of the family, Osbert son of Torger, William nephew of Warner, William son of Robert nephew of Warner, and Giles son of Osbert, gave Lincoln lands or rents to the Fosse Nunnery. Another member of the family was the incumbent of All Saints, Torksey: in 1219 Bishop Hugh de Welles appropriated this church to the nuns, saving the right of Stephen Hundegate, then holder of it, who as long as he lived was to pay the nuns a yearly pension of two marks, one to be used for their clothing and the other for their kitchen.[4] When Reiner son of John granted rent from houses in St Lawrence's parish in Lincoln to the nunnery, the grant was witnessed by Stephen de Hundegate, clerk, and his brother Giles.[5]

The priory of St Leonard also had close associations with Lincoln citizens, though not so many details are available. The canons of St Leonard had land in St Peter at Pleas parish in Lincoln.[6] Master Stephen of Lincoln, son of Osbert, witnessed a grant to the canons of Torksey, and other grants to the same canons were witnessed by his brother John son of Osbert.[7]

The foundations of the two religious houses in Torksey and the benefactions which have been noticed seem all to belong to the second half of the

[1] *C.P.R.* 1330–4, p. 215; *Monasticon*, IV, 242; Cole, op. cit. p. 493.

[2] Ralph son of John of Lincoln gave to the church of Lincoln two tofts in Torksey, saving 2*d*. to the king. *R.A.* IV, 2.

[3] See Appendix v, p. 388.

[4] Cole, op. cit. p. 467.

[5] D. & C., Dii, 75/2/3.

[6] D. & C., Dii, 80/3/11.

[7] *R.A.* II, 266, 267, 270, 271, 272. The prioress of Fosse is returned as having an annual rental in Lincoln of £4. 14*s*.; the prior of Torksey £4. 17*s*. *R.H.* I, 312b.

twelfth and the first half of the thirteenth centuries, and this seems to be the period of the town's greatest post-Conquest prosperity. It is no surprise to find that it prospered when Lincoln did. The privileges of the Lincoln gild merchant were being asserted, probably on the whole with success, and foreign merchants wishing to trade in Lincolnshire were going to Lincoln. The only hint that is forthcoming as to the volume of traffic passing along the Fossdyke is given in a complaint in the Hundred Rolls. Robert of Donham, bailiff of William of Valence, was levying, wrongly, it was complained, a toll of a halfpenny (more or less) per ship passing from Lincoln by Fossdyke to Dunham, a village on the Trent above Torksey, and in one year his receipts amounted to half a mark;[1] this suggests 160 ships in the year, and the figure would not include ships passing downstream from Torksey.

The town had a position of privilege on the Trent. To its lord belonged certain tolls, called 'thourthtoll' and 'overthuertoll' from which men of London, Lincoln, Nottingham, York, Beverley and Torksey were exempt. The rule was laid down that any man might have his goods exempt if he swore that they were not merchandise or if he kept them a year and a day; and if the cargo of a ship paid duty, the ship itself was free. The town was protected from competition within a considerable stretch of the Trent: all goods coming up the Trent from Gainsborough and all goods going down from Newark were to unload nowhere before reaching Torksey.[2]

Even so, Torksey owed much to its position on the Fossdyke, and by the end of the thirteenth century the canal was beginning to fail it. For example, in 1299 and following years the bursar of Durham Priory bought cloth and other goods at Boston fair. The usual route by which the goods were sent home was by boat from Boston to Lincoln; thence not by the canal but in carts to Torksey, and by the Trent and the Ouse to York and Boroughbridge.[3] In the middle of the fourteenth century wool was being taken by road from Lincoln to Barton on Humber instead of to Torksey, and thence by boat to Hull.[4]

The silting of the Fossdyke was a serious matter for Lincoln, and indeed for the whole district; and as might be expected, loud complaints are heard of its condition. In July 1335 the men of the county of Lincoln petitioned the king and council, setting forth that the Fossdyke from Lincoln to the

[1] *R.H.* I, 320a. The Lady Devorgilla of Torksey was also taking toll there.

[2] Gras, *Early English Customs System* (Harvard, 1918), p. 155, quoting B.M. Rot. Cott. II, 14.

[3] *Durham Account Rolls* (Surtees Society), II, 495–6, 512, 532. When purchases at Boston were resumed in 1336 after an interval of 20 years the goods went from Boston to Newcastle by sea. Barley, op. cit. p. 17.

[4] Pelham in *Historical Geography of England before* 1800 (ed. Darby, 1936), p. 264.

Trent was so obstructed that the passage of boats and ships was no longer possible; and a commission was issued to survey the dyke, to inquire how and when it became obstructed, and to compel interested parties to cleanse it.[1] It was quickly reported that certain men of the counties of Lincoln and Nottingham had received divers sums of money for removing an obstruction of the dyke from those who caused it, but had converted the greater part to their own use; and the commissioners were bidden to inquire further.[2] Thirty years later, the citizens of Lincoln, declaring that they spoke not only for themselves but also for merchants of York, Nottingham and Kingston upon Hull and elsewhere, asserted that the dyke, which used to carry ships and boats with merchandise and victuals, was obstructed by those with lands on both sides of it, who in summertime drove their cattle over it to their feedings, as well as by an unusual growth of grass and the rising of the sand in it, with the result that there was then no passage; and new commissioners were ordered to make the persons responsible do their duty.[3] On another complaint in 1376 the citizens claimed to be speaking for the merchants of Newcastle on Tyne as well as those aforementioned.[4] This complaint followed upon a presentment by a Lincoln jury in the Michaelmas term, 1375, that the Fossdyke, which was once open and full of water so that ships from Nottingham, York, Kingston on Hull and elsewhere could come thereby from the Trent to Lincoln and thence to Boston, was stopped; that the prior of Torksey, the town itself, the prioress of Fosse, John bishop of Lincoln, Gilbert earl of Angus and his tenants, Ralph Daubenay knight and his tenants, the abbot of Newstead, the tenants of the lands of Gilbert de Brydeshale and Hugh de Normanton in Saxilby, the Lady Katharine de Swynford of Lincolnshire, John Bret of Thorney (Notts), Ralph Paynell knight and all other lords whose lordships abutted on the dyke, ought to and were wont to clean, empty and repair the said dyke according to an old established rate; and that the stoppage had continued for thirty years to the damage of the king, the country, and the city, of £1,000.[5] A like commission of 1384 had upon it some weighty persons. It included John of Gaunt, John bishop of Lincoln (himself a riparian owner), Henry Percy earl of Northumberland, Sir Michael de la Pole the great Hull merchant, clergy, gentry and citizens.[6] The last complaint of the series, it appears, was made in 1432, and among the com-

[1] *C.P.R.* 1334–8, p. 148. [2] Ibid. p. 203.

[3] 8 February 1365. *C.P.R.* 1364–7, p. 138. [4] *C.P.R.* 1374–7, p. 322.

[5] Flower, *Public Works in Medieval Law* (Selden Society), I, 292. In 1354 it was presented before the king at Lincoln that the south part of Fosse bridge by Torksey was destroyed, and ought to be repaired by the township of Fenton. The township acknowledged liability (ibid.).

[6] *C.P.R.* 1381–5, p. 500.

missioners appointed were William bishop of Lincoln, the duke of Norfolk, the earl of Northumberland, and Sir Ralph Cromwell.[1] The wording of the complaints was generally the same, and it would seem that after each complaint something was done, perhaps very little, and that within a few years the navigation was blocked again. The struggle seems to have been given up, for though there were still complaints about the Witham there were no more about the Fossdyke.

A new attempt to restore the dyke was made in 1518, when the king appointed commissioners of sewers for the district between Torksey bridge and Brayford at Lincoln.[2] One of them was William Atwater, bishop of Lincoln, who entered upon his duties with zeal, issuing an indulgence to all who would aid the work of restoration, declaring that:

> The city of Lincoln, which once, with very few exceptions, excelled the other cities of this England not only in the company of people who had their lawful abode there, but also in the richness and art of its buildings and the wealth of its resources, the adornment of its churches, and the other possessions which embellish it, has now come to such indigence and disaster, that unless it is speedily aided by the singular devotion of men who support it with their labours, diligence, and outlay, will come to greater and almost irreparable decay. But certain men of experience and skill with whom the bishop has taken counsel are of opinion that it would be greatly to the advantage of the city and its citizens and the people of the neighbourhood if a certain dyke, called Foss Dyke, which begins at the river Trent near Torksey, and runs towards Lincoln were dug out and made deeper, wider and longer as far as Lincoln. For, as it is stated, merchants, as well native as foreign, would bring their goods to Lincoln at less cost, and also the citizens and inhabitants of Lincoln would be able more easily and safely to convey their commodities and saleable goods to other places.[3]

The common council of Lincoln was active in collecting funds, and the aid of the archdeacons of Lincoln and Stow was invoked.[4] Unhappily Atwater's death in 1521 brought the work to an end.[5]

Lincoln's other waterway was the river Witham. It is surprising that there are so few complaints of the obstruction of the river. The earlier ones relate, not to silting, but to the improper activities of riparian owners. It was complained that the lay brethren of St Katharine's Priory at Lincoln had encroached on and turned the course of the upper Witham, so that ships could no longer pass; the abbots of Kirkstead and Peterborough, the prioress of Stainfield, Earl Warenne and others had like charges made against them.[6] From the earlier part of the fourteenth century the river

[1] *C.P.R.* 1429–36, p. 202.
[2] *Letters and Papers, Henry VIII,* II, ii, no. 4131.
[3] *R.A.* II, 135–6.
[4] C.C.M., 1511–41, ff. 80, 92b, 93.
[5] Leland, *Itinerary* (ed. Toulmin Smith), I, 29.
[6] *R.H.* I, 311, 317, 319.

banks were supervised by the commissioners of sewers.[1] In 1363 obstructions in the upper river from Claypole to Lincoln were reported; the Knights Hospitallers, owners of the east mill of Bracebridge, were found guilty of obstructing the course of the river, and were ordered to remove the mill.[2] The upper river was still choked in 1375.[3] There seems to have been no general complaint about the river below Lincoln until 1491. In that year the bishop of Lincoln, the abbots of Bardney, Barlings, Kirkstead, the chancellor of the cathedral, Sir Edward Burgh and Sir Thomas Fitzwilliam, with William Bele, mayor of Lincoln, and Hamo Sutton, Thomas Knight and John Stanlowe, citizens (the first two of the last group being described as 'esquire') were appointed justices of sewers, for the removal of obstructions from the river, 'to survey the water and the great river called "le Brayford" which extends from the town of Waryngton' (*rectius* Waddington) 'to the city of Lincoln, and the great river passing through the city of Lincoln; also the great river called "le Wethom" extending from the city of Lincoln to the water of Dokdyke, in Lyndesey and Kesteven'.[4]

When Lord Cromwell was building his castle and college at Tattershall his servants made great use of water carriage. In 1457–8 they bought 84,000 tiles at Boston, and brought them up the Witham to Dogdyke, and thence up the tributary river Bain to Tattershall. Timber was bought at Lynn, Skegness, Newark and Hull. Ancaster stone from the quarries at Wilsford and other places was carted to Appletreeness, thence down the river to Dogdyke and so to Tattershall.[5] And when Louth church spire was being built between 1500 and 1515, the stone came from Wilsford by the same route to Dogdyke, whence it was carted to Louth.[6]

In the days following the Conquest there had grown up near the mouth of the river a town even more significant in the history of Lincoln than Torksey. The city's struggle to maintain its commerce was conducted chiefly with the lords of Boston, who in addition to having a favourable position for their town had the advantage of being among the greatest magnates of the realm: for Boston, or the chief part of it, belonged to the honour of Brittany and Richmond.

Boston is not mentioned in Domesday Book. It is surrounded, east of the Witham, by Skirbeck, and in 1086 was evidently comprised therein. It formed part of the vast grants made by the Conqueror to his nephew Count Alan of Brittany: and Professor Stenton has pointed out that the

[1] Dugdale, *History of Imbanking and Draining of the Fens* (1662 ed.), p. 168.

[2] *C.P.R.* 1361–4, p. 371.

[3] *C.P.R.* 1374–7, p. 151.

[4] *C.P.R.* 1485–94, p. 394.

[5] *H.M.C. Report on MSS. of Lord De L'Isle and Dudley*, I, 198–9, 213–15, 228. Barley in *L.A.S.R.* (n.s.), I, 18.

[6] Dudding, *First Churchwardens' Book of Louth*, 1500–24 (see index).

Breton colony founded by Alan 'can still be traced, late in the twelfth century, by the personal names which give a highly individual character to records relating to the country round Boston, itself a town of Breton creation'.[1]

The early stages of the history of the town can be only dimly discerned. Alan gave the church of St Botolph (whence Botolph's town took its name) with its appurtenances and a carucate of land and the site of a mill to the abbey of St Mary of York, and his gift was confirmed by William II.[2] The gift of a church, a piece of land, and a mill site suggests a village, but the next grant makes a significant addition. Count Stephen, in 1125–35, confirmed the previous grant, and added that in the time of the fair at Boston the monks might carry on trade in all their land in the town both within and without the cemetery of the church.[3] In 1156–8 Conan, duke of Brittany and earl of Richmond, confirmed to the men of the soke of Holland all the tenures and liberties they had in the time of Count Stephen his grandfather;[4] and between 1181 and 1201 Duchess Constance confirmed to Sibton Abbey in Suffolk the gift which Richard Pinchard had made of the empty wine casks at Boston fair, given to him by her father Earl Conan.[5]

The dynasty of Brittany was interrupted in its possession of the honour of Richmond when the honour was forfeited in 1200 by Duchess Constance, because of her attempt to secure Brittany, Maine, Touraine and Anjou for her ill-fated son Arthur, who was universally believed to have been murdered by his uncle King John. In consequence the honour was in the king's hand, and the Pipe Rolls preserve a record of its revenues. These rolls have a few interesting references of earlier date. 'Botulvestan' is mentioned in the roll of 1130.[6] Earl Conan was dead in 1171, when £62. 4*s*. 5*d*. was paid into the Exchequer for his honour.[7] In 1172 Ranulph de Glanville accounted for £430. 11*s*. 2*d*. from various sources for the year, and in addition for £67. 1*s*. 6*d*. from Holland fair.[8] The next two years are dealt with together on account of the war: the revenue from Holland fair had fallen heavily to £22. 2*s*. 5*d*. and £10. 6*s*. 1*d*.[9] The receipts then grew from £61. 7*s*. 2*d*. in 1175 to £91. 15*s*. 4*d*. in 1182 and £104. 19*s*. 5*d*. in 1183.[10] After Michaelmas 1183 the financial administration of the honour of Richmond, or part of it including Holland, devolved on Duke Geoffrey,

[1] *First Century of English Feudalism* (1932), pp. 25–6.
[2] Farrer, *Early Yorkshire Charters*, I, 265.
[3] Ibid. IV, *Honour of Richmond*, ed. Clay, p. 10.
[4] Ibid. IV, 35.
[5] Ibid. V, 351.
[6] P.R. 31 *Henry I*, p. 120.
[7] P.R. 17 *Henry II*, p. 117.
[8] P.R. 18 *Henry II*, p. 5.
[9] P.R. 20 *Henry II*, p. 49.
[10] P.R. 21 *Henry II*, p. 4; 28 *Henry II*, p. 47; 29 *Henry II*, p. 57.

who had married Constance, daughter of Earl Conan.[1] The roll of escheats at Michaelmas 1190 has, however, an entry of the land of the count of Brittany which Warin de Bassingeburne had in custody, and among the receipts are the following: from the farm of Washingborough £40. 5*s.* 0*d.*; from the town of St Botolph 76*s.*; from the farm of the soke of Holland £67. 18*s.* 2*d.*; from the pence of the pigs of Holland for the third year 30*s.* 5*d.*; from the fair of St Botolph £50. 7*s.* 7*d.*; from Washingborough mill 12*s.* 8*d.*[2] In 1196 Simon of Kyme, then sheriff of Lincolnshire, owed 500 marks as a fine to the king for the ships and merchandise of foreign merchants which he allowed to go away from Boston fair.[3] Of the statement of receipts in 1200 on the forfeiture of Duchess Constance the material items are as follows:

Assized rent of the soke of Holland	£64.	16*s.*	0*d.*
Assized rent of the town of Holland (½ year)	£8.	0*s.*	5*d.*
Payment of stalls therein	£1.	4*s.*	6*d.*
Issues of Boston fair, previous year	£54.	5*s.*	5*d.*
The like, this year	£71.	0*s.*	0*d.*
Perquisites of the soke of Holland	£5.	6*s.*	0*d.*[4]

In 1241 Henry III granted to the queen's uncle, Peter of Savoy, the earldom of Richmond with the town of Boston with its soke and markets, and other parts of the honour of Richmond in the county of Lincoln, to be held by Peter and his heirs or any brothers or kinsmen of his to whom he might assign the same, for a fee of five knights.[5] Peter died in 1268, when John of Brittany recovered the earldom, and with it, apparently, Boston. In 1308 another John of Brittany was granted a weekly market on Saturdays at Boston,[6] and an inquisition of 1331 records that John held his fair at Boston the previous year from St Botolph's day (17 June) to the quinzaine of Michaelmas (13 October); though in past times it had been held from St Botolph's Day sometimes to St Bartholomew (24 August), sometimes to the Exaltation of the Holy Cross (14 September), and sometimes to Michaelmas (29 September).[7]

The principal part of Boston, including church and market place, is situate on the east side of the river Witham; and the *Book of Fees* records that all of the town to the east of the river was held of the king in chief by

[1] See Mr Clay's appendix on 'Finances of the Honour' in *Early Yorkshire Charters*, IV, 112.

[2] P.R. 2 *Richard I*, p. 5.

[3] P.R. 8 *Richard I*, p. 248.

[4] P.R. 2 *John*, pp. 88, 89.

[5] *C. Chart. R.* I, 259.

[6] *C. Chart. R.* III, 123.

[7] *Cal. Inq. Misc.* II, no. 1221. Bishop Grosseteste advised the countess of Lincoln to buy her wines, wax and wardrobe at the fairs of Boston, Southampton, or Bristol, and her robes at St Ives. 'Les Reules Seynt Roberd' in *Walter of Henley's Husbandry* (ed. Lamond), p. 144.

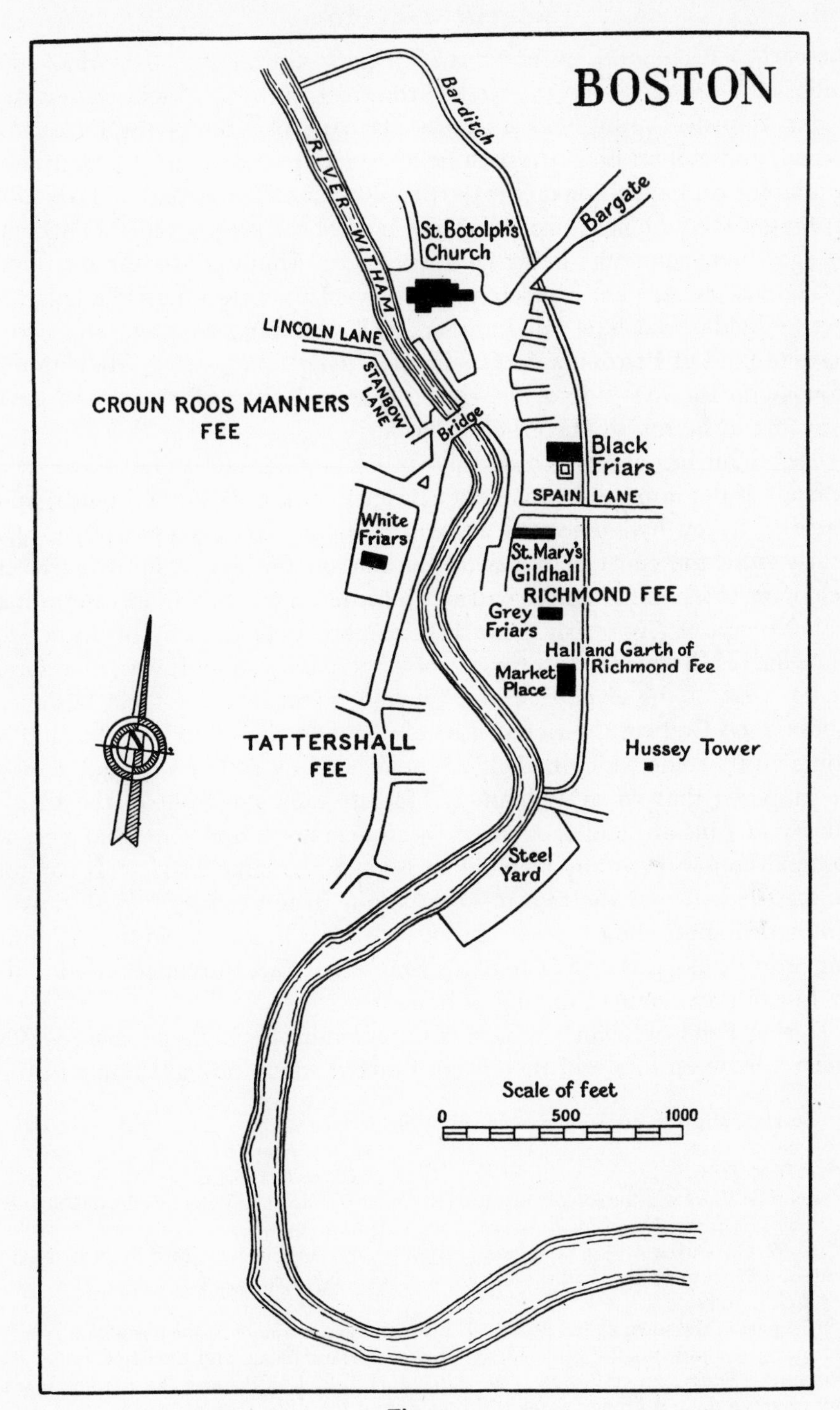
BOSTON
Barditch
RIVER WITHAM
Bargate
St. Botolph's Church
LINCOLN LANE
STANBOW LANE
CROUN ROOS MANNERS FEE
Bridge
Black Friars
SPAIN LANE
White Friars
St. Mary's Gildhall
RICHMOND FEE
Grey Friars
Hall and Garth of Richmond Fee
Market Place
TATTERSHALL FEE
Hussey Tower
Steel Yard
Scale of feet
0
500
1000

Fig. 21.

the earl of Richmond, except a twelfth part of a knight's fee, which the abbot of York had.[1] To the west of the river, however, there were other lords. Alan de Danby held a twenty-first part of a fee of the honour of Croun, and Robert of Tattershall held the like part of a fee of Lambert of Moulton.[2] An inquisition on the death of Robert of Tattershall adds details. In Boston town he held two bovates of land of the king in chief for which, by agreement sometime made with Thomas of Moulton, Robert answered to Thomas' heirs, whenever scutage was levied, for a twentieth of a knight's fee; he held also a house of Lambert of Bicker, rendering 2*d*., and three acres of land of Petronilla de Croun, rendering 12*d*. yearly.[3] He claimed tronage on the west side of the river.[4] A later Robert of Tattershall gave his court in Boston to Haverholme Priory.[5]

Boston fair belonged to the honour of Richmond, but it must have been difficult, if not impossible, to restrict business to the Richmond lands, and Peter of Savoy had therefore an arrangement whereby he received £5 yearly from the court held during the fair on the west side of the river belonging to Robert of Tattershall and John de Vaux.[6] Still more interesting is the receipt of £10 yearly from the commonalty of Lincoln for licence to trade during the fair on the property of Robert and John.[7] It was, therefore, to the west of the river that the Lincoln merchants did their business. About 1200 Godwin the rich of Lincoln gave to the monks of Durham a house on that side which he held of the fee of Guy de Croun;[8] and it may be supposed that when William of Holgate took stone out of the king's quarry at Lincoln, had it squared by stonemasons, and sent it to Boston to build houses there,[9] he planned to use it in the same district. It cannot be an accident that the most northerly lane in this part of the old town, almost facing the church across the river, is Lincoln Lane, and that at right angles to it, along the river bank, is Stanbow Lane, so named, no doubt, by Lincoln merchants thinking of home.[10]

During Peter of Savoy's tenure of the honour of Richmond there was a quarrel between him and the city of Lincoln which brought home to the

[1] *Book of Fees*, p. 1010. The abbot held of the earl, p. 1478.

[2] Ibid. p. 1011.

[3] *Cal. Inq. Henry III*, p. 35.

[4] *R.H.* I, 348b.

[5] *C. Chart. R.* IV, 416.

[6] John de Vaux was the son of Petronilla de Croun by Oliver de Vaux her third husband.

[7] Gale, *Registrum Honoris de Richmond* (1722), App. p. 39.

[8] D. & C., Durham, 3/3/Ebor no. 4, from a copy supplied by Mrs Stenton. John Pynson, a Lincoln citizen, had land at Boston. *Cal. Inq. p.m.* IV, 432.

[9] *R.H.* I, 399a.

[10] 'A part of the town called Stonbow' is mentioned in a note in the Crowland Abbey Cartulary, f. 138d, no. 1. For Lincoln Row, Newland Place and Stanbow Lane, see Thompson, *Boston*, pp. 128, 129, 253. Nichol Hill, in Louth, near the market place, may preserve the old French name of Lincoln, and for a like reason.

citizens the disadvantage which they suffered by living many miles up the river, whilst Boston was near the mouth. In 1263 Peter brought the bailiffs of Lincoln before the justices in eyre and complained that for twelve years they had taken toll of his men in Lincoln, although the men of the honour of Richmond were quit of tolls throughout England. The tolls were a penny for each horse sold or bought, a halfpenny for each ox, twopence for each cart, fourpence for a ship, a penny for twenty-four sheep, a penny for a quarter of corn: the damages claimed were £500. The bailiffs replied that they took only such tolls as the king had taken when the city was in his hand. Peter denied that his men had ever paid until twelve years ago. The bailiffs refused to put themselves on a jury without invoking the king, because, they said, the tolls belonged to the king, and were only farmed by them. In the end the parties came to terms. The bailiffs agreed that the men of the honour of Richmond should be quit within the bounds of the city of all things produced, fed or grown within the honour, or things bought for the support of men of the honour; but for things bought in the way of trade reasonable toll must be paid. The men of the honour were to pay for each ship with helm rudder coming within the bounds of the city twopence, and each ship with hand rudder a penny.[1]

In 1265 it was the turn of the citizens to complain. The king issued letters patent directing inquiry into their complaint that whereas they and their ancestors, in the time of all the lords of the town of Boston, had paid to the lords half a mark only for every year for tronage, during the last seven years Peter of Savoy and John de Vaux had been extorting £10 a year.[2] The story of this £10 was told by the jurors of the Hundred Rolls. They said that William son of Giles, then mayor of Lincoln, by counsel of Jordan son of Giles, Walter Brand, Thomas son of Robert, Thomas de Beaufou, and Alexander son of Giles, without the consent of the other citizens, came to terms with the bailiffs of Peter of Savoy, and entered into a composition granting to Peter a farm of £10 a year, out of money which the king ought to receive from the city of Lincoln.[3] When they were attached by their fellow-citizens in the city court for this transaction, the mayor's brother Jordan declared that he would rather have given £10 out of his own property than lose his Boston fair.[4] The principal Lincoln merchants, at whatever cost to the community, were determined to maintain their footing at Boston, and in the light of this incident the above-

[1] Birch, p. 62. In 1349 the citizens were held to be quit of tronage and pesage in Boston as throughout England, except when their goods were exposed for sale. *Cal. Inq. Misc.* II, no. 2074; *C.C.R.* 1349–54, p. 75.

[2] *C.P.R.* 1258–66, p. 481. Thomas de Cantilupe, the chancellor, had it noted that he did not consent to this letter.

[3] *R.H.* I, 313b.

[4] Ibid. 320a.

quoted action of a later mayor, William of Holgate, in building houses at Boston, gains new significance.

Another Lincoln complaint against Peter of Savoy illustrates the difficulty which the city was having in trying to enforce its monopoly of foreign trade within the county. It was said that for sixteen years Peter had been appropriating the customs owing to the city from all ships coming from Norway to Boston, as provided by the grant of Henry II: the jury of great men put the damage at 60*s.*[1] It was apparently not being claimed as against Boston that all foreign trade in Lincolnshire owed toll to Lincoln, perhaps because the honour of Richmond was presumed to be outside the shire of Lincoln, perhaps merely because such a claim was so obviously unenforceable; but it was claimed that Henry II's specific writ to the men of Norway trading to Lincolnshire ports, ordering them to pay customs to the king's bailiffs of Lincoln, was still in force.

Yet in other parts of Lincolnshire the city's monopoly of foreign trade was still being asserted. The city *abbrokeurs*, official agents and perhaps inspectors appointed to supervise the woollen trade, were required to swear not to suffer any foreign merchants to trade outside the city.[2] In 1262 letters were procured from the king warning the abbots of the Cistercian order and other religious men in the county that in causing wool and other things to be brought in parcels (*particulatim*) by their lay brethren in divers places of the county, and in afterwards causing these to be sold to merchants from beyond seas and others, together with their own wool, they were carrying on business contrary to the duty of honesty (*debitum honestatis*) of their order, and to the impoverishment of the city of Lincoln and other of the king's market towns in that county, whereby the farm and customs due to the king were fraudulently withdrawn; wherefore the king commanded them to desist from this kind of business, or he would lay the hand of correction upon them not lightly.[3] In 1302 the commons of Lincolnshire complained that men of religion drove a wool trade, not only in the produce of their own sheep, but also by sending their lay brethren about the county to buy cheap and sell dear.[4]

There are several instances of dispute with the other market towns in the county. In a quarrel with Louth and Sleaford the citizens relied on letters patent of Henry III, which, they said, granted that purchases and sales of any merchandise by foreign merchants in boroughs and markets of Lincoln-

[1] *R.H.* I, 309b.; the middling jurors said 40*s.* (p. 316a); the lesser men said 20*s.* (p. 323a).

[2] Birch, p. 37. For the functions of the brokers, see Gras, *Evolution of the English Corn Market* (1915), p. 158.

[3] *C.P.R.* 1258–66, p. 203.

[4] *Rot. Parl.* I, 156–7. And see Coulton, *Five Centuries of Religion*, III, 269.

shire outside Lincoln should be made by parcels (*particulares*); on the other hand the good men of Louth and Sleaford claimed that time out of mind they had been accustomed to make purchases and sales freely anywhere in the county. This practice the citizens would not tolerate, and they distrained the men of Louth and Sleaford to render to them a sum of money 'by occasion of a gild merchant provided amongst themselves', to which, said the Louth and Sleaford men, neither they nor their ancestors had been accustomed to contribute. The king (at the suit of the other parties) had commanded the citizens by letter to desist from such grievance, but the citizens, whether from recklessness or because they were sure of their case, continued to molest the men of Louth and Sleaford. In 1271 the king referred the matter to the justices in eyre in the county of Lincoln to see that justice was done.[1]

The Hundred Rolls contain similar complaints. The Louth jurors said that the mayor and citizens of Lincoln had for eight years distrained the men of Louth in the name of the gild to the amount of 100 marks; that Roger son of Benedict, mayor of Lincoln, in the name of the gild, took from Alan de Helgelofe half a mark before he could remove his hides in the king's way of Lincoln, causing 8*s*. damage; that Roger attached Simon of Alvingham and Richard son of Walter of Lynn with their goods, in the name of the gild, unjustly and against the king's peace, causing 100*s*. damage. William, another mayor of Lincoln, came to Boston fair and attached Simon of Alvingham and Walter of Louth market with their goods, by pretext of the gild, to their loss to the extent of 100*s*. They were delivered by the seneschals and merchants of the court of Boston gathered there from many regions. When Gilbert Rosel of Louth was coming to Louth at the royal command for the gaol delivery, the said Roger took his horse from him in the king's highway of Lincoln and kept it for two days until the king's bailiffs delivered the horse: all this by pretext of the gild.[2] The Grimsby men said that William of Holgate, sometime mayor of Lincoln, unjustly took from the burgesses of Grimsby horses, pledges, money and the like for gildwite to the value of 10 marks contrary to the charter of King John and the royal power.[3]

[1] *C.P.R.* 1266–72, p. 569; Gross, *Gild Merchant*, II, 378.

[2] *R.H.* I, 332–4; Gross, op. cit. II, 147.

[3] *R.H.* I, 291 b; Gross, op. cit. II, 147. Apparently because these exactions, made by the mayor in the name of the gild, were denounced as unjust, Gross infers that there were distinct officials of the gild who should have taken the money instead of a civic official like the mayor (op. cit. I, 63). It is clear, however, that the men of Louth and Grimsby were complaining, not because they were distrained by the mayor of Lincoln instead of the alderman of the gild merchant, but because they were being made to pay anything to anybody in Lincoln at all. For the relations between court and gild, see supra, pp. 186–7.

In 1284 it was the citizens who were complaining. The sheriff was commanded that whereas foreign merchants set out their merchandise in neighbouring places to the hurt of the city, he was to have their bodies to answer the contempt of the king and the damages to the citizens.[1] It seems probable that the gild merchant claim to monopoly of foreign trade within the county was abandoned by the end of the thirteenth century; three reasons suggest themselves for such a change of front on the part of the citizens of Lincoln. In the first place, there was the growing difficulty of enforcing it, and indeed the complete failure so far as Boston was concerned; secondly, English merchants were establishing themselves in overseas trade, and the city was not quite so dependent on the foreigner; and thirdly, the institution of the staple gave Lincoln a position comparable with that once secured by its gild merchant. The staple was, however, not to be relied upon: it could be removed at the royal pleasure, and when it finally left Lincoln in 1369 the city was in a sad plight.[2] When, years after, the citizens petitioned Richard III, they recalled that his progenitors had granted that merchant strangers or 'Esterlyngez northweyz' who brought merchandise to sell in Lincolnshire should bring it whole to the said city, and sell it in no other town, on pain of forfeiture; and they sold, bought and bartered with cloth, whereupon there was great clothmaking and occupation for the people.[3] Edward IV's charter recites that a great number of foreign merchants used to come to trade in the city, whereby it was greatly enriched.[4]

These foreign merchants came from many parts of Europe. The trade with Scandinavia has already been mentioned.[5] The Hundred Rolls record that when the export of wool to Flanders was forbidden certain merchants of Ypres and Germany obtained letters from the king allowing them to pass and repass overseas, and produced them to the sheriff to prevent him from attaching their goods: the sheriff received payment for forbearance. Merchants from Cambrai, Douai, Lübeck and Lombardy are also mentioned.[6] When an inquiry was made into the rates of lastage, or seacoast tolls, taken at Skirbeck (Boston) in 1323, it was noted that certain groups of merchants, such as those of Norway, Jutland, 'Fryseby' in Friesland, Scotland, Ireland, Cologne and London, were exempt as well as individual merchants.[7] It has been noted that by the end of the thirteenth century native merchants were claiming a share in the foreign trade: already in the

[1] *Dyer's Reports*, p. 279. Birch (p. xxi), who quotes Dyer *via* Merewether and Stephens, *History of Boroughs and Municipal Corporations*, I, 525, has confused his references.

[2] See p. 250.

[3] *H.M.C. Lincoln*, p. 263. The document is among the Grimsby papers.

[4] Birch, p. 132. It is confirmed by Richard III.

[5] See pp. 174–7.

[6] *R.H.* I, 314a, b, 321b, 327a.

[7] Gras, *Early English Customs System*, p. 207.

Hundred Rolls William Cause of Lincoln is reported as having taken 40 sacks of wool and more and 30 measures of lead overseas.[1]

Some of the conditions and the difficulties of the Lincoln merchants are illustrated by their appeals for royal aid. Stephen de Stanham (mayor in 1303) acted as agent for the king in a large wool purchase in 1298;[2] and having bought for him from both English and foreign merchants at Boston goods and merchandise was charged with converting it to his own use, with oppressing the merchants of Lincoln, and, with Walter bishop of Coventry and Lichfield, converting money received from tax collectors in the county.[3] It was complained in 1323 that Hugh Tyler (mayor in 1325) had delivered £200 sterling to William Bondeleti, the changer of St Omer, to exchange in London on the security of the mayor and *échevins* of the town. William secretly left the town without satisfying Hugh. The mayor and *échevins* admitted liability and asked for a long time in which to pay. The king then wrote asking for payment with a threat of another remedy. The mayor and commonalty reported that the mayor and *échevins* scorned and tore the king's letters. The king therefore granted letters of reprisal, ordering the sheriffs of London to arrest goods and merchandise of the men of St Omer to the value of £200, and to keep the same until Hugh was satisfied.[4]

In 1303 John of Blvton and Walter Beynes complained that John duke of Brabant owed them £47. 13*s*. 4*d*. which he ought to have paid long ago, and for which the king had requested payment. The king ordered the sheriff of Lincoln to seize the goods of merchants of the land and power of the duke to the value of the debt: another example of reprisals. The sheriff returned that the bailiffs of the city of Lincoln had done so, and the king ordered that the goods be delivered to Blyton and Beynes upon their finding security to answer to the king for the goods or their value.[5]

A group of leading citizens, John of Blyton, Walter of Bayeux, Henry of Severby, Richard of Scarle, Walter of York and Robert of Oxford, with Nicholas of Thimbleby of Lindsey, complained that malefactors of the towns of Kampen, Lübeck and Hamburg and elsewhere in Eastland, in the summer of 1311, took and carried away a ship laden by them at Boston with wool and other goods to the value of £1,244. 10*s*. 0*d*. whilst voyaging to Brabant. The king wrote to the *consules* and *schöffen* of the said towns asking for justice for the merchants; but the latter did nothing save that the *schöffen* and council of Kampen, having obtained a safe conduct for their envoys to come to England to treat with the king and his council as

[1] *R.H.* I, 321b.
[2] *C.P.R.* 1292–1301, p. 335.
[3] *C.P.R.* 1307–13, p. 36.
[4] *C.C.R.* 1318–23, p. 650.
[5] *C.C.R.* 1302–7, p. 22.

to damages, sent two envoys, who later declared that they were sent only to receive information, and asked for a long delay. They then secretly went home: wherefore the king, considering that the envoys were trying to defraud the merchants by frivolous delays and excuses, ordered the sheriff of Lincoln to arrest goods of the men of the said towns to the extent of a third of the damages, like sums being ordered to be raised in Norfolk and Yorkshire.[1]

In Parliament at Stamford in 1309 an agreement had been reached upon matters in dispute between the king's subjects and William count of Holland and Seland and lord of Friesland. The count's envoys were to give security to Walter le Keu of Lincoln and his partners in the sum of £954; and to merchants of Yarmouth in other sums. Roger of Buslingthorpe, one of Walter's partners, and another, were given leave to levy in specified ports and towns from merchants of the count.[2] The sheriff and other officers of Norfolk and Suffolk were ordered to prevent obstruction of the collection by fishermen or mariners of the count.[3] Proceedings were once stayed, no doubt in hope of a settlement,[4] but ordered to be resumed, as the king was informed that attempts were being made to avoid payment by the trans-shipping of goods at sea.[5] The bailiffs of Yarmouth were suspected of collusion,[6] and a writ of aid was issued for Walter le Keu and Roger of Buslingthorpe, and Robert Elys of Yarmouth, the sheriffs being ordered to make proclamation against persons attempting to hinder or practise fraud in the collection of tolls.[7] These tolls were being levied by consent of the count of Holland upon the merchants, fishermen and mariners of his dominions coming into the realm. Some of the magnates and the men of Great and Little Yarmouth complained, however, that if such levy were made in the fishing season, the count's fishermen would withdraw, to the loss of those towns and the disturbance of the next fairs there.[8] The first complaint was made in 1321, and the money was still owing to the aggrieved merchants in 1325.[9]

In 1375 the mayor and bailiffs of Lincoln instituted reprisals on behalf of certain merchants of the city against Florentine merchants named Peter Mark, Nicholas Luke and Matthew Johan, of the society of the Albertini, and also against John Credy and Francis Johan of the society of the Strossi, on account of debts due from Lombard merchants named Blancard and Johan. As the former had never been in partnership with the offenders, and had found security to answer the Lincoln merchants, the king ordered that

[1] *C.C.R.* 1313–18, pp. 26, 27.
[2] *C.P.R.* 1317–21, pp. 106–7.
[3] Ibid. pp. 171–2.
[4] Ibid. p. 112.
[5] Ibid. p. 365.
[6] Ibid. p. 463.
[7] Ibid. p. 481.
[8] *C.P.R.* 1321–4, pp. 55, 56.
[9] *C.P.R.* 1324–7, p. 140.

the arrested goods be restored. There followed an agreement between the Lincoln men and the Florentines by which the latter were to recover debts due to the former by the Strossi and Albertini of Florence, who had escaped suddenly out of the realm with merchandise to the value of £10,000 without payment; which would ruin the city of Lincoln if no remedy were obtained.[1]

Though the Lincoln merchants dealt mainly in wool, they dealt also in cloth produced by the weavers, fullers and dyers of the city. In 1181–2 the sheriff of Lincoln bought, presumably in Lincoln, 9 ells of blanket (*blanchet*) for the use of the brethren of the Chartreuse, for 27*s.*; 90 ells of scarlet for £30; 12 ells of green say for 36*s.*; and 9 ells of grey say for 15*s.*[2] The scarlet cloth was the most costly, at 6*s.* 8*d.* (half a mark) for an ell, the blanket and the green say each cost 3*s.* and the grey say 1*s.* 8*d.* The scarlet cloth of Lincoln was a speciality, and became famous at home and abroad. In 1240 the guardians of the bishopric of Winchester were bidden to buy at Winchester fair two pieces of Lincoln scarlet cloth for the use of the queen of Norway, as a gift from the king.[3] In 1310–11 the agent of Durham Priory bought 7 ells of Lincoln say for the prior and his fellows, for 43*s.* 1*d.*[4] Black cloth and cloth of mixed colour are mentioned in an assize roll.[5]

'Lincoln green' has been preserved in the popular memory by the tales of Robin Hood. Doubt has long been cast on the historicity of the popular hero; but Professor Owen has lately called attention to a piece of record evidence which seems to be decisive on the point. In the Pipe Roll for 1230 there occurs an entry that the sheriff (of Yorkshire) owes 32*s.* 6*d.* in respect of the chattels of Robert Hood, fugitive (*Roberti Hood fugitivi*).[6] The position of the entry points to the West Riding, recalling that Robin is associated with Barnsdale as well as with Sherwood.[7]

The rhymes of Robin Hood were current in the days of Langland,[8] and in *A Lytell Geste of Robyn Hode* (*c.* 1510) occur the lines

> Whan they were clothed in Lyncolne grene,
> They kest away theyr graye.[9]

[1] *C.P.R.* 1374–7, p. 196; *C.C.R.* 1374–7, pp. 472–4; 1381–5, pp. 21–2; *Rot. Parl.* II, 350–1.
[2] P.R. 28 *Henry II*, pp. xxvi, 50, and see P.R. 26 *Henry II*, p. 48.
[3] *Cal. Liberate Rolls, Henry III*, 1226–40, p. 493.
[4] *Durham Account Rolls* (Surtees Society), p. 506.
[5] P.R.O. Assize Roll 523, m. 1, 2.
[6] P.R. 14 *Henry III*, p. 274.
[7] *The Times Trade and Engineering*, February 1936. Professor Owen writes that 'the scarlet dye was derived from the "grain" (greyne) = *alkermes*, an insect resembling cochineal: see *Oxford Dictionary* (*Shorter*) under Grain III, graine = the kermes or scarlet grain. It seems thus to be possible that one, perhaps the earlier, of the Lincoln greens is this grain or scarlet'. An article in *The Dyer and Textile Printer*, 31 December 1937, scornfully rejects the suggestion that these men of the woodland were dressed in an expensive grain red.
[8] *Vision of Piers Plowman*, l. 3277.
[9] Ritson, *Robin Hood* (1885 ed.), p. 75.

Spenser's *Faerie Queene* has

> All in a woodman's jacket he was clad
> Of Lincolne greene, belay'd with silver lace,[1]

and Drayton refers to

> Swains in Shepheard's gray and Girls in Lincolne greene,

adding in a marginal note that

> Lincolne anciently dyed the best greene of England.[2]

Almost the only evidence of the size of the Lincoln cloth industry comes from letters patent of 1348. The weavers were then in difficulties and were asking for relief. They asserted in the Exchequer that Henry, sometime king of England, had granted the weavers of the city a charter to the effect that none should make cloth, dyed or rayed, within a circuit of twelve miles of the city unless he were of the gild, for which privilege they rendered £6 yearly to the king: but that these liberties had not been observed although the annual payment for them continued to be made. On these representations the treasurer and barons of the Exchequer reported that, in searching the rolls and memoranda, they found in the roll for the third year of Henry II the weavers' payment of £6 for their gild recorded; from subsequent rolls they found that payment continued to be made until 1321, since when arrears had accumulated to the sum of £160. 13*s.* 4*d.* Between 1321 and 1331 there were no weavers working in the city and its twelve-mile radius, and from 1331 to 1345 only a few working spinners. By contrast, in the time of Henry II there had been more than 200 spinners, who were wealthy and powerful. Their gild had been constituted in honour of the Holy Cross, and every weaver contributed proportionally to the farm. Their charter had, however, been burned at 'Letherplace' in the suburb of Lincoln in time whereof there was no memory. The few spinners then charged with the farm and its arrears had represented to the king that many citizens kept hired weavers working cloths for sale, and other weavers refused to contribute towards the farm because the charter was wanting; and they prayed the king to order the charter to be renewed in due form, or to discharge them from their liability for the farm and its arrears. The king, having regard to the immemorial possession by the crown of the farm, and willing to do justice both to himself and to the weavers, confirmed the grant of Henry II, and granted that no weaver should exercise his calling

[1] VI, ii, 5.

[2] *Works*, Shakespeare Head Press, IV, 517. See also Henderson, *Complete Works of John Skelton*, p. 100.

in the city or within twelve miles of the same unless he were of the gild and contributed proportionally towards the farm.[1]

The special position of the weavers' gild was acknowledged by the common council in the sixteenth century when they were revising the charters of the craft gilds; they did not interfere with the weavers, who rested on the royal grant. Thomas Sympson noted in 1737 that the only companies then subsisting were those of the cordwainers and the weavers, these being the only ones ever incorporated by royal charter: the others had been established by licence under the common seal of the city.[2] Little is known about most of the gilds before the sixteenth century save for the gild certificates of 1389.[3] These returns give in some instances the dates of foundation of the gilds, or of their statutes; nearly all are in the fourteenth century. The dual function of many of the gilds, spiritual and industrial, is illustrated by the ordinances of the tilers, which were sealed with the seals of the mayoralty of the city and of the deanery of Christianity (the rural deanery covering the city);[4] and by those of the sailors, which direct that no brother or sister who has quarrelled with another in word or deed should plead before the mayor or bailiffs or the dean of Christianity until he should have submitted to the graceman of the gild.[5] The craft ordinances relate to the control of journeymen and apprentices, and the trade monopoly of the gild brethren within the city. This was the great source of the power of the gilds, and it is illustrated by a royal order, issued in 1401 on the petition of citizens of Lincoln who traded as mercers there, to the sheriff of the county. If he were assured that the custom had been used time out of mind, the sheriff was to cause proclamation to be made forbidding any strange or 'foreign' mercer at his peril to sell or expose for sale any wares within the city or suburbs. The complaint showed that though no such mercers ought to sell or offer wares in the public market except in time of the fair or prescribed market days, yet great numbers of them had done so, to the great loss of the Lincoln mercers.[6]

At the Reformation, the gilds, shorn of their religious functions, were remodelled as companies. They seem mostly to have disappeared in the seventeenth century; when they could no longer enforce their right of search or their monopoly of trade it was not worth the craftsman's while to pay his contributions.

[1] *C.P.R.* 1348–50, pp. 120–1. For places in Lincoln where the trade was carried on, see Appendix I, sub Tentercroft, Cleumarket, Drapery, Walkergate.

[2] Adversaria, p. 290.

[3] Some of these are given in Toulmin Smith, *English Gilds* (1870), pp. 172–85; and see appendix to Westlake, *Parish Gilds of Medieval England* (1919), pp. 167–75.

[4] Gild Certificates, no. 157.

[5] Ibid. no. 158.

[6] *C.C.R. Henry IV*, I, 384.

CHAPTER XVI

FIELDS AND PASTURES

ACCORDING to Domesday Book there were $13\frac{1}{2}$ carucates of land in the fields of the city, and as one of the carucates belonged to a manor of the bishop it is convenient to follow the example of the Domesday clerks and deal with it first. They wrote:

> Bishop Remigius has 1 little manor (*maneriolum*) with 1 carucate (of land) near the city of Lincoln with sake and soke and with toll and team (over it); and likewise over 3 messuages, and over 2 churches, and likewise over 78 messuages, except for the king's geld which they give with the burgesses. Of these messuages 20 are waste. Of the 3 messuages aforesaid one is quit of all things, but two geld with the burgesses.[1]

Canon Foster has linked this little manor of Remigius with the *burgum* in the city of Lincoln which is called *Willigtorp* in the bull of Pope Honorius II in 1126.[2] The bull of Pope Innocent II (1139) supplies another name for it: 'Westgate with its appurtenances as well outside the walls of the same city as within'.[3] Two bulls of Eugenius III (1146 and 1149) mention 'the manor of Lincoln to wit Willingtorp', and so also a bull of Alexander III (1163).[4] Canon Foster adds:

> The name of Willingthorpe has been found only in one other context, namely a confirmation by Robert II bishop of Lincoln to William son of Fardain of four dwellings (*mansiones*) in Willingtorp at the north side of Willingtorp, with all that belongs to them, free and quit of all service except *burgagium*, a service which points to the tenement being in the city of Lincoln.[5]

Although the names of Willingthorpe and Westgate are not found again, the bishop's manor does not disappear. Another bull of Alexander III (1163), addressed not to the bishop but to Adelmus the dean and the canons of Lincoln, refers to churches in Lincoln, including St Stephen, and St Faith in the bishop's soke, and also to a carucate of land in the fields of Lincoln with tithes of the carucate.[6] An unfinished charter of the abbot and convent of Barlings gives a clue to the later name of the manor. They acknowledge that they owe to Bishop Hugh (of Welles) and his successors four shillings a year for certain land of the bishop's fee in the parish of St Faith in Newland, which John son of Richard son of Sigerith of Newland

[1] Appendix II; supra, pp. 61–2.
[2] *R.A.* I, 188–9.
[3] Ibid. p. 190.
[4] Ibid. pp. 194, 196, 202.
[5] Ibid. p. 190; *D.C.* p. 343.
[6] *R.A.* I, 205.

gave them.[1] During the vacancy in the see of Lincoln the accounts of the bishopric appear on the Pipe Rolls. In 1180–1 there occurs this entry:

And in the waste of Newland which Robert Chode held, 5*s.* 2*d.* And in small repairs of the houses of the bishopric and vineyards and orchards, 54*s.* 5*d.*[2]

The district surrounding old St Faith's church lies on the lower part of the hillside to the west of the city, rather to the north-west of the modern Newland, and considerably to the south-west of Westgate. Perhaps the name of Westgate was given to the manor by the bishop's men, accustomed to approach it by way of the west gate of the upper city (the Bail), whereas royal officers and citizens would reach it from the lower city by way of Newland. About 1300 the bishop's garden is mentioned in a summary of portions of tithes in churches which did not themselves belong to the chapter: this refers to land under the hill towards Newland behind the castle called the bishop's garden, tithe from it being worth 5*s.*, and to tithe from a certain small *cultura* of arable under St Bartholomew's Hill, which is called the bishop's garden, and worth 18*d.* or more.[3]

The archives of the dean and chapter contain many charters relating to land in Newland. Thomas the goldsmith of Lincoln sold to Gilbert de Innocentibus, dean of the city, for four silver marks, land in the parish of St Faith in Newland which Robert the goldsmith his brother had held of Hugh de Bussey, situate between land of Hawis the Fleming and land formerly of William Helije. Gilbert's nephew, Thomas son of Henry de Bathele, sold the land to Bishop Hugh II for 20*s.* and renounced all claim in the bishop's court.[4] Grimward son of Andrew son of Ketelbern sold to Bishop Hugh II land in St Stephen's parish in Newland between land of Peter of Paris and land formerly of Robert Ledman: he must have held this of the bishop, because the latter released some arrears of rent, paying him a sum of money in addition.[5] Hugh Fardhayn, son of Warner Fardhayn, sold to Bishop Hugh II, for 3*s.*, two tofts and two half tofts, which Hugh held of the bishop, between land of Brian the mercer on the east and land of Peter of the Bail on the west.[6] Also next to Brian the mercer's land was that of Walter son of Godfrey, who sold it to Bishop Hugh II for 5*s.*[7] The bull of Innocent II mentions that the bishop's manor had appurtenances

[1] *R.A.* II, 85. For a confirmation to Barlings by Sibman of Newland see Barlings Cartulary, f. 59b.

[2] P.R. 27 *Henry II*, p. 64, and see 28 *Henry II*, p. 60. Algar *de nova terra* is mentioned in 1163–6. *D.C.* p. 343.

[3] *R.A.* III, 376–7.

[4] D. & C., Dii, 81/1/1, 6.

[5] D. & C., Dii, 81/1/9.

[6] D. & C., Dii, 81/1/14. Warner son of Fardein appears as a principal citizen in 1206. *Earliest Lincolnshire Assize Rolls* (L.R.S.), no. 1448, and infra, Appendix VI.

[7] D. & C., Dii, 81/1/16.

within the city as well as without: a piece of land in St Mary Crackpole's parish in Hungate was sold to Bishop Hugh II and forsworn in his court.[1]

The bishop also bought rents from the prior and convent of Haverholme, paying them four silver marks.[2] Evidently he was engaged in buying out his tenants and taking his land into his own hands. The proximity of the city would ensure substantial money rents for accommodation pasture, and it would seem that he was enclosing his land. In 1317 the hospital of St Giles without Lincoln obtained confirmation of a garden in the parish of St Faith in the fee of the bishop of Lincoln;[3] closes in St Faith's parish are mentioned in 1505;[4] a terrier of 1664 describes five rows of closes, containing respectively (counting from the waterside) five, nine, nine, four and two closes;[5] and Thomas Sympson noted that 'the grounds hereabout are now old enclosure'.[6]

The dean and chapter were laying together lands in the bishop's manor. William son of Giles of Hungate took a lease of a place of theirs in St Faith's parish next to land of Master Stephen of Hungate.[7] In St Stephen's parish they granted to Alan the palmer land which Osbert the brother of Warner gave to St Mary for the soul of his wife.[8] A terrier of St Martin's parish (to which St Stephen had been united), of date 1605, indicates that land adjoining Cause Manor lay in the parish;[9] and a terrier of lands of the prebend of St Mary Crackpole, dated 1652, mentions that Cawsey Farm adjoined the ancient churchyard of St Stephen.[10] It seems that some of the lands gathered by the dean and chapter were put together and known as Cause Manor: they may have had to do with the Cause chantry whose chaplain had land in St Stephen's parish in 1487.[11] The chantry had an income of £7. 3*s.* 2*d.*, and paid thereout 19*s.* 10*d.* in rent to the bishop, and 16*s.* 2*d.* to the chapter. By the Lincoln Enclosure Award some 56 acres 2 roods 33 perches were allotted to the dean and chapter for Cause Manor and Farm, and 10 acres 2 roods to the prebendary of St Mary Crackpole for tithe of Cause Farm.[12]

Besides the bishop's carucate there were 12½ carucates of land in the fields outside the city: there are mentioned in addition 231 acres of arable

[1] D. & C., Dii, 75/1/1.
[2] D. & C., Dii, 81/1/19.
[3] *C. Chart. R.* III, 364.
[4] *Lincoln Wills* (L.R.S.), I, 25.
[5] Terrier of St Mary le Wigford at Diocesan Record Office. One of the closes was owned or occupied by Serjeant Callis, the author of *Reading on Sewers*.
[6] Adversaria, p. 287.
[7] D. & C., Dii, 81/1/3.
[8] D. & C., Dii, 81/1/12.
[9] Diocesan Record Office.
[10] Lincoln Public Library.
[11] White Book, ff. 99b–100. In 1378–9 Agnes widow of Sir Thomas Cause and Geoffrey le Scrope had licence to grant messuages, a dovecote and land in Lincoln and its suburb to the dean and chapter. *Inq. A.Q.D.* (P.R.O. Lists and Indexes), p. 612.
[12] The Enclosure Act wrongly stated that this tithe belonged to the dean and chapter.

and 100 acres of meadow.[1] The Latin word *carucate* conceals the Old English word *plogsland*, the amount of land which could be tilled by one plough team. There were eight oxen to a plough team, and the *bovate*, or oxgang, was one-eighth of a carucate.[2] Professor Stenton has assembled a body of evidence from the twelfth century to show that the standard acreage of the bovate in Lincolnshire was 20 acres.[3] It is clear that its area sometimes departed from the standard: about 1250 Richard son of Herbert of Newport granted seven bovates in the Lincoln fields to the dean and chapter. One contained 17 acres ½ perch, another 16½ acres, and a third 15½ acres 1 perch.[4] There is no evidence of a lower standard than 20 acres; but variations make the calculation of areas uncertain. Assessments of land in carucates were often made in round figures, such as 12 or 24, though the Lincoln figure of 12½ carucates, plus the bishop's, looks like an attempt at accuracy.

Assuming that a carucate was 160 acres, the area in the fields (excluding the bishop's carucate) was 2,000 acres, plus 231 acres of arable and 100 of meadow, a total of 2,331 acres. When in 1803 the Lincoln Enclosure Act was passed, the fields and pastures were estimated to contain 1,800 acres, apart from certain small parcels of land called Lammas grounds; and the award itself, made in 1811, allotted a total area of 1,734 acres 2 roods 36 perches. The difference between the estimate based on the Domesday evidence and the later figures may be due to an original over-estimate in carucates, though it may equally well be due to a gradual encroachment on the fields by enclosures. The whole of the Monks Liberty (with an area of nearly 300 acres) had by 1803 become 'old enclosure', and was omitted from the operations of the enclosure commissioners, though it certainly was once included in the fields.

The fields lay round the city in a semicircle, resting to the west of the city on the Fossdyke, and reaching on the east to the Monks Liberty, which rested on the Witham: that is to say, they were all to the north of the waterways. Those who dwelt to the south of them had no part or lot in the city fields. Though the citizens who dwelt in the transpontine suburb of Wigford acquired rights of common of pasture elsewhere, they never acquired any arable. Their settlement being wholly urban in origin, perhaps they never felt the need of it.

The boundaries of the city and liberties on the north have, it seems, remained unchanged from early times to the present. The fields marched with those of Burton, Riseholme, Nettleham and Greetwell. It has already

[1] Appendix II.
[2] *D.C.* pp. xx et seq.
[3] Ibid. p. xxviii. There are, however, a few deviations, as is shown by the existence of small bovates (*bovati parvi*) at Gate Burton and Owmby by Spital. *R.A.* IV, 29–30, 32–3.
[4] D. & C., Dii, 82/2/103.

been noticed[1] that the fields were no larger than those of many villages, and it is clear that by the time of Domesday the great majority of citizens cannot have had any interest in arable cultivation. The citizens had, however, a close interest in the meadows, and in rights of common over the arable between harvest and seed-time and when the land lay fallow. Thus it is that the minutes of the common council have much to say about rights of common, and something about relations between the commoners and the 'husbandmen', or tillers of the arable, concerning these rights, but practically nothing about the arable itself.

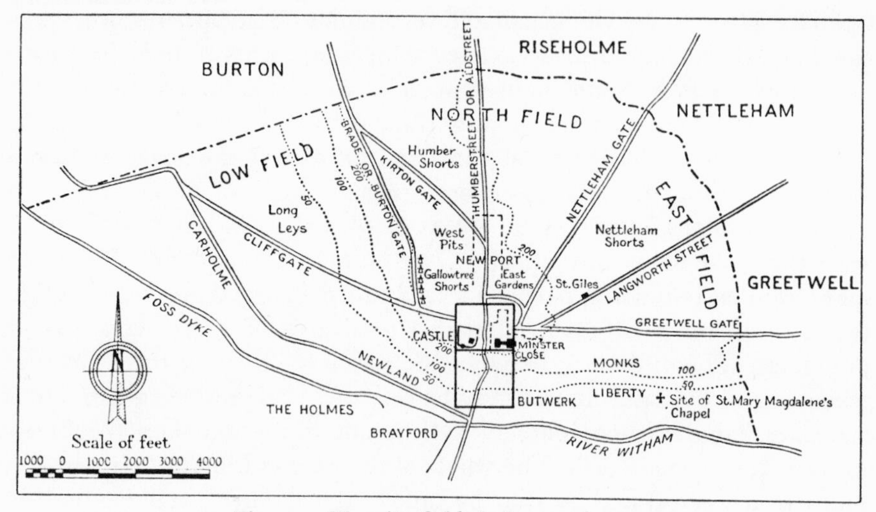

Fig. 22. The city fields before enclosure.

There is in the minutes, however, a single hint of the system of cultivation in the fields. In 1546 the common council appointed a committee to hear and determine whether the Wong should be several and enclosed two years together, that is, from Lady Day (25 March) to St Peter *ad vincula* (1 August) and a third year to lie open to the commons according to the rote of the fields next adjoining, or whether it ought or might be taken in and continually kept several and enclosed.[2] Evidently there was a three-field system in operation: that is to say, the arable was divided into three roughly equal areas, and every year two of them were cultivated and the third lay fallow. Deeds of land indicate that the same system was in operation about 1300. There was the east field, including all between Greetwellgate and Langworth Street, and between the latter and Nettlehamgate, these latter lands being called Nettleham Shorts. West of Nettlehamgate were the East Gardens and Langdales, and west of Humber Street (the Ermine Street, now Riseholme Road) were the Humber Shorts. All these, it seems, belonged

[1] Supra, p. 62.

[2] C.C.M. 1541–64, f. 37.

to the north field. Probably the present Burton Road, west of which the ground falls away sharply (this is the Cliff), was for the most part the western boundary of the north field, though some of the low land belonged to this field. Most of the land west of Burton Road and below the Cliff was in the south field, sometimes called the low field (*sub clivo*), or the nether field. The permanent pasture was on the west side of the city, scattered about on the hillside or in the region of the low field: there were the Carholme, the Long Leys, the Short Leys, the Oxpasture.

Professor Stenton's examination of a great number of charters has led him to the conclusion that there is no definite evidence of the three-field system in Lincolnshire before 1300; and that the earlier evidence points to a two-field system, in which half the arable was fallowed every year.[1] Nothing has been found to suggest that Lincoln was an exception to the general rule: but a definite conclusion upon the system of cultivation of the city fields before 1300 must await a further examination of the evidence.

If they ever existed, the days when a number of citizens had symmetrical holdings—with so many acres in each field, so that every year they had the same area under the plough—had ended before the thirteenth century. In the deeds that have survived, the bovates and the acres were not assigned in multiples of three or two. The parcels of land transferred were irregular, and a man might hold land in the east field without holding any in the other fields at all. But such a fact tells nothing about the actual cultivators, for cultivation by the owners was becoming exceptional. Great numbers of strips of land were passing into the hands of religious bodies as endowments of masses and chantries, and the priest entitled to the revenue from them was interested only in the money rent. The tillers of the soil, the 'husbandmen', were the smallholders who made a living from the fields, bringing their produce to the city markets.

To calculate the amount of land belonging to the dean and chapter, the several prebendaries and the city churches at the time of the enclosure would give no indication of the total area of land in the fields which had passed into mortmain by the end of the Middle Ages, for the lands of religious houses and chantries were secularised at the Reformation. There has, however, survived a terrier of lands in the fields belonging to the dean and chapter, St Giles' Hospital, the Malandry Hospital, several prebendaries, and a number of chantries, including those of Roger son of Benedict in St Peter in Eastgate, Sir William Blyton in St Stephen, and Alexander son of Martin in St Lawrence.[2] Much of the terrier is now illegible, having been damaged by water, but it runs to 22 folios, and there are about 30 selions of land per page; so that some 1,320 selions belonged to these religious

[1] *D.C.* p. xxxi.

[2] In the collection of Captain W. A. Cragg, F.S.A.

persons and bodies. It is not easy to translate this figure into acres, because the selions vary between a perch and two acres in area, but the total gives some idea how widespread was the ecclesiastical interest in the fields: the more so when is added the land which belonged to other religious houses. It may well be that before the dissolution of the monasteries half of the arable had passed into mortmain.

It was with the pasture land and the straying of cattle that the citizens as a whole were chiefly concerned. Clearly the husbandmen must have some rights in the pasture, but their rights were strictly defined by the common council, who had chiefly at heart the interests of the ordinary freemen and inhabitants pursuing urban avocations but wishing to keep a horse or a cow or more on the commons. In 1581 an agreement was made between the mayor, sheriffs and commonalty of the one part, and the dean and chapter and other freeholders and the husbandmen of the city of the other part. It laid down that the ancient stint of seven beasts for a plough, three for every citizen (that is, every freeman), and one for every foreigner (or non-free inhabitant), with one follower under a year old for every cow, and no more, should be observed and kept as well in Carholme, Long Leys, Lowfield and other pastures commonable on the west side of Lincoln.[1] The number of ploughs at work in the fields cannot have been very great, and it is evident that the cattle of freemen and foreigners predominated in number over those of the husbandmen. For the advantage of the former it was resolved in 1580 that according to ancient custom no oxen should be kept amongst the kine or beasts, nor come into Carholme or the Fen, except to the waithes to drink; and therefore the husbandmen were confirmed in a piece of land formerly set out by agreement near Burton field in the Long Leys to be their oxpasture after Lammas for evermore. Furthermore, no sheep were to come down to any of the pastures beneath the clay-pits on the hillside under the western mills before the morrow after All Hallows Day (2 November). The husbandmen were to maintain prescribed fences, and if through their default any citizens' cattle escaped, the cattle were to be set free without payment other than a penny to the common pinder impounding the same 'unless it were some unruly beast which for the second default shall make amends'. This settlement was the result of a conference between six citizens and the husbandmen.[2] Earlier, in 1566, the husbandmen were granted common of pasture in Carholme and Wymark Close yearly with sheep from St Andrew's Day (30 November) to Candlemas (2 February) for seven years, at a rent of £4 yearly, the rent to be devoted towards dykes and fences.[3]

[1] C.C.M. 1565–99, f. 124.
[2] Ibid. f. 116b.
[3] Ibid. f. 14b. The rent was reduced to £3. 6*s*. 8*d*., f. 16b.

The protection of the freemen and inhabitants against the husbandmen continued to concern the common council to the end. In 1733 it was complained that the husbandmen brought down their sheep on the west commons contrary to the articles of 1581, to the prejudice of the citizens and commoners;[1] and in 1800 that the farmers had meadowed the Oxpasture, which had been used as pasture from time immemorial.[2]

The trespass of citizens' cattle on the arable is heard of in 1657. It was then agreed, at the request of the Newport husbandmen, that as cattle trespassing in the fields had been impounded in private yards, to the damage of owners not knowing where to repair for them, the husbandmen should be allowed at their own charges to erect a common pound on the west of Newport green, which they were to maintain.[3]

In the early years of the sixteenth century a conflict of interest arose between the owners and tenants of the arable on the one hand and the common council on the other upon the subject of enclosures. The common council was permitting the enclosure of part of the common pasture, and receiving the rents therefor in relief of the common chamber; and in so doing was reducing the area of land which could be commoned by the husbandmen's cattle. Compromise was reached in 1511 by the mediation of the bishop, William Smith; it related to the commons on the south as well as on the north of the city, and the agreement was stated to be made between the dean and chapter, the prior of St Katharine's, the master of Burton Lazars and others of the one part and the mayor and commonalty of the other part. So far as related to the commons north of the river, it was declared that the closures in the tenure of Robert Wymark and John Taylboys should be laid open for ever; any other enclosures made by the mayor and commonalty within the preceding five years were to remain enclosed, but no other enclosures were to be made within the common pastures within the walls, which the mayor and commonalty must suffer to lie open for ever.[4]

The agreement did not last long. In 1518 a close at Bishopbridge was let for 60 years.[5] The same year Robert Wymark was given in farm common ground beyond Bishopbridge between the Fossdyke and John Hutchinson's close, for 20 years at a rent of 40*s*. yearly: Wymark was to discharge the common council against the dean and chapter of 'all former grants awards judgments arbitraments and compositions heretofore made'.[6] The council

[1] C.C.M. 1710–1800, p. 185. [2] Ibid. p. 905.

[3] C.C.M. 1655–1710, p. 66.

[4] White Book, f. 79b. The authorised closes were apparently in the neighbourhood of Bishopbridge, which was built *c*. 1475. Hill, 'Three Lists' in *A.A.S.R.* XXXIX (1929), p. 238.

[5] C.C.M. 1511–41, f. 79b. [6] Ibid. f. 94.

wished to go further in 1524, when the mayor was bidden to have communication with the dean and chapter for the enclosing of the commons round Bishopbridge 'that the profit might be to the aiding of the common chamber'.[1] This is the origin of Waves Farm, 'old enclosure' of the award of 1811, and it is clear that the council's motive for enclosure was the need of revenue.

On the edge of the common pasture, near the enclosures in the parish of St Faith which have been identified as part of the bishop's little manor, was the Wong. Apparently it was part of the arable, and the selions of which it had consisted had come into the same ownership. Like the rest of the arable it was subject to rights of common between Lammas and Lady Day; and in every third year, when it lay fallow, it also lay open between Lady Day and Lammas. In 1537 the common council, still in pursuit of revenue, agreed to allow the tenants of the Wong to enclose it the whole year for a term of 31 years, at a yearly rent of 33*s*. 4*d*.[2] Perhaps the lease was not executed, for in 1546 a committee was bidden to inquire whether the Wong ought to lie open every third year according to the rote of the fields adjoining.[3] A dispute about rights of common there was proceeding in 1607[4] and in 1618 arbitrators between the citizens and the husbandmen, concerning commons for sheep, were appointed.[5] It was complained in 1637 that Mr George Walter had ploughed up the Shooting Leys (another piece of Lammas land) and the Wong, parcel of the west commons, to the prejudice of the commoners, and it was ordered that counsel be consulted.[6] Twenty-one years later it was proposed to exchange with Mr Walter the city's right of common on the Wong for his right and interest in the Shooting Leys, to be by him conveyed for the benefit of the city and the freemen for ever: but Walter had first to obtain the consent of all the husbandmen under their hands and seals,[7] and it seems that this was not forthcoming. Thereafter the Wong was let every third year, the rent being shared between the city and the husbandmen.[8] In 1722 complaint was made that Mr Edward Brefford had taken in several pieces of ground, which time out of mind had been common every third year, and sown them with corn. 'This being the third year yet he impounds the goods of several freemen which were upon the said ground and makes them pay.'[9] It is not surprising that so inconvenient a system by which land was sometimes several and enclosed, and sometimes common, gave rise to conflicts.

On the crest of the hill, to the west of the castle, was other ground the precise status of which was in doubt. There was in 1530 a close 'at the

[1] C.C.M. 1511–41, f. 167. [2] Ibid. f. 259b. [3] C.C.M. 1541–64, f. 37.
[4] C.C.M. 1599–1638, f. 51. [5] Ibid. f. 153. [6] Ibid. f. 277.
[7] C.C.M. 1655–1710, p. 74. [8] Ibid. pp. 619, 638. [9] C.C.M. 1710–1800, p. 82.

castle mills' west of St Bartholomew's chapel, which the dean and chapter claimed to have 'as toft and croft', that is, in severalty: the leet jury of the city made gaps in the hedge by way of claiming common of pasture to the commons of the city in open time. The matter was deferred until the dean and chapter could show why the close should not be laid open in open time. Agreement was reached that the chapter should have licence to enclose as well in open time as in several time, in exchange for a rent of 12*d.* yearly: in the event of non-payment, the close was to be cast open according to old use and custom.[1] In 1562 it was agreed that a close under the hill near St Bartholomew's chapel should be cast open unless the tenant would take a new lease of it.[2] Here, as before, the common council's incentive to enclosure was revenue.

The early plans of Lincoln all show a row of mills between the edge of the hill and the Burton road to the west of the city, several of which continued to stand within living memory. A 'new wind mill set' on the west side of the city is mentioned in 1507.[3] The row of mills is referred to in 1555, when they failed the city for five weeks because there was no wind. No wheat could be ground, and the bakers could not bake. Wheat was sent out to horse mills and water mills, and querns were brought into use. Even horse bread gave out, and the poor suffered severely.[4] This incident is a reminder of the important part played by the mills in the life of the city. They existed for the common good, and apparently none was disposed to query the right of the miller to set up on the common land. That his legal right to do so was not beyond doubt is indicated by a resolution of the common council in 1716 to grant a lease of a piece of land whereon a new mill was built 'so far as in them lies'.[5]

With the Enclosure Award of 1811 all the land allotted as arable passed into several ownership. The lords of the manors—the dean and chapter for Newport Manor and Cause Manor and the corporation for the rest—and the tithe owners were compensated, and the rights of common over the arable were extinguished. The rights of the husbandmen, tenants of the arable, over the pasture were also extinguished, leaving the freemen and the non-free inhabitants living north of the waterways (including those in the Bail and Close) and the senior and junior vicars and the patent officers of the cathedral to enjoy their pasture rights over the remaining pasture, which became known as 'the west common'. Their rights were defined in 1836; householders could pasture one head of cattle each, and freemen two, or, if householders, three.[6] These rights of pasture over the west

[1] C.C.M. 1511–41, ff. 219, 222.
[2] C.C.M. 1541–64, f. 175b.
[3] *Lincoln Wills* (L.R.S.), I, 34.
[4] C.C.M. 1541–64, f. 89b.
[5] C.C.M. 1710–1800, p. 39.
[6] Council Minutes, 16 February 1836.

common (and the south common to be mentioned later) were extinguished by the Lincoln Corporation Act, 1915. Compensation was paid to the freemen for the loss of their rights: and the corporation were empowered to let rights of pasture to inhabitant householders upon terms therein specified.

This same report of 1836 mentions the Holmes Common, and describes it as being exclusively a freemen's common. Here the 'foreigners' who dwelt in the city, the non-free inhabitants, never established themselves: the common came into being late, and the freemen suffered no encroachment on their preserves. The Holmes were situate to the south of Brayford: they were always liable to flood, being in the low marshland between Brayford and Swanpool. No doubt the reason why this tract was within the liberties and not in the adjoining parish of Boultham was that for a great part of the year it was under water and formed part of Brayford. It was apparently first mentioned in 1554, when it was ruled that no man was to keep more than two beasts or cattle (and no sheep) there.[1] The following year the West Holme was let for 80 years to a syndicate (who were to set willows about it) for a lump sum of £30 and a rent of 10*s*.[2] Clearly the common council was as usual in need of ready money, though whether the lease took effect is uncertain.

Access to the Holmes was difficult. It was complained in 1610 that the freemen had been hardly dealt with by the farmers of the water of Brayford—that is, the tenants of the fishing rights—for the carriage of cattle into the Holmes, and the carriage of servants evening and morning for milking. One man was appointed for this traffic, and a tariff of charges fixed for him; a penny for every horse and beast, and twopence for the carriage of one servant going to milk per week.[3] The following year the charge for cattle was reduced to a halfpenny, and staithes, or wharves, were ordered to be built for the safe landing of cattle.[4]

Part of the Holmes Common was taken by the Great Northern Railway in 1849, and the sale of the remainder was authorised by the Lincoln City Commons Act, 1870. The proceeds of sale were invested for the benefit of freemen and their widows.[5]

At a date very soon after the Norman Conquest the monks of the great Benedictine abbey of St Mary of York had begun to acquire lands on the

[1] C.C.M. 1541–64, f. 109.

[2] Ibid. f. 122.

[3] C.C.M. 1599–1638, f. 70.

[4] Ibid. f. 76b. For a claim to the grounds called Far Holmes and Hither Holmes, see f. 115b.

[5] For the Holmes Common see *Mayor & c. of Lincoln* v. *Overseers of Holmes Common, Law Reports*, 2 Q.B. 1867, p. 482. The corporation were owners and occupiers of the common, but were not liable to poor rate because the common was subject to a profit *à prendre* in the freemen which exhausted the whole value of the occupation.

hillside to the east of the city, and to put together the estate which is still known, though it is now broken up and built over, as the Monks Liberty. In 1120–2 Henry I confirmed to the abbot and monks the land near Lincoln called 'Inland' and 'Calvecroft', with meadow adjoining, and all the pasture between Calfcroft and the bounds of Greetwell, extending to the middle of the Witham, with toll and team, infangthief and other free customs; and all men were forbidden to pasture animals there without leave. The gift thereby confirmed had been made by Romfar, who had given land in Winterton, Usselby and Osgodby to the same house before the Lindsey Survey was made (that is, before 1115–18).[1] Calfcroft was situate between the suburb of Butwerk and the cell built by the abbot and monks, and it is evident therefore that the gift of Romfar included the site of the cell itself, which was dedicated to St Mary Magdalene. It is apparent from the reference to rights of pasture in this charter and in later documents that the monks' lands had formed part of the common lands of the city.

Romfar's grant was quoted by the abbot of St Mary in the course of a dispute upon the abbot's tenure of his land. It was alleged on behalf of the king that one Romfarus of Lincoln was formerly seised in his demesne as of fee of a plot built upon in the suburb of the city then called 'les Blakmunkes' with lands adjoining, in which was a chapel dedicated to St Mary Magdalene, which plot Romfarus had held of the king in burgage by the service of a penny yearly; and that he granted the plot to the abbot and convent of St Mary of York under condition of finding two monks, chaplains, continually dwelling on the plot to celebrate divine service in the chapel for the souls of Richard I, Romfarus, their progenitors and heirs; and that if the monks should be absent and divine service stopped for one whole year, pestilence excepted, the king and Romfarus and their heirs might enter upon and retain the plot: that Romfarus died without heir, and the plot should pertain to the king, because since Michaelmas 1392 no monk had dwelt on the plot and no divine service had been celebrated in the chapel, and the plot was let to laymen and pigs were herded in the west end of the chapel, and the abbot and convent had collected the rents and refused to deliver them to the king's escheator. The abbot rebutted the claim that he held by tenure of divine service, and declared that Romfarus granted the land to the convent in frankalmoign—free of all rent service—his grant being confirmed by Henry I. The abbot and convent, who had been dispossessed, recovered possession.[2] The abbot was presumably right

[1] *C. Chart. R.* III, 120; Lindsey Survey in *L.D.* 1/16, 7/9; Farrer, *Early Yorkshire Charters*, I, 275, 358.

[2] *C.P.R.* 1405–8, p. 249; *C.C.R.* 1405–9, p. 162. *Cal. Inq. p.m.* III, 222. The cell had an 'establishment' of a prior and two monks. *V.C.H. Lincoln*, II, 129–30.

in his law, but the allegations of fact would hardly have been made without some justification. The remains of the chapel, which are perpendicular in style, suggest that it may have been rebuilt after this period of neglect.

Other acquisitions of land by the abbot and convent are specified in a general confirmation by Henry II in 1156–7. Picot son of Colswein gave the church of St Peter[1] and two houses, land and four acres in the fields, and the 'Hevedland'; Gocelin gave eight houses, Auca, Aschatillus Siwata and Osbert Goldrun one each; Suaneburg three houses and Alexander his son one. There was land which Gerard and Costard held; and two strips of land in Lincoln which Hugh nephew of Romfar held; and a house which Gurred, Hugh's brother, gave in Lincoln, and two houses there which Ailric their brother gave;[2] and one piece of land which Redni gave, and one which Alan son of Wigot gave, which lay between the abbey lands.[3]

The Monks Liberty, as it is known in modern times, became a compact territory stretching from the east of the suburb of Butwerk to Greetwell boundary, and from the river on the south to the hilltop on the north. In addition there were lands between Greetwellgate and Langworthgate, and from thence to Nettleham Road, which were old enclosure at the time of the Lincoln Enclosure Award.[4]

But the abbot and convent did not enjoy their lands in severalty. The citizens had their rights of pasture, of which they were tenacious, and it may well have been due to a dispute on the subject that Henry Bere and other citizens assaulted one of the monks of St Mary of York at the cell of 'la Maudeleyne', carried him to Lincoln and imprisoned him.[5]

A great number of matters in dispute came to a head in 1455, when an agreement was entered into by the abbot and convent of the one part and the mayor and citizens of the other. Any claim by the citizens to rights of pasture over the site of the cell was abandoned; much of the land to the east and south of it was confirmed to the convent, a right of pasture for all animals but pigs being reserved thereover to the mayor and citizens. The citizens were given leave to make a watering-place in Greenpasture. The Inland, between Bagerholmgate and Greetwellgate, was to be enjoyed by the monks as Lammas land, being laid open from Lammas to Lady Day.

[1] Supra, pp. 133–4.

[2] Cf. *R.A.* I, 118, 119: Henry II commanded the reeves and citizens of Lincoln that Siward the canon should hold his lands in the city, and especially that which was Gurret the moneyer's and Ailred his son's; and also land which was Guthred his kinsman's near the gate of the Bail. Gurret (or Godric) coined under Henry I, Stephen and Henry II.

[3] Dugdale, *Monasticon Anglicanum*, III, 548–50; Farrer, op. cit. I, 275.

[4] Hence the Monks Manor Estate, so named from the mansion built by the late Joseph Ruston and now demolished. Lee Road, Massey and Mainwaring Roads take their names from modern owners of the Monks Liberty.

[5] *C.P.R.* 1307–13, pp. 419, 420, 471.

The abbot was to have a 96-years lease of Calfcroft; and the land below, extending west to the Stamp, was to belong to the city, subject to rights of pasture for the abbot and convent and their tenants and farmers. For the sake of consolidation of their domain the convent gave up their selions in Bagerholm Wong and St Hugh Croft and other plots, and they surrendered four houses in St Mark's parish in Wigford, opposite St Mark's church. Various rights of way were prescribed, one up the east side of the Cheviot Wall, from Monks Road to the present Lindum Terrace; this has been open ever since.

Some of the most interesting passages in the deed of 1455 relate to Blackdyke. The abbot and convent granted to the city the ditch of that name, bounded by two stones at its north end, with the willows, thorns and other trees upon its banks, as the citizens had had it of old time, for the purpose of loading and unloading their ships and boats. A modern map of the Monks estate shows a long narrow close running north and south and touching the river, which may represent Blackdyke: it may also be the Monkhouse Lock shown on Armstrong's map. The city granted to the convent free passage in and out of Blackdyke, but the rights of fishing and fowling in common waters were withheld, save by leave of the mayor.[1]

The cell was dissolved in 1539, and soon the mayor and citizens were involved in disputes with the secular successors of the Black Monks. Richard Deyncot, the farmer of the house late called the Black Monks, enclosed a piece of common, and the mayor and others were bidden by the common council to cast down the close and assert the commonalty's right to common of pasture: Deyncot was to be warned that he might pasture only such cattle as he kept in Lincoln field, and not any from Greetwell.[2] In 1554 it was resolved that if any freemen's cattle were impounded at the late priory they were to be released by Mr Mayor.[3]

Presently there began trouble with a later occupier, Mr Sapcote. In 1562 it was ordered that his sheep be impounded if they were found in St Hugh Croft.[4] No doubt for reasons of finance it was agreed in 1566 that Mr Sapcote should have the Greenpasture to the east of the Black Monks, with all the pasture and swarth-ground above the highway going towards Greetwell, to be enclosed at his charge, at a rent to be agreed.[5] This at once led to complaints by citizens deprived of their rights of common from Lammas to Lady Day: and the commoners secured their right to put their horses and other beasts (swine excepted) in the meadow grounds and leas

[1] The deed is calendared in *H.M.C. Lincoln*, p. 15. It was claimed in the nineteenth century that a free fishery in the Witham was appurtenant to the manor or reputed manor of the Black Monks.

[2] C.C.M. 1511–41, f. 278b.

[3] C.C.M. 1541–64, f. 109b.

[4] Ibid. f. 176.

[5] C.C.M. 1565–99, f. 10b.

during the winter half of the year, and in the Greenpasture throughout the year by staffholding or tethering. At the same time it was recalled that the 96-year lease of Calfcroft had expired, which land was ordered to be thrown open to the beasts and cattle of the city.[1]

In 1571 negotiations opened with Mr Sapcote which led to legal proceedings, and the following year Lord Dyer, one of the judges of assize before whom the city's action was expected to come, suggested arbitration. Some compromise seems to have been reached, as letters of attorney to the city's agents were annulled.[2] The dispute broke out again with Sapcote's successor Robert Smith. The common council resolved in 1581 to maintain their commons and common of pasture, and sent three aldermen to report whether any hedges hindered the commons of the freemen.[3] Proposals for arbitration followed, and at the Michaelmas leet, 1582, at which a great number or the most part of the freemen were present by commandment of the mayor and his brethren, they all agreed that the mayor, the recorder, the aldermen and common council should take order with Smith for common of pasture at the Monks and the watercourse, and what order should be taken the freemen would be therewith content.[4] After repeated postponements the arbitrators agreed upon a piece of land to be handed over to the corporation of the city in lieu of all rights of common within the Monks Liberty, and this was ordered to be dyked, quickset, enclosed and fenced.[5]

The award itself declared first that the city should have undisturbed possession of a watercourse through the monks' lands which supplied the city conduits, and which had been acquired by the citizens on the dissolution of the Grey Friars; all rights of common of citizens and inhabitants over the monks' lands were abolished; the soil of Blackdyke was vested in Smith, subject to an existing lease, but the mayor and citizens were given power to repair the dyke and make it passable for any boats or otherwise for landing of goods, with free egress and regress to carry and recarry goods between the city and the dyke or to the banks of the Witham, a convenient way being provided and kept up by the city. Part of the Inland or Monks Leas was allotted to the city in severalty in compensation for the loss of common rights, with other land which has not been identified. Smith gave up all claim to tithe from St Hugh Croft or any other city lands: the tithe, no doubt, he had claimed as having belonged to the church of St Peter at Welles.[6]

[1] C.C.M. 1565–99, f. 29.

[2] Ibid. ff. 54b, 62, 62b, 64, 66b, 72, 73b.

[3] Ibid. ff. 116, 118b.

[4] Ibid. f. 131b.

[5] Ibid. f. 149b (4 September 1585).

[6] *H.M.C. Lincoln*, p. 16.

The Monks Leas so appropriated became the Monks Leys Common. The common council reserved it exclusively for freemen, each of whom might stock this and other commons with two head of cattle in right of the freedom.[1]

By the Lincoln City Commons Act, 1871, it was declared that it would be greatly for the benefit of the inhabitants of the city if part of the Monks Leys Common were converted into a public park or pleasure ground, and the remainder sold and the proceeds devoted towards such conversion. All rights of common thereover were extinguished, the consideration being a perpetual yearly rent to the freemen's committee of £200. The public park is the present Arboretum.

The commons on the south of the High Bridge have a wholly separate history. Between the suburb of Wigford, the villages of Bracebridge and Canwick and the river Witham lay a large tract of land which was important because the great roads from the south and the south-west converged and met upon it a few yards to the south of Bargate. Encroachments upon this expanse, licensed or otherwise, began to reduce its area within a few years of the Norman Conquest, and occupation and payments of rents and tithe gradually defined the parishes or liberties to which the occupied parts belonged: but of the residue, now represented by the south common, it was still possible to say in the Canwick Enclosure Act in 1786 that it was not known in which parish or parishes the said common did lie.

To the east of the highway, between Bargate and the foot of Cross Cliff Hill, there early appeared a leper hospital, the hospital of the Holy Innocents, or the Malandry, whose enclosure, now cut through by the line of the London and North-Eastern Railway, is still clearly marked on the map, being occupied by school buildings and St Botolph's vicarage house. The foundation of the Malandry is ascribed by Giraldus to Bishop Remigius,[2] who, he says, endowed it with 13 marks of rent. An inspeximus charter of Henry IV recites a charter of Henry II which confirms, *inter alia*, a grant by Henry I of rent of the church of Lincoln;[3] later records show such a sum to have been charged on the manor of Nettleham, a manor which belonged to the bishopric, though not, it seems, until after the death of Remigius.[4] The honour of foundation remains uncertain, but it is at least clear that the leper hospital was in being in the early years of the twelfth century.[5]

A charter of Henry II shows that the Malandry at once attracted local endowments: William son of Fulk gave an oven, and Everard of Hungate

[1] Council Minutes, 16 February 1836 (p. 32).
[2] *Opera* (R.S.), VII, 18.
[3] Dugdale, *Monasticon*, VI, 628.
[4] *R.A.* I, 18.
[5] See Brooks, 'Hospital of Holy Innocents without Lincoln' in *A.A.S.R.* XLII (1934–5), pp. 157 et seq.

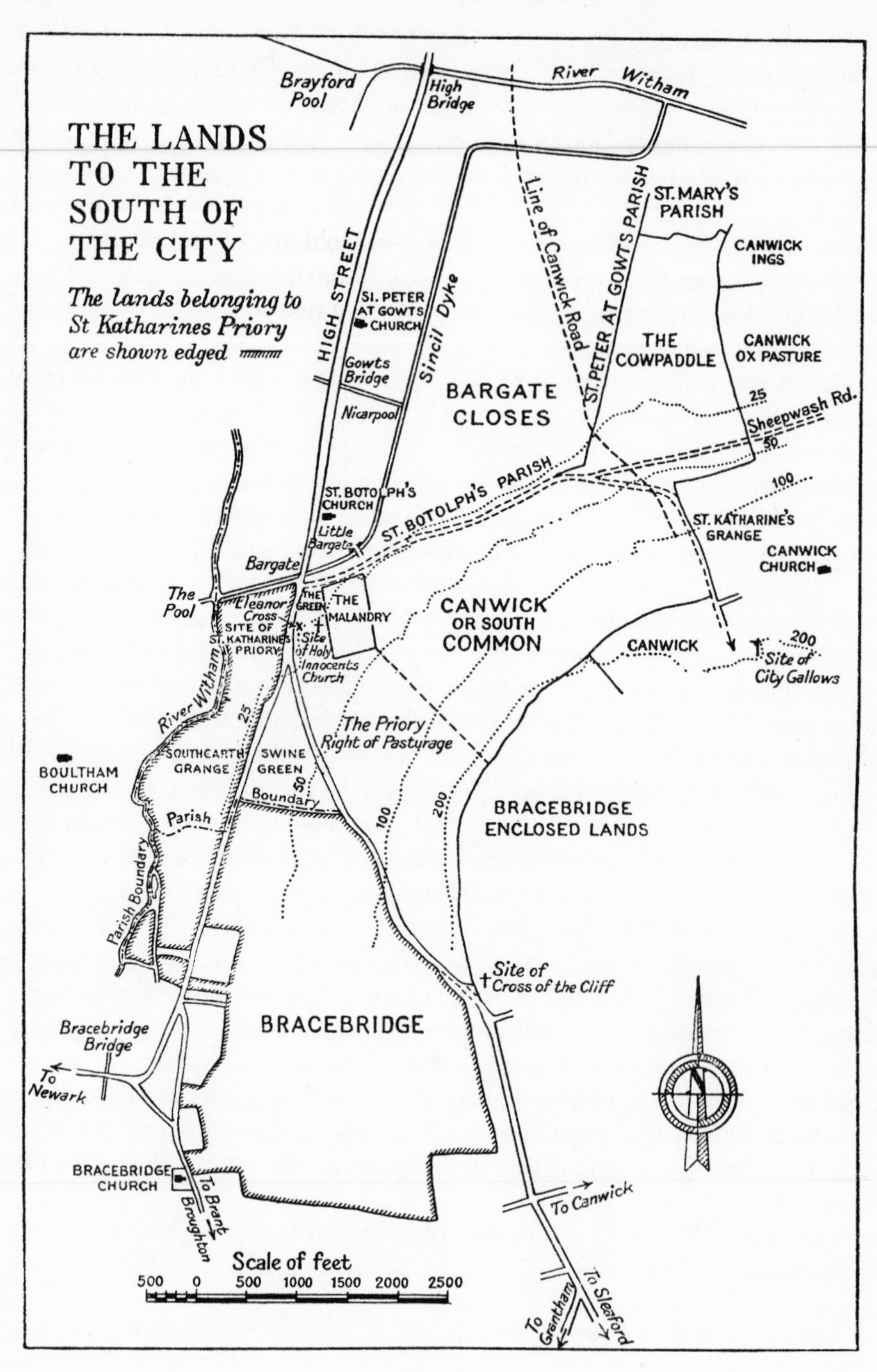
THE LANDS TO THE SOUTH OF THE CITY
The lands belonging to St Katharines Priory are shown edged
Brayford Pool
High Bridge
River Witham
HIGH STREET
Sincil Dyke
Line of Canwick Road
ST. PETER AT GOWTS PARISH
ST. MARY'S PARISH
CANWICK INGS
ST. PETER AT GOWTS CHURCH
THE COWPADDLE
CANWICK OX PASTURE
Gowts Bridge
BARGATE CLOSES
Nicarpool
Sheepwash Rd.
ST. BOTOLPH'S PARISH
ST. BOTOLPH'S CHURCH
Little Bargate
Bargate
ST. KATHARINE'S GRANGE
CANWICK CHURCH
The Pool
Eleanor Cross
THE GREEN
THE MALANDRY
SITE OF ST. KATHARINES PRIORY
Site of Holy Innocents Church
CANWICK OR SOUTH COMMON
CANWICK
Site of City Gallows
River Witham
The Priory Right of Pasturage
BOULTHAM CHURCH
SOUTHCARTH GRANGE
SWINE GREEN
Boundary
Parish
BRACEBRIDGE ENCLOSED LANDS
Parish Boundary
Site of Cross of the Cliff
BRACEBRIDGE
Bracebridge Bridge
To Newark
BRACEBRIDGE CHURCH
To Brant Broughton
To Canwick
Scale of feet
500 0 500 1000 1500 2000 2500
To Grantham
To Sleaford
25
50
100
200

Fig. 23.

land in Lincoln. Alan son of Elsi, a brother, gave 5*s.* of rent from his house in St Cuthbert's parish. Ranulph earl of Chester gave 2½ marks yearly from his mill at Bracebridge.[1] Later the brethren acquired two bovates and two acres of meadow in Branston, ten acres in Canwick, and land and rents elsewhere. One item of revenue records an act of charity which they performed on the open land near Canwick village: the Master of the Preceptory of the Hospitallers of Maltby paid them 6*s.* 8*d.* yearly for burying all persons hanged on the city gallows on Canwick Hill, and for inscribing their names in the book of the 'Fraternity of St John the Baptist'.[2]

Houses were built on 'le grene', either the land between the hospital and the highway, or part of the Malandry close itself, paying rent to the warden and the hospital;[3] and there was also a church of Holy Innocents 'on the green', to which the brethren presented in 1253.[4] On the green, in front of the Holy Innocents and opposite St Katharine's, was raised the first of the Eleanor Crosses by Edward I,[5] described by Leland as 'very fair and large'.[6] To the rights of pasture of the Malandry it will be necessary to return.

On the west side of the highway, and probably just without Bargate and the Sincil Dyke, was founded, by Bishop Bloet (1094–1123), the hospital of the Holy Sepulchre. When the adjoining priory of St Katharine was founded, the care of the hospital was vested in the prior, and the two foundations were so knit that they were often confused. The brethren of the hospital, however, continued to hold their separate estate.[7]

St Katharine's was the most important of the religious houses founded in the vicinity of Lincoln. It was a Gilbertine house and one of the largest of that purely English order. The founder of the order, Gilbert of Sempringham, had settled its first members on his ancestral estate at Sempringham, near Folkingham in Lincolnshire: he was rector of the church there and also of that at West Torrington. He must have been well known in the diocese of Lincoln, having served as a clerk in the household of Bishop Bloet, and stayed on in the court of his successor Bishop Alexander. When Gilbert returned to Sempringham he began to gather his community. Gilbert de Gant, his feudal lord, granted him three carucates of land at Sempringham to build a priory, and other endowments came in. Before the death of King Stephen, Gilbert had built eleven monasteries. In

[1] Dugdale, op. cit. VI, 628. [2] Brooks, op. cit. p. 163. [3] *Cal. Inq. Misc.* I, 1939.

[4] *Rotuli Roberti Grosseteste* (L.R.S.), p. 128. Probably the church of '*Grene juxta Linc*'' which the bishop conferred in 1272, as suggested by Venables. *Rotuli Roberti Gravesend* (L.R.S.), pp. 51, 277; Venables in *A.A.S.R.* XIX (1888), pp. 329–30.

[5] Many of the gild certificates of 1389 direct that if a brother or sister goes on pilgrimage to Jerusalem, or Rome, or Compostella, the brethren and sisters shall accompany him or her to this cross (the Queen's Cross) and meet him or her there on return.

[6] *Itinerary* (ed. Toulmin Smith), I, 30. [7] *V.C.H. Lincs*, II, 189.

planning for their future his thoughts turned to the Cistercian order, but at a general chapter of that order the abbots decided that they could not rule over another order, especially as some of Gilbert's houses contained women. At Citeaux, however, Gilbert met St Bernard of Clairvaux, who helped him to compile the Institutes of the Order of Sempringham, which were confirmed by Pope Eugenius III in 1148.[1]

Soon after that date Robert Chesney (bishop of Lincoln from 1148 to 1166) founded the priory of St Katharine's without Lincoln, and provided as endowment the prebend of Canwick, land in Wigsley and Balderton, the churches of Bracebridge, Newark, Norton Disney, Marton and Newton on Trent, houses and land at Newark and a chapel in Newark Castle, and the custody of St Sepulchre's Hospital. The grant was confirmed by charter of Henry II, which declared that it was made with the assent of the chapter;[2] but generosity at the expense of the see and the cathedral church brought severe criticism on the bishop.[3] A charter of St Hugh, however, shows that there was spiritual compensation: the canons of the hospital of Lincoln of the order of Sempringham promised to maintain a clerk to minister in the church of Lincoln, and Roger, prior of Sempringham, had granted the full brotherhood of his order to all canons of Lincoln, so that there might be done for them, living or dead, as the canons of the order were wont to do for their own members.[4]

The buildings of the priory and St Sepulchre's Hospital occupied the area between Sincil Dyke to the north, the Witham to the west and the highway to the east, and they reached southwards to a point some way beyond the foot of Cross Cliff Hill. The buildings have long since vanished, but modern building operations on the site have uncovered two Norman capitals and pieces of zigzag moulding, which probably belonged to Chesney's original church, and a large quantity of Early English vaulting rib stones, some bell capitals and other fragments. These latter pieces point to further building in the thirteenth century.[5]

Such near neighbours of the city as the prior and canons could hardly avoid contact with the citizens, and there was often friction between them. The prior and convent owned about £30 worth of land in the city, far more than any other religious foundation except the cathedral. Here was

[1] See Graham, *St Gilbert of Sempringham and the Gilbertines* (1903), ch. i.

[2] *R.A.* I, 120. Bracebridge church can only have been in the hands of the church of Lincoln a short time. Ibid. p. 89. Wigsley, Balderton and Newark are in Nottinghamshire: the other places in Lincolnshire.

[3] Giraldus wrote that, by alienating a prebend and churches which his predecessors had been wont to confer on their chaplains, he had done serious damage to the church of Lincoln and his successors. *Opera* (R.S.), VII, 34.

[4] *R.A.* II, 40.

[5] *Arch. Journ.* XXXIII (1876), p. 189.

scope for argument, and in addition there were disputes about the use of the river: the Hundred Roll jurors complained that the prior and canons had encroached on the king's water of Witham to a depth of from 8 to 12 ft. along the whole length of their courtyard and garden, and the prior had made a private chamber there to the detriment of the city. Of the lay brethren of the hospital the jurors had many complaints, which Canon Cole has summarised:

They had appropriated to themselves a portion of the common pasture of Lincoln, stretching in length for fifty five perches from the southern gate of the priory, and from sixteen to thirty two perches in width, and on this they had built granges, cowsheds and other buildings, causing an annual loss of £3 or £4 to the city, which had still to pay the ferm in full to the king. They had raised a windmill also on the common pasture, damaging the city to the amount of ten shillings a year by depriving its millers of so much of their trade. They had ploughed up for their own use thirty acres of this common pasture on which the citizens' cattle used to graze. They had turned the course of the Witham and narrowed it, so that vessels that used to bring down turf and faggots and other things for the city's use, were no longer able to pass. Beyond the right course of the Witham they had taken possession of three islands, containing two acres or more, and had placed curtilages and houses there. On the west of these islands they had fixed a fish-garth in the river, prejudicing the king and the city to the amount of ten shillings a year. Yet another island to the west of R. de Wykford's wall had been appropriated by them, containing more than two acres, which the bailiffs had formerly let in aid of the city's ferm, so that thus too a loss was caused of ten shillings a year to the city. The brethren also in conjunction with 'Dominus' John de Bracebridge had appropriated another portion of the common pasture between the king's highway running towards Bracebridge and that which passed under the gallows, twenty four perches in length and twelve in breadth northwards from the mill, damaging the city to the amount of six marks a year or more. Further they had appropriated to themselves a certain court or courtyard royally built (*curia regaliter edificata*), fifty five perches long, at its southern end thirty three perches and at its northern end sixteen perches in width, reaching from the king's highway to the water of Witham. Yet another piece of land on the north of their infirmary, 'reaching northwards as far as the king's dyke, about seven perches in breadth and extending lengthways down to the Witham in shape of a bishop's rochet (*ad modum birri*)' had been appropriated by them. Finally they had built a house and wall, twelve feet in breadth and two hundred feet in length, from the eastern part of the king's wall in the parish of St Botolph. All these appropriations and encroachments, the jurors state, had been made by the brethren of the hospital for various periods within the last fifty years, and without any warrant so far as they knew.[1]

[1] Cole, 'Priory of St Katharine without Lincoln' in *A.A.S.R.* XXVII (1904), pp. 277–8. *R.H.* I, 285–6, 311–27. In 1265 a commission was issued to Gilbert de Preston and William de Ingleby to inquire into a complaint made on behalf of the commonalty of the city, that certain religious men and others in past times, by the negligence and connivance of certain bailiffs and citizens, had made trespasses by occupying common pastures belonging to the city, raising houses and mills there, bringing pastures into cultivation and

These are, of course, *ex parte* statements, and not the findings of an impartial tribunal; but the process by which the priory and hospital consolidated and extended their land holdings is sufficiently shown by them and by later evidence. In 1284–5 the prior and convent sought leave to erect a windmill on a green outside the priory gate towards the east, and it was granted.[1] In 1292 they had leave to enclose a plot adjoining the priory;[2] and in 1306 they obtained licence to lead water from a well in Canwick field by conduit to their house.[3] Later Henry Cotty of Canwick and others granted them land in Canwick, in other villages and in Lincoln.[4]

Such extensions, whether authorised or not, were apt to cause bad feeling. In 1375 it was presented by a jury of Flaxwell and Langoe wapentakes that the prior had built a wall and blocked a common road between Branston and Lincoln within the prior's grange at Canwick. The prior contended that the road only existed there by his will, and that, owing to damage done by men passing through to his own animals and those of other persons enclosed therein, he had built a stone wall where there used to be a gate, as he had power to do. A jury upheld the prior, but the court was not then fully advised.[5]

On the dissolution of the priory its lands were surveyed and valued. To the south of the priory buildings was Southgarth Grange, which might be called the home farm. There were demesne lands, meadows and pasture, between the priory and Goldyngdales, 17 acres; Marshland 9 acres and Moor close 10 acres; in Bracebridge between the cliff top and the Witham 74 acres; arable land on the cliff 156 acres; a fishery below the priory and in Bracebridge. At Canwick, in the grange there, were 30 acres of meadow, of which 24 were in the marsh; 24 acres of enclosure of which 20 were on the heath; 246 acres of arable, of which 120 were on the heath or near it; and there was the tithe of corn, with some house rent. The total Canwick revenue was £22. 2*s*. 4*d*., from which deductions were payable: an annual pension of £7. 16*s*. 10*d*. out of the tithe of hay to the dean and chapter; a payment to the prebendary of All Saints Hungate for the prebend of Can-

appropriating them to themselves, narrowing the course of the river by building houses and planting trees; obstructing the (Sincil) dyke which for the defence of the extra-mural part of the city used of ancient time to be broad and deep, and building houses there; making weirs therein and appropriating the fishery thereof; and raising foreign chambers beyond the water to the nuisance of the inhabitants of the city. *C.P.R.* 1258–65, p. 479.

[1] *Inq. A.Q.D.* (P.R.O. Lists and Indexes), p. 15; *C.P.R.* 1281–92, p. 160.

[2] *Inq. A.Q.D.* (P.R.O. Lists and Indexes), p. 32; *C.P.R.* 1292–1301, p. 53.

[3] *Inq. A.Q.D.* (P.R.O. Lists and Indexes), p. 91; *C.P.R.* 1301–7, p. 482.

[4] *Inq. A.Q.D.* (P.R.O. Lists and Indexes), pp. 312, 335, 390.

[5] Flower, *Public Works in Medieval Law* (Selden Society), I, 276. The prior was also indicted for appropriation of a common fishery called Le Pole and for extortion of money from named persons.

wick, £1. 6s. 8d.; with other payments and pensions amounting to £11. 3s. 4d. At Bracebridge the tithe of corn was worth £4. 13s. 4d., and house rents came to £2. 17s. 10d.[1]

It is evident that the priory, situate to the west of the common land, and having interests in the parishes to the east and south thereof, would have ample scope for disagreement with commoners living in the city, because rights and boundaries were uncertain. Not only had the mayor and citizens rights of common over the waste now represented by the south common, but even before they became lords of the manor of Canwick[2] they had rights of common over the fields in Canwick parish, just as the Canwick men had rights of common over the waste.

Disputes upon a variety of subjects came to a head in an arbitration made at the house of the Carmelites in Lincoln in 1447. The mayor complained that the monks had depastured and trodden down the common pasture with their cows, which they had no customary right to do, and agisted on the common the cattle of men from Boultham, Bracebridge and North Hykeham; on which it was ruled that their cows to the number of five or six might go from the infirmary to the pasture. It was said that they had disseised the mayor and citizens of a fishery called Le Pole in the Witham near Henyngs; they were allowed a fishery with a 'garthnet' seven yards long in the fishgarth near Henyngs. It was said that for 30 years the monks had refused to pay a rent of 1s. a year for the site of a windmill which their predecessors had paid from time immemorial, and that for a like period the mayor and citizens had been deprived of common pasture from Lammas to Lady Day in certain meadow and marshland in Lincoln. On the other hand the prior said that the citizens had disseised the convent of right of pasture in 40 acres belonging to free tenements of the prior at Canwick, and of tithe there.

Upon the subject of enclosures the arbitrators ruled that the mayor and citizens had rights of pasture over the priory meadow land in Canwick from Lammas to Lady Day, and that the prior must not enclose against them; but a close made by the citizens, called the New Meadow, on the south and east sides of the Old Ee (or Sincil Dyke) must also be thrown open, so that the prior and convent might have their rights of pasture for oxen, cows and calves at any time of the year as far as the Old Ee.[3]

[1] *Valor Ecclesiasticus*, IV, 30; Cole, op. cit. p. 328 et seq. [2] Supra, p. 273.

[3] In 1409 the mayor and commonalty demised to Thomas Archer, citizen and mercer, for 20 years, a plot of the common soil called the south part of the new meadow lying within the ditches of the enclosure of the same, viz. from a lake called 'le Gulle' to the new ditch of the enclosure of the said meadow by Nykarpole, at a rent of 20s. yearly. Archer obtained letters patent confirming the lease. *C.P.R.* 1408–13, p. 137. This is the first hint of the enclosure of the fields later called the Bargate closes.

Other rights were granted to the prior and convent. They were to be allowed to drive their pigs from Southgarth to Canwick fields by the king's street without interruption, and, much more important, they were given common pasture for their 'foreign' sheep on the common to the south of the city at the time of shearing and washing (*loconis*) for one month from the Vigil of St Barnabas (11 June) to the Translation of St Thomas the Martyr (7 July). For this pasture for sheep, the site of the windmill and some other rights the convent was to pay the city 11*s.* yearly: this suggests that the pasture for 'foreign' sheep could hardly be regarded as a matter of right. Apparently as an afterthought the award added at the end that the mayor and citizens might clean out and deepen the city ditch from West Bargate to the 'Pole' as often as they thought fit, throwing the soil to the south bank (the priory side) with leave to use the soil in time of war for the protection of the city.[1]

The most interesting of these provisions is that relating to the pasture of 'foreign' sheep for a month at shearing time. It meant that the prior might bring his sheep from lands to which rights of pasture on the south common did not attach: these were 'foreign' sheep. As in other ways, the Gilbertine houses followed the Cistercian example in entering upon the wool trade, and St Katharine's was no doubt one of those houses of whose trade practices the citizens bitterly complained.[2] With other houses of the order, it is clear, St Katharine's traded in wool: and the name of 'Santa Chaterina de Nicchola' appears in an Italian list of English monasteries dealing in wool. Its wool was priced at 22½ marks per sack on the Flemish market, a price exceeded only among Lincolnshire houses by Kirkstead and Barlings (24 marks) and Stainfield, which, with Tintern and Abbey Dore on the Welsh border, heads the list of prices with 28 marks. The cheapest wool made only 7 marks.[3]

In 1511 there was another arbitration. It related to all the city commons, the parties being the dean and chapter, the prior of St Katharine's, the master of Burton Lazars (who had succeeded to the Malandry) and others of the one part, and the mayor and commonalty of the other part. It was awarded that one close on the south side of the city lying next to Canwick was to be laid open for ever; another near by was to be divided, one half at the choice of the dean and chapter to be laid open, the other to be kept several by the city. Apart from one other close, all closures made by the mayor and citizens within the preceding five years were to be undisturbed.

[1] White Book, ff. 77–9. Cole, op. cit. pp. 305–7, is not quite accurate in a few details.

[2] Supra, p. 320.

[3] Cunningham, *Growth of English Industry and Commerce* (1915 ed.), I, 628, 636. Power, *Wool Trade in English Medieval History* (1941), p. 23. A mark equals 13*s.* 4*d.* and a sack 26 stone.

No swine or sheep were to be put on the common pasture by any party, on penalty of having such swine and sheep kept until amends were made: but the rights of the prior of St Katharine's and his successors to pasture for *sherne* sheep at shearing time were expressly reserved.[1]

Five years later the prior's right of pasture for sheep was under discussion again. The prior offered to give up his right at clipping time and have it instead from St Andrew's Day (30 November) to Lady Day (25 March). The citizens suggested Christmas to Lady Day, but the prior disagreed, and his suggestion was adopted. The recorder was directed to put the agreement into writing; and the right of pasture was to be exercised between the high street and 'the path that goeth up to the myllne against the malandry on the south end'.[2]

The convent's wool trade and its interest in sheep pasture at the shearing season was probably on the wane at the time of the arbitration of 1447. By 1516 the prior was prepared to give up his summer rights. Emphasis had shifted to subsistence farming. Winter keeping was the problem of the time, and it was perhaps in order to secure pasture for four winter months (an extension of time) that the prior agreed to a limitation of the area within which the rights might be exercised.

After the dissolution of the priory the secular occupants of the house were soon in dispute with the city. In 1568 the common council declared that Edmund Yarburgh (farmer of St Katharine's) was foddering his sheep on the city commons between the Queen's Cross and the common ground of the city in his occupation, which was farther than was warranted, and the mayor sent his officer to bid Yarburgh remove them.[3] This and other points continued in dispute until 1595, when the mayor and citizens agreed with Vincent Grantham, then owner of St Katharine's, that Grantham should have yearly, in satisfaction of his summer-time sheepgates, and to the exclusion of others, common of pasture for his sheep from St Andrew's Day to Lady Day over the ground from the top of the hill in the corner by the late Cross of the Cliff unto the thorn tree at the Vicar's Garth. The boundary is evidently the same as that laid down in 1516, as also are the pasture rights themselves and the reserved rent of 11*s*.[4]

To complete the history of the St Katharine's sheepgates: in 1834 Major Colegrave, then the owner, offered the St Katharine's estate for sale. Rights of pasturage over 70 acres 2 roods 14 perches were included, and a plan indicates a boundary in accordance with the agreements above quoted. It seems, however, to have been the practice for the owner or his tenant to pasture his sheep upon the whole of the common; and to complaint of this

[1] White Book, f. 79b.
[2] C.C.M. 1511–41, f. 60 (28 August 1516).
[3] C.C.M. 1565–99, ff. 29b, 31.
[4] Ibid. f. 228.

practice was added another that though Grantham's award only permitted the pasture of *his* sheep, other sheep were taken in.

Presently a movement was made by the city council to buy out private rights of common, and it transpired that the St Katharine's rights had been bought by the town clerk. This investment by the city's legal adviser provoked some plain speaking. One newspaper correspondent pointed out that the pasture rights had been severed from the site of St Katharine's itself, and that there could be no right of common in gross (that is, existing independently) without stint (or limitation of number): though the Commons Committee of the council found in 1836 that the owner of St Katharine's had a right to stock with a given number of sheep. Another correspondent suggested that pieces of the common should be sold and the proceeds devoted to drainage and general improvement of the remainder, adding that the improvement would be an ample equivalent to all parties having private rights of pasture for the little curtailment of space. The principal private owner was 'our excellent Town Clerk.... I know enough of this gentleman to venture the assertion that he would not allow any *little* rights of his own to interfere with the carrying out of a measure calculated to effect a great public good'.[1]

The Lincoln Corporation (Canwick Common) Act, 1868, recited that (among others) John Thomas Tweed (the town clerk) in respect of rights formerly appendant or appurtenant to an estate called Saint Catherine's, claimed rights of common according to certain rates or stints, and empowered the corporation to buy the rights and hold them without their becoming merged in the larger estate of the corporation as lord of the manor in the common. The corporation regularly let these grazing rights until all rights were extinguished in 1915.

The corporation did not seek to provide in the Act of 1868 for the purchase of the Malandry rights of common, as they did for St Katharine's.[2] At that time the rights were vested in the vicars of Normanby and Canwick and the Great Northern Railway Company. After the dissolution of religious houses William Cecil had received a grant, in 1553, of the capital messuage, cottage and garden in 'le Mallandrye' with five cottages there, and a cottage in the parish of St Cuthbert.[3] In 1767 the Malandry was conveyed to the Governors of Queen Anne's Bounty for the augmentation of the vicarages of Normanby and Canwick and the rectory of Snarford. Perhaps the corporation acquired the pasture rights by private treaty, for in 1869 they invited tenders for the Malandry rights in the south common.[4]

[1] Newspaper cuttings in Ross Scrap-Books at Burton Hall, Lincoln (Lincoln City ii).
[2] Council Minutes, 17 December 1867.
[3] *C.P.R. Edward VI*, v, 182.
[4] Council Minutes, 6 September 1869.

Not much is heard of these rights. In 1699 the parishioners of St Botolph certified what commons belonged to the owners of the Malandry, and the common council ordered that they should have their commons and gates as theretofore, and two horse and beast gates for every cottage and parcel of land belonging to it. If a cottage were demolished, the gates would still go with the land, but they must not be let.[1] In his account of the Malandry, Dr Cookson, writing in 1841, said that the rector of Snarford had seven beastgates from Old Mayday to Old Lady Day, and forty sheepgates from Old St Andrew's Day to Old Lady Day (the same as the St Katharine's sheep pasture). The vicar of Canwick had six oxgates, and the vicar of Normanby eight.[2]

The closes (called the New Closes) which were left undisturbed by the arbitration of 1511 were evidently some of those known later as the Bargate closes. These eventually extended into five rows, bounded on the west by the Sincil Dyke, on the south by other part of the common, and on the east by that part of the common called the Cowpaddle. In 1515 one of the tenants ploughed up and sowed a piece of the commons without East Bargate, and the common council ordered one or two mowers to mow the corn off to the use of the common chamber, or else that cattle should forthwith be put on the ground to eat it off.[3] The offence lay, not in the enclosure, but in the conversion of common pasture temporarily enclosed (presumably on the theoretical ground that existing rights of common could be satisfied without it) into arable.

The marshland farther north, in the angle formed by the Sincil Dyke as it turned eastwards, was not enclosed in the same trim way. In the angle was Chequers in the Myres, and farther to the east was Coultham or Coltholme: in 1518 both were ordered to be let to the highest bidder.[4] About the same time the 'aley' from St Mary's Lane end to Gowts Bridge (or Nickarpool)—presumably land along the bank of the Sincil Dyke—was being let.[5] The cleansing of the dyke was a matter of importance. In 1518 a common day was set for the 'sewing of the eye', and every able person from the farthest ends of St Mary's parish to the other end of the city was bidden by himself or his servant to cleanse the same, every man to make his stath on his own ground, and all other persons in Wigford cleansing and cutting the 'eye' against their tenements;[6] and in 1528 all frontagers from East Bargate to the Stamp were ordered to raise their banks before St Martin in winter (11 November), and every farmer to cut sedges and

[1] C.C.M. 1655–1710, p. 552.
[2] *Lincolnshire Topographical Society*, 1841, 1842, p. 48.
[3] C.C.M. 1511–41, f. 42b.
[4] Ibid. ff. 94, 107, 110.
[5] Ibid. f. 59b; 1541–64, f. 109b.
[6] C.C.M. 1511–41, f. 91.

other things growing in the stream at the usual time of the year after the king's proclamation.[1]

Just as the mayor and citizens had rights of common over the Canwick fields between Lammas and Lady Day, so Canwick men had rights over the south common. But not all Canwick men: no such right attached to Sheepwash Grange at Canwick, which was parcel of the abbey of Kirkstead. In 1527 the sheriffs of Lincoln pinned the sheep of Hamon Sutton, the farmer of Sheepwash, for pasturing without the South Bargate. The sheep died of the rot, and Sutton threatened to sue the sheriffs.[2] In 1570 the common council resolved that if Humphrey Wilson, then farmer of Sheepwash, put sheep on the south commons they were to be impounded until he replevied them.[3]

There is an interesting entry on the council minutes in 1543, when it was resolved to build a house on a toftstead in Canwick belonging to the common council, and lay it to a meadow in Canwick belonging to the Great Gild, rent being paid to the gild.[4]

The boundaries between the south common and Canwick were uncertain, and several attempts were made to define them. A committee was set up for the purpose in 1542;[5] and in 1559 ancient and young persons with certain of the last leet inquest were to be appointed to set boundstones outside the commons down to Canwick meadows nigh the watering-place there;[6] boundstones were ordered to be set again in 1563;[7] and division made once more in 1569.[8]

The pasture rights of individual commoners also gave rise to difficulties. In 1576 a stint was agreed upon by the common council, but deferred as the tenants and inhabitants of Canwick would not agree.[9] Apparently agreement followed, for later in the year it was laid down that the stint for freemen below St Bennet's Lane (that is, south of the river Witham) should be three beasts, and for other inhabitants one, and this not to be exceeded on penalty of impounding and amercement by the justices. Every inhabitant and farmer in Canwick (except those of Sheepwash) having a ploughland within the fields of Canwick, answering for all payments and assessments for twenty years, might keep on the south commons of the city six beasts,

[1] C.C.M. 1511–41, f. 209b.

[2] Ibid. f. 196b; and see C.C.M. 1541–64, f. 178b.

[3] C.C.M. 1565–99, f. 47b. Wilson was the elder brother of Thomas Wilson, one of Queen Elizabeth's Secretaries of State, and M.P. for Lincoln, 1571 and 1572. The Sheepwash lands apparently had rights of common in the Canwick Oxpastures. In 1680 the owner of Sheepwash claimed 17½ beast-gates in the south common. Lincoln Public Library MSS. 4690, 4695.

[4] C.C.M. 1541–64, f. 16b.

[5] Ibid. f. 10.

[6] Ibid. f. 148b.

[7] Ibid. f. 180b.

[8] C.C.M. 1565–99, f. 31.

[9] Ibid. f. 93b.

and so in proportion. Cottagers might keep two beasts. The Canwick men were allowed in severalty, for their oxpasture and for draught cattle from Lady Day to Lammas, a piece of ground between 'willow row' and Sheepwash wherein the citizens and freemen of the city had time out of mind had common of pasture for kine and horses at all times of the year. After Lammas the freemen and inhabitants of the city (south of the river) were to have common of pasture through all the fields of Canwick for the number of beasts above mentioned.[1]

When in 1579 the fences and hedges needed repair the council directed a bustage of the commoners, at the rate of 2*d.* per beast, to be collected by the parish constables. The Canwick husbandmen were to pay 6*d.* for the assessment of a plough, and every cotter 2*d.* per beast. Poor men not keeping their stint were to pay according to the number of cattle they kept.[2]

A dispute arose in 1583 between Sir Thomas Cecil, on behalf of young Mr Grantham the queen's ward, and the citizens and freemen, and the council appointed arbitrators in accordance with a commission issued out of the Court of Wards and Liveries concerning common of pasture in Canwick.[3] The arbitrators' award was made in the following year, and may be summarised as follows:

1. The Oxpasture at Canwick to be enjoyed in severalty by the Canwick husbandmen from Lady Day to Lammas, and then to be common as well to the inhabitants of Canwick as to the freemen and inhabitants of Lincoln as heretofore.

2. The stints upon the south common for the Canwick husbandmen to be, for every ploughland there, six kine and young beasts, or four kine and young beasts and two horses at all times of the year, and for every Canwick cottager two kine and no more.

3. The stints for inhabitants of Lincoln living between High Bridge and Bargate to be, for freemen three kine or three horses, and for denizens not free, one cow or horse. No other person to keep any cattle on the south common at all, and no beastgate or horsegate to be sold or let to any other person.

4. The Canwick Ings to be kept several from Lady Day to Lammas, except that Mr Mayor and his brethren and the commonalty and the inhabitants of the town of Canwick may by consent break the same sooner; and then the Ings to be eaten only with oxen and horses, according to the stints aforesaid.

5. If any person of the city exceeds his stint, it to be lawful for any of the Canwick inhabitants to distrain and impound any such beast or

[1] Ibid. f. 99b.

[2] Ibid. f. 111; and see f. 192.

[3] Ibid. f. 137b.

horse found there, and to take upon such impounding 4*d.* to the use of the impounder and 8*d.* to the churchwardens of Canwick to the use of the poor. Any Canwick man so offending to be subject to the like penalty, 4*d.* to the impounder and 8*d.* to Mr Mayor to bestow on the poor inhabiting between High Bridge and Bargate.[1]

When the Canwick Enclosure Act was passed in 1786 it was recited that there were about 2,000 acres in the open fields of Canwick with the ox-pastures and the meadows or ings and about 240 acres in the Canwick or south common, but that it was not known in what parish the common lay. The common was commonable at certain seasons of the year according to certain rates or stints, as well to proprietors in Canwick as to freemen and inhabitants of and living in certain districts of Lincoln and to other persons by reason of their property in or near the common. The mayor, sheriffs, citizens and commonalty of the city of Lincoln were lords of the manor of Canwick; and the wardens and commonalty of the London Mercers' Company were seised of the rectory impropriate, and as such entitled to tithes of corn and hay arising and growing within the parish except lands belonging to Robert Padley called the Grange (evidently Sheepwash), and the Mercers were patrons of the vicarage and parish church. The vicar had certain glebe lands and rights of common and the tithe of wool and all other small or vicarial tithes from all the lands (including the Grange) in the parish.

The chief purpose of the Act, so far as it concerned the city, was referred to in the recital that 'it would be a great convenience and advantage to all persons and parties interested' if the common were assigned as a common for the freemen and inhabitants of the city resident as aforesaid and for the other persons having rights of common thereon, except the proprietors within the parish of Canwick, and the common divided from the parish altogether; and if as compensation to the Canwick proprietors the rights of common of the freemen and inhabitants of the city and owners of property in or near the common over the common fields, meadows, pastures and waste lands of Canwick parish were extinguished, and the lands in the parish were enclosed.

These purposes were effected by the Act, and lands were allotted to the corporation of Lincoln in lieu of their rights in the common fields of Canwick, and also in satisfaction of their rights as lords of the manor. The city sewage farm now occupies lands on both sides of the Washingborough (formerly Sheepwash) Road so allotted.

[1] C.C.M. 1565–99, f. 150b. By 1605 a new dispute arose about the freemen's right of common within Canwick fields, and the common council resolved to uphold the freemen. C.C.M. 1599–1638, f. 42.

The south common then included not only the present common but the Cowpaddle, which lay between the Canwick boundary to the east, the Bargate closes to the west, and lands in the parish of St Mary le Wigford to the north. The district has been altered out of recognition. Formerly a highway ran across the common from Newark road just south of Bargate to the western end of the Washingborough Road. The present Melville Street, Pelham Street, and Canwick Road to the foot of Canwick Hill was made about 1860; part of the Cowpaddle was conveyed to the Burial Board for a cemetery in 1856; the Great Northern Railway line cut through the Cowpaddle, the present common, the Malandry closes and the Swine Green in 1864; by an exchange with the engineering firm of Messrs Robey and Co. 6¾ acres of Cowpaddle was given up and 17½ acres of land in Canwick parish laid thereto instead. In consequence of all these changes the Lincoln Corporation (Canwick Common) Act, 1868, was obtained. The Act diverted the road across the common to a line which is now the South Park, and authorised the sale of pieces of common severed from the main area by the railway, including the fringe of land on which the houses on South Park now stand. It is said that the reason for this severance was that the commoners feared that their horses and cattle at pasture would be frightened by the noise and smoke of passing trains. The proceeds of sale of the various pieces of common so alienated were apportioned between the corporation and the commoners: the share of the latter was invested for the benefit of the freemen, and now forms one of the Freemen's Funds.

There were no city rights of common in the Bracebridge fields as in those of Canwick. From time to time the mayor and brethren, in the course of their annual perambulation, found it necessary to make orders for the making of hedges or fences upon the boundary;[1] or for the erection of boundstones by ancient persons.[2]

The city had, however, a share of the liability for the maintenance of the great bridge at Bracebridge. In 1565 Alderman Thomas Fulbeck was granted the city's right and interest of the water of a half part of the great bridge for 70 years without rent, he and his executors standing charged with all repairs of such of the said bridge and arches as appertained to the city; provided he did not set nets or leips to take fish in the water there for the stopping of water, or make any garmouths.[3] Apparently this arrangement was not satisfactory, for two years later the council decided that as much part of the Bracebridge great bridge as was within the liberties of the city and appertaining to the same should be amended, and the recorder was asked to advise on the city's interest in the water and fishing.[4] In 1600 the

[1] C.C.M. 1511–41, f. 244b.
[2] C.C.M. 1541–64, f. 180b.
[3] C.C.M. 1565–99, f. 4.
[4] Ibid. f. 18.

repair of the east half of the middle arch of the bridge was directed;[1] perhaps this was all that needed repair. Liability for the bridge generally was later repudiated,[2] but in 1739 the city undertook the repair of the part of the bridge belonging to the city to uphold, and in 1751 the city repaired the middle arch.[3]

In his famous *Reading on Sewers*, Robert Callis drew on his experience as a commissioner in Lincolnshire to illustrate his points, and he records:

> in 14 Jacobi Regis it was found by inquisition taken at the city of Lincoln in the Guild-Hall there, before Sir Thomas Grantham knight, and myself, and other Commissioners of the Sewers, that the great Bridge at Bracebridge near the city of Lincoln, and standing upon the River of Wytham thirty miles from the Sea, was fallen into great decay, whereby carts, carriages and men on horse-back could not pass over the same, as in times past had been used, in defect of Henry Sapcote Esq. who ought to repair a part thereof by reason of his Mannor of Bracebridge; and of Bartholomew Gregge, who by reason of his house standing at the Bridge foot, called the Hermitage, on the North side of the river, ought to repair another part; and of the Corporation of Lincoln, who was to repair a part thereof; and of the country of Moreland, who used to repair another part: And the same was decreed accordingly.

An appeal from the Exchequer Chamber by Mr Sapcote, on the ground that the bridge being far from the sea the Commissioners had no jurisdiction, failed.[4]

Callis' account is amplified by Edward Trollope. There were formerly seven arches. The two eastern ones belonged to the city of Lincoln until the Municipal Reform Act of 1835, when they passed to Kesteven. The third arch was said to have been built by a former lord of the manor of Bracebridge, and was repaired by his representatives. The fourth belonged to the corporation of Lincoln. The fifth, called the 'Abbot's arch', was built by the abbey of St Mary of York, the former proprietor of certain lands in the parish forming (in 1857) the 'Gregge Hall Farm', also of that small piece of land adjoining the bridge in the parish of Boultham, having a public house upon it. The sixth and seventh arches, called the 'Moorlands Arches', belonged to the parts of Kesteven, and had been filled in.[5]

[1] C.C.M. 1599–1638, f. 5.
[2] Ibid. f. 113.
[3] C.C.M. 1710–1800, pp. 244, 329.
[4] (1st ed.), p. 65.
[5] *Handbook to Excursions of Lincolnshire Architectural Society* (1857), p. 71. For indictments of inhabitants of the county of the city of Lincoln for non-repair of the eastern arches, see *Lincoln, Rutland and Stamford Mercury*, 17 July 1818, 19 March 1824. The central arch belonged to the corporation of Lincoln as distinct from the inhabitants. In the charter granted to the Lincoln Cordwainers' Company by the justices of assize *temp.* James I, it was provided that fines imposed under the charter were to be divided, half to the chamberlain of the south ward towards the repair of the Bracebridge in the county of the city of Lincoln, and the other half to the wardens of the company. Cordwainers' MS. Lincoln Public Library.

APPENDIX I

SOME PLACE-NAMES IN THE CITY OF LINCOLN

This list is far from exhaustive. It consists only of names which have been noted in the course of reading, and could be greatly lengthened by further research. Many names whose meaning is obvious have been omitted. The notes are mostly contributed by Professor Stenton.

ME. = Middle English	ON. = Old Norse
OE. = Old English	OS. = Old Scandinavian
OF. = Old French	

ALDUSSTYGH in parish of St Peter *ad placita*, 1349. B.B. f. 192 b. Aldusa was a ME. feminine name, used as a short form of some OE. compound name in *Eald-* (Ealdgyth or Ealdgifu); *stygh* is OE. stīg, 'path'.

AMSEGATE, 1324. B.B. f. 100.

ARNALDGARE, 1275. *R.H.* I, 310 b. A *cultura* in the fields. 'Arnald's *gāra*.' Arnald is continental-Germanic; *gāra* here probably means a three-cornered field.

BAGGERHOLM. Bagg'holme, *c.* 1260. D. & C., D ii, 76/1/53. Baggerholm, *c.* 1330. *R.A.* III, 403. Bagerholmgate, Bagerholmwong, Oldbagerholm-gate, 1455 deed. Apparently 'bag-makers' *holm*. ME. *baggere* is not well, if at all, recorded, but it is a normal sort of formation from ME. *bagge*, 'bag'; *holm* means, presumably, a piece of wet, low-lying ground. Cf. Beggargate, formerly Baggergate, in York.

BAILGATE is not found until the nineteenth century. It was formerly 'the Bail'. *Bail* is an importation from OF. *baille*. See Chapter v.

BARGATE. Barra regis, late twelfth century. *D.C.* 47–9. Portam barream orientalem. Thurgarton Cartulary, f. 162. West Bargate and postern near East Bargate, Blickling Homilies, p. 75. OF. *barre* in this context seems to have meant simply 'bar'—a length of timber thrust out to block a road through a gate. In York the word *bar* was used as early as the twelfth century to denote the gate itself. The adjectival use in *porta barrea* is interesting and precisely accurate.

BATTLEPLACE. La Batailplace, 1275. *R.H.* I, 312 a. Croft on west side of *la Batalplace*, abutting towards the north on cemetery of St Bartholomew. 1358. B.B. f. 235. Common pasture called Bataylplace. Blickling Homilies, p. 37. The plot on which trials by battle took place. This was a necessary appendage to a court of justice so long as trial by battle remained a method of judicial proof.

BAXTERGATE, *c.* 1230, in parish of St Peter at Arches, to north of Saintmarystigh. D. & C., D ii, 80/3/41. Bakestergate, D ii, 80/3/23. Probably Guildhall Street. 'Bakers' street.' ME. *bakkestere*. Wheelergate in Nottingham was originally Baxtergate, *vicus pistorum*.

BEAMUND RENT, 1530. *Lincoln Wills* (L.R.S.), II, 198. Beamond Rent, 1512. C.C.M. 1511–41, f. 6. Hill 'Manor of Hungate' in *A.A.S.R.* XXXVIII (1927), p. 190. Named from the Beaumont family; supra, p. 241.

BELE COTTI, 1275. *R.H.* I, 310 b. A *cultura* in the fields.

BEREGECLOSE. 1455 deed.

BESOMPARK. Bysyngpark in St Mary Crackpole, 1343. B.B. f. 159 b. Besom Park, 1576. C.C.M. 1565–99, f. 97. Cf. Besingate, York. ME. personal name *Besing*, well recorded but still of uncertain origin.

BIGHT. *c.* 1250, *in orientali Bictrio*, D. & C., D ii, 78/1/80, *c.* 1254, *in orientali Bictho*, D ii, 78/1/82, *c.* 1280, Est Bigth in *Registrum* is rendered *le Quaterbyhoe* in D ii, 78/1/108. OE. *byht*, 'bend', 'angle'. The Lincoln example is a test-case for the meaning of the word when used in local names.

BISHOPBRIDGE (made 1474–5), 1587. Closes there, C.C.M. 1565–99, f. 162.

BLACKINGARTHES. 1600 deed. Close in Newland.

BLAKEDIKE. 1455 deed. The Black Dyke was in the Monks Liberty.

BOTHEMES, *c.* 1270. D. & C., D ii, 82/1/21. In the fields. OE. *botm*, *boþm*, 'bottom'. The meaning here is probably 'hollows'.

BOUERN LANE, 1363. B.B. f. 255 b. In St Augustine's parish.

LE BOUNE, *c.* 1270. D. & C., D ii, 78/3/77. Lane leading from Minster Yard to Greestone Stairs.

BOUNGARTH, 1382. *Lincoln Wills* (L.R.S.), I, 14. Apparently the western part of Vicars Court.

BOWERHILL, 1349. B.B. f. 201 b. 1533. C.C.M. 1511–41, f. 233. Waste plot in St Michael on the Mount. Probably Bowyers' Hill.

BRADEGATE, *c.*1270. D. & C., D ii, 82/1/21. Bradgate. B.B. f. 100. In the fields. Broadgate, 1580. C.C.M. 1565–99, f. 118 b. 'Broadway.'

BRANCEGATE. Brantegate, 1226–8. *Book of Fees*, I, 365; 1257, *C. Chart. R.* I, 460. Brancegate, 1258. D. & C., D ii, 82/2/133. Brauncegate, 1341. B.B. f. 149 b. This seems to be a compound of *gata* and OS. *Brand.*

BRAYFORD. Braidemere, ? 1228. D. & C., D ii, 76/3/3. Braytheforde, *c.* 1316. D ii, 76/3/16. Aqua de Bradeford. Goxhill Leiger, f. 295. Bradeford, Braydeford. Welbeck Cartulary, ff. 105 b, 106. Originally identical with the familiar name Bradford, i.e. a compound of OE. *brād* and *ford.* Presumably this 'broad ford' was across, or more probably adjacent to, the 'broad pool' referred to in Braidemere (OE. *mere*). The interest of the name lies in the gradual, but at last complete, substitution of the Scandinavian *breiðr* 'broad' for the OE. *brād.*

BRIGGATE. Briggegat, *c.* 1180. D. & C., D ii, 80/3/48. Brigegate, D ii, 80/3/33. 'Bridge street', cf. Briggate in Leeds. Here, 'bridge' probably stands for Scandinavian *bryggja* rather than OE. *brycg.*

BUTTERCROSS. Buttur crosse, 1507. *Lincoln Wills* (L.R.S.), I, 35. Lately cast down, 1572. C.C.M. 1565–99, f. 70 b. In Newland. Cf. Butter Cross in Nottingham. Cross at which dairy produce was sold.

BUTWERC, 1185. Lees, *Templars*, p. 82. Butewerk, *c.* 1220. D. & C., D ii, 76/1/53. Butwerk, 1296. *Lincoln Wills* (L.R.S.), I, 4. Botewerk, 1349. B.B. f. 187 b. Butwark, 1383. *C.P.R.* 1381–5, p. 303. Literally 'outside the work', an OE. compound presumably applied to a piece of land, perhaps of considerable extent, outside the city wall. The name occurs again at Stamford.

CALFCROFT. Calcroft, 1349. B.B. f. 187b. Calfcroft, 1455 deed. 'Calf-enclosure.'

CARHOLME. Karholm, *c.* 1270. D. & C., D ii, 82/1/21. Probably 'holm', or low ground, by the marsh. 1270 is an early date for the Scandinavian *Kiarr* to appear in a local name as *Kar* (instead of *Ker*). But this objection does not really override the evident meaning of the name.

CHEVIOT CLOSE. Chiviot wall. 1455 deed.

CLASKETGATE. Clachislide, ? 1240. D. & C., D ii, 74/2/17. Claskytgate, 1527. C.C.M. 1511–41, f. 197 b. Claxslete gate, 1578. C.C.M. 1565–99, f. 106 b. Claxledyate, Blickling Homilies, p. 72. Scandinavian *Klakks hlið*. Klak is a well-recorded *East* Scandinavian (not ON.) personal name (found in Claxby, etc.). *hlið* is the Scandinavian *hlið*, 'door', 'gate', found in a number of names in York.

CLEUMARKET, 1349. B.B. f. 189 b. Holy Trinity in Cleumarket. Cleumarketh, 1331. Fosse Charter.

CLIFGATE, *c.* 1270. D. & C., D ii, 82/1/21. 1324. B.B. f. 100. The road along the Cliff.

COCKEPLACE, 1294. D. & C., D ii, 75/1/22, 24. Street called le cokplace, 1369. B.B. f. 269. In St Mary Crackpole, subsequently St Martin. Apparently 'place used for cock-fighting'.

COKROWE, 1342. B.B. f. 157. House in Briggate on le Cokrowe in St Benedict.

COLTHOLME, 1517. C.C.M. 1511–41, f. 75. Coltham causey. 1707 deed. Preserved in Coultham Street, off Canwick Road.

CORNMARKET. Stalls *ad forum bladi* in St Cuthbert, 1310. D. & C., D ii, 74/3/14.

COUFOLDES, Kufaldes, 1275. *R.H.* I, 310 b, 318 a. 'Cow-pens.'

COUNBOYE, 1275. *R.H.* I, 317 b.

CRACKPOLE. Krakepol, *c.* 1290. D. & C., D ii, 75/1/13. Crapole, 1594. C.C.M. 1565–99, f. 217 b. Contains Scandinavian *Kráka*, often meaning 'crow'. Probably 'water-crake'. The district to the north of Brayford Pool.

CRIKELGATE, 1314. B.B. f. 149. In St Peter *ad placita*. It is difficult to get any firm meaning for *crikel* (as in Cricklewood). The most likely derivation connects it with a ME. dialectal *crickel* meaning 'bend' or the like. If so, this will be 'crooked road'.

CROKEDSTIGH, 1353. B.B. f. 223 b. In St Benedict. 'Crooked path.'

DANESGATE. Danssegate, *c.* 1200. D. & C., D ii, 76/1/12. Danissegate, Daynesgate, 1226–8. *Book of Fees*, I, 363–4. Danisgate. Welbeck Cartulary, f. 105 b. This seems to be 'Danes' street'. If so, presumably it denotes the site of a medieval Danish colony.

DERNSTALL. Dernestall, *c.* 1288. D. & C., D ii, 75/1/25. Dernstall, 1317. B.B. f. 81. 1389. Gild Certificate, no. 144. Danstallak, 1610. C.C.M. 1599–1638, f. 71. For ballads of Little St Hugh, see supra, pp. 230–1. Butcher market in place called Dernestall, Blickling Homilies, p. 237. Literally 'hidden place' from OE. *dierne*, *derne* and *steall*.

DRAPERY. Parmentaria, 1210. *C.R. Rolls*, VI, 67. Forum Draperie, 1257. *C. Chart. R.* I, 467. Draperia, 1275. *R.H.* I, 322 b. The drapers' market.

DRULINLIDE, in or near parish of St Edmund, *c.* 1190. D. & C., D ii, 76/1/13.

EASTGATE. Estgata, 1147. *R.A.* I, 262. Barra de Estgate. Barlings Cartulary, ff. 62, 62 d.

EEL ROW. 1722 deed. Little tenement on north side of river leading to Brayford, in St Benedict.

EXCHEQUERGATE appears to be a modern form. La escheker, 1389. Chapter Acts, Liber VI, f. 22 d. Shops and chambers within lescheker, 1407. Ibid. f. 28. Escheker, Leland, *Itinerary*, v, 122. 'The said Chequer with buildings round about.' Duchy of Lancaster Surveys, James I, f. 142. Chequer gate. D. & C. lease 1623. Chequer square occurs in 1823: it was the name of the quadrangular court formed by two gatehouses (the western one demolished *c.* 1795), St Mary Magdalene's church on the north, and a row of houses on the south.

FLAXENGATE. Flaxgate, 1661. White Book, f. 285.

FOSSDYKE. Fosdig', Fossedike, 1275. *R.H.* I, 310 a, 317 a.

FROSKHOLM, 1344. B.B. f. 165 b. A lane in St Augustine's parish.

FYNKELSTRETE. 1455 deed. Perhaps Rosemary Lane. The meaning is uncertain. *Fenkel* may be a variant of Latin *faeniculum*, street where fennel was sold; or it may be the northern dialect word *fenkl*, a bend or elbow, meaning a corner street. Finkle Street occurs in York, Hull, Carlisle, Nottingham, Oakham and elsewhere.

GARBREDES. D. & C., D ii, 82/2/21. A field name.

LE GARE, 1275. *R.H.* I, 310 b. In the fields.

GOLDERIUMSTYGH, 1336. B.B. f. 130 b. In St John in Wigford's parish.

GOLDINGLAND, 1330. B.B. f. 122. In parish of Holy Cross in Wigford.

GOWTS. Gotes, *c.* 1230. D. & C., D ii, 76/2/32. Ponts de Gotes, 1275. *R.H.* I, 322 a. Le Goytts, 1507. White Book, f. 94 b. Gawt bridge, 1521. C.C.M. 1511–41, f. 128 b. West gote bridge, 1566. C.C.M. 1565–99, f. 12 b.

GREESEN. At the grece foote, 1512. C.C.M. 1511–41, f. 6. Gresse foytt, 1528. *Lincoln Wills* (L.R.S.), II, 84. Greeseing stairs, 1708. C.C.M. 1655–1710, p. 636. The Stairs.

GRESGROUND. Lease of tenement with le Gresgrounde in Holy Trinity in Wigford, 1550. *Chapter Acts* (L.R.S.), III, 43.

LE GULLE, lake called, 1409. *C.P.R.* 1408–13, p. 137.

HALIWELGATE, 1275. *R.H.* I, 310 a. 'Holy-well-road.'

HARALDSTIGH. Haraldsti, temp. John, D. & C., D ii, 80/3/54. Haraldstigh, *c.* 1299. D ii, 75/2/25.

HEMPGARTH. 1455 deed.

HERMIT STREET is named from Henry Chaplin's Derby winner of 1867, which was kept in a field there.

HIGH BRIDGE. Pons magna, 1146. *R.A.* I, 200. High bryg, 1527. *Lincoln Wills* (L.R.S.), II, 56.

HIGH MARKET. Land *in alto mercato*, *c.* 1220. D. & C., D ii, 76/2/4. *In alto foro*, 1226–8. *Book of Fees*, I, 365.

HIGH STREET. Vicus magnus, 1146. *R.A.* I, 198.

HOLGATE. Hollegate, 1308–9. B.B. f. 199. In Holy Trinity on the Hill. See Pottergate. A hollow road under the city wall.

HORNERGATE, 1324. B.B. f. 100.

HORNESTY, 1226–8. *Book of Fees*, I, 363, 366.

HUDEKIN CROFT, 1275. *R.H.* I, 317 b.

HUMBERSTREET. Humberstrete, *c.* 1270. D. & C., D ii, 82/1/21. Humbrestret, 1328. B.B. f. 107 b. Land in Humberscot, 1324. B.B. f. 100. The road to the Humber: Ermine Street.

HUNGATE. Hundegata, 1126. *R.A.* 1, 188. Hundegate, 1228. D. & C., D ii, 75/2/2. 'Hounds' street', found at York and Nottingham.

KIRTONGATE. Kirketongate, 1324. B.B. f. 100. In the fields, apparently now represented by Burton Road. Road to Kirton in Lindsey.

KRINGLES, *c.* 1270. D. & C., D ii, 82/1/21. A field name. 'The circles', from OS. *Kringla.*

LANGWATHSTRETE, 1275. *R.H.* 1, 318 a. Langwithgate, *c.* 1536. P.R.O. Lists and Indexes, xxv, E 315, vol. 397, f. 106. Street (Roman road) going to Langworth.

LANNERSTITH, 1347. B.B. f. 178 b. In St Martin.

LEWYNSTIGH, *c.* 1270. D. & C., D ii, 75/1/11. Adjoined land which once belonged to William son of Ralf son of Lewyn. Probably Mint Street district. OE. Lēofwine.

LONGDALES. Langedales, 1324. B.B. f. 100. 'Long strips' in the open field, from OE. *dāl*, 'share', 'lot'.

LUCY TOWER. Lewcie Tower, 1611. Register of Leases, Corporation MSS. refers to small tower north of Brayford; supra, p. 86.

LUMNOUR LANE, 1366. B.B. f. 260 b. Probably in St Rumbold or St Augustine.

MAKHATSTIGH, 1535–6. White Book, f. 113 b. Makeheytstith, *c.* 1624. Ibid. f. 244.

MARY BRIDGE, 1589. C.C.M. 1565–99, f. 190 b. Over Sincil Dyke in the present St Mary Street (in St Mary le Wigford).

MICKLEGATE. Mikelgate, 1228. D. & C., D ii, 75/2/2. Myckelgate, *c.* 1250. D ii, 75/2/6. Mikklygate in St Peter at Arches, 1343. B.B. f. 159 b. 'Great road.'

MIDHERGATE, *c.* 1230. D. & C., D ii, 81/1/10. St Stephen's church stood here. Probably Orchard Street.

MISTERSTALL, 1324. B.B. f. 97.

MOTSTON. St Peter ad motston. Thurgarton Cartulary, f. 157 b. Usually appears as St Peter *ad placita*. OE. *mōt stān*, the moot stone.

NETELHAMGATE, 1275. *R.H.* 1, 310 b. The road to Nettleham.

NEWGATE, 1349. B.B. f. 193. Messuage in Hungate abutting on Newyat north. Newyate, 1564. Lease of Saffron garth (between west city wall and the modern Spring Hill) lying next the newyate. C.C.M. 1541–64, f. 190.

NEWLAND. Nova Terra, 1163–6. *D.C.* p. 343. 1202. *Earliest Lincs Assize Rolls* (L.R.S.), p. 167. Constancius de Neweland, 1206. Ibid. p. 261. Le Neuland in the suburb, 1331. B.B. f. 127 b. Land north of Brayford, reclaimed from the pool.

NEWPORT. Neuportia, ? *c.* 1150. D. & C., D ii, 77/2/40. Neuporth, Neuport, Niweport, 1202–6. *Earliest Lincs Assize Rolls* (L.R.S.), pp. 162, 167, 261. Supra, p. 169.

NICHORPOOL. Nykarpole, 1409. *C.P.R.* 1408–13, p. 137. Nycharpool, 1549. C.C.M. 1541–64, f. 104. Nicopoole, 1619. Register of Leases, Corporation MSS. 'Pool of the water-sprite.'

NORTHGATE, 1349. B.B. f. 199 b.

OLDHUNGATE. Aldhundegate, 1275. *R.H.* 1, 321 a. Oldhundegate, 1369. B.B. f. 269. In St Mary Crackpole, apparently the old name for the street called Beaumont Fee.

ORDEPIT WELLE, 1275. *R.H.* I, 310 a.

PANTENERSTRETE, 1349. B.B. f. 195 b. In the fields.

PARCHEMINGATE. Welbeck Cartulary, f. 106. In parish of St Peter (Stanthaket). Street of the parchment-makers.

LES PETTES, 1324. B.B. f. 100. The pits.

PIKENHOUPIT, *c.* 1270. D. & C., D ii, 82/1/21.

POTTERGATE. Poteregate, 'Vita S. Hugonis', in Giraldus Cambrensis, *Opera* (R.S.), VII, 133. Potteregate, Richard I, *D.C.* p. 17. Pottergathe, *c.* 1215. D. & C., D ii, 79/1/131. Pottergate, *c.* 1230. D ii, 79/1/102. Holgate or Potergate, *c.* 1620. Register of Leases, Corporation MSS.

POULTRY HILL. Pultria in St Martin, 1345. B.B. f. 171. Le pultri, 1349. B.B. f. 198. Pultry Hill, 1554. C.C.M. 1541–64, f. 115 b. Polther Hill in St Michael on the Mount, 1601. White Book, f. 196 b. Steep Hill. Poultry market.

PRIORYGATE. This arch was so misnamed in the nineteenth century, following the adoption of the name 'the Priory' by occupants of the house to the east of it. The Priory estate is mentioned in 1824.

PYTING LANE, 1331. B.B. f. 124 b. In St Swithin.

ST FAITH'S LEYS, 1539. C.C.M. 1511–64, f. 274. Near St Faith's church.

ST GILES GATE. Seyntgiligate, *c.* 1225. D. & C., D ii, 79/3/70. In St Peter in Eastgate. The road leading to St Giles' Hospital.

ST HUGH CROFT. St Hewecroft. 1455 deed. Hugh Croft, 1505. *Lincoln Wills* (L.R.S.), I, 25. South of Monks Road, so called because St Hugh's fair was held there.

ST JOHN'S WONG. 1455 deed. Probably now the site of the County Hospital.

ST MARY STIGH. Saintemariestich, temp. John. D. & C., D ii, 80/3/55. Saintemaristig, *c.* 1230. D ii, 80/3/41. Sayntmaristygh, 1329. B.B. f. 113. St Mary's Stigh, 1685. C.C.M. 1655–1710, p. 397. In St Peter at Arches, now Much Lane; supra, p. 132.

SALTERGATE, *c.* 1260. D. & C., D ii, 76/1/32. 1346. B.B. f. 176 b.

SAPERGATE. Thurgarton Cartulary, f. 157 b. Soper lane, 1330. Birch, p. 55. 'Soap-maker street.'

SASTANGATE. Sextonesgate in St Nicholas, 1226–8. *Book of Fees*, I, 364. Sostancgat, 1253. *R.A.* II, 109. Saxstangate, 1303. *Cal. Inq. Misc.* I, no. 1939. This looks like 'Seaxstān's street', from an OE. personal name Seaxstān, and if the first form is correct, no other meaning seems possible.

SCHOLEGATE. Skolegate, 1328. B.B. f. 109 b. 1516. C.C.M. 1511–41, f. 59 b. Scholegate, 1601. White Book, f. 196 b. In St George, later St Michael on the Mount.

SILVERBRIGG, 1308. Chapter Acts, Liber I, f. 13 v. Silverbreg, 1349. B.B. f. 189. A bridge over the Witham.

SILVERDYKE, 1348. B.B. f. 182.

SILVER LANE, 1328. B.B. f. 109 b. Tenement in St Cuthbert, bounded by Silver Lane on the south, 1361. B.B. f. 246 b.

SINCIL DYKE, 1539. C.C.M. 1511–41, f. 273 b. Synsell dyke. Foster Library, seventeenth century. Also called Silverdyke, and, earlier, *le old eye,* 1513–14. White Book, f. 96.

SKYNNERGATE, 1347. B.B. f. 178 b. In St Martin.

SNEKEDIKEWALL. 1455 deed.

SPAROWE LANE. 1455 deed.

SPITAL STREET, Spitil Stret, 1509. *Lincoln Wills* (L.R.S.), I, 39.

SPITEL GRENE, 1275. *R.H.* I, 327 b.

SPOUTELANE, 1360. B.B. f. 244. Land in St Bavon, abutting on the cemetery of St Peter *ad fontem* to the east and Spoutelane to the west. 1354. P.R.O. Lists 5, Ministers' Accounts, Pt I, Bundle 913, no. I.

STAGGARTHES, 1352. B.B. f. 220 b. Plot of land in St Clement in Butwerk.

STAMP. Wall called the Stamp. Stamp causeway. 1455 deed. 1521. C.C.M. 1511–41, f. 132. Banks at Stamp End, 1630. C.C.M. 1599–1638, f. 240.

STANTHAKET (St Peter). Stanteked, *c.* 1200. D. & C., D ii, 80/3/8. Stantheked. D ii, 80/3/5. Stanheghet. Late twelfth century? D ii, 80/3/3. Lapide coopt. 1259. D ii, 80/3/1. Monasterium Sancti Petri in Lincolnia quod vocatur Petra tectum. Henry of Pytchley, Liber Cartarum, unnumbered folio between 13 and 14. 'Stone-thatched.'

STAYNEGATE, 1226–8. *Book of Fees*, I, 363. 'Stone street', with OS. *steinn* as the first element; cf. Stonegate, York, where the first word was originally *steiun.*

STODFALDES, *c.* 1225. D. & C., D ii, 78/2/50. From OE. *stōd*, 'stud', and *falod*, 'fold'.

STONEBOW. Stanboge, late twelfth century. D. & C., D ii, 80/3/49. Houses in 'la Stanbegh', 1231. *Final Concords*, I, 240. OS. *stein-bogi*, arch of stone.

STUBCROSS. 1455 deed.

TENTERCROFT, *c.* 1616. Register of Leases, Corporation MSS. Now Tentercroft Street in St Mark. Tentergarth in St Martin in Newland, bounded by city wall on the west, 1575. White Book, f. 164. Another Tentergarth near Clasketgate, 1623. White Book, f. 242 b. Named from frames for stretching cloth.

THORN BRIDGE. 'Pons de Thorn', *c.* 1230–40. D. & C., D ii, 76/1/26.

THORNGATE. Thornegate, late twelfth century. D. & C., D ii, 82/2/129. (See *R.A.* I, 277.)

TOFTSTEDES, *c.* 1270. D. & C., D ii, 82/1/21.

TOWERGARTH, 1573. C.C.M. 1565–99, f. 73 b. At junction of eastern city wall with river bank.

WAINWELLSTIGH. Waynwellgate, *c.* 1220. D. & C., D ii, 78/2/57. Waynewellestifh, *c.* 1260. D ii, 79/3/73. Winnowsty Lane. Path for carts or wains.

WALBURPIT, *c.* 1270. D. & C., D ii, 82/1/21.

WALKERGATE, 1241. Thurgarton Cartulary, f. 160. Walker's Lane, in St Peter at Arches, leading down to Brayford Head, 1693. C.C.M. 1655–1710, p. 486. The street of the fullers of cloth. Probably Water Lane.

WARKDYKE, *c.* 1296. D. & C., D ii, 74/2/19. 1527. C.C.M. 1511–41, f. 197 b. OS. *virki*, OE. *geweorc*. The ditch near the fortification: i.e. the ditch outside the east wall of the lower city, now levelled and become Broadgate.

WATERGANG, *c.* 1230. D. & C., D ii, 76/2/32. In St Michael in Wigford.

WATERGANGSTIGH, 1328. B.B. f. 108 b. Watergangstreet, 1275. *R.H.* I, 326 a. Lane leading from the modern Saltergate to the Waterside.

WAXSCOPES, 1349. B.B. f. 194 b. Near St Martin's churchyard.

WIGFORD. Wikeford, 1146. *R.A.* I, 200. Wikeforda, Wickeforda, late twelfth century. *D.C.* pp. 51, 147. Wicheford, twelfth century. Giraldus Cambrensis, *Opera* (R.S.), VII, 155. Supra, p. 35.

WILLINGTHORPE. Willigtorp, 1126. *R.A.* I, 188. Willingtorp, 1163–6. *D.C.* p. 343. Supra, p. 328.

WINGARTH. Vinea, *c.* 1103. *R.A.* I, 22. Wingarth in parish of St Margaret, *c.* 1221. D. & C., D ii, 79/1/122. Wyngard, *c.* 1260. D ii, 76/1/53. Vineyard.

WINTREGATE. Wintregat', 1275. *R.H.* I, 317 b.

WITHAM. Withma, late twelfth century. *D.C.* p. 52.

WONG, 1537. C.C.M. 1511–41, f. 260.

APPENDIX II

LINCOLN IN DOMESDAY BOOK

The text and translation are taken from the *Lincolnshire Domesday*, edited by C. W. Foster and T. Longley for the Lincoln Record Society (1924). The passage quoted occurs at folios 336, 336 d in the Record Commission's edition of *Domesday Book*, and at pp. i and ii of the facsimile edition (Lincolnshire volume) published by the Ordnance Survey Office (1862).

⌈ ⌉ These signs indicate that the words or letters which they enclose are interlined.

⌊ ⌋ These signs indicate that the words or letters which they enclose have been added to elucidate the text.

T.R.E. means *Tempore Regis Edwardi*, i.e. A.D. 1066.

[CIVITAS LINCOLIA]

1. In CIVITATE LINCOLIA . erant tempore regis Eduuardi nouies centum et lxx . mansiones hospitate . Hic numerus anglice computatur . i. centum pro . c^{tum} xx^{ti}. In ipsa ciuitate erant . xii . lageman . idest habentes sacam et socam . Hardecnut . Suartin . filius . Grimboldi . Vlf filius Suertebrand . qui habuit thol et theim . Walrauen . Aluuold . Britric . Guret . Vlbert . Godric . filius . Eddeue . Siuuard [presbyter] . Leuuine [presbyter]. Aldene [presbyter].

2. Modo sunt ibi totidem . habentes similiter sacam et socam . [.i.] Suardinc loco Hardecnut patris sui . [.ii.] Suartinc . [.iii.] Sortebrand loco Vlf patris sui . [.iiii.] Agemund loco Walrauen patris sui . [.v.] Aluuold . [.vi.] Goduinus filius Brictric . [vii.] Normannus Crassus loco Guret . [.viii.] Vlbert frater Vlf adhuc uiuit . [.ix.] Petrus de Ualonges loco Godric filii Eddeue . [.x.] Vlnodus presbyter loco Siuuard . presbyteri . [xi.] Buruolt loco patris sui Leuuine qui modo . est monachus . [.xii.] Leduuinus filius Rauene loco Aldene presbyteri.

3. Tochi filius Outi habuit in ciuitate .xxx. mansiones pręter suam hallam . et ii. ęcclesias et dimidiam . et suam hallam habuit quietam ab omni consuetudine . et super alias xxx. mansiones habuit locationem . et pręter hoc de una quaque unum denarium idest landgable . Super has .xxx. mansiones habebat rex theloneum et forisfacturam . ut burgenses iurauerunt . Sed his iurantibus contradicit Vluiet presbyter . et offert se portaturum iudicium quod non ita est sicuti dicunt . Hanc aulam tenet Goisfridus Alselin . et suus nepos Radulfus . Remigius episcopus tenet supradictas .xxx. mansiones in ęcclesia Sancte Marię . ita quod Goisfridus Alselin nichil inde habet . neque scangium neque aliam redditionem . Isdem Goisfridus habet .i. mansionem extra murum . unde habet landgable . sicut habuit Tochi.

4. Radulfus Pagenel habet .i. mansionem quę fuit Merlesuen . quietam ab omni consuetudine.

5. Ernuin presbyter habet .i. mansionem Morcari [comitis] cum saca et soca . et sic de rege tenet sicut Morcar habuit . ut ipse dicit.

6. Gislebertus de Gand habet .i. mansionem . Vlf . cum saca et soca . et aliam mansionem unde habebat .i. denarium . et iterum .i. mansionem . Siuuard quietam ab omni consuetudine.

7. Comes Hugo habet .i. mansionem comitis Heroldi . cum saca et soca . et ii. mansiones unde habet landgable.

8. Rogerus de Busli habet .i. mansionem Suen . filii . Suaue . cum saca et soca.

9. Judita comitissa . habet .i. mansionem Stori sine saca et soca . et hanc calumniatur Iuo Taillebosc per burgenses.

10. Remigius episcopus habet .i. maneriolum cum .i. carucata contiguum[1] ciuitati[2] Lincolię[3] . cum saca et soca et cum thol et theim . et super iii. mansiones similiter . et super .ii. ęcclesias . et super .lxx viii. mansiones similiter . pręter geldum regis quod dant cum burgensibus . Ex his sunt .xx. mansiones wastę .

[1] *contiguum* has been interlined by way of correction above *in*.
[2] *ti* has been interlined by way of correction above final *te* of *ciuitate*.
[3] *ę* has been interlined by way of correction above the final *a* of *Lincolia*.

[THE CITY OF LINCOLN]

1. In the CITY of LINCOLN there were T.R.E. 970 inhabited messuages. This number is reckoned according to the English method, 100 counting for 120. In the same city there were 12 lawmen, that is ⌊men⌋ having sake and soke: Hardecnut; Suartin son of Grimbold; Ulf son of Suertebrand, who had toll and team; Walraven; Alwold; Britric; Guret; Ulbert; Godric son of Eddeve; Siward [the priest]; Lewine [the priest]; and Aldene [the priest].

2. Now there are as many there having sake and soke in like manner: [1] Suardinc in the place of his father Hardecnut; [2] Suartinc; [3] Sortebrand in the place of his father Ulf; [4] Agemund in the place of his father Walraven; [5] Alwold; [6] Godwin son of Brictric; [7] Norman Crassus in the place of Guret; [8] Ulbert, brother of Ulf, who is still living; [9] Peter of Valognes in the place of Godric son of Eddeve; [10] Ulnod the priest in the place of Siward the priest; [11] Buruolt in the place of his father Lewine who is now a monk; [12] Ledwin son of Ravene in the place of Aldene the priest.

3. Tochi son of Outi had in the city 30 messuages besides his hall and 2½ churches. And he had his hall quit of all custom. And with respect to other 30 messuages he had by way of letting; and in addition to this ⌊he had⌋ from each ⌊messuage⌋ one penny, that is 'landgable'. Upon these 30 messuages the king used to have toll and forfeiture, as the burgesses made oath. But Ulviet the priest gainsays what they say thus upon their oath, and proffers himself to prove by the ordeal of fire that it is not as they say. Geoffrey Alselin holds this hall, and his *nepos* Ralf. Bishop Remigius holds the aforesaid 30 messuages in respect of the church of Saint Mary, so that Geoffrey Alselin has nothing therein either by way of exchange or other render. The same Geoffrey has 1 messuage outside the wall, wherefrom he has 'landgable', as Tochi had.

4. Ralf Pagenel has 1 messuage, which was Merlesuen's, quit of all custom.

5. Ernuin the priest has 1 messuage ⌊which was⌋ [Earl] Morcar's, with sake and soke; and he holds it of the king in the same way as Morcar had ⌊it⌋, as he himself says.

6. Gilbert of Gant has 1 messuage, ⌊which was⌋ Ulf's, with sake and soke; and another messuage wherefrom he used to have 1 penny; and yet again, 1 messuage, ⌊which was⌋ Siward's, quit of all custom.

7. Earl Hugh has 1 messuage, ⌊which was⌋ Earl Harold's, with sake and soke; and 2 messuages wherefrom he has 'landgable'.

8. Roger de Busli has 1 messuage, ⌊which was⌋ Suen the son of Suaue's, with sake and soke.

9. Countess Judith has 1 messuage, ⌊which was⌋ Stori's, without sake and soke; and Ivo Tailleboisc claims this through the burgesses.

10. Bishop Remigius has 1 little manor with 1 carucate ⌊of land⌋ near[1] the city of Lincoln with sake and soke and with toll and team ⌊over it⌋; and likewise over 3 messuages, and over 2 churches, and likewise over 78 messuages, except for the king's geld which they give with the burgesses. Of these messuages 20

[1] See nn. 1–3, p. 368.

De tribus superioribus mansionibus est .i. quieta ab omnibus rebus . duę uero sunt in geldo cum burgensibus.

11. In campis Lincolię extra ciuitatem sunt xii. carucatę terrę et dimidia . prętor carucatam episcopi ciuitatis . De hac terra habent rex et comes .viii. carucatas in dominio . Ex his dedit unam rex Willelmus cuidam Vlchel pro una naui quam ab eo emit . Ille uero qui nauim uendidit mortuus . est . et hanc carucatam terre nullus habet nisi rege concedente . Pręter has .viii. carucatas . habet rex et comes cc et xxx.i. acras terrę arabilis inland . et c. acras prati.

12. De reliqua terra idest .iiii. carucate et dimidia: T.R.E. habuit Vlf .i. carucatam . nunc habet filius eius Sortebrand.

13. Aliam carucatam . T.R.E. habuerunt Siuuard presbyter et Outi . et vi . acras terrę quas tenet Vluiet presbyter . Nunc habet Alfnod medietatem huius carucatę . et Norman filius Siuuard presbyteri alteram medietatem . Hanc uero predictam medietatem istius terre . et uxorem Siuuardi presbyteri inuasit Vnlof presbyter dum erat in saisitione regis propter .xl. solidos quos ipsemet rex imposuerat super Siuuardum presbyterum.

14. Terciam carucatam habet Petrus de Valongies . quam habet Godricus T.R.E.

15. Quarta carucata adiacuit in ęcclesia omnium sanctorum . T.R.E. et xii. toftes . et iiii. croftes . Hanc ęcclesiam et terram ęcclesię et quicquid ad eam pertinet . habuit Godricus filius Gareuinę . Sed eo facto monacho . abbas de Burg[1] obtinet . Burgenses uero omnes Lincolię dicunt quod injuste habet . quia nec Gareuin nec Godricus filius eius nec ullus alius dare potuerit extra ciuitatem nec extra parentes eorum . nisi concessu regis . Hanc ęcclesiam et que ibi pertinent clamat Ernuin presbyter[1] hereditate Godrici consanguinei sui.

16. Residuam dimidiam carucatam terrę habuit et habet sancta Maria de Lincolia . in qua nunc est episcopatus.

17. Inter ęcclesias Lincolię et burgenses . habuerunt . xxx. vi. croftes in Lincolia . exceptis .xii. et dimidia carucatis terrę quę [supra] enumeratę sunt.

18. Ex predictis mansionibus quę T.R.E. fuerunt hospitatę . sunt modo waste .cc. anglico numero .*id.* cc.xl. et eodem numero septies centum et lx. sunt modo hospitatę.

19. Hi subscripti non dederunt geldum regis sicut debuissent . Terra sancte Marie in qua Tedbertus manet in magno uico . non dedit geldum . neque terra episcopi ad sanctum Laurentium posita . non dedit geldum de .i. domo.

Abbas de Burg de .i. domo et de .iii. toftis non dedit geldum . Hugo [comes] de omni terra sua non dedit geldum . neque Turaldus de Greteuilla . neque Losuardus . neque Chetelbertus . Hugo . filius . Baldrici non dedit geldum de .ii. toftis . Neque Goisfridus Alselin . similiter de .ii. toftis.

Neque Gislebertus de .iii. domibus dedit geldum . Neque Petrus de Ualonges de sua domo . Neque Judita [comitissa] de sua domo . Neque Radulfus Pagenel de .i. domo . Neque Radulfus de Badpalmas de sua domo . Neque Ertaldus de sua domo.

[1] There is a blank space here of about a quarter of an inch.

are waste. Of the 3 messuages aforesaid one is quit of all things, but two geld with the burgesses.

11. In the fields of Lincoln outside the city there are 12½ carucates of land, besides the carucate of the bishop of the city. Of this land the king and the earl have 8 carucates in demesne. Of these King William gave one ⌊carucate⌋ to a certain Ulchel for a ship which he bought from him. But he who sold the ship is dead, and no one has this carucate of land unless the king grant ⌊it⌋. In addition to these 8 carucates the king and the earl have 231 acres of arable land ⌊which is⌋ inland, and 100 acres of meadow.

12. Of the rest of the land, that is 4½ carucates, Ulf had T.R.E. 1 carucate: now his son Sortebrand has it.

13. Siward the priest and Outi had another carucate T.R.E., and 6 acres of land which Ulviet the priest holds. Now Alfnod has a moiety of this carucate, and Norman son of Siward the priest has the other moiety. But Unlof the priest invaded this aforesaid moiety of this land and Siward the priest's wife, while it was in the seisin of the king on account of ⌊a fine of⌋ 40 shillings which the king himself had laid upon Siward the priest.

14. Peter de Valognes has the third carucate, which T.R.E. Godric had.

15. The fourth carucate belonged to the church of All Saints T.R.E., and 12 tofts and 4 crofts. Godric son of Gareuine had this church, and the church's land, and whatever belonged to it; but, on his becoming a monk, the abbot of Peterborough obtains it. But all the burgesses of Lincoln say that he has it unjustly, because neither Gareuine nor his son Godric nor any one else could give it outside the city or outside their kindred, except by grant of the king. This church and what belongs thereto Ernuin the priest claims by inheritance from his kinsman Godric.

16. Saint Mary of Lincoln, in which the bishopric now is, had and has the remaining half carucate of land.

17. The churches of Lincoln and the burgesses had among them 36 crofts in Lincoln, excepting the 12½ carucates of land which are enumerated ⌈above⌉.

18. Of the aforesaid messuages which were inhabited T.R.E., there are now waste 200 by English reckoning, that is 240; and by the same reckoning 760 are now inhabited.

19. Those written below have not paid the king's geld as they ought:
The land of Saint Mary on which Tedbert dwells in the high street has not paid geld; nor has the bishop's land situate at Saint Laurence's paid geld in respect of 1 house.

The abbot of Peterborough has not paid geld in respect of 1 house and 3 tofts.

⌈Earl⌉ Hugh has not paid geld in respect of any of his land; nor ⌊has⌋ Thorold of Greetwell (Lawress), nor Losuard, nor Chetelbert.

Hugh son of Baldric has not paid geld in respect of 2 tofts; nor Geoffrey Alselin likewise in respect of 2 tofts.

Nor has Gilbert paid geld in respect of 3 houses. Nor has Peter de Valognes in respect of his house. Nor ⌊has⌋ the ⌈Countess⌉ Judith in respect of her house. Nor ⌊has⌋ Ralf Pagenel in respect of 1 house. Nor ⌊has⌋ Ralf of Bapaume in respect of his house. Nor ⌊has⌋ Ertald in respect of his house.

20. Domum de qua abbas de Burg ut dictum est non dedit . geldum; ipsam clamat Normannus [Crassus] de feuo regis . Ipsam enim habuit Godredus antecessor suus in uadimonio pro tribus markis argenti et dimidia.

21. Colsuen habet in Lincolia ciuitate .iiii. toftes de terra Cole nepotis sui . et extra ciuitatem habet xxx. vi. domos et ii. ęcclesias in quibus nichil adiacet . quas hospitauit in wasta terra quam rex sibi dedit . et quę nunquam ante hospitata fuit. Modo habet rex omnes consuetudines ex eis.

22. Aluredus nepos Turoldi habet .iii. toftes de terra Sybi . quam rex sibi dedit . in quibus habet omnes consuetudines . pręter geldum regis de monedagio.

23. Abbas de Elyg habet dimidiam mansionem de terra Edstan.

24. Hugo . filius . Baldrici . habet .ii. toftes quas rex sibi dedit.

25. De predictis wastis mansionibus . propter castellum destructę fuerunt c.lx.vi. Relique .lxx.iiii. wastatę sunt extra metam castelli . non propter oppressionem uicomitum et ministrorum⁝ sed propter infortunium et paupertatem . et ignium exustionem.

26. T.R.E. reddebat ciuitas Lincolia regi .xx. libras . et comiti .x. libras. Modo reddit .c. libras ad numerum . inter regem et comitem . Moneta uero reddit .lxx.v. libras.

20. The house in respect of which the abbot of Peterborough has not, as they say, paid geld Norman [Crassus] claims [as] of the king's fee, for Godred his predecessor had it in gage for 3½ marks of silver.

21. Colsuen has in the city of Lincoln 4 tofts of his *nepos* Cole's land; and outside the city he has 36 houses and 2 churches to which nothing belongs, which he built on the waste land that the king gave him, and that was never before built upon. Now the king has all the customs from them.

22. Alfred, Thorold's *nepos*, has 3 tofts from Sybi's land, which the king gave him, in which he has all customs except the king's geld in respect of minting.

23. The abbot of Ely has half a messuage from Edstan's land.

24. Hugh son of Baldric has 2 tofts which the king gave him.

25. Of the aforesaid waste messuages, 166 were destroyed on account of the castle. The remaining 74 are waste outside the castle boundary, not because of the oppression of the sheriffs and officers but by reason of misfortune and poverty and the ravage of fires.

26. T.R.E. the city of Lincoln used to render to the king 20 pounds and to the earl 10 pounds. Now it renders 100 pounds by tale between the king and the earl. The mint, however, renders 75 pounds.

APPENDIX III

SOME MINSTER NOTES

(1) *The tombs of Remigius*

According to Giraldus, who wrote about 1200, Remigius was buried in his cathedral before the altar of the Holy Cross. He also says that during a fire about the year 1124, while the flames were raging in the cathedral roof, some fragments, falling to the ground, broke in the middle the stone which was laid over his body; the body had then been removed from its original resting-place before the altar of the Holy Cross because it was subject to the too-frequent tread of persons passing over it, and buried at the north side of the altar (*Opera* (R.S.), VII, 25, 26). The account of a fire about 1124 is open to suspicion: but such a mishap to the tombstone might have occurred at another date. Nothing more is known of the original burial place of Remigius.

About 1857 the Rev. G. A. Poole found in the cathedral cloisters a coffin lid, carved with a Jesse tree, and broken across the middle, which he claimed to identify as that of Remigius: 'everything, date, size, character, the very marks of a singular accident, is repeated in this stone' ('The Tomb of Remigius' in *A.A.S.R.* XIV (1877), pp. 21–6). Mr Poole's theory was officially adopted. In 1872 the coffin lid was brought into the nave, and raised on two slabs to the north of the altar there: this was presumed to be its former position. Upon the upper slab was placed an inscription from the pen of Bishop Wordsworth. Unfortunately for Mr Poole's claim, the carving upon the stone cannot be dated before the later part of the twelfth century, and the work cannot have been carried out when Remigius died, or even in time to be broken in the fire described by Giraldus (Clapham, *English Romanesque Architecture after the Conquest* (1934), p. 159, and an opinion expressed by Sir Alfred Clapham to the writer; see also Watson, *Early Iconography of the Tree of Jesse* (1934)).

After the Restoration of Charles II Bishop Fuller erected a tablet on a tomb on the north side of the high altar, and adjoining the Easter Sepulchre, recording that there were the remains of Remigius the founder; an identification not accepted by the late Precentor Venables, and not proved, as is generally supposed, by a recent opening of the tomb. (See the account of the opening written by Bishop Hine in *A.A.S.R.* XXXVIII (1926), p. vii, and the comment of the Rev. Algernon Curtois on p. lx.) Probably Fuller was relying upon the evidence of Robert Sanderson, his predecessor in the see, who, describing the cathedral monuments, said

> On the north side [of the high altar] two tombs, not known. But it is famed one of them is Remigius; whose bare sheet of lead is now (MDCLVIII) to be seen. No inscription, coat, or other mention of any one. (Peck, *Desiderata Curiosa* (1779), p. 300.)

The only other evidence adduced to support this identification of Remigius' tomb comes from the *Customs of Divine Service* in the Black Book of the dean and chapter. This document directs the censing of the high altar, the tomb of

Remigius, the altar for the mass of the Blessed Virgin Mary, and the tomb of St Hugh in that order (*L.C.S.* I, 368). Such a sequence suggests that the tomb of Remigius was near to the high altar. It is to be noted, however, that the *Customs* were compiled about the year 1260; the Angel Choir—the part of the cathedral east of the lesser transepts, including the high altar and the tombs near it—was not completed before 1280; and the tomb in question, on architectural grounds, can hardly be earlier than 1300. The argument would therefore imply that Remigius' tomb occupied a position near to the high altar in St Hugh's apse; this may be so, and it may also be that a new tomb was given a like position in the new choir. Yet there is no evidence other than the *Customs* that the remains of the bishop rested near the high altar, and indeed there is no proof that they were ever moved from the north side of the altar of the Holy Cross.

For a time after his death Remigius enjoyed a local reputation as a saint, but his shrine was eclipsed in popularity by that of St Hugh, and later also by that of Grosseteste. The wardrobe accounts of Edward I record the giving of alms in the cathedral at the shrine of St Hugh the bishop, the head of the same saint, the tombs of the saints Remigius and Robert Grosseteste the bishops, and of Hugh the Martyr. Prince Edward's offerings were made at St Hugh's shrine, the saint's head, the tomb of St Robert and the high altar (*Liber Quotidianus Contrarotulatoris Garderobae*, pp. 37, 39). There were keepers of the tombs or shrines of St Hugh and St Robert (Grosseteste), and in 1322 there were complaints of the falling off of customary offerings there (*L.C.S.* I, 122, 335–9). There is no sign of a keeper of the tomb of Remigius (Wordsworth, *Notes on Mediaeval Services*, p. 295). The offerings at shrines in the accounts for 1420–1 include 45*s.* at the image of Blessed Mary on the south side of the choir, and 11*d.* in offerings on the north side of the choir (ibid. p. 109): the accounts do not refer to the tomb of Remigius as being there.

(2) *The Church of St Mary Magdalene*

John de Schalby, a canon of Lincoln who was registrar to Bishop Oliver Sutton (1280–99), says in his *Lives of the Bishops of Lincoln* that Remigius built his cathedral church on a site on which had stood the church of St Mary Magdalene in the Bail of Lincoln; that the parishioners of St Mary Magdalene heard divine service in a certain part of the cathedral, their children were baptised in the cathedral font, and their dead buried in the cathedral cemetery; and that a certain priest, deputed by the dean and chapter, ministered to them. Later, in his account of Bishop Sutton, Schalby says that the parishioners had used the western part of the cathedral; and that for the peace of the choir and the security of the church Sutton built a church for them in the cathedral churchyard (Giraldus Cambrensis, *Opera* (R.S.), VII, 194, 209; and see *L.C.S.* II, p. lxxii). The church he built was St Mary Magdalene, and it stood on the site still occupied by the church of that name.

Schalby's evidence of the activities of Bishop Sutton is of high authority, but for the state of things when Remigius planned his new church, 250 years earlier, his evidence is of less value. He says that the church removed by Remigius was St Mary Magdalene, implying that the bishop made an entirely fresh start with his new church of St Mary. His statement has been accepted by modern local historians (e.g. Sympson, *Lincoln*, p. 328); and it has obscured the pre-Conquest history of St Mary. That St Mary of Lincoln existed before the bishop transferred his seat to it is conclusively proved by Domesday Book (supra, p. 67). There was no church of St Mary Magdalene until Bishop Sutton built it.

The new dedication was, however, coming into use before the church was built. About 1218 W. archdeacon of Buckingham, being about to cross the sea, made over to the dean and chapter his houses in the churchyard of the church of Lincoln for division between two of the canons. A later endorsement upon his charter notes that the document refers to two houses near the church of St Mary Magdalene in the corner towards the north which the vicars then held (D. & C., D ii, 81/1/46). About 1248 Alice, wife of Geoffrey the cooper, released to the fabric her dower in land between Simon the carter's and Alan the spicer's in the Bail in the parish of St Mary Magdalene (D. & C., D ii, 81/1/34; these were probably stalls in the churchyard; see also D ii, 81/1/38, and *R.H.* I, 312 a, where seventeen stalls in the churchyard of the mother church are mentioned).

The explanation of this reference to St Mary Magdalene before the building of the new parish church is given in a note in the *Registrum Antiquissimum* of the dean and chapter, written in a hand which Canon Foster has identified as that of John de Schalby. The note refers to the chapel of Magdalene which was formerly within the church and afterwards, by order of Bishop Oliver Sutton and the dean and chapter, placed outside the church in the churchyard, for the peace of the choir and the security of the church, and the convenience of parishioners for divine service in time of need and otherwise (*R.A.* III, 403). Canon Christopher Wordsworth was inclined to place the Magdalene chapel in the cathedral in the north-west corner of the nave (*L.C.S.* II, pp. lxx, cclxii; *Mediaeval Services in England*, p. 183); and when it is recalled that the nave was being built from about 1230 to 1250 it will be seen how Schalby's note fits the charter evidence. The building of the nave provided an opportunity of moving the parishioners into a side chapel, which may presently have acquired the reputation and status of a parish church. Thereafter they were moved to a new church in the old churchyard. The witness clauses of charters illustrate these stages: about 1250 appears Godred, vicar of Magdalene, and about 1275 John de North Leverton, rector of the church of St Mary Magdalene (D. & C., D ii, 77/3/2, 11).

Leland, writing about 1536, had part of the story right. He said that Bishop Gwyney (no doubt meaning Gynwell, though herein he was wrong) builded a great chapel of St Magdalene without the very north wall, but joining on the north side of the cathedral church, and founded five chantries; and that this church was afterwards translated into the north side of the *esheker* (*Itinerary*, V, 122). There is no evidence of a dedication to St Mary Magdalene before the chapel at the north-west corner of the nave was built, and this is not surprising, for it is not a dedication found in early times.

An incident in the life of St Hugh suggests a possible reason for the adoption of the dedication. St Hugh obtained pieces of a bone of the saint by biting them from a bone belonging to the abbey of Fécamp in Normandy, to the wrath of the abbot and monks (*Magna Vita Sancti Hugonis* (R.S.), p. 317). Perhaps these relics were placed in the new chapel.

(3) *References to bishops of Lincoln before the transfer of the See*

In his profession to Archbishop Lanfranc, Remigius described himself as bishop of Dorchester, Leicester, Lincoln, and the other provinces of his predecessors (Giraldus Cambrensis, *Opera* (R.S.), VII, 151). It may be that the title of bishop of Lincoln was sometimes used by or of the bishop in matters relating to Lincolnshire before the transfer from Dorchester was made in 1072–3. Several post-Conquest references to bishops of Lincoln have been noted: these may be so accounted for, though they may be due merely to a reading back into pre-Conquest times of a post-Conquest state of things. Yet there is also some evidence that the title was used before 1066:

(*a*) In two charters of 1050–60, Bishop Wulfwig signed as *Lincolniensis episcopus* and *Lincoliae antistes* (Kemble, *Codex Diplomaticus*, IV, 140, 143; Dugdale, *Monasticon*, I, 385).

(*b*) William the Conqueror's charter to Peterborough is attested by *Wilwinus Lincolniensis episcopus*, though Wulfwig died in 1067 (Dugdale, *Monasticon*, I, 383; Davis, *Regesta*, no. 8). Henry of Pytchley's *Liber Cartarum* reads *Dorcestrensis*, but in making this correction it also omits William the earl (*E.H.R.* XXXVIII (1923), p. 155).

(*c*) Remigius produced to the Domesday clerks a writ by which King Edward gave a certain Leofric with his land to the bishopric of Lincoln (*D.B.* I, 208 b).

(*d*) Florence of Worcester refers under 1012 to Ednoth bishop of Lincoln, who with Alfhere bishop of London interred the body of Archbishop Alphege in St Paul's London; under 1034 to Eatheric bishop of Lincoln; under 1052 to Ulf bishop of Lincoln, and writes that in 1057 Eadnoth bishop of Lincoln built St Mary of Stow (*Chronicon*, ed. Thorpe, I, 165, 189, 210, 216). On p. 203 he records the death of Eadnoth bishop of Dorchester and the succession of Ulf. Freeman, *Norman Conquest*, I, 354, and Page, *London, its Origin and Early Development*, p. 57, alter Lincoln to Dorchester.

(*e*) Ralph de Diceto gives the founder of St Mary of Stow as *Elnoth Lincolniensis* (*Opera Historica* (R.S.), II, 211).

(*f*) Roger Howden, under 1012, mentions *Ednoth Lincolniensis* and under 1052 Ulf bishop of Lincoln (*Chronica* (R.S.), I, 76, 100).

(4) '*The Mother Church of Lincoln Minster*'

The suggestion that Stow might be Sidnacester, the seat of the Anglo-Saxon bishopric of Lindsey, was made by Edmund Gibson in his edition of Camden's *Britannia*, which he published in 1695 when he was 26 years of age. But Gibson himself was more cautious than his followers. After mentioning that Camden had in general settled the ancient Sidnacester in the Gainsborough district, but without determining it to any particular district, he goes on 'if one should take the liberty of a conjecture, and settle it at Stow, there would not want several probabilities to warrant it'. He notes the resemblance between Dorchester and Stow; that like St Margaret's Leicester (thought to have been the seat of the see of Leicester) Stow was a peculiar, a prebend, and an archdeaconry; that it was famous before Lincoln was a bishop's see; and "'tis a common notion in those parts, both of learned and unlearned, that Stow was anciently the mother-Church to Lincoln'. He acknowledges that the claim that the see of Lindsey belonged to the archbishops of York was an objection to his theory (Gibson's *Camden*, 1st ed. col. 480). In his second edition (1722), col. 572, Gibson was still more guarded. He begins: 'They who have been for setling it at Stow have argu'd thus....' He suggests an alternative site on the hills above Lea and Gainsborough.

No hint of such a 'notion' is found prior to Gibson (1695). Leland does not mention Stow at all; he does mention 'Stratton on the Streate' in Stow parish, but only to refer to the street (Tillbridge Lane) itself (*Itinerary*, I, 32). De la Pryme is silent. Holles in his *Church Notes* merely says that Stow church was built minster-like and was first founded by Leofricus and his Countess Godiva, who likewise founded an abbey which was afterwards transferred to Eynsham ((L.R.S.), p. 70). Of writers later than Gibson, Bishop Wake noted that 'the church is a very ancient and large structure, built in manner of a Cathedral' (*Speculum Dioeceseos Lincolniensis* (L.R.S.), p. 172); and William John Monson, who made his notes on Stow church in 1835, confined himself to copying inscriptions (*Lincolnshire Church Notes* (L.R.S.), p. 345).

Gibson's suggestion and reference to tradition was repeated in Gough's edition of the *Britannia* (II, 279). For his Lincolnshire material Gough drew upon the minute books of the Society of Antiquaries of Spalding, and the papers of Dr Gordon, precentor of Lincoln (Preface to Gough's *Camden*, I, p. viii). The theory received a new lease of life from the local historian Adam Stark, who set it forth in his history of Stow (2nd ed. 1843) and later in his *History of the Bishopric of Lincoln* (1852). His argument was based on the assumption that Lindisse was a town, to be identified with Stow and Sidnacester (see title-page of his *Bishopric of Lincoln*, and p. 351; for Stark, see H. G. Gamble in *Lincs Magazine*, II, 87). The claim was quoted with approval by Archdeacon Stonehouse in 1845 (*A Stow Visitation*, ed. N. S. Harding (1940), p. 82, and see p. 98). About the same time the devoted incumbent of Stow, the Rev. George Atkinson, who was instrumental in procuring the restoration of the church by Mr Pearson, was proclaiming 'the uniform tradition prevailing all the country round, from time immemorial, that Stow church is "the mother of Lincoln Minster"' (*A.A.S.R.* I (1851), p. 315; and see his *Notes, Historical and Architectural, on Stow Church*, Louth and Lincolnshire Architectural Society, 3rd Report, 1846). An appeal for funds, made with the sanction of 'the highest ecclesiastical authority', for further restoration, carries the 'history' back to 672, when Etheldreda, queen of Northumbria, is said to have rested there on her flight to Ely.

Syddensis has still to be identified; it is now impossible to say whether there was a tradition in Gibson's time, though if there were its value as evidence must have been small. But the claim that Stow was famous before Lincoln was a bishop's seat implies that the author did not know of the pre-Conquest existence of St Mary of Lincoln. This greatly weakens his whole argument. There is no evidence, documentary or architectural, that there was a church at Stow before 1000.

APPENDIX IV

EARLY CIVIC OFFICERS

Date	Bailiffs	Reference
1154–55	Aubrey	*Red Book of the Exchequer*, II, 657
1163–64	William of Paris Ailwin Net	P.R. 10 *Henry II*, p. 23
1164–65	Walter s. Radewi Warner	P.R. 11 *Henry II*, p. 39
1165–66	William of Paris (*Prepositi* mentioned)	P.R. 12 *Henry II*, p. 5
1166–67	William of Paris	P.R. 13 *Henry II*, p. 50
1167–68	Warner s. Turgar William s. Ailsi	P.R. 14 *Henry II*, p. 75
1168–69	Walter s. Redwi Ralf the villein	P.R. 15 *Henry II*, p. 16
1169–70	William of Paris Warner	P.R. 16 *Henry II*, p. 153
1170–71	Warner Ralf the villein	P.R. 17 *Henry II*, p. 109
1171–72	Warner Ralf the villein	P.R. 18 *Henry II*, p. 94
1172–73	Warner Ralf the villein	P.R. 19 *Henry II*, p. 139
1173–74	Aulfwin Net	P.R. 20 *Henry II*, p. 104
1174–75	Ailwin Net	P.R. 21 *Henry II*, p. 156
1175–76	Warner s. Turstin	P.R. 22 *Henry II*, p. 87
1176–77	Warner s. Turstin John nephew of Richold	P.R. 23 *Henry II*, p. 117
1177–78	Ralf de Colecr' Alan s. Romphar	P.R. 24 *Henry II*, p. 8
1178–79	John s. Suaue Alan s. Rumfar	P.R. 25 *Henry II*, p. 47
1179–80	Robert s. Juhel Ædmund	P.R. 26 *Henry II*, p. 58
1180–81	Alan Multun	P.R. 27 *Henry II*, p. 62
1181–82	Alan Multun	P.R. 28 *Henry II*, p. 58
1182–83	Alan Multun Hugh the Fleming	P.R. 29 *Henry II*, p. 70
1183–84	James of Holm	P.R. 30 *Henry II*, p. 21
1184–85	Robert s. Martin William of Beaufo	P.R. 31 *Henry II*, p. 94
1185–86	Walter nephew of Lichtwin Gerard the tailor	P.R. 32 *Henry II*, p. 80
1186–87	William of Beaufo William nephew of Warner	P.R. 33 *Henry II*, p. 76
1187–88	Hugh the Fleming Hugh Parnell	P.R. 34 *Henry II*, p. 81
1189–90	William nephew of Warner	P.R. 1 *Richard I*, p. 73

Alderman	Date	Bailiffs	Reference
Adam s. Reginald	*c.* 1185–90	—	D. & C., D ii, 75/1/26, 40
Adam the alderman	Late 12th cent.	—	*D.C.* p. 51
,,	31 Aug. 1201	John Fleming Richard s. James	D. & C., D ii, 76/3/9
Adam s. Reginald the alderman	1202	Thomas of the Bail Hamo of Wicford (Hamo s. Lambert)	D. & C., D ii, 77/1/3, 8 *Earliest Lincs Assize Rolls*, no. 1012
John de Holm	3 Nov. 1217	—	Madox, *Firma Burgi*, p. 14

Mayor	Date	Bailiffs	Reference
A mayor	1206	—	*Earliest Lincs Assize Rolls*, no. 1448
,,	1206	Richard Clerk Wigot s. Wigot	*C.R. Rolls*, IV, 209
Adam	1210	—	Madox, *Exchequer*, p. 352
,,	1212	Thomas of Paris Ralf s. Lefwine	Madox, *Firma Burgi*, p. 182 note b (and see D. & C., D ii, 79/2/26, and 81/2/25)
,,	*c.* 1212	Hugh de Merston James s. Brand	D. & C., D ii, 79/1/107, 80/3/5 (and for J. s. B. see 77/1/5)
,,	1214	Roger Robert	D. & C., D ii, 80/3/7
,,		Walter Cause Nicholas s. Gunnilda	D. & C., D ii, 80/3/11
	30 Dec. 1216	William nephew of Warner Peter of the Bail	*Rot. Lit. Pat.* p. 162
William nephew of Warner	6 Oct. 1217	—	*Patent Rolls*, 1216–25, p. 100. *C.P.R.* 1216–25, p. 20
Peter of the Bridge	1218	—	*C.P.R.* 1216–25, p. 160
,,	1221	—	D. & C., D ii, 78/2/58
,,	(Prob. 1221)	Robert s. Ywain William s. Walter	D. & C., D ii, 76/3/12, 79/1/124
,,	1222	Reginald son of the priest James Bern	D. & C., D ii, 82/1/13 Lib. Cant. no. 518
,,	—	Fulk s. Rembald Robert s. Ywain	D. & C., D ii, 76/2/22
,,	(Before 1223)	Ralf Michael	D. & C., D ii, 77/2/14
,,		Peter of Paris	*Sempringham Charters*, no. 5
,,	(Undated)	—	Harl. Cart. 47 H 39
		Robert s. Eudo	*Bracton's Note Book*, II, 121

Mayor	Date	Bailiffs	Reference
Robert s. Ywain	? 1225	Robert s. Roger Henry Cotty	D. & C., D ii, 79/1/140 (and see D ii, 79/1/138, 139)
Peter of the Bail	1224–26	—	*R.A.* III, 68
John s. Osbert	? 1226	Richard Cause William Champennais	*F.C.* II, xiv
John of Paris	Election confirmed 21 Nov. 1227		*C.P.R.* 1225–32, p. 171
"	1227	Martin s. Eudo Norman of Wikeford	D. & C., D ii, 75/2/45, 46
"	—	Ralf the tailor Henry Cotty	D. & C., D ii, 74/1/3, 75/2/5
"	—	Robert John s. Robert	D. & C., D ii, 76/3/7, 77/2/20
"	—	Adam John (John s. Wlstan)	D. & C., D ii, 77/2/56 D. & C., D ii, 76/2/32 (and see 75/2/47, 76/3/4)
Peter of the Bail	1233	Adam s. Herbert (of Newport) Godfrey at the hall	D. & C., D ii, 74/2/17, 77/2/46
"	1240	—	*R.A.* IV, 68
"	1241	Richard s. Arnald Adam s. Robert	Thurgarton Cartulary, no. 1079
"	1243	Robert of Kyrketun Hyvo Flavus	Goxhill Leiger, nos. 300, 305. Lib. Cant. no. 243
"	1245	Richard s. Alfred Adam s. . . .	Lib. Cant. no. 215 D. & C., D ii, 76/2/21
(Peter s. Thomas of the Bail)	—	Giles s. Osbert William of Paris	D. & C., D ii, 76/1/25
William of Paris	? 1245–50	John Long William Brand	D. & C., D ii, 74/3/1 (and see 81/2/26, 81/2/42. *R.H.* I, 313 a)
Richard of the Bridge	*c.* 1245–50	—	*R.A.* IV, 280
Thomas of Beaufou	1249–50	Thomas the Bouef Thomas the skinner	D. & C., D ii, 76/1/22, 76/3/22
"	—	John s. Martin Robert of Belton	D. & C., D ii, 75/3/13, 75/2/42
"		Ralf de Guagi John of Lincoln	D. & C., D ii, 76/1/1, 76/2/61
"	—	Alan	D. & C., D ii, 76/3/14
"	June 1253	—	Lib. Cant. no. 273 (and see D. & C., D ii, 77/3/21, 78/1/133, *R.H.* I, 313 a, b)
"	*c.* 1255	—	D. & C., D ii, 79/1/141
William s. Giles	—	Ralf of Gayton John of Greiby (? Grey)	D. & C., D ii, 74/3/18. *R.H.* I, 313 b

Mayor	Date	Bailiffs	Reference
William s. Giles	May 1259	Peter Rabuck Hugh Fairweather	D. & C., D ii, 76/2/59, 82/1/32, 79/1/116
Peter of Paris	—	—	*R.H.* I, 313 a
Walter Brand	—	—	*R.H.* I, 313 a, 398 b
		Adam of the Hospital Nicholas Stonle Lucas of Neuland Hugh of Leir Simon the changer Jordan of Amecotes Henry Gopil Gregory Bolur	*R.H.* I, 313 b
John of Louth	7 April 1263	Jordan s. William Gilbert Peck	*R.A.* III, 304
Osbert s. Giles	—	William of Borton	D. & C., D ii, 75/2/52
Thomas s. Robert	—	Gilbert of the Bridge William Cause	D & C., D ii, 75/1/24
Thomas Shanfoyl	—	—	*Gilbertine Charters* (L.R.S.), p. 44
Thomas of Beaufou	1266	—	D. & C., D ii, 75/3/13, 74/2/22. *V.C.H. Lincs*, II, 313
William of Holgate	In his first year	Richard of Bultham Walter le worthi (Lefwordi)	D. & C., D ii, 74/1/21, 74/2/9, 74/3/17
,,	Second roll of mayoralty 1268–69	—	D. & C., D ii, 80/3/21
,,	1272	Andrew Cause Andrew of Horkstow	D. & C., D ii, 75/1/9, 77/2/10. Harl. Cart. 43 A 67. Welbeck Cartulary, f. 106
,,	1273–74	Matthew Dogneck (the draper) Robert of Dunham (the tanner)	D. & C., D ii, 74/3/28, 75/1/8. *Lincoln Wills*, II, 218
,,	—	(Robert Leper	*R.H.* I, 398 b)
,,	—	Jordan s. Giles William of Hepham	D. & C., D ii, 74/1/29, 76/1/32, 77/1/24, 82/1/21. Goxhill Leiger, nos. 295, 299, 303. *R.H.* I, 313 b
,,	—	Walter of Fiskerton John of Burg	D. & C., D ii, 82/1/22. *R.H.* I, 313 b
,,	—	John of Kirkstede Gernegan of Newport	D. & C., D ii, 76/1/16. *Lincoln Wills*, II, 217
Roger s. Benedict	1274	Martin the cordwainer Symon Unwyn	D. & C., D ii, 75/2/36, 39. *R.H.* I, 313 b, 314 a, 398 b

Mayor	Date	Bailiffs	Reference
Roger s. Benedict	Mayor for the second time	Simon Cansor Jordan Aureis	D. & C., D ii, 74/2/1
,,	c. 1275	—	D. & C., D ii, 77/3/57
,,	1280	—	D. & C., D ii, 77/3/54
,,	—	William Jalkes (Galkes) Ivo the glover (le Gaunter)	D. & C., D ii, 75/1/5, 20
,,	—	Alan biwestcastel Peter of Thornhawe	D. & C., D ii, 75/2/33, 34, 78/3/77
,,	—	Hugh tregetur Ivo the cordwainer	D. & C., D ii, 75/3/1
,,	—	Gilbert of Thorp William of Canwick	Lib. Cant. no. 307
James of the Bridge	c. 1277–78	—	Lib. Cant. no. 410
,,	c. 1279–80	—	D. & C., D ii, 77/3/15
	1279	William Cause	*C.C.R.* 1272–9, p. 538
Richard of Beaufou	1284	Hugh s. Robert William Hunwyn	Lib. Cant. nos. 91, 143
Ralf of Gayton	c. 1287	—	Bodleian MS., Lincs, ch. 354
Henry Gopyl	1288–90	Thomas of Wolingham Simon of Wymbylthorpe	D. & C., D ii, 75/1/25
	—	Robert de Hicham	Goxhill Leiger, no. 297

Keeper	Date	Bailiffs	Reference
Robert le venur	1291	Alexander s. John s. Martin (*or* Alexander s. Martin) Adam Cokerel	D. & C., D ii, 74/2/26, 75/1/17
,,	1293	William de Paris Robert ad Fontem	D. & C., D ii, 75/1/13–15
William Cause	1298	Walter Bayhous John Rothinger	D. & C., D ii, 74/2/52
Dom. William Cause[1]	1299	John de Normanton Ralf Russell	D. & C., D ii, 74/2/25

Mayor	Date	Bailiffs	Reference
William Cause	—	John of Bliton John ad fontem	D. & C., D ii, 74/2/18
,,	—	Geoffrey de Hampton John Bere	D. & C., D ii, 75/2/32, 35
Stephen de Stanham	1303 (Trinity)	Hugh Thorn Richard de Severby	D. & C., D ii, 75/1/18
,,	1305	Gilbert Rodyng Geoffrey de Lenne	D. & C., D ii, 75/1/37

[1] William Cause is described as a knight, 1299, in D. & C., D ii, 77/3/14.

Mayor	Date	Bailiffs	Reference
Alexander s. Martin	1306–7	—	D. & C., D ii, 74/2/50. *C.C.R.* 1302–7, p. 485 (15 Feb. 1307)
John of Amcotes	1307–8	—	D. & C., D ii, 74/2/51
John of Blyton	1308	—	*C.C.R.* 1307–13, p. 87
Gilbert le Blake	1310	John the ironmonger Geoffrey de Kew	D. & C., D ii, 74/3/14, 74/2/49
Alexander s. Martin	1311	William de Brayland Thomas Fayrinou	D. & C., D ii, 74/3/12, 75/2/24
Osbert le Lung	1312	Adam de Hibaldstowe Hugh Bacon	D. & C., D ii, 74/2/48, 75/2/18

At this point the lists already printed begin. See Hill, 'Three Lists of the Mayors, Bailiffs and Sheriffs of the City of Lincoln,' *A.A.S.R.* xxxix (1929), pp. 217–56.

For corrections and additions see *Registrum Antiquissimum of the Cathedral Church of Lincoln* (L.R.S. 1958), edited by Kathleen Major, vol. viii, appendix.

APPENDIX V

SOME LEADING FAMILIES

It seems fitting to begin with the family to which Adam, the first mayor, belonged. His grandfather Eilsi (OE. Ælfsige) is the earliest recorded member of the family. He is called Eilsi of Wigford, and his wife Alviva gave three acres of land in St Bartholomew's parish to St Mary (*L.C.S.* II, p. ccxl). Eilsi seems to have had five sons:

(1) David, whose fee is mentioned in the Thurgarton Cartulary (f. 158). He had a son who had a wife Agnes, and of whom Adam his kinsman held land in the parish of St Peter in Wigford (Kirkstead Cartulary, ff. 61, 61 d).

(2) Thomas (Kirkstead Cartulary, f. 47).

(3) William, bailiff in 1167–8 (supra, p. 378), who witnesses with his brother Reginald in 1156–7 (*Gilbertine Charters* (L.R.S.), p. 48).

(4) Roger (Bardney Cartulary, f. 248 d).

(5) Reginald, who witnesses in 1163–6 (*D.C.* p. 343, and Kirkstead Cartulary, f. 47); Reginald elsi de elsi de Lincoln witnesses *c.* 1155–77 (Lees, *Records of the Templars in England in the Twelfth Century*, p. 268; *Early Yorkshire Charters*, v, 339). He was fined 4 marks for changing his plea, 1176–7 (P.R. 23 *Henry II*, p. 118). With William of Paris he supervised the repair of the gaol in the castle, 1187–8 (P.R. 34 *Henry II*, p. 67). Reginald had issue Adam and two daughters, Matilda and Margery.

Adam had contacts with St Hugh. Giraldus tells of the cure by the bishop of a dumb boy of Wigford, who had been brought up in the house of Adam the mayor, Reimbald the rich, and other leading people of Wigford (*Opera* (R.S.), VII, 131). Adam was a benefactor of the cathedral. With the assent of James de Holm (husband of his sister Matilda), he gave to the common of the canons his stone house in Hungate in the parish of St Peter Stanthaket which Simon the butcher had held of his father: it was already subject to rent charges in the canons' favour, his father having given them 4*s.* yearly and Adam himself 1*s.* yearly for the souls of his father and mother, his ancestors and successors (D. & C., D ii, 80/3/9).

He also held land in the Bail, which he had granted to a tenant subject to a yearly rent, and when his tenant granted it to the canons of Barlings, Adam confirmed the grant (Barlings Cartulary, ff. 56 d, 57 d). He bought from Ralf son of Lefwine land in Mikelgate in the parish of St Lawrence subject to rents of 2*s.* to the heirs of Ralf de la Mare, 12*d.* to Robert de Areci, and 12*d.* to the heirs of Hubert son of Ralf; and a rent of 3*s.* from land which Reyner son of John held of Ralf in St Edmund's parish, paying him a pair of white gloves and the sum of 9 marks with which Ralf redeemed his land from the Jews. Later Adam granted to the abbey of Kirkstead for the maintenance of a chaplain the land and rent he had bought from Ralf, together with land which he held of his cousin William son of David in St Peter in Wigford; half a mark of rent in Mikelgate in St Lawrence's parish, subject to payment of 12*d.* yearly to holders of land formerly of Richard son of Outi, and a pair of white gloves to William son of David; and land which he had of Rumfar son of Lambert in St Mary

Crackpole's parish, subject to payment of a pair of white gloves to Rumfar. The grants were confirmed by William son of David so far as they concerned him (Kirkstead Cartulary, ff. 59 d, 60 d, 61, 61 d).

After his deposition from office Adam seems to have retired to Branston, for there are several grants of land in the Branston fields to Adam 'late of the city of Lincoln' or 'late mayor of the city of Lincoln'. He bought 20 acres from Robert Patric of Branston, 6 acres from Robert Attebec, and 3 acres and 1 perch from Haimo son of Wdefat; and he later granted these parcels to the monks of Kirkstead to maintain a chaplain (ibid. ff. 58 d–59 d). He was dead by 1231 (*F.C.* I, 240).

Adam's sister Matilda, who seems to have been his elder sister, because her husband figures as Adam's heir, married James de Holm, or *Flandrensis*. There are a few persons described as Flemings; Hugh the Fleming was city bailiff in 1182–3 and 1187–8, and Marcius the Fleming his son-in-law witnesses a charter with him (*D.C.* p. 369); both held land in Lincoln of the Templars in 1185 (Lees, *Templars*, pp. cciv, 82). The comparative rarity of the description suggests, however, that not many Flemings had settled in the Lincoln district. At any rate it was sufficient to identify James, though the name 'de Holm' gradually displaced it. The family's land holdings indicate that this name derived from Holm in the parish of Beckingham (*L.D.* p. lviii; *F.C.* II, p. lx). James was bailiff of Lincoln in 1183–4. In 1185 he held a house in Lincoln of the Templars at a rent of 2*s.* (Lees, *Templars*, p. 82). He gave 100*s.* worth of land in Albodesle and a carucate in Holm which Roger son of Reinfred his lord had granted to him to Kirkstead Abbey, mentioning his wife Matilda (Kirkstead Cartulary, f. 47), and land which he received of William Bigot in the fields of Langton by Wragby to the same house (f. 161). He also gave 10*s.* rent from land which Peter *novus magister* held of him in the parish of St Mary *de capella*, and confirmed land in the parish of St Edward, to Kirkstead (f. 47). The confirmation by James' son John shows that the former land was situate in Wigford *ex west platee parte* in St Mary *ad capellam* (f. 52).

His son John de Holm, who married Agnes, and was dead by 1231, had a son Adam de Holm, who had a son Peter de Holm, and it is convenient to deal with their lands collectively. John de Holm was succeeded in a house in Wigford by John the farrier, who sold it to Henry III for 60 marks in 1228 (*Cal. Liberate Rolls*, 1226–40, p. 79). John gave 10 acres of his lordship in Langton, and confirmed other gifts, and also granted a windmill in the fields of South Langton on the south of the road from Strubby to Bardney, to Kirkstead (Kirkstead Cartulary, ff. 163 d, 165, 166).

The Holms were also benefactors of Bardney. John Fleming son of James de Holm released to them land in the parish of St John in Wigford which he held of the abbot and monks, and William the fuller held of him, in exchange for which they remitted half a mark yearly from land which he held of them for a mark yearly: this land was in the parish of St Mary Crackpole in Walkergate (Bardney Cartulary, f. 246). John also granted them a toft in Sutton in the parish of Beckingham (f. 212 d). Adam, John's son, confirmed a gift of half a mark which John had given for the soul of Adam's mother Agnes from the same land in St Mary Crackpole (f. 247), and he granted to the abbot a right of way through his wood and land in Langton by Wragby to the abbot's manor of Brethage, a manor in the parish of Langton extending to the parish of Hatton

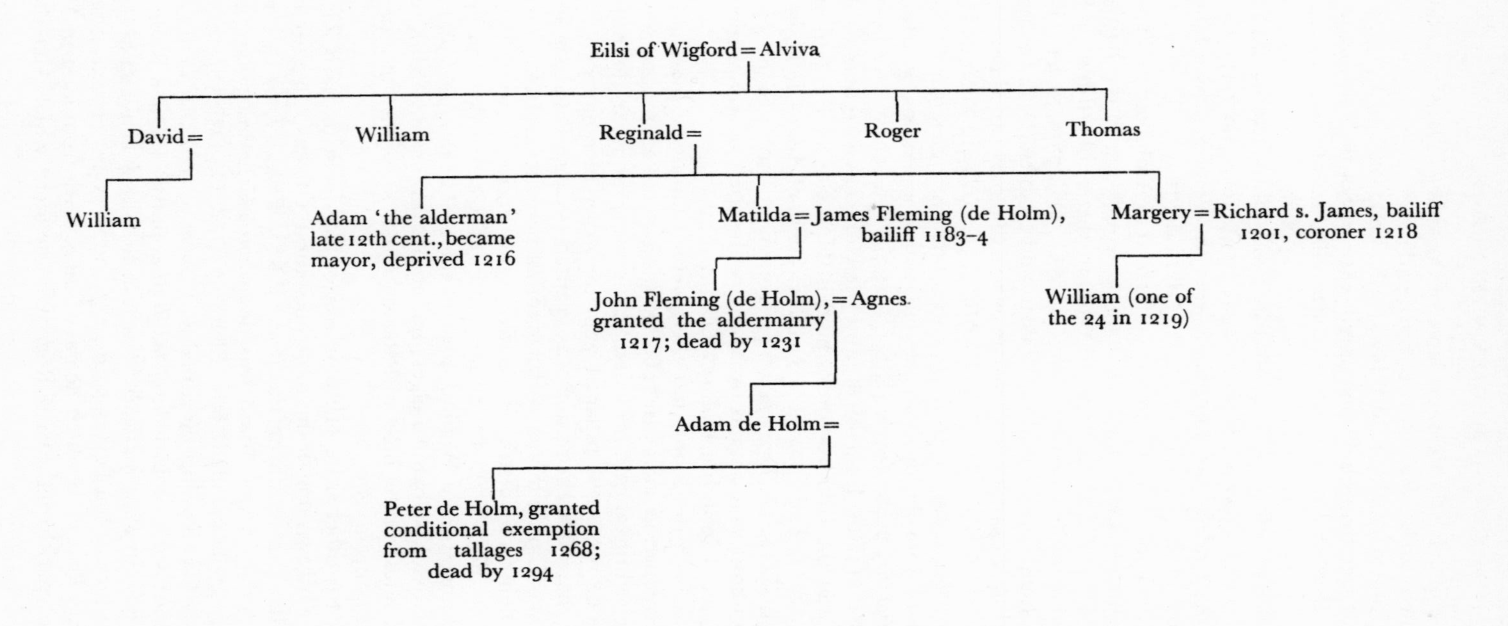
Eilsi of Wigford = Alviva
David =
William
Reginald =
Roger
Thomas
William
Adam 'the alderman' late 12th cent., became mayor, deprived 1216
Matilda = James Fleming (de Holm), bailiff 1183–4
Margery = Richard s. James, bailiff 1201, coroner 1218
John Fleming (de Holm), = Agnes. granted the aldermanry 1217; dead by 1231
William (one of the 24 in 1219)
Adam de Holm =
Peter de Holm, granted conditional exemption from tallages 1268; dead by 1294

(f. 90; *F.C.* II, p. lxiv; the demesne lands of the abbey in Bardney and 'Brethagh' are mentioned in *Cal. Inq. Misc.* II, no. 344).

In 1212 John de Holm held 6 bovates in Langton and in 1242–3 Adam de Holm and Roger Bygot held one knight's fee in South Langton of Marmion of Scrivelsby (*Book of Fees*, I, 173; II, 1062). The family seem also to have had associations with Canwick. James Fleming appears with Canwick witnesses in a Kirkstead charter (*D.C.* p. 143), and in 1202 John Fleming was appealed for breaking house at Canwick (*Earliest Lincs Assize Rolls*, no. 997).

Most of the lands so far mentioned were the Flemings' own lands: others in Lincoln came to them by succession to Adam the mayor. They succeeded to his interests in the Bail. Adam de Holm confirmed to Archibald nephew of Geoffrey Scot land which Geoffrey had once bought from Peter of the Bail and given to Archibald (D. & C., D ii, 77/3/1). William the scabbard-maker held land of Peter de Holm, of the fee of Durham (D. & C., D ii, 77/3/70, 71). Peter released his right in houses in the Bail to the dean and chapter (D. & C., D ii, 78/1/133) and granted to Alexander de Claypole part of his court called Durham fee within the east gate of the Bail (D. & C., D ii, 78/1/135). In 1312 Peter de Holm appears in a list of the tenants of the bishop of Durham, he having formerly held tenements in the Bail of Lincoln by homage and fealty, rendering yearly an almsgift (*Registrum Palatinum Dunelmense* (R.S.), I, 263). Peter must have been dead some years before that date. John son of James de Holm gave a rent of 2*s.* to the church of Lincoln and the Common from land in Hungate for the soul of his mother Matilda (D. & C., D ii, 75/1/38). Land was held of Adam de Holm in St Rumbold's parish (D. & C., D ii, 74/2/14). Tenements in 'la Stanbegh' within the walls and without were shared by Margery the sister of Adam son of Reginald and Adam son of John [de Holm] (*F.C.* I, 240).

There can be little doubt that they were a family of merchants: Peter de Holm is mentioned as such. In 1268 he was granted exemption for life from all tallages assessed in Lincoln provided he did not practise trade in the town; but if he did so he was to be tallaged with the other merchants (*C.P.R.* 1266–72, p. 203). Perhaps this exemption was granted because Peter was in difficulties. He owed large sums of money to Isaac son of Benedict Gabbay, as was found in 1275 after Benedict's death, amounting apparently to over £130 (Rigg, *Exchequer of Jews*, II, 266–7). In the mayoralty of Richard Beaufou Peter sold the house of his ancestors in Wigford, next to the hall of the great gild of St Mary, to Peter of Goxhill (Goxhill Leiger, no. 298). Ralph de Goxhill was found to have held a house of the heirs of Peter de Holm by service of a penny in 1294 (*Cal. Inq. p.m.* III, no. 209).

Margery, the other sister of Adam son of Reginald, married Richard son of James. Richard was one of the most substantial citizens. In 1191 he was fined 10 marks after the assault on the Jews (P.R. 3 *Richard I*, p. 15), and in 1201, when his brother-in-law Adam was described as the alderman, he served as bailiff with his wife's nephew John Fleming (D. & C., D ii, 76/3/9). In 1203 he was fined 20*s.* for an unjust plevin (P.R. 5 *John*, p. 102). In 1218 he was one of the four coroners (Stenton, *Rolls of the Justices in Eyre* (Selden Society), no. 21). He had a house in *Parmentaria*, held of him first by Joceus son of Ave the Jew, and then by Joceus' son Peytevin (*Book of Fees*, I, 365). He was a benefactor of Sempringham Priory, to which he gave half a mark from land in Mikelgate in St Lawrence's parish, of the fee of Roger Montgomery, which Alan the goldsmith

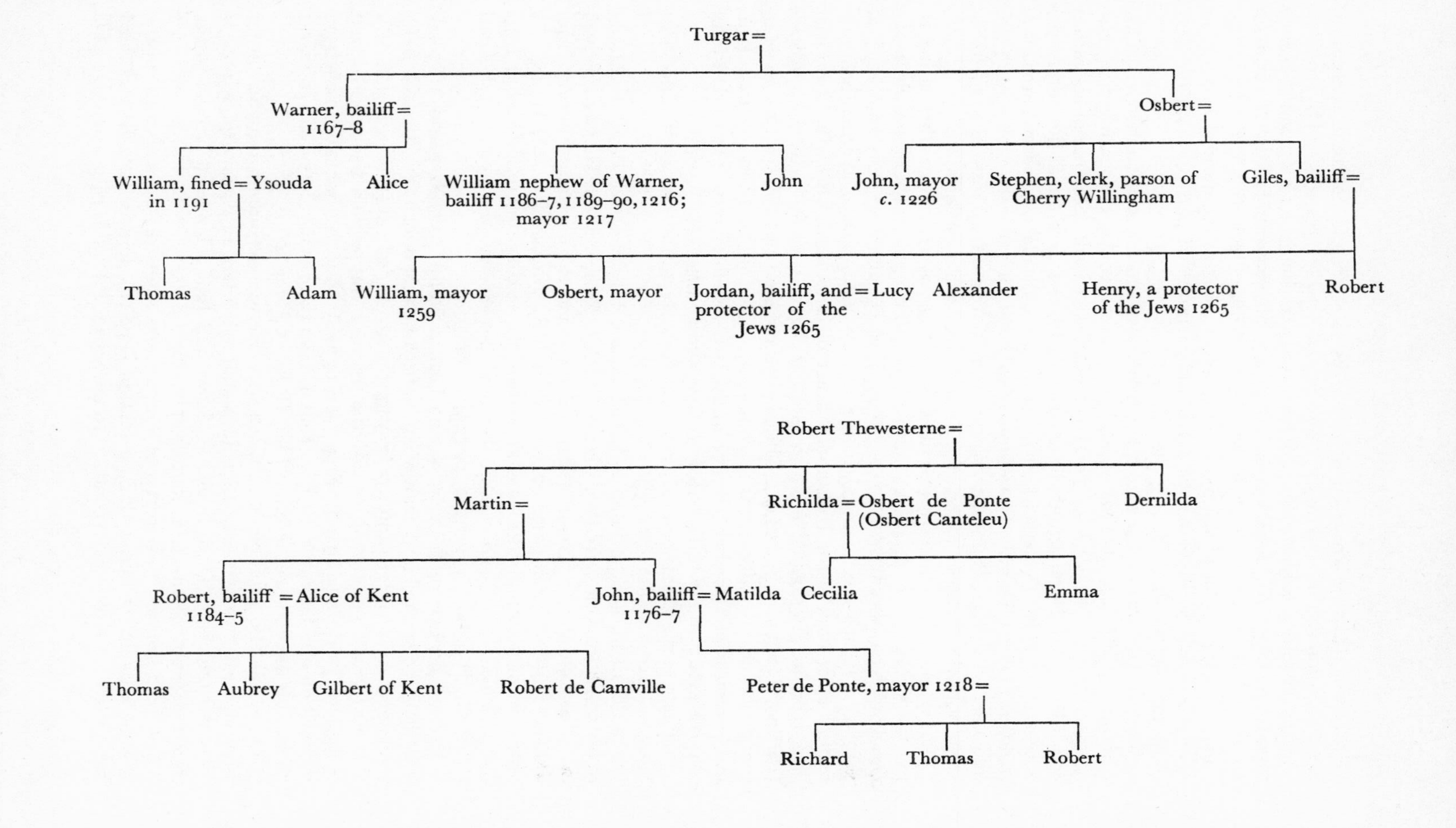
Turgar=
Warner, bailiff=
1167–8
Osbert=
William, fined=Ysouda
in 1191
Alice
William nephew of Warner,
bailiff 1186–7, 1189–90, 1216;
mayor 1217
John
John, mayor
c. 1226
Stephen, clerk, parson of
Cherry Willingham
Giles, bailiff=
Thomas
Adam
William, mayor
1259
Osbert, mayor
Jordan, bailiff, and=Lucy
protector of the
Jews 1265
Alexander
Henry, a protector
of the Jews 1265
Robert
Robert Thewesterne=
Martin=
Richilda=Osbert de Ponte
(Osbert Canteleu)
Dernilda
Robert, bailiff =Alice of Kent
1184–5
John, bailiff=Matilda
1176–7
Cecilia
Emma
Thomas
Aubrey
Gilbert of Kent
Robert de Camville
Peter de Ponte, mayor 1218=
Richard
Thomas
Robert

held of him; and he witnessed the grant by Godwin the rich of a carucate in Sempringham to the same house (*Sempringham Charters*, pp. 2, 3). He probably lived in the parish of St Swithin, for Margery lived there after his death (Bardney Cartulary, f. 260 d). This fact suggests that his interests lay on the river, a conclusion supported by the fact that his son William had land in Torksey, from which he gave a rent of 2*s.* and 8 cocks and 2 hens to the nuns of Fosse there (Fosse Charter). William also held land in St Rumbold's parish, which was near the waterside (D. & C., D ii, 74/2/17).

When Adam was deposed from the mayoralty there was appointed as bailiff and mayor William nephew of Warner (see p. 200). His grandfather was Turgar. When (*c.* 1150) Ranulph II earl of Chester in the presence of his barons in his house at Lincoln granted a charter to Robert de Folinuc the butler, the witnesses included Turger of Lincoln (*D.C.* p. 363). Warner son of Turgar was bailiff of the city in 1167–8, and apparently also in 1169–70, 1170–1, 1171–2, and 1172–3, though as another Warner, son of Turstin, appears in 1175–6, the identity of the bailiff in the intermediate years cannot be certain.

The family is frequently described as being 'of Hungate', their Lincoln properties being mainly in that district, in All Saints Hungate and St Mary Crackpole's parishes (D. & C., D ii, 75/1/7, 8, 16, 29) and St Martin (D. & C., D ii, 75/2/51). It has been noticed before that William son of Warner held the rectory of St Paul in the Bail, and Warner of Lincoln and his wife Christiana gave land in Thorngate, in which Gordon Blacgris lived, to Bardney Abbey (Bardney Cartulary, f. 258 d). Christiana gave land in St Mary Crackpole to the same house (f. 248 d), and their daughter Alice added 2*s.* of rent from land by the church of St Benedict, and half the land which Henry Neht held of John son of Rumfar in the same parish (f. 247, and *C. Chart. R.* IV, 240).

William son of Warner held half a knight's fee of the bishop of Lincoln at Stow in 1210–12 (*Red Book of the Exchequer*, II, 515). With Robert Spicer and Richard Villein, he was found to have disseised Jocelin son of Peter of London of his house in Boston, and was in mercy (*C.R. Rolls*, I, 271). He was involved in the assault on the Jews in 1191, and was fined the enormous sum of £100, much the largest fine imposed on any citizen (P.R. 3 *Richard I*, p. 16). He appears in the list of principal citizens who guaranteed a tallage in 1206 (*Earliest Lincs Assize Rolls* (L.R.S.), no. 1448). He held the rectory of St Paul in the Bail (D. & C., D ii, 80/2/17; supra, p. 103).

William nephew of Warner, having been a bailiff in 1186–7 and 1189–90, must have been an elderly man when he became mayor in 1217. In 1201 King John fined him 60 marks and a palfrey for the royal goodwill (P.R. 3 *John*, p. 18). The next year he paid nothing into the treasury, but he paid 20 marks by writ to the king in his chamber (P.R. 4 *John*, p. 228). Another fine must have been imposed on him later, for the Pipe Roll of 1230 records that he owed 150 marks for having the goodwill of King John (P.R. 13 *Henry III*, p. 301).

There was also John nephew of Warner. He was defendant in an action for a half share in two houses in Lincoln, a stall and a half in *Parmenteria*, a quarter of a stall and half of two houses in Stow, and half a house in Lenton in the county of Nottingham (*C.R. Rolls*, VI, 67).

Warner's brother, Osbert son of Turgar, was assessed for the assault on the Jews at a modest 5 marks (P.R. 3 *Richard I*, p. 16), and in 1203 he was fined half a mark for selling wine contrary to the assize (P.R. 5 *John*, p. 102). He gave land in St Faith in Newland to Bardney Abbey (*C. Chart. R.* IV, 241). He had three sons, Giles, Stephen and John.

The family had links with Torksey. Osbert son of Torger of Hungate gave land in St Edmund's parish and a rent of 12*d.* from land in St Faith in Newland to the nuns of Fosse there, and his son Giles gave land in the parish of St Ed(mund?) to them; William nephew of Warner gave them 2*s.* worth of rent from his garden which he bought from the wife of Ralf son of Orgar the fuller in St Stephen's parish (Fosse Charter).

Stephen son of Osbert went into the church. He is described as a clerk (D. & C., D ii, 75/2/3), and also as 'magister' Stephen of Hundegate (*R.A.* IV, 77; Harl. Cart. 53 D 43). He was the parson of Cherry Willingham when Bishop Hugh de Welles appropriated the church to the Fosse nunnery (*Rotuli Hugonis de Welles* (L.R.S.), III, 95; Cole, 'Royal Burgh of Torksey' in *A.A.S.R.* XXVIII (1906), p. 467).

John son of Osbert had rent from land in St Margaret in Wigford (D. & C., D ii, 76/3/12, 13). He was mayor about 1226. His brother Giles son of Osbert had land in St Andrew on the Hill (Welbeck Cartulary, f. 105 b). Giles was bailiff when Peter of the Bail was mayor. He had six sons. William son of Giles was mayor in 1259, and held office for at least two years; Osbert son of Giles held the same office, and he and his brothers Henry and Jordan were among the chief citizens ordered by the king to protect the Jews in 1265 (*C.P.R.* 1258–66, p. 421). Osbert son of Giles was one of the Christian chirographers of the chirograph chest (Rigg, *Exchequer of Jews*, I, 124). Jordan was a bailiff. Osbert and Henry witness together in Harl. Cart. 44 A 41.

Several of the family were involved in a transaction of which the juries of both the greater men and the *mediocres* complained in the Hundred Roll inquests. The citizens of Lincoln had been free of customs at Boston fair. Fourteen years earlier the bailiffs of Peter of Savoy, lord of the fair, took goods from the Lincoln men, and attached them, to the city's great damage. William son of Giles, then mayor, by consent of Jordan son of Giles, Walter Brand, Thomas son of Robert, Thomas of Beaufou and Alexander son of Giles, without the consent of the other citizens, made a certain composition with Peter of Savoy's bailiffs which gave Peter a farm of £10 a year: and Jordan, the mayor's brother, told the court of the commonalty of Lincoln that he would give £10 of his own money rather than lose his Boston fair (*R.H.* I, 313 b, 320 a). Jordan was at one time a bailiff of Peter of Savoy (ibid. 398 b).

There was also a Robert son of Giles (*F.C.* II, p. xiv). In the systematic encroachments on the waste in Newland there were complaints that Jordan and Osbert had squatted on plots of land to the damage of the king and therefore of the city (*R.H.* I, 312 a). William son of Giles gave a rent of 20*s.* from two lands in Thorngate in St Swithin's parish to the house of St Giles of Lincoln (*C. Chart. R.* III, 365). Jordan's widow Lucy had dower in land in North Carlton and Burton (ibid. IV, 7).

There was a large and important group of citizens bearing the name of 'Paris'; and though it cannot be proved that all of them were related, many of them were members of the same family. William of Paris was bailiff in 1163–4, 1165–6, 1166–7, 1169–70. In 1181–2 he bought lands belonging to the old moneyers; and in the same year he brought an action in respect of scarlet cloth against Everwine of Lincoln at the same time as Everwine brought one against him and his son-in-law John (P.R. 28 *Henry II*, pp. 55, 57). Three years later he sought an inquiry into the truth of an appeal that John the Norwegian brought against him (P.R. 31 *Henry II*, p. 89). In 1187–8, with Reginald son of Eilsi, he supervised the repair of the castle gaol (P.R. 34 *Henry II*, p. 67). He had a brother Thomas of Paris (*D.C.* p. 210) and two daughters Matilda and Hawise, who held a tenement at Canwick granted by Richard I to Richerus the butler (Kirkstead Cartulary, f. 50). Two sons of a William of Paris, Geoffrey and William, appear in the cathedral obituary (*L.C.S.* II, pp. ccxxxvi, ccxli).

In 1200 King John granted to Peter of Paris the advowson of the chapel on the bridge of Lincoln (*Cartae Antiquae, Rolls* 1–10 (P.R.S.), no. 144). About 1231 Peter of Paris was presented by Peter of Paris, citizen of Lincoln, to the church of Aunby (*Rotuli Hugonis de Welles* (L.R.S.), I, 231); and in 1232 Ralf Arsic acknowledged the advowson of Aunby to be of the right of Peter, with six bovates (*F.C.* I, 249).

A William of Paris had four sons, John, William, Peter and Thomas (D. & C., D ii, 76/3/14; *R.A.* II, 35, 37). John was coroner in 1218 (*Lincs Justices in Eyre*, no. 21), and mayor about 1227–32. William (perhaps this one) had 12 bovates of land in Glentworth which his grandfather Peter of Paris had held (*R.H.* I, 250 b). Peter had a son John who held land in Fillingham (*R.A.* IV, 98). This Peter can hardly be the Peter of Paris of whom the Hundred Roll jurors declared that 20 years before (which, taken strictly, would mean about 1255) Peter, then a man of great authority, married a Beverley woman, and that by her influence the Beverley men escaped from payment of customs in his mayoralty (*R.H.* I, 309 b). Peter of Paris son of John granted half a house in Lincoln to Barlings (Barlings Cartulary, f. 64 d).

Thomas, son of William of Paris (*R.A.* III, 254), was dead by 1226, when Mary his widow had a dispute with the dean and chapter and others (*C.P.R.* 1225–32, p. 71). Mary was the daughter of Godwin the rich who will be mentioned later. Thomas' son, William of Paris, was a notable man. He was a moneyer in 1244 (*Red Book of the Exchequer*, III, 1075), and mayor about 1245–50. He held 3 carucates of land in Humby in 1242–3, and the third part of a knight's fee at Burton of Ralf of Bracebridge from year to year, and the third part of a fee of Gilbert of Gant in Winceby (*Book of Fees*, II, 1037, 1063, 1065, 1069, 1085). He was appointed to buy cloth for the king in 1245 (*C.P.R.* 1232–47, p. 449). He gave rent and land in Burton and Bracebridge to Bardney Abbey (Bardney Cartulary, ff. 204 d, 205), and (before 1217) a rent of 12*d.* to the common of the canons of Lincoln from land in St Peter in Eastgate for the souls of himself, Mary his wife, and their ancestors and successors (D. & C., D ii, 79/2/42). It was perhaps this same William of Paris, described as a citizen of Lincoln, who presented to the church of Somerby near Grantham in 1250–1; John of Paris, citizen of Lincoln, presented in 1287, and John of Paris, of Humby, in 1310–11 (*Lincs N. & Q.* IX, 251).

Godwin the rich owed £20 to Walter of Grimsby, brother of Dreu son of Ralf, sheriff of Lincoln, in 1176–7 (P.R. 23 *Henry II*, p. 119). In 1185–6, Outi the chaplain bought a writ of right against Godwin and William son of Engelbert in respect of four hawks and four falcons (P.R. 32 *Henry II*, p. 80). Godwin was fined 5 marks for his share in the assault on the Jews in 1191 (P.R. 3 *Richard I*, p. 15). In 1198–9 Thomas de Aresi claimed a house in Wigford against Godwin the rich in the king's court (*Roll of the King's Court, Ric. I* (P.R.S.), p. 215). As his daughter was called Mary of Wigford it seems that Godwin's town house, like that of other leading citizens, was south of the river.

He may have been the Godwin who gave Boicroft to St Mary of Lincoln (*L.C.S.* II, p. ccxlii). He gave a carucate of land at Sempringham, of the fee of Alice de Gant, to the priory of Sempringham (*Sempringham Charters*, p. 2). He founded the priory of St Saviour, Bridgend in Horbling, known as Holland Bridge, for the Order of Sempringham, in or before 1199; as early as 1177 he was received by St Gilbert, founder of the Order, into full fraternity. At Bridgend he gave the chapel of St Saviour and certain lands and tenements for the maintenance of a house for canons, and bound them, after providing for their own support, to keep in repair the causeway through the fens called Holland Bridge and the bridges over it as far as the new dyke near Donington (Dugdale, *History of Imbanking and Drayning* (1662), p. 225; *V.C.H. Lincoln*, II, 198; Darby, *Medieval Fenland* (1940), p. 116). His daughter Mary (who had married Thomas of Paris) confirmed her father's grant of a house in Lincoln to the prior of Holland Bridge in 1231 (*F.C.* I, 226). Godwin the rich gave land at Broughton near Brigg to the Templars (Lees, *Records of the Templars*, p. 102).

Apparently Godwin had interests in Torksey, for he was a benefactor of the Fosse nunnery there. With Alice his wife he gave them half a toft which Henry the smith held of them in Mikelgate, Lincoln; and Alice gave land in her fee in Walkergate in St Mary Crackpole. Godwin also gave 3½ bovates of land in the Fulbeck fields (Fosse Charter).

Godwin is also to be found at the other end of the Lincoln waterway, for he had a house in Boston. He gave it to the monks of St Cuthbert of Durham. It stood on the west of the river Witham, where the Lincoln colony dwelt, being 16 ft. by 14 ft., held of the fee of Guy of Croun. The most famous of the witnesses to this charter is Roger, parson of Howden, the historian, with him being notable Lincoln citizens, namely Reginald son of Ailsi, William of Paris, James of Holm, William son of Warner, and Osbert brother of Warner, all of them members of the families abovementioned (D. & C., Durham, 3/3 Ebor no. 4, from a copy kindly supplied by Mrs Stenton).

Godwin held land of Thurgarton Priory in Holy Trinity within the walls of Lincoln (Thurgarton Cartulary, no. 1086). His daughter Mary received rent from land in St Peter in Eastgate, a grant of which was confirmed by Mary's son Martin to the convent of Ormsby (*Gilbertine Charters* (L.R.S.), pp. 43, 44).

Among Godwin's contemporaries was Reimbald, also called 'the rich'. Reimbald son of Ralf ranks as a witness next after Reginald son of Eilsi, 1163–6 (*D.C.* p. 343). After the assault on the Jews in 1191 he was fined 20 marks (P.R. 3 *Richard I*, p. 16), and in 1202 he paid tallage of 20 marks (P.R. 4 *John*, p. 240). He is one of the group of 24 principal citizens in 1206 (see p. 398). He is sometimes described as being 'of Wigford', and with Adam son of Reginald he helped to maintain the dumb boy of Wigford healed by St Hugh (supra, p. 385). There is a casual reference to his toft in the parish of St Peter in Wigford (*Sempringham Charters*, p. 4). He was held as a hostage by King John in 1216 (supra, p. 199). Robert of Kent quitclaimed to Barlings Abbey a mill in Lincoln of the fee of T. son of Rambald; and Peter of Paris, chaplain, and Thomas son of Raimbald came to terms about a mill built near Peter's stone houses in Sapergate, Peter agreeing to indemnify Thomas against damage (Barlings Cartulary, ff. 64 d, 65 d). In 1219, Thomas son of Reinbald claimed a house in

Lincoln against the prior of Lenton (Mrs D. M. Stenton, *Rolls of Justices in Eyre for Lincs and Worcs* (Selden Society), no. 810).

The family which took its name from the Bail (*de Ballio*) presents difficulties in the construction of a pedigree. Thomas of the Bail was bailiff in 1202. He had a son Peter (D. & C., D ii, 76/1/25) who was bailiff with William nephew of Warner in 1216, and mayor several times.

Thomas gave Ramsey Abbey lands in the churchyard of St Peter Stanthaket between the land he held of Stixwould Convent and land of William of St Bartholomew; and also a half share of land in St Andrew on the Hill, the other half being held by Gilbert the priest: his sons Peter and William gave a release of the premises. William his son farmed all the said lands of Ramsey Abbey, paying one mark yearly by chirograph dated 1205; when the rent was in arrear in the time of the war in King John's time, he gave the abbey the other half of the land which his father Thomas had given, and his brother Peter released it (*C.A.D.* I, 164).

Either Peter had a long public career, or there were two Peters. A Peter of the Bail was mayor about 1226, and several times, if not continuously, between 1233 and 1245. He was for some years keeper of the cathedral fabric jointly with one of the canons (*R.A.* IV, 95–100, supra, p. 113).

Elias the fat once held a house in Brancegate of Peter of the Bail for 10*s.* yearly (*Book of Fees*, I, 365). About 1260 a Peter son of Thomas of the Bail sold the great garden in East Bight to Canon Geoffrey Scot (D. & C., D ii, 77/3/34). Perhaps this was the holding in the Bail from which the family took its name. Peter had a house in Mikelgate in St Martin's parish, extending westwards to Hungate, between land formerly of Moses the Jew and land which Thomas Aldman held of St Mary, which he granted to Adam Haring (D. & C., D ii, 75/2/15).

Thomas of the Bail had land in St Cuthbert (D. & C., D ii, 74/3/7). Peter had a son Robert, mentioned about 1240 (*R.A.* IV, 68). Fulk son of William and nephew of Peter of the Bail granted land in St Peter at the skin market (Stanthaket) to Robert son of Godred and Helevisa his wife (D. & C., D ii, 80/3/38). William son of Geoffrey son of Johel of the Bail granted land to the rector of All Saints in the Bail (D. & C., D ii, 77/3/8). In 1250 William de Wendover and Matilda his wife, who was the daughter of Peter of the Bail, assigned 2½ bovates of land and half a house in Carlton to the dean and chapter, for the soul of Peter and the fabric of the Minster (*Lincs N. & Q*, VII, 192). In 1258 there was a Thomas of the Bail who was a monk of St Mary's cell at Lincoln belonging to the abbey of St Mary of York (*Chronicle of St Mary's Abbey, York* (Surtees Society), p. 4).

This family had apparently, unlike the others mentioned above, no interest outside Lincoln. They do not figure among the magnates of Wigford. They come from the Bail, and have a link with the Minster, though trade has brought them into the lower city to the market districts.

There was another important family with its roots in the Bail. Its various surnames make it more difficult to construct a family tree, but the evidence appears to be as follows:

Charters of land in the Bail show that Thomas son of Robert son of Martin, and Peter son of John nephew of Richilda, alias Peter of the Bridge, were holding land jointly. Thomas no doubt acquired his share from his father Robert, and Peter through his father John from his great aunt Richilda, taking with it

Richilda's husband's name 'of the Bridge'. They were chief lords, and their land lay in the corner between Bailgate and West Bight. Record of it is due to the fact that Thomas' brother Gilbert of Kent was busy acquiring plots of land and laying them together both in Bailgate and in Eastgate, in order to endow a chaplain at the altar of St Thomas or some other altar in the cathedral for the souls of himself, his ancestors and all the faithful (*L.C.S.* III, 440).

John nephew of Richold was bailiff in 1176–7, and Robert son of Martin in 1184–5. In 1185–6 Robert son of Martin and his brother John accounted for 40 marks and five hawks for having the land of William son of Fulk whose heirs they were (P.R. 32 *Henry II*, p. 76), having in 1179–80 owed 20 marks to the Exchequer for a writ of right against William (P.R. 26 *Henry II*, p. 51). Robert owed £5. 6*s*. 6*d*. to Walter of Grimsby (ibid.).

Members of the family apparently held land in St Peter Stanthaket (D. & C., D ii, 80/3/6, 8, 10), St George (D ii, 76/1/12), St Edmund (D ii, 76/1/13), perhaps St Swithin (D ii, 76/1/30), St Margaret in Wigford (D ii, 76/3/12, 13), and All Saints Hungate or St Mary Crackpole (D ii, 75/1/5, 9, 10). Robert son of Martin granted land in St George's parish, confirmed by his son Thomas, to Bardney Abbey; and the abbey granted to Robert son of Peter of the Bridge land on which part of Robert's hall stood in the waterside district of Thorngate, 1250–8 (Bardney Cartulary, ff. 251, 251 d, 259 d). John nephew of Richilda gave land in St Augustine's parish to Stainfield Priory (D. & C., D ii, 74/1/1).

Peter of the Bridge was one of the leading citizens in 1206 (*Earliest Lincs Assize Rolls* (L.R.S.), no. 1448). He was held as a hostage by King John in 1216 (supra, p. 199). He was confirmed by the king in the office of mayor in 1218 in succession to William nephew of Warner. He was mayor in 1221 and 1222, and to judge by the number of bailiffs with whom he witnessed charters he must have held the office for four or five years at least. He gave a rent of 11*s*. from land in Walkergate to Thurgarton Priory (Thurgarton Cartulary, no. 1079). He had a meadow in Ingham (*R.A.* IV, 38).

His son Richard of the Bridge held a third of a knight's fee of the bishop of Lincoln in 1242–3 (*Book of Fees*, II, 1076). He was a moneyer for Lincoln in 1244 (*Red Book of the Exchequer*, III, 1075) and was mayor about 1245. Richard and Thomas his brother witness together (Harl. Cart. 44 A 41).

William de Ponte was deprived by the Legate of the church of St Peter at Pleas (*Rotuli Hugonis de Welles* (L.R.S.), I, 105). There was a Robert son of Peter *de Ponte* (Bardney Cartulary, f. 259 d). It may have been the latter's son Thomas son of Robert who was mayor about 1260. James of the Bridge (son of Peter, D. & C., D ii, 67/1/4) was a Christian chirographer of the Jewish Exchequer in 1274 (Rigg, *Exchequer of Jews*, I, 123–4), and mayor about 1278. He appears with Gilbert *de Ponte* as a witness about 1250 (D. & C., D ii, 74/3/30). About 1290 a Peter of the Bridge acted as attorney of his sister Matilda the daughter of Gilbert, and here appears for the first time the surname concealed by the Latin *de Ponte*: it is 'Attebrig'.

Thomas of Beaufou was mayor during all or most of the years between 1250 and 1258. He had half a knight's fee in Silk Willoughby of the bishop of Lincoln, worth £10 yearly (*R.H.* I, 241). He may be the Thomas de Bello Fago who had 12 quarters of oats taken from half a bovate of land of his at Hundleby after the battle of Evesham (*Cal. Inq. Misc.* I, 778). Perhaps he was a farmer and corn merchant: in 1303 a later Thomas de Bello Fago had a house in St Cuthbert's parish, which was by the corn market (*Cal. Inq. Misc.* I, 1939). Richard of Beaufou was mayor in 1284.

Of William of Holgate who was mayor from 1267 until *c.* 1273, a hint of his business interests is given by the charge that he took stone from the king's quarry at Lincoln and sent it, squared by stonemasons, to Boston to build houses there (*R.H.* I, 399; supra, p. 318). When in 1265 the king was seizing the lands of rebels, William of Holegate served as one of the collectors in the city (*Cal. Inq. Misc.* I, 773).

APPENDIX VI

SOME CITIZEN LISTS

Fines imposed on Lincoln men for assault on Jews, 1191 (P.R. 3 and 4 *Richard I*, pp. 15–16, 242–3).

Gosçelin the long	½ mark
Robert son of Rumfare	½ m.
Baldwin the tanner	10 m.
Ralf de Merston	1 m.
Hugh son of Ralf	40*s*.
William son of Ougrim	4 m.
Walter son of Wulmer	½ m.
William de Kyrkested	½ m.
William son of Brictiue	1 m.
Hugh son of John	½ m.
Wiger the tailor	20*s*.
Roger son of Brand	10 m.
William the tailor	1 m.
Gundred the tanner	3 m.
Turgot the tanner	4 m.
Richard Suaue	10*s*.
Godwin the rich	5 m.
Richard the long	1 m.
John son of Suaue	2 m.
Thomas de Paris	10 m.
Fulk the tanner	2 m.
Roger the weaver	20*s*.
William son of Lambert	100*s*.
Robert son of Suartebrand	3 m.
Simon son of Toke	3 m.
Alan son of Brand	6 m.
Robert nephew of Goscelin	1 m.
Nicholas son of Gunnilda	2 m.
Martin son of Ædric	15 m.
Wigot son of Wigot	20*s*.
Ærnulf the little	3 m.
Richard son of James	10 m.
Yuo son of Brand	3 m.
Ralf son of Lambert	40 m.
Gamel canum	20*s*.
Alan the dyer	½ m.
Roger son of the smith	2 m.
Hamo son of Lambert	6 m.
Robert son of Aumund	20*s*.
Leuric de Potteregate	½ m.
William pes leporis	2 m.
William de Fiskerton	15 m.
Robert son-in-law of Lambert	2 m.
Richard son of Ase	2 m.
William Collecnape	1 m.
Robert son of Alnad	1 m.
Fulk son of William	2 m.
Robert of St John's churchyard	5 m.
William nephew of James	½ m.
William son of Walter	4 m.
Roger brother of William	3 m.
Miles the porter	4 m.
Peter son-in-law of Lefric	½ m.
Robert de Legerton	5 m.
Herbert de Neweport	1 m.
Hugh Painel	5 m.
Siward de Neweport	2 m.
Martin son of Joscelin	1 m.
Fulk the mercer	1 m.
Arnulf the tailor	½ m.
John son of Walter	20*s*.
Ulf de Hundegate	12 m.
Osbert son of Turgar	5 m.
Ralf son of Walter	4 m.
Robert son of Emma	20*s*.
Adam Blund	2 m.
Robert de Bongeia	½ m.
Arnulf the weaver	1 m.
John son of Hugh	3 m.
Marsilius the Fleming	4 m.
Lefwin the moneyer	40 m.
Norman the weaver	½ m.
Reinbald of Wicheforde	20 m.
Simon son of Alan	1 m.
Constantius	20*s*.
Hugh the Fleming	20 m.
John Ruffus	20*s*.
William son of Gladew'	½ m.
Lambert the draper	4 m.
Bonefacius	1 m.
Gerard the tailor	5 m.
Ewan son of Walter	½ m.
Richard son of Sirild'	6 m.
Robert de Geiton	½ m.
Thomas son of Gode	½ m.
William son of Orgar	3 m.
Walter Dod	4 m.
Gilbert Gay	2 m.
Robert son of Gamel	2 m.
William son of Warner	£100
Richard the villein	½ m.
Warin the tailor	½ m.
Arnald the sailor	½ m.
Goscelin de Neweport	½ m.
Peter Thore	½ m.

Citizens who answered for the commonalty in the king's court in 1201 (*C.R. Rolls*, I, 418).

Adam son of Reginald	Roger son of Walter
Thomas of the Bail	Richard the villein
William Warneri	Richard son of James
Peter son of John	John the Fleming

Keepers of measures in 1202 (Mrs D. M. Stenton, *Earliest Lincs Assize Roll* (L.R.S.), no. 1016).

Constancius de Newland	John the villein
Osbert son (*or* brother) of Warin	Warin the barber
Richard de Neuport	Ralf de Rouen
Girard the skinner	Martin the mercer
Ralf Lodein	Robert the mercer
Hamo son of Lambert	

Twenty-four principal citizens in 1206 (ibid. no. 1448).

William nephew of Warner	Gilbert the tailor
Reinbald the rich	Gregory le roser
John de Benniworth	Alan son of Brand
Peter de Ponte	Nicholas son of Gunnilda
William son of Warner	Simon de Araz
Hugh de Marston	Hamo son of Lambert
Richard de Newport	Richard his brother
Herbert de Newport	Richard the bailiff
James son of Brand	Wigot son of Wigot
Constancius de Newland	Hugh Blund
William the carpenter	Roger son of Walter
Warner son of Fardein	Adam de Colchester

Coroners in 1218 (Mrs D. M. Stenton, *Rolls of Justices in Eyre for Lincs and Worcs* (Selden Society), no. 21).

John de Paris	Richard son of James
Peter of the Bail	Robert son of Iwein

Officials of the Mint in 1244 (*Red Book of the Exchequer*, III, 1075).

Moneyers:	William de Paris
	Richard de Ponte
	William Brand
	John de Luda
Keepers:	Alan de Gaytun
	John Berne
	John son of Marenni (? Martin)
	Henry Cocus
Assayers:	Thomas de Beaufou
	John the goldsmith
Clerk:	Hugh son of John

Witnesses on the part of the commonalty to the agreement with the dean and chapter, 7 April 1263 (*R.A.* III, 304).

John de Luda, mayor
Thomas de Beaufou
Osbert son of Giles
Robert Totti, coroner
Jordan son of William, bailiff
Gilbert Peck, bailiff
Walter Braund
William son of Giles
James de Ponte
Gilbert de Ponte
John de Lincoln
William de Hollegate
Peter son of Maurice
Ralf de Gayton
Germagan

Twenty-four principal citizens in 1265 (*C.P.R.* 1258–66, p. 421).

Thomas de Fou
Walter Braund
William Braund
Gilbert de punt
Roger s. Benedict
John de Luda
Osbert s. Giles
John de Paris
James del punt
Jordan s. Giles
Henry s. Giles
Thomas s. Robert
Peter s. Robert
Henry Gupil
Walter de Croyland
Nicholas Munde
Nicholas Stoyle
William de Holegate
William de Hepham
John Coiti
Thomas the tailor
John de Lincoln
John del Soler
Martin le cordwaner

HUNDRED ROLL JURORS

Great men:

Ralph Gayton
Adam of the hospital
Walter of Croyland
Robert Scot
Robert Cott
Roger Gupil
Gilbert of Lissington
Roger at the pump
Nicholas of Chester
Alan at the gate
Henry Deynus
Adam Tornholm

Middling men:

William Cause
John Cotti
Richard s. Robert
Richard Bedford
Roger s. Ralph
Peter Botild
Richard medicus
William Scowle
William de Boston
Ralph de Greigham
Richard of Stowe
Symon in Anglo

THE MAYOR'S COUNCIL OF TWENTY-FOUR

(From the margins of the Blickling Homilies)

	c. 1303 p. 2	*c.* 1306 p. 140	*c.* 1307 p. 4	*c.* 1308 p. 6	*c.* 1310 p. 10	*c.* 1311 p. 200	*c.* 1313 p. 40	*c.* 1314 p. 220	*c.* 1315 p. 38	*c.* 1316? p. 66	12 in 1314 (supra, p. 298)
William Cause	*	*	*	*	*	*	—	*	*	—	o
Alexander fitz Martin	*	Mayor	*	*	Mayor	*	*	*	*	*	—
Osbert le Long	*	*	*	*	*	Mayor	—	—	—	—	—
John de Blyton	*	*	Mayor	*	*	*	*	—	*	*	o
John de Roderham	*	*	*	—	—	—	—	—	—	—	—
James Berne	*	*	*	*	*	*	*	*	*	—	o
Adam fitz Martin	*	*	*	—	—	*	—	—	*	—	—
Simon de Edlynton	*	*	*	*	*	*	*	Mayor	*	*	o
Hugo de Thorn	*	*	*	*	—	—	—	—	—	—	—
Walter Bayus	*	*	*	*	*	*	*	*	—	—	o
John de Normanton	*	*	*	*	*	*	—	—	—	—	—
John de Amcotes	*	*	*	Mayor	*	*	*	*	*	—	—
Eustace le Hanser	*	*	—	—	—	—	—	—	—	—	—
Ralf Russell	*	*	*	*	*	—	—	—	—	—	—
Robert de Bynington	*	*	*	*	*	—	—	—	—	—	—
Geoffrey de Thornhagh	*	—	*	*	*	—	—	—	—	—	o
Robert ad Fontem	*	—	—	—	—	—	—	—	—	—	—
John ad Fontem	*	—	—	—	—	—	—	—	—	—	—
Ralf de Fillingham	*	—	*	*	*	—	—	—	—	—	—
Henry Bere	*	*	*	*	*	*	Mayor	*	*	*	o
Gilbert de Atherby	*	*	*	*	*	*	*	*	Mayor	*	o
John de Hadington	*	*	*	*	—	*	*	—	—	—	—
Geoffrey de Keworth	*	*	*	—	*	—	—	—	—	—	—
Simon de Wymbelthorpe	*	—	—	—	—	*	—	—	—	—	—
Stephen de Stanham	—	*	—	—	—	—	—	—	—	—	—
Gilbert le Neyr (Blake)	—	*	*	*	*	*	—	*	—	—	o
John le Neyr (Blake)	—	*	*	*	—	—	—	—	—	—	—
Gilbert Rothing	—	*	*	*	*	*	—	—	—	—	—
William de Fillingham	—	*	—	—	?	—	—	—	—	—	—
John Good	—	*	*	*	—	—	—	—	—	—	—
John fitz Thomas	—	—	*	*	*	*	*	—	*	—	—
John Gernun	—	—	*	*	—	*	*	—	—	—	—
Robert Oxford	—	—	*	*	*	—	*	—	*	*	—
John de Newcastle	—	—	*	—	—	*	*	*	*	*	o
. . . Glover	—	—	—	*	—	—	—	—	—	—	—
John Kemp	—	—	—	*	*	*	*	*	—	—	—
Nigel Sistrik	—	—	—	*	—	—	—	*	—	—	—

Name											
John? le Ironmonger	—	—	—	—	*	—	—	—	—	—	—
Walter de Momby	—	—	—	—	*	—	—	—	—	—	—
Richard Blakeden	—	—	—	—	*	*	*	*	*	*	o
Robert de Bardney	—	—	—	—	—	*	—	*	*	*	—
Richard de Scarle	—	—	—	—	—	*	—	*	—	—	—
John Paternoster	—	—	—	—	—	*	—	—	—	—	—
Alan Faukes	—	—	—	—	—	*	—	—	—	—	—
John Pinzon	—	—	—	—	—	—	*	—	*	—	—
Alexander fitz Richard	—	—	—	—	—	—	*	—	—	—	—
Stephen de Norton	—	—	—	—	—	—	*	*	—	—	—
Adam de Hibaldstow	—	—	—	—	—	—	*	*	*	*	—
Symon de Grantham	—	—	—	—	—	—	*	*	—	—	—
Peter Wynstan	—	—	—	—	—	—	*	—	—	—	—
Walter de Burgh	—	—	—	—	—	—	*	*	*	*	—
Walter de York	—	—	—	—	—	—	*	*	—	—	—
Hugh Russell	—	—	—	—	—	—	*	—	*	*	—
Walter de Hauvill	—	—	—	—	—	—	*	—	*	—	—
Hugh de Edlington	—	—	—	—	—	—	—	*	*	*	—
Hamo Skinner	—	—	—	—	—	—	—	*	—	—	—
Robert Hare	—	—	—	—	—	—	—	*	—	*	—
John de Leicester	—	—	—	—	—	—	—	*	—	—	—
Henry Lavender	—	—	—	—	—	—	—	*	—	*	—
Hugh Tyler	—	—	—	—	—	—	—	*	*	—	—
Henry de Broune	—	—	—	—	—	—	—	*	—	—	—
John de Tame	—	—	—	—	—	—	—	*	*	—	—
Robert Dughty	—	—	—	—	—	—	—	*	—	—	—
Henry de Outhorpe	—	—	—	—	—	—	—	*	*	*	—
Walter Dainyot	—	—	—	—	—	—	—	*	*	—	—
William Russell	—	—	—	—	—	—	—	—	*	*	—
Henry Stoyle	—	—	—	—	—	—	—	—	*	*	—
Richard Lewordy	—	—	—	—	—	—	—	—	*	—	—
Robert de Humberston	—	—	—	—	—	—	—	—	*	*	—
David le Taverner	—	—	—	—	—	—	—	—	*	*	o
Geoffrey de Lynn	—	—	—	—	—	—	—	—	*	*	—
. . . le parmenter	—	—	—	—	—	—	—	—	*	—	—
Richard piscator	—	—	—	—	—	—	—	—	*	—	—
William de Hakethorn	—	—	—	—	—	—	—	—	—	*	—
Thomas Russell	—	—	—	—	—	—	—	—	—	*	—
Richard Little	—	—	—	—	—	—	—	—	—	*	—
Hugh Bacon	—	—	—	—	—	—	—	—	—	*	—
Henry de Severby	—	—	—	—	—	—	—	—	—	*	—
John de Spridlington	—	—	—	—	—	—	—	—	—	*	—
Alan de Hodelston	—	—	—	—	—	—	—	—	—	*	—
William Ryvett	—	—	—	—	—	—	—	—	—	*	—

* Indicates membership of the twenty-four in the year at the head of the column.   o Indicates membership of the twelve in 1314.

APPENDIX VII

PROVISIONS FOR THE GOVERNMENT OF THE CITY, *c.* 1300

(From MS. account of the Lincoln Charters, compiled in 1785 by Samuel Lyon, Town Clerk. See supra, pp. 290–1. Lyon writes 'There is amongst the city records an ancient writing in the Latin language, upon a single skin of parchment, purporting to be part of an order of the common council of the said city, or of an exemplification thereof...the conclusion and date which appear to have been wrote upon a second skin with the city seal annexed to the whole are torn away.')

THE WRITING CALLED PROVISIONS

These are provisions made together with the underwritten articles by the mayor and whole commonalty of the city of Lincoln for keeping the peace of our Lord the King and for the perpetual observance of the liberties and improvements hereunder mentioned (that is to say)

That the commonalty shall by their common council elect a mayor from year to year of their own election; and that no mayor shall be elected unless he shall before be assessed to the public taxes, with other citizens of the said city; and that the mayor shall remain in his mayoralty so long as it pleases him and the commonalty; And that the same mayor shall be discharged of all taxes dues and talliages and of all other customs belonging to the city so long as he shall be mayor (saving the precept of our Lord the King in all things); And also that it shall be lawful for such mayor to take his hansels within the city and without, except of the citizens of Lincoln and their sons, and all those who pay scot and lot in the said city and who ought not to be anselled within the county of Lincoln;

And further it is provided that the commonalty with the advice of the mayor shall choose twelve fit and discreet men to be judges of the said city, but that those twelve men shall be assessed to the public taxes and dues, and to all royal customs with other citizens of the said city;

And it is further provided that the said citizens shall have bailiffs every year of their own election, and that those bailiffs shall faithfully discharge the fee farm rent of our Lord the King at the end of the year; And if they dont do so the mayor and commonalty shall distrain such bailiffs by their lands and chattels until the fee farm rent of our Lord the King be fully paid; And that if any damage happens to the city thro' default of paying the fee farm rent of our Lord the King such damage shall be made good to the city out of the chattels of the said bailiffs; And those bailiffs ought to have two clerks and four sergeants who shall be presented before the mayor and commonalty at the feast of St Michael;

And that there shall be no weigher of goods unless he is elected by the common council and that the persons so elected shall take their corporal oath upon the holy Evangelists faithfully and firmly to fulfil all these things and to keep and observe the customs of the city;

And if it shall happen that the mayor or any bailiff shall be called into question unjustly for supporting the rights of the city the commonalty shall defend them within the city and without to the utmost of their power; And also shall faithfully restrain the mayor and bailiffs within their own liberties of the said city;

And it is further provided that four men worthy of trust shall be elected from amongst the citizens by a free election at the feast of St Michael to keep an account of outgoings talliages and arrears belonging to the city; and that they have one chest and four keys; And that they shall render up their account to the city at the end of the year;

Also it is provided for the keeping the peace of our Lord the King that they who ought shall appoint two men out of each parish of the city worthy of trust to search their own parishes once a month; And that no person shall lodge a stranger more than one night unless he shall bring him forth to public view on the morrow if it shall be necessary; And if any person in any parish shall be suspected and he cannot find pledges he shall be sent out of town until he can find pledges; And if the said two men will not search their respective parishes as aforesaid, they shall remain in the mercy of the city, and the names of the aforesaid men shall be set down in writing, to be in the keeping of the mayor, and at the feast of St Michael there shall be other two such men appointed to succeed to the said office; And if a disturbance of the city and a tumult and clamour happens, and the mayor and bailiffs attend, all the commonalty ought to prosecute them to the keeping of the peace of our Lord the King, and of the city;

And it is further provided that those who choose to defend themselves by the liberty of the city shall be assessed, together with the commonalty, to all taxes dues and royal customs belonging to the city; And if any person of the city shall oppose the mayor and commonalty concerning any matter of a public nature by them enacted, he shall be in the mercy of the city; And it shall be lawful for the mayor and citizens to distrain him for his amercement until he shall make them satisfaction according to the greatness of his offence; And if reasonable summons's have been issued by command of the mayor and commonalty, he who withdraws himself, and does not appear, shall be amerced to the amount of 2*s*., unless he can suggest some reasonable cause by way of excuse;

Also it is provided that no foreign merchant shall remain in the city more than forty days for selling his merchandizes, unless he shall have licence of the mayor and commonalty; And it is further provided that no foreigner shall have the freedom of the city unless he shall receive it in the presence of the mayor and commonalty; Also it is provided that no foreign merchant of any kind of merchandize ought to be admitted to sell it within the city by retail; Also it is provided that if any broker of the city shall lead a foreign merchant out of town to buy wool, or any other thing, which is contrary to the liberty of the city, he shall remain in the mercy of the city; And if he shall a second time be convicted of the like offence, he shall lose his freedom, until he shall make satisfaction to the commonalty; And if any citizen shall deal with him, he shall be in the mercy of the city; And if any merchant citizen shall associate himself with a foreign merchant to make any kind of merchandizes within the city he shall be in the mercy of the commonalty, and the property of the foreigner shall be seized, and be in the mercy of the city; Also it is provided that if any worker of wool, man or woman, shall go out of the city to work at their trade (except at markets) he or she shall be in the mercy of the city; and if again convicted of the same offence, no one shall employ them in their business;

Also it is forbid that anyone do go out of the gates of the city to buy anything that is coming towards it, and if anyone do so, he shall be in the mercy of the mayor and bailiffs of the city, and the thing bought shall be seized to the use of the city;

Also it is forbid that anyone shall exercise his right of common in the common pastures but in a reasonable degree as he ought; and that any hog shall be suffered to enter thereon to the injury of the pasture;

And it is provided that it shall be lawful for every citizen to distrain his foreign debtors found within the city for their known debts, without any denial of the bailiffs, except in the times when the judges shall be holding pleas in the city, and proceeding from thence into the county, and also except as to men coming to market with their merchandizes;

Also so that no weaver or dyer shall dye the wool or cloths of foreigners, nor fuller full the same against the liberty of the city, and if he does so, and is thereof convicted, he shall be in the mercy of the city, and if he shall be again convicted, he shall forfeit his right of a citizen, until he shall submit and promise amendment, And if anyone shall knowingly hold communication with him, he shall be in the mercy of the city, and the wool or cloth shall remain in the mercy of the mayor bailiffs and commonalty of the city, And it shall be lawful for any citizen to seize such wool or cloth as aforesaid without cause until he can show it to the mayor and bailiffs; And it is provided that no merchant of the city shall buy cloth made out of the city to dye within the same; And if anyone shall be convicted of this offence, the cloth shall be in the mercy of the city, and the seller also; And further that neither the dyer, the weaver, or the fuller, ought to dye any cloth for their own use; and if they shall be thereof convicted the cloths shall remain to the use of the commonalty; And it shall be lawful for any citizen without cause to seize any such cloths, wheresoever he shall find them, until he shall show them to the mayor and bailiffs; Also it is provided that if any citizen shall find his cloth injured thro' the default of the fuller, the fuller shall make good the damage to him whose cloth it shall be, by the view of lawful men; Also it is provided that the dyers and weavers shall be punished in like manner if their works are ill done;

And also that no regrator of flesh or fish shall buy any flesh or fish to sell which the Church of Lincoln refused before it was offered to the mayor, and that it shall be lawful for any citizen to arrest the person and the thing so bought, and bring them before the mayor, if any one shall be found so to do;

And it is provided that no fisherman ought to fish in the free waters of the city, unless with nets provided and made by the consent of honest men of the commonalty of the said city, and if anyone shall do so, he shall be in the mercy of the said city, and if he shall again be convicted thereof, he shall be in the mercy of the city, and his nets shall be forfeited;

Also it is provided that if any citizen of Lincoln shall be arrested out of the town for any debt of another citizen of Lincoln, it shall be lawful for the mayor and commonalty to distrain him, by whom he is arrested, by his chattels, until the streets of our Lord the King shall be made free to the citizens of Lincoln;

Also it is provided that if any seller of wool shall sell any false wool to a merchant, by reason of which sale complaints shall come to the mayor or commonalty, the seller of such wool shall remain in the mercy of the city, and the false wool shall be burnt in any place the mayor and commonalty please; and be it known that all false merchandize, as in cloths, shoes, tanned leather, and all other merchandizes, found to be false, which ought to be subject to a like penalty, shall be punished by a like penalty as false wools;

'Here this writing ends, the second skin containing the conclusion and date with the seal annexed being wanting as was before observed.'

Lyon's Marginal Notes

N.B. I have compared the writing in this skin of parchment with a specimen given by Mr Astle in his late publication upon *Origin and Progress of Writing*, p. 150, plate 27, No. 19 (which was taken from a record wrote in the year 1280) and find that in character and style of writing they nearly resemble each other.

Hansells were a customary present made to the mayor out of a commodity brought by strangers into the city for sale, and I believe still exists, at least in the article of oysters.

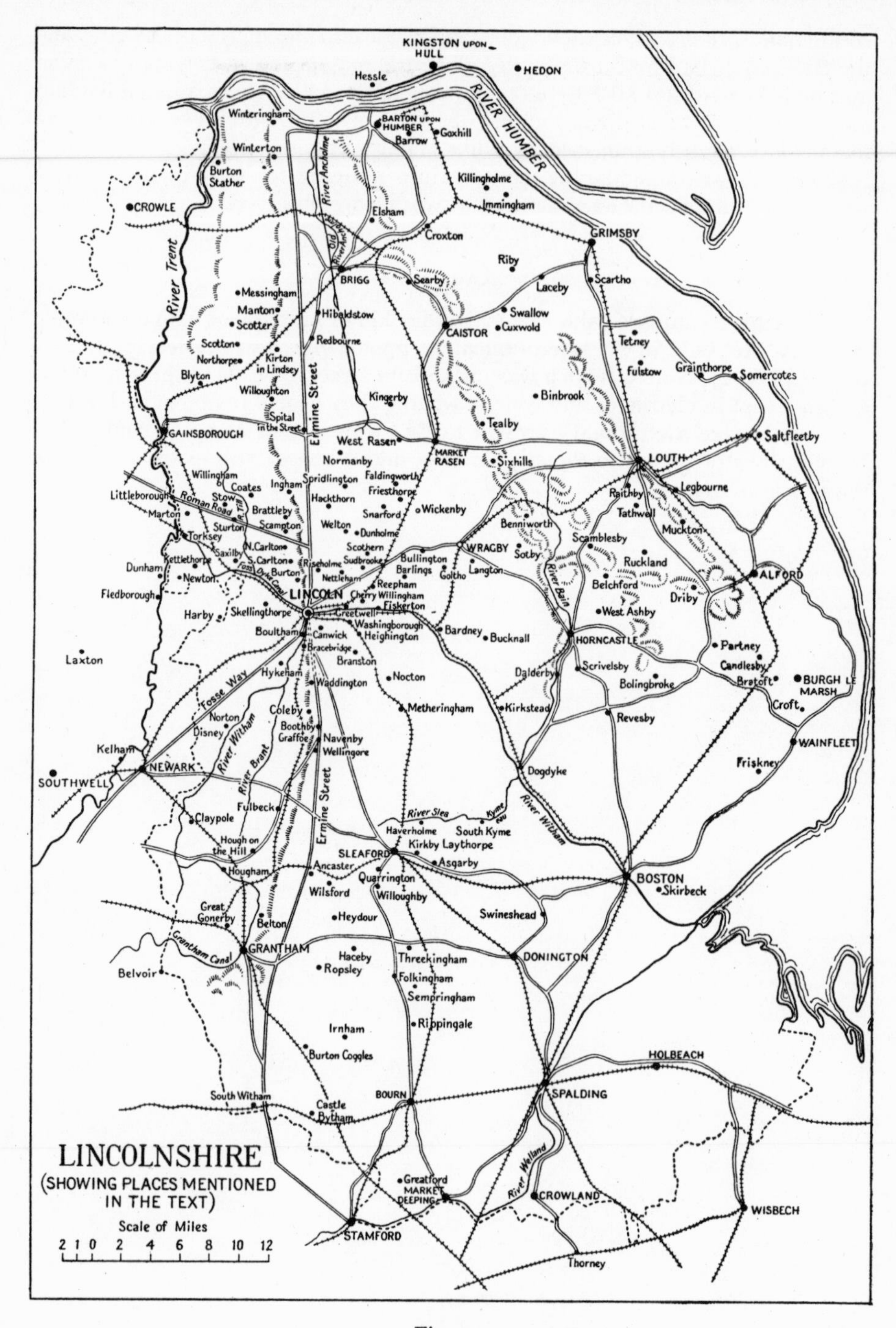
LINCOLNSHIRE
(SHOWING PLACES MENTIONED IN THE TEXT)
Scale of Miles
2 1 0 2 4 6 8 10 12
KINGSTON UPON HULL
HEDON
Hessle
RIVER HUMBER
Winteringham
BARTON UPON HUMBER
Barrow
Goxhill
Winterton
Burton Stather
Killingholme
Immingham
CROWLE
River Trent
River Ancholme
Old River Ancholme
Elsham
Croxton
GRIMSBY
Riby
BRIGG
Searby
Laceby
Scartho
Messingham
Manton
Scotter
Hibaldstow
Swallow
Cuxwold
CAISTOR
Redbourne
Scotton
Northorpe
Kirton in Lindsey
Tetney
Fulstow
Grainthorpe
Somercotes
Blyton
Willoughton
Kingerby
Binbrook
Tealby
Spital in the Street
Ermine Street
GAINSBOROUGH
West Rasen
MARKET RASEN
Saltfleetby
Normanby
Sixhills
LOUTH
Willingham
Stow
Coates
Ingham
Spridlington
Faldingworth
Friesthorpe
Hackthorn
Legbourne
Raithby
Tathwell
Littleborough
Roman Road
R. Till
Marton
Brattleby
Scampton
Snarford
Wickenby
Sturton
Welton
Dunholme
Benniworth
Muckton
Torksey
Saxilby
N. Carlton
S. Carlton
Scothern
Sudbrooke
WRAGBY
Sotby
Scamblesby
Ruckland
Kettlethorpe
Dunham
Newton
Foss Dyke Canal
Risholme
Burton
Nettleham
Bullington
Barlings
Goltho
Langton
River Bain
Belchford
ALFORD
Fledborough
LINCOLN
Reepham
Cherry Willingham
Fiskerton
Driby
Harby
Skellingthorpe
Greetwell
West Ashby
Boultham
Canwick
Washingborough
Heighington
Bardney
Bucknall
HORNCASTLE
Laxton
Bracebridge
Branston
Partney
Scrivelsby
Candlesby
Hykeham
Nocton
Dalderby
Bratoft
BURGH LE MARSH
Waddington
Bolingbroke
Fosse Way
Coleby
Metheringham
Kirkstead
Croft
Norton Disney
Revesby
River Witham
Boothby Graffoe
Navenby
Wellingore
WAINFLEET
Kelham
NEWARK
Dogdyke
SOUTHWELL
Friskney
River Brant
Ermine Street
Fulbeck
River Slea
Kyme Eau
Claypole
Haverholme
South Kyme
Hough on the Hill
SLEAFORD
Kirkby Laythorpe
Asgarby
Hougham
Ancaster
Quarrington
BOSTON
Skirbeck
Wilsford
Willoughby
Great Gonerby
Heydour
Swineshead
Belton
Grantham Canal
GRANTHAM
Haceby
Threekingham
DONINGTON
Belvoir
Ropsley
Folkingham
Sempringham
Irnham
Rippingale
Burton Coggles
HOLBEACH
South Witham
Castle Bytham
BOURN
SPALDING
Greatford
MARKET DEEPING
River Welland
CROWLAND
WISBECH
STAMFORD
Thorney

Fig. 24.

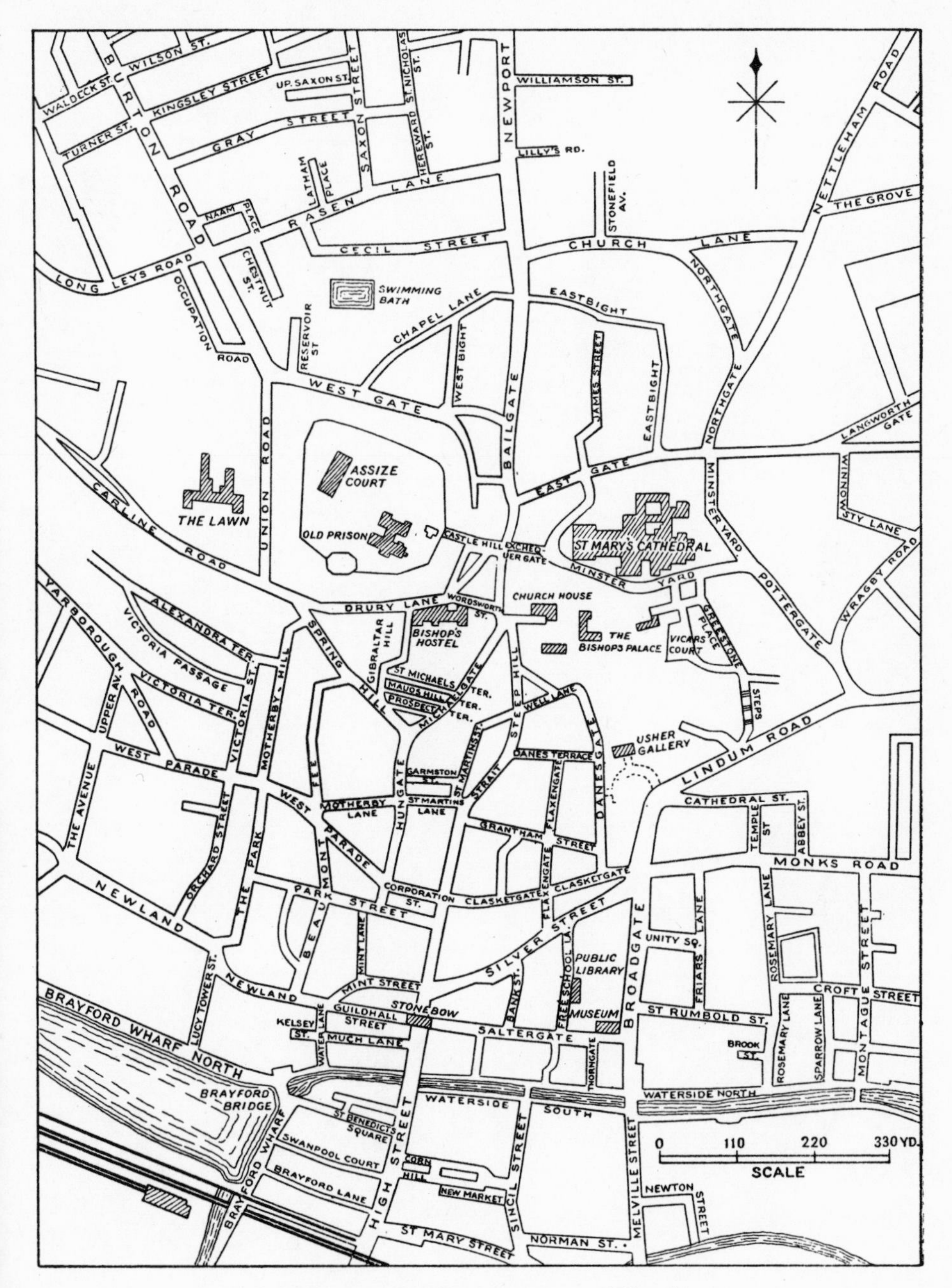

Fig. 25. Modern street map of Lincoln.

INDEX